MILTON'S LEVELLER GOD

Milton's Leveller God

DAVID WILLIAMS

McGill-Queen's University Press
Montreal & Kingston · London · Chicago

ISBN 978-0-7735-5033-9 (cloth)
ISBN 978-0-7735-5034-6 (paper)
ISBN 978-0-7735-5035-3 (ePDF)
ISBN 978-0-7735-5036-0 (ePUB)

Legal deposit second quarter 2017
Bibliothèque nationale du Québec

Printed in Canada on acid-free paper that is 100% ancient forest free (100% post-consumer recycled), processed chlorine free

This book has been published with the help of a grant from the Canadian Federation for the Humanities and Social Sciences, through the Awards to Scholarly Publications Program, using funds provided by the Social Sciences and Humanities Research Council of Canada.

McGill-Queen's University Press acknowledges the support of the Canada Council for the Arts for our publishing program. We also acknowledge the financial support of the Government of Canada through the Canada Book Fund for our publishing activities.

Library and Archives Canada Cataloguing in Publication

Williams, David, 1945–, author
Milton's leveller God / David Williams.

Includes bibliographical references and index.
Issued in print and electronic formats.
ISBN 978-0-7735-5033-9 (cloth). – ISBN 978-0-7735-5034-6 (paper). – ISBN 978-0-7735-5035-3 (ePDF). – ISBN 978-0-7735-5036-0 (ePUB)

1. Milton, John, 1608–1674 – Criticism and interpretation.
2. Politics in literature. 3. God in literature. I. Title.

PR3592.P64W55 2017 821'.4 C2016-907783-7
C2016-907784-5

Set in 10.5/13.5 Minion Pro
Book design & typesetting by Garet Markvoort, zijn digital

IN MEMORY OF

Joseph Frank and Philip J. Gallagher

CONTENTS

PREFACE

OVER A CENTURY AGO, English scholar Sir Walter Raleigh famously called *Paradise Lost* "a monument to dead ideas."[1] Ever since, Milton's detractors have been at pains to explain what brought on the rigor mortis. Resisting the "monotony" of the "Grand Style" in *Paradise Lost*, the New Critic F.R. Leavis (1933) hinted that the poem was substantially empty, and that "we surrender at last to the inescapable monotony of the ritual."[2] And the high priest of modernism, T.S. Eliot (1936) claimed "that Milton writes English like a dead language" and "may be said never to have seen anything." Worse yet, his epic affords little more than "a glimpse of a theology … in large part repellent, expressed through a mythology which would have better been left in the Book of Genesis."[3] While Eliot didn't say whether dead language was a cause or a result of dead ideas, William Empson (1961) had not the slightest doubt that "God's absolute claims"[4] in *Paradise Lost* were symptomatic of the dead hand of Calvinism. To Empson, the existential protest of Satan against universal tyranny was the one idea in the poem that had any life. And while J.B. Broadbent (1960) denied moral grandeur to Satan, he, too, found little in Milton's "vicious" deity to mitigate the effects of "a legalism indigenous to Judeo-Christianity."[5]

Milton's defenders soon rallied to bring his ideas back to life, if only to recover a solid prop of their religion. By 1942, C.S. Lewis had made *Paradise Lost* over into a broadly "catholic" work inspired by, but also re-inspiring, the whole long heritage of Augustinian Christianity.[6] Despite the glaring heterodoxy of Milton's theology in his *De Doctrina Christiana*, William B. Hunter, C.A. Patrides, and J.H. Adamson (1971) reaffirmed Milton's doctrinal orthodoxy in *Bright Essence*,[7] with Hunter (1998) even bidding to "disprove" Milton's authorship of the heretical *De Doctrina Christiana*.[8]

Meanwhile, less doctrinal critics like Denis Saurat (1925) tried to explain Milton's heterodoxy through his absorption of Jewish mysticism via the Kabbalistic tradition of the *Zohar*.[9] Subsequently, Maurice Kelley issued a broadside in *This Great Argument*[10] (1941) against any and all attempts to fit Milton to a Procrustean bed of orthodoxy concerning the Trinity, *creatio ex nihilo*, and a host of other "dead ideas." Finally, in his *Milton's Good God*[11] (1982), Dennis Danielson freed Milton from the Reformed orthodoxy of Calvinism, and so from the shadow of an "evil deity" in his epic poem. In rapid succession, Hugh MacCallum (1986)[12] explained the relevance of Milton's anti-Trinitarianism to his radical vision of "the Sons of God," and John Rumrich (1996)[13] unveiled some of the more radical implications of Milton's materialist heresy in *Paradise Lost* that equated matter with the divine substance. Contrary to Hesiod's primeval "*Χαος*," Milton's Chaos was not God's arch-enemy.

The problem, as this brief survey suggests, is that we are left to debate Milton's merits in a culture that is largely post-Christian. To those for whom "dead ideas" remain dear, *Paradise Lost* rises like a tropical island out of a vast sea of scientific secularism, cultural pluralism, and "militant" feminism. If that atoll of faith were to subside beneath an all-encompassing sea, the note of resignation heard in several Milton sessions at MLA 2015 would surely turn to despair. For those who once tended the poet's shrine at or near the peak of Mt Parnassus have every right to be anxious about literary studies in America. Only Shakespeare still commands a single-author course in many universities, since the Bard of Avon's concerns are "closer" to our own. Shakespeare is supposed to be more "humane," more "catholic" in his sympathies, and more generous in his treatment of women and other disempowered and dispossessed persons. In short, Shakespeare's dramas are still relevant; although many of his ideas are "medieval," his characters live on. While such a judgment comes close to caricature, the fact remains that what makes Milton relevant today – his doctrine of liberty – is based on an idiosyncratic theology.

In one of the more important studies in recent decades, Nigel Smith's *Is Milton Better Than Shakespeare?* (2008) argues that "the reach of Milton's achievement is far greater than Shakespeare's," given that "Milton's interrogations of free will, liberty, and the threat to it are more riveting" than "Shakespeare's grasp of humanity or poetry, his troubling displays of power, and his wonderful and delightful exposure of sexual identity."[14] In short, Smith shows that the major ideas governing Milton's prose and poetry are still very much alive. In separate chapters on Miltonic themes of divorce, free will, tyranny and kingship, free states, creation, and love, Smith presents a longitudinal study of the development of most of the grand ideas that govern his prose and poetry. The result is a crystalline view of how Milton's theology of free will continues to be a great cornerstone of Western liberal democracy, which could so easily have collapsed without his timely contributions to debates on the separation of church and state and "the history of toleration," rather more "than might at first appear to be the case" (Smith, 131). And yet the shortcoming of most longitudinal studies is that great ideas are isolated from the works in which they appear, and are too easily distorted by the logical rigour of the ideas themselves, not the dramatic logic of the works which come to embody them.

Take Benjamin Myers's recent book, *Milton's Theology of Freedom* (2006), which admirably demonstrates Milton's "continuity and discontinuity with post-Reformation theological discourse."[15] Here, a familiar problem obtrudes: the theology of free will is a religious myth to most readers, not a philosophical ground of human rights. Rather than showing, as Nigel Smith does, how Milton's theology has been secularized, or how he has largely become "a postreligious writer" (Smith, 13), Myers clings to esoteric changes within theology itself as a result of pressure put on it by Milton and other reformers. Perhaps the most vital notion in Myers's book appears at its outset, where he outlines the bitter religious divisions (2–5) informing two opposing camps in Milton studies, helping to explain if not to condone the unexploded minefield between them. Conservative Miltonists tend to be orthodox, while radical Miltonists focus on his religious "heresies."

Nigel Smith's recent contribution to *The Oxford Handbook of Milton* (2009), in fact, is titled "*Paradise Lost* and Heresy." Yet even here, Smith never really answers the key question posed in his prior work. If Milton had hoped in his prose for a better world, and in his poems "for better poetry," then "why didn't he make God a republican?" (*Is Milton*, 108). The short answer is that he made God a democrat, which puts me in the "heretical" camp, since "Leveller" is about as radical as it gets in Milton studies. But, rather than introduce his Leveller ideas at this point – ideas by which we still live today – I simply insist for now that his social and political heresies are linked, as Smith has claimed, to his religious heresies. It is *critical* heresy nonetheless to write what has oft been thought, but rarely seen in print in Milton studies – that finally he is not a classical republican,[16] given to political "elitism" (Smith, 120), but is increasingly a social egalitarian. Nor is "gender prejudice," which Smith sees "as inevitable given the time and context in which Milton lived" (81), really germane to his work. Least of all is he a Puritan "oligarch," rejoicing in "the triumph of the Saints."[17] To recognize his populism, rather than his "contempt for vulgar opinion" (Smith, 123), and to allow for sexual equality as the very axis of his egalitarianism, is to see him bridge the vast gulf between the mental world of the seventeenth century – 95 per cent of that world, at least – and our own world, dispelling some old and invidious stereotypes about his poetry, such as its religious intolerance, its gender bias, and its social conceit. Milton could at last emerge from his work as the great liberator he claimed to be in a famous passage of *Second Defense of the English People* (1654),[18] in which he expresses the hope to free his nation from civil, religious, and domestic tyranny.

To obsess, however, about the endless dogmas and doctrines that have come to encase his work is also to lose sight of Raleigh's solution to concerns about "a monument to dead ideas." "The *Paradise Lost*," he wrote, "is like the sculptured tombs of the Medici in Florence; it is not of Night and Morning, nor of Lorenzo and Giovanni, that we think as we look at them, but solely of the great creator, Michael Angelo" (88). Raleigh's purpose was to explore the artistry of the *monument*, not to disinter the bones it concealed. And he saw very clearly why Milton's epic had to be viewed as a timeless monument: "He flies in the face of the Athanasian Creed by representing the Son's generation as an event occurring in time – 'on such day as Heaven's great year brings forth'" (86). Narratives of time take place in a world on the cusp of change, not in a timeless world; in consequence, the static figure of an unchanging God rules out all possibility of drama. Raleigh's solution was to reduce an "impossible" narrative of timeless change to one of spatial form. In "*Paradise Lost*: The Scheme," he very nearly suceeded in transforming the poem into a timeless monolith featuring the carved faces of angels on a marble tomb.

Nevertheless, what Milton criticism has ignored to its peril in its ongoing quest to resurrect his "dead ideas" is the living drama of *Paradise Lost*.[19] Rare is the critic like Nicholas von Maltzahn who recalls its origins in "'Adam unparadiz'd' in the Trinity Manuscript," or who speaks of a "return to the work in 1658" that was initially conceived as drama.[20] Nigel Smith offers a telling reminder that "Milton knew and loved Renaissance drama; he picks up the heretical dynamism of Christopher Marlowe's compelling characters and makes much more of them, and in doing so he also moves far beyond the doubts that define but also limit Hamlet" (*Is Milton*, 11–12). But Smith's own method prevents him from showing how Milton submits his "ideas" to the test of drama, by which each is modified or qualified in the epic. I share his liberal sense that Milton is one of the greatest dramatists in the language, and yet he is rarely taught that way in the classroom. What gets in the way of his dramatic method is the looming "presence" of an eternal, unchanging God who has no dramatic part to play in the poem except as the author of our human drama. And to members of the Holy Trinity – who share the total omniscience of the godhead – there can be no surprises, and so no drama, apart from "all that play-acting of the persons of the godhead,"[21] as Milton scoffed in an anti-Trinitarian chapter of his heretical theology. Being timeless, the heavens are quite as immune to change as the Trinity is to surprise. The assumption of immutability – deriving from the Thomistic privileging of essence over existence – thus excludes drama from a world of infallible beings. Raleigh accepts the only gambit left to him: to eternalize the monument.

What this move inevitably closes off is the riveting drama of a non-Trinitarian godhead that is "omnipresent" in Milton's theology and his poetry. For the Son doesn't know what the Father intends and so must struggle to interpret his will; the angels, too, are forced to *read* him aright; and Satan and his cohort turn out to be wilful readers in their Fall. Everywhere, the drama plays out in a literal animation of "eternity." So if some well-meaning angel – deserving, say, of the sobriquet "the winged Hierarch" – should chance to blunder and cause the first man to doubt his dialogue with God about an "equal" partner; or should his wife, who *is* the equal the man had requested and received of God, then happen (as in a stage drama) to overhear the archangel lay down the law of "hierarchy" to her husband, and find him utterly changed in the Separation Scene – not at all the man he used to be – we would find ourselves plunged into a tremendous drama, forced to read aright where even angels struggle to do so. And if the road to hell should be paved with good intentions, what would we say about the wife's need to regain what was lost in a needless "exaltation" of her husband over her? Only the divine dramatist could foresee the outcome of such events, and he alone might see the point of it all, although he sends another angel at once to dramatize the problem of foreknowledge, thereby leaving Adam to grieve that "by my foreknowledge," all humans will suffer "Birth / Abortive, to torment me ere thir being / With thought that they must be" (*PL* 11.768–70).[22] Adam is thus brought to share in the divine quandary of omniscience, raising the curtain on a peerless drama of divine *and* human history where we, too, are left to wonder why "they must be," in spite of "all our woe" (*PL* 1.3)? In the process, we stumble into something much greater than a tragedy, let alone a pointless exercise.

I sketch in brief this plot to prepare readers for a contingency in the method: there is a danger of misreading *any* scene where part is linked to part as closely as an articulated joint, and where, since the cosmic drama turns into *historical* drama, any failure to hear the thrilling chorus of echoes that resounds with living voices of the English Revolution cuts us off from the poem's context. What follows may sound to some readers like a surfeit of echoes. Rest assured that all these phrasal repetitions are structured as speaking parts in a dramatic narrative. As a practicising novelist, I aim to recreate the historical dialogue in a form that comes as near as possible to a form of fiction. But as a cultural historian, I insist on the "truth" of the known, as well as many unknown facts, adhering to the referent as my historical method obliges me to do. What this method demands of readers is to hear familiar lines ("old chestnuts," one of my readers called them) as if for the first time, and thus to discover the great, unheard story that will require us to *unhear* much of what we think we know, and to hear instead those reasonable harmonies between the poem's daring religious and social heresies. For it is ultimately the renewal of those astounding echoes that can justify the poet's "ways to men." More importantly, it must justify them "to women," who, until the nineteenth century at least, had possessed the cultural resources, as Joseph Wittreich demonstrates, to read Milton as their strongest ally, a feat that is beyond most ordinary readers today.[23]

The unheard story in *Paradise Lost* largely concerns an hermaphroditic deity who brings a universe into being out of the divine body, who genders *metaphysically* feminine the will of creatures liberated from "his" divine being. With one stroke, Milton overturns the ontological hierarchy of soul/body that has traditionally justified the social hierarchy of male/female and a political hierarchy of ruler/ruled. But having liberated the creature from "his" own body, the material deity still courts the love and faith of his creatures in a union of wills, figured as a marital union in which the faculty of will must outweigh the faculty of reason. Female readers before the twentieth century often sensed, even where they failed to articulate, such factors at play in the fate of a creation that literally turns on a paradisal plot of marriage. In that epoch of advancing liberalism after the Great Reform Bill of 1832 and John Stuart Mill's classic argument *On Liberty* (1859), it was not only possible but natural to think of Milton as the supreme champion of political and social freedom. This book, then, is a call to all those who are at least willing to conceive of an historical Milton whose epic poems are more radical in their liberalism than it has been possible to assume for well over a century now.

A RESPONSIBLE PREFACE should satisfy four distinct requirements: offer a thumbnail sketch of the work to come; say something about the method of its production; give some account of its birth in the author's imagination; and thank those who have assisted at the birth. As I turn to these latter functions, I confess that Milton has long been a substitute for the lost religion of my boyhood; he haunts my imagination as an unflinching scripturalist who wrote the biblical story as it should have been written in the first place. Here, I am surely on the same page as Nigel Smith who claims that "the achievement of the poetry and of *Paradise Lost* in particular is to offer to the reader a new Bible" (166). But it is my settled conviction that we continue to get that story wrong – Miltonists as much as anyone – because we fail to read him as a superb *dramatist*, let alone a man who is closer to publicans and sinners than his likeness on the marble face of that monolith.

This conviction began in my early formation with Joseph Frank, that most genial and sociable of mentors at the University of Massachusetts, who remarked with a smile one day to our crowded seminar that his face had been rearranged by a Japanese grenade. Joe taught me more about print culture and seventeenth-century history than anyone before or since. Yet this courageous man, who had written so daringly about Lilburne, Walwyn, and Overton in the era of Joe McCarthy, saw little or no connection between the Levellers, the subject of his writing, and Milton, the subject of his teaching.

In that graduate seminar at Amherst in 1970, I sat next to my friend Phil Gallagher, who was still struggling to reconcile his Thomistic education with his reading of Milton. One day, Phil confided his fear that he didn't feel the text with the same intensity that I did, to which I responded with my own fear that he grasped the philosophical issues far better than I. Both of these dear friends are long gone, and I miss them greatly, although I chance to meet them now and again in a line or phrase about which we once contended mightily.

I also thank my university for allowing me to teach Milton through more than four decades, even when my publications went on appearing in twentieth-century studies. In ways that have kept me more hopeful, even "youthful" perhaps, my students have responded to Milton's great story in ways that I cherish, as much for the cogency and passion of their debates as for the professionalism of their papers, often far in advance of their years, some appearing in journals while they were still undergraduates.

Most vividly, I recall Martin Kuester coming as a doctoral student from Germany to study at the University of Manitoba with our beloved colleague, the Canadian novelist Robert Kroetsch, only to find himself assigned by Kroetsch and his entrance committee to fill an historical gap in Milton. "I came here to study Canadian literature," he grumbled initially, though in the end he returned to Germany to write his *Habilitation* on Milton – now available in translation as *Milton's Prudent Ambiguities: Words and Signs in His Poetry and Prose* (Academic Press of America, 2009). Just as vividly, I recall Reinhold Kramer, who, a year or two before Kuester, spoke with growing brilliance in our Milton seminar and later, as a tenured professor, wrote two stimulating essays on my own debt to *Paradise Lost* in fiction. Both of these good friends credit Milton as I do for giving us an uncommon perspective on literature from Homer to last week's bestseller.

Once again, to Dr Reinhold Kramer, professor of Canadian literature and film at Brandon University, and to Dr Robert Smith, professor of theatre and drama at the University of Manitoba, I am grateful for their reading of this book at every stage of its production. Their generous criticisms and words of encouragement have come to me so often like breaths of fresh air, bearing life-giving oxygen to my tired literary blood. I am more grateful to them than these few words can say.

I am indebted as well to my former mentor and academic advisor John J. Teunissen who introduced me to Milton half a century ago. Last but not least, I want to express my gratitude to my editor and helmsman Jonathan Crago, who brought this vessel safely through the clashing rocks and swirling eddies of Scylla and Charybdis.

I wish it were possible to name the several readers for the press who shared their vast wealth of knowledge. Responsibility for any remaining errors is mine alone.

A NOTE ON ARCHIVAL SOURCES, ABBREVIATIONS, AND SPELLINGS

MOST OF MY QUOTATIONS FROM Leveller booklets and pamphlets come from originals that are available online from the British Library through Early English Books Online (EEBO). A copy of the first edition of William Walwyn's *The Compassionate Samaritan* (July 1644) was very kindly provided to me by Stephen Tabor, curator of early printed books at the Huntington Library in San Marino, California. All Leveller documents are noted in the text or endnotes, either by their date of publication, or else by their known date of acquisition by George Thomason, the London bookseller and friend of John Milton.

The weekly journalism of Marchamont Nedham, appearing over the better part of two decades in *Mercurius Britanicus* (from 12 September 1643 to 18 May 1646); in *Mercurius Pragmaticus* (21 September 1647 to 1 May 1649); and in *Mercurius Politicus* (13 June 1650 to 12 April 1660), has likewise been obtained through EEBO from online copies made available by the British Library. I abbreviate the titles of these weekly newsbooks as follows: *Britanicus*; *Pragmaticus*; and *Politicus*.

Attribution of several Leveller pamphlets remains contested. Space does not allow for resolution of these questions in my text; the reader will find answers in a dozen or so endnotes, all of which are locatable in the Index, where "authorship" is a recurrent entry for titles such as *Regall Tyrannie Discovered*, *Vox Plebis*, and *Tyranipocrit*.

The Yale edition of *The Complete Prose Works of John Milton* (abbreviated *CPW* and volume number) remains the definitive edition, at least until completion of the Oxford edition, under the general editorship of Laura Lunger Knoppers.

The text I have chosen for its fidelity to Milton's poetry is *The Riverside Milton*, ed. Roy Flannagan (Boston and New

York: Houghton Mifflin, 1998), notwithstanding its priscian concern at times about minor questions of punctuation.

Seventeenth-century spellings in all their variant forms have been retained in quotations from documents peculiar to the era. This orthography mimics the experience of a world in flux where older, hierarchical forms of mediation in Church and state were beginning to be challenged by new reading communities, and where novel forms of political and religious communion were finding progressive embodiment in print.

MILTON'S LEVELLER GOD

The increasing influence of print has been reflected in republicanism with the bias toward constitutions and documents and guarantees of freedom of the press and of the right of the individuals.

Harold Innis, *The Bias of Communication*

We now live in the early part of an age for which the meaning of print culture is becoming as alien as the meaning of manuscript culture was to the eighteenth century.

Marshall McLuhan, *The Gutenberg Galaxy*

The various degrees of difference in the languages from the same stock, would have to be expressed by groups subordinated to groups, but the proper or even only possible arrangement would still be genealogical; and this would be strictly natural, as it would connect together all languages, extinct and modern, by the closest affinities, and would give the filiation and origin of each tongue.

Charles Darwin, *On the Origin of Species*

INTRODUCTION

IN THE SUDDEN VACUUM of legitimate authority in England in 1647–49, the Levellers came quite close to enshrining *An Agreement of the People*[1] as the written constitution of the republic, guaranteeing government by consent, legal and political equality, and religious freedom. "Common to all versions of the *Agreement* was a call for a broadened franchise, electoral redistribution according to population, liberty of conscience in religious matters, the dissolution of the Long Parliament, fresh elections every one or two years, and a list of powers that were reserved by the people to themselves."[2] David Wootton describes the result as an original attempt "to construct a liberal state," where ideas of "government by consent" and "inalienable rights" nearly overturned an ancient culture of social deference based on historical precedent.[3] But lingering social differences in the Army Debates at Putney in 1647 rendered the first *Agreement* stillborn; thereafter, men of property contrived to out-manoeuvre enlistees from a volunteer army and an emerging class of urban migrants. Both of these latter groups belonged to a changing social order where "egalitarian principles made sense" (Wootton, 81), and where men were "free to choose their masters, and free, in principle, to become employers themselves. And this," as Wootton sums up the turbulent decade of the 1640s, "was characteristic of the Leveller movement as a whole: it demanded a right to choose its rulers, rather than to rule" (82). Or, as the royalist newsbook *Mercurius Pragmaticus* phrased it, "the word *People* admits all in general to have *voices* in *selection,* which utterly destroyes all ancient *Order.*"[4]

But the English harbingers of Jefferson, Paine, and Voltaire were three centuries or more ahead of their time,[5] and Cromwell crushed them with the same ferocity that he unleashed against Irish Catholics in 1649–50. So these populist republicans dropped out of sight and were largely forgotten until the twentieth century. And yet their radical ideas and language survive in the most unlikely place – in the epic poems of John Milton, the man whom David Masson, Milton's nineteenth-century biographer, sought to portray on the model of Oliver Cromwell as an "heroic Puritan." As Catherine G. Martin recalls in *Milton Among the Puritans*, "Thomas Carlyle popularized the highly romanticized portrait of the 'Puritan Revolution' that inspired Masson, Carlyle's great admirer and disciple." She specifies that, "He accomplished this primarily through his immensely influential edition of Cromwell's letters and speeches (1845), which … is a literally fictional 'Cromwelliad,' a German Romantic, anti-democratic, and far from accurate portrait of the faith of Carlyle's forefathers."[6] From the state letters that Milton wrote for Cromwell to foreign powers, Masson somehow imagined that "one hardly knows which is speaking, the secretary or the ruler. Cromwell melts into Milton and Milton is Cromwell eloquent and latinizing."[7]

A more accurate portrait of Milton might be better drawn on the model of Wootton's Levellers, at least to the extent that both insisted on the necessity of choice in public and private matters, and each broke with Cromwell (one more publicly than the other) on the crucial issue of liberty of conscience.[8] Milton's argument for freedom of the press, for instance, assumes that God entrusts man "with the gift of reason to be his own chooser … for reason is but choosing."[9] As for liberty of individual conscience, God himself declares in *Paradise Lost* that "(Reason also is choice) / Useless and vain, of freedom … despoild" (3.108–9).[10] "Not free, what proof could" any "have givn sincere / Of true allegiance, constant Faith or Love" (3.103–4)? As for people's freedom to choose their own rulers, Milton argued in his first major polemic, *Of Reformation in England* (1641), that "the ancient election of Bishops … could not lawfully be without the consent of the people," and that, "This voyce of the people to be had ever in Episcopall elections was so well known … even to those that were without the Church, that the Emperor *Alexander Severus* desir'd to have his governours of Provinces chosen in the same manner."[11]

As in the church, so in the state: Milton would later argue in *The Tenure of Kings and Magistrates* (1649) that "all men naturally were borne free" and that, despite "*Adams* transgression," "either to one, … or to more then one whom they thought of equal deserving … they chose above the rest … Not to be their Lords and Maisters … but, to be thir Deputies and Commissioners."[12] By contrast with other nominally "Puritan" writings, both Milton's prose and his poetry demonstrate a "comparatively cool suspension of judgment," Catherine Martin explains, "that marks what critics frequently call Milton's 'poetics of choice'" (3). Together with the Leveller social heresy[13] about humanity's "right to choose its rulers, rather than to rule," Milton advocates for religious heresy (Gk. *hairesis*, "choice") – where believers are required to give a *reasoned* account of their beliefs – an idea which is fundamental to his poetics of choice. Calling *Paradise Lost* "a heresy machine," Nigel Smith recalls how his poetics grew out of Milton's "very position on heresy – in itself unusual in his time – as the act of choosing by the believer when confronted by the evidence in the first and second scriptures: the Bible and the Book of Nature."[14] Axiomatically, then, Milton's views on liberty of conscience and religious toleration elevate the act of choosing to the status of *true heresy*.

Even under Cromwell, Milton held fast to "liberty of conscience" and freedom of choice as the *sine qua non* of toleration. David Masson, that unabashed Cromwellian, still had to admit of the sonnet "To the Lord General Cromwell, May 1652" that it was "an expression of Milton's utter dislike of the Church policy" of Cromwell's former chaplain John Owen "and his colleagues as urged in their Fifteen Proposals" for an established church with clergy to be maintained by the State. "The closing lines of the Sonnet leave little doubt," Masson observes, "that it was precisely the policy of Absolute Religious Voluntaryism, entire disconnexion of Church and State, that Milton ventured to recommend to Cromwell."[15] In the end, however, Cromwell would opt for religious uniformity in a state church "with such fervour of conviction and such persistence of effort that History has now to remember the conservation of a Church Establishment in England as one of the distinctions of the Oliverian Protectorate" (Masson, 228). In large part the republic was sacrificed on the altar of religious uniformity. So one word must be added to Martin's otherwise just conclusion that Milton's "dedication to fuller religious toleration [further] distanced him not just from Cromwell, his Independents, and the Army, but also from the Puritan establishment in both church and state which had so disappointed his hopes" (87). A year after Cromwell's death, Milton's disaffection with the Protector remained on public display in *The Likeliest Means to Remove Hirelings Out of the Church* (August 1659) – "hireling" echoing his old friend Roger Williams (1652) in support of "Religous Voluntaryism" in *Hireling Ministry None of Christ's* (227).

Toleration had been a bone of contention between Army officers and the Levellers even before Pride's Purge. A Committee of Sixteen (four each from the Levellers, the Army, Parliament, and City Independents) met "whole nights together" in late November 1648 at Windsor Castle, clashing with Cromwell's son-in-law Henry Ireton in tense debates "*about Liberty of Conscience, and the Parliaments punishing where no law provides*," before reaching what Lilburne thought was "*an absolute and final conclusion … But alas, poor fools, we were meerly cheated and cozened.*"[16] Reconvening at Whitehall[17] in the wake of Pride's Purge (6 Dec. 1648), Lilburne wrote, "[T]here came the *General, Cromwel*, and the whole gang of Creature-Colonels, and other officers, and spent many dayes in taking it all in pieces" (*Legal*, 39).[18] In debate, the civilian Leveller John Wildman "argued that the reason why the magistrate should not be allowed to choose the religion of his subjects was simple: there was no reason to be confident he would choose aright. Such choices were best left in the hands of each and every individual" (Wootton, "The Levellers," 76). But, as Barbara Taft recalls, Ireton was "defeated, 27:17, on the proposal to give the representative final judgment in 'Morall' as well as in 'civil' matters, although he carried a majority opposed to including religion among the reserved rights, 37:12."[19] Most of the junior officers at Whitehall valued liberty of conscience above the Grandee project of religious uniformity – one of the many reasons why Oliver Cromwell, MP, never moved to discuss the Officers' *Agreement* after its submission to the House on 20 January. Ian Gentles rightly judges that it "represented the most radical constitutional position that the New Model Army officers would ever take" in its unstated assumption that England would be "a republic without a king, house of peers or coercive established church."[20] Yet it was set aside by the Rump as unwarranted meddling in its affairs.[21]

Had Milton been appointed in time to take part in the Whitehall Debates, his principles would have put him on the side of civilian Levellers and junior officers, but his government post was still three months off. Yet his principles clearly overlap with those of the Levellers in at least two key areas: freedom to choose one's secular and spiritual leaders; and liberty of conscience. Though other people – Roger Williams and Henry Vane come to mind – shared the same principles, they left no hint of their Leveller sympathies. Only Milton is suspected on occasion of harbouring such sentiments,[22] although the evidence has remained elusive. In personal terms, he neither wrote, nor mentioned, nor spoke to the jailed Lt-Col John Lilburne, nor to Richard Overton, printer, nor to William Walwyn, merchant, these three being widely acknowledged as the leaders of a proto-democratic political movement in London at the time. So why do echoes of their language and ideas resound in Milton's political prose in the same way that Nigel Smith says Milton's prose "echoes originally in the voices of Adams and Jefferson," as well as in "the American constitution"?[23]

Areopagitica (Nov. 1644) was the first of his prose works to resonate with echoes of the future Leveller William Walwyn from *The Compassionate Samaritan* (July 1644). Since Walwyn's defence of the sectaries' right to speak and worship freely was published four months before *Areopagitica*, it deserves to be recognized as an important source for Milton's great argument "for the liberty of unlicens'd printing" (see Chapter 1 below), the hybrid character of which actually unsettles David Norbrook's formalist claim that the "tension on [Milton's] title-page between the democratic implications of the Theseus speech and his idiosyncratic title, *Areopagitica* … serves as a reassurance that this new polity need not lapse into complete chaos, that it possesses controls on pure democracy." Recalling that "the Areopagus was a vestigial element of an older, aristocratic constitution, a body which censored morals and served as a counterweight to the democratic Assembly,"[24] Norbrook takes Milton's title page as the political equivalent of a civic form by which the wise "few" could bridle the wild impulses of the "many."

Milton's highly allusive and deeply learned argument for freedom of speech suggests the opposite, however, in making the monarch confer a right to speak on "*free born men.*" Particularly in London, where John "Lilburne himself had been nicknamed 'free-born John' at the time of his earliest public defiance of the authorities in 1638,"[25] "free born" is a loaded phrase, spurring an evolution of identity from subject to citizen. Equally telling is the context of the phrase translated from Euripides's *The Suppliants*: "*This is true Liberty, when free born men / Having to advise the public may speak free, / Which he who can, and will, deserv's high praise.*"[26] Access to humanist learning, like "differential access"[27] to reason for the ancients, need not confer a monopoly of power. The native abilities of "free born men" – those sectaries and vernacular-Bible readers whose political rights Walwyn defends in *The Compassionate Samaritan* – are deemed to be of "public" worth. Even an Athenian king speaks like a republican: "What can be juster in a State then this [to speak freely]"? The politics of translation thus transforms what Norbrook, in *Writing the English Republic*, calls "the public implications of all speech" (11) by setting demotic speakers among the classical elite. A Greek ruler joins the English populist John Lilburne and a bible-reading Walwyn in a discourse on *res publica*, in which vernacular voices become as free and equal as any in Latin and Greek. And the persistence in Milton's political prose and epic poetry of these demotic, vernacular voices offers a subtle if tenacious challenge to the accepted notion of an "aristocratic republic" in Milton's writing where "concessions to radical groups would be counterbalanced by the political influence of aristocratic magnates" (158).[28]

As Jonathan Scott rightly comments, "No seventeenth-century republican wrote in one political language only, and most combined several, spanning the intellectual terrains of humanism, Christianity, science and law."[29] So a purely "linguistic methodology" (36) is not likely to reveal more than "the form of a contemporary text" (9). Norbrook's reading is thus premature in its assumption that, because "The printed press has made possible an equivalent of the classical forum" (129), "the classical *polis*" appears in *Areopagitica* "as a realm where modern divisions between public and private, between individual and state, were overcome (for the free male, at least) in the forum" (141). For, if the Areopagus is truly a formal "counterweight," free speech is only a formal pretense.

These social tensions are not reduced but magnified for Scott by the "historiographical disassociation between" the "classically informed political republicanism" of the English revolution "and its religiously inspired social radicalism" (xi). Most historians of classical republicanism tend to view it as a logically superior, "secular, or secularising, ideological force," although "the late Christopher Hill, had ideological preoccupations" as a Marxist "which led him to be less interested in classical republicans than in plebeian sectaries. The eventual exception to this rule was Milton, portrayed by Hill as a plebeian 'heretic' rather than a Christian humanist" (xi). Scott attempts to bridge these class divisions, both ancient and modern, by making the bible, as much as Plato, Aristotle, and Cicero, the cradle of English republicanism, thus revealing in the work of Milton and others a synthesis based not merely "upon political language, or constitutional form, but upon Christian humanist moral philosophy applied in the practical context of an attempted radical reformation of manners" (x). In countless examples, Scott shows that English republicanism defined "itself primarily in relation, not to constitutional structures, but moral principles" (151). And most of these principles – arising equally from the bible and rational Greek moral philosophy – invariably constellated "a politics of virtue" (9, 170).

For such reasons, Paul Rahe takes Milton to be the paradigmatic classical republican in England, inasmuch as "he presented himself as a Christian Aristotelian who believed not only that Christian virtue and the moral virtues prized in pagan times could be made compatible, but that together they provided the only proper foundation for the political virtue required in a republic" (119). Rahe supposes that it is not the bible but Christian Aristotelianism that matters most in Milton's *res publica.* For Aristotle, it was "man's capacity for reasoned speech (*lógos*)" (23) that created "a political community distinct from a household" by enabling a shift from "*res privata*" to the "middle ground" of *res publica* "within which to deliberate concerning the transcendent common good" (29). If *res publica* were firmly set upon a foundation of reason and speech, it would be futile to challenge the humanist principle of "the unequal distribution of reason among men and the significance of this distribution with regard to their capacity for political speech … In both *De inventione* and in *De oratore*, Cicero stresses that, in developing his potential for *ratio et oratio*, such a *vir sapiens* can come to 'surpass' other human beings in the very sphere in which they are most superior to the other animals" (24).

In "so fervent a believer in the power of *ratio et oratio*" as Milton was "to create and shape a community of moral discourse … transcending mere material interest," Rahe maintains, a populist politics is surely precluded by "the classical republican principle of differential moral and political rationality" (107). This classical principle had been firmly buttressed in the late Middle Ages by Christian teaching when Marsilius of Padua worked out the definitive Christian Aristotelian "apology for the secular power against the divine-right claims of the papal monarchy" by appealing, as Milton also did, "to the principle of popular consent" (112). But Marsilius "circumscribed" the "democratic potential" of popular consent "by conferring on the people's '*valentior pars*' – their sturdier, healthier, more vigorous, more resourceful, and weightier part – a right to legislate on behalf of the whole" (113). This was the argument, Rahe rightly claims, that Milton would employ in *Defensio*, where "he insisted that 'the true power of the people resided' at the time of Charles I's execution in 'the better qualified, that is the more reasonable, part of the legislature (*Senatûs pars potior, id est sanior*)'" (110). "Whatever John Milton may have been," Rahe bluntly concludes, "he was not a modern populist" (118). Yet others have noted a pervasive element of collective ennoblement in the classical principle of differential moral and political rationality. As Jonathan Scott says, "Morally it centred upon an idea of rational self-government, within the commonwealth and the soul, present from Plato to Sallust, Cicero, and Tacitus. This was combined by English writers with a Christian natural law language with its own emphasis upon the moral implications of human rationality" (Scott, 152). No matter the possessor, it was this collective expression of human rationality that had invariably dignified classical republican rule.

For Rahe, however, English classical republicanism was offset by Marchamont Nedham, a disciple of Niccolò Machiavelli who saw the "cause of moral virtue" (168) as a sham. The Machiavellian republicanism of Nedham differed, Rahe believes, from the "high-minded" classical republicanism of his friend John Milton by "the spirit of political distrust" (237) resulting from the Florentine's premise that "all men are wicked" (235). Indeed, "the guardianship of the people" over "the general good" was defensible only because "ordinary folk possess a defect in appetite" for domination and acquisition. Populist republican rule is thus possible "simply and solely because the general good is … indistinguishable from" the common people's "'own interest.' Such a coincidence of their own self-interest and the good of the whole cannot, however, be attributed to the grandees" (236). In this deeply sceptical philosophy, "the many" are not better by virtue of "their moral superiority" over an aristocratic "few," but rather by close regard for their "own self-interest." Lacking in ambition, the *many* thus serve as a curb on the ambitious *few*. So Milton, unquestionably the champion of the virtuous few, Rahe assumes,

> was himself a political moralist of the sort most abhorrent to Machiavelli: whatever doubts he may privately have entertained, to the public, he presented himself as a Christian Aristotelian who believed not only that Christian virtue and the moral virtues prized in pagan times could be made compatible, but that together they provided the only proper foundation for the political virtue required in a republic. (119)

If Milton believed in a politics of virtue as the basis of English republicanism, so did his friend Sir Henry Vane, as well as others like Algernon Sidney, Edmund Ludlow, and John Streater. In his *Defense of the English People* (1651), Milton argued that "Plato in the *Laws* says it is law which ought to be the most powerful in the state, and in his *Letters* praises that form of government where law is ruler and king over men; and not men, tyrants over the law."[30] But Jonathan Scott recalls that such ideas were just as readily adopted by the advocates of popular sovereignty: "Thus Levellers as well as republicans juxtaposed the 'Lusts and wills of tyrants' imposing 'insufferable bondage and slavery,' to the 'originall reason' of government by 'Law'" (152). If it is Law, and not men, that rules under good government, and if reason, not persons, is the sole legislator, then "the many" would surely have reason to choose the "best" to rule them, while retaining their inherent power to consent, dissent, or question rulers by virtue of their collective reason.[31]

The Leveller *Regall Tyrannie Discovered* (6 January 1647) says as much in an abstract

> shewing that all lawfull (approbational) instituted power by GOD amongst men, is by common agreement, and mutual consent. Which power (in the hands of whomsoever) ought alwayes to be exercised for the good, benefit, and welfare of the Trusters, and never ought other wise to be administred: Which, whensoever it is, it is justly resistable and revokeable; It being against the light of Nature and Reason, and the end wherefore God endowed Man with understanding, for any sort or generation of men to give so much power into the hands of any man or men whatsoever, as to enable them to destroy them. (1)

The surprise is not that populists could share with republicans this moral value drawn from rational Greek moral philosophy that, "To replace kingship, and with it dependence upon the will of fallen man, by the self-government of God-given reason, was the nearest mankind could come to the government of God" (Scott, 60). It is rather that Milton's *The Tenure of Kings and Magistrates* (Feb. 1649) would sound so much like the Leveller tract, not only in its moral principle of self-government by "God-given reason" but in most of its arguments from history, its proof-texts from scripture, and even its specific wordings.

Supposedly written by Lilburne,[32] *Regall Tyrannie* is premised on Parliament's theory of natural law[33] in its *Book of Declarations* – in reality two large tomes published in 1643 and 1646, from which "John Lilburne quoted," as Ann Hughes recalls, "almost as much as from the Bible."[34] By contrast, "The lawfulness of resistance to tyrants" in Milton's *Tenure* "was illustrated not only from scripture, from ancient Greece and Rome, and from the history of England, but from the works of Buchanan, Grotius and Hotman" (Scott, 194). Yet, despite its broader range of reference from humanist sources, Milton's opening paragraph sets the same tone as the opening of *Regall Tyrannie.* Although Merritt Y. Hughes would admit that "In *The Tenure* there is much that recalls the political slogans and thinking of the Levellers," he still hedged his bet: "How deeply Milton was moved by the abuse of the Levellers' appeal to the people as arbiters of the application of the law of reason (or simply reason itself) to the reform of the laws and the constitution is an unanswerable question."[35] And yet, from its opening sentence onward, *The Tenure* does manifest his sympathy with a Leveller version of the appeal to reason:

> If men within themselves would be govern'd by reason, and not generally give up thir understanding to a double tyrannie, of Custom from without, and blind affections within, they would discerne better, what it is to favour and uphold the Tyrant of a Nation. But being slaves within doors, no wonder that they strive so much to have the public State conformably govern'd to the inward vitious rule, by which they govern themselves.[36]

Milton even exceeds the Leveller political calculus by exposing a "double tyrannie" of "Custom from without, and blind affections within," both of which are surely fatal to self-government via the faculty of God-given reason. Being "slaves within doors" to their own lusts, Milton asks, is it any wonder that they should become slaves to "the 'Lusts and wills of tyrants' imposing 'insufferable bondage and slavery,'" as the Levellers had likewise maintained, "to the 'originall reason' of government by 'Law'" (Scott, 152).

It was the sheer abundance of Leveller echoes in Milton's prose that drove me to read through the British Library's massive collection of Leveller documents online (EEBO), together with others from the Huntington Library. By typing up my own copies of each work, I compiled a searchable database that makes it possible to track countless verbal echoes, conceptual links, and summary arguments from Leveller sources in Milton's prose. The surprise is that his epic poetry contains rather more of them. Still, as Jonathan Scott warns, "to identify the terminology deployed by a writer is not thereby to determine the use to which it was being put" (9). I then have two reasons in Chapter 1 for tracing verbal and conceptual parallels between Walwyn's *Samaritan* and Milton's *Areopagitica,* between the anonymous *Regall Tyrannie* and Milton's *Tenure*, and between the two parts of Lilburne's *Englands New Chaines* and Milton's two-headed *History of Britain*, with its unpublished "Digression": first, to fathom the notable depth of Milton's sympathy with Leveller principles; and second, to assess his dramatic use of such language in his epics. In a moment of historical drama that represents his own and the nation's moment of crucial choice, I attempt to explain why Milton opted in that instant for a classical, rather than a Leveller, version of the English republic, a choice he would come to regret.

By 1650 or 1651, Milton was linked to that quondam Leveller and sometime Machiavellian republican, Marchamont Nedham, some of whose views, as Blair Worden shows,[37] were shared by Milton. Here, it is expedient to read, as Worden does, the prose of both men as classical republicans who, like Sallust, challenged the rise of a military dictator such as Sulla or Julius Caesar. In a second database, compiled from well over a decade's worth of journalism by this "great crony of *Milton*,"[38] I find startling evidence that Nedham and his licenser, the great defender of the English people, were warning readers on a weekly basis from October 1651 through January 1652 of a mounting threat to the young republic from the new "Caesar." In Chapter 2, I offer an original account of why Milton lost his job as a state "censor," not as is commonly supposed for having licensed the heretical *Racovian Catechism*, but for having attempted through two dozen issues of *Mercurius Politicus* to depose Cromwell before he could usurp the "throne."

Nedham, an Oxford man, had already made common cause with the Levellers in the summer of 1646, soon after he was sacked by Parliament as the editor of *Mercurius Britanicus*.[39] His friendships with both Lilburne and Milton temper any temptation to reduce the poet to that "plebeian 'heretic'" which Scott (xi) says Christopher Hill made of him, although Milton was rather more radical than Hill had supposed, yet largely failed to demonstrate, in *Milton and the English Revolution* (1977). David Norbrook (1998) makes a contrary, if self-contradictory, case for Milton as both a classical[40] and a Machiavellian republican following the principle set out in the "*Discourses* that: 'For the maintenance of a Religion or Commonwealth long in being, it is necessary oftentimes to reduce them to their first grounds'" (97). For Milton, as Rahe insists, was never a Machiavellian republican (104), nor ever attempted a "divine reduction to first principles"[41] in *Paradise Lost.* Not surprisingly, since Norbrook's view of Milton as a Lucanian iconcoclast and anti-Augustan makes him into a classical republican, Norbrook's reading of the poem typically marginalizes Adam and Eve, much as the "classical republican principle of differential moral and political rationality" (Rahe, 104, 107) had always marginalized the masses. By contrast, Worden argues for Milton's definitive repudiation of the rule of the "best" – Cromwell &

Co. – by 1654, while tracing some of the radical effects of Milton's literary collaboration with Nedham.

Jonathan Scott deepens the case for Nedham as the missing link between Milton and the Levellers in noting that, "before he became a royalist and then a republican journalist, he was a Lilburne-associated pamphleteer" (245). As Scott recognizes, it is the "broader function of both Milton's and Nedham's writing during the 1640s to underline the close relationship between Leveller and republican ideas" (248). What my database from Nedham's journalism suggests is that his Leveller brand of republicanism survived well into the 1650s, and helped (for Milton, at least) to mitigate the disaster of the Restoration by transforming his deep ambivalence in prose about classical or Leveller republicanism into an active, if discreet, dramatization in his epic poetry of God as the head Leveller.

In this context, I must add that Joad Raymond's chapter on Marchamont Nedham in *The Oxford Handbook of Literature and the English Revolution* (2012) makes no mention of collaboration between Nedham and Milton in the 1650s. Raymond, whose doctoral work was supervised by David Norbrook, explains Nedham's fluid political allegiances as a logical consequence of his "support of religious toleration,"[42] while staying clear of what Worden maintains is hidden collaboration between the journalist and his licenser. In any event, Worden deals mostly with Milton's prose in relation to *Politicus* and avoids the major poems, apart from *Samson Agonistes.* So I pick up the thread of the epic poetry in Chapter 3 and after to braid it with the Leveller prose, in order to depict an unrecognized champion of liberal democracy whose theological heresies were for a long time hidden in the glare of his epic grandeur, and whose social and political heresies went unnoticed as well, despite his radical theology of sonship (Smith, *Is Milton Better*, 129–30), his metaphysics of liberty, his world-altering materialism, and his Leveller-inflected vision of natural equality.

Since other readers have been sceptical of Worden's case for Milton as a defender of the English republic against the Lord Protector, they are less likely still to see him as a Leveller republican. Paul Stevens, for one, is aghast at "the speed with which" classical republican critics have adopted this new "orthodoxy" that Milton renounced Cromwell before the Lord Protector's death in 1658.[43] In particular, he takes issue with an article by Martin Dzelzainis arguing for Milton's return in the spring of that year to the company of republicans like Bradshaw and Vane, whose principles had forced them to retire from politics in 1653. Rejecting the traditional view that Milton effectively fell silent for five years – from February 1654, the publication date of *Defensio Secunda* with its panegyric of Cromwell, until February 1659, when the protectoral regime of Oliver's son Richard began to crumble – Dzelzainis argues that Milton's edition of *The Cabinet-Council*, in reality an unattributed Elizabethan compilation, was published in early 1658 to offer "the Protector an image of what he had become."[44] As "an advice book to Cromwell," supposedly written by Sir Walter Raleigh, it was actually meant to operate ironically "as a mirror for the prince." Since "*The Cabinet-Council* was … corrupt advice for a corrupt prince … the point of publishing it may in part have been to reassure doubters that he had indeed remained true to his earlier commitments" (Dzelzainis, 201).

Stevens does have some reason to doubt the "tenuous" nature of the evidence used by Dzelzainis to turn Milton's edition of "Raleigh's" *Cabinet-Council* (1658) into public notice of his return to the republican fold. For Stevens is able to show that the Latin epigraph that Milton took from Horace actually works to praise, not to criticize, the military commander, since it evidently "refers not to Cromwell but to Raleigh" (373). Stevens further suggests that the "national" figure of Raleigh better reflects "the unfolding drama of England's providential history" (380) through the "necessity" (379) of a defensive war in 1658 with Spain; and that most of the pithy maxims, adapted from the *Discorsi* of Machiavelli, are the same ones "recorded with so much enthusiasm by Milton in his *Commonplace Book* in 1651–52" (384). So it is not Milton's supposed republicanism, Stevens insists, but rather his "Protestant nationalism … that best explains … his loyalty to Cromwell and his decision to publish a book of aphorisms by Sir Walter Raleigh in the midst of a war against England's enemies" (392).

While Stevens may have a strong case for Raleigh and his "cabinet-council" in the context of England's war with Spain, his larger target is the mode of interpretation that underwrites the premise of a "republican" Milton. As he notes in his preamble, "One of the essays that seems to have helped confirm Worden and other republican critics in the accuracy of their interlinear speculations is what Worden describes as Martin Dzelzainis's 'remarkable' article on Milton's subversive publication of Sir Walter Raleigh's *Cabinet-Council* in 1658" (364). Oddly, however, Stevens is just as guilty of assuming his conclusions as he supposes "republican critics" to be. Dismissing Dzelzainis's "interlinear speculations" which are "tenuous" if "crucial piece[s] of evidence for Milton's renunciation of Cromwell" (365), Stevens proceeds to pair the names "Milton and Cromwell," as if to imply an equivalence in their thought: for example, "One of the many convictions that Milton and Cromwell inherited" (373); "While both Milton and Cromwell were secular enough" (374); "At the center of Raleigh's great providential drama, in a way that always seems to inhibit the secular and pragmatic responses of Milton and Cromwell, is the ideological significance of Spain" (376). My point is not that Stevens is mistaken in what Spain represented to the Lord Protector or even to the Latin Secretary, but rather that his own rhetorical method of paralleling texts by Cromwell and Milton is a covert version of the same "interlinear speculations" that he rejects in the work of others. In defence of this rhetorical pairing of "Cromwell and Milton," he even quotes Milton's biographer (or is it hagiographer?) David Masson to the effect that, "in so many of these letters, 'one hardly knows which is speaking, the secretary or the ruler. Cromwell melts into Milton and Milton is Cromwell eloquent and latinizing" (381).

Contrary to this rhetorical method, the "interlinear" method of Dzelzainis is at least in keeping with a very respectable "list of those who think that Milton did renounce, if not necessarily Cromwell himself, then at least his works," placing him firmly in the company of a number of important twentieth-century critics that "includes J.S. Smart, Don M. Wolfe, Barbara Lewalski, Michael Fixler and, most recently and persuasively, Austin Woolrych" ("Protectorate," 183–4). But for Stevens, there can only be one "key essay in this critical movement," the "recent" one by "Austin Woolrych" (364, n2). Stevens thus aims to insert himself into the critical lineage of Masson, whose Victorian mythologizing left us with the haloed portraits of seventeenth-century Puritan "saints."

Whatever its Horatian failings regarding Raleigh, the case of Dzelzainis for Milton's "renunciation" of the Lord Protector in 1658 is worth another look. From the appearance of *The Cabinet-Council* in the spring until Cromwell's death on 3 September, Dzelzainis shows that Milton was occupied with preparing a new edition of *Defensio*, in order "to voice opposition to the retrograde tendencies of the Protectorate, and to warn against the drift back to monarchical forms." This "did not require a reformulation of his views: all that it required was a reiteration of views he had previously held."[45] As fate would have it, Cromwell died before the edition was published, making it seem less a critique of the Protectorate than a sign of Milton's desire to return to the republican fold. To Stevens, however, Milton must be counted as one of Cromwell's greatest admirers, sharing his vision of "England's providential history" as a godly check on the Spanish

Anti-Christ. Stevens makes Milton a traditional Protestant nationalist, "longing for a national hero"[46] on the model of Raleigh, or (better yet) Cromwell, or (briefly) George Monck. Stevens thus depicts a Milton more along the lines of Cromwell himself, whose "sanctification or providential *virtù* is understood as ... a function of his moral education." This Milton is almost scandalously willing to assert the need of "a strong hand" to realize "the potential of the English people to be educated into true liberty, and so realize their destined end, in the custody of the Lord Protector."[47] The "imagined community"[48] of Stevens's Milton requires, in no uncertain terms, "an educated elite"[49] to form a moral aristocracy of virtue.

To such readers, a populist Milton, as compared to this more aristocratic[50] avatar, will be no more acceptable than Worden's Milton, who degenerates into a rank "collaborator" with Nedham, the turncoat journalist. Having dismissed "interlinear speculations" out of hand, the party of "virtue" is most unlikely to accept "the highly circumstantial and speculative nature of the evidence"[51] presented in Chapter 2 below of Milton's dismissal as Nedham's licenser for political, not for religious reasons. My argument, however, neither stands nor falls on that likely inference, although it does radicalize Worden's portrait of Milton by advancing the date of his break with Cromwell to *before* the Protectorate.[52] For that ultimate rejection of Cromwell, whatever its date, helps to explain why the portrait of Satan in *Paradise Lost* resonates with a distinctly Leveller language of "hatred and mistrust" of Cromwell, and why its opposing portrait of God pulsates with suggestions of Leveller decentralization and political liberalization. Chapter 1 then explores that deeply revealing moment in 1649 when Milton stood at the foot of his own Tree of Good and Evil, forced to choose between the Levellers – with whose ideas and language he was in sympathy, but who stood arraigned on capital charges of treason – and his good friends on the Council of State like John Bradshaw and Sir Henry Vane, who at least held out some hope of stable republican government. While it may not equate to Eve or Adam's "apple" moment in paradise, the evidence of Milton's *History of Britain* and both his epic poems will suggest that the greatest poet of the age had made a decision that he came to rue.

Before we turn in Chapter 1 to that fraught moment, however, where Milton is forced on the instant to choose between classical and Leveller forms of republicanism, there is a second problem of method to address. In view of Milton's vast learning and extraordinary range of citations – many in quotation marks, many more not – how is it possible to show that these

Leveller ideas and phrases that echo throughout Milton's work are not Leveller-*like* conclusions that he arrived at, as one of my readers would ask, by "alternative routes"?[53] This problem becomes more acute with respect to Milton's epic poetry, since Leveller prose rarely scans in blank verse; anyway, was Milton not blind for fifteen years before *Paradise Lost* was published? The best answers are usually writ large in plot, and it is Milton's plot that bears the clear signature of his Leveller thought. One flourish of this Leveller "hand" is the materialist heresy that he adapted from his reading of the future Leveller Richard Overton's *Mans Mortalitie* (1644) to affirm the intrinsic goodness of matter in its extraction from the "body" of God. Contrary to what Jonathan Scott thinks, Milton's faith in rational Greek moral philosophy was deeply shaken by the Restoration, and the story that he later recounted of Creation in Book 7 of *Paradise Lost* systematically undermines Plato's account of creation in the *Timaeus*, where pre-existent matter, "although possessing some traces" of its "own nature," such "as everything is likely to be in the absence of God," can only be made good by receiving its Form from the divine Reason. Of course, this fundamental ground in the humanist tradition on which the Idea of the Good rests crumbles as usual at the border of Form and Matter.

Matter without Reason in Plato's account of the Creation is no more than a rude lump until the forming hand of God can make it Good. As Plato's Timaeus describes created things, "God constructed them, so far as He could, to be as fair and good as possible,"[54] even if the materials of creation, suffering an elemental lack, are deficient in themselves. Such will be the case in all dualist philosophies where the Good is imposed from without, and matter (the masses, in political terms) is then constrained by external means. By contrast, the monist materialism of Milton's story of the origins of matter guarantees its inherent goodness by its "birth" from the divine "body." Here, a universe of created beings comes into existence through liberation from God's own matter. And it is the goodness of this "God-stuff," as Nicholas McDowell describes it, that "secures the natural liberty" of every individual who possesses it.[55] Nothing in the natural law theory which Parliament had adapted from Cicero[56] and his Stoic sources remotely resembles the heretical materialism that reaches *Paradise Lost* via Milton's reading of Overton's *Mans Mortalitie* and his adaptation of its vitalist materialism to the theology of *creatio ex Deo* in his *De Doctrina Christiana.*[57] Equally, it is categorically opposed to Machiavelli's universe, where "chaos is natural and the norm," in a world "constituted solely by matter in motion" where "order is as fragile as it is artificial."[58] If Lucretius's *De rerum natura* taught the Florentine Secretary the political lesson that a "spirit of political distrust" is necessary to control *grandi* ambition, Milton's vitalist philosophy of matter assured him that divine law and the law of nature are essentially the same.[59] So if the goodness of God is woven into the very warp and woof of matter, all of humankind must share in it. And this is only the first, most obvious, flourish of Milton's Leveller signature in the poem.

For classical English republicans, the fly in the ointment of the story of creation had to be the Fall, the failure of individuals and nations to preserve "self-government in the city and the soul" (Scott, 153). Supposedly for Milton and other classical republicans, "the loss of English liberty is the result of moral failure; of wickedness and vice; above all, of ignorance. This signalled the failure of the republican educational project; of the attempt to instil the public preference for substance over appearance, for virtue over vice; to equip a people for self-governing rationality" (Scott, 185). Yet Milton's story of the Fall climaxes in regeneration, while the very title of his sequel declares "paradise regained." So we need to ask whether the faculty of will matters more in his drama of "restoration" than the faculty of reason, that irreducible ground of rational Greek moral philosophy?

Here, one recognizes a second flourish of Milton's Leveller signature that, while shared by sectarian antinomians, had also been repurposed to political ends by Nedham in *Vox Plebis* (1646).[60] For the Fall is henceforth rendered "without consequence" by God's gift of "free grace,"[61] thereby neutralizing the toxic doctrine of original sin. "By denying that any were predestined to damnation," David Wootton concludes, "and by insisting that even sinners could be saved, it [the doctrine of free grace] opened the way to a new sense of the equality of all men in God's eyes, and thus made a democratic political theory plausible" ("Democracy," 437). Or, as Nedham had put the case with the logical elegance of a syllogism, "For as God created every man free in *Adam*, so by nature are all alike freemen born; and are since made free in grace by Christ: no guilt of the parent being of sufficiency to deprive the child of this freedome" (*Vox*, 4). The only question is whether fallen beings are able to accept the gift of "free grace." Here, in the estimate of another Leveller tract, it is truly the faculty of will, not reason,[62] that is decisive in the reception of free grace, at least insofar as "religion must bee a joyning of two free-wils in one."[63] But if human will is both in fact and deed free to unite itself with God's gift of grace, then the original moral failure in Eden need not be permanent. So, too, the moral failure of the republic may be as readily redeemed by the restorative power of "free grace."

This second flourish of a Leveller signature in Milton's epic poems has long been obscured, however, by a critical assumption of the poet's "pessimism concerning the personal qualities of parliamentarians and 'people'" (Scott, 276). Even in Worden's estimate, "The cast of Milton's mind is always ethical" as compared to "Nedham's," which is "always practical" (*Literature and Politics*, 226). That is why "Nedham is for the most part without Milton's pessimism. He still thinks it 'probable enough' that, 'after the death of Caesar,' the Romans 'might then have recovered their liberty.' What thwarted them was not the degeneracy of the majority but a practical error. They allowed power to remain in the triumvirate of Octavius, Antony, and Lepidus" (Worden, 235).

Although Scott and Worden's judgments are recent, this is the standard twentieth-century view of Milton's "commonwealth principles" established by Don M. Wolfe in *Milton in the Puritan Revolution* (1941). At the end of this influential work, Wolfe had concluded that "The bitterness and despair of 1660 confirmed and intensified the more aristocratic of Milton's political convictions."[64] For Wolfe, these convictions had nothing to do with a Leveller-inspired "consent of the governed" (344). To the contrary, Wolfe had imagined the disillusioned older poet moving towards a "conception of the rule of the virtuous" in all three realms of the "government of heaven" (343), the "government of the home" (344), and "man's government of himself." In the main, this relentlessly "puritan" conception of rule is "colored by the domination of superior virtue and wisdom" (345). So, Wolfe concludes, "Believing that 'Orders and Degrees jar not with liberty, but well consist,' that one's happiness lies in placing himself willingly under the government of reason or superior beings, Milton unhesitatingly ascribed the failures and tragedies of life to violations of his principle of government by the best" (346). The irony is that this moral judgment is thoughtlessly based on a *dramatic* speech of Satan, that quintessential aristocrat, who is made to represent *Milton*'s political philosophy not just in the polity of Hell but also in Heaven and on Earth, thereby fostering an enduring view of the "puritan" revolutionary so deeply disillusioned by the Restoration that he ended as a quietist, ultimately turning his back on politics to write of eternal, unchanging verities.

But Wolfe and his standard-bearers have failed to explain what makes Satan a reliable judge (in heaven or anywhere else) of "Orders and Degrees." Today, most critics take for granted the aristocratic politics of *Paradise Lost*, without realizing its *dramatic* bias. It is almost unthinkable in Milton studies to challenge "the winged Hierarch" for bringing his outdated, Trinitarian system of Neoplatonic thought to Eden. It is much easier to choose from obvious instances of *natural* inequality and egalitarian sentiments in Milton's early, "liberal" prose works than it is to explain why God would send an old-school "hierarch" to an egalitarian Eden. Wolfe deferred in his very title, of course, to the royalist caricature of a "Puritan Revolution," accepting its corollary that "sin meant also the victory of sex over reason" (348). In the end, the great editor of the Yale *Complete Prose* merely affirmed the validity of a profoundly anti-feminist, aristocratic philosophy[65] transplanted to paradise by "the winged Hierarch": "Raphael warns Adam against allowing the 'dear delight' of sense to overwhelm love" (345). The result is a reading quite as fatal for women as it has been for popular sovereignty: "In Milton's judgment of Adam we may trace his analysis of mankind's woes, including the suffering of his fellow-countrymen under a restored monarchy" (346).

And yet, despite his bleak conclusion that *Paradise Lost* offers better "justification of man's punishment" (350) than of "God's ways to men," Wolfe returns almost compulsively at the close of his study to Milton's "revolutionary fervor" of the 1640s, especially to those more hopeful arguments of *Areopagitica* "that would open all creeds to pitiless criticism, leaving no institution unchallenged, no social assumption static or secure" (351). But was it Milton or Wolfe who wrote better than he knew – sensing more, anyway, than his evidence could yet support – that, "In his justifications of democratic ideals, though he was not consistent or realistic in their application, he spoke best from the riches of his humanistic knowledge, arguing better than he knew for the 'miscellaneous rabble' of the Levellers and the Diggers" (351)?

Ernest Sirluck, who agreed with Wolfe about Milton's pessimism, would come to a similar conclusion that, "The poem's resumé of human history contains pathetically few traces of decent earthly happiness," attributing the lack to Milton's experience of a failed "work of reformation. To this he had sacrificed first his poetic plans, then his tranquility, many of his friendships, most of his fortune, his sight, and even his safety; and what was the result? God's commonwealth in England had failed, rather betrayed from within than overcome from without."[66] To be fair, Sirluck adds, "We grant the essence of Milton's justification to us of God's ways: if man's existence is to have significance he must be free, and all that he suffers is the result of his own abuse of this freedom" (27). Although Milton's defence of free will shows his moral and intellectual courage in "declining to seek final refuge in mystery" (28), Sirluck is "aware of the price Milton has paid for his refusal to take refuge in the always-available inscrutability of God's will" (27). He has no good answer to the question, "[W]hy should a God who needs nothing, being infinitely perfect, have insisted upon the work of creation" when "the vast majority will in fact be damned?" The lessons of history are demoralizing; the end will not justify the means.

In unexpected ways, however, *Paradise Lost* controverts that end once we recognize the poem as its own means of creating its imagined community.[67] For each time that it finds a "fit audience … though few" (7.31), and every time that its "fit audience" hears the poet "Sing with mortal voice, unchang'd / To hoarce or mute, though fall'n on evil dayes" (7.24–5), the more it appears that all is not lost, that the deathless hope of that "voice" arises out of the "song" itself. In the event, *Paradise Lost* turns into a song that reverberates with a multitude of echoes sounding above "the barbarous dissonance / Of *Bacchus*" and "that wilde Rout that tore the Thracian Bard / In *Rhodope*" (7.32–5). But it is no longer that tragic echo of Orpheus that once sounded in *Lycidas* – "And all their echoes mourn"[68] – but rather the echo of a far different history, one that has *yet to be imagined.* And this imagined community, as we know from Benedict Anderson, takes its shape, as much as its enduring vitality, from the birth of the newspaper and the novel.[69]

Among recent historians and critics, Blair Worden is unique in showing how such hopes for the nation were tied to the newsbook whose publication Milton supervised. According to Benedict Anderson (although Anderson's bias towards America and the eighteenth century forces him to overlook earlier developments in England), the printing press, the printman, and the invention of the newspaper were what first brought the modern nation into view (Anderson, 61–5), leaving readers to bring new national "communities" into existence. For Worden, the decisive factor was Milton's long-time collaboration with Marchamont Nedham in the fascinating story he unearths of Milton's efforts in prose to preserve a classical republican community free of a "single ruler." In Chapter 2, I explore further Milton's collaboration with Nedham on *Mercurius Politicus*, offering evidence of their astonishing attempt in 1651–52 to depose Cromwell and put the English republic back on a safer course. But it is in Milton's epic poetry where a new imagined community takes shape in terms shared both early and late with the London Levellers, but that he would be forced to compromise by his choice in 1649 of a "classical" over a "Leveller" republic, and then see turn remote by his continuing service to the Protectorate after 1653.

It is the prose writer, not the epic poet, however, who emerges from Worden's book on *Cromwellian England* (2007) as being much more radical than Worden had been willing thirty years before to credit in his review of Hill's book on networks of influence in Milton's political development.[70] The only person (though Worden doesn't say so) who was ever in a position to encourage Leveller sympathies in Milton was Nedham, whom he had befriended in his official capacity as his state licenser.[71] As Joad Raymond remarks of the appointment of this repentant royalist to a government post, "Nedham's value to the Commonwealth in 1649–50 involved his former sympathies with Levellers and royalists: he understood their perspectives, and knew their arguments and loyalties" ("Marchamont Nedham," 382). But since Raymond is silent on the effects of this appointment on Milton, it is Worden's book that constitutes the opening chapter in a yet-to-be-told story of Milton's radicalism – not in the 1640s but 1650s – in his daring resistance to Cromwell's monarchical tendencies in church and state – and then, more profoundly still, in his epic poetry begun before, but only completed after, the Restoration. Although Worden's book inaugurates a radical rethinking of Milton in relation to Cromwell, to the Council of State and the Protectoral regime, it stops well short of portraying his friend Nedham as a Leveller sympathizer.

After Nedham was jailed by Parliament in May 1646 for *lèse-majesté* and relieved of the editorship of *Mercurius Britanicus* – the parliamentary newsbook of the first civil war – he turned to a theme deeply critical of his former employers, writing two unsigned tracts in defence of the jailed Leveller leaders – *Vox Plebis* (19 November 1646) and *Regall Tyrannie Discovered* (6 January 1647).[72] The former appealed, as we have seen, "to free grace against feudal bondage,"[73] while the latter reprinted that seminal image of Adam and Eve which had graced the "Postscript" to Lilburne's *Free-Mans Freedome Vindicated* (23 June 1646), a source which continues today to reverberate in Book 4 of *Paradise Lost*. Other echoes of Leveller writings have also gone unheard for centuries in Milton's epic poems. To a point, I then follow the method Worden uses in juxtaposing a number of memorable phrasings and key terms in the various writings of Milton,

Nedham, and Andrew Marvell,[74] in order to trace the recurrence, as well as particular uses, of a host of echoes in Milton's epic poems from the writings of Lilburne, Overton, Walwyn, and Wildman, those original advocates of "*Common Right* and *Freedom.*"[75]

Among some of the more innovative rights and freedoms called for in the Levellers' second *Agreement of the People* (December 1648) was a pressing need "to prevent the many inconveniences apparently arising from the long continuance[76] of the same persons in authority," to ensure equitable distribution of representatives, to extend considerably the franchise, to guarantee equality before the law, and to reserve certain powers[77] to the people that would free them from compulsion in religion[78] or from military impressment. Far more radically, the third *Agreement*, issued on 1 May 1649 from the Tower of London, sought "to abolish all arbitrary Power and to set bounds and limits both to our Supreme, and all Subordinate Authority."[79] While it aimed to block the restoration of a political system of landed hierarchy,[80] based on hereditary right, it aimed as well to forestall an oligarchy of the saints by means of popular sovereignty rooted in natural law. For what the Levellers were "opposed to," as David Wootton says, "was any measure which would reserve power in the hands of the self-selected godly" (76).

Apart, however, from one brief chapter on "Milton and the Levellers" in *Modern Political Thought: A Reader* (2000) that parallels brief excerpts from the *Agreement* with others from *Areopagitica* and *The Tenure of Kings and Magistrates*,[81] there is nothing in the various discourses of literature, history, and political theory to suggest that Milton, the epic poet, let alone Milton the republican revolutionary, was ever a fellow-traveller with the Levellers. And yet *Paradise Lost* is suffused by their principles, to a point that Milton's Heaven and his God evolve in ways surprisingly like (and unlike) the English republic, moving from a feudal, if not absolute, monarchy toward a popular democracy. This fact alone ought to take us beyond "pessimist" critics to say with a reader like Hugh Jenkins, that when Milton had "laid down his history of England" in the mid- to late 1650s, "he took up his universal history of mankind, *Paradise Lost,* which offers a broader and more hopeful definition of the human character and the nature of its fall."[82]

Even so, the demands placed on readers by this progressive political evolution on earth (let alone heaven) are considerable. Yet any aristocratic turn in the poet's final vision is far more apparent than real, once an equivocal voice of irony begins to sound in scene after scene. This equivocal mode of narration ultimately derives from the divine voice itself in its method of posing dramatic choices for angels as well as for human beings. Free will, in fact, is only possible if the creature *cannot* know what the creator knows, where the epistemic distance requisite to free will is only formed in the gap between appearance and reality. At that point, free choice is not only possible but necessary, particularly where readers face many of the same choices that characters have to make in the poem. Much like Milton's Christ of the divorce tracts, who "meant not to be tak'n word for word," the poet "requires a skillfull and laborious gatherer" of his work "who must compare the words he finds, with other precepts,"[83] as he explained his own biblical hermeneutics in *The Doctrine and Discipline of Divorce* (2nd ed, February 1644).

The Levellers had similar expectations of their readers, as Rachel Foxley points out.[84] Given that they, too, were "fundamentally optimistic" about "human nature and human potential in this life," part of their purpose in writing "was to stimulate people to recover the use of their reason and come to a full and proper understanding of themselves and of their true human nature and potential" (280). While the dismal events of 1649 meant that "the Levellers came to have a more disillusioned view, recognizing the corrupting effects of power as almost universal," Foxley thinks that their faith in human goodness remains a cardinal point of difference between them and the epic poet. "Where Milton," she says, "withdrew his trust from the mass of the people, seeing them as dangerously inconstant and corruptible, and placed it in the godly few, the Levellers continued to place their faith in the people as the only possible safeguard against the corruption of the few" (281).

Since this has long been *the* critical consensus on Milton, I need to show in great detail, through choice after dramatic choice, how the poetry invariably turns on "right reading" (as a reflex of "right reason"). Not the least of these choices in the "laborious gatherings" of the reader is to locate just where the epic voice is inflected by hope or by disillusionment – even as it sings of having "fall'n on evil dayes, / On evil dayes though fall'n, and evil tongues; / In darkness, and with dangers compast round, / And solitude, yet not alone" (7.25–8). Yet "More safe I Sing," the epic narrator intones, "with mortal voice, unchang'd / To hoarce or mute" (7.24–5), just before that great and aching admission, "though fall'n on evil dayes." And "yet not alone," the beautiful counter-movement begins to swell, "while thou / Visit'st my slumbers Nightly" (7.28–9).

The more we are attuned to a hopeful language of levelling in Milton's paradisal poems, the more we are likely to accept his "heavenly" Muse as being *this*-worldly as much as she is *other*-worldly. For the vision of paradise in both epics is informed, like the "commonwealth principles" of the Levellers themselves, by a rich confluence of classical and scriptural influences.[85] Particularly from the writings of William Walwyn, as well as a great glut of scriptural quotations and images from Lilburne's late writings, Milton took inspiration for his gospel of political, social, and sexual equality. Nor was Milton alone in falling on "evil dayes"; few ever fell on "evil dayes" more than did John Lilburne.

By the time *Paradise Lost* was published in 1667, the Leveller leader had been ten years in his grave. Although a jury of his peers acquitted him on charges of treason in October 1649, a new parliamentary trial in January 1652 convicted him of criminal libel, a verdict swiftly elevated by Parliament to the level of treason, condemning him to exile in perpetuity from the Commonwealth. Returning to England on pain of death from the Low Countries in June 1653 after the dissolution of the Rump Parliament (thinking the force of Parliament's judgment had expired with that extra-judicial body), Lilburne was tried again in July for his life. Once again, a jury of his peers acquitted him, although he remained a prisoner of the Lord Protector for the rest of his life in Dover Castle, dying of a fever in 1657 during a leave to visit his pregnant, long-suffering wife, Elizabeth.

Emulating their ink-stained hero, a surprising number of army radicals had also "fall'n on evil dayes" in 1649 because of their support for Lilburne's *Englands New Chains*[86] and their agitation for implementation of *An Agreement of the People*. One such group was drummed out of the army in March; a second was executed for mutiny at Burford in May; and a third was swiftly suppressed after a failed mutiny at Oxford in September.[87] By the end of 1649, the entire Leveller movement, it seemed, had "fallen on evil dayes," it being common today to hold that "the arrest of the Leveller leaders and the defeat of the army mutinies" are "normally taken as marking the effective end of the Levellers as an organised political movement." Yet, for years after the Restoration, "Contemporaries … were less sure. They saw the spectre of the Levellers in popular political agitation out-of-doors throughout the reign of Charles II."[88] Among other instances, Tim Harris recalls the rioting "apprentices [who] took to the streets to pull down brothels in Easter Week of 1668" (219). Although this incident occurred several months *after* the publication of *Paradise Lost* in ten books, it is revealing of the climate in which Milton composed his poem. As Harris explains, "[T]he fact that they marched behind green banners (the colour of the Levellers) and made demands for liberty of conscience and further reformation sounded alarm bells for the government, who became convinced that the riots had been instigated by republican conspirators bent on overthrowing the monarch" (219–20).

For a poet likely to sympathize with these demands for liberty of conscience and further reformation, who had recently repurposed Leveller sentiments in a first edition of *Paradise Lost*, the watchword was still caution – not just for the sake of self-protection, but for the safety of all those, like the London apprentices, ready to fling caution to the wind. Aside from the classic principle of *salus populi suprema lex* – the safety of the people is the supreme law – Milton's appeal to the Muse invoked a second, unstated, principle on which the Leveller movement had depended from its inception: a nation of political equals has usually been imagined in print before it is realized in the home or church or state. So, the poet pleads, "[S]till govern thou my Song, / *Urania*, and fit audience find, though few" (7.30–1), since that "fit audience … though few" is going to be called on to perform the same action that the narrative performs – of gathering a community of silent readers into a new community of equals mediated by the Word. This is ideologically similar, as Rachel Foxley suggests, to the Leveller's own program of printing: "Whatever their own political manoeuvres, the Leveller leaders knew that their political visions could only be realized, in the end, by their readers" ("Levellers," 283–4).

Suffice to say that the role of a "Leveller" reader does not resemble that monocratic version of "humiliation" and forced re-education envisioned by Stanley Fish,[89] nor is it quite the militant role encouraged by Sharon Achinstein of "revolutionary readers" taught by the poem "to prepare and keep watch in the meantime,"[90] to be ready to catch the next wave of the Revolution. Rather, it is through the ongoing acts of readerly choice that an imagined community[91] of Leveller republicans is realized, as readers *become* the Word they read. The change is thus inward and private before it ever turns outward and public; it only comes into being through the mediation of the "Word" in the most literal sense.

And here, it turns out, is one final flourish of Milton's Leveller signature in both of the epics. For it is not Lilburne's constitutional proposals, but rather his use of *mass* communications[92] that is the real measure of Milton's Leveller design in the epics. Fearing imminent death as the result of his approaching trial for treason, Lilburne presents his literary remains in *The Innocent Man's second-Proffer* (22 October 1649) by naming in print most of those pamphlets he had written but never owned as author, as well as listing the others "Since his first Contest with the Bishops" (sixteen titles); "Since my Contest with the Lords" (twenty titles); and "Since his Contest with the Counsell of State" (nine titles). In effect, Lilburne gives up his textual corpus to the full punishment of the state in a manner reminiscent of John Foxe's Book of Martyrs. Crucially, Lilburne had "intreat[ed]" his readers three weeks earlier, in *Strength out of Weaknesse* (30 September 1649), "that if I should die in this contest … that this *Epistle* may live, and many Thousands of them be printed, and seeing by their new pretended Act about Printing they cannot be sold, they may be thrown away, and given, and sent all up and down the Nation" (25). He might as well have written, "This is my body; take and eat." For the distribution of his textual "body" among an imagined community of readers is really tantamount to a new form of political communion. His readers, in fact, are urged to discover what Adam will finally learn at the end of *Paradise Lost* — "by things deemd weak / Subverting worldly strong, and worldly wise / By simply meek" (*PL* 12.567–9). In this context, it is profoundly telling of the Leveller movement that Richard Overton should have made his living as a printer, and that Lilburne, the long-suffering martyr, should have invited his readers to join his Leveller communion of print.

In the end, each of Milton's Levelling doctrines is fleshed out in the Incarnation of a truly human Son in *Paradise Regain'd*, where we find a more "English" Jesus – not that impatient and impetuous Lilburne, it must be said – who brings together disciples he will inspire through their reading of the gospels and the *Actes and Monuments* of John Foxe – Lilburne's culture hero.[93] For it is Foxe's theology of reading, which Milton had also absorbed from the *Actes and Monuments* (or so-called Book of Martyrs), that supplies the definitive print model of how readers can be gathered – in their own acts of "labourious gathering" – into a "Leveller" community of equals. Again, it is Foxe who supplies the largest answer to David Wootton's far-reaching question: "For why was the idea of starting a state *de novo*, which had simply never been considered by previous thinkers, who had assumed that legitimacy derived from past undertakings, rapidly embraced by the Levellers?" ("Democracy" 435). In fact, Foxe's kindly "old Bishop" in the Book of Martyrs had said more than he knew – or anyone could foresee – in seeking to spare the life of one of the Marian martyrs: "[G]ood young man," the inquisitor had urged, "you must be taught by the church, and by your auncients, and do as your forefathers haue done before you."[94] For in Foxe's martyrology, it was literally those "forefathers" who had corrupted the primitive Church by overwriting "those written Records pure" (*PL* 12.513) in scripture.

In the same week that Charles I's trial opened before the High Court of Justice, and "the General Council of the Army subscribed the *Agreement for the people*," a London newsbook began its "news" report with the story that the Earl of Pembroke in the reign of Elizabeth had "desired that his examination might not be put in writing, because he could not write himself; neither if it should come to the view of the common people could many of them understand it." The editor adds, "Then were men rather guided by the tradition of their Fathers, than by acting principles in reason and knowledge: But to the contrary in these our dayes, the meanest sort of people are not only able to write, &c. but to argue and discourse on matters of hightest concernment." The newsbook thus explains why it has "committed to writing, and made publique" such "remarkable events."[95]

It was evidently print that had given the Levellers authority for their radical belief that the past ought not to bind the present, leaving them "determined to throw off the dead hand of precedent" (Wootton, "The Levellers," 80). More specifically, the *Actes and Monuments* had established a popular, if very untraditional, precedent for challenging age-old hierarchies in the Church and State. And Milton, like the Levellers before him, was finding untraditional ways to imagine a revolutionary new form of community.

PART I

A Levelling History

· 1 ·

The Levellers and the Council of State

FATEFUL CHOICES

"LILBURNE AND THE LEVELLERS ARE never mentioned by name anywhere in Milton's work," Merritt Y. Hughes once noted, "and he was silent about them even though he may have been present in the Council of State on March 28, 1649, when Lilburne, Walwyn, and Prince were committed to prison for agitating against the new government."[1] His silence is all the more intriguing when one recalls that Milton was "appointed," by an order-in-council of 26 March, "to make some observations upon a paper lately printed called old & new Chaines."[2] This duty was assigned to him just six days after he was inducted into office as the Secretary for Foreign Tongues on 20 March 1649.[3] So it might be folly, as Martin Dzelzainis says it is, to "underestimate the extent to which even reluctance to comply with the Council's order, let alone outright refusal, would have struck Milton's colleagues as irresponsible and quixotic. The Levellers, after all, posed a clear and present danger to the stability of the new regime." Would it not "be simpler," Dzelzainis inquires drily, "to decline the Council's offer of a job"?[4]

A larger claim, however – that, "while … the Levellers posed a threat to the unity of the Army in the spring and early summer of 1649, the suppression of the mutiny at Burford by Fairfax and Cromwell in mid-May meant they were almost a spent force" (Dzelzainis, "History," 275) – nullifies the threat (15 May) before there is time to make "some observations," thus rendering the whole exercise redundant. And yet, "a clear and present danger" to the regime was revived in the revolt of the Oxford garrison in September.[5] While the failure of this latter revolt may suggest that Army Levellers were now a "spent force," civilians continued in their thousands to rally around Lilburne at his trial in October, and to elect him on 21 December 1649 to the Common Council of London, a result the Rump swiftly revoked.[6] As Lilburne's banishment two years later suggests, the threat of popular revolt was likely to continue so long as Lilburne remained in England.

Dzelzainis is on firmer ground in disputing the claims of nineteenth-century historians like S.R. Gardiner that Milton "felt too much sympathy with Lilburne's vindication of personal liberty to care to enter the lists against him."[7] Yet Milton had good reason to feel compunction about the arrests of William Walwyn and Richard Overton.[8] Although it is not well known, he was deeply indebted to Walwyn for many phrasings, examples, and concepts he had borrowed, recycled, and reworked five years before in his *Areopagitica*. Milton's plea "For the Liberty of unlicenc'd Printing" was so close, in fact, to Walwyn's plea "for liberty of conscience" in *The Compassionate Samaritan* that he could, like the older man (b. 1600), also be suspected – though neither had published a word – of supporting Lilburne's *The Second Part of Englands New-Chaines Discovered* (24 March 1649).

Later, he would be equally indebted to Richard Overton's *Mans Mortalitie* (1644), the heretical materialism of which was to inform his thinking about original matter in *De Doctrina Christiana* and thus his portrait of creation in Book 7 of *Paradise Lost*. But for the moment he had other reasons to feel kinship with Overton as a victim of what today are called "attack ads." The most virulent of these came from the poison pen of the Puritan lawyer and moralist William Prynne, who, on 16 September 1644, had railed against "the late dangerous increase of many *Anabaptisticall, Antinomian, Hereticall, Atheisticall opinons, as of the soules mortality, divorce at pleasure, &c.* lately broached, preached, printed in this famous City."[9] Then, "In early May, 1645, Ephraim Pagitt listed Williams, Overton, and Milton as notorious 'Atheists [who] … preach, print, and practise their hereticall opinions openly: for books, *vide* the bloudy Tenet, witnesse a Tractate of divorce, in which the bonds [of marriage] are let loose to inordinate lust: a pamphlet also in which the soul is laid asleep from the hour of death unto the hour of judgement.'"[10] By now, Milton must have wondered how he had joined the suppressors.

Some self-questioning would have been inevitable, given the persecution the Levellers had endured, not only in their arraignment by the Council of State but in the Lords' and Commons' abuse of them. Obviously, the council had taken Lilburne's questions about its legitimacy as a threat. But the Rump's refusal to debate the Army version of the *Agreement of the People* (submitted to Parliament on 20 January) had also weakened that legitimacy; so in the first part of the Leveller's *Chains*, Lilburne reprinted the *Agreement* as a written constitution to legitimate government by popular subscription. Was the Rump's bid to sit for six months, and an unelected council[11] to rule in its absence for eighteen months, not a provision for unelected tyranny? The fear of Cromwell "having command of all Forces by Sea and Land" was palpable in the *First Part of Chains* (2) before Lilburne took the fatal step of publishing *The Second Part* (24 March), in which he accused Army Grandees of bargaining in bad faith with an ad hoc committee of Leveller, Army, Commons, and City Independents in the month leading up to Pride's Purge (6 December 1648). At this point, Lilburne decided, like the hothead he was reputed to be, that these difficult negotiations had been little more than a temporizing measure, "when it's evident by the *contents*, they did it only to stop the mouths of their *souldiers* & to amuze them into a *pleasing dream*, whilst they go on with their *designe* of absolute *domination*" (15). So Lilburne, together with Overton and Prince, set out to rip the mask from the face of the "martiall power" (14) hiding behind the facade of the Council of State.

By mid-April, the "Free people of England" would be asked to judge the truth of these allegations in "A full Narrative of the late Extra-Judicial and Military Proceedings Against Them" in *The Picture of the Councel of State* by "Lieut. Col. *John Lilburn*, Mr *Thomas Prince*, and Mr *Richard Overton*." As usual, Lilburne assumed a right to have the first word: "On *Wednesday* the 28. of *March* 1649. about foure or five a clock in the morning, my Lodging at *Winchester-house* was beset with about a hundred or two hundred armed men, Horse and Foot" (1). William Walwyn,[12] who had had no part in either instalment of *Englands New-Chaines*, and yet who had with alacrity obeyed the messenger's summons to appear before the council, now found himself dragged "through the streets" by "armed Victors," who intended, in Lilburne's words, to "carry us, like three conquered Slaves, making us often halt by the way, that so their men might draw up in good order, to incounter with an Army of Butter-flies, in case they should meet them in the way to rescue us their Captives from them" (2). Thomas Prince was more serene in his recollection of the event: "I laught heartily to see so many armed men come for me … And I also told, my name is *Prince*, and that it was usual for Princes to have great attendance" (51).

Marched to a common assembly point near "*Pauls* Church," even Lilburne was aghast at what he saw: "We could not but wonder at the apprehending of M. *Walwin* about that, he having for some moneths by past (that ever I could see, or hear of) never bin at any of our meetings" (2). What grieved Walwyn more than the fact of his arrest was the manner of it, given how he was "so well known to most of the Gentlemen there present, that neverthelesse I should be sent for with a party of horse and foot, to the affrighting of my family, and ruine of my credit."[13] Of course, this was the point of such political street theatre – by an overwhelming show of force, to intimidate, humiliate, frighten, and even convict in the court of public opinion by means of spectacle. In the event, an untried government seems to have felt threatened on all sides – on the right by royalists; on the left by Levellers; and in between by every shade of public opinion.

In this context, it hardly matters whether Milton did or did not stand behind members of the council, facing the four Levellers brought in for examination each in his turn. Lilburne was in his element, like a ham actor returning to the stage: "I marched into the Room with my hat on, and looking about me, I saw divers Members of the House of Commons present, and so I put it off; and by Sergeant *Dendy* I was directed to go neer M. *Bradshaw*, that sate as if he had bin Chairman to the Gentlemen that were there present" (3). Had Milton not been there, doubtless his good friend John Bradshaw would have told him about Lilburne removing his hat before members of the Commons, whom he still regarded as "the original of all just Powers." But Milton was almost certainly present; Barbara Lewalski remarks that, "On March 28, Milton attended the council to receive a commission relating to Ireland, and so may have heard the Leveller authors – Lilburne, Walwyn, Overton, and Thomas Prince – examined, charged with high treason, and sent to the Tower."[14] Since he was already in the building, he would be summoned to witness their response, if only for better information in making "some observations upon a paper lately printed called old & new Chaines." And this is where Milton was certain to have seen himself reflected in the eyes of Walwyn, Overton, and Lilburne, now feeling the sting of his own wise counsel in *Areopagitica*: "Beleeve it, Lords and Commons, they who counsell ye to such a suppressing, doe as good as bid ye suppresse your selves."[15]

Particularly in the face of Walwyn, if he did see him there, there would be confusion about his allegiances, given that Milton's soaring eloquence in *Areopagitica* had built upon Walwyn's arguments in *The Compassionate*

Samaritan, a tract published on 29 July 1644, some four months before the appearance of *Areopagticia*[16] on 23 November. There, Walwyn had argued, "Truth was not used to feare colours, or to seeke shifts or stratagems for its advancement. I should rather thinke that they who are assured of her should desire that all mens mouthes should bee open, that so errour may discover its foulnesse, and truth become more glorious by a victorious conquest after a fight in open field."[17] Milton then reversed the order and expanded the two sentences by half:[18]

> [T]hough all the windes of doctrin were let loose to play upon the earth, so Truth be in the field, we do injuriously by licencing and prohibiting to misdoubt her strength. Let her and Falshood grapple; who ever knew Truth put to the wors, in a free and open encounter … For who knows not that Truth is strong next to the Almighty; she needs no policies, nor stratagems, nor licensings to make her victorious, those are the shifts and the defences that error uses against her power. (*CPW* 2: 561, 562–3)

Here is but one of the countless turns of phrase that Milton adapted from Walwyn's tract.

Just as important as these verbal echoes are the shared assumptions in both works about ordinary people's judgment and their capacity for reason. Walwyn claimed that "Hee that bade us try all things, and hold fast that which was good did suppose that men have faculties and abilities wherewithall to try all things" (*Compassionate*, 26). Milton wrote: "Read any books what ever come to thy hand, for thou art sufficient both to judge aright, and to examine each matter" (*CPW* 2: 511). While Milton's argument in favour "of reading Books, what ever sort they be," and of Moses, Daniel, and Paul reading "Books of all sorts" (*CPW* 2: 507–8), clearly follows Walwyn's wording on "Liberty of Conscience of what opinion soever" (5), his imagination was consistently fired by Walwyn's book, from its subtitle, "Liberty of Conscience asserted, and the Separatist vindicated," through to its peroration: "That the Presse may be free for any man that writes nothing scandalous or dangerous to the State. That so this Parliament may prove themselves loving Fathers to all sorts of good men" (76). Just as Walwyn's argument in the front matter is addressed "To the Commons of *England*" (A3), so the title page of *Areopagitica* announces "A Speech of Mr. *John Milton* … To the Parlament of *England*." Much of this "speech" can be described as an epigrammatic restatement of Walwyn's basic arguments for liberty of conscience and toleration of difference, while "The formal articulation," as Ernest Sirluck has observed, "is that of regular deliberative rhetoric,"[19] likewise the mode of *The Compassionate Samaritan*.

While some of these stylistic and formal similarities are likely incidental, the faith of both men in the dignity of reason is not. Walwyn, who was less likely than Milton to have read Plato or Cicero, sounds almost like a Socratic in praising "the Brownist and Anabaptist" as "rationall examiners of those things they hold for truth" (8), admiring their practice of "objecting … by which meanes the weakest becomes in a short time much improved" (10). Milton's insistence that "God uses not to captivat under a perpetuall childhood of prescription, but trusts him with the gift of reason to be his own chooser" (514), parallels Cicero's insistence in *De legibus* that, "nothing is better than reason, and since it [is] in both human being and god, the primary fellowship of human being with god involves reason."[20] Even so, the fellowship of man and god depends on man's maturation in reason, or "nature fully developed."[21] Else, as Milton develops this idea, "What advantage is it to be a man over it is to be a boy at school, if we have only scapt the ferular, to come under the fescu of an *Imprimatur?*" (CPW 2: 531). Milton applauds "reading, trying all things, assenting to the force of reason and convincement" (554) to arrive at right reason, or "nature fully developed." In "proposing any doubt whereof any one desires to be resolved," Walwyn avers, the reason-loving sectaries are "every one able to give an account of their tenets (not relying upon their Pastors as most men in our congregations doe)" (*Compassionate*, 10). "A man may be a heretick in the truth," Milton turns to logical paradox to underwrite his argument, "and if he beleeve things only because his Pastor sayes so, or the Assembly so determins, without knowing other reason, though his belief be true, yet the very truth he holds, becomes his heresie" (CPW 2: 543). Since reason is godlike, it is surely the true ground of religion.

This emphasis on *reasoned* religion also informs both men's arguments for liberty. The first of Walwyn's "Reasons" for defending "Liberty of Conscience" is the faculty of "*Reason*" itself: "Because of what judgement soever a man is, he cannot chuse but bee of that judgment, … and so man is by his owne reason necessitated to be of that minde he is" (6–7). Milton is equally clear on the link between reason and freedom, for, "when God gave" Adam "reason, he gave him freedom to choose, for reason is but choosing; he had bin else a meer artificiall *Adam*, such an *Adam* as he is in the motions [or puppet shows]" (527). Free reason also entails the duty, however, to be sceptical of mere authority. Complaining of clerical resistance to biblical translation, Walwyn says "they have thereby made it a difficult thing to be a Minister, and so have engrossed the trade to themselves, and left al other men by reason of their other professions in an incapacity of being such in their sense" (31–2). "I never found cause to think," Milton bluntly insists, "that the tenth part of learning stood or fell with the Clergy: nor could I ever but hold it for a sordid and unworthy speech of any Churchman who had a competency left him" (531).

Pastors who deny reason are pilloried by both authors for constraining conscience and denying choice. Walwyn mocks those who claim "a succession from the Apostles," and reduces their "profession" to a trade: "They would not have us to thinke that a Minister comes to be so, as another man comes to be a Merchant, Bookseller, Taylor, &c. either by disposall of him by his friends in his education, or by his owne making choice to be of such a Trade" (24). Milton mocks the "wealthy man" who "resigns the whole warehouse of his religion, with all the locks and keyes into his custody; and indeed makes the very person of that man his religion … He entertains him, gives him gifts, feasts him, lodges him; his religion comes home at night, praies, is liberally supt, and sumptuously laid to sleep, rises, is saluted, and [then] walks abroad at eight," leaving "his kind entertainer in the shop trading all day without his religion" (544–5). Walwyn, a London merchant who had, by virtue of royal charter,[22] to compete with "Monopolising merchants,"[23] lumped them together with "the Divines" who also enjoyed exemption from liberal competition. Milton similarly trivializes their phony "wares": "Truth and understanding are not such wares as to be monopoliz'd and traded in by tickets and statutes, and standards" (*CPW* 2: 535).

For both, the enemy seems cut from the same black cloth. Walwyn is slightly acerbic in his claim that "the tyrannie over conscience that was exercised by the Bishops, is like to bee continued by the Presbyter: that the oppressors are only changed, but the oppression not like to bee removed" (17). Milton is much more caustic about "some who but of late were little better then silenc't from preaching," complaining that, if they "shall come now to silence us from reading, except what they please, it cannot be guest what is intended by som but a second tyranny over learning: and will soon put it out of controversie that Bishops and Presbyters are the same to us both name and thing" (*CPW* 2: 539). Sneering at lordly attitudes "that none must be heard, but whom they like" (566), he sounds like Walwyn carping “that nothing may come to the Worlds view but what they please, unlesse men will runne the hazard of imprisonment (as I now doe)” (39).

In either pamphlet, it is clearly the Presbyterians who are cast in the role of villains, whether before or after they gained legislative power. “Is it so long since the yokes were broken off these mens necks,” Walwyn asks more tenderly, “that they forget the burthen and injustice of them, or that assistance they had from their separatist Brethren in breaking those yoakes, that now so soone as they are got into reputation, they should suppose a time of suffering for their Brethren for doing what to them appears to be their duty” (55–6). Most thoughtful people “beginne to feare that some bad ends of their owne were aimed herein, and not so much the liberty of the people, as that they might get up into the Chaire and become to them in stead of a Lord Bishop, a ruling Presbyter” (19–20). Milton is less tender, if rather more pithy in his observation

> that while Bishops were to be baited down, then all Presses might be open; it was the peoples birthright and priviledge in time of Parlament, it was the breaking forth of light. But now the Bishops abrogated and voided out of the Church, as if our Reformation sought no more, but to make room for others into their seats under another name, the Episcopall arts begin to bud again, the cruse of truth must run no more oyle. (541)

Pity largely informs Walwyn’s complaint “that whilest the Presse was o[p]en no men undertooke the Anabaptists, and that now their adversaries have bound their hands they begin to buffet them; what can they doe else but necessarily suspect that our Divines have not the truth, or that they are not able to defend it” (59). Milton is more comical, even scatological in “voiding” Bishops from the body politic while railing against these “new forcers of Conscience.”[24] Pitying the human flesh rotting within whitewashed sepulchres, Walwyn holds out hope of the resurrected body to such as even these: “so long as ye propose dominion and the sway over your Brethren for your ends, which our Saviour said his followers should not doe, you must give men that are unwilling to bee deceived leave to think that ye have yet but the forme and shew of Religion, but want the inward sweetnesse and most excellent fruits and effects thereof” (62–3). By contrast, Milton pillories every hypocrite in the Westminster Assembly who wants power but has only the “forme and shew of Religion”: “This is not, Yee Covnants and Protestations that we have made, this is not to put down Prelaty, this is but to chop an Episcopacy, this is but to translate the Palace *Metropolitan* from one kind of dominion into another" (*CPW* 2: 540–1). Walwyn's similar denunciation of this devilish drive for clerical power was still five years off when, adopting something of Milton's satiric tone, he had published in Rotterdam an anonymous pamphlet called *Tyranipocrit.*[25] A decade later, his keen analysis of the tyrant-hypocrite would return to inform Milton's analysis in *Paradise Lost* of the exercise of power.

But in 1644 the most noticeable difference between these two great essays on liberty still has to do with their differing nuances on toleration. Walwyn is unequivocal in his assertion "that every man ought to have Liberty of Conscience of what opinion soever," unless "it be dangerous to the State" (5). "To compell mee against my conscience," he says, "is to compel me against what I beleeve to be true, and so against my faith; now whatsoever is not of faith is sin; to compell me therefore against my conscience, is to compell me to doe that which is sinfull" (42–3). With characteristic humility, Walwyn then pleads, "Ith' meane time I wish with all my heart we could all put on the spirit of meeknesse, and rather endeavour to rectifie by argument and perswasion one anothers infirmitie" (9–10). For it is "The uncertainty of knowledge in this life" which ensures that "no man, nor no sort of men can presume of an unerring spirit" (11); "since there remaines a possibility of error, notwithstanding never so great presumptions of the contrary, one sort of men are not to compell another, since this hazard is run thereby, that he who is in an error, may be the constrainer of him who is in the truth" (11–12). Equally aware that Truth "may have more shapes then one" (*CPW* 2: 563), Milton turns to an architectural metaphor to show that, "when every stone is laid artfully together, it cannot be united into a continuity, it can but be contiguous in this world" (2: 555). Extrapolating from the mixture in Gothic styles, he maintains that "the perfection consists in this, that out of many moderat varieties and brotherly dissimilitudes that are not vastly disproportionall arises the goodly and the graceful symmetry that commends the whole pile and structure." On formal as well as moral grounds, he will conclude that it "doubtles is more wholsome, more prudent, and more Christian that many be tolerated, rather then all compell'd" (2: 565).

Not *all*, however, can be tolerated; Milton draws the line at "tolerated Popery, and open superstition, which as it extirpats all religions and civill supremacies, so it self should be extirpat, provided first that all charitable and commpassionat means be us'd to win and regain the weak and the misled: that also which is impious or evil absolutely either against faith or maners no law can possibly permit, that intends not to unlaw it self" (565). His premise and conclusion differ, and critics have long been at pains to explain why.[26] The best explanation to date is the pragmatic one of Ernest Sirluck, who sees Milton appealing to prejudices on the political left and right in order "to split the Presbyterian majority."[27] Seeking to build a tolerationist coalition, he "finds a patron for his proposals from each of the major groups he wishes to bring together, citing the leading Erastian in the Commons, Selden, as a believer in unrestricted reading, and the late leading Independent in the Lords, Brooke (now a martyr of the Parliamentary cause), as a believer in religious toleration. No Presbyterian is cited" (Sirluck, "Introduction," *CPW* 2: 177). Were Milton speaking in the Commons or negotiating a backroom deal, this might suffice. But no one in Parliament was to pay him any mind, let alone seek alliances on this model.

The real stop, it seems, was in Milton's mind; the lessons he needed to learn from Walwyn were radically incomplete. Only in his portrait of Adam disputing with God for a mate in *Paradise Lost* did he confront at last the implications of intolerance as urged by the self-appointed heresiarch, Thomas Edwards. In an unguarded moment, the author of *Gangraena* warned "how[,] if a toleration were granted," chaos were indeed come again, for husbands and masters "should never have peace in their families more, or ever after have command of wives, children, servants."[28] Once married, Adam is hardly an Edwardian "master"; he strongly encourages his wife to express her opinions. But what could Milton say on that March day in 1649 about Walwyn and the terrible misfortune that had befallen him, save that his own plea for "Liberty of Conscience" now threatened to turn Milton's judgment back on himself? For, "it would be no unequall distribution," Milton had insisted, "to suppresse the suppressors themselves; whom the change of their condition hath puft up, more then their late experience of harder times hath made wise" (*CPW* 2: 568–9). In this fateful moment of deciding the future direction of the Republic, how could he possibly fail to see his own condemnation in the face of Walwyn?

Conscience-stricken as he must have been at Walwyn's arraignment, Milton had to be mortified by Overton's arrest. Not five years ago, they had been lumped together and publicly named by the Stationers' Company for unlicensed printing of subversive doctrines. Responding to the Stationers' petition to hold both men accountable, the Commons Committee for Printing had authorized the complainants "diligently to inquire out the

Authors, Printers, and Publishers, of the Pamphlet against the immortality of the Soul, and concerning Divorce."[29] That Milton should now be asked to join the attack on Overton was bad enough; that the Leveller was soon to publish an account of his wife's sufferings in "*The Proceedings of the Councel of State against* Richard Overton, *now prisoner in The Tower of* London"[30] was even more humiliating. There, Overton would report how a military officer, appearing at the head of "a partie of Horse and Foot" (25) of a hundred or more men, had made scurrilous accusations against him in his own home of violating the marriage bond, and insisted publicly at Whitehall, how "*it was now an opinion amongst us* [the Levellers] *to have community of women*" (29). This cyncial agent of the council appeared to accuse the Leveller leader of sharing Milton's "shameful" views on marriage.

Finding Overton in the same room as a "*Gentlewoman who then sate suckling her childe*," the commanding officer of the arresting troop, one Lt-Col. Axtel, asked Overton whether she "*were not one of my* [i.e., Overton's] *wives*, and averred *that she and I lay together that night*" (26). Hearing from the woman's outraged husband "*that he and I lay together that night*" in a crowded house with a lamentable shortage of beds, Overton recounts how "the Lieutenant Colonel, out of that little discretion he had about him, took the Gentleman by the hand, saying, *How dost thou, brother Cuckold?*" (27). Then the officer "gave it out in the Court and Street, amongst the souldiers and neighbours that *it was a Bawdy-house, and that all the women that lived in it were whores, and that he had taken me in bed with another mans Wife.*" Whether it was the officer's private conceit or a strategy of the Council of State to make the word *Leveller* synonymous with adultery and polygamy,[31] his abuse could only redound on the author of *The Doctrine and Discipline of Divorce* as the original "divorcer at pleasure," who had evidently influenced his fellow heretic. After this, how could Milton expect any justice from "the compassionate Samaritan's" plea that he who was without sin should cast the first stone?

Facing Lilburne, Milton had further reasons to ask himself by what right he stood behind, and not in front of the council table? Lilburne was supposed to be the author of *Regall Tyrannie Discovered* (6 January 1647), a booklet that had two years earlier largely anticipated his *Tenure of Kings and Magistrates*, published just six weeks before (13 February 1649).[32] It was Milton's friend George Thomason, the bookseller, who took Lilburne to be the author of *Regall Tyrannie*, although Lilburne had responded at once that "some of my friends, or well-wishers have done it excellent well for me, in those two notable discourses called, *Vox Plebis*, and *Regall Tyranny discovered*, which will live when I am dead; and be (I hope) as good as winding sheets unto the Lords."[33]

To further complicate matters, John Bradshaw – elected President of the Council of State a fortnight before – had served as Milton's "attorney in 1647 in the Powell affair,"[34] not long after providing legal "counsel in John Lilburne's hearing before the House of Lords"[35] about indemnities owed to him for his persecution ten years before by Star Chamber. It was Bradshaw who must have nominated Milton to the post of Secretary on the basis of his *Tenure of Kings and Magistrates*, where he had exposed the laughable ignorance of Presbyterians about "the proceedings now in Parlament against the King," which they said "are without precedent from any Protestant State or Kingdom."[36] Nor was Bradshaw really above boasting of his friend's strengths as a controversialist: "Why, he's read them all, this Milton ... Germans, Genevans, Scots, he knows more than the lot of them put together! Who among them dares any longer to repeat this nonsense that 'Kings are accountable to none but God'?[37] When even our ancient Ancestors 'thought it no way illegal to depose and put to death thir tyrannous Kings.'"[38]

Here, the difficulty was that Milton's arguments were much too close for comfort to *Regall Tyrannie.*[39] Although the Leveller pamphlet was concerned with regal tyranny since the Conquest, and Milton's tract focussed on classical precedents for deposing a tyrant, they were very much alike in their principles, their scriptural proof-texts, and even in some of their phrasings. The sovereignty of the people is the overriding principle of *Regall Tyrannie*: "though the *King* be the Supream Officer, which is all, and the most he is; yet he is not the supreame Power: for the absolute Supream Power is the People in generall, made up of every individuall."[40] The author says "*That the people in generall are the originall sole legislaters, and the true fountain, and earthly wellspring of all just power*" (99), much as Milton says that "the King or Magistrate holds his autoritie of the people, both originaly and naturally for their good in the first place, and not his own" (*CPW* 3: 206).

For both writers, the logical corollary is government by consent. The author of *Regall Tyrannie* stipulates that "all lawfull (approbational) instituted power by God amongst men, is by common agreement, and mutual consent" (1). Still more largely he declares, "Power is originally inherent in the People, and it is nothing else but that might and vigour, which such and such a Society of men contains in it self, and when by such and such a Law of common consent and agreement, it is derived into such and such hands,

God confirmes the Law" (40–1). More largely still and also more powerfully, Milton writes that "No man who knows ought,[41] can be so stupid to deny that all men naturally were borne free, being the image and resemblance of God himself, and were by privilege above all the creatures, born to command and not to obey." After the Fall, however,

> they agreed by common league to bind each other from mutual injury ... This autoritie and power of self-defence and preservation being originally and naturally in every one of them, and unitedly in them all, for ease, for order, and least each man should be his own partial Judge, they communicated and deriv'd either to one, whom for the eminence of his wisdom and integritie they chose above the rest, or to more then one whom they thought of equal deserving: the first was call'd a King; the other Magistrates. Not to be thir Lords and Maisters (though afterward those names in som places were giv'n voluntarily to such as had been Authors of inestimable good to the people) but, to be thir Deputies and Commissioners, to execute, by vertue of thir intrusted power, that justice. (*CPW* 3: 198–9)

As Roy Flannagan suggestively comments, "Putting both kings and magistrates in his title, with the 'and' to connect them, Milton levels the two ranks and derives their position from the consent of the people they are elected to govern."[42]

But Milton is far closer to "levelling" principles than a mere sleight of grammar. He and the Leveller author both turn to natural law theory[43] to prove a people's right of resistance to unjust rulers. In terms adapted from Cicero, the author of *Regall Tyrannie* states: "It being against the light of Nature and Reason,[44] and the end wherefore God endowed Man with understanding, for any sort or generation of men to give so much power into the hands of any man or men whatsoever, as to enable them to destroy them," which "is justly resistable and revokeable" (1). Milton seconds this idea, arguing that "the power of Kings and Magistrates is nothing else, but what is only derivative, transferr'd and committed to them in trust from the People, to the Common good of them all, in whom the power yet remaines fundamentally, and cannot be tak'n from them, without a violation of thir natural birthright" (202). Popular sovereignty is a birthright from nature.

But if by nature people enjoy the right to choose their rulers, they also enjoy the right to depose a tyrant. In the words of *Regall Tyrannie*, "if Parliaments be the most high and absolute power in the Realm ... Then much more may they disthrone or depose, these Lordly prerogative Innovators and Intruders" (98); and yet, "the betrusted Commissioners of the Commons of *England, now assembled in Parliament*, have not faithfully discharged their duty to their Lords and Masters, the people, their impowerers, till they have effectually and throughly done it" (98). Avoiding particulars (like Charles I) to argue not from historical precedent but natural law (though not referring directly or even indirectly to Cicero's theory of natural law), Milton says that, "since the King or Magistrate holds his autoritie of the people, both originaly and naturally for their good in the first place, and not his own, then may the people as oft as they shall judge it for the best, either choose him or reject him, retaine him or depose him though no Tyrant, meerly by the liberty and right of free born Men, to be govern'd as seems to them best" (*CPW* 3: 206).

In fact, the rights of "free born men"[45] are named so often in *Tenure* that Lilburne could have pointed to a second "Free-born John" in the bosom of the Council. And "free-born" wasn't the half of it; other terms echo just as loudly, terms like "common right"; "intrusted powers"; "cov'nant"; and "consent."[46] At times, *The Tenure* reads like a précis of what it had taken the author of *Regall Tyrannie* 108 pages to develop. But the gist of each argument is also writ large in their choice of scriptural proof-texts. *Regall Tyrannie* traces the history of kingship in biblical Israel for evidence that monarchy is not of divine but of heathen origin: "And therefore they knowing that when he possessed the Land of *Canaan*, they would reject him, and desire a King (like all the rest of the Heathens, and Pagans) to reign over them: Yet they being dear unto him, he would not wholly reject them, but gave them a *Law* for the chusing of a *King* and his behaviour, which we find in Deut. 17. 14, 15, 16, 17, 18, 19, 20. in these words,"[47] and so forth. Milton drew a like conclusion from "*Deut.* 17.14. *When thou* [Israel] *art come into the Land which the Lord thy God giveth thee, and shalt say I will set a King over mee, like as all the Nations about mee*," glossing it as follows: "These Words confirme us that the right of choosing, yea of changing thir own Goverment is by the grant of God himself in the People" (206–7).

From 1 Samuel 8, *Regall Tyrannie* inferred the right of any people to reject their rulers: "But *the people of Israel like foolish men, not being content with the Government of their Soveraign by Judges*," rejected "their Liege Lord" and chose "one of their own; namely, a *King*, that so they might be like the *Pagans and Heathens ... which Act of theirs, God plainly declares was a rejection of him, that he should not reign over them*, 1. Sam. 8.7."[48] Milton remarks that, "when they desir'd a King … and though thir changing displeas'd him, yet he that was himself thir King … would not be a hindrance to what they intended, furder then by perswasion, but that they might doe therein as they saw good, 1 *Sam.* 8. onely he reserv'd to himself the nomination of who should reigne over them" (207). But where the author of *Regall Tyrannie* ultimately rested his case on the prophet Hosea – "And therefore the Scripture saith, He gave them a King in his anger, and took him away in his wrath, *Hosa* 13.11" (14) – Milton based his own case on a logical deduction from scripture: "since God ascribes as oft to himself the casting down of Princes from the throne," then "if the peoples act in election be pleaded by a King, as the act of God, and the most just title to enthrone him, why may not the peoples act of rejection, bee as well pleaded by the people as the act of God, and the most just reason to depose him?" (211).

Although *Regall Tyrannie* uses scripture more extensively than Milton, Nedham, its likely author, still depends on reason to justify a fundamental principle that, "amongst the *Sons* of *Men*, that live in mutuall society one amongst another in *nature and reason*, there is none above, or over another, against mutuall consent and agreement … [who] becomes a *Soveraign Lord* and *King*" who is *not* subject to "what rules they judge convenient; alwayes provided, they be consonant to the *Law of God, Nature,* and *Reason*" (11). The first words of *Tenure* also affirm this primacy of reason in the exercise of sovereignty: "If men within themselves would be govern'd by reason, and not generally give up thir understanding to a double tyrannie, of Custom from without, and blind affections within, they would discerne better, what it is to favour and uphold the Tyrant of a Nation" (190). Nonetheless, in his claim that "none can love freedom heartilie, but good men; the rest love not freedom, but license; which never hath more scope or more indulgence then under Tyrants" (190), critics see Milton as privileging virtue over reason, as opposed to the "modern" view of Machiavelli, who had argued that, since "all men are wicked," the common folk are superior to aristocrats only by virtue of their common "self-interest."[49]

While Barbara Lewalski admits that Milton does echo "Leveller theories of popular sovereignty in vesting the power to choose and change governments and governors in the people generally, not in inferior magistrates as Calvinist resistance theory had it,"[50] she insists nonetheless that he is "unlike the Levellers." In her view, "Milton adapts his republican theory to the exigencies of the time as well as to his underlying assumptions about slavishness and citizenship, arguing that good men who love liberty (e.g., the truncated Commons, the army, and the commissioners) may rightfully act as 'the people' in these extraordinary circumstances" (232). In other words, Lewalski characterizes Milton as a typically classical republican, preferring aristocratic to "mob" rule.[51] By contrast, Jonathan Scott notes that the Levellers share these classical republican ideas, including the nobility of virtue.[52] The author of *Regall Tyrannie* says, "I am absolutely of *Catoes* mind, to think, that *no man can be an honest man, but he that is a free man, And no man is a free man, but he that is a just man*" (*Regall*, 11). Is this not identical to Milton's claim that "none can love freedom heartilie, but good men; the rest love not freedom, but license" (*CPW* 3: 190)?

Even so, Stephen Fallon writes recently that the *Tenure* is fractured by two contrary arguments about men who "are governed either by 'reason' or an 'inward vitious rule'"; only "those who are governed by reason do not need to be constrained by kings and magistrates."[53] Fallon conseqently reads the "unravelling of the republican experiment in the years to come" solely in terms of Milton's contradictory "political calculus" (251), by which he grants unfettered freedom to "the uprighter sort" (244), while reserving curbs and halters for the rest. But *Regall Tyrannie*'s insistence on "honest" and "just" men who form the ground of liberal society is based on the same political calculus. What Fallon terms "an arresting shift of argument in the pages added in the second edition" of *Tenure* may well be a sign of "the shifting political landscape" (244) in late 1649. Indeed, Martin Dzelzainis[54] and Go Togashi[55] both notice that, in the second edition of *Tenure*, Milton restores to the "inferior magistrate" the right of judgment he had formerly denied him. Donning this mantle of magistracy, the Rump may then deny sitting or having ever sat as "private persons." The Presbyterians, who refuse that magistracy, are thus the ones reduced to "private persons," clamouring to bring the Rump to judgment. But a better explanation for Milton's logical about-face is that, by the end of 1649, he had begun, like the Levellers, to doubt the rule of the self-appointed "godly." Like Lilburne in the first part of *Englands New Chains*, he had become sceptical of anyone seeking power.

A more intractable problem, however, for demonstrating Milton's Leveller sympathies has to do with his *History of Britain* (not published until 1670). Nicholas von Maltzahn rightly notes in his authoritative study of the *History* that "Milton's residual doubts about the Saxon Church" in the third and fourth books "surface in the telling silence on original Saxon laws in *The Tenure of Kings and Magistrates*." So, "Against the Leveller support for Magna Carta," he reasons, "Milton now seems close to the radical parliamentarians' hostility to the statute." For von Maltzahn, "His failure to consent to the exaggeration of Saxon laws and liberties further distinguishes his position from the Levellers' acceptance of this historical myth."[56] In part, this reading depends on a doubtful date for *History's* composition; von Maltzahn is forced to argue that Milton wrote books one to four (of six) soon after finishing *The Tenure* (late January 1649), and before taking up his duties as Secretary to the Council of State (16 March). But Milton's nephew Edward Phillips, still at that time a member of his household, dated the *History*'s inception to 1647, when they moved from "his great House in *Barbican* … to a smaller in *High Holbourn*," "not long after the March of *Fairfax* and *Cromwel* through the City of *London* with the whole Army, to quell the Insurrections" of August 1647 (Darbishire, *Early Lives*, 68).[57] So a commencement date of February 1649 leaves von Maltzahn to argue that two-thirds of Milton's second-longest prose work were written in six weeks "as advice literature to the nation," and that, "at the crisis of the revolution, as he wrote the *History* in the weeks following the execution of the king, Milton had doubted the national character, and had seen the confusion in English politics as a sure sign of the same shortcomings that Gildas had denounced over a thousand years before" (22, 132). If 1647 were the more likely start date, however, Milton's obvious reticence about the Leveller myth of Saxon liberties could then be read as a necessary corrective to the myth that English tyranny had originated with the Norman Conquest – which was the claim of *Regall Tyrannie* in its history of the Norman Yoke,[58] with examples drawn from the reign of every English king from William the Conqueror down to Charles Stuart.

"Milton's anti-Normanism in *The Tenure of Kings and Magistrates*" could actually be more, rather than less, consistent with Leveller ideology, and not what von Maltzahn takes to be "a reaction to the increasing Leveller commitment to Magna Carta in 1648 and 1649" (206). In *The Just Mans Justification* (10 June 1646), Lilburne had called William the Conqueror "a *perjur'd Tyrant*" who "never observed any of his oaths, and the same (saith *Daniel Fol.* 43.), did *Henry* the first, *Henry* the second, and King *John &c*, … and though there may be some veines issuing from former originals, yet the main stream of our Common law, with the practice thereof, flowed out of *Normandy*, notwithstanding all objections can be made to the contrary, *and therefore I say it came from the* Will *of a* Tyrant" (13). While von Maltzahn admits that "a historian like Samuel Daniel could, in support of civil law, propose that Conquest had been disruptive of earlier institutions, and that the apparent respect of the Norman line of kings for the laws of Edward was a sop to the people to disguise the loss of 'their auncient customes and liberties'" (205), he fails to mention Lilburne's barbed quotation from Daniel to refute the claims of Coke and the common lawyers about the historical continuity of English law, thus misconstruing "Leveller support for Magna Carta" (209) as a claim for Norman confirmation of those liberties. David Wootton recalls that "when Lilburne did this in 1645, Walwyn corrected him. The oppressed are in error when they 'with one consent, cry out for Magna Carta … calling that mess of pottage their birthright, the great inheritance of the people.' This is 'to call bondage liberty, and the grants of conquerors their birthrights'" ("The Levellers," 78). Milton and the Levellers were really on the same page, it would seem, about the Norman Yoke.

Similarly, Milton recalled in *The Tenure* the reign of that tyrant "*Eglon*," who "by the Jewes had bin acknowledged as thir Sovran; they had serv'd him eighteen yeares, as long almost as we our *William* the Conqueror" (*CPW* 3: 215). Although he was quite as anti-Norman as von Maltzahn claims, this does not mean that "The *History* shows none of the Levellers' faith that things had once been better; instead, the Saxons are barbarians who did little to improve their status during the troubled centuries of the Heptarchy" (219). If things *had* once been better for Milton, it had not been under the Saxons. Citing Gildas, Milton says that the ancient Britons had been "re-invested" by the departing Romans "with thir own original right, about the year 446," and "both elected them Kings, whom they thought best (the first Christian Brittish Kings that ever raign'd heer since the Romans) and by the same right, when they apprehended cause, ususally depos'd and put them to death" (*CPW* 3: 221). As von Maltzahn has to admit, "Milton already values Gildas for his testimony that British sovereignty originated in popular consent" (130).

Is it not probable, then, that Milton extends and enlarges upon rather than refutes the Leveller myth of "ancient" liberties? For him, the most relevant "Conquest" dates from "*Cæsars* acts here, whether it were esteem'd a Conquest, or a fair Escape";[59] otherwise, he needlessly recalls that "*Julius* before his Death tyrannously had made himself Emperor of the *Roman* Common-wealth, and was slaine in the Senate for so doeing" (61). And yet the tyrant "*Julius Cæsar* … having subdu'd most part of *Gallia*," failed to subjugate the ancient Britons who, "not tarrying to be assail'd, ride in among the Waves to encounter, and assault the *Romans* eev'n under thir

Ships; with such a bold, and free hardihood, that *Cæsar* himself between confessing and excusing that his Souldiers" had "to stand in water heavy arm'd, and to fight at once, denies not but that the terrour of such new and resolute opposition made them forget thir wonted valour" (CPW 5.i: 44–5).

That it took the Romans a century to invade and subdue even a part of Britain pushes the Leveller myth of native liberty back to time immemorial. Fighting the invading forces of Claudius under the Roman general Plautius, the ancient British hero "*Caractacus* … continually went up and down, animating his Officers and Leaders, *that this was the day, this the field either to defend thir Libertie, or to die free*; calling to mind the names of his glorious Ancestors, who drove *Cæsar* the Dictator out of *Britain*, whose valour hitherto had preserv'd them from bondage, thir Wives and children from dishonor" (70).[60] Here, Milton pointedly ignores his own principles of historical writing in reporting the speech assigned by Tacitus to the British leader to illustrate the "nobleness of his bearing" before the Roman Senate, where "*Cæsar* mov'd at such a spectacle … gave him pardon, and to all the rest" (72). He thus flouted "his favored classical historians," including Polybius, who had insisted "on adhering to the truth of the facts and not operating like the tragic poet who imagines the probable utterances of his characters."[61] This adaptation of the Leveller myth of liberty now puts in a very different light Milton's "reaction" in the first book to "the uncritical reception of the British myths" (von Maltzahn, 103). The first book begins to look like a joke at the expense of that blatant apologist for the Conquest, Geoffrey of Monmouth,[62] and his justification of Norman empire as the continuation of a mythical "Trojan empire."

Martin Dzelzainis hears a further, "darkly comic" joke in the final books. Here, the jest is "at the expense of the Danes and Normans, blithely unaware of the literally self-defeating nature of their conquests," since Normans are really Danes who had conquered other Danes. Such a "joke makes a mockery of conquest theory as such, and with it the myth of the Norman Yoke."[63] But Dzelzainis has no warrant for a further claim that "if the *History* is not geared to the anti-Norman myth, neither does it make any serious attempt to reconstruct the lineaments of 'Anglobritannia'" (Dzelzainis, 287). Quite the opposite is claimed by Hugh Jenkins, who finds that Milton gives "a relatively favorable depiction of the English" through the first four books, at which point he leaves off writing to take up the duties of a public servant. If the *History* is "Milton's reply to the Levellers," it then contains "two answers to the Levellers' view of history." The first is indeed an "Anglobrittania," but the second, written in very different political circumstances, finds the English to be "worthy of their yoke(s), past and present."[64] In distinguishing between an "early," hopeful *History* and a "later," darker one, Jenkins opens up a much deeper correspondence between Leveller and Miltonic history. For, "Throughout the early books of his *History*, … Milton examines the concept of the 'foren yoke' in a way that often parallels that of the Levellers. In equating the 'Roman yoke' with that of the Presbyterians and the Long Parliament, and with civic (and … religious) compulsion in general, Milton's *History* agrees with many of the more radical Leveller claims" (318).

In *The Second Part of Englands New-Chaines Discovered* (24 March 1649), Lilburne arguably arrived at similar conclusions about the waste of English liberty that Milton, unbeknownst to Lilburne, had already reached (probably in 1648) in the third book of his *History*. Ostensibly, Milton recounts the Saxon invasions of the fifth and sixth centuries, though recent parallels (such as to Naseby) evidently emerge in the telling: "But as for this Battell of Mount *Badon* where the *Saxons* were hemm'd in," Milton insists that the Britons, "contented with the quiet they had from thir Saxon Enemies … fell to civil Wars at home"; and "by this Victory at *Badon*," they "receav'd no great annoyance from the *Saxons*; but the peace they enjoy'd, by ill using it, prov'd more destructive to them then War" (*CPW* 5.i: 168, 170, 174). "For what was more incredible," writes Lilburne in *The Second Part* of *New-Chaines*, "than that a Parliament trusted by the people to deliver them from all kinds of oppression, and who made so liberal effusion of their bloud, and waste of their estates (upon pretense of doing thereof) should yet so soon as they were in power, oppress with the same kind of oppressions" (1). "And thus," Lilburne concludes despondently, "the most hopefull opportunity that ever *England* had for recovery of our *Freedome*, was spent and consumed" (9).

Against this parallel with the Independents' failure, Milton contrasts the tolerant Saxon king Ethelbert, who, "convinc't by [the] good life & miracles" of the Britons, "became Christian, and was baptized." And yet Ethelbert "compell'd none" of his Saxons to join him in baptism: "For so he had bin taught by them who were both the Instructors and the Authors of his faith, that Christian Religion ought to be voluntary, not compell'd" (189). It is a lesson forgotten by the English in 1643 in establishing the Westminster Assembly to advise Parliament on religious reform, and imposing on all and sundry the Larger Westminster Catechism of 1648.[65] But if "Milton's response to the yoke of compulsion is more complex than the Levellers'"

(Jenkins, 318), his response to Saxon militarism repeats the Leveller view of the Army's failure. The Saxon story is largely one of endless "Wars, but for what cause wag'd, or by what Councells carried on, no care was had to let us know" (229). Until "The year 800. made way for great alteration in *England*, uniting her seaven Kingdoms into one, by *Ecbert* the famous *West-Saxon*" (247–8). Yet a "great alteration" in the form of government is pointedly reduced to a mere tale of Ethelmund, a nobleman "passing over with the *Worcestershire* men," who "was met by *Weolstan* another Nobleman with those of *Wiltshire*, between whom happ'nd a great fray, wherin the *Wiltshire* men overcame, but both Dukes were slain, no reason of thir quarrel writ'n; such bickerings to recount, met oft'n in these our Writers, what more worth is it then to Chronicle the Wars of Kites, or Crows, flocking and fighting in the Air" (248–9). For Milton, the only Saxon legacy was endless civil war, not native liberties.

Although David Loewenstein reminds us in his *Milton and the Drama of History* that "We should … be wary of assuming that Milton's sense of history evolves in a completely consistent manner, that it develops in a predictable fashion from energetic optimism to profound disillusionment as we move from the early to the later revolutionary prose," he fails to heed his own advice in arguing that "the *History of Britain* seems not to offer a way out of the labyrinth of history: there is no iconoclastic gesture which breaks its cyclical pattern, that transforms history dramatically. Rather its story of failed historical promise reinforces a sense of historical repetition" (87). Nicholas von Maltzahn is equally pessimistic, finding that "Milton's 'firm confidence' lay not in the English people at large, but in God and, at first, 'our Supreme Magistracy'" (47). But this Milton is more an aristocratic than a Leveller republican, hostile to the "many" and favouring "'the few" who, "in Milton's mind, are likely to have been those who pushed through the Purge and the execution of the king" (40). For such reasons, von Maltzahn concludes that, "After the crisis of the Revolution in 1649, Milton had written first a defence of England, then a defence of the Council of State, and then a defence of himself" (175–6), the "few" being continually whittled down toward the vanishing point. "Later the 'fit audience' of *Paradise Lost* is an even smaller remnant than the *saniores* who were to have benefited from Milton's historical instruction in the 1650s" (176). This, of course, is to assume that the true "crisis of the English Revolution in January–March 1648/9" (von Maltzahn, viii) was the readmission of "the secluded MPs" (37), where the "delay and compromise" suggested "to him that this republican *occasione* was being squandered within a month of the execution of Charles" (31). Yet for Milton, the more likely crisis was a fateful choice he had to make between the Council and the Levellers.

How could four ordinary men of the middling sort threaten the new republic?[66] Were they not more of a threat to those who, as Lilburne warned, "endeavoured to grasp the power of the Army into their hands, thereby to enforce their Tyrannie upon us; insomuch that it was almost too late to give check to their wicked intentions" (*Second Part*, 2). English history could just as easily degenerate into another chronicle of wars of "Kites, or Crows, flocking and fighting in the Air." And yet there had been progress – God's judgment on a wicked king, for one thing; for another, a bill before the Commons to abolish the monarchy and the House of Lords; for a third, some hope of religious toleration. There was also much to hope for in the Levellers' idea of "an *Agreement of the People, upon grounds of Common Right*," as Lilburne had described it, "*for uniting of all unprejudiced people therein*" (6). Could that not be the basis for a stable government? Were authority now to devolve to the people, would that not make it harder for kings and lords to be restored? Yet how many people would subscribe to the Leveller program?

Milton's own failure at this point to produce "some observations" on the Levellers can best be understood as his despairing reluctance "such bickerings to recount." There were also other strenuous demands on him to answer "the King's book" (Feb. 1649), which he did in *Eikonoklastes* (October 1649). And, after that, there was his ringing answer to Salmasius's *Defensio Regia*, comprising two "epic" *Defenses of the English People* (February 1651; May 1654), and his *Pro Se Defensio* (August 1655). Yet Blair Worden also finds in *Defensio Secunda*[67] an implicit critique of another "great alteration" in the form of government (the Protectorate; see Chapter 2), that helps to explain his darkening view of history after the "Danish Conquest," when he took up his *History* again in the mid-1650s.[68] "Here," Jenkins says of these last two, if not the earlier "Leveller" books of the *History*, "we see all the pessimism von Maltzahn and others have attributed to Milton throughout; here we see a people for whom foreign yokes become not potential means for reformation of the national character but instead just punishments for its failings" ("Shrugging Off the Norman Yoke," 321). Taking these last books to be a "long-delayed answer to the Levellers," Jenkins thereafter traces a complete reversal in the *History*, from his Roman Yoke theory to a "more providential and pessimistic view of history," in response to the naive "claims of the Levellers" (322).

By the time Milton did resume his writing of the *History*, the Rump was two years dissolved; its successor, the Nominated Assembly, had resigned after five months; and the republic had been replaced by the Protectorate. As Worden concludes of this trying period in his life, "Milton himself has hope. But he has, as far as *Defensio Secunda* allows us to see, no optimism. After his unequivocal endorsement of Cromwell in the period following the dissolution of the Rump, his earlier suspicions of him have returned. In the years ahead the hope would dissolve, and the suspicions would turn to anger and revulsion. Cromwell became, not a flawed hero, but a villain."[69] This view is certainly writ large in the opening paragraph of book five of the *History*, written in 1655 or 1656:

> The summe of things in this Iland, or the best part therof, reduc't now under the power of one man; and him one of the worthiest, which, as far as can be found in good Authors, was by none attain'd at any time heer before unless in Fables; men might with some reason have expected from such Union, peace and plenty, greatness, and the flourishing of all Estates and Degrees: but far the contrary fell out soon after, Invasion, Spoil, Desolation, slaughter of many, slavery of the rest, by the forcible landing of a fierce Nation. (257)

This implied judgment on Cromwell for having brought the republic "under the power of one man; and him one of the worthiest," was also implicit in the conclusion to the Fourth Book: "Mean while the *Northumbrian* Kingdom of it self was fall'n to shivers; thir Kings one after another so oft'n slain by the people, no man dareing, though never so ambitious, to take up the Scepter which many had found so hot, (the only effectual cure of ambition that I have read)" (255).[70] Like Worden's take on *Defensio Secunda,* the *History*'s early part seems to have been "[w]ritten as counsel" to the British people, while the later books "appeared as a testament to the cause that Cromwell has betrayed" (297).

The fall of "the *Northumbrian* Kingdom" cries out to be read as commentary on the fall of the republic. *Cromwell, our cheif of men*, indeed, *who through a cloud / Not of warr onely, but detractions rude.* Had the Lord Protector chanced to seize Milton's papers in 1654 along with those of his friend Robert Overton – who was corresponding at the time with the Leveller John Wildman – he would have found "detractions" quite as rude as any in *Englands New-Chaines.* For, aside from Milton's sardonic "cure for ambition," there is also his bitter "Digression," intended for insertion near the beginning of the Third Book, but suppressed, if not actually withdrawn, upon publication of the *History* in 1670.[71] This aside – left unpublished in Milton's lifetime – turns out to be very close in its themes and language to *The Second Part of Englands New-Chaines*, where Lilburne had railed against military and parliamentary leaders for whom "all obligations" are "Transitory and Ceremoniall," and "every thing is good and just only, as it is conducing to their corrupt and ambitious Interests. And thus," the Leveller leader ends in visible darkness and growing despair, "the most hopefull opportunity that ever *England* had for recovery of our *Freedome*, was spent and consumed, in such their uncertaine, staggering motions, and *arbitrary, irrational Proceedings*" (9).

Does it matter that Worden takes the "Digression" to be "late work,"[72] and not, as is so often assumed, a work of 1648?[73] The headnote to the manuscript copy – "made at some time after the publication of the *History*" (Worden, 414) – does instruct the printer as follows: "The Digression. / in Miltons History of England./ To come in Lib. 3. page 110. after these words. / [from one misery to another.]"[74] Written long after events, the "Digression" has all the clarity of hindsight. But the opening of the Third Book – which Worden sees as revised to suit the style and matter[75] of the "Digression" – sounds much closer to "the late civil broils" of 1648 that "had cast us into a condition not much unlike to what the *Britans* then were in" (*CPW* 5.i: 129) after the Romans had departed. "This third Book, having to tell of accidents as various and exemplary, as the intermission or change of Government hath any where brought forth," hints at the birth of the republic; so it would "deserve attention more than common, and repay it with like benefit to them who can judiciously read,"[76] since it conjures up the hope of possibilities yet to be realized. The immediacy of the events it describes is also evident in the sequel,

> when the imperial jurisdiction departing hence left them to the sway of thir own Councils; which times by comparing seriously with these later, and that confused Anarchy with this intereign, we may be able from two such remarkable turns of State, producing like events among us, to raise a knowledg of our selves both great and weighty,

> by judging hence what kind of men the *Britans* generally are in matters of so high enterprise. (129–30)

French Fogle, the *History*'s modern editor, believes that "Milton's references to 'the intermission or change of Government,' to 'the late civil broils,' and to 'this intereign' all suggest a period after the first civil war was over and before any new form of government had been established in place of the old."[77] But this is doubtful: the king was not yet charged with treason until after the second civil war; and "intereign," as von Maltzahn maintains, better fits the period after Pride's Purge, by which the Treaty of Newport and the king's restoration to the throne were prevented (22). "Intereign" points rather to the interval when royal power was at an end but the Commonwealth had yet to be proclaimed. Instead of reading the "Digression," however, as contemporaneous with Book 3, as von Maltzahn does, reading it as a late "Digression" inserted into the earlier *History* evokes the anxiety of that "intereign" by likening it to the ancient "Anarchy."

Since "the imperial jurisdiction departing hence" already points to the monarchy's end, the "Digression" then asks "why the Britans having such a smooth occasion giv'n them to free themselves as ages have not afforded, such a manumission as never subjects had a fairer, should let it pass through them as a cordial medcin through a dying man without the least effect of sence or natural vigor" (441)? This juxtaposition indicates as well that the English have wasted their liberty on other occasions. Now, "so neare a parallel betweene their state and ours in the late commotions" grows almost palpable, since ancients and moderns alike "had set before them civil goverment in all her formes, and giv'n them to bee masters of thir own choise," yet "were not found able after so many years doeing and undoeing to hitt so much as into any good and laudable way that might shew us hopes of a just and well amended common-wealth to come" (441).[78]

If the Britons of Book 3 are those who were "at first greedy of change," and so

> to be thought the leading Nation to freedom from the Empire, they seem'd a while to bestirr them with a shew of diligence in thir new affairs, some secretly aspiring to rule, others adoring the name of liberty, yet so soon as they felt by proof the weight of what it was to govern well themselves, and what was wanting within them, not stomach or the love of licence, but the wisdom, the virtue, the labour,

> to use and maintain true libertie, they soon remitted thir heat, and shrunk more wretchedly under the burden of thir own libertie, than before under a foren yoke. (130–1)

Here, the use of participles like "leading," "aspiring," "adoring," and "wanting" evokes a continuing action, while the failure of modern Englishmen in the "Digression" is set in a remote past perfect: "For a parlament being calld," as the "Digression" puts it, "and as was thought many things to redress, the people with great courage & expectation to be now eas'd of what discontented them chose to their behooff in parlament such as they thought best affected to the public good, & some indeed men of wisdome and integritie" (443). Tonally, the ensuing verdict suggests a judgment made from on high against the baser impulses of a democracy: "Some who had bin calld from shops & warehouses without other merit to sit in supreme councel[s] & committies, as thir breeding was, fell to hucster the common-wealth" (445). So "Thir votes and ordinances which men look'd should have contain'd the repealing of bad laws & the immediate constitution of better, resounded with nothing els but new impositions, taxes, excises, yearlie, monthlie, weeklie[,] not to reck'n the offices, gifts, and preferments bestow'd and shar'd among themselves" (445). "The Army," adds von Maltzahn, was "so suspicious of MPs that it set up a committee to invesitage corruption on 1 January 1648/9, and the Digression has been compared with the Leveller tracts in this regard" (33). The reach of Milton's verdict is thus very close to the judgment made by that more obvious democrat, John Lilburne.[79]

For one thing, the tone of continuing possibility at the outset of Book 3 of the *History*, set against the distant tone of the "Digression," recalls Lilburne's change of tone between the First and Second Parts of *Englands New-Chaines.* The first part concluded with a speech made by Lilburne to Parliament in February 1649, urging present action and further possibility: "*M. Speaker, We own this honorable House (as of right) the true Guardian of our Liberties and Freedoms; and we wish and most heartily desire, you would rouse up your spirits (like men of gallantry) and now at last take unto your selves a magnanimous resolution, to acquit your selves (without fear or dread) like the chosen and betrusted Trustees of the People.*"[80] Yet, having "once more unburdened our hearts before you," Lilburne was to write in *New-Chaines* four weeks later, "and faithfully discharged our duties to our Country, giving timely warning of the most dangerous thraldom and misery that ever threatned this much wasted Nation, and much we doubt not, wil, by wisdom mixt with som honest resolutions, be timely prevented," he holds out only the despairing hope that, "after so many yeers of sorrow, the people may at length be comforted, and the Land enjoy her rest; and that all the world may be enforced to confess, That *There is a reward for the righteous,* and *that there is a God that judgeth the earth*" (18). As a judgment made from on high, it is no less harsh than Milton's "Digression."

The tonal distance between the two parts of *Englands New Chains* approximates the distance that likewise opens up between Milton's "Third Book" and his "Digression." The only difference is that it would take Lilburne a month, and Milton much longer, to get there.[81] While von Maltzahn regards the *De excidio* of Gildas as the model for the "jeremiad" that supposedly "distinguishes [Milton's] historiography" (69), the alarm sounded by Lilburne in *The Second Part of Englands New-Chaines* resembles more closely the jeremiad of the "Digression." Like Milton, Lilburne pronounces God's judgment on England's shameful waste of liberty. With his usual acuity, Jonathan Scott notes that "Milton's savage indictment" in the "Digression" (which he assumes was written in the early months of the Republic) "echoed the Levellers. Like them he found the seeds of the revolution's failure in the moral failings, not of the 'rabble,' but of those chosen in good faith to be their leaders."[82] What remains to be said is that Milton was far more willing than Lilburne to implicate himself in that waste. Although Milton's wrath may sound like a judgment from on high, he does not shrink from a share of the blame.[83] For, finding the "Britans" to be sorely wanting throughout Book 3 in "the wisdom, the virtue, the labour, to use and maintain true libertie" (131), he assigns that later failure in the "Digression" to "causes equally belonging both to ruler, priest, and people" (443). In the next chapter, we will see how, in his collaboration with Marchamont Nedham in *Mercurius Politicus* in 1651–52, he repeats Lilburne's warning of the ambition of "some secretly aspiring to rule" (131), athough such a caution is really of no more consequence than the Leveller's jeremidad. Yet, with the Rump restored to power, Milton once more dares to hope that there "is now again by a new dawning of Gods miraculous providence among us," "after a short but scandalous night of interruption."[84]

Since "causes equally belonging both to ruler, priest, and people" divides the blame among the Rump, the Westminster Assembly, and the people in general, Milton might conclude, as Jenkins says he did, that the English people "prove themselves worthy of their yoke(s), past and present" (310). And yet the people, Milton appears more truthfully to say, were betrayed by their leaders before they ever betrayed themselves:

> The people therefore looking one while on the statists, whom they beheld without constancie or firmness labouring doubtfully beneath the weight of thir own too high undertakings, busiest in pettie things … Then looking on the Church-men most of whom they saw now to have preach't thir own bellies, rather then the gospel … they who but of late were extolld as great deliverers, and had a people wholy at thir devotion, by so discharging thir trust as wee see, did not onely weak'n and unfitt themselves to be dispencers of what libertie they pretented [*sic*], but unfitted also the people, now growne worse & more disordinate, to receave or to digest any libertie at all. (449)

So where did Milton really stand in the crisis – with the people or with their governors? While he had doubtless endeavoured to "fit" the people for liberty, he had also chosen to do so from within the government. In this context, the *History* turns into an admission of his own failure to save a "people wholy at thir devotion" rather than a rejoinder to the Levellers about a people not worth saving. Yet where Lilburne appears as a self-righteous prophet of judgment, Milton speaks as one who, in the "discharging [of] thir trust," had ultimately failed in that trust to gauge the drift of events. The real crux had not been the dissolution of the Rump nor even the establishment of the Protectorate.[85] The greater crisis loomed here and now in the Hobson's choice Milton would be forced to make. To side with the Rump – thirty-four of the forty counsellors were MPs – or with the unelected Levellers? Who was more deserving of his trust? Two years later, there could be no doubt. "Employed by the new government," von Maltzahn recalls, "Milton now spoke even of its members in … disparaging terms." For, "Ample evidence of his misgivings about the majority of MPs may be found in the 'Tagebuch' of his acquaintance Hermann Mylius, in entries from February 1651" (43). This is the moment when he first assumed responsibility as state censor for *Mercurius Politicus.* In the next chapter, we will encounter the doubts he now expressed about his choice of a government. It was a choice that he would continue to dramatize in one form or another throughout his *History* and his later poetry.[86]

The author of the *Tenure*, however, had yet to defect from Lilburne's declaration of 26 February 1649 to Parliament, "*That for the most part of us, we are those that in the worst of times durst own our Liberties and Freedoms, in the face of the greatest of our adversaries; and … never shrunk from the owning of our Freedoms, in the most temptestuous times, nor changed our Principles.*"[87] He, too, must suffer "*The serious apprehensions of a part of the People, in behalf of the Commonwealth*,"[88] about how "Parliaments for the future are to continue but 6. moneths, and a Councel of State 18. In which time, if they should prove corrupt, having command of all Forces by Sea and Land, they will have great opportunities to make themselves absolute and unaccountable" (2). Milton still had reason to favour Lilburne's expedient of "cast[ing] themselves upon an *agreement of the People* for the future settlement of the *Peace of the Nation*,"[89] rather than watching it be set aside and ignored as a defensible ground of political legitimacy. Yet persistent references "to the undesirability of the 'rude multitude' having the vote, the secularity (natural liberty) of the *Agreements* against the Godly interest and to the novelty of the *Agreements*' constitutionalism, all indicate that many contemporaries perceived that they proposed a shocking transformation of the constitution."[90]

Being Secretary for Foreign Tongues also made it more difficult now for Milton to support the notion that "those specious pretenses, and high Notions of Liberty" in the Army *Agreement* were "directed by some secret powerful influences, the more securely and unsuspectedly to attain to an absolute domination over the Common-wealth."[91] Only when it was too late would he finally agree with Lilburne.[92] And yet, in one telling phrase from the third book of his *History* – "some secretly aspiring to rule" – he had anticipated Lilburne's "secret powerful influences."[93] Still, the broken faith of the Army leadership, documented in *The Second Part of Englands New-Chaines*,[94] did not yet persuade him of the hypocrisy of those "secretly aspiring to rule." "And as for *Peace*," Lilburne had sounded reasonable enough, "whilst the *supream Officers of the Army* are supream in your *House*, in the *Councel* of *State*, and all in all in the *generall Counsell of the Army*, when the *martiall power* is indeed *supream* to the *Civill Authority*, what *Peace* can be expected?" (14).

Still, it wasn't exactly peace that Lilburne was seeking as he doffed his hat before the seat of the President. Bradshaw even had to repeat the question that Lilburne had previously refused to answer on grounds of self-incrimination, "*Whether you made not this Book, or were privie to the making of it or no.*" To which Lilburne retorted: "My late Actions need no covers nor hidings, they have bin more honest than so, and I am not sorry for what I have done, for *I* did look well about me before I did what I did, and I am ready to lay down my life to justifie what I have done; and so much in answer to your question."[95]

They were not strangers: Bradshaw had once acted as Lilburne's solicitor in a suit to recover indemnities voted him by the House to compensate for the treatment he had endured at the hands of the Court of Star Chamber. Perhaps Lilburne's mounting anger at Bradshaw sprang from the intransigence of the House to repay that debt to him. Or perhaps it was the memory of being "whipped from the Fleet to *Westminster*, with a 3.fold knotted Cord[,] receiving at least 200 stripes." That scalding memory had not even begun to cool years later, in one of his endless petitions, as he told of "arriving at Westminster" and being "set on the Pillary the space of 2. houres (and over and above the censure of the Court at the Warden of the Fleets command was gagged about an houre and halfe) after which most cruell sufferings was againe returned into the Fleet close Prisoner."[96] Perhaps it was simply his skin and nerves talking, that horribly flayed skin, those frayed and jangled nerves, erupting instantaneously in a towering rage:

> But if for all this, you shall send me back to the Military sword again, either to White-hall, or any other such like garison'd place in England, *I do solemnly protest before the Eternal God of Heaven and Earth*, I will fire it, and burn it down to the ground, if possibly I can, although I be burnt to ashes with the flames thereof; for Sir, *I* say again, the souldiers have nothing to do to be my Goalers.[97]

Was it an idle threat, or did he intend to act? And what choice did he leave Bradshaw but to return him from whence he strode moments ago like an actor taking the stage? His three accomplices were brought in singly to answer the same question. And one by one they refused to respond. The door had no sooner closed on the last of them than the Lt-General slammed his fist on the table. It is only from a Leveller pamphlet that we know what Lilburne claimed to hear with his ear pressed up against the door:

> *I tel you Sir, you have no other way to deale with these men, but to break them in pieces*; and thumping upon the *Councel Table* againe,

he said, Sir, *let me tel you that which is true, if you do not breake them, they will break you; yea, and bring all the guilt of the blood and treasure shed and spent in this Kingdom upon your heads and shoulders; and frustrate and make voide all that worke, that with so many yeares industry, toile and paines you have done, and so render you to all rationall men in the world, as the most contemptible generation, of silly, low spirited men in the earth, to be broken and routed by such a despicable contemptible generation of men as they are; and therefore Sir I tel you againe, you are necessitated to break them.*[98]

No one else inside that room has left corroborating evidence of this haunting scene. One imagines an assembly of gaping men looking around and asking themselves which of these two players in the scene had just renounced reason?

By the slimmest of margins, the vote went in Cromwell's favour to proceed on a capital charge of treason. Had Lilburne not threatened to burn things down, would he have won the single vote he needed for a stay of proceedings? Would Cromwell still have blustered and bullied? Or would "all rationall men in the world" have honestly judged them "the most despicable, contemptible generation of men," simply because they were loath to "breake" such mean and "low spirited men" as these?

It was a question on which the "great alteration" was about to turn.

· 2 ·

Milton and Politicus

DEPOSING CROMWELL

IN THE UNSETTLED AND UNSETTLING summer of 1647, the emerging Leveller leader John Lilburne had publicly broken with his good friend Oliver Cromwell in a series of private letters sent from the Tower and published in pamphlet form.[1] Conscious of his debt to his old mentor, which is "to me," he admits, "so large an Obligation that I thinke while I live it will be engraven upon my heart as with the point of a *Diamond*," he recounts[2] having been set free in 1640 "*from the long and heavy Tyranny of the Bishops and Starchamber*" (2) by means of Oliver's maiden speech in the Commons. As a prisoner of war in Oxford in 1642–43, he had been unable to repay his debt to his benefactor until an exchange of prisoners set him free from a royalist threat to hang him. Accepting Col Cromwell's invitation to join his cavalry regiment in the army of the Eastern Association, Lilburne became his "bedfellow"[3] and confidant, loyally supporting Cromwell's effort to convict their general, the Earl of Manchester, of treason in his dilatory conduct of the war.[4] Thrown once more into prison by Manchester – who had resigned his military post in 1645 and resumed his role as Speaker in the House of Lords – Lilburne laments that, "for my zeale to truth and justice," the earl had "got the gallowes, if you had followed him with as much vigour and strength as you should, and I was made beleeve you would. But you pluckt your head out of the coller, and I was catched in the bryers" (9).

Lilburne's misgivings are clearly more than personal, since he casts himself in the role of Jonah, the biblical prophet reluctant to speak God's truth to Nineveh. Cromwell, he fears, has been corrupted by Nineveh – money from the Commons – and is working to undermine the Engagement of the

Army. He confesses that, "if the Army doe disband before they petition, I and all such as I am, must truly lay the whole blame upon you, and truly declare the House of Commons bribe *Cromwel* to betray the liberties of *England* into their tyrannicall fingers" (4). The danger is that Cromwell has become another Manchester; so the rank and file must oppose him. In a "Postscript" dated 16 July, Lilburne is clear: "I can doe no lesse then publish the fore-going Letters as an Alarum to all the privat Souldiers in the Army, and to all their honest Officers, that really, cordially, and heartily desire the settlement of all mens just interest in *England*" (15).

Such a warning was not unwarranted; at best Cromwell was lukewarm to the "Solemn Engagement" made by the Army at Newmarket on 5 June 1647, refusing to disband until Parliament paid their arrears and agreed to a settlement of the nation that did not enshrine conservative interests of property and religion. There was also reason to think that a Presbyterian majority in the Commons, led by "*Hollis* and *Stapleton* (both now impeached): and the rest of that bloody and devouring faction, ... hath designed us to utter ruine and destruction, and this land and kingdome to vassalage and slavery" (*Jonahs Cry*, 3). Apart from the rhetoric, the facts were dire enough: the Presbyterians wanted a state church to impose Calvin's creed on all and sundry, and to impose strict censorship, ending demands for liberty of conscience and freedom of expression.

By December, Lilburne's associate John Wildman was publicly insisting that Army Grandees had intended all along to betray their "Solemn Engagement" of that spring: "I shall not prejudge the singlenesse of *Cromwells* or *Iretons* hearts as to publique good, in their first associating with the Army at *Newmarket*, but its worth the knowing, that they both in private opposed those gallant endeavours of the Army for their Countries freedom."[5] Lilburne's second letter[6] to Cromwell in *Jonahs Cry* sounds even more prophetic. Even though "my soul [y]earnes towards you," he admits, "I cannot but once again ... write two lines unto you, to tell you that I canot sit still though I dy for it, and see you that are reputed honest conscientious men be the betrayers and destroyers of your poore native Countrey, and the lawes and liberties thereof" (6).

In a fourth letter dated 1 July, Lilburne warns, "I know your practices of old." Cromwell is indeed behaving like those who "*will sell Christ, their Country, friends, relations, and a good conscience for a little money or worldly honour*" (10). In publishing his private reproach, Lilburne takes the part of an honest friend who "must as a faithfull plaine dealer tel you, that I am necessitated wholly to withdraw my present good thoughts from you and others with you, and *must and will print my conceptions to the view of the world, that so you may delude*, and destroy *honest simple hearted, plain dealing men no longer*, cost it what it will, I valew it not." He has finally made good on the warning sent previously to the Lt-General on 25 March: "But Sir, if these Army newes be true, I must bid you for ever *Farewell*, and must hereby declare my selfe an avowed enemy to your selfe-pecuniary interest, … and unmask you to my friends, then my adversaries the tyrannicall and arbitrary Lords." For the moment, however, he maintains a jocular, if chilling, hope of renewing their former intimacy: "doe the worst you can to my throat, which you used jestingly to say, you would cut so soon as ever I fell out with you" (4).

The sorrow of his falling out with Cromwell is all the more poignant in view of the final letter he appends to *Jonahs Cry*, a relic of happier days (9 December 1645) when he had refused Cromwell's invitation to join his command because of "the soyles, affronts, and undermining usages that I met with (not from you but others [Manchester] of more quality then honesty, when I was last in the Army" (12). Though "I highly honour your selfe," Lilburne movingly admits, "and could willingly (if I know my owne heart) lay downe my life for you, your honour and reputation, as soone as for my father that begot me, *or the dearest friend I have upon the face of the earth*) … give me leave without passion, to tell you, that I saw your self harbour in your brest a Snake or Snakes [Manchester again], although you will not know it."

Later, after Fairfax and Cromwell's brisk suppression of Leveller hopes at Putney to extend the franchise and to guarantee popular sovereignty, Lilburne's measured and temperate supporter, William Walwyn, offered this analysis of the many factors in play:

> [T]he great ones of the Army, what ever they pretended, are of nearer relation, and more strongly contracted to the Lords and great ones of the Nation, then to the Commons or such faithfull patriots as Mr. *Lilburn*; which being discerned by him sooner then by other men … he spares neither paines, cost nor hazard, forthwith to discover their delusion … to the world, and finding his old friend *Cromwell*, to have been a chief instrument in destroying the ends of their engagement, he neither flatters nor spares him nor any other, but layes all their actions naked to the view of the world, fore-shewing that which since is come to passe, and which now every man sees and many feels, though then few or none would believe.[7]

What is "discerned by him sooner then by other men" now looms large in the "Postscript" to *Jonahs Cry*, where the language[8] of "agreement, or solemn engagement" (14) fires Lilburne's imagination with the idea of "An Agreement"[9] of every soldier in the Army. Given that hereditary right has been exposed for a chimera, and that soldiers "hold their swords in their hands for their own preservation and safety, which both Nature, and the two Houses practices and Declarations teaches them to doe," it is clear that "the principles of Saifety, flowing from Nature, Reason, and Justice" ought to be "agreed on by common consent and mutuall agreement amongst themselves; in which every individuall private Souldier, whether, Horse or Foot, ought freely to have their vote, to chuse the transactors of their affaires" (13). Parliament's ingratitude may be fuelling the move to popular sovereignty, but Parliamentary consent theory is the real ground on which it moves.

Consent theory still had multiple meanings at the time. Rachel Foxley recalls that, to royalists, power was supposed to pass directly from God to the monarch, to whom the subject must consent, whereas, for Presbyterians, power passed from God to the monarch by popular "designation" of the magistrate or consent of the representative. To Henry Parker and other exponents of parliamentary sovereignty, the people were originally "free and equal," but consented to delegate their power to the monarch. But to the Levellers, a "free and equal" people delegated their power only to parliament, with right of revocation and reservation of certain powers.[10] The Levellers were thus able "to fuse two very different strands of parliamentarian thought: the supremacy of Parliament and the appeal to the people" (Foxley, 64). Lilburne's claim that it is "by these words in their agreement, [that] you see the foresaid position proved, that they act by mutuall consent, or agreement" (14) assumes that the Army does reserve a right to resist Parliament's attempt to disband them.[11] That the Army was not a democratic polity became obvious at Ware where, four days after "the great ones of the Army" put a period to the Putney debates, Fairfax and Cromwell snuffed out the revolt by summarily executing one man. So Lilburne probably did see "sooner then … other men" how Army Grandees were "more strongly contracted to the Lords and great ones of the Nation, then to the Commons."

It was not the prescience of the prophet but the machinations of Cromwell and his son-in-law Henry Ireton that John Wildman would subsequently emphasize in *Putney Projects*, where the generals had "painted in the most lively colours to the peoples eyes" a "domineering, tyrannicall faction" in the Commons who had invaded "the peoples freedome," and

"Petitions to the Generall … drawn by *Cromwell* himself, were sent to some Counties to subscribe, and then the most mellifluous enamouring promises were passed to petitioners of clearing and securing their rights and liberties" (7). Hereafter, the portrait sketched by every Leveller writer identifies Cromwell with "the *Apostate*" and "fallen star" Lucifer. Walwyn says flatly that Cromwell has "fallen like *Lucifer*, yea, and all that steere his unsteady course, doe they not stagger and reele up and downe like so many drunken men, and finde no certain path wherein to walke, or set their feet, since they forsooke the streight way of this just and impartiall man, Mr. *Lilburne*."[12]

Marchamont Nedham, like Wildman a Leveller defender[13] of Lilburne in the winter preceding the latter's denunciation of Cromwell in July 1647, was so suspicious of the Lt-General's motives that he turned coat, begging pardon from Charles I and becoming editor of the royalist newsbook *Mercurius Pragmaticus* in September 1647, where he now jeered at Lilburne's own shifting political aims. In the wake of the failure of Army radicals at Putney and Ware in November, Nedham wrote that the Lords begin to see

> that His Majesty being once beaten downe, the next fatall Blow must be at themselves; which is the very reason why *John Lilburne* lies so quiet and still now in the *Tower*; he being satisfied at length, that the reason why he hath been kept so long a *Prisoner* is, that he may not onely have *Reparations* for himselfe, but when time serves, be ready to give a *stroke* toward the Ruine of the House of *Peeres*.[14]

A year later, Nedham offered more anxious comment still on Lilburne's *Englands New Chains*, which had expressed "*The serious apprehensions of a part of the People*" about "the dominion of a Councel of State; a Constitution of a new and inexperienced Nature, and which they fear, as the case now stands, may design to perpetuate their power."[15] Of a sudden, *Pragmaticus* now began to jest in earnest: "What? *Iohn Lilburn* that divine piece of Singularity is it seems turn'd from a *Brewers* Clark to a *souldier*, from that to a *Councellor*, and now at last to a *Smith* to make *chaynes* of Government to the whole *Kingdome*, truly 'tis a pretty *project* but not well taken amongst the *Westmin. Cut-throats*."[16] Although he speaks in jest, Nedham does rally to the cause of Lilburne who

> is sory that he hath no more lives to loose in opposing their *Illegall power*, and vindicating the *People* in their dying *Liberties*: for the reviving of *which*, all this while he hath been so great a *Stickler*,

> that by his meanes the *agreement* of the *People* was promoted and brought to *perfection*, and now when it ought to be put in execution, he finds it layd aside and an *Arbitrary rule*, much like or worse then that of *Kings*, endangered as be exercis'd upon his freeborn *fellows* of England as may appear, by the *Comittee of States* who are to be in authority 18. *Moneths*, and all succeeding representatives but 6. *Moneths.* (5–6; unpaginated)

For such reasons, it is fair to say with Jonathan Scott that Nedham's entire "'royalist' phase conforms closely, ideologically, to this broader Leveller trajectory,"[17] not least in his urging that the Agreement of the people be adopted. For their mutual mistrust of Cromwell had driven Nedham and Lilburne both to prefer a king to a military dictator.

Awaiting trial for treason, Lilburne wrote "*To all the Affectors and Approvers* in England, *of the* London *Petition of the eleventh of* September, 1648," that "you may justifiably, before God or man, Joyn with the Prince himself (yea, I am sure a thousand times more justly, then the present ruling men … who if we must have a King, I for my part had rather have the Prince, then any man in the world, because of his large pretence of Right."[18] Two years before, Nedham had switched sides for much the same reason, claiming that Lilburne had unfolded "the *mysterie* to be a designe of Mr. *Cromwel's*," which is "but in plaine termes to tell the people of *England*, that there is no need of a King any longer, but that the government of *old Israel* shall be set up in our *new*, while *Crumwell* and *Peters* goe in and out before them like *Moses* and *Aaron*."[19] Even in the midst of dreadful animosities during the second Civil War, Nedham can still write,

> But who is able to recount the noble *Acts* or sing, all the *praises* due unto *Nol. Cromwell*? This is the great *Lucifer*[20] that furnish't the *Cause* with all the *new-lights* of this *last* Reformation; whereby having quite banish't *Presbitery*, he bids defyance to the *Gyants* of the *Covenant* beyond the *River*; and sayes they shall have as little mercy as the *Welsh*: Among whom this man of God and his Troopers fought like *Michaell* and his *Angells*, and plaid the Dragon to boot.[21]

On the day before the Leveller leaders were arrested and charged with treason, Nedham even trumpeted the alarm that Lilburne had sounded in the Second Part of *Englands New-Chaines*, that the Council of State "are resolved to proceed and goe forward in their Change of *Government.* And to that end have sent abroad a *Paper-Kite* call'd an *Act*, for the abolishing all *Kingly government* in *England* and *Ireland* … for the future, wherein their *Devilships* make all men *Traytors* and *Rebels* (to them and their proceedings) who shall be ayding, abetting, or promoting the cause of our lawfull *King* Charles *the second*."[22] Even in his royalist guise, Nedham clearly confirms Scott's judgment that, subsequently, "as editor of *Mercurius Politicus* Nedham was to play a key role in the incorporation into republican ideology of Leveller ideas" (247). Indeed, Nedham had already been moving in that direction as the royalist editor of *Mercurius Pragmaticus*.

So the Council of State issued a warrant for Nedham's arrest on 18 June 1649. "Five days later," Milton "was ordered to examine *Mercurius Pragmaticus* for suspicious utterances."[23] Far more evidence of treason filled the pages of *Pragmaticus* than appears in *Englands New-Chaines*. For "promoting the cause of our lawfull *King* Charles *the second*," Nedham was certain to be convicted on the charge of treason. That Milton made no such recommendation speaks volumes about his own reluctance to write against the Levellers, even after Nedham had given his jailers the slip, remaining on the lam until 14 August. Milton must have played a key role, then, in his release on 14 November on condition of "first takeing the test,"[24] the Oath of Engagement to the Commonwealth. Even though Nedham wrote to a friend that it was John Bradshaw, president of the Council, "whose 'favour hath once more turned the wheel of my fortune; who upon my single letter hath been pleased to indulge me my liberty,'"[25] who else, apart from Bradshaw's friend John Milton, had the literary discernment to recognize the talent of the era's most widely read journalist, and turn it to advantage? "The fact that Milton and Nedham became friends soon after this suggests that Milton may have helped," concludes Barbara Lewalski, "in the effort to recall Nedham to his earlier republican allegiance."[26]

The release of the Leveller leaders from the Tower on 8 November 1649 likely played a part, as well, in Nedham's own release six days later. Doubtless, the Council had reason to fear a public backlash at the prospect of another treason trial, although a few months later, they did convict and execute Christopher Love, the Presbyterian conspirator and minister, for treason. A plausible inference is that Milton, who was far more qualified than anyone to judge the writings of Nedham, had persuaded Bradshaw of the journalist's supreme value to the republic, now threatened on all sides. Nedham had been a Leveller propagandist before he was a royalist; so who was better situated than he, and better able to reconcile its enemies to the new regime? At the same time – and this would have been no small consideration – Nedham might even be persuaded to fulfill the terms of Milton's unfulfilled commission "to make some observations" regarding the Levellers.

What issued from Nedham's hand five months later in *The Case of the Commonwealth of England, Stated* (May 1650) differs in many respects from the soaring eloquence of Milton's prose. Dispassionate, plain-spoken, and relentlessly rational, *The Case*[27] argues for submission, rather than resistance to the established power. In a manner absolutely unique in polemics of the era, Nedham "drew upon Sallust and Guicciardini, but above all Machiavelli," in deploying "the interest theory established by the *Discorsi* Book 2, Chapter 1. Moreover Machiavellian interest analysis is a more or less consistent feature of Nedham's writing from 1645 to 1660."[28] Among a multitude of interests now opposed to the government of the republic, Nedham selects for analysis those of "the Royal Party" (53–70), "the Scots" (71–86), "the English Presbyterians" (87–95), and "the Levellers" (96–110), demonstrating in each case "the great improbability of effecting their designs," and "the grand inconveniences which must needs follow, in case either of them be effected, to the prejudice of the whole nation" (51). The harm certain to follow from the success of any one of these opposing interests was enough to convince recalcitrant segments of the population that it was in their best interest to support the republic. As for those who scrupled to deny old loyalties, both biblical and classical history proved "That Governments Have Their Revolutions and Fatal Periods" (7–14); "That the Power of the Sword Is, and Ever Hath Been, the Foundation of All Titles to Government" (15–29); "That Nonsubmission to Government Justly Deprives Men of the Benefit of Its Protection" (30–3); "That a Government Erected by a Prevailing Part of the People Is As Valid *de jure* As If It Had the Ratifying Consent of the Whole" (34–40); and "That the Oath of Allegiance and Covenant Are No Justifiable Grounds to Raise a New War in, or against, the Commonwealth of England" (41–50). As "the Florentine Secretary" (35) had written more than a century before (and Nedham now proceeded to expound), it is no "mere gallantry of spirit which incites men to the love of freedom; but experience tells us it is the most commodious and profitable way of government, conducing to the enlargement of a nation every way in wealth and dominion" (116).[29] To Nedham, a Commonwealth was no more, but also no less, than the common interest of the people.

To those who see only an aristocratic Milton, Nedham's interest theory and ethic of self-interest are surely at the farthest possible remove from a godly republic under the "rule of the virtuous."[30] And yet, in view of what

Milton proposed in *The Tenure of Kings and Magistrates* as the main end of government, it appears "that the power of Kings and Magistrates is" none-theless "transferr'd and committed to them in trust from the People, to the Common good of them all, in whom the power yet remaines fundamentally" (CPW 3: 202). Sharing a common vocabulary with *The Case*, Milton also appeals to Aristotle's authority to show that "the best of Political writers have defin'd a King" as "him who governs to the good and profit of his People, and not for his own ends." Resorting to Aristotle's definition of "the two main ends of all civil communion" as being "public safety" and "public equity, for the administration of justice, encouragement of virtue, and punishment of vice" (*Case*, 30–1), Nedham is likewise indebted to Aristotle's argument that "the best of governments" is "by experience known to be most conducing to the advancement of a nation every way in honor, profit, and dominion; having ever produced many more excellent heroes than any other form upon the stage of action, as is evident in the Grecian, Roman, and modern stories" (123). Nedham's faith in the improving effects of a free state on popular morality were anticipated by Milton, who argued that, "from the murmurs of new discord," the majority will "heark'n rather with erected minds to the voice of our Supreme Magistracy, calling us to liberty and the flourishing deeds of a reformed Common-wealth" (CPW 3: 236). Nor is moral improvement alien to Nedham's interest theory; he quotes Machiavelli's friend Francesco Guicciardini claiming that "free states are most pleasing to God because that in them more regard is had to the common good, more care for impartial distribution of justice to every man, and the minds of men are more inflamed with the love of glory and virtue and become much more zealous in the love of religion than in any other form of government whatsoever" (*Case*, 117).

In both *The Tenure* and *The Case*, the transformative power of liberty is a major determinant of political morality. To Milton, it is "the liberty and right of free born Men, to be govern'd as seems to them best" (CPW 3: 206). "And not to have in our selves, though vanting to be free-born," he adds in *Eikonoklastes* (October 1649), "the power of our own freedom, and the public safety, is a degree lower then not to have the property of our own goods. For," as Milton expatiates, "liberty of person and the right of self-preservation, is much neerer, much more natural, and more worth to all men, then the propriety of thir goods, and wealth" (CPW 3: 454). "Yet it is a wonder to see," Nedham expands on this idea, "how lightly men prize this invaluable jewel of liberty which hath cost the Commonwealth so much blood and treasure" (*Case*, 111). Therefore, "when the Romans had lost that ancient virtue which purchased their liberty and an empire over the world, being softened in their manners and conquered by their vices whose dominions they had conquered," Nedham cites Milton's favorite historian Sallust, "they soon bowed under the yoke of imperial tyranny" (113). Nedham, the exponent of interest theory, sounds like a classical republican[31] in making liberty first and foremost an *ethical* value.

Milton argues similarly that it was those "Patriots" who, "endu'd with fortitude and Heroick vertue," were foremost in "the deliverance of thir Countrie" (*CPW* 3: 191). Nedham also claims "that if the Commonwealth had not a party of its own throughout the nation, men of *valor* and *virtue, free from those corruptions* of excess and riot, and sensible of liberty, it were then in reason to be expected they could not long maintain their station" (114, emphasis added). To Milton, such "proceedings" of "Heroick vertue" really do "appeare equal to what hath been don in any age or Nation heretofore, justly or magnanimouslie" (*CPW* 3: 194). And Nedham hails "this necessary and magnanimous act" (*Case,* 89) by which the "invaluable jewel of liberty" was obtained by those worthy of it, contrary to those caged "beasts" that, "if they be let loose, yet they will return in again because they know not how to value or use their liberty" (111–12). In the same way, Milton had argued in *Eikonoklastes* (1649) that they "would shew themselves to be by nature slaves, and arrant beasts; not fitt for that liberty which they cri'd out and bellow'd for, but fitter to be led back again into thir old servitude, like a sort of clamouring & fighting brutes, broke loos [from thir copyholds,] that know not how to use or possess the liberty which they fought for" (*CPW* 3: 581).

According to both writers, the impediments to liberty are not external to "free born men" but are first formed within by shackles of custom, idolatry, and licence (or luxury). Milton's *Tenure* opens with a ringing assertion that, "If men within themselves would be govern'd by reason, and not generally give up thir understanding to a double tyrannie, of Custom from without, and blind affections within, they would discerne better, what it is to favour and uphold the Tyrant of a Nation" (*CPW* 3: 190). *The Case* inveighs with equal strength against the "impression" made "by education and custom from the cradle, even upon men that are endued with reasonable souls, that they choose to live in those places and customs of government under which they have been bred rather than submit to better which might make more for their content and advantage" (112). In *Eikonoklastes,* Milton had lamented that "the People … are prone ofttimes not to a religious onely, but to a civil kinde of Idolatry in idolizing thir Kings; though never more mis-tak'n in the object of thir worship" (*CPW* 3: 343). Nedham recalls the biblical story of Nimrod, who "became the first tyrant in the world and therefore was called a mighty hunter, as having used his power to no other end but to lay the foundations of idolatry and tyranny" (15).

To both commentators, men are easily courrupted by the worship of idols both "civil" and "religious," not to mention their own excess in love of luxury. "For indeed none can love freedom heartilie," Milton says, "but good men; the rest love not freedom, but license" (*CPW* 3: 190). Guicciardini is "very pertinently to our purpose," Nedham adds, "that 'many times when a people have got loose from the yoke of a tyranny or kingly government out of a desire of liberty, they proceed from one extreme to another … and except they be restrained, run headlong to licentiousness; which also may be rightly called a tyranny'" (100). Finding examples of excess not "only in Greece," but "also among the Roman levelers" (107), Nedham says the ancient prejudice against unbridled democracy applies just as much to the English Levellers, who have "disseminated such strange principles of pretended freedom among the common sort of soldiery and people that it became evident to all the world they sought not liberty but licentiousness" (96).

Nedham, as Elliot Vernon shows, was not above linking "the political demands of the Levellers to fears of social dissolution. Citing Aristotle's *Politics* amongst other works, Nedham argued that classical history and philosophy provided countless precedents of the political trajectory of the type of settlement announced in the *Agreement.*"[32] And the trajectory of such "levelling" is invariably downward: "An equality of political right ultimately led to an equality of property and social levelling; this, in turn, would see the 'brutish multitude,' 'being void of reason,' establish tyranny and crush liberty."[33]

That the majority of people are inclined to slavery because of their lack of vigour is also basic to Aristotle's *Politics*, a lesson that Milton had repeated the year before in *The Tenure*, claiming that "the people of Asia, and with them the Jews also, especially since the time they chose a King against the advice and counsel of God, are noted by wise Authors much inclinable to slavery" (*CPW* 3: 202–3). So, "in Asia and other countries," Nedham is quick to echo both Aristotle and Milton, "where civility hath degenerated into effeminacy, they ever have lived and do for the most part continue in miserable slavery at the will of imperious tyrants" (113). If "effeminacy" is an ever-present threat to republican virtue, then masculinity[34] – the *vir* of *virtus* or moral worth that Cicero had defined as *prudentia*, *justitia*, *fortitudo*, and *temperantia* (wisdom, justice, courage, and temperance)[35] – is the strongest support of a classical republic. Five years before, Milton had remarked similarly in *Areopagitica* that "such a steepe disadvantage of tyranny and superstition … as was beyond the manhood of a *Roman* recovery" was a direct consequence of the state policy prohibiting "unlicenc'd Printing" (*CPW* 2: 487, 486). (By these lights, Nedham ought to have warned Milton that Adam's "subjection" to Eve was fatal to classical republican *virtus* – if either had ever been a classical republican.)

Paul Rahe shows that Nedham turned his back on classical republicanism with its "emphasis on man's capacity for moral and political rationality," emulating Machiavelli rather in his view that "moral virtue" was "a sham."[36] Since "all men are wicked" (235), reasoned Machiavelli, then the only feasible way to preserve "the general good" (236) was to prevent its seizure by "the few" in securely "placing the guardianship" of "the common good" – meaning liberty – "in the hands of the people" (235). The reason was clear: "no matter how 'good a patriot' a particular individual may be, 'yet if his power be prolonged, he will find it hard to keep self from creeping in upon him, and prompting him to some extravagancies for his own private benefit" (236). Therefore, "Frequent popular elections and a 'due and orderly succession of power and persons' are … 'the only remedy against self-seeking, with all the powerful temptations and charms of self-interest.'" Even if Nedham does support the Levellers on occasion, Rahe says, it is with a Machiavellian twist on their "noble" populism. For Nedham had "been quite friendly to John Lilburne and to the Leveller cause" (234) in 1645 and had even "contributed a laudatory preface, signed M.N., to Lilburne's *An Answer to Nine Arguments*. In 1646, the two are thought to have co-authored[37] at least one pamphlet, *Vox Plebis*, if not more; and, as we have had opportunity to observe, Nedham had occasionally made common cause with the Levellers" (213). In this respect, Rahe concludes, Nedham's political outlook is obviously at the antipodes from his state licenser and friend John Milton. For, "Whatever John Milton may have been, he was not a modern populist" (118).

This variance in the politics of the two men is less obvious, however, in view of a typical passage from *The Case*: "For shame or fear then, if not for love, let men forbear an opposition and consider what an honor it is to be in the list of that party which have ennobled themselves by their own virtue and the love of liberty. For as Cato saith in Plutarch, even the greatest kings or tyrants are much inferior to those that are eminent in free states and commonweals" (115). Evidently, "the Excellency of a Free State above a Kingly Government" (111), as proclaimed in Nedham's closing chapter title, inheres in that nobility which "virtue and the love of liberty" confers on citizens. "And though now the very name of liberty is grown odious or ridiculous among us, it having been a stranger a long time in these parts," Nedham exhorts, "yet in ancient time nations were wont to reckon themselves so much the more noble if they were free from the yoke of regal tyranny; which was the cause why there were then so many free states in all parts of the world" (115) The "self-interest" of the common people is then no more than a negative virtue holding the "self-interest" of "the few" in check; for there is still a positive "virtue" in liberty that ennobles those who feel its transforming power.

Furthermore, the use of that phrase "yoke of regal tyranny" is not likely to be a slip of Nedham's pen, but rather a sly reference to his part in the publication of the Leveller tract *Regall Tyrannie Discovered* (January 1647).[38] If such is indeed the case, a number of echoes of Milton's *Tenure* in Nedham's *Case* begin to sound like Nedham's witty echo of himself, given that *The Tenure* had also resounded with wordings and arguments[39] from *Regall Tyrannie*. Yet, in present circumstances, Nedham is supposed to be taking aim at the Levellers as enemies of the "virtuous" few. Or so it would seem, as he brings the authority of Aristotle's *Politics* to bear on those "not improperly called 'Levellers'" to support a charge that "this plea for 'equality of right' in government at length introduceth a claim for 'equality of estates'" (98). The joke is that Nedham had himself argued in *Vox Plebis* for a "Roman" agrarian law to prevent the concentration of wealth. Therefore, as Scott concludes with mordant irony, "When Nedham attacked the Levellers for seeking to introduce an agrarian law he apparently did so with the full authority of an author of that campaign."[40]

Rather than swallow hook, line, and sinker the rather dubious proposition that "John Milton's defense of the English commonwealth was characteristically high-minded," and that Marchamont Nedham chose the "opposite course, eschewing high-mindedness when he published his defense of the republic" (Rahe, 187–8), we need to reconsider the close relationship of these two writers in light of the reception of their intertwoven defences. For "his service already done to the Commonwealth,"[41] Nedham was awarded £50 and the editorship of a government newsbook he proposed. According to the prospectus that he submitted to the Council on

"June 8," he planned to "entitle it Politicus, because the present Government is vera πολιτεία [literally *state*] as it is opposed to the despotick forme."[42] Whether from its inception or later on is not clear,[43] but for such reasons, Milton was appointed to supervise the content of *Politicus.*

Given the strictures of the Press Act of 20 September 1649, Nedham was very fortunate to have for his licenser[44] one whose vocabulary and arguments were so close to his own. Who actually wrote what in *Politicus* has been a subject of some speculation since Masson (1877) first remarked a shift in the style of *Politicus* 16 (26 September 1650), after fifteen initial issues consisting of "disconnected, slangy jibes at the Royalists." "With number 16," J.M. French (1936) admits, "comes so marked a change as to suggest a new author."[45] David Masson had in fact made it a real problem of attribution: "I have not seen anything," wrote the Victorian biographer, "of his [Nedham's] of a serious kind nearly so good as the best leaders in *Mercurius Politicus* through the year 1651, or in a spirit so high and religious."[46] French, however, realized that material from *The Case* had been recycled in issues from numbers sixteen to sixty-nine, if "with some gaps."[47] Only recently have readers noticed that none of these editorials contains material recycled from *The Case*'s attack on the Levellers. As Rahe explains this omission, "Nedham's *Case of the Commonwealth of England Stated* had been a job application: in it, as one would expect, he was willing to give his prospective employers every benefit of the doubt" (213). Echoing Rahe's claim that Nedham "omitted the material on the Levellers" because "the *Case* was written as Nedham's 'job application' to his future employers,"[48] Rachel Foxley refuses to speculate on whether the omission suggests his renewed support for the Levellers, or whether Nedham simply regarded them as having shot their bolt.

Whatever the case with the jettisoned materials, French also realized that, "Beginning with number 70 a new method appears" in the lead editorials of *Politicus.* "Instead of plagiarism from previous books Needham now reversed the process and collected the editorials into a book."[49] In the event, he waited four years to publish *The Excellencie of a Free State* (1656), the mordant irony of which lies, as we shall see, in the change of political circumstance.[50] As for the question of attribution, the later materials in *Excellencie* had only Milton's imprimatur. So much for numbers 70 to 114; they clearly belong to Nedham. Yet "So much," too, says French, "for numbers 1–69" from *Politicus,* most "of which are stale and second-hand. From most of them Milton's pen is now definitely absolved, unless the whole affair is more of a hoax than I am willing to believe" (242).

That the author of *Areopagitica* could be party to a "hoax" might have given readers pause, had Elmer Beller (1942) not been more concerned that French "leaves the door ajar for the supposition 'that Milton's participation was limited to occasional paragraphs which he added to articles already written or for which he supplied Nedham with suggestions and facts.'"[51] In at least one sentence of *Politicus* 91 (4 March 1652), French thought he did hear Milton speaking in his own voice: "First for *Kings*, give me leave to shew (what I once published upon another occasion) that tis no new thing for Kings to be deprived, or punish'd with death for their crimes in government." As French says, "This, almost the only personal statement in the editorials, sounds very suspiciously like John Milton alluding to his own *Tenure of Kings and Magistrates.* Little if any of Needham's writing could be mentioned in these terms. With considerable temerity," he then concludes, "I venture to claim this one sentence for Milton's bibliography" (245).

Beller slammed the door shut on this idea, however, noting that Nedham had already promised in *Politicus* 49 to supply a "Treatise" from "Holy Writ and secular history, of wicked kings punished for their crimes" (486). "Unfortunately," Beller admitted, "it has not been possible to find the 'Treatise' promised [!] in No. 49." But by identifying "units" of thought in sequences of leads matching arguments from *The Case*, and by showing that Nedham had previously used "Miltonic word[s]" himself, Beller saw "no satisfactory evidence of collaboration" between the two authors. As he confessed with artless candour: "Perhaps it is best so. We should prefer to think that the position of the author of *Areopagitica* as 'licenser' was purely nominal" (487). Milton, the champion of freedom of the press, could not be allowed to dirty his hands with censhorship. French went even further, making it "conceivable that his licensing was perfunctory, and hence that he did not follow carefully what his colleague was doing." For, "In comparison with a Latin Tome which should make all Europe ring from one end to the other, the vulgar little weekly Mercuries were petty things not worth a serious thought" (246). Thus, the whole question of attribution appears to hinge on the sort of Milton one is willing to imagine.

For seventy years, no one dared to question this idealized image of Milton until Blair Worden (2007) showed that "There are in fact many parallels or near-parallels of phrasing, which Masson and Gardiner did not record, between Milton's tracts and passages of *Politicus* that had not appeared in *The Case.*" But, as Worden admits, "there is, or may be, a simple explanation of them. Milton wrote his tracts of 1649–51, in which most of the moments of his prose that correspond to passages of *Politicus* are to be found, before the analogous material appeared in the newsbook. Nedham, we can or could infer, simply took material from his colleague's work."[52] Worden is keenly aware all the same that his "interlinear" speculations better fit the big picture, where "Milton and Nedham stood together until the last breath of the Puritan Revolution, which helps to explain why a number of tracts linked their names and why their enemies called for them to die by the same rope. Just how far they collaborated in that time it is hard to be sure" (348). Worden will not refrain, however, from referring to "a creative partnership" (181), and even "a close working partnership between Milton and Nedham" (207).

The problem, of course, is that most readers have not been "willing to believe" in Milton the literary hack: "If the thought of Milton stooping to collaboration with Nedham requires mental adjustment, an acclimatizing example of it may help us," Worden coaxes (41). Since *Politicus* 91 had indeed appeared to David Masson to speak directly in the voice of Milton, Worden remarks of this unattributed "*I*" that it is here "we learn" as well

> that "the greater part" of men "was ever inclined to adore the golden idol of tyranny," and there too that we are informed, in words so close to those of *Eikonoklastes* and *Defensio*, that "in the monuments of the Grecian and Roman freedom we find those nations were wont to heap all the honours they could invent, by public rewards, consecrations of statues and crown of laurel upon such worthy patriots; and as if all on earth were too little, they enrolled them in heaven among their deities." This does not mean that the whole editorial was written by Milton. (206)

And yet, as Worden justly concludes, "The prose of the two writers has, by some process intertwined." Indeed, "Cicero, recalls Milton, recorded that the Greeks 'ascribe divine worship to men who have killed tyrants.' The Greeks and Romans, *Politicus* 91 reminds us, 'enrolled' the slayers of tyrants 'in heaven among their deities'" (182). Evidently Milton's voice begins to sound in more than just a single personal pronoun.

As for other instances of pronominal usage, Worden notes that "The same 'I' appears to have spoken in another editorial in *Politicus*, ten months earlier, on 15 May 1651. That editorial, too, vindicates the regicide" (206). Even more remarkable is the probability that "the letter from Leiden which appeared in *Politicus* in September 1652, and which Milton used in 1655 in ascribing *Clamor* to Alexander More" (208), was written by Milton. "For if the passage about More was written, not in Holland, but in England, then there is one man who answers to the description of its author as a man of 'learning and prudence,' 'very well known to myself,' and – thanks to the impact of *Defensio* there – 'very generally known in Holland': Milton himself" (212). By these lights, it is almost certain that the author of *Areopagitica* was happy to be party to "a hoax," rather more so than some are "willing to believe" (French, "Milton, Needham," 242).

Then there is the problem of "important gaps" that French clearly glossed over in his catalogue of reprints from *Case* in numbers 16 to 69 of *Politicus*, none more troubling than 66 (11 September 1651), that great hymn of thanksgiving to God for Cromwell's victory at Worcester (3 September 1651). Here, the style soars of a sudden into the language of providential history, unlike anything yet seen from Nedham, with the possible exception of one sentence in *The Case* lauding the New Model Army's "special protection from heaven, God having sealed them for his own by many miraculous victories and successes to the wonder of the whole world" (77). Yet the voice that celebrates the stunning victory at Worcester is far more lofty, making it prudent to describe the author as "Politicus," and to catch him in the act of sounding now like Nedham, now like Milton:

> It was a loud *Declaration* from Heaven at *Naisby*, when by a despised Company it pleased God to decide the controversie; … but his loudest *Declaration* of all was mightily set forth in the late sudden Revolutions and Actions, before, and at *Worcester*; whereby he unquestionably appears to have given a full and finall Decision of the controversie, and seems as it were with his own Finger, to point out to all the world his Resolutions for *England*. (1045–6)

Ten pages later, the epic voice dwindles to a sly reference to triumph on another field of battle, if modestly restricting our view to the figure of a second opponent vanquished:

> The reason why *Salmasius* left *Sweden* was, because *Milton's* book having laid him open so notoriously, he became thereby very much neglected, the Queen not having sent for him, nor seen him for the space of two moneths; so that perceiving a decay of her favor, he

> came himself and desired leave of departure, which was very readily granted, the Queen having at length understood, how impolitick it is for any Prince, to harbor so pernitious a *Parasite*, and Promoter of Tyrany. (1056)

Given the manner in which God "owned this *Cause*" (1046), both at home and abroad, the voice speaking the language of prophetic truth is best heard as a duet of Milton and Nedham hymning God's praise in accents that properly belong to Politicus.

This prima facie reading of *Politicus* 66 dates back to Masson's late-Victorian *Life*, where, in two pages of volume 4, he had reprinted the editorial in full, before saying:

> I can *conceive* the article on Worcester Battle to have been a hurried composition or dictation of Milton, lowering his habitual style somewhat, to adapt it to Needham's journal. So, in others of the articles, … I have come upon passages of such a Miltonic strain that I could *suppose* them possibly Milton's. On the other hand, in no complete article or long continuous passage have I felt positively sure, from the internal evidence, that I was reading Milton, while at the same time there is the adverse evidence, of whatever worth it may be, lying in the fact that we have no attestation anywhere by Milton himself that he contributed to Needham's journal, and in the fact that Needham was always identified with *Mercurius Politicus* by his contemporaries, and credited with what appeared there. But then, if Needham did write the article on the Battle of Worcester and other similar articles, it must have been Needham greatly metamorphosed. (334–5)

Though Nedham was without peer in the art of changing shape, it would require a marvel on the order of Ovid to metamorphose his logical prose into the epic register of Milton. And a "miracle" greater than the victory at Worcester was most unlikely.

There is a more mundane problem, however, in attributing that passage to Milton; he was absent from London for several weeks before 15 October, at the very time when issue 66 appeared, although Barbara Lewalski thinks that he may have been no farther afield than at Hammersmith (*Life*, 259). During that painful year of increasing blindness and frequent headaches, Milton was not obliged to write propaganda, but only to translate occasional letters of state. Apart from this single duty, there was his nephew's work to supervise, John Phillips's *Responsio* to John Rowland's (anonymous) *Apologia* "for the king and people of England."[53] And his normal habits of supervision do point to what Nedham could have expected from his supervising editor. "According to [John Phillips's] brother Edward," recalls Worden, "Milton committed the writing of the book to John, 'but with such exact Emendations before it went to the Press, that it might very well have passed for his, but that he was willing the person that took the pains to prepare it for his Examination and Polishment, should have the Name and Credit of being the Author'" (215–16).[54] The case for attributing every word to Nedham that appeared in issues 70 to 114 is thus fundamentally weakened, since his reprinting of the editorials in book form in *The Excellencie of a Free State* (1656) says next to nothing about their original composition.

More likely, then, is Worden's claim that, with *Defensio* "completed by the end of 1650," Milton began to collaborate with Nedham as early as mid-January 1651 (181), meaning that, during his Septmeber rest cure (if that's what it was), he welcomed a visit from Nedham to Hammersmith. Great things were afoot in the land, after the rout of the royalist cause at Worcester, although there were growing indications that the royalist threat had infiltrated the republican cause, now that "the lord general sat with his family in the royal pew in the chapel of Whitehall at a service of thanksgiving for the victory."[55] The immediate public response from *Politicus* was a primer in commonwealth principles that came out weekly for the next ten months to educate the public. Most likely this is the project that Nicholas von Maltzahn found described in the so-called "Digression" of Milton's *History of Britain*, where he affirms "his belief that only education will repair his countrymen's natural failings as citizens of a free state" (1). For, starting with issue 68 (25 September), the prophetic voice gives way to the witty, aphoristic style of Nedham and his custom of quoting maxims from the *Discorsi*, that venerable bible of pragmatic republicans: "It is a noble saying, though *Machiavel's; Not he that placeth a vertuous government in his own Hands, or Family, but he that establisheth a free and lasting Form, for the peoples constant security, is most to be commended*" (1077).

In fact, Worden takes this whole series of editorials (70 to 114) as Milton's own education in Machiavelli's rules of republican citizenship and civic responsibility as the ground of any "free state." For "England's new government," Worden notes, was "far removed, in Nedham's eyes, from the republican ideal of Machiavelli" (220). Indeed, it was in "the months between November 1651 and February 1652" that Milton seems to have recorded his first maxims from the *Discorsi* in his Commonplace book, revealing "preoccupations close to the editorials in *Politicus* in and around those very months" (222). "He approvingly noted," for instance, "that Machiavelli 'much prefers a republican form to a monarchy' [CPW, 1] (477). He endorsed Machiavelli's principle, which is a basic premiss of Nedham, that republics need to be renewed at their source 'by restoring the control of things to the decision of the people' (475–7)" (223). Here, too, in the pages of the newsbook is covert development of the principles of Machiavellian populism,[56] and reasons why "the People" are invariably "the best Keepers of their own Liberties."[57]

First and foremost of a dozen reasons offered by Politicus for popular government is "because it is ever the Peoples care to see, that Authority be so constituted, that it shall be rather a Burthen than a Benefit to those that undertake it" (1222), an echo of Machiavelli's idea that common self-interest is a good brake on private self-interest.[58] Another reason is

> because as the end of all Government is (or ought to be) the good and ease of the People, in a secure enjoyment of their Rights ... so questionless, the People, who are most sensible of their own burthens, being once put into a capacity and Freedom of Acting, are the most likely to provide remedies for their own relief. They onely know where the *Shoe wrings*, what grievances are most heavy, and what future fences they stand in need of, to shelter them from the injurious assaults of those powers that are above them. (1287–8)

Above all, "it is very observable" from the example of Rome, "that this *Commonwealth* ever thrived best, when the People had most power, and used most moderation" (1111). But, "when the *Senate* afterwards worm'd the People out of Power, as that design went on by degrees, so *Rome* lost her Liberty, the *Senate* domineering over the People, and particular *Factions* over the *Senate*," until "hee that was head of the Paramount surviving Faction, by name *Cæsar*, took occasion to usurp over all; swallowing up the Rights and Liberties of the *Romans*, in the Gulph of a *single Tyrannie*."

Doubtless, Rahe is correct to insist that Nedham "really was intent, as he had been in 1651 and 1652, on instructing his compatriots in the logic underpinning the modern republic" (*Against Throne and Altar*, 233). But Rahe's choice of *The Excellencie of a Free State* (1656) over the weekly journalism of

1651–52 to present that instruction suggests his fidelity to a book-history of the idea (Machiavellian republicanism) at the expense of the weekly drama emerging from the editorials in those critical months. Of course, my choice of the newsbook to represent these ideas reveals my own predilection for drama; for the challenge that Politicus offers to the Rump on 9 October 1651 is nothing if not dramatic, claiming it has "worm'd the People out of Power," and left the nation in danger of falling into the gulf "of a single Tyrannie." Even though the English "bee born as free as any people under Heaven, yet naturally they are of a supple humour and inclination," Politicus cautions, "to bow under the ignoble pressures of an *Arbitrary Tyranny*," and so are "utterly unapt to learn what, *True Freedom is*: It is an inestimable Jewell, of more worth then your Estates, or your Lives" (1095). For that reason, he is just as eager as Lilburne to hold Parliament accountable to its declarations in this political standoff: "the People have been solemnly acknowledged and declared to be the *Original and Fountain of Supremacy*," and ought to taste "all the sweets of *Soveraignty*" (1125).

What is of indisputable importance is Worden's conclusion that Nedham's "editorials of that time clothed Leveller thinking in arguments drawn from the history of classical antiquity" *(Literature and Politics*, 29). But to what extent did his licenser share in such "Leveller thinking" if and when it wore a Roman toga? Here, Worden wants to differentiate Nedham's Machiavellian pragmatism from his censor's "classical" republicanism, arguing that Milton "took his political values as much from Greece as from Rome," and that, "The cast of Milton's mind is always ethical, of Nedham's always practical" (225–6). Scott says something similar about the ethical strain of Milton's thought, as compared to the pragmatism of Nedham, "whose less severe approach to matters of personal morality was accompanied by a far more developed interest in constitutions" (136). Good men supposedly matter less than good states to Nedham; the "virtue" inheres in the form. By contrast, good government for Milton is supposed to come from within; men must govern their passions before self-government can ever work in the state. For Worden, "the public struggle between 'liberty' and 'licence,' or between 'discipline' and 'licence,'" in Milton's world view, "is the extension to the state of the struggle between reason and passions for the sovereignty of the individual soul" (226).[59] Neither historian is "willing to believe" that Milton could be of two minds about "classical" and "Leveller" republicanism.

For instance, issue 69 (2 October 1651) of *Politicus* makes education the keystone in the republican arch. Citing Machiavelli, Nedham still seems as dependent as Milton is supposed to be on a Platonic epistemology:[60] "Wee who have been educated under a *Monarchy*, may very fitly be resembled to those Beasts, which have been caged or coop't all their lives in a Den, where they seem to live in as much pleasure as other Beasts that are abroad; and if they be let loose, yet they will return in again, because they know not how to value or use their Liberty" (1093). While liberty awaits in the light of the sun outside the cave, those who emerge wearing blinkers of custom are just as blind as those who have never left the cave. In *The Tenure*, Milton argued similarly that "If men within themselves would be govern'd by reason, and not generally give up their understanding to a double tyrannie, of Custom from without, and blind affections within, they would discerne better, what it is to favour and uphold the tyrant of a Nation" (*CPW* 3: 190). Custom is liberty's enemy, blinding even those who do escape from Plato's cave, leaving them hostage to "blind affections within." In this blatant echo of *The Tenure*, Politicus adds, "So strong an impression is made likewise by education and custome from the Cradle, even upon men that are endued with reasonable souls, that they chuse to live in those places and customs of government, under which they have been bred, rather then submit to better, which might make more for their content and advantage" (1093).

Eikonoklastes (October 1649) had railed in similar terms against those "who through custom, simplicitie, or want of better teaching, have not more seriously considered Kings, then in the gaudy name of Majesty, and admire them and thir doings, as if they breath'd not the same breath with other mortal men" (*CPW* 3: 338). Only "reasonable souls" are ever free to choose the good, and only when they are able to recognize what they see. For Nedham, it seems, as much as for Milton, the politics of choice requires the underpinning of a moral philosophy "centered upon an idea of rational self-government, within the commonwealth and the soul, present from Plato to Sallust, Cicero, and Tacitus."[61] It is precisely this sort of education that Milton had proposed in a pamphlet by that name in 1644, and had a few months later elaborated in *Areopagitica* into a genuine metaphysics of choice, based on the freedom to read books, "what ever sort they be" (*CPW* 2: 507). For God has entrusted man "with the gift of reason to be his own chooser" (*CPW* 2: 514); "for reason is but choosing" (*CPW* 2: 527). Given a manifestly Socratic ethic of testing,[62] even bad books may be useful "to a discreet and judicious Reader," since they "serve in many respects to discover, to confute, to forewarn, and to illustrate" (*CPW* 2: 512–13).

Politicus offers another warning against political error in a second civics lesson of 9 October 1651, aiming to ensure the preservation of republican virtues: "When *Rome* was once declared a *Free-State*, the next work was to establish their *Freedom* in some sure and certain way: And in order to this, the first business they pitcht upon was, not only to engage the People by an *Oath* against the Return of *Tarquin's* Family to the Kingdom, but also against the admission of any such Officer as a *King* for ever" (1109). From the outset of the republic, the Rump had demanded an Oath of Engagement from its own ranks, as well as from members of the Council of State, to ensure loyalty to the Commonwealth. But it had "to learn with a shock" in 1649 "that its own Captain-General, Lord Fairfax, was among the first who refused" (Brailsford, *The Levellers*, 606). In early 1650, with a Scottish war on the horizon, the loyalty oath was required of every adult male in England. In this respect, Roman history offered a means "to discover ... and to illustrate" best practices in a classical republic. A more oblique intent "to discover, to confute, to forewarn" awaited a fifth civics lesson (23 October) upon Milton's return to London, where "It is observed, that when *Kings* were driven out of *Rome*, though they were declared and called a *free-State*; yet it was a long time ere they could be *Free* indeed, in regard that *Brutus* cheated them with a meer shadow and pretence of *Liberty*" (1141).

Here is evidence to suggest that the rise of an English Brutus was of concern not only to Nedham but to his licenser who allowed his words into print. For liberty, Politicus suggests, is yet possible under the Council of State[63] presided over by Nedham's and Milton's friend, John Bradshaw. But issue 72 (23 October) hints at a tense power struggle with more relevance to Cromwell than to Lucius Junius Brutus, the founder of the Roman republic.[64] After the Lord General's return to Westminster,[65] the Council began to lose its radical bent, offering little but a "shadow and pretence of Liberty." As Politicus implies, "He [Brutus-Cromwell] had indeed an Ambition high enough, and opportunity fair enough, to have seized the *Crown* into his own hands; but there were many considerations that deterred him from it: For, he well perceived how odious the name of *King* was grown: Besides, had hee sought to inthrone himself, men would have judged it was not love to his Country that moved him to take Arms, but desire of Dominion" (1141). The need of displacing events to antiquity was familiar, of course, to all Renaissance readers who understood the risk of spelling things out. "It was necessary therefore," Politicus remarks of the English Brutus, "that hee should think of some other Course more plausible, whereby to work his own ends and yet preserve the love of the People; who not having been used to *Liberty*, did very little understand it, and therefore were the more easily gull'd[66] out of the *substance*, and made content with the *shadow*" (1142). One could not say more about Cromwell's design in the wake of Worcester and expect to go on publishing a weekly civics lesson.

The question was whether Politicus could sail closer to the wind before capsizing? By reference to Greek antiquity, readers were now reminded of those "*leading Grandees*, more potent than their fellows," who "took occasion ... to assume the power into their own hands, to the number of *Ten persons*. This form of Government was known by the name of the *Decemvirate*, wherein these *new Usurpers* joyning Forces together, made themselves rich with the spoils of the People" (1142). Ever since *Jonahs Cry* (1647), Lilburne had used "Grandee"[67] to refer to Cromwell, as he did more frequently after Putney, jeering at the House of Lords' "tyrannical *Lords*, and masters, *Cromwel* and *Ireton*, and the rest of their confederat, *Grandees of the Armie*."[68] Mere weeks after this outburst, Lilburne would trumpet on the title page of *The Prisoners Plea* how "he is like to be murdered in the Tower, by *Crumwell* and his tirannicall fellow Grandees."[69]

Pragmaticus (Nedham in his royalist phase) had reported at the time with evident glee on the Leveller leader's use of this term "Grandee" to upbraid the tyrant Cromwell:

> *Iohn* proceeds, flings *wild-fire* among the States, and extream *Dudgeon* throwes the nickname of *Levellers* in the very face of *Oliver*, and like a flie about the *Candle*, playes with the flames of his *Nose*, without all fear of *sindging*; telling him, that he *and his Grandee faction are the only* Levellers, *who have in good earnest* de facto, *levelled all our Lawes and Liberties, to their own corrupt lusts and wills, and made* England, *already like* Turkey, London *like* Constantinople.[70]

That Politicus dared to use the epithet of Pragmaticus in a republican civics lesson shows how anxious "he" now was about Cromwell's ambition. That Nedham remained above suspicion was literally by virtue of his licenser, the great defender of the English republic, the little "English David," who had just this year (1651) slain Salmasius, widely reputed to be the foremost Latinist in Europe. Nor could Nedham afford to forget that his former licenser, Capt. Thomas Audley, had been thrown in jail[71] (before the editorialist) when Nedham had deliberately crossed the line in *Mercurius Britanicus* in May 1646, depicting Charles "as a tyrant" and warning "that he was endeavouring to set the two crowns of England and Scotland against each other."[72] Would he not warn his "particular friend"[73] Milton, then, about that injury to his previous licenser and contributing editor? And here is where his licenser and likely collaborator seems to have paid him no heed.

Although the word "Grandee" never appears in Milton's attested writings of this era, the newsbook's allusion to "some *leading Grandees*" whose "form of Government was known by the name of the *Decemvirate*" (1142) directly recalls his use of *decemviri* earlier that year in *Defensio*. Speaking of the Roman magistrate's duty to obey the Senate as the expressed will of the people, Milton wrote, "The best example of this might be the decemvirs, for though they enjoyed consular power in the highest sense they were still one and all, despite any resistance, compelled to yield to the authority of the Senate" (CPW 4.i: 464).[74] *Politicus* (23 October 1651) repeats the same lesson: the usurpers, "not caring by what unlawfull means they purchased either profit or pleasure," grew "every day more insupportable," until "they were in the end by force cashiered of their *Tyranny*" (1142).

There is one important difference, however, between these two accounts. The newsbook aims to incite mutiny in the Army and rebellion in the street: "That they who were *Lords* abroad should be *Slaves* at home" was so galling to Romans that "they resolved to be riden no longer under fair shews of *Liberty*," and "raised a Tumult under the conduct of their Tribune *Canuleius*; nor could they by any perswasions be induced to lay down Armes, till they were put in possession of their Rights and Priviledges" (1143). Thus, Politicus concludes, "Now, and never till now, could they be said to be a *free State* and *Commonwealth*, though long before declared so." Nor was Milton nearly so euphemistic as his eighteenth-century translator endeavoured to make him concerning the struggle of the *decemviri* "to retain [!] their Government"; instead, he justifies the rebellion as follows: "We are also told that certain consuls, even before the end of their terms, were judged to be enemies of the state and were opposed by force of arms. For none supposed that he who acted as an enemy was still a consul" (CPW 4.i: 464). The changed political context after the Battle of Worcester had by now supplied its own referent for this seemingly prophetic sentence of *Defensio*. It is Cromwell, Politicus implies, who is on his way to becoming that "Consul, who acted as an Enemy."[75] The warning could not be clearer.

Solely on Milton's authority, Politicus was left to hammer away week after week on the theme of "Grandee" ambition, fashioning an abundance of classical analogies to fit the new circumstance. At the end of November, Politicus writes in Machiavellian fashion that "the People are the best *Keepers of Liberty* because they are not ambitious; They never think of usurping over other mens rights, but minde onely which way to preserv their own, wheras the case is far otherwise among *Kings* and *Grandees*, as all Nations in the world have felt to some purpose" (1222–3). As Paul Rahe rightly observes, Nedham grounds "his defense of the guardianship of the people on the Machiavellian assertion that ordinary folk possess a defect in appetite" (*Against Throne and Altar*, 235). The inference is clearly topical: "Such another *Triumverate of Grandees* was that of *Augustus*, *Lepidus*, and *Antonie*, who agreed to share the world between themselves, and traced the same paths, as the other did, to the top of worldly Tyranny, over the ruins of their Countries Liberty" (1223). But if the epithet "Triumverate of Grandees" shies away from Lilburne's explicit yoking of "Caesar" to "Cromwell," the claim that "a *Free*-State (or a *Government by the People)* to be much more excellent than the *Grandee*, or the *Kingly Power*" (1237) is familiar. It is the old warning, repeated in so many Leveller pamphlets before the regicide, against the ambition of the Lt- (now Lord-) General. Whether he co-wrote or licensed such sentiments, Milton was allowing his early political sympathies to resurface.

Cropping up twice at the end of November, the word "Grandee" appears three more times in the first issue of December, during a week when Milton's "last appointment had lapsed," and he "was without any official status in the Government." His chief twentieth-century biographer, W.R. Parker, surmised that, "On his forty-third birthday, 9 December, the poet probably felt himself finished as a public servant, if not as a useful citizen."[76] But something else was surely contributing to this anxiety: John Bradshaw had just been rotated out of the Presidency of the Council[77] – by "a *Grandee-Cabinet* or *Junta*" (1238), Politicus says brazenly. While the term "Junta" certainly pins the tail on the military donkey, the theme of this issue – that, "as *Motion* in bodies *natural*, so *Succession* in *Civil*, is the grand Preventive of Corruption" (1237) – provides a minimum of cover for their suggestion that replacing Rump and Council both would be a better "Preventive of Corruption" than removal of its temporary president. The former is revealed as their actual policy when Politicus opines that the People must either "yeeld to the pleasure of the *Grandees* or be broken by Them" (1238). Nedham had surely not heard these words repeated by the eavesdropper Lilburne, but Milton had probably witnessed that infamous speech in the arraignment of the Levellers – "If you do not break them, they will break you."[78] The echo is every bit as deliberate as the next one that follows in *Defensio*: "By these practices, they produced that upstart *Tyranny* of the *Decemviri*, when *ten men* made a shift to enslave the *Senate*, as well as the People" (1238).

In the subsequent issue (11 December 1651), the word "Grandee" appears only once, if in a damning context where history's verdict upon "the *ten Grandee Usurpers*, with *Sylla*, and *Caesar*, and the names of others" had made them "as odious upon the *Roman* Record, as the name of *Stuart* will be in our modern Chronicle, to all posterity" (1257), a verdict meant to render the usurping Cromwell faction equally odious. And "grandee" is used again in incendiary fashion in issue 81 (25 December 1651), "In pursuance of our *Position*, That a *Free State is much more excellent then a Government by Grandees, or Kings*" (1287). Though Milton's reappointment to the Council of State had to wait four days yet to be approved,[79] Politicus scorned to moderate his attack on "*Grandees* in a *standing Senate*,"[80] looking to Roman antiquity to show how citizens, when the republic was in danger, "neglected all the *Grandees* and *Gallants* of *Rome* to make choice of this poor man," Cincinnatus, to subdue "the Enemy," after which he returned to "following his plough in a poor rustic habit" (1305). The implied comparison, of course, is to Cromwell, who had not withdrawn to his rural estate after Worcester.

At the same time, there is increasing emphasis on the plural authorship of *Politicus*: "*Our* Design [italics added] is still to prove," the authors write on 8 January 1652, "That a *Free-State Government* is much more excellent then any other form ... Because it is the people onely that are concerned in the point of *Liberty*; For, whereas in other *Forms*, the main Interest and Concernment both of *Kings* and *Grandees*, lies either in keeping the people in utter ignorance of what *Liberty* is, or else in allowing and pleasing them onely with the name and *shadow* of Liberty in stead of the *substance*" (1319). Here, "Grandee" occurs three times in a context where public judgment must not be left to posterity, no more than it was "during the War of *Peloponesses*, where the people having been rook't of their Liberty by the slights [*sic*] power of the *Grandees*, and afterwards by the assistance of the Free-Stae [*sic*] of *Athens* recovering it again, took occasion thereupon" – and here the cautionary tale takes a more ominous turn – "to clap up all the *Grandees*, and chopt off ten of their heads at one time" (1320). Only three years before, a king had for a similar crime suffered the same fate. The warning to the "Grandees" on Council is so graphic that tensions are bound to come to a head.

Even so, the crisis is delayed the following week (15 January 1652) as Politicus offers "to prove, that a Form thus qualified, is much more excellent than that of *Kings*, or *Grandees*," reminding us that "we are still upon the account of Reason" (1333). "Reason" gives way to invective, however, in four swift references to "Grandees," before we return to "the ten *Grandees* … after whose deposition, Liberty and Sobriety began to breath again, till the days of *Scylla, Marius*, and the other *Grandees* that followed down to *Caesar*" (1335). Here at last is the "deposition" that Politicus has hinted at all along, if now with a Lilburne-like urgency. For Politicus rails against grandees (seven times) and their disdain for classical republican virtues "that could be raked out of the ashes of the old *Roman* Discipline and Freedom" (1335). Not least of these is the familiar Miltonic pairing of temperance with liberty, now joined to Machiavelli's populist pairing of restraint with lack of ambition. Insofar as the people "are the more free from luxurious courses, they are likewise free," Politicus sums up the crisis, "from those many oppressive and injurious practices which *Kings* and *Grandees* are most commonly led, and often forced unto, to hold up the Port and Splendor of their tyranny" (1334). The old warning that Milton had directed to leaders of the republic at the end of *Defensio* has now been repeated as a judgment.

Four months later, Lilburne dared, in a pamphlet published in exile, to repeat that warning at the end of *Defensio*, "commend[ing] unto the serious and hearty consideration of the LORD GENERALL and his Confederates the Advice of their valiant and learned Champion Mr. MILTON." And then Lilburne reprints the warning to the English people

> "to make it appeare to all the World, that you are as well able in the middest of peace and disarmed, most valiantly to conquer *Ambition, Avarice, Mammon* and those corruptions of manners that attend prosperity; wich are wont to conquer other Nations and generations of men; as you have bin to vanquish your Enemies in a time of Warr; and to shew forth as much *Iustice, Temperance* and *Moderation* in the preservation of your Liberties, as ever you have manifested courage in casting the *yoake of bondage* from of your necks" … and soe far for Mr. *Miltons* excellent and faithfull advice to them.[81]

It is a qualified, though grateful, endorsement of Milton from the exiled Leveller leader, and a likely sign that Lilburne had read between the lines of

Politicus and understood the message. Whatever guilt by association with the "Grandees" Milton may now share, his Leveller republican credentials have been recognized and hailed by "free-born John."[82]

Whether he wears the hat of author or licenser matters little as Politicus ends his issue 84 (15 January) with the fate of "the *ten Grandees*" (1335). But if a sixth and even seventh instance of "Grandee" is not sufficient provocation – or the repeated mention of Caesar not incendiary enough – Politicus, ever mindful of Bradshaw's marginalization by Cromwell, recalls all those republican virtues that were enumerated at *Defensio*'s end, in writing that "onely *Cato* remained as a monument of that Temperance, Vertue, and Freedom, which flourished under the Government of the people. But that you may know what it was, take here the copy of old *Catos* countenance, as it was drawn by *Lucan*."

Cato's celebrated declamation is the climax of *The Civil Wars*, a work of profound relevance to English republicans as a republican epic poem (65 CE) by Lucan, the nephew of Seneca the Younger. As David Norbrook explains, "Lucan was the central poet of the republican imagination, and his traces can be found again and again amongst leading Parliamentarians."[83] While the poem was obviously designed to be "an anti-epic, vandalizing the conventions of Augustan imperial art" (33), it ended at book ten (two books short of Virgil's *Aeneid*), for the simple reason that the poet had been sentenced to death for conspiring to depose the emperor Nero. So Lucan died like a Roman, slitting his wrists in his bath. And, "In reciting lines from his own poem while he was dying – a moment illustrated on the title-page of May's translation – Lucan enacted the process by which republican poetry was suppressed by imperial power" (Norbrook, 30).

The Civil Wars will not take us far, however, in understanding the subtle politics of Milton's God, or in following an evolution from feudal monarchy to republican rule in Heaven, much less in explaining the relevance of the marriage plot in *Paradise Lost*. To take Lucan's elegy for republican Rome as the model for Milton's epic even has the negative effect of making Cromwell seem magnanimous, since he was more lenient than Nero had been. In the event, Milton lost his job as the licenser of *Politicus*; even then, the judgment would be delayed for a week. If "Milton's" final issue[84] now seems more genial than anything in a month's worth of threats of judgment, Politicus still makes a principled attack on "the grandeur of any *standing Power* whatsoever" (1349) as being fatal to that merit "which makes men aspire[85] unto great actions, when reward depends not upon the will and pleasure of particular persons, as it doth under all *standing Powers*; but is conferr'd upon men … according to merit, as it ever is, and ought to be in *free States* that are rightly constituted" (1350). So why did the Council of State not welcome the turn from stick to carrot? Because antiquity, it would seem, has "come nearer [and more riskily] home" (1351). Even as it invites readers to "witness at present the valiant Swisses, the Hollanders, and also our own Nation; whose high atchievments may match any of the Ancients, since the extirpation of Tyranny, and a re-establishment of our Freedom in the hands of the People" (1352), the belatedness of such praise after so much criticism more likely says how little the English have achieved of what the Swiss or Hollanders now enjoy. It resembles a promissory note about to fall due more than any true praise or even flattery. And, as we know from Lilburne's example, tying the political commentary too closely to present circumstances can be dangerous indeed.

This was the final issue (22 January) of *Politicus* to be "Entred … under the hand of Master Milton" (French, *Life Records*, 3.155). No announcement was made, no reason given; the Council of State was not eager to publicize the sacking of its chief defender. Modern historians, however, have been misled by a coincidence – a most fortunate one for the government – that, two days before the issue of *Politicus* 86 on 29 January 1652, "William Dugard printer" was "arrested for handling the Racovian Catechism about which Milton was later to be questioned" (French, 3.157). Biographers have always taken this to be the reason for Milton's removal as the licenser for *Politicus*; his connection to Dugard was the smoking gun.[86] Milton seems to have written a note on 10 August 1650 (although it was never found) that may or may not have authorized Dugard[87] to print the heretical Socinian treatise. Yet theological heresy was hardly as urgent as blatant political heresy, although it could serve as a cloak for the latter. Two days after Dugard's arrest, was the government really ready to sack its most famous public defender for religious error without having all the evidence in hand, and with a full public hearing still months away?[88] In the event, Milton would not be examined "Before April 2" (French, 3.212).

In terms of the timeline alone, it is quite absurd to conclude that Milton's "hand" was expunged for religious reasons from *The Stationers' Register* on 29 January, less than forty-eight hours after a printer with no relation to the newsbook had been apprehended. Neither the machinery of printing nor that of government moved that swiftly, not even in the urgent matter of Leveller "treason."[89] In view, then, of the cleverly subversive subtext of

Politicus over many weeks and months, is it not reasonable to suppose that hardliners on Council, who supported Cromwell over Milton's friend John Bradshaw, had begun to harbour serious doubts about their former champion? Would it not not be more expedient to dismiss the censor in total silence than be forced to admit to political heresy within the bosom of Council? If asked, the government could always pretend that the licenser had to be sacked on grounds of religion, although the issue was not raised by anyone. But how could Milton be allowed to keep his post if his political heresy were publicized? He wrote no more propaganda, *ever*, at the behest of the Council. And when his *Second Defense* did come out two years later, it was neither commissioned by the Council nor praised under the Protectorate.

In the meantime, the Council moved quickly, on 2 February 1652, to appoint Lewis Rosin as their French translator. Then, on 11 March, "the council called out of retirement Milton's predecessor as Latin Secretary, Georg Weckherlin, appointing him assistant secretary to the Committee for Foreign Affairs."[90] Innocuous in isolation, what these several signs reveal in their new configuration is the Council's need to neutralize "blind guides."[91] While moderates on Council might accept the expediency of keeping watch on their Latin Secretary, no one wanted to dispense with the great prestige that the elegant Latin of their "Champion" brought to state correspondence in foreign affairs.

In the same week that Milton was cashiered as a government licenser, the Rump Parliament convicted John Lilburne of libelling Arthur Haslerig, MP, and passed an act (30 January 1652) banishing him in perpetuity from the Commonwealth.[92] Obviously, Nedham had now to proceed more cautiously with his civics primer. Although the word "Grandee" appeared once more in *Politicus* (29 January), it was surely too late to catch it in the wake of his collaborator's sacking. And there is only one more instance of its use over the next two months. On 26 February 1652, Politicus uses it to refer to *Lords* of old: "whereas under Monarch and *Grandees*, it hath been ever seen that … they arrogate all [power] unto themselves" (1425). Stylistically, however, Politicus gains a new pronominal signature, in this distinct "I" emerging out of the former "we": "And withal remembring, that we are now put into a better course, upon the *Declared Interest of a Free State or Common-weal*, I conceived nothing could more highly tend to the propagation of this *Interest* … then to manifest the Inconveniences and ill Consequences of the other *Formes*, and so to root up their Principles" (1457). This new "I" reappears as well in the next issue (91), where Milton appears to speak in the first person.[93] Textual evidence, both circumstantial and verbal, suggests that Milton, lately cashiered, has just re-emerged as the defiant author, unable to hide his mounting frustration at Cromwell's hypocrisy. In effect, Milton lets the mask slip, daring the Council to look upon the face of its critic. While not exactly Lilburne's form of frontal assault, it does indicate Milton's growing alienation from the great apostate and betrayer of English republicanism.

In this context, the "heroic" sonnet "To the Lord Generall Cromwell May 1652" looks decidedly less heroic. While J.S. Smart concedes that, "On the occasion when the Sonnet was written, Cromwell and Milton met on common ground as supporters of religious toleration, and Cromwell's greatness is nobly commemorated," he qualifies this estimate, insisting that, "The relationship between them was not so close, nor Milton's adherence so unreserved, as is sometimes imagined."[94] As Blair Worden remarks, there is also a revealing contrast between Milton's sonnet to Sir Henry Vane in July 1652 and this one in May on the question of liberty of conscience: "Since Vane 'knows' as well as Milton the proper boundaries of Church and state, he has nothing to learn from him. Cromwell has much to learn" (*Literature and Politics*, 245). Indeed, Milton "dwells only on Cromwell's military exploits" in the poem, "not on his performance in parliament. That performance troubled Milton," hence the "reticence of the sonnet" (246).

At the very least, the diction suggests a profound ambivalence about, if not an active distrust of, "our cheif of men, who through a cloud / Not of warr onely, but detractions rude, / Guided by faith & matchless Fortitude / To peace & truth thy glorious way hast plough'd" (1–4).[95] As E.A.J. Honigmann notes, "The implications of Milton's appeal to Cromwell have never been fully explained by his editors, who overlooked his use of a once-popular catch-phrase" among "supporters of the Parliamentary party [who] signed themselves in a multitude of pamphlets 'by a lover of *peace and truth* (or, of truth and peace).'"[96] For Honigmann, the phrase merely explains the poet's choice of particular victories, not against English troops but against the Scots at "Darwen stream" (Preston, 1648), "Dunbarr feild" (1650), and Worcester (1651), tying Cromwell's military exploits against the Covenanters to his resistance to the Assembly in its plan to impose a national church on non-Presbyterians. "It is against this background of recent invasions from the north," Honigmann maintains, "that we must judge Milton's approval of a general who had ploughed his *glorious way*, to all intents, through the *blood of Scotts*" (148–9).

Four years before, at the volte of the sonnet to "the Lord Gen. Fairfax at the seige of Colchester," Milton had asked, "[W]hat can Warrs but endless War still breed"? (Flannagan, 290, line 10). In such a context, what stands out in the sonnet to Cromwell is not "thy glorious way" but the verb "plough'd," highlighting the brute force of conquest in relation to the attempt of the "Commtee for Propagation of the Gospell," led by Cromwell's former chaplain John Owen, to impose "fifteen 'fundamentals' of belief" (Worden, 248) on the nation. Honigmann likewise recalls Milton's changed political views in 1654, when "he no longer regarded Cromwell as a fellow-Tolerationist, a believer in Absolute Voluntaryism in matters spiritual, for the Protector had at last made manifest his sympathy with John Owen and the Independents, and was publishing ordinances to halt the move towards Church-Disestablishment" (149). But Cromwell's susceptibility to Owen must have been clear in the sacking of the licenser for *Politicus*. "On 10 February 1652," Owen, "Bridge, Goodwin, Nye and Simpson and others anxious to set up an Established Church, submitted various documents on this subject to Parliament and also a copy of the Racovian Catechism" (145). While it took the Independent ministers two weeks more to express their repugnance to Milton's tolerationism, Cromwell and the Council of State had seemingly anticipated them. In the sonnet, Milton thus reveals himself almost openly to be a part of that "cloud … of detractions rude" through which the Lord General "hast plough'd."[97]

Throughout the remaining weeks of the spring of 1652, Politicus continued to deal with Cromwell's relentless rise to power, as well as a growing inclination among MPs to go to war[98] with the United Provinces of the Netherlands, a truly perverse war between two new republics. It is difficult to know if Politicus speaks here with one or two voices. On 3 June, he still has some hope, given that "in the Turn from a *Free-State* to a Monarchy again, we see with what difficulty *Cesar* met, in setling his own Domination over a People that had been educated in a Free-state and in principles of Freedome."[99] Yet "Caesar's" influence over the Council, where he had begun to hold near total sway, and his continuing influence in the Rump – apart from war with the Dutch – was to frustrate this last forlorn hope. Then, a petition from junior Army officers on 2 August, asking the Rump to dissolve their sitting and call for elections, was rebuffed by a majority, who, as Bulstrode Whitelocke wrote, viewed "it as improper, if not arrogant, for the officers of the army to petition the parliament their masters."[100] On 5 August, throwing caution to the wind, Politicus reprinted Chapter 18 of Machiavelli's *The Prince*, "*In What manner Princes ought to keep their words*" (1770). To the Florentine's cynical wisdom about when to play the Lion and when the Wolf, Politicus adds one unmistakably personal sentence: "A Prince there is in these days, whom I shall not do well to name, that preaches nothing else but peace and faith; but had he keept the one and the other, severall times had they taken from him his state and reputation" (1772). It is the Lord General who has just been publicly identified as the Wolf.

So the line in the sand approached on 22 January – "To come nearer home" – has been crossed for good, although a week is allowed to pass with a new editorial (12 August 1652) explaining the "*Ninth* and last *Error in Policie*, observable from the Practice of most Times and Nations," which "hath been the *persecuting and punishing of men for their opinions in Religion*" (1785). Supposedly, it will be for meddling in the tolerationist controversy that Nedham is banned henceforth from printing editorials (they will not appear again in the seven years the newsbook has left to run). But the trajectory of the crime, like that of its punishment, follows exactly the same pattern as the licenser's offence. In either case, a religious pretext is made to mask a political cause. The outcome is so laughably similar in both instances that joint authorship of *Politicus* is exposed almost by default.

No one, of course, had chanced to notice "Mr. Milton" using the voice of Politicus after his abrupt, if unpublicized, dismissal in January. Yet here is the Miltonic "I" still speaking distinctly on 4 March 1652: "First for *Kings*, give me leave to shew (what I once published upon another occasion)" (1443). And if on 4 March, then why not on 11 March? On this date, Politicus assumes his plural voice again to counter a common objection to popular sovereignty – "That the erecting of such a Government would be to set on *Levelling* and *Confusion*. For *Answer*, if we take *Levelling* in the common usage and Application of the Terme in these daies, it is of an odious signification, as if it levell'd all men in point of Estates, made all things common to all, destroy'd *Propriety*, and introduced a community of enjoyments among men" (1458). Politicus replies that it

> is a scandal fastned by the cunning of the *common Enemy* upon this kinde of Government, which they hate above all others; because

were the People once put in possession of their *Liberty*, and made sensible of the great benefits they may reap by its injoyment, the hopes of all the *Royal sticklers* would be utterly extinct, in regard it would be the likelyest means to prevent a return of the *Interest* of *Monarchy*.[101]

Nothing in the style or content of the rebuttal ties it to Milton, save for the fact that the "we" of the previous week appears again as this Miltonic "I." Notable as well is the earnestness of the "I's" defence of "Levelling," bearing no trace of Nedham's former jocularity in having written in the inaugural issue of *Politicus* (13 June 1650) that, "This day the *Parliament* resolved into a *grand Committee*, to consider of the Form of an *equal Representative*, and the regulating of *Elections*. Tis not the wild *Levelling Representative*; Alas, that *Project* is at an end, since *John Lilburn* turned off the Trade of *State mending*, to take up that of *Sope-boyling*."[102] At that time, Nedham was still accustomed, in his recent guise as the royalist *Pragmaticus*, to jibing at "free-born John's" expense. But by March 1652, under the rising star of Cromwell and in the wake of Lilburne's summary conviction and banishment, the joke must have stuck in his throat (if he were the sole author of these paragraphs on Levelling). But whether Nedham or Milton, singly or together, composed that sober apology of 11 March for "Levelling," Politicus did not – could not – unsay his original preference for a Levelling republicanism. Indeed, he reminds his readers yet again that "all determinations being carried in this Form by common consent, every mans particular interest must needs be fairly provided for against the arbitrary disposition of others. Therefore, whatever is contrary to this, is Levelling indeed, because it placeth every mans right[103] under the will of another" (1459).

In view of mounting tensions with the Dutch,[104] Politicus further advises "that such as have commenced war, to serve the lusts of Tyrants against the People's interest, should not be reckoned any longer a part of the People, but may be handled as *Slaves* when subdued … because by their Treasons against the *Majesty of the People* … they have made forfeiture of all their Rights and Priviledges, as Members of the People."[105] As *Vox Plebis* (1646) had long ago shown, Nedham was ready and able to defend Lilburne's principles. Did the Miltonic voice now demur, or did it co-operate in this defence? How was it even possible to disentangle it from that straightforward and sober apology for Levelling? Whatever one is "willing to believe" about Milton's collaboration with Nedham, a canny ventriloquist named Politicus was seeking to "depose" Cromwell, if in a manner rather more reminiscent of Machiavelli's wolf than of Lilburne's lion. In view of the newsbook's subtext and the context of its production, sceptics have to be wilfully blind to doubt that Milton, as much as Nedham, was really essaying to depose Cromwell before he seized power, although both remained in the employ of the Council of State.

Not even the military coup eight months later, with its expulsion in April 1653 of the do-nothing Rump, exposed the face of Caesar. The Nominated Assembly – made up of "140 delegates," with "one-third" of them "drawn from the traditional ruling élites of their regions" – quickly "passed twenty-six ordinances" that promised to reform church and state alike. In August, in a move that should have eased lingering doubts in the mind of the author of *Doctrine and Discipline of Divorce*, an ordinance was passed requiring "that all marriages be performed not by the clergy but by a justice of the peace." Other ordinances mandated "the compulsory civil registration of births, marriages and deaths within each parish; greater protection for lunatics and their estates, and provision for the relief of impoverished debtors and prisoners."[106] But when "A bill calling for the abolition of the rights of patrons to appoint clergymen to livings and to reform the gathering of tithes was rejected by only two votes," moderate members now "regarded the attack on patronage as a threat to the rights of property owners." On 12 December, Cromwell connived in the voluntary "resignation" of the Assembly, and on 16 December accepted the title of "Lord Protector." Neither Nedham nor Milton had any further reason to doubt their prophecies about the rise of Caesar. Even so, Nedham would wait another thirty months to publish "a daring attack on the protectorate" in *The Excellencie of a Free State* (June 1656). As Worden demonstrates, he had "made slight adjustments to his earlier text" in *Politicus* 70 to 114, amending the wording of his advice to the Council of State, for example, "to keep close to the rules of a free state, for the barring out of monarchy," by changing it to "the turning out of monarchy." With similar intent, he elected to "commend founders of commonwealths 'who shall block up the way against monarchic tyranny, by declaring for the liberty of the people'" (Worden, 309–10).

But Milton, it seems, had beaten Nedham to the punch by two years in revising his *Defensio Secunda*, a work in progress since at least August 1652, to offer a scathing critique of the Protectorate. As Worden plausibly insists, "The very act of publishing in defence of 'the people of England' assumes an ironic aspect now that Cromwell has turned his back on the principle of popular sovereignty" (294–5). Here, in a text that nobody had asked for, written mostly under the Rump and largely preserving its republican ethos, a number of anachronisms surely begin to sound more and more ironic in view of each of those military coups in the previous year. "Why did he not remove or alter statements that had become anachronistic?" Worden asks rhetorically.

> He cannot have been unaware of the effect of the anachronisms, which is to give the work the character of dramatic irony. The stark … recognition that Cromwell, the "patron of liberty," might "violate" it; the eulogy of Milton's hero John Bradshaw, who so defiantly accused Cromwell of having done that very thing … the contrast between the retirement of the first leader of the new model army, Fairfax, who shunned ambition, and his successor, who after his elevation in December 1653 was so widely charged with it: those passages stand in ominous assessment over the protector. (294)

Why else would Milton warn, after the fact, "that if 'our republic' ('nostra republica'), 'which has sprung up with so much glory' – that is, with the regicide – 'should vanish as soon as it has arisen, no equal disgrace and shame could fall upon this nation'" (269)?

Such passages written under the aegis of the Commonwealth and published six months into the Protectorate are now repurposed as ironic commentary, given that "our republic" had vanished within months of the writing of such counsel. In it, the Lord General is praised as "the greatest and most glorious of our citizens, the director of the public counsels, the leader of the bravest armies" (285), if only by virtue of his refusal of a title. Except that Cromwell has just been described as assuming "something like a title, resembling most that of the father of your country." As Worden drily remarks:

> The wording is strange. Why should the office of lord protector, from which he derived his power, be referred to, and only referred to, as "something like a title"? Milton may have had some aversion to the title of protector, which at no point in his writings did he bring himself to name … But there is another reason. It lies in the preceding passage, which Cromwell's assumption of the protectorate contradicts, and which must have been written before it. There Cromwell is

> lauded on the very ground that, even though he is "the greatest and most glorious of our citizens, the director of the public counsels, the leader of the bravest armies," he refuses a title. (285)

The acceptance of "something like a title," followed by a lionizing of him for refusing a title, exposes the hypocrisy of Cromwell's "republican" virtue. Milton implies that he has seen it all before; the Protector is just another Princeps claiming to be *primus inter pares*. Though Worden doesn't say so, such ironies largely anticipate the political lesson repeated by Adam at the end of *Paradise Lost* – "by things deemd weak / Subverting worldly strong" (12.567–8). It is a statement that can only belong to the author, not to his character. For it is ultimately irrelevant to Adam's condition, though it speaks clearly to despondent republicans who have witnessed the rise of an English Caesar, as well as to Levellers who had warned of the rise of an English Satan.

What Worden adds with great precision, not to mention enormous reach, is

> that in 1650–2 Nedham [had] hinted at parallels … between Cromwell, whose sword threatens to end the English republic, and Julius Caesar, whose sword killed the Roman one; and that he used the analogy of Caesar to indicate Cromwell's strategy of wooing the people by portraying himself as the friend of their liberty … It was with Cromwell in mind that *Politicus* contrasted Caesar, who "pretends" to be the "patron" of "liberty," with the frugal Pompey, that "true patron of the people's liberty," who "both in peace and war … approved himself the grand patron of public liberty." A parallel point is made in *Defensio Secunda*, which asks whether Cromwell, who has been the champion of liberty in war, will be its friend or enemy in peace. (260)

Even before the debates at Putney, Lilburne had warned of the rise of "King *Cromwell* and his Son Prince *Ireton*," as gleefully reported by *Mercurius Pragmaticus*[107] (Nedham again in his royalist phase). And Lilburne would do so once more while awaiting trial on a capital charge of treason, brazenly ramping up his attack on Cromwell and the Council. With Walwyn and Overton still imprisoned with him in the Tower in the summer of 1649, he caused to be printed in the margin of the second edition of *The Legal Fundamental Liberties* (4 August 1649) – right next to Cromwell's name

– the title "*New King of* Ireland, *the next step by election of his Army* (Caesar *like) to be King of* England" (3). A page later, Lilburne explained why the republic was now without foundation: "Of all which crimes and charges, and all your others against the King … I know not three of them, but *Cromwel* and his Confederates in your pretended House and Army, *are as guilty of the like in kinde*, though under a new name and notion, as the King was of the forementioned" (4). English republicans have only jettisoned the *name*, but not the *thing* of kingship.

In the end, it is still misleading to call Milton the prose writer an unequivocal Leveller. Only after the disaster of the Restoration did the epic poet begin to imagine the kingdom of God evolving into a Leveller republic. Where Nedham had asked readers in *The Excellencie of a Free State* to choose between tyranny and republican liberty, Milton had by that time retreated into deafening silence. After *Pro Se Defensio* (1655), he published very little under Oliver's Protectorate. And when he did resume writing his *History of Britain*, there was only the darkening vision of the last books, together with the "Digression," about the "headstrong and intractable" character of the English people both then as now, but nowhere more so than in their abysmal failure to understand "true civil government: Valiant indeed and prosperous to winn a field, but to know the end and reason of winning, unjudicious and unwise, in good or bad success alike unteachable."[108]

Having lost immediate hope of a classical or a Leveller republic, Milton's challenge in the dark days of the Protectorate was not to become lost in loss itself.

PART II

Paradise Lost

· 3 ·

"The Tyranny of Heaven"

REPUBLICAN LANGUAGE IN HELL

THE DEATH OF Oliver Cromwell on 3 September 1658 was the likely trigger for Milton to begin his epic poem to "justifie the wayes of God to men" (*PL* 1.26). Later, his nephew Edward Phillips recalled how, "All the time of writing his *Paradise lost*, his veine began at the Autumnall Æquinoctiall and ceased at the Vernall or thereabouts (I believe about May) and this was 4 or 5 yeares of his doeing it. He began about 2 yeares before the K. [King] came-in, and finished about 3 yeares after the K's Restauracion."[1] Since Charles II landed at Dover on 25 May 1660, Milton would have started in the winter of 1658 to compose his "adventrous Song," were he not occupied in readying two prose works for the press. Before May, he had begun work on a manuscript in his possession to publish an edition of *The Cabinet Council*, a book of aphorisms supposedly by Sir Walter Raleigh. And for the rest of that spring and summer, he laboured over "a new and revised edition of *A Defence of the People of England*"[2] which pointed to the "vast abrupt" between the English Republic and the Humble Petition and Advice of 25 May 1657. This latter had contained provisions for a second parliamentary chamber, for hereditary succession, and even for a crown, all of which were fiercely opposed by senior Army officers, sectaries, and republicans alike. As Martin Dzelzainis sums up, "It follows from this that for Milton to voice opposition to the retrograde tendencies of the Protectorate, and to warn against the drift back to monarchical forms, did not require a reformulation of his views: all that it required was a reiteration of views he had previously held."[3] But the unexpected death of the Lord Protector put a sudden period to Milton's renewed vein of prose.

For two reasons, it is probable that Milton began to compose scenes of a "parliament in hell"[4] during the autumn of 1658. Firstly, the issue of *Politicus* for the week (18–25 November) of Cromwell's funeral neatly juxtaposes the reissue of Milton's republican *Defensio* to the regality of the event; secondly, the immediacy of the funeral makes itself felt in the way that Satan's republican rhetoric is set in apposition to the regal panoply of Book 1. Since the newsbook puts the poem's opening in a new light, it deserves examination at this point. A page before its account of the Lord Protector's obsequies begins, Nedham points an editorial finger in the margin of "*Advertisements of Books lately published*," to draw attention to "Joannis Miltoni Angli pro Populo Anglicano Defensio contra *Claudii Anonymi*, alias *Salmasii* Defensionem Regiam. Editio correctior & auctior, ab Autore denuo recognita."[5] We are thus put on notice how to read Nedham's story of a glittering state occasion where the deceased, who had barely resisted a crown in life, contrives to wear that crown in death, republican pretences be damned.

The long sentence that opens Nedham's narrative is datelined "*Somerset-house Novemb, 23*," from whence "the Effigies of his Highness" were borne down the Strand a mile or more to Westminster Abbey, in a procession so elaborate that it took seven hours to complete.[6] Nedham says of "the Effigies of his Highness" (30) that when

> the time came that it was to be removed into the Carriage, it was carried on the *Herse* by ten of the Gentlemen of his Highness forth into the Court, where a Canopy of state very rich, was born over it, by six other Gentlemen of his Highness, till it was brought and placed on the Carriage, at each end whereof was a Seat, wherein sate two of the Gentlemen of his Highness Bed-chamber, the one at the head the other at the feet of the Effigies. The Pall being made of Velvet and fine linen, was very large, extending on each side of the Carriage, to be born by persons of honour, appointed for that purpose; the Carriage it self was adorned with Plumes and Escutcheons, and was drawn by six horses, covered with black Velvet, each of them likewise adorned with Plumes of Feathers. (30–1)

Confessing to a "shortness of time," the journalist feigns regret that he cannot supply "The manner of the Proceeding from hence along the Strand, towards *Westminster* ... in all its particulars" (31), although he does manage, in a paragraph of twenty-one lines, to catalogue the full range of "persons of all qualities" taking part in this dead march where, "on each side the Streets, the Soldiers were placed without the Rails" to control the throngs of spectators. Besides "all the Servants of his Highness, as well inferior and superior, as well those within his houshold as without," there passed "the servants and officers of the Lord Major of the City of *London*," as well as the "Gentlemen attendants on publick Ministers and Ambassadors," the latter followed by "poor Knights of *Winsor*; Secretaries, Clerks, and other officers belonging to the Army, Admiralty, Treasury, Navy and Exchequer." From bottom to top, Protectoral society was on display:

> Judges of the Admiralty ... Baron of the Exchequer, Judges of both Benches, Lord Major of *London,* persons allied in blood to his late Highness; the Members of the Lords House, publick Ministers and Ambassadors of Foreign States and Princes, Lords Commissioners of the Great Seal, Lords Commissioners of the Treasury, the Lords of his Highness privy Council, the chief Mourner and those persons of honor that were his Assistants. (31)

"The Reader," Nedham insinuates, "is to excuse the not naming these in order, the purpose being onely to declare the quality of the persons that attended" (32), although the procession is clearly designed to be majestic, its order strictly hierarchical, given how, "in their passage," they were all "disposed into several Divisions, each Division being distinguished by Drums and Trompets, a Standard or a Banner, born by a person of honor and his Assistant, and a horse covered and led, of which horses four were covered with black cloth, and seven with Velvet, these being passed in their order." Even today, one watches them passing, the plumed and escutcheoned

> Carriage with the Effigies; on each side of the Carriage were born the Banner-Roles being Twelve in number by Twelve persons of honor; and several pieces of His Highness Armor were born by honorable persons, Officers of the Army eight in number. After those noble persons that supported the Pall, followed *Garter* principal King of Arms attended with a Gentleman on each side bareheaded; next him the chief Mourner; and those Lords and noble persons that were Supporters, and Assistants to the chief Mourner. Next followed

the Horse of Honor in very rich Equipage, led in a long Rein by the Master of the Horse. (32)

London had not seen its like since the funeral of James I in May 1625. But truth be told, although "All was performed with great magnificence" in 1625 for the Stuart monarch, on that occasion all had been "very confused and disorderly."[7] To compare great things with small, Julius Caesar could not have hoped for a funeral more befitting of an emperor than this dazzling pageant which took place in the late autumn of 1658. Such, at least, is the impression that Nedham feigns to leave. The royalist John Evelyn more crudely admitted that "it was the joyfullest funeral that ever I saw, for there was none that Cried, but dogs, which the souldiers hooted away with a barbarous noise; drinking, & taking *Tabacco* in the streets as they went."[8] The modern editor of Evelyn's diary even allows as how "some trouble was caused by a pig getting in among the chief mourners" (de Beer, 224, n4), adding a note of Laurel-and-Hardy comedy to the din of royalist scoffing and soldier-talk in the Strand. Nedham, however, makes no mention of his former "licenser" and "collaborator"[9] in the editorials of 1651–52, the republican John Milton, passing by with other mourners, though now stone-blind and needing the help of a guide. From the *Diary of Thomas Burton esq.*, we can still locate the Latin Secretary's place in the order of 380 named mourners among the thousands more identified by occupation or rank.[10] In the van of sixteen Army majors and thirteen lieutenant colonels there walked the "Secretaries of the French and Latin tongues, Mr. Dradon [Dryden], Mr. Marvel, Mr. Sterry, Mr. John Milton, Mr. Hartlibbe, Sen."[11] By his position next to Milton in the sentence, Samuel Hartlib, who had published his *Of Education* in 1644, seems to have been the friend who took his hand, leading the blind man amidst a blare of trumpets and rattle of drums through the raucous gauntlet of soldiers holding back the throngs of mourners.

There is no record of what passed through the mind of the Republic's great defender during those seven hours. It is tempting to think that the opening of *Samson Agonistes* was conceived on that day: "Ask for this great Deliverer now, and find him / Eyeless in *Gaza* at the Mill with slaves."[12] Was that not what these scoffers were, slaves to an old idol of kingship? As for "the better, the sound part"[13] of the people, it would have sounded as if all of them were lining the Strand to stand in awe of another idol trundling along at the end of the procession. Here were "the Effigies of his Highness," "the most Serene and Renowned *Oliver* Lord Protector," now "vested with royal Robes, a Scepter in one hand, a Globe in the other, and a Crown on the head."[14] Whether anyone else in that throng remembered or not, Milton could not have forgotten his words in the preface to *Defensio*: "For what majesty of an high-enthroned king ever shone with brilliance such as that which flashed forth from the people of England when they had shaken off this ancient and enduring superstition, and caused the king himself ... to be caught in the meshes of his own laws and to tremble at the bar of justice?"[15] And where was the brilliance of that majesty now? Draped over a dummy, a crown set on its head and a sceptre stuck in one hand.

Nor was the author of *Defensio* likely to forget his proud retort to Salmasius, the leading Latin scholar in Europe, that, yes, it truly was the people who had rid themselves of the idol of kingship, "and by that act they freed their necks from the well-nigh unbearable yoke of slavery" (*CPW* 4.i: 457). He had even taunted the Frenchman, "Let us see whether the Gospel, God's proclamation of our freedom, subjects us to the slavery of those kings and tyrants from whose wilful despotism the old law, though it countenanced slavery to some degree, had set God's people free" (*CPW* 4.i: 374). Now here he was, "Eyeless in *Gaza* at the mill with slaves."

It wasn't that he and Nedham had not dared to warn the nation of the rise of a new Caesar. But others, like the Leveller Richard Overton, had risked more in ripping off the mask of the hypocrite to expose the naked tyrant: "You shall scarce speak to *Crumwell* about any thing, but he will lay his hand on his breast, elevate his eyes, and call God to record, he will weep, howl and repent, even while he doth smite you under the first rib."[16] The same had happened to Milton's friend Robert Overton (no relation to Richard), after Cromwell's spies had searched the Major-General's papers in 1654, and found the words "ape of a king." For that incriminating phrase, the former Army officer had been forced to rot in the Tower, then in a Jersey prison, even when the "ape" was dead and gone.

IN *PARADISE LOST*, Satan is portrayed as that "ape of a king," if never the rib-smiting, howling penitent. The only difference is in the presentation. For the devil gets to tell his story first in the poem and, to an unusual degree, he is self-deceived.[17] Satan is obliged, for example, to defend his failed attack on "the Tyranny of Heav'n," although there is a curious discrepancy between his memories of "the happy Realms of Light" (*PL* 1.85) and his diatribe against "our grand Foe, / Who now triumphs, and in th' excess of joy / Sole reigning holds the Tyranny of Heav'n" (1.122–4). Does he mean to say that the "happy Realms" were less happy than their present sorry state? How could "happy Realms" be corrupted by an "excess of joy"? And what would happiness mean under "the Tyranny of Heav'n"? How could tyranny exist in "the happy Realms of Light"?

Despite, or perhaps because of, his troubling contradictions, Satan's apologia is obviously based on recent British history. "If he whom mutual league, / United thoughts and counsels, equal hope" – his auditor is reminded to keep the goal in mind, even when eclipsed by a dire result – "And hazard in the Glorious Enterprize, / Joynd with me once, now misery hath joynd / In equal ruin" (1.87–91). Apart from his equivocal use of "equal," Satan sounds convincing in his claim that the reward was equal to the risk, even if "mutual league" had ended in "equal ruin." If it seems odd that Satan's locution should echo Milton's *Tenure*, the phrase seems intended to recall the latter's own account of the origins of kingship and its raison d'être: "Till from the root of *Adams* transgression, falling among themselves to doe wrong and violence … they agreed by common league to bind each other from mutual injury, and joyntly to defend themselves against any that gave disturbance or opposition to such agreement" (CPW 3: 199). By virtue of an unnamed "transgression," the denizens of heaven have thus banded together for common protection; Satan's "mutual league" is already linked to some sort of Fall.

In fact, Satan's "league" is a defence of kingship as old as Aristotle's *Politics*,[18] since, "for ease, for order, and least each man should be his own partial Judge," as Milton had glossed the idea in *Tenure*, "they communicated and deriv'd either to one, whom for the eminence of his wisdom and integritie they chose above the rest, or to more then one whom they thought of equal deserving: the first was call'd a King; the other Magistrates" (3: 199). It is precisely this claim that Satan will soon make from a throne in Hell, that his followers *chose* him to head their league against "the Tyranny of Heav'n": "Mee though just right, and the fixt Laws of Heav'n / Did first create your Leader, next free choice / With what besides, in Counsel or in Fight, / Hath bin achievd of merit" (PL 2.18–21). Supposedly, theirs was a defensive league to protect them from the will of a tyrant.

In 1643, Parliament offered a similar view of the Solemn League and Covenant to Englishmen, proposing to establish a national Presbyterian church in exchange for military support from the Scots against a tyrant. Royalist newsbooks had denounced it as a league with the devil to make war on Heaven's anointed King: "And we dare the Devill and all the *Covenanters* to shew so much as one Peece of Ordnance, one Colour, or one Carriage of Ammunition, Armes, or Baggage that you gained in this service."[19] The court messenger made lively propaganda out of the qualms of many on Parliament's side who hesitated at this unholy alliance with the ancient enemy: "And since this is that religion the pretended *Houses* would make us sweare to, no wonder if some *Lords* have stumbled at the *Covenant* (as this day we were advertised they did) desiring time to consider, for of three Lords that were in the *House* but Two refused it, *viz. Denbigh* and *Lincolne*, being somewhat unwilling to make a bargaine with the Devill."[20]

The "Devil," of course, takes a very different view of the bargain, as does Milton's Satan, recalling the "Innumerable force of Spirits arm'd / That durst dislike his reign, and me preferring, / His utmost power with adverse power oppos'd / In dubious Battel on the Plains of Heav'n, / And shook his throne" (*PL* 1.101–5). He holds to the populist principle already familiar from Milton's *The Tenure of Kings and Magistrates*,

> that since the King or Magistrate holds his autoritie of the people, both originaly and naturally for their good in the first place, and not his own, then may the people as oft as they shall judge it for the best, either choose him or reject him, retaine him or depose him though no Tyrant, meerly by the liberty and right of free born Men, to be govern'd as seems to them best. (*CPW* 3: 206)

The same principle had been expressed with equal force in the founding document of the Leveller movement, addressed to Parliament some thirty months before Milton's *Tenure*:

> Wee are your Principalls, and you our Agents; it is a Truthe, *That* you cannot but acknowledge: For if you or any other shall assume, or exercise any Power, that is not derived from our Trust and choice thereunto, that Power is no lesse then usurpation and an Oppression, from which wee expect to be freed.[21]

In their unsolicited *Remonstrance* in support of John Lilburne, unjustly thrown in prison by the Lords, Richard Overton and William Walwyn expressed their firm conviction that "we are the men of the present age, and ought to be absolutely free from all kindes of exorbitancies, molestations or *Arbitrary Power*; and you wee chose to free us" (5). The fact that Parliament had grievously failed to free them, much less to ignore the claim of precedent, was a betrayal of their "Power of trust, which is ever revokable" (3).

Appealing to broadly republican principles, Satan thus asserts in Milton's own words the right of angels to choose or reject whomsoever they please as their leader, to retain or depose God himself if they so choose, "though no Tyrant," but only "to be govern'd as seems to them best." Noting Milton's own republican principles in Satan's campaign to depose a tyrant, William Empson finds "the basic claim of Satan's faction" to be their sense "that God has been cheating the angels out of their equal status with him."[22] Empson therefore concludes "that Satan's cause is just" (44), based on his critique of the "infinite malice" (38) of omnipotence, amounting to a "metaphysical claim against God" that he rules by force, not by principles of equity and justice. Satan's "heroism" is his willingness to bear "any privation rather than endure the presence of God, *Whom reason hath equall'd, force hath made supreme / Above his equals*" (39). For Empson, his position resembles that of an early-modern Sartre or Camus in maintaining, much like these existentialists, that, "If the rebels prove that they are not nothing in comparison to God, then they have disproved God's absolute claims, and to remind him for ever that he is known to be false would be a moral victory" (50).

The "existentialist" critique of omnipotence has found new currency of late in Michael Bryson's critique of the monarchy of God, where he holds, in *The Tyranny of Heaven* (2004), that "*Paradise Lost* forces its readers to stare directly into the face of a God conceived in terms of military might and kingly power, presenting a God who is obsessed with his own power and glory, manipulative, defensive, alternately rhetorically incoherent and evasive, and an arranger of political dialogues designed to mold angelic opinion."[23] Contrary to Empson, however, Bryson admits that "Satan aspires to that very monarchical and military model of divinity" (25). So he tries to read the poem as another "*Eikonklastes* designed to break not the king's image, but the King's image" (18), thereby making it Milton's design to shatter an idolatrous image of God conceived as a king, in order to "demonstrate that kingship, *both on earth and in heaven*, is part of the larger problem of how God has been misconceived" (29). Specifically, Bryson argues that "Satan speaks in the language of a magistracy-based theory of rebellion" (37), initiated by Calvin in the sixteenth century and thereafter advocated by other Reformed theologians like John Knox. From the vantage point of

Satan as a lesser magistrate, "The objection [he] makes to the raising of the Son is clothed in terms of unjust usurpation of power: God is he who 'Sole reigning, enjoys the Tyranny of heaven'" (Bryson, 37).

But Satan is rather closer to the first edition of Milton's *Tenure* than he is to Calvin's notion of a "lesser magistrate." His exact phrase, "Sole reigning," bristles with republican hostility to the rule of a "single person," such as the "personal rule" of Charles I from 1629 to 1640. Appealing to St Basil, Milton had even defined a tyrant as one who, "whether by wrong or by right comming to the Crown, is he who regarding neither Law nor the common good, reigns onely for himself and his faction."[24] *Solely reigning* "onely for himself and his faction," Satan appeals, as it were, to Milton for a definition of tyranny. And Milton calls on Aristotle, who "writes in the fourth of his politics chap. 10. that Monarchy unaccountable, is the worst sort of tyranny; and least of all to be endur'd by free born men."[25] "Monarchy unaccountable" is the heart of the matter, both historically and dramatically. Within living memory (mere weeks before Milton was graduated BA from Cambridge), Charles I had opened "*His Majesty's* Declaration *to all his loving Subjects, of the Causes which moved him to dissolve the last Parliament*, March 10, 1628" with a declaration that came to define his reign: "Princes are not bound to give Account of their Actions, but to God alone."[26] It is against this absolutist principle that Satan objects, intending to hold him to account who "Sole reigning holds the Tyranny of Heav'n."

Empson also makes Satan's objection "identical with that of persons such as Milton who had dared to deny that Charles I had Divine Right; identical morally, though Milton believes that God actually had it and Charles hadn't. Whether the rebels deserve blame for their initial doubt of God's credentials, before God had supplied false evidence to encourage the doubt, is hard for us to tell; but once they have arrived at a conviction they are not to be blamed for having the courage to act upon it" (46–7). Satan's quarrel with Heaven thus recapitulates the failure of English republicans to do away with absolutism, making "the tragedy of Satan" (90) equivalent to the tragedy of Milton: "As Macaulay said in his review of the *De Doctrina*, indeed considered the chief thing to say," writes Empson, "the Divine Right of Kings was a Renaissance development, related to the improved weapons and increased wealth which gave them a standing army capable of putting down popular revolt; it was decisively important that the English, almost alone in Europe, succeeding in resisting this new absolutism" (78). Yet royalists "were astonished that his [Milton's] life was spared" for advocating resistance, Empson says, and were only reconciled to his inclusion in the Act of Oblivion when they "found him meekly ascribing to Satan his own political opinions" (82).

What Empson misses, as did Milton's contemporaries, is a more tangled system of identifications in the poem. How, for example, are we to read Satan's defiant refusal

> To bow and sue for grace
> With suppliant knee, and deifie his power,
> Who from the terrour of this Arm so late
> Doubted his Empire, that were low indeed,
> That were an ignominy and shame beneath
> This downfall. (1.111–16)?

Aside from its echoes of Lilburne's refusal to kneel before the Lords, Satan's speech appears to reverberate with the language of *A Remonstrance of Many Thousand Citizens, and other Free-born People of England, To their owne House of Commons* against that body's insistence that, "*The King can doe no wrong*." The remonstrants even accuse Parliament of "begging and intreating him in such submissive language, to returne to his Kingly Office and Parliament, as if you were resolved to make us beleeve, hee were a God, without whose presence, all must fall to ruine, or as if it were impossible for any Nation to be happy without a King."[27] The irony is that Milton's Satan proposes to deify "the terrour of this [his] Arm," while feigning the courage to deify a God of "power."

On one hand, Lilburne's spectacular defiance of the power of the Lords lends an aura of popular resistance to Satan's righteous quarrel with "the tyranny of Heav'n." As Lilburne rehearses their mistreatment of him in *An Anatomy of the Lords Tyranny* (1646):

> I was called into their House: and being by them commanded to kneele at their Barre; I absolutely refused to doe it, unlesse they would by force compell me thereunto: which, if they did, I told them, it would bee no act of mine. And I shall (with your favour) give you one reason, which with some others, that made me I did not kneele; and it was this: I knew, by Law the Lords had no jurisdiction over me, and accordingly I had performed my duty to my selfe, &c. in protesting against them.[28]

There is a huge – and hugely ironic – difference, however, between these two gestures of defiance. As Lilburne rightly claimed, the Lords had no power, save by inheritance, to demand a commoner's obeisance; even then, their inherited titles were solely in the gift of a king. Satan's own title derives, however, from what he prefers to term "the fixt Laws of Heav'n" (*PL* 2.18). And yet his rebellion now proposes to undo those same "fixt Laws."

Empson has not ignored the irony, conceding that, "The point was very clear to Milton and his first readers; after a hint that Satan was like a Norman baron, they could imagine him expressing his views on kingship at greater length" (77–8). The problem, of course, is that such views are brimming with self-interest. On the one hand, Satan proposes to depose the very King who granted him his title and to usurp his throne, thereby raising doubt about his claim that God is a usurper. On the other hand, he styles himself a populist who rejects the Lords' authority. Even Satan's lieutenant finds it hard to suppress disbelief.

"O Prince, O Chief of many Throned Powers" (1.128), Beelzebub blurts out, exposing the hypocrisy of opposing in Leveller fashion "the Lords usurpations and incroachments upon our common rights" ("Anatomy," 22), while yet defending a title and even seeking a crown. Satan is merely another "Prince," like "the Grand Prerogative-men" mocked by Lilburne because they "ruled and governed by no other law, then that of their own will" ("Anatomy," 19). Then again, is Satan so different from the "republican" Cromwell pretending to good "Common-weal principles,"[29] much less a monarch like Charles I pretending to "Divine Right"? Has he not claimed that divine right for himself? Milton does indeed portray Charles I as a hypocrite, one who stole prayers from Sidney's *Arcadia* to bolster his image as the royal martyr to which he had pretended in *Eikon Basilike* (1649): "[T]he worst of kings … for ought we know, have still pray'd thir own, or at least borrow'd from fitt Authors. But this King, not content with that which, although in a thing holy, is no holy theft, to attribute to his own making other mens whole Prayers, hath as it were unhallow'd, and unchristn'd the very duty of prayer it self, by borrowing to a Christian use Prayers offer'd to a Heathen God."[30] Merritt Y. Hughes recalls how "Milton's resentment of them [the purloined prayers] breaks out in his comparison of Charles to Shakespeare's Richard III cheating his way to tryannic power by 'speaking in as high a strain of pietie, and mortification, as is utterd in any passage of this Book.'"[31] Worse, says Milton, who "knows not that the deepest policy of a Tyrant hath bin ever to counterfet Religious"?[32] In Satan, he then manages to conflate Cromwell, a hypocrite in politics *and* religion, with that other religious and regal hypocrite, Charles Rex, thereby exposing the *double* fraud of Satan's political position. The real question is whether Satan's critique of omnipotence is based on merit or on disguised self-interest?

Beelzebub does complain that he and his fellows were misled: "Too well I see and rue the dire event, / That with sad overthrow and foul defeat / Hath lost us Heav'n" (1.134–6). True monarchist that he is, he holds to the law of Conquest as the basis of any legitimate polity. To say otherwise would confirm the Leveller objection to conquest as the just ground of government: "The History of our Fore-fathers since they were Conquered by the *Normans*," Overton and Walwyn[33] had lamented in *A Remonstrance*, "doth manifest that this Nation hath been held in bondage all along ever since" (4). So by his own logic, the royalist is now reminded to accept the rule of conquest:

> But what if he our Conquerour, (whom I now
> Of force believe Almighty, since no less
> Then such could have orepow'rd such force as ours)
> Have left us this our spirit and strength intire
> Strongly to suffer and support our pains. (1.143–7)

Like the Anglo-Saxons subdued by William the Conqueror, Beelzebub accepts the doctrine that Might Is Right, given that Satan's recklessness has exposed their lack of both. What Beelzebub cannot accept, however, is a Leveller-like insistence that "we remain under the *Norman* yoke of an *unlawfull Power*, from which wee ought to free ourselves; and which yee ought not to maintaine upon us, but to abrogate" *(A Remonstrance*, 13). The power that has defeated them is by definition *lawful.* So Beelzebub has reason to fear that Hell is not the worst they face, that "mightier service" may be required of them "as his thralls / By right of Warr" (1.149–50). Although Milton's colleague Nedham had used the same language, it had been to justify the people's rights, not those of the conqueror: "That if a *King* may thus by *Right of warr*, lose his Share and Interest in Authority and Power, being conquered, then on the other side, by *Right of warr*, the *whole* must needs reside in that part of the *people* which prevailed over him, there being no *middle power* to make any Claim."[34] Beelzebub's speech points to his dawning awareness that the royal prerogative is not only lost, but fairly lost, to the almighty force that has conquered them.

Satan answers his shattered lieutenant with all the haughtiness of a true "Prince" – "Fall'n Cherube, to be weak is miserable / Doing or Suffering" (1.157–8). Here, it is the language of Charles I, not the language of Cromwell, that echoes throughout a second speech of thirty-five lines. For Satan's rebuke echoes a famous letter sent by Charles I to his nephew and military commander, Prince Rupert, from Cardiff on 3 July 1645. "Read it over," Nedham had chortled as he prepared to parse the intercepted missive line by line in a full issue of *Mercurius Britanicus*, "and you will find it was written since the Battel of *Naseby*; for the old *confident stile* droops now into *despaire*; A man may observe *Terror* in every *line*, though drawn by the hand of a *King*."[35]

In fairness to Charles, he does chide his nephew in this captured letter for his evident defeatism after the disaster of Naseby, managing to preserve at least a face of royal dignity in defeat. Otherwise, the evidence on balance supports Nedham's judgment that, "If you will see *self-opinion* and *obstinacie* shut *reason* out of dores, read on: See here the *King* confessing a *probability* of *Ruine* in that way he goes, and yet resolved to pursue it: But having no hope here below, he again takes heart, and *casts anchor* in *Heaven*, upon pretence of GODS *Cause*" (953). Even on the burning lake in hell, Satan is quite as obstinate as Charles I, and just as willing as the king to "shut reason out of doors." He urges Beelzebub to seek "What reinforcement we may gain from Hope, / If not what resolution from despare" (1.190–1). Ignoring his principle that, "To be weak is miserable," Satan now projects an image of stoic indifference to circumstance, of his unconquerable will to continue fighting even against hopeless odds. What he rejects is defeatism, even if Beelzebub has given him every reason to despair.

Addressing Rupert just as curtly as Satan will address Beelzebub, Charles had written: "*NEPHEW*, This is occasioned by a *Letter* of yours, that the Duke of *Richmond* shewed me yesternight" (954). Though Rupert's letter is lost, the king's tone suggests that Rupert was guilty of the same type of defeatism that Beelzebub expresses. The king does not try to hide from his nephew how desperate things are: "I confesse, that either speaking as a meer *Souldier* or *States-man*, I must say there is *no probability* but of my *Ruine*." In parentheses Nedham comments "that Pr. *Rupert* was inclinable to an *Accommodation*, and had counselled his *Uncle* accordingly; in answer whereunto, the *King* disclaims such Advice as prejudiciall to his *Religion, Crown*, and *Friends*" (955): "But observe how *inveterate* the King is against *Accommodation*, the only meanes of *Peace*, when he construes *Composition* with his *Parliament* to be an absolute *Submission* to them. But by this it appears, he means to continue so averse to the desires of his *People*, as not to descend, compound, or yield to them in any *Particulars*" (*Britanicus*, 956).

Nedham reprints the King's letter to show that he is impervious to reason, that he will accept ruin before he will compromise his regal image: "And whatsoever *personall* punishment it shall please [God] to inflict upon me, must not make me repine, much lesse give over this *Quarrel*; and there is as little question, that a *composition* with them at this time is nothing else but a *Submission*, which by the grace of *God* I am resolved against whatsoever it cost me." Charles proves in practice what he had affirmed in theory to be his Divine Right: "Princes are not bound to Account for their Actions, but to God alone." Even Nedham has to admit that, "Not to repine at *Gods* punishment is commendable," for it confirms the king's accountability to God; "yet," the journalist adds, "no good *Inference* hereupon that this *Quarrel* must be maintained" (956). The truth is that it is obstinacy, not fate, that has defeated him. A like obstinacy on Satan's part turns into self-defeating logic: "but of this be sure" (1.158), he says, adding a curious qualification – "Which oft times may succeed" – and then another qualification, "if I fail not" (1.166–7), in the hope that God "Perhaps hath spent his shafts" (1.176). *Of this be sure*, indeed!

Charles frankly admits in this letter that the cause is hopeless, and that Rupert is within his rights to surrender the besieged city of Bristol (as he will shortly do). But the King is now prepared to die to defend his stubborn principle of royal absolutism; in fact, he signals his deathless wish to martyr himself to the "heroic" image of his own majesty:

> Indeed, I cannot flatter my selfe with expectation of *good successe* more than this, to *end my days with honour* and a *good Conscience*, which obligeth me to continue my endeavours, as not despairing that *God* may yet in my time avenge his own *Cause*, though I must avow to all my *Friends*, that he that will stay with me at this time, must expect and resolve either to die for a *good Cause*, or (which is worse) to live as miserable in maintaining it, as the violent rage of *insulting Rebels* can make him. (956)

Likewise, what Satan proposes to Beelzebub is less about what "we may gain from Hope" and more about clinging to a paradoxical idea of "resolution from despare."

When we look again at Satan's "heroic" fortitude in his opening speech, we need to weigh it against the obstinacy of his second speech. Initially, Satan said that, "not for those, / Nor what the Potent Victor in his rage / Can else inflict, do I repent or change, / Though chang'd in outward lustre" (1.94–7). It is "that fixt mind / And high disdain, from sence of injur'd merit" (1.97–8), he says, that does entitle him to ask, "What though the field be lost? / All is not lost; the unconquerable Will, / And study of revenge, immortal hate, / And courage never to submit or yield" (1.105–8). Yet the irony of Satan's rhetoric is that his second speech asserts at the outset that "to be weak is miserable," though he ends that speech by proposing to find "resolution" in "despare." The first thing to say about "heroic" fortitude of this sort is what Nedham had said about regal obstinacy: "the sole *observation* arising is this, that there is no hope of reclaiming the *King* from these *courses*, by any means whatsoever, having vowed them to the death" (956).

The language of Hell, then, is not exactly the idiom of English republicans, nor should we expect it to be. "Republicans" like Cromwell and Ireton had negotiated in secret with the king throughout the summer and autumn of 1647, while he was still in Army custody at Hampton Court.[36] But, after the king's death on the block and Ireton's death in Ireland in 1650, Cromwell set his sights on a much higher position than that of an honest member of the republican Council of State. The conjunction of a republican- *and* regal-sounding Satan in these first two speeches has thus fatally damaged both images: the Lord General and Lord Protector-to-be is now tied directly to monarchy; and the king's "heroic" defence of his regal image is exposed as a death wish.

In his third speech a "regal" Satan then turns the charge of tyranny back on God, presenting himself as their last, best hope of liberty and equality. "Be it so," he says, "since he / Who now is Sovran can dispose and bid / What shall be right: fardest from him is best / Whom reason hath equald, force hath made supream / Above his equals" (1.245–9). Satan dismisses the very principle Beelzebub had maintained, "By right of Warr," adopting instead a Leveller-inspired principle of resistance by "natural right" to the Norman Yoke. Claiming equality with God in reason, if not in power, Satan preaches what sounds like egalitarian doctrine, but shades into something more like a protectoral regime in Hell, where he defends his followers' freedom from the Heavenly Tyrant: "Here at least / We shall be free; th' Almighty hath not built / Here for his envy, will not drive us hence: / Here we may reign secure" (1.258–61). The problem is that Satan shifts from the plural and egalitarian

"We shall be free" to the *royal we* of "Here we may reign secure." Mastery of rhetoric is surely more useful to the tyrant than mastery of logic.

And the "devil" is literally in the details – in this case the pronominal details – as we watch Satan slip from the first-person plural to an "impersonal" infinitive construction – "and in my choyce / To reign is worth ambition though in Hell" (1.261–2) – to end in another infinitive construction, a maxim without a grammatical subject: "Better to reign in Hell, then serve in Heav'n" (1.263). What has been presented as a form of power sharing, or withering of state power, turns out to be nothing of the sort. Satan aims at nothing less than "single-person" rule: "The mind is its own place, and in it self / Can make a Heav'n of Hell, a Hell of Heav'n. / What matter where, if I be still the same?" (1.254–6). While he insists that his is "A mind not to be chang'd by Place or Time" (1.253), it is a mind that, by self-definition, refuses to learn from experience. It is most like the obstinate mind that berates Prince Rupert in all its suicidal "dignity." Despite his claim to an "unconquerable Will" and "courage never to submit or yield" (1.106, 108), Satan does not mean to be inclusive, only to *sound* that way in "Here we may reign secure." But the royal "we," both by metonymy and custom, is only ever singular.

What passes for inclusion in Satan's rhetoric is finally exposed in a mocking series of litotes that he employs in a fourth speech to rouse his troops from their stupor:

> Princes, Potentates,
> Warriers, the Flowr of Heav'n … have ye chos'n this place
> After the toyl of Battel to repose
> Your wearied vertue …
> Or in this abject posture have ye sworn
> To adore the Conquerour? (1.315–16, 318–20, 322–3).

The pageantry which follows is another series of negatives stated as positives, except that the ranks of devils who process in front of Satan tend to reflect the majesty of "Thir great Commander" more than their own glory, once "Godlike shapes and forms / Excelling human, Princely Dignities, / And Powers that earst in Heaven sat on Thrones" (1.358–60).

The narrator leaves no doubt, in his subsequent invocation to the Muse, that we are plunged into a polity that, in its structure, is fundamentally regal and hierarchical:

Say, Muse, thir Names then known, who first, who last,
Rous'd from the slumber, on that fiery Couch,
At thir great Emperors call, as next in worth
Came singly where he stood on the bare strand,
While the promiscuous croud stood yet aloof? (1.376–80)

Ordered hierarchies are literally the basis of a *system* of monarchy: "First *Moloch*, horrid King besmear'd with blood" (1.392), heralds the cannibal nature of precedence in these descending ranks of aristocrats down to "*Belial*" who "came last, then whom a Spirit more lewd / Fell not from Heaven" (1.490–1). Their highly ordered, ranked procession is just as socially constitutive as the Homeric roll call of ships in *Iliad* 2, or Virgil's roll call in *Aeneid* 7, as the latter's Muses are invoked "to tell what kings / Were stirred to war, what troops in each command,"[37] who support or oppose the survivors of ruined Troy.

Quite the opposite of Homeric events in a distant, absolute past, however, Satan's procession has all the immediacy and urgency of Cromwell's funeral procession. What seems to have been taking shape in Milton's imagination during the weeks and months of poetic composition surrounding the event was the death grip that monarchical forms still had on the English people. He had said as much in his indictment of the regal hypocrite:

> Such Prayers as these may happly catch the People, as was intended: but how they please God, is to be much doubted, though pray'd in secret, much less writt'n to be divulg'd. Which perhaps may gaine him after death a short, contemptible, and soon fading reward; not what he aims at, to stirr the constancie and solid firmness of any wise Man … but to catch the worthles approbation of an inconstant, irrational, and Image-doting rabble.[38]

Despite the heroic efforts of Politicus to educate citizens in republican principles, the English people have indeed remained like children craving freedom from responsibility, "chusing them a captain back for *Egypt*," as Milton was to write in *The Readie and Easie Way* (1660) as "the last words of our expiring libertie."[39] In the meantime, the impossible had come to pass: Richard, heir and successor to the Lord Protector, meekly accepted the ultimatum of the Major-Generals to resign. And the Army restored the Rump to power, at least for the interim. Writing in 1659 "after a short but scandalous night of interruption," Milton would consign the entire six (or even ten) years past to oblivion, for there "is now again by a new dawning of Gods miraculous providence among us."[40]

That dawning hope of "reviving liberty" was still months away, however, when Milton turned to composing his poem's next book. What now loomed large was the threat of seeing "Th' Imperial Ensign" (1.536) raised again; it always seemed to be just a single funeral procession away. So the most he could hope for at this point was to break the grip of the dead hand of custom, even if it took the devil himself to expose its power. It is evidently such a hope that underwrites the argument of Satan's last speech in Book 1:

> But he who reigns
> Monarch in Heav'n, till then as one secure
> Sat on his Throne, upheld by old repute,
> Consent or custome, and his Regal State
> Put forth at full, but still his strength conceal'd
> Which tempted our attempt, and wrought our fall. (1.637–42)

It is a speech that depends on one of the most basic principles that Milton and Nedham had advanced in their republican editorials:

> That as in the *government of the people,* the successive revolution of Authority by their consent, hath been the only bank against Inundations of Arbitrary Power and Tyranny; so on the other side it is as sure, that all *standing Powers* have and ever do assume unto themselves an Arbitrary exercise of their own Dictates at pleasure, and make it their only Interest, to settle themselves in an unaccountable state of Domination.[41]

What could be more damaging to republican freedoms dependent on a continuous, consensual revolution of Authority than the image of an *eternal* deity designed to maintain a permanent, standing power in the state?

Of this *sine qua non* of republicanism, Empson acknowledges that, "A reader who has completed the poem can hardly deny that this is true; and presumably the comfort of the reflection, though Satan is mainly concerned to win their hearts with the pathos of the thing, is that such tricky behaviour is not what one would expect of total Omnipotence; so that there is probably yet hope of circumventing God by trickery, as is being proposed" (47). Despite the trickiness of his reasons for "hope," the justice of Satan's question is obvious. Is God's eternal power a matter of custom – that is to say, of mindless consent – or does it call for reasoned consent? For Empson, the answer is implicit in the claim, "Whom reason hath equald." For it is here that "we get the first of a number of hints, cumulatively strong, that he had held an actual debate on the rights of God, for senior angels only, before the crisis which made him call them out for immediate military action" (39–40). It is then fair to judge in Empson's terms the merits of such a claim according to reason, not authority. "This seems an important point," as Empson notes in another context, "because it lets us recognize their theological opinions as rationally considered, and the leadership of Satan as one which our minds can understand" (59). Reason is most certainly the ground of any theodicy worthy of the name.

At the same time, Empson has to concede "that, both for Milton and Satan," there "is partly sophistry and partly truth" (73) in his hellish speeches. Satan is most sophistical in accusing God of "tempting our attempt" by concealing "his strength." For, in making the result ("our attempt") into a punning cause ("tempted"), he undercuts his own claim of rational equality with God ("Whom reason hath equald," 1.248). His credibility is further undermined by his admission – verging on self-parody – that anyone "who overcomes / By force, hath overcome but half his foe" (1.648–9). Having failed at "force" himself, Satan then dismisses it as illegitimate. And yet the panoply of majesty to which he resorts in summoning his troops is nothing less than a ritual display of such power.[42] The sophist who accuses his opponent of sophistry is neither so innocent nor just himself.

In fact, Satan's enitre critique of Divine Right – implicit in the formula, "till then as one secure / Sat on his Throne, upheld by old repute, / Consent or custome" (1.638–40) – is about to recoil on him. It is the same republican critique made by Nedham and Milton on the basis of "Till then," the moment when events expose the real illegitimacy of "old repute," "custome," and habitual "Consent." The parade of "Princely Dignities" (1.359) before "Thir great Commander" – taking a third of the first book to accomplish – exposes the falsity of Satan's claim, since no one here objects to the force of "old repute, Consent or custome." Instead, an entire society falls back on the validity of received forms, as "the winged Haralds by command / Of Sovran power, with awful Ceremony / And Trumpets sound throughout the Host proclaim / A solemn Councel" (1.752–5).

In their concerted attempt to inculcate Commonwealth principles in readers of their editorials in 1651, Milton and Nedham explained this behaviour as a conditioned political reflex: "Wee who have been educated under a *Monarchy*, may very fitly be resembled to those Beasts, which have been caged or coop'd all their lives in a Den, where they seem to live in as much pleasure as other Beasts that are abroad; and if they be let loose, yet they will return in again, because they know not how to value or use their Liberty."[43] The devils, it seems, are no more able to escape the conditioning of their "education under a *Monarchy*" than caged animals are able to enjoy freedom on being set at liberty.

The very architecture of the "great consult" (1.798) further exposes a pretence of democracy in this hellish assembly where, to accommodate the multitude, some beings

> to smallest forms
> Reduc'd thir shapes immense, and were at large,
> Though without number still amidst the Hall
> Of that infernal Court. But far within
> And in thir own dimensions like themselves
> The great Seraphic Lords and Cherubim
> In close recess and secret conclave sat
> A thousand Demy-Gods on golden seat's,
> Frequent and full. (1.789–97)

The scene pointedly recalls the sardonic Leveller portrait of seating arrangements at Putney, where enlisted men had come in 1647 to dispute as equals with their military superiors, with the latter resenting their social presumption:

> And being thus seated, even before they were well warmed in their places, they begin to stomack the sitting of the private souldiers in Council with them … with two Commission Officers and two soldiers to be chosen for each Regiment; but a Councell thus modelled, was not sutable to their wonted greatnes and ambition, it was somewhat of scorn to them, that a private soldier (though the Representour of a Regiment) should sit cheek by joll with them, and have with an Officer an equall vote in that Councel: This was a thing favoured too much of the peoples authority and power, and therefore inconsistent with the transaction of their lordly Interest.[44]

Satan has learned from the Army Grandees' error, as it were, for henceforth he shows naught but disdain for the realities of the democratic process, pretending to "equality" without compromising in the least his own regal space. Lords will be lordly, whatever else they might ask us to believe. And hypocrites display their hypocrisy in what they do, more than in their honeyed words. It is in this "architechtonic" duplicity of Satan, the pretended democrat, that Cromwell and Charles I each finds his true match. In this one respect, at least, Satan has earned a right to be considered their "royal" equal.

But the larger question raised by Satan (that will also take somewhat longer to answer) is whether the hypocrite's betrayal of liberty in hell as on earth has much of value to say about political forms in Heaven? Are we to assume that Satan's critique of omnipotence really equals Milton's critique of God? Or is it hardly more than Satan's projection onto God of his own Cromwellian ambition and Stuart sense of entitlement?

· 4 ·

"The Great Consult"

FROM PUTNEY TO PANDÆMONIUM

THE "GREAT CONSULT" in Pandæmonium is modelled on a military institution of the English civil wars[1] that would lead to a political struggle for the heart and soul of England's future in the debates at Putney in 1647. The cloistered events in Putney Church have left their trace – not of specific speeches or particular speakers, but of attitudes and social types – that would be a model for Milton's dramatic debates in Hell. The General Council of the Army, a quasi-democratic assembly made up of two elected representatives and two officers from each regiment, met about a dozen times from July to October 1647, before convening a special session at Putney from 28 October to 8 November, after which it was suspended out of the High Command's alarm at the depth of radical, populist forces unleashed in the debates. But a more immediate inspiration and motive force for Milton's "great consult" was the logical weakness of his *Pro Populo Anglicano Defensio* (February 1651), his public answer in Latin prose to the great Salmasius, which he was commissioned to write in early 1650 by the Council of State.[2]

Salmasius had attacked Milton's *Tenure* where he was most vulnerable: his conflation of the *people* with the *Army* as England's governing power. The "fanatics of England," the French scholar mockingly called political naïfs like Milton who claim that the people are "the source and origin of all power and authority." In consequence, they fail to understand and distinguish between several types of government, because they claim "it is for the people to establish any kind of government – both kingly and aristocratic and popular."[3] "But whatever those depraved men say and teach about popular rule," the "form of government which they have introduced is quite new and was unheard of in former times. It is not popular, nor kingly, nor aristocratic, but military" (CPW 4.ii: 989).

Salmasius catechizes Milton by a set of questions whose answers are as obvious as they are damning: "Who ejected the class of nobles from Parliament? Was it the people? The army with their leaders did this." The catechist is trenchant: Who purged the lower house? The common people? No. "The leaders with their own soldiers did this."

> Who dragged the king from prison to prison? Who set up a court of justice for condemning him to death? … Who finally condemned him and handed him over to the executioner? Was this the crime of the people? Was it the crime of anyone who received this power from the people? This was the deed of the soldiers and the leaders of the party. Who now rules the people of England with more than kingly power? … Who filled the city with armed men? Who seized the public treasury? Was it the people? All these are acts of the army which perpetrated them by order of its own leaders. (CPW 4.ii: 989)

Milton's sixth chapter – following a time-honoured method of refuting point by point the opponent's discourse – begins abusively, as if to mask a logical weakness: "After your vain treatment and foolish discussion of the law of God and the law of nature, which merely made you equally notorious for ignorance and vice, I fail to see what you can do in this royal defence but turn to trifles" (4.i: 453). But it is less *what* Milton says than *how* he says it that betrays his anxiety: "'Whatever things those wretches say,' you claim, 'are to deceive the people.' You knave! Was it for this that a degraded grammarian like you wanted to interfere with our government … to bury us in your barbarous solecisms?" (CPW 4.i: 457). Neither the bullying tone nor the name-calling is worthy of a noble mind. "'The form of government introduced by them is not popular but military.' I suppose that crew of renegades paid you a few pennies to write this; and so I must direct my answer not to you who prate of things you quite fail to understand, but to those who hired you." Yet, neglecting to mention that he too now writes as a paid civil servant, he falls back on the tired old tactic of scornful repetition and negation: "Who 'drove out the nobles from Parliament? The people?' Yes, the people; and by that act they freed their necks from the well-nigh unbearable yoke of slavery" (CPW 4.i: 457). And yet he can't even free his own neck from the iron truth: *it was not the people; it was the army with their leaders who did this.*

Still, he will find his footing for the space of a sentence or two, ceasing to flail about: "The soldiers to whom you ascribe the act were themselves not foreigners but citizens, forming a great part of the people, and they acted with the consent and by the will of most of the rest, supported by Parliament" (*CPW* 4.i: 457). Here, he relies on one far-reaching, if totally unforeseen, consequence of Parliament's declarations in their struggle with the king, on which Lilburne had also capitalized as a true achievement of the Revolution – the idea of the citizen-soldier.[4] Quoting the call to arms in *Englands Birth-Right Justified* from "the 150. *page.* of the Booke called, An exact Collection of the *Parliaments* Remonstrances, Declarations, &c."[5] (24 March 1642), Lilburne says, "I left my trade, *and in iudgment and conscience* girded my sword unto my thigh, with an honest resolution to spend my heart blood for the preservation of the lawes and liberties of my native country, which then the Parliament by their Declarations, made me and the Kingdome beleeve was indeavoured to be distroyed by the King and his evill Councell."[6]

Lilburne claims to represent the grievances of citizen-soldiers against an ungrateful Parliament for which he had ventured his life. And he portrays his difficulties, first with the Commons in 1645, then the Lords in 1646, as a foretaste of Parliament's treatment of the Army in 1647, after the Scots had handed over the king. "Their motives, in planning as they did for the reduction of the home forces and the reconquest of Ireland," Austin Woolrych remarks, "were transparently political, and resentment of this fact was strongly to colour the debates at Putney."[7] Indeed, the soldiers were encouraged by their officers to petition the Lord General, Sir Thomas Fairfax, to secure arrears of pay and indemnities for damages relating to the war, before agreeing to disband. Furious at its insubordinate creature, Parliament issued on 29 March 1647 its "Declaration of Dislike." As Edmund "Ludlow tells the story, Denzil Holles scribbled a declaration on his knee which the Commons at once adopted. The Lords adhered to it next day and it went down to the Army as the challenge of all Westminster."[8] The New Model must cease petitioning, or else it "shall be looked upon as enemies of the state and disturbers of the public peace."[9]

One MP from the Army, Cromwell's son-in-law Henry Ireton, was so enraged by the insult that he challenged Hollis to a duel; they had to be forcibly restrained by fellow MPs. In his *Memoirs*, Hollis later expressed what no one said but was well understood by everyone in 1647, "that what was at issue between the Presbyterians and the Army was the ascendancy of his [Hollis's] class: 'The wisest of men saw it to be a great evil that servants should ride on horses and princes walk as servants on the earth.'"[10] Worse still, Hollis described the soldiers themselves as nothing more than "a mercenary army raised by the Parliament, all of them … not able to make a thousand pounds a year lands, most of the colonels and officers mean tradesmen, brewers, tailors, goldsmiths, shoemakers and the like, a notable dunghill, if one would rake into it, to find out their several pedigrees: these to rebel against their masters" (quoted by Brailsford, *The Levellers*, 177).

Commissary-General Ireton had anticipated this social sneer in the Army's Declaration of 14 June 1647, which he wrote to justify their grievances: "Especially considering that we were not a mere mercenary army, hired to serve any arbitrary power of a state, but called forth and conjured by the several declarations of Parliament to the defence of our own and the people's just rights and liberties."[11] Indeed, here was a widely available image of the *people* conflated with *Army*; for citizen-soldiers *had* sacrificed life and limb to secure the common right. And Milton does describe fairly accurately in his tenth chapter of *Defensio* this singular development of 1647, noting that "there were found some in Parliament itself who hated our invincible army, from jealousy of its great accomplishments, and, after it had deserved so much, wished to disband it in disgrace" (4.i: 510). Were this the whole story, we could take Milton at his word that "The soldiers … were themselves not foreigners but citizens, forming a great part of the people, and they acted with the consent and by the will of most of the rest, supported by Parliament." Except that this final clause – "supported by Parliament" – gives the lie to all the rest.

In July 1647, the Presbyterian majority in the Commons had incited the London mob to demand the King's restoration to his Parliament. Milton's account is vague on details:

> At the behest of certain traitorous ministers … they seized the moment when many of those they knew differed heartily from them had … gone off to the provinces to settle the swelling revolt of the Presbyterians, and with strange fickleness, if not actual treachery, they decreed that this deep-dyed foe, who was king in name alone, should, without giving any real satisfaction or guarantees, be restored to the city and reinstated in the full dignity and power of office as though he had done great things for the state. (4.i: 510)

In the event, there were "violent disturbances in London, where the army was widely hated and feared."[12] The Speakers of both Houses, with eight peers and fifty-seven MPs, including Cromwell, fled the city on 26 July to the safety of the Army.

Coincidentally, it was also the day on which *Jonahs Cry out of the Whales Belly* appeared in London bookstalls. Lilburne's "Postscript" of 16 July called on the Army, "being now thereby dissolved" by Parliament's perfidy "into the originall law of Nature," to "hold their swords in their hands for their own preservation and safety, which both Nature and the two Houses practices and Declarations teaches them to doe" (13). He had begun to envision another "agreement," based on the Army's "Solemn Engagement," in which the soldiers had agreed to "act by mutuall consent, or agreement" (14).[13] Here was that image of rule by *the people and the Army* to which Milton resorted in 1651 to refute the claim that England was a military dictatorship. In August 1647, Richard Overton had also maintained that the rank and file wanted to speak "not only as *Soldiers* for the good and safety of the Army; but as *Commoners*, for the peace, freedome, and liberty of the Kingdome."[14] So what went wrong? Why did the imagined ideal fail to materialize?

Parliament's resort to mob violence with the goal of purging Independents from the Commons was one factor. But, as Milton read the result, "there is surely no reason to censure the army for marching to the city at the call of Parliament and carrying out its orders, putting down with ease the royalist riots and revolt which more than once threatened that assembly itself … With the help of the army, it was possible for us to keep our freedom and save the state" (*CPW* 4.i: 511). A mere show of force was enough to disperse the mob. "The Army assigned to Rainsborough the conduct of an encircling movement," and "The Levellers of Southwark opened the gates of their borough to him with a welcome" (Brailsford, 248). Rainsborough pointed "his guns at the defences of London Bridge," and "the resistance of the City collapsed. The former Speakers, with their followers, took their seats as before, and on 7 August the Army, horse and foot, with laurel leaves in their hats, made a memorable march through the City, 18,000 strong."[15]

The Army was now united in its conviction that Parliament must impose a settlement limiting the King's power to interfere with the rights and liberties of all, not merely the rights and liberties of Parliament. Thereafter, a General Council of the Army held at Kingston on 18 August proposed "a purge of 65 Members in addition to the notorious Eleven [including Hollis]. Cromwell shared the views of his men, and would have done then what Colonel Pride did more than a year later, had not Fairfax thwarted him by delaying day after day his signature of the necessary orders" (Brailsford, 248). It was finally at this point that Cromwell and Ireton decided on a flanking move to beat the Parliament at its own game, while reducing a call for rights to professional grievances.[16]

John Wildman, the civilian author[17] of the first *Agreement of the People* at Putney, would later write how "In the time of *Cromwells* and *Iretons* straights, when *Hollises* and *Stapletons* faction domineered over them, and intended to dethrone them, then were their words smoother then oyle their words dropped like the honey Comb, into the mouths of the hungry, oppressed people."[18] And the soldiers took them at their word: "Thus common right and freedome was visibly the choice object of all their actions and intentions, that was seemingly the golden ball of their contention, the ultimate end of their hazardous race" (5). But all was mere pretence: "And what Eagle eye could at first discerne, that this glorious cloathing was but painted paper?" (6) "[F]rom that time the King had his Emissaries at the Head Quarters"; "Kings flatteries proved like impoysoned arrowes, which infected all the blood in *Cromwels* and *Iretons* veins" (11).

Incredibly, the *Heads of the Proposals*, drafted by Ireton and presented to the General Council on 17 July as the Army's minimum settlement, was quickly given to the King for amendment. As Wildman says, "When these Proposalls were roughly drawn, IRETON IN A PRIVATE CONFERENCE WITH THE KING, INGAGED HIMSELF TO SEND HIM A COPY,[19] and though at the first some of the other Generall Officers opposed it, yet *Ireton* professed he was fixed in his resolution to fulfill his INGAGEMENT, though the General should hang him" (13). As a result, "the PROPOSALLS WERE ALTERED in five or six particulars, NEERLY RELATING TO THE KINGS INTEREST" (14).[20]

The upshot, according to Wildman, was "*That the estates, liberties, and lives of the whole Nation*" once again became the King's "*RIGHT and PROPERTY*" (20, italics in original).[21] And "let every Impartiall iudgement, passe his sentence upon the question," Wildman insisted further, "whether *IRETONS* and *CROMWELLS* (or as they are called the Armies) *PROPOSALLS*, doe not confirme that *foundation of tyranny*, the Kings first enslaving principle? viz. *that all power and authority in this nation, is fundamentally seated in the Kings WILL*" (32). So "Now (my deare Countrymen) I have shewn you the pictures of your *new Saviours*, drawn with their own Pencill," Wildman warns:

> you have seen them as they entered the Field, when justice and freedome, appeared to be as a golden chaine about their necks, a Bracelet on their Armes, the only Motto in all their Colours, the Banner

> under which they would encounter with every ruling *Nimrod*, and proud *Haman*, who would over-top their bretheren, and make them bow the knee to their raging lusts. (42)

Similar suspicions of Grandee double-dealing were expressed in a pamphlet presented to Fairfax on 18 October by Army "Agitators," *The Case of the Armie Truly Stated.* Speaking "in their dual capacity as soldiers and Englishmen,"[22] the authors[23] advise the Lord General that, "Whereas the grievances, dissatisfactions and desires of the army, both as commoners and soldiers, has been many months since represented to the Parliament … we not only apprehend nothing to have been done effectually, either for the army or the poor oppressed people of the nation, but we also conceive that there is little probability of any good without some more speedy and vigorous actings."[24] Ian Gentles notes that *The Case* demanded a "written constitution" giving sovereignty to "the whole body of the people" in "[f]reely elected parliaments," and guaranteeing that "The practice of religion must be free, with no compulsion and no tithes."[25]

In a subsequent *Cal to All the Soldiers of the Army*, Wildman was much more pessimistic: "Those of you, that use your thursday general-Councels of late, might have observed so much of this kind of *jugling, false-hood*, and *double dealing*."[26] And he puts most of the blame on one senior officer: "*Ireton* (yee know) hath already scandalized the *Case of the Army* in the generall counsel where, by his owne, and his confederats craft and policy, he raigneth as sole master" (*Cal*, 7). The authors of *The Case* had in fact been fairly prescient about the dangers lurking in the protracted political impasse between a devious monarch, a jealous Parliament, and the Army Grandees: "First, the love and affection of the people to the army … is decayed, cooled and near lost. It's already the common voice of the people, 'What good have our new saviours done for us? What grievances have they procured to be redressed? Wherein is our condition bettered?' or 'How are we more free than before?'"[27] The situation was becoming insupportable: "So that now the people begin to cry louder for disbanding the army than they did formerly for keeping us in arms because they see no benefit accruing" (*Case*, 36). Unless they acted soon, the growing gulf between the people and the Army would be unbridgeable.

"Fairfax and his advisers recognised the seriousness of this challenge and decided," notes Austin Woolrych, "that it must be put before the General Council, if only to flush its real authors out into the open and rebut their accusations" ("Debates," 67). Referred to the next regular meeting on Thursday 21 October, it was not discussed. In the meantime,

> The new agents and their mentors jumped at this opportunity, for which they may have planned, to make the General Council their captive audience. They responded not with a mere defence of their recent manifesto but with an entirely fresh document, drafted for the occasion. This was no less than the original *An agreement of the people*, which was approved by the new agents' meeting on the 27th and brought to headquarters that same day by Trooper Robert Everard of Cromwell's own regiment. (Woolrych, 67)

Here, in essence, was the document that should have justified Milton's claim that the army and the people were one. In fact, as Rachel Foxley remarks, this was a proposal that "appears, rather tellingly, as an agreement *between* the army and the people."[28]

It was this document on which Henry Ireton chose to focus relentlessly during the General Council the next day, a session that would last almost two weeks. The Putney debates pitted egalitarian democrats against defenders of the ancient constitution (property and tradition). It featured sharp clashes between the two camps, and stirring eloquence that continues to echo down the centuries, since it turns, in the stenographic record of William Clarke, on contested issues of earned citizenship and universal manhood suffrage (another bone of contention in the *Agreement* on which Ireton would gladly pounce). While twelve of the fifty agitators spoke on behalf of their regiments in the course of three days of recorded debate, five spoke "only once, and very briefly" (Woolrych, "Debates," 73). Edward Sexby, Thomas Rainsborough, and Wildman (soon to be christened Levellers by the king, if not Cromwell himself)[29] squared off against those prototypical country squires, Cromwell and his son-in-law Ireton.

On behalf of the "ancient constitution," Ireton manipulated the agenda to focus on the social heresy that poor people had "a permanent fixed interest in this kingdom." On the populist side, Rainsborough drew on Lilburne's own assertion that "the poorest that lives, hath as true a right to give a vote, as well as the richest and greatest"[30] – to say as grandly,

> that the poorest he that is in England hath a life to live, as the greatest he; and therefore truly, sir, I think it's clear, that every man that is to

> live under a government ought first by his own consent to put himself under[31] that government; and I do think that the poorest man in England is not at all bound in a strict sense to that government that he hath not had a voice to put himself under.[32]

As Michael Mendle justly comments, "Ireton's callous (and incomprehensibly tactless) assimilation of the case of the propertyless to that of the foreigner," and his "unrelenting ridicule of the claims of birthright (the more painful, perhaps, for the cruel truth of some of his jibes)" were "literally and, much more poignantly, psychologically alienating."[33]

The defenders of birthright countered Ireton's language of legal precedent and the "ancient constitution" with a language of native,[34] even earned, rights. Sexby declaimed:

> We have engaged in this kingdom and ventured our lives, and it was all for this: to recover our birthrights and privileges as Englishmen … There are many thousands of us soldiers that have ventured our lives; we have had little propriety in the kingdom as to our estates, yet we have had a birthright. But it seems now, except a man hath a fixed estate in this kingdom, he hath no right in this kingdom. I wonder we were so much deceived. If we had not a right to the kingdom, we were mere mercenary soldiers. (Woodhouse, 69).

Responding to Ireton's objections to this novel claim of rights *earned* by citizen-soldiers, Rainsborough argued just as pointedly: "I see that it is impossible to have liberty but all property must be taken away. If it be laid down for a rule, and if you will say it, it must be so. But I would fain know what the soldier hath fought for all this while? He hath fought to enslave himself, to give power to men of riches, men of estates, to make him a perpetual slave" (Woodhouse, *Puritanism and Liberty*, 71). (It is the same case Milton makes against Salmasius.) The *army* and *people* together, if Sexby is their measure, do claim a right of populist rule.

Here, Milton's case for equating *people* with *army* in his *Defensio* seems justified, particularly in view of Ireton's dogmatism and lack of sympathy with the rank and file. Austin Woolrych recalls that, "late in that famous meeting on 29 October a motion was carried, with only three dissentients, to give the vote in parliamentary elections to all men except servants and beggars, and that the General Council confirmed this four days later"

("Debates," 77). There was now "pressure to call the army to a general rendezvous, doubtless in the hope of carrying *An agreement of the people* by acclamation, as the *Solemn engagement* had been carried in June; Rainborough [*sic*] had already urged such a course on 29 October" (76). But the Lord General ordered the agitators back to their regiments to rendezvous in three separate locations. The Grandees feared a vote by acclamation that would tie the Army and the soldiery to an *Agreement of the People*. The interests of the people were more closely linked to the Army than Milton knew.[35]

At one stage of the debate, Colonel Thomas "Harrison, uncontrollable fanatic as he was, burst out into a cry that the King was a man of blood, and declared that 'they were now to prosecute him.'"[36] But Cromwell, resisting calls on 1 November from officers and men to do away with the king as well as his throne, responded that the king

> was King by contract. Let him that was without sin amongst them cast the first stone at him. If they and the Parliament had been free from transgression towards the King, they might justly require that he should be cut off as a transgressor, "but, considering that we are in our own actions failing in many particulars, I think there is much necessity of pardoning of transgressors." (Gardiner, *Civil War*, 4: 3).

Nevertheless, the king's flight from Hampton Court on 11 November – rather oddly just as the Lord General was cutting off debate in the General Council and ordering men back to regiments for a general rendezvous – began to favour the radical faction at Putney.

Fairfax and Cromwell's suppression of a rising mutiny four days later at Corkbush Field near Ware was ominous for several reasons. Here, the Grandees were confronted by Col. Thomas Rainsborough, who "presented a petition urging the army to embrace *An agreement* ... The most dangerous moment of the day came when Colonel Thomas Harrison's regiment turned up uninvited and without their officers. They wore copies of *An agreement* pinned provocatively to their hats, bearing the slogan 'England's freedom, soldiers' rights.'"[37] Historians are generally agreed that Cromwell rode into their midst, snatching copies of the *Agreement* from their hatbands and ripping them to shreds, but "there is no mention of it in the contemporary accounts of the rendezvous. Legends always grow up round the towering figures in history. Fairfax was the general in command at this review, and it was officers of his staff who rode in among the mutineers" (Brailsford, 297).

Legends, however, are more true at times than fact: "England's freedom" simply meant Parliament's rights to Cromwell, while "soldiers' rights" were clearly unrelated to "freedom." The Army was one thing to the Grandees; and "the people" were quite another, with no mutual, let alone overlapping, identities.

Within a twelvemonth, the road from Corkbush Field would lead to Westminster and the purging of the lower house, just as Salmasius had described it, and to the king being taken from prison in Carisbrooke Castle to Windsor, and then to the extra-judicial High Court of Justice, before the scene ended on the scaffold in front of Whitehall. Overton describes a general revulsion from the Army when, by military force, Cromwell,

> called a Court of *Mock justice* by his own Authority, against the peoples will, or advice: and hired knaves to cry *Justice, justice*; directly against the Law of God, and his own former Oathes and Protestations, took off the Kings head, abolished Monarchy, erected a Popular Government of himself, his hired Servants, and combined Creatures … and so having usurped *Gods Authority*, as well as the *Kings*, hath establisht a Monstrous *Government*, without *head* or *tayle; rule* or *President; law* or *Reason*; and commanded all *People* under pain of *high treason*, to acknowledge just, and be subject unto it.[38]

By contrast, Milton's account in Chapter 10 of *Defensio* recalls for the most part the bitter feelings in the Army and Independent faction at the prospect of a second civil war:

> The conquered leaders of the royalists had indeed laid down their arms, though unwillingly … [so now] the Presbyterians, after they saw that they were forbidden to tyrannize over everyone in church and state … became so embittered as to sell themselves once again to the king rather than share with their brethren that freedom which they too had bought with their blood. A return to the mastery of that tyrant stained with the blood of so many citizens, who was already burning with rage against those who yet survived, and who had planned his revenge, seemed to them preferable to allowing their brothers and friends a position of just equality with themselves. Only those called Independents knew how to be true to themselves until the end and how to use their victory. (CPW 4.i: 511)

In view of what happened in 1648, every line in Milton's account is justified, apart from that final sentence. What it hides is the brutal suppression, first of citizen-soldiers at Corkbush Field who were demanding "England's freedom, soldiers' rights"; then of the five enlisted men drummed out of the Army in early March 1649 for their Levelling petitions; and finally the four Leveller leaders haled before the Council in late March for protesting against "Englands new chains." Nowhere does Milton recall the military revolt that was put down (with three soldiers lined up against a wall and summarily shot) at Burford on 15 May 1649. If the Independents were "true to themselves," the plain truth was that they were tyrants. In the end, they simply "use[d] their victory" to rule in the interests of their own faction, and then later on, in the interests of a new "single person," the Lord Protector.

Soon after Milton finished writing *Defensio* in December 1650, he was assigned, as we saw in Chapter 2, to license Nedham's *Mercurius Politicus*, in order "to imprint such Principles in Mens minds, as might actuate them with an irreconcileable enmity to the former Power, insomuch that the very name of *King* became odious."[39] The trouble was that the road from Corkbush Field to Whitehall was thronged with troops who were no longer in agreement with the people, having by now taken over Whitehall Palace. By the time *Defensio Secunda* was published in May 1654, the Rump had been barred from the Commons for more than a year, a new Nominated Assembly had been "invited" to resign in December 1653, and the Lord Protector had been installed, despite the dire warnings of *Politicus*. In spite of Milton's jibes at Salmasius's expense in 1651, it should have been clear by now "that the act of the better, the sound part of the Parliament, in which resides the real power of the people," was not, and never had been, a legitimate power. It was in fact a military tyranny. "The leaders with their own soldiers did this."

Salmasius had predicted that the road to Ireland must lead to another tyranny. "Who," he asked rhetorically, "when he was recently about to undertake an expedition to Ireland, went out from London with the appearance of a conqueror, with regal pomp, conveyed in a six-team carriage, drawn by white horses, accompanied by an escort of eighty nobles? Was it not one of the leaders, who did not receive this power from the people, but from the soldiers and the military council?" (*CPW* 4.ii: 989). Lilburne came to a similar conclusion in *As You Were* (1652) about the course of Cromwell's career and his deception of the people: "The gulled, cheated & abused peoples lives, really & truly being of no more value with him or them, then so many dead doggs, serving him or them for no other end, but to be his foote-steps to climbe up to the top of absolute and arbitrary Power & pretended Authority, *or unlimited & unbounded Kingship*" (3).

In more trenchant language than either Salmasius or Lilburne would use, Overton remarked how, "no sooner was he in the House of *Commons*," than Cromwell appeared

> like *Belzebubb* amongst the inferior *Devils*, and sent out his *Agents* and *spies* to work *mischief*; he first got the Earl of *Essex* to be poysoned, and wone *Fairfax* to be *Head of his Faction*, till he had brought his *Plots* to perfection; he hath taken the Oath of his Allegiance, Supremacy, the Solemn League and Covenant; look'd up to Heaven, call'd God to behold his Hypocrisie, and the Angels to witness his perjury.[40]

Not until Milton was losing his eyesight did he really see the hypocrisy that he denied in *Defensio*. In an equivocal voice of irony, he set out to correct his errors of vision, firstly, through his association with *Politicus* in 1651–52;[41] then by subtle revisions of *Defensio Secunda*[42] in 1653–54; and lastly, in his portrait of "the great consult" in Pandæmonium, very likely begun under the reign of Richard Lord Protector during the winter of 1659.

THEN HOW MUCH of the Putney debates was public knowledge in the autumn of 1647? The transcripts of these debates made at the generals' behest by William Clarke, Secretary of the General Council, were not published in his lifetime, and not even found by C.H. Firth until 1890 and published in a Royal Historical Society edition. So it is not likely that the speeches of Milton's devils in "consult" refer to particular speeches made at Putney.

Dramatic and rhetorical situations are another matter, however. In *A Cal to All the Soldiers of the Army* (29 October 1647), John Wildman characterized as follows the speeches in Putney Church on Thursdays, beginning 9 September 1647: "One of the surest markes of deceivers, is to make faire, long and eloquent speeches … whiles in the meanetime, under the vizards of great professions, gilded with some religious actions, they both deceive the world, and bring their wicked designes and selfe-interests to pass."[43] That description could serve as a stage direction for Satan's opening speech in Book 2:

> Powers and Dominions, Deities of Heav'n,

> For since no deep within her gulf can hold
> Immortal vigor, though opprest and fall'n,
> I give not Heav'n for lost. From this descent
> Celestial vertues rising, will appear
> More glorious and more dread then from no fall,
> And trust themselves to fear no second fate. (2.11–17)

Satan's pretence of religion is evident in his continued use of the social titles of Heaven, as well as in his mention of "Celestial vertues rising," the latter a blatant tautology.

"Take heed of crafty polititians and subtill *Machiavelians*," Wildman warned in *A Cal*, "& be sure to trust no mans painted words" (4). Those at the "grand consult" in Hell should likewise have looked beyond Satan's "painted words" to where he sat, "High on a Throne of Royal State" (*PL* 2.1). For the tyrant's need to justify his position in embarking on this sham debate is self-evident in Satan's positioning of himself "in a safe unenvied Throne / Yielded with full consent" (2.23–4), where none can "envy whom the highest place exposes / Formost to stand against the Thunderers aim / Your bulwark" (2.27–9). Satan knows his followers well enough to warn: "where there is then no good / For which to strive, no strife can grow up there / From Faction," since "none, whose portion is so small / Of present pain" "Will covet more" (2.30–5). It is a wise general who appeals to memories of former "union and firm Faith," not to mention the present "firm accord, / More then can be in Heav'n," where "we now return / To claim our just inheritance of old, / Surer to prosper then prosperity / Could have assur'd us" (2.36–40). There is nothing specifically Cromwellian in the speech of this heroic stockbroker assuring clients tautologically that they are *surer* to *prosper* than *prosperity assures* them. Here is hardly more than the hypocrite's "gilded" promise to initiate "open" debate on the means of attack, whether by "open Warr or covert guile, / We now debate" (2.41–2). In a single speech, Milton thus manages to evoke the essence of Cromwellian politics, which Wildman had crisply defined in print more than a decade before as the pretence of holding

> forth the *white flag of accommodation and satisfaction*, and of minding the same thing which yee mind, and to be flesh of your flesh, and bone of your bone, and to invite you to their head-quarters, where they hope either to worke upon you as they have most lamentably

> done upon others, even to betray your *trust*, confound both your understandings and Councels, corrupt your judgements, and blast your actions. (*A Cal*, 5–6)

A second source of echoes heard in "the great consult" is Nedham's *Mercurius Pragmaticus*. Having defected in 1647 to the royalist cause out of mistrust of Cromwell, Milton's future friend very publicly warned advocates of property and of birthright "that I have a *Familiar* that *creeps* into all your *Conventicles* and *Counsels*."[44] A full three weeks before *A Cal* appeared, Nedham had already offered this sketch of Cromwell's methods, if relating more to his conduct in the Commons than in the Army's General Council. Here, Nedham satirizes a mind-boggling conflict of interest between Lt-General Cromwell and Oliver Cromwell, MP, the one feigning no relation to the other:

> And because King *Cromwell* (as *Iohn Lillburne* cals him) will not be seen to have a hand in it, as the *primum Mobile* of the design, the *plot* was laid thus, that he should receive at *Westminster*, as it were at *second hand*, a *Letter* from the *Army* directed to himselfe, which bespeakes him to this effect, as if he (harmlesse man) knew nothing of it before; that he would be pleas'd to represent unto the *Parliament* the great *distresse* lying upon the *Army* for want of Money.[45]

It is a perfect gloss on Satan's dramatic situation in "the great consult" as "the *primum Mobile* of the design," who, "(harmlesse man) knew nothing of it before," and consults his constituency to know the public will. That this sketch of Cromwell would be familiar to Milton is most likely, given his close association with Nedham throughout the 1650s.

A week later, *Pragmaticus* satirized Cromwell in terms that offer a witty preview of the debaters in Pandæmonium; for Lilburne "gives the *Adjutators* to understand, how that *Oliver* and his Son *Ireton*, begin to play *Rex*, and are become as *Apocryphall* as *Bal* and the *Dragon* in their late proceedings, and so no more to be worshipped in the *Assembly of Saints*."[46] Nedham's wording cuts multiple ways, first by laying bare Ireton's complicity in putting Cromwell on the throne; next by exposing each as a false idol; and finally, by rousing sympathy for the soldiers whose only "sin" was to have doubted God's loyal spokesperson (Abdiel-Lilburne). Overton's retrospective account in *The Hunting of the Foxes* (21 March 1649) of the

Grandees' coup against the "agitators" makes a final chapter in what were likely to have been the print sources available to Milton for his scene of the debate in Hell: "Hence followed secret murmurings & *whisperings* amongst the *Prerogative Officers* against the session and power of the *Agitators*, and at length palpable endeavors broke forth to suppress them ... [T]hen it was openly given out, *That they stood as souldiers, only to serve the State, and might not as free Commons insist upon their liberty*" (Overton, 3).

In this context, it is obvious that the first of Satan's generals to speak – "*Moloch*, horrid King besmear'd with blood / Of human sacrifice, and parents tears" (1.392–3) – is from "the 'war party,'" or those wanting "to defeat the king militarily."[47] At Putney, there was an appetite for revenge on Charles Stuart as "a man of blood" who preferred to fight another war rather than compromise his "divine right" to the throne. Nedham wrote in the first issue of *Pragmaticus* of the simmering fury at the weekly meetings in the church: "A mad-man in the generall Councell at *Putney*, said, There was now no *visible* Authoritie in the *Kingdome*, but the *power of the Sword.* But whatsoever this man said, I am sure few wise men can see any else as yet; yet the *Councell* did doe well to declare against it."[48] "My sentence is for open Warr" (2.51), "*Moloc*" begins his own furious speech in Hell. Presented as "the strongest and the fiercest Spirit / That fought in Heav'n" (2.44–5), the "Scepter'd King" sets a tone as fierce as anything reported by Nedham. He is nonetheless opposed by every speaker for what even he admits is suicidal belligerence, "happier farr / Then miserable to have eternal being" (2.97–8). Without objection from the chair, Belial and Mammon are left to oppose alone a headlong assault on the "monarchy" of Heaven, in spite of Moloch's vainglorious claim that they will find "perpetual inrodes to Allarme, / Though inaccessible, his fatal Throne: / Which if not Victory is yet Revenge" (2.103–5).

Belial, the second to speak, has no counterpart in contemporary reports by Nedham or Wildman, but his retort to Moloch points to a peer of the realm speaking in the House of Lords: "I should be much for open Warr, O Peers" (2.119), says a "graceful and humane" (2.109) Belial as a prelude to his strategy of accommodation. For the same strategy, the Earl of Manchester had been impeached in 1644 by Cromwell, who later dropped the suit, to the consternation of Lilburne, who complained endlessly[49] of "the Earl of *Manchesters* ... treachery to his Countrey."[50] Of Manchester it could be said nonetheless that he was "a sweet meek man."[51] Milton could not know what we know, that Sir Philip Warwick later described him as possessed "of a debonair nature, but very facile or changeable."[52] But he apparently knew enough by common report to say of Belial that, "A fairer person lost not Heav'n: he seemd / For dignity compos'd and high exploit; / But all was false and hollow" (2.110–12).

The falsity of Belial's strategy of accommodation in Hell is immediately apparent in the answer he gives to his question, "[I]s this then worst, / Thus sitting, thus consulting, thus in Arms?" (2.163–4). For "when we fled amain, pursu'd and strook / With Heavn's afflicting Thunder, and besought / The Deep to shelter us[,] this Hell then seem'd / A refuge from those wounds" (2.165–8). Indeed, "This is now / Our doom: which if we can sustain and bear, / Our Supream Foe in time may much remit / His anger" (2.208–11). Belial sounds like a repentant royalist regretting present company.[53] Still, he pretends to hope that "Our purer essence then will overcome / … Or chang'd at length, and to the place conformd / In temper and in nature, will receive / Familiar the fierce heat, and void of pain" (2.215–19). His passivity makes him a true foil to Satan, who had rebuked Beelzebub, claiming that "to be weak is miserable, / Doing or Suffering" (1.157–8). And yet Belial's ethic of suffering still poses a moral danger, since it is a "hollow" version of what Adam eventually learns: "that suffering for Truths sake / Is fortitude to highest victorie" (12.569–70). When Belial claims that, "To suffer, as to doe, / Our strength is equal" (2.199–200), he thereby cloaks Manchester's do-nothing policy in the garments of active virtue – bearing witness unto death to the cause of Truth. "Warr therefore, open or conceal'd, alike / My voice disswades" (2.187–8), Belial quavers, leaving the narrator to condemn his "ignoble ease, and peaceful sloath, / Not peace" (2.227–8). That Manchester's private royalism had long been public knowledge was due in part to John Lilburne. In the first of many narratives about the Earl's "sloth," he writes, "After my deliverance, I served under my Lord of *Manchester*, where and with whom I adventured my life as freely as any man in the Army, & the best requital that I got at his hand, was an earnest endeavour by him to hang me, for taking *Tickel* Castle from the Cavaleers."[54]

But Belial's "passivism" is strongly opposed by Mammon's advocacy of "Hard liberty before the easie yoke / Of servile Pomp" (2.256–7), an argument which could be used to justify Milton's claim in *Defensio* that the *people* and the *army* are one and the same. Yet Mammon sounds more like Lilburne prosecuting Manchester for treason to the cause of freedom. Most of all, his populist appeal resembles Wildman's *A Cal to All the Souldiers of the Armie by the Free People of England* to stand firm in the great cause for which they had enlisted. For the soldiers in John Wildman's army had doubtless fought in the name of the *people* to be citizens, not subjects.[55] Even were their "king" to forgive their revolt against the "ancient constitution" and his regal authority, who among them would now choose to bend the knee again and return to an abject state of subjecthood?

> Suppose he should relent
> And publish Grace to all, on promise made
> Of new Subjection; with what eyes could we
> Stand in his presence humble, and receive
> Strict Laws impos'd, to celebrate his Throne
> With warbl'd Hymns, and to his Godhead sing
> Forc't Halleluiah's. (2.237–43)

Or again, when Mammon urges, "Let us not then pursue / By force impossible, by leave obtain'd / Unacceptable, though in Heav'n, our state / Of splendid vassalage" (2.249–52), he makes the same argument that Lilburne had first used in *The Just Mans Justification*, exposing "that which is the greatest mischiefe of all, and *the oppressing bondage of England* ever since the *Norman yoke*, [which] is this, I must be tryed before you by a Law (called the Common Law) that I know not, nor I thinke no man else, neither do I know where to find it, or reade it; and how I can in such a case be punished by it, I know not."[56] In *A Remonstrance*, Overton and Walwyn wrote as well that, "The History of our Fore-fathers since they were Conquered by the *Normans*, doth manifest that this Nation hath been held in bondage all along ever since by the policies and force of the Officers of Trust in the Common-wealth."[57] So "we remain under the *Norman* yoke of an *unlawfull Power*," they said, "from which wee ought to free ourselves" (13).

Two weeks after *The Just Mans Justification*, Lilburne added the term "vassalage" to his Norman Yoke theory, sounding the alarm against the Lords' design "to enslave the free People of *England*," who "will scorn to be made slaves & vassals, by the meer Creatures of their Creature *the King*."[58] A few weeks later, in *An Alarum To the House of Lords*, Overton adopted this term "vassalage" to lament the ongoing loss of rights and freedoms of free-born Englishmen: "But by this We may discerne your most insufferable encroachments upon our *Common Rights*, daily increasing upon us; which in time, if not prevented, will wholly enslave and Vassallage us all."[59] Mammon, in fact, is never more a Leveller than when he invokes the

"Norman" Yoke. The whole tenor of his argument is that he and his fellows would "rather seek / Our own good from our selves, and from our own / Live to our selves " (2.252–4). It is he who advises the council "how in safety best we may / Compose our present evils, with regard / Of what we are and were, dismissing quite / All thoughts of warr: ye have what I advise" (2.280–3).[60] And then "Such applause was heard / As *Mammon* ended, and his Sentence pleas'd" (2.290–1), evidently carrying with ease the popular vote. Here, in a word, is full vindication for Milton's bold assertion in *Defensio* that "the people and the army" were one. For here, if anywhere, the classical republic approached reality – in Hell.[61]

The problem is nonetheless transparent: *this* classical republican idiom is the real thing, unlike Satan's use of republican language to clothe his reactionary politics in the garment of liberty. Mammon's call is at least made to the soldiers of a citizen army. So why does Milton situate the people's cause in Hell? The answer is simple. A number of the English people had been receptive to the politics of virtue in a classical republic.[62] A few were receptive as well to Nedham's appeal to self-interest, the cynical ground of a Machiavellian republic.[63] But just as clearly, they had by now failed the test of republican freedom – whether it be conceived of as a "politics of virtue," or as a "politics of vigilance" against the ambition of the great ones – in returning to the worship of old idols. Mammon evidently speaks for recent English history. For the problem is not only the rhetor's classical message but his changeable audience: the rank and file exhibit no more steady principles in Hell than the English could muster to save the republic. And then Beelzebub thwarts the popular will by scorning the whole republican project.

Wildman's *A Cal* was not the sole source, but only the first on record, to predict how the popular vote was likely to be abused. After the first day of debate, he wrote how

> most that have beene there have been deluded, to our great griefe, which appeareth by the unreasonable proceedings of that Court, as in many things, so especially in their debates about the aforesaid *Case of the ARMY*, now published and subscribed by you.
>
> Wherein though the *Generall* was so ingenuous, as to move for the publike reading thereof, yet the Commissary Generall *Ireton*, and Lieutenant Generall *Cromwell*, yea, and most of the Court, would and did proceed to censure & judge both it and the Authors and promoters thereof, without reading it, and ever since doe impudently boast and glory in that their victory. (*A Cal* 4–5)

The generals' contempt at Putney was public knowledge, and evidently Milton's immediate source for Beelzebub's haughty scorn:

> Thrones and Imperial Powers, off-spring of heav'n,
> Ethereal Vertues; or these Titles now
> Must we renounce, and changing stile be call'd
> Princes of Hell? for so the popular vote
> Inclines, here to continue, and build up here
> A growing Empire. (2.310–15)

The only difference between Ireton and Beelzebub is that the latter speaks to actual "Peers," not Commoners, upbraiding them for voting to renounce their place-based titles.

Another printed source for the rigging of the vote in Hell had long been available to Milton in *The Hunting of the Foxes* (21 March 1649), Overton's mocking account of the Army's evolution from a democratic General Council to a military dictatorship:

> When *Cromwell* and *Ireton*, and their faction of self interested Officers thought they had got the souldiery fast by the brain, as to dote sufficiently upon their transaction and conduct of busines, they then decline the Agitators, decline the *Engagement*, sleight their *Declarations* and *Promises* to the people and Army, rendring the Agitatours but as ciphers amongst them, corrupting some with places, over-ruling and overawing others. (5)

Milton likely recalled Lilburne's post-mortem, too, of the suppression of populist sentiments and crushing of Leveller hopes after Putney in *Legal Fundamental Liberties*. Although Lilburne refers to the Whitehall debates on the *Agreement of the People* of 1648, his synopsis of methods and principles also reflects Grandee strategies at Putney:

> That no tye, promises, nor engagements were strong enough to hold the grand Juglers, and Leaders of the Army … was now made clearly manifest, for when it came to the Councel, there came the *General, Cromwel*, and the whole gang of Creature-Colonels, and other officers, and spent many dayes in taking it all in pieces, and there *Ireton* himself shewed himself an *absolute King*, if not an *Emperor*, against whose will no man must dispute.[64]

In view of so much public information about the conduct of the "people" and the "Army" in both debates at Putney and Whitehall,[65] Milton surely knew the players well enough to be able to script characteristic speeches for them in setting his scene in Pandæmonium.

Beelzebub is just as "absolute" as Ireton in demolishing the arguments brought against him, sneering at Belial's indolent "dream" while they sit "And know not that the King of Heav'n hath doom'd / This place our dungeon, not our safe retreat" (2.315–17). Mammon's idea, like that of the Levellers, is soon relegated to the trash heap of history:

> For he, be sure
> In heighth or depth, still first and last will Reign
> Sole King, and of his Kingdom loose no part
> By our revolt, but over Hell extend
> His Empire, and with Iron Scepter rule
> Us here, as with his Golden those in Heav'n. (2.323–8)

As for Moloch's suicidal folly, why do "we need / With dangerous expedition to invade / Heav'n, whose high walls fear no assault or Siege, / Or ambush from the Deep" (2.341–4), "if we find / Some easier enterprize" (2.344–5)? So Beelzebub-Ireton ends: "Advise if this be worth / Attempting, or to sit in darkness here / Hatching vain Empires" (2.376–8).

The narrator's comment further echoes Leveller commentary on the whole stage-management of the Grandee design: "Thus *Beelzebub*," says Milton, "Pleaded his devilish Counsel, first devis'd / By *Satan*, and in part propos'd" (2.378–80). In like fashion, Overton had exposed Ireton's pretense of negotiating a new *Agreement of the People* when the Grandees had needed popular support in November 1648, and "by this means they so far prevailed over the most constant and faithful friends to the People, as to beget an acquiescence in them for a season, till they in the mean time so far effected their business, as to the introduction of an absolute platform of Tyranie, long since hatched by *Ireton*" (*Foxes*, 8). It is not the first (or last) time that Milton echoes Overton; but it is the first time that the Leveller's voice distinctly sounds in the voice of the epic narrator. By contrast, Beelzebub speaks as a loyal foot soldier, exalting his "heroic" commander by exaggerating all the difficulties he must face: "But first whom shall we send … whom shall we find / Sufficient?" (2.402–4). In conjuring up the dangers, he leaves no room for anyone else to act: "who shall tempt with wandring feet / The dark unbottom'd infinite Abyss" (2.404–5), who shall "spread his aerie flight / Upborn with indefatigable wings / Over the vast abrupt, ere he arrive / The happy Ile" (2.407–10)?

The answer is seated directly in front of them, "High on a Throne of Royal State" (2.1). And Satan's rhetorical mastery outdoes even that of his lieutenant in slipping from pronouns of inclusion to those of exclusion – broadly from "us" to "me," by way of the bridge of the impersonal pronoun "any" and the non-person "he": "With reason hath deep silence and demurr / Seis'd us" where, in "Our prison strong, this huge convex of Fire … immures us round" with "gates of burning Adamant / Barr'd over us" that "prohibit all egress" (2.431–7). And yet, "These past, if any pass," there is still "the void profound / Of unessential Night" waiting to "receive him next / Wide gaping, and with utter loss of being / Threatens him, plung'd in that abortive gulf" (2.438–41), where, "If thence he scape … what remains him less / Then unknown dangers and as hard escape" (2.442–4). So we pass from "us" to "him" to a teasing glimpse of the emperor's new clothes:

> But I should ill become this Throne, O Peers,
> And this Imperial Sov'ranty adorn'd
> With splendor, arm'd with power, if aught propos'd
> And judg'd of public moment, in the shape
> Of difficulty or danger could deterr
> Mee from attempting. (2.445–50)

Overton had satirically asked, "O *Cromwel! whither art thou aspiring*? … [H]e that runs may read and fore-see the intent, a *New Regality!* And … by their *Machiavilian* pretenses, and wicked practices, they are become masters and usurpers of the name of the Army, and of the name of the Parliament; under which Visors they have levell'd and destroyed all the Authority of this Nation" (*Foxes*, 9). Satan is just as adept as the Machiavellian politician who had posed at Putney, and again at Whitehall, as the selfless Protector of his people, even when he is exposed in the act of assuming a new regality:[66]

> Wherefore do I assume
> These Royalties,[67] and not refuse to Reign,
> Refusing to accept as great a share
> Of hazard as of honour, due alike
> To him who Reigns, and so much to him due

> Of hazard more, as he above the rest
> High honourd sits? (2.450–6)

Offering "ethical" proof of his right to reign, Satan (Cromwell) thus offers to "prove" that monarchy is both necessary and self-evident, the only legitimate form of government. The result is to make those who talked of "seek[ing] / Our own good from our selves" the true egotists, bent on being "to none accountable," unlike their humble Lord Protector.[68]

Lilburne had offered a like conclusion concerning the debates at Putney, where the Grandees aimed "so [to] modelize their Army, that it in due time might totally become slavish by obeying without dispute what-ever their great Officers command them, and so unanimously elect, and impose *upon the people their present generall for their King*, as the onely fit, able, and best deserving man in England for that *sovereign Place*."[69] Barely a year later, Cromwell was already planning "to cut off the Kings head … and so take him out of his way that he might be absolute King himself, as now he is, and more then ever the King was in his life."[70] So, as "the sequell shews," Lilburne concludes, all the negotiations toward a new *Agreement of the People* at Windsor in November, and again at Whitehall in December 1648, had been a cheat, nothing more:

> [T]hey undertook meerly to quiet and please us (*like children with rattles*) till they had done their main work; (*viz.* either in annihilating or purging the House to make it fit for their purpose, and in destroying the King; *unto both which they never had our consents in the least*) that so they might have no opposition from us, but that we might be *lull'd asleep in a fools paradise* with thoughts of their honest intentions, till all was over; and then totally lay it aside, as they have done, as being then able to do what they pleased whether we would or no: for if they ever had intended an *Agreement, why do they let their own lie dormant in the pretended Parliament ever since they presented it?* (*Legal Fundamental Liberties*, 41)

In comparing "the General and his Councel" to the biblical rebels Corah, Dathan, and Abiram, and to the historical rebels John of Leydon, Jack Straw, and Wat Tyler, Lilburne judges military types to be the worst. His staccato series of questions, like the ones posed by Salmasius a few months later, will leave the Army leaders without moral or legal defence. "And I will *undertake the task upon my life*," Lilburne maintains,

> *to make good every particular of this I now say, to the Generals face.* For did any, or all of them fore-mentioned, ever rebell against their Advancers, Promoters, and Creators, as these have done two severall times? Did ever any, or all of them *chop off* (without all shadow of Law) a KINGS and NOBLES HEADS? *Ravish and force* a Parliament twice? *Nay, raze the foundation of a Parliament to the ground?* and under the notion of performing a trust, *break all Oaths, Covenants, Protestations and Declarations* … and under pretence of preserving their Laws, Liberties, and Freedoms, destroy, annihilate, and tread under their feet all their Laws, Liberties, Freedoms and Properties? (*Legal Fundamental Liberties*, 42–3)

Milton's placement of Satan's speech – acceding to a "new Regality" in Hell to dispense with the older "regality" in Heaven – turns into an admission of his own error in *Defensio* and thus invites a reading as his belated, if heartfelt, expression of regret, along the lines of Wildman in *Putney Projects*, or of Lilburne's quotation of Wildman in *As You Were*:

> And what Egle-eye could at first discerne, "that this glorious cloathing, *was but painted paper*?" what jealous heart could have imagined, "that these promiseing Patriots, *were only sweet mouthed dissemblers*?" Who could have harboured the least suspitions that these seeming visible starrs of heaven, "*were but blazing Comets*?" that would quickly *turne their backs* as they have perfectly done upon all these glorious promises and declarations, and prove the *vilest apostates* that ever the earth bore?[71]

More touchingly, Milton's scene in Pandæmonium ends on a note of keen regret that "the *people* and the *army*" in Hell are able to achieve a unity of purpose that had eluded honest debaters and dissemblers at Putney: "O shame to men! Devil with Devil damn'd / Firm concord holds, men onely disagree / Of Creatures rational" (2.496–8). It is a sad commentary on events that Cromwell's ambitions were twice enhanced by Lilburne's impulsive decision to ignore the series of compromises made on the *Agreement* in Committee – the negotiated agreement reached on the weekend of 30–31 October 1647 and presented to the General Council on 1 November – and to publish his own version:

> The committee's draft bore signs of a compromise between the Leveller *An agreement* and the grandees' *The heads of the proposals.* It silently rejected the Levellers' original and revolutionary concept of an unalterable written constitution brought into being by the signatures of the people. Yet it embraced the almost equally revolutionary concept of powers reserved from parliament – religion, impressment, and indemnity for things said or done in the late war.[72]

"By 3 November" 1647, however, "*An agreement of the people* (as presented to the General Council on 28 October) was on the bookstalls in London, carrying the boast of 'the general approbation of the army.' It was as if the laborious work of compromise by the General Council's committee had never taken place" (Gentles, "Agreements," 154).

Lilburne did the same thing again a year later, as debate continued to rage at Whitehall over liberty of conscience and Parliament's right to punish where no law existed (a genuine crux if one plans to try a king for treason). "On 15 December [1648] John Lilburne jumped the gun by publishing, with the help of an obscure printer, his slightly amended version of the Committee of Sixteen's text of the *Agreement of the people*" (Gentles, 159–60). By appealing to popular opinion over the heads of negotiators, Lilburne's rash action undermined his own cause again by proving the inconstancy of the "giddy multitude," and ensuring the eventual installation of "Hells dread Emperour with … God-like imitated State" (2.510–11) on the throne at Whitehall. Except that Milton, unlike Lilburne, had the grace to acknowledge his error in judgment. The debates in Pandæmonium are unimaginable without consideration of what was left on the public record. And they are still the best evidence we have of the profound understanding to which Milton came over what had been missing in his arguments against Salmasius regarding military and social unity in a form of government that was supposed to be of and by and for the people.

· 5 ·

"All Power I Give Thee"

KINGDOM OF GRACE

THE DRAMA OF THE "grand consult" enacts what was simply described at the outset of that scene where, "High on a Throne of Royal State … Satan exalted sat" (*PL* 2.1, 5). Appealing anxiously to "just right, and the fixt Laws of Heav'n," "free choice," and "merit" (2.18–21) to justify his "Royal State," Satan has by scene's end transcended a merely elective state: "Wherefore do I assume / These Royalites, and not refuse to Reign, / Refusing to accept as great a share / Of hazard as of honour?" (2.450–3). The mask of the hypocrite slips just enough to reveal the usurper doing what he had so reviled in him "who reigns / Monarch in Heav'n" by "old repute, / Consent or custome" (1.637–40). Then, "Towards him they bend / With awful reverence prone; and as a God / Extoll him equal to the highest in Heav'n" (2.477–9). Contrary to Empson, Michael Bryson does recognize that "the Tyranny of Heav'n" has been exposed as Hell's autocracy: "Satan does not go on from rejecting the 'Tyranny of Heav'n' to rejecting all tyranny, in fact, to rejecting *kingship itself*; Satan merely sets himself up as an alternate monarch, another tyrant, another king" (*The Tyranny of Heaven*, 109).

But the despot's prior claim about "the Tyranny of Heav'n" is doubtful. While Bryson supposes that "The Son … takes a significant turn away from the models offered by the Father and Satan, mirror-image monarchs whose concerns are for power, glory, and reign" (132), Satan's challenge to despots is soon beside the point in the scene that ends, "[A]ll Power / I give thee" (3.317–18). For the Father's *renunciation* of power initiates a reversal of authority in Heaven that becomes a faithful mirror image – literally the inversion – of Satan's consolidation of power in Hell. God, it turns out, is less interested in the exercise of power than in its devolution. "Love," he declares of the Son's noble willingness to sacrifice himself, "hath abounded more then Glory abounds" (3.312). Here is the beginning of a tense counter-drama where Tyranny shall be no more.

If the plot is millenarian, is it really adaptable to quotidian life? It seems to be so in the most radical document from any Leveller writer, William Walwyn's *Tyranipocrit*.[1] In his "Epistle Dedicatory," Walwyn recalls the central paradox of the Christian message: "[T]hou knowest that Christ ruled as a servant, and tooke the burden of the people upon him; but our Rulers do rule like Lords, and cast their burden upon the poor people" (3). In consequence, the Leveller writer dares "to prate of an equallity of goods and lands, amongst such false Christians as inhabit *Europia*," though tyrants are bound to object, "[L]et him die without mercy, because hee is a disturber of the tranquilitie of Tyranipocrit" (33). But the enemy, a Tyrant-Hypocrite is bound to triumph unless we "consider how the devil doth strive to erect his kingdome of sinne and impiety, in the same place where God will have his kingedome of grace, namely, in the free will of man" (9). For in this hybrid devil, Walwyn cautions, "are included al sinnes, for hypocrisie is the chiefest sinne against God, and tyranny is the greatest sinne against man" (14).

What Walwyn sees as a marriage of the devil's "*daughter Hypocrisie*" to "*his great friend Tyranny*" (14) adds another gloss on that scene where Satan had assumed God's "royalties." For the devil, Walwyn warns, "hath gotten such great power in the world, for the world adoreth tyranny and hypocrisie ... and yet so cunningly doth the world know how to carry this kinde of Idolatry, that he will not, and others must not say that hee is an hypocrit" (5). Idolatry is the heart of the matter for Walwyn, as it is for Milton. Yet "al this were little," Walwyn explains, "if the devil did appeare in his owne colours, blacke as he is, but the hypocrit hath made him a great white Surplus, so wide as a Bishops Cassoack, embroidered with Atheistry, laced with partiality, and lyned with hypocrisie" (5). Indeed, the "white devil" is much worse than "a blacke devil" (31), he says, because "the [white] devil being thus bravely set forth, hee telleth the world, that hee is God, Christ, and al in al" (5). Responding to those seven Baptist and Independent ministers who had attacked him in *Walwins Wiles* (23 April 1649) as the secret leader of the Levellers, Walwyn thus sets out in *Tyranipocrit, Discovered with His Wiles* to expose the sanctified hypocrisy of those who cunningly pervert the truth of Christianity.

This "dissembling white devil" (18) who "telleth the world, that hee is God" (5) is no more than "a pestilent doctrine" of "unmercifull men," Walwyn avers, who "maintaine, that God hath predestinated one man to salvation more then another" (11). The unnamed "white devil" can only be the God of Calvin and English Presbyterians, who "preach and teach an uncertaine doctrine, of an absolute predestination in God of man, without man, which is contrary to Gods nature, for God cannot bee partial, neither can God do the works of a tyrant, as that doctrine would have him to doe" (24). So pernicious is this doctrine that it really amounts "to say[ing] that God is a hater of unborn children," which "is a most impious saying: but, say they, it is written as we say. True," he responds, "but it was not written that thou shouldest construe it to make God a tyrant" (Walwyn, 12).

Calvin, it is true, was obliged in his *Institutes* to defend his doctrine of election from several strong objections, the first (949) being that it "*makes God a tyrant*";[2] the "*Second*" (953) that "*the doctrine of election takes guilt and responsibility away from man*," given how predestinated souls "are not rightfully punished on account of those things of which the chief cause is in God's predestination" (*Institutes*, 3.23.6); and "*Third*" (958) that "*the doctrine of election leads to the view that God shows partiality toward persons*" (*Institutes*, 3.23.10). In the end, Calvin still insisted (926) that "all are not created in equal condition; rather, eternal life is foreordained for some, eternal damnation for others" (*Institutes*, 3.21.5). To preserve God's eternal majesty, Calvin is thus reduced to making God the author of everlasting inequality.

It is this image of God in *Paradise Lost* that Empson insisted was "astonishingly like Uncle Joe Stalin."[3] At the height of the Cold War era, J.B. Broadbent also doubted the possibility of divine justice from such a deity, since he "speaks as judge, counsel, and plaintiff in one,"[4] and fails to recuse himself as an interested party. Michael Bryson, the latest heir to Empson's critique, also finds that "Milton constructs a God who is nearly indistinguishable from Satan" (25). Making "Milton's Rejection of God as King" the best measure of his republicanism, Bryson argues that he "uses the Father as a foil, a negative to the positive that Milton envisions in the Son" (39). What this version of God the Father represents – though Bryson doesn't say so – is more like an updated version of Walwyn's "white devil." Ultimately, Bryson sees the Son much as the Leveller had done in urging readers to "consider a little better of the nature and power of God, for God is love without hate" (11). Calvin's loveless doctrine of election is more like a chimera that we ourselves "have invented, and which wee doe intend to maintaine so long as wee can" (24).

Milton's colloquy in Heaven is thus designed to show God the Father as being utterly unlike Calvin's puppetmaster, and more like an actor in the drama. Rare indeed is the critic who, like Michael Lieb, will identify "Milton's 'Dramatick' Constitution" in "The Celestial Dialogue." As Lieb reads it, this colloquy is constructed on the model of Abraham contending with God to spare Sodom (Genesis 18), and Moses contending with God to spare Israel (Exodus 32; Numbers 14). For such reasons, Lieb is not deceived by appearances, even though "The language in which that utterance is cast is harsh and uncompromising: it grates, it repels, it provokes. The word 'ingrate' itself is enough to cause any reader to bristle."[5] Because it is typical of God's speech-acts in scripture, it is typical of "Milton's 'Dramatick' Constitution" in the colloquy of Book 3. God dares the Son, as it were, to call him a "white devil" (although Lieb does not use this term):

So will fall,
Hee and his faithless Progenie: whose fault?
Whose but his own? ingrate, he had of mee
All he could have; I made him just and right,
Sufficient to have stood, though free to fall. (3.95–9)

God's accusing tone, his affective rhetoric, and his indignation at being betrayed could hardly leave a worse impression on the reader. So Satan does have reason, it seems, to denounce "our grand Foe / Who … Sole Reigning holds the Tyranny of Heav'n." "Ingrate," the stage villain hisses, indifferent to the fact that neither the man nor his wife has yet to sin. Then what they say must be true: "God hates unborn children."

Indeed, were God to be "partial" – electing whomever he prefers to salvation and damnation – it could not be otherwise. But this would be merely to take appearance for reality, as Milton's God instantly opens a window on a very different reality:

Freely they stood who stood, and fell who fell,
Not free, what proof could they have givn sincere
Of true allegiance, constant Faith or Love,
Where onely what they needs must do, appeard,
Not what they would? (3.102–6)

It is a declaration that resonates with the language of *Tyranipocrit*, where "God gave unto man a free power, which wee call *will*," and that "God so framed man, that hee is capable of divine wisdome, not by compulsion, but by reason; not by force, but free-will" (8). As Walwyn further maintains, "man must desire to bee good, or God cannot make him good, because it is contrary to Gods nature to force a man to bee good" (9). Mankind had otherwise "servd necessitie, / Not mee" (3.110–11), adds the God of *Paradise Lost*, "As if predestination over-rul'd / Thir will, dispos'd by absolute Decree" (3.114–15). Milton's God is no more disposed than Walwyn's deity to impose on man's free will. "[F]or that which God gave unto man," the Leveller invokes the Free-Will Defence, "was a sparke of his own essence, and it doth participate of Gods nature, and because it is one with God, and free as God, therefore God placed Religion in it" (8). In the end, this is "where God will have his kingedome of grace, namely, in the free will of man, for the devil knoweth that God will have nothing of man, if hee have not his wil and desire, which are one" (9).

The only problem for Walwyn is the typically Calvinist misreading of God's character. For, Walwyn insists, "where God is, there is love, *& Amor vincit omnia*," using the Latin poet Virgil to gloss the "Apostle's" assurance "*that God is love* … and hee hath all that hath God, for hee is in al, and over all, and will turne all to the best for them that doe love him, and keepe his loving commandement" (20). But if God *is* Love, why does Milton's God seem so much less a loving parent than an offended monarch who accuses, convicts, and condemns his *subjects* of a crime yet to be committed?[6] His foreknowledge does not entail necessity – both Calvin and Augustine[7] are clear on this point – yet Milton's deity seems anxious to clear himself of blame:[8] "[T]hey themselves decreed / Thir own revolt, not I: if I foreknew, / Foreknowledge had no influence on their fault, / Which had no less prov'd certain unforeknown" (3.116–19). It is difficult to temper the judgment that Milton creates a "Father who is profoundly disturbing" as "an illustration of what can and will go wrong with deity imagined in absolutist and monarchical terms" (Bryson, 115). At best, this God is a cavilling legalist, it seems; at worst an emotional bully. Yet he ends his speech on a grace note that is anything but ornamental, since the accusing rhetoric and its forensic logic unexpectedly give way to a non sequitur of mercy:

> The first sort by thir own suggestion fell,
> Self-tempted, self-deprav'd: Man falls deceiv'd

> By the other first: Man therefore shall find grace,
> The other none: in Mercy and Justice both,
> Through Heav'n and Earth, so shall my glorie excel,
> But Mercy first and last shall brightest shine. (3.129–34)

The grace note really is "grace,"[9] and yet it comes so unexpectedly that the Son is rattled. He even slips into tautology: "O Father, gracious was that word … grace" (3.144–5).

While Lieb maintains that "Six lines of praise are followed by seventeen lines of challenge that call into question the very promise of grace that the first six lines made a point of extolling" (228), the speech comes less as praise than as relief. For an instant, the Son doesn't know what to say; bracing for the worst, he had been prepared to appeal the "sovran sentence" of an absolute monarch. Yet his *four* (not six) lines of praise are hardly the words of a sycophant, as Lieb demonstrates from the next seventeen lines. No matter how tactful the Son is in framing his questions in the conditional mood, he shows that he would be the first to shout "white devil" at a God who damned his creatures by decree.

And yet the Son never doubts the Father's goodness, willing as he proves himself to be to cry "Tyrant" at *anyone* adhering to a doctrine of arbitrary predestination:

> For should Man finally be lost, should Man
> Thy creature late so lov'd, thy youngest Son
> Fall circumvented thus by fraud, though joynd
> With his own folly? that be from thee farr,
> That farr be from thee, Father, who art Judg
> Of all things made, and judgest onely right. (3.150–5)

Walwyn had likewise recalled in *Englands Lamentable Slavery* how "*Abraham* reasoning with God, was bold to say to that Almighty power, Shall not the Judge of all the earth doe right?"[10] And Lieb clearly sees how "the Son's locution, 'that be from thee farr, / That farr be from thee' … derives from Abraham's statement to God: 'That be far from thee to do after this manner, to slay the righteous with the wicked: and that the righteous should be as the wicked, that be far from thee: Shall not the Judge of all the earth do right?' (Gen. xviii, 25)" (232–3). But Milton's repetition of this line is even more emphatic – and more dramatic – than Lieb appears to realize: the syntax of "that be from thee farr" shifts to "That farr be from thee." By putting "farr" at the greatest possible remove from "thee," the repetition performs the very action that the Son describes by keeping the "tyrant" as far as possible from the paternal deity, if only to ensure that the "Judg / Of all things made" will continue to be the supreme being who "judgest onely right."

The Son's next question indicates his equal concern for the Father's omniscience, lest divine justice should defeat itself: "Or shall the Adversarie thus obtain / His end, and frustrate thine, shall he fulfill / His malice, and thy goodness bring to naught?" (3.156–8). It is a sharp reminder that prudence[11] is the soul of jurisprudence, and that the exercise of one entails the exercise of the other, lest the Law fail and the Adversary triumph where he had least right. And the Son's third question shows his deepest concern for Man, whose intercessor he becomes by choice, not decree: "or wilt thou thy self / Abolish thy Creation, and unmake, / For him, what for thy glorie thou hast made?" (3.162–4). His concern for his Father's greatness proves his desire to make God truly worthy of that praise "wherewith thy Throne / Encompass'd shall resound thee ever blest" (3.148–9).

Here, Lieb is unquestionably right: "The intensity of the drama at this point could not be greater, an intensity that the language of the challenge does much to reinforce: 'So should thy goodness and thy greatness both / Be questioned and blaspheam'd without defence'" (229). The Son's challenge impresses him so much that Lieb will repeat it four times in two pages, commenting further on each occasion: "Consider the implications of the Son's challenge. Warning that if his Father's decree is not executed in a manner consistent with his promise of mercy, the Son charges that his Father's actions would render him defenseless"; "One senses in the challenge that the Son himself would be foremost among the reprobate in excoriating the Father, should the father fail to heed his Son's warning" (229); "To have the Son proclaim that his Father's actions might be justifiably 'questiond' is one thing. To have him proclaim that his Father's actions might be 'blaspheam'd without defence' is quite another" (230); "In an epic that purports to justify the ways of God to men, Milton creates a circumstance in which the very theology upon which that justification is founded threatens to undermine its own cause. I know of no other instance in the history of either dramatic or epic poetry in which a poet has undertaken such risks" (230–1). Except that the risk is more apparent than real; "O Son, in whom my Soul hath chief delight," the Father exults, "Son of my bosom, Son who art alone / My word, my wisdom, and effectual might, / All hast thou spok'n as my thoughts are" (3.168–71). The Father has merely played the scene in accents of rage in order to create the requisite conditions of freedom for the Son to act. Only the absolute freedom provided by a non-Trinitarian deity could allow the Son to respond as a free creature.

Were Milton in fact a Trinitarian – or were the Son to coexist with the Father from all eternity, and so, by virtue of divine omniscience, know the Father's full intent – the scene would simply be another rigged council like the one in Hell. It would then be lumbered, as Milton had quipped in his chapter on the Son in *De Doctrina Christiana*, with "all that play-acting of the persons of the godhead" (*CPW* 6: 213), reducing Christian doctrine to ritual, not reasoned belief. To Milton, scripture was nonetheless "clear that the Father alone is a self-existent God: clear, too, that a being who is not self-existent cannot be a God" (6: 218). Human reason likewise compels us to believe that, "The God to whom we were reconciled, whoever he is, cannot, if he is one God, be the same as the God by whom we were reconciled, since that God is another person." The intercessor who speaks on behalf of mankind should not be the person who judges, lest the scene turn to farce or worse: "If he is the same, then he is his own mediator between himself and us, and reconciles us to himself by himself: a quite inexplicable state of affairs!" (6: 218).

What emerges from the dramatic action of the poem, as well as the poet's lucid theology, is the strongest possible assurance that this God is nothing like the God of Calvin whose "*justice*" (951), as the Genevan insisted, is "*not subject to our questioning*" (*Institutes*, 3.23.4). Calvin may "say with Paul" (952) that we ought not to seek any reason for it [divine providence] because in its greatness it far surpasses our understanding [cf. Romans 9: 19–23]"; and, "With Augustine I say: the Lord has created those whom he unquestionably foreknew would go to destruction. This has happened because he has so willed it. But why he so willed, it is not for our reason to inquire, for we cannot comprehend it" (*Institutes*, 3.23.5). But where the Trinitarian Calvin is obliged to insist on the Son's omniscience, Milton's God, by contrast, is delighted by the deeply human, inferential reasoning of the Son. The mask of a manipulative deity has been ripped away to reveal a loving Father.[12]

Moreover, the Son's challenge allows us to remark sharper differences in these mirroring scenes where Satan and God reveal themselves in word and deed. Where Satan poses as a democrat in order to seize a throne, God poses as a tyrant to test the faith and love of his creatures. It is not the God of Love, but the "white devil" – the God of Calvin – that Milton adapts from

Tyranipocrit to dramatic ends. For Walwyn, like the Son in the colloquy in Heaven, is quick to challenge all who continue to worship this "white devil": "[W]ho hath taught thee to pay God with an external show of holinesse, when he will have internall holinesse, and to show him the figure of the law, without the substance and meaning of the law, and to maintaine lovelesse law, when the whole law is love" (*Tyranipocrit*, 8).

Even now, the trial of the Son's love in *Paradise Lost* has only just begun. Yet Lieb's quotation from Torah ends the scene before we meet the Christian Son: "And the Lord repented of the evil which he thought to do unto his people" (Exodus 32: 14). Lieb, who accuses Irene Samuel of "depriv[ing] the dialogue of just that drama which would otherwise bring it to life" (216), inexplicably fails to bring the drama to life. Ironically, Samuel's reading is more full than Lieb's drama, since it includes three more acts. As Samuel says, only "The speaker" of the first act knows where the action is leading, since he alone is "omniscient: none of his hearers is."[13] Samuel sees how, "beyond working out a plan for man's redemption, the dialogue of the council in Heaven has shown in dramatic process the Son's growth to what the Father himself calls virtual equality" (609).[14] Her recognition of Milton's "Arianism" (though she will retract the term) rightly points her in the direction of what Hugh MacCallum has termed "an earned Godhead."[15]

And yet Samuel fails to explore the dramatic function of God's next speech — the third in a five-act drama — apart from suggesting that God distinguishes himself from Satan by "not pretend[ing] to seek advice" (605). Praising the Son for speaking his mind, why would the Father suddenly reverse his direction? "Man," he declares, "shall not quite be lost, but sav'd who will, / Yet not of will in him, but grace in me / Freely voutsaft" (3.173–5). While the problem is more apparent than real, it appears to renege on that gift of free will by which the Son had reconciled God's "goodness" to his "greatness." Now human agency virtually disappears: "Yet not of will in him," the "white devil" rears its ugly head again, it seems, to determine every action of the creature: "once more I will renew / His lapsed powers, though forfeit … / yet once more he shall stand … / By me upheld … and to me ow / All his deliv'rance, and to none but me" (3.175–82). The speech is doctrinally convenient - avoiding the Pelagian heresy of man saving himself - but it is most *in*convenient in terms of drama, since it now reduces everyone but the Father to a state of total passivity. And yet an unexpected drama begins to emerge from the Father's pretense of meeting the second objection to Calvin's doctrine, that it breeds fatalism, and thus renders human action meaningless, since the outcome is predetermined.

At first, it might seem that Milton's God has left no room for the sort of religion Walwyn claimed "must bee a joyning of two free-wils in one" (9). Most humans lack even the pretense of choice: "Some I have chosen of peculiar grace / Elect above the rest," the deity declares; "so is my will" (3.183–4). The demands of biblical typology might explain why Enoch, Noah, Abraham, and others are predestined to salvation; but the value of their example pales beside the fact that grace comes with what looks like insuperable difficulty to everyone else. As God outlines this process, "The rest shall hear me call … while offerd grace / Invites; for I will cleer thir senses dark, / What may suffice, and soft'n stonie hearts" (3.185–9). Over some thirty-five lines, an all-seeing, supposedly all-controlling Father resorts to "I," "mee," and "mine" twenty-three times. He is neither inclusive in his diction nor dramatic in his syntax, sounding every bit as arbitrary as he is narcissistic: "and to me ow … and to none but me (3.181–2); "for I will cleer … and soft'n stonie hearts" (3.188–9); "And I will place within them as a guide"; "But hard be hard'nd, blind be blinded more, / That they may stumble on, and deeper fall; / And none but such from mercy I exclude" (3.201–3). Were it not for his previous expression of "grace in me / Freely voutsaft," Act 3 couldn't even pretend to underwrite a genuine drama of free-willed choice.

But once again, Walwyn's Leveller understanding of "free grace" is crucial to understanding what has been "Freely voutsaft" to humankind. "For as God created every man free in *Adam*," Nedham, the Leveller author[16] of *Vox Plebis* (19 November 1646) had argued on behalf of the imprisoned Lilburne, "so by nature are all alike freemen born; and are since made free in grace by Christ: no guilt of the parent being of sufficiency to deprive the child of this freedome."[17] "This argument," David Wootton observes, "is an elegant one. By denying that any were predestined to damnation, and by insisting that even sinners could be saved, it opened the way to a new sense of the equality of all men in God's eyes, and thus made a democratic political theory plausible." It is this "appeal to free grace against feudal bondage" that allows the Levellers to "treat the law of nature and the law of grace as identical, as if the Fall had been without consequence."[18] In advance of the climactic reversal to the drama that he has initiated, Milton's God now invokes the third clause of the Leveller patent of freedom: "since made free in grace by Christ." For, although the law does demand that, "He with his whole posteritie must dye, / Dye hee or Justice must; unless for him / Som other able, and as willing, pay / The rigid satisfaction, death for death" (3.209–12), the Father's declaration that man should "ow" his salvation "to none but me" nonetheless requires another person to accomplish that end: "Say Heav'nly powers, where shall we find such love, / … Dwels in all Heaven charitie so deare?" (3.213–16). In the space of a phrase, God has now dropped the mask of the narcissist to ask, Do I have a volunteer?

Even on its face, the Father's behaviour is dramatic; only this time, he rips off the mask of the determinist – or the traditional assumption that the creature is powerless to change a thing. Here, it is all the "Heav'nly powers" whose love and faith is tested, to the point of being asked to volunteer to be "mortal to redeem / Mans mortal crime" (3.214–15). Is it any wonder that "all the Heav'nly Quire stood mute / And silence was in Heav'n" (3.217–18)? Given the immensity of the demand and this option to refuse, everyone is shocked into silence. Obviously, we are supposed to remember that earlier scene in Hell, where the devils had also stood mute on the lip of the abyss. But the two scenes are truly the reverse of one another. For an "all-controlling" Father waits on the will of the Other to speak and act, whereas Satan makes the difficulties seem insuperable before he invites others to act. And even then he swiftly "prevented all reply" lest others might win "cheap the high repute / Which he through hazard huge must earn" (2.467, 472–3).

After the slightest hesitation, the Son enacts Walwyn's definition of religion as "a joyning of two free-wils in one" (9). "Behold mee then," he says after a thoughtful pause, "mee for him, life for life / I offer" (3.236–7). The Son is the sole *creature* in Heaven willing to give his life to save other creatures. And he does so in real uncertainty about the means, progressing from declarative to interrogative verbs: "Father, thy word is past, man shall find grace; / And shall grace not find means, that finds her way, / The speediest of thy winged messengers?" (3.227–9). Rather than slip into the Satanic rhetoric of interrogative declaration – "Wherefore do I assume / These Royalties?" – the Son even makes himself the grammatical object: "Behold mee then, mee for him, / … on mee let thine anger fall; / Account mee man" (2.236–8). Three times, he employs "mee" as the object of the verb, twice as a prepositional object – "on mee let thine anger fall; on me let Death wreck his rage" – thereby performing the act he describes of making himself a legal substitute, of submitting to Death in the place of the Other. While the Son's choice thus makes the faculty of will the decisive faculty in the divine life, it does not exalt will above reason as does Calvin's theology; rather, it begins to dismantle the dualist hierarchy of reason over will by asserting an equivalence between the two.

The Son's self-sacrifice is a political, as well as a moral instance of the Leveller claim "that Christ ruled as a servant, and tooke the burden of the people upon him" (Walwyn, 3). For, instead of insisting on his feudal, hereditary right to rule, the Son enacts the celestial equivalent of a "Self-Denying Ordinance,"[19] with one difference from the ordinance of 1645: the Son does more than resign a military commission, like Manchester returning to his hereditary place in the House of Lords, or like Cromwell, who kept his seat in the Commons while accepting the parliamentary Army's commission as Lt-General. The Son's "self-denying ordinance" is the sacrifice of his life without promise of compensation. And, contrary to Satan, the Son has nothing to rely on but the Father's dramatic proclamation in a prior scene: "Under his great Vice-gerent Reign abide / United as one individual Soule / For ever happie" (5.609–11).

Acting on the basis of "For ever happie," the Son has only the Father's word on which to rely. For the "union" that God had proclaimed was broken before the night had even passed. And beyond this one ambiguous example, there is no private assurance, no backroom deal like the one made in the "grand consult" of Hell.[20] The Son must literally wager his life on a wing and a prayer: "[T]hou has given me to possess / Life in my self for ever, by thee I live, / Though now to Death I yield" (3.243–5). In what is no more than a faithful inference of God's goodness, the Son nonetheless expresses his perfect trust in the Father: "But I shall rise Victorious, and subdue / My vanquisher" (3.250–1).

His act of "Freely put[ting] off" glory – the only life the Son has ever known – is all the more remarkable for his uncertainty about the outcome. He expects that he "Shall enter Heaven long absent, and returne, / Father, to see thy face, wherein no cloud / Of anger shall remain" (3.240; 261–3).[21] Contrary to Calvin, who held that "the Son of God descended from heaven in such a way that, without leaving heaven, he willed to be borne in the virgin's womb, to go about the earth, and to hang upon the cross; yet he continuously filled the world even as he had done from the beginning!"[22] (2.13.4), Milton's Son of God foresees only his "long absen[ce]" from Heaven, and the deprivation of "this glorie next to thee" that he will "Freely put off." No hint of Trinitarian equivocation lurks in his declaration of what it will cost him to earn his way back to Heaven.[23] Even after his long-delayed return "with the multitude of my redeemd" (3.260), he actually foresees nothing more than universal "peace assur'd, / And reconcilement; wrauth shall be no more / Thenceforth, but in thy presence Joy entire" (3.263–5).

But he is about to discover the "rule of God in Christ" that Walwyn had identified as the "servant-Ruler." Elaborating on this inverted rule, Walwyn (56) insists that, "In the power of God in Christ, every man should be a

King and a Priest, and then what need is there of ceremoniall Kings and Priests." What the "rule of Christ" more largely suggests is a devolution of God's sovereignty to humankind.[24] For, if Christ "sum'd up all the commandements in love: then consider how this loving law should be stated, for love is all in all, because God is love, and therefore to love God and man, or God in man, that is the fulfilling of the whole law" (49). In view of the Son's willingness to make himself a ransom for all mankind, it is not surprising that "Admiration seis'd / All Heav'n, what this might mean, and whither tend / Wond'ring" (3.271–3)? And yet neither the angels nor the Son can see as yet the full extent of God's design. "O thou in Heav'n and Earth the only peace / Found out for mankind under wrauth, O thou / My sole complacence!" God says with unbounded praise: "well thou know'st how dear / To me are all my works, nor Man the least … / that for him I spare / Thee from my bosom and right hand, to save, / By loosing thee a while, the whole Race lost" (3.274–80). Having admitted that the Son has had to intuit the true character of the Father, he will not don the mask of the "white devil" again; it has only been used as a dramatic instrument to ensure a genuine trial of the Son, whose Love is the sole source of his identity with the Father.[25]

This identity, however, begins to expand exponentially in the Father's promise that human nature will be joined to the divine nature: "Thou therefore whom thou only canst redeem, / Thir Nature also to thy Nature joyn; / And be thy self Man among men on earth, / Made flesh, when time shall be" (3.281–4). This is close to the orthodox view of the Incarnation, where the divine is also joined to a human nature: "Be thou in *Adams* room," the Father says, "The Head of all mankind, though *Adams* Son," so that, "As from a second root, shall be restor'd, / As many as are restor'd, without thee none" (3.285–6; 288–9). Further, it is a conventional restatement of the doctrine of the Atonement, since "Man, as is most just, / Shall satisfie for Man, be judg'd and die, / And dying rise, and rising with him raise / His Brethren, ransomd with his own dear life" (3.294–7). But, in a seventeenth-century context, what is most revolutionary is the deity's promise of *universal* atonement,[26] as opposed to Calvin's insistence on a limited atonement. For it guarantees God's impartial love for each of his creatures, as expressed on earth through the career of the Son: "So Heav'nly love shall outdoo Hellish hate" (3.298).

The point at which Milton's God departs most radically from orthodox doctrine, however, is in his implication of a levelling Incarnation. While the divine nature is not corrupted by its descent into human nature – "Nor shalt thou by descending to assume / Mans nature, less'n or degrade thine owne" (3.303–4) – the divine nature forms the radical ground of a change that God says will utterly transform human nature: "Here shalt thou sit incarnate, here shalt Reign / Both God and Man, Son both of God and Man, / Anointed universal King" (3.315–17). What is most remarkable in this implicit formulation is that all of humanity, in the person of this "Son both of God and Man," is then destined to put on the divine nature as "Anointed universal King." For "thy Humiliation," God declares, "shall exalt / With thee thy Manhood also to this Throne" (3.313–14). In the person of the Son, humankind has just been set on the path of rising into the godhead.

Almost as extraordinary is the further implication that status and station will no longer be determined by heredity, but rather by merit. As God explains this principle:

> Because thou hast, though Thron'd in highest bliss
> Equal to God, and equally enjoying
> God-like fruition, quitted all to save
> A World from utter loss, and hast been found
> By Merit more then Birthright Son of God,
> Found worthiest to be so by being Good,
> Farr more then Great or High (3.305–11)

The merit of "one greater Man" promises to do more than simply "Restore us" (1.4–5) to Eden; it literally proposes to set "thy Manhood" on the throne of the "universal King."

For Empson, this is the sole redeeming feature of Milton's God, the idea "that Milton did expect God to abdicate. At least, that is the most direct way to express the idea; you may also say that he is an emergent or evolutionary deity" (130).[27] To Empson, whose image of the Father is rather closer to Walwyn's White Devil than to Milton's deity, "It is a tremendous moral cleansing for Milton's God, after the greed for power which can be felt in him everywhere else, to say that he will give his throne to Incarnate Man, and the rhythm around the word *humiliation* is like taking off in an aeroplane" (137). This, Empson maintains, is more like the penance that God owes himself — an admission that the Son needs to atone for the sins of his Father as much as for the sins of mankind: "I had long felt that this is much the best moment of God in the poem, morally as well as poetically, without having any idea why it came there. It comes there because he is envisaging his abdication, and the democratic appeal of the prophecy of God is what makes the whole picture of him just tolerable" (137).

While he has no doubt of the Father's goodness, Hugh MacCallum does gather in his *Milton and the Sons of God* that a transfer of authority is taking place: "Now all power is conferred on the Son until that time when the 'regal Sceptre' shall no longer be needed for 'God shall be All in All' (340–1). Power is thus put in its place as the effect rather than the cause of the Son's victory, and as an instrument rather than the goal of providence" (106). This is to begin to realize that God does not mean, nor has ever meant, to actualize the White Devil's model of centralized power.[28] The Son, if he has his wits about him, would do well to dwell on the Father's example: "all Power / I give thee, reign for ever" (3.317–18). For what does "Power" mean when the Father equates it with the law of Love? Or, as Walwyn expresses this same paradox, "O Christian world, how contrary art thou to Christ! nothing can bee more rediculous to the world, then the rule of Christ. Who will give his coat after his cloake, and turn one cheek to bee smitten, after the other? Who will sell all to follow Christ?" (40). Does God himself not suggest a more humble conception of "rule" that equates to a type of "self-denying ordinance"?

Furthermore, what does "reign for ever" mean when it is foreshortened on the instant to "Then thou thy regal Scepter shalt lay by, / For regal Scepter then no more shall need" (3.339–40)? As Empson remarks, "[A] reader who noticed the change of grammar from shalt to shall could only impute the old construction: 'Authority will then no longer be needed' – not, therefore, from the Father, any more than from the Son" (134).[29] David Norbrook remarks similarly that, "This episode is closely parallel to a king's abdicating and showing solidarity with his people" (475).[30] Observing that the Son "is crowned from merit, not mere hereditary right," Norbrook goes on to say that "within a few lines we are looking forward to his final apocalyptic triumph and then his abdication." Such a drastic reduction of the time required to alter the structures of power suggests that sovereignty is now transferred to the whole creation, where "God shall be All in All" (3.341).

The latter wording is scriptural, as Christopher Hill recalls in *Milton and the English Revolution*, since it recalls St Paul: "And when all things shall be subdued unto him, then shall the Son also himself be subject unto him that put all things under him, that God may be all in all" (1 Corinthians 15: 28). As Hill elaborates, "[T]he emotional content, recalls Servetus: 'All reason for ruling will then end, all power and authority shall be abolished, every ministry of the Holy Spirit shall cease, since we shall no longer need an advocate or mediator because God will be all in all'" (303). Since Servetus was put to the stake in Calvin's Geneva for denying the Trinity, this gloss on "All in All" would be sure to resonate with Milton.[31] Anti-Trinitarians were often regarded as seeking to subvert social hierarchies, given that Kings, Lords, and bishops were also categorical reflections of Father, Son, and Holy Ghost, from whom all worldly authority derives. But the dramatic context of the scene implies "how this loving law should bee stated," as Walwyn said, "for love is all in all, because God is love, and therefore to love God and man, or God in man, that is the fulfilling of the whole law" (49). The Leveller view differs little, in fact, from Hill's millenarian conclusion that, "For the radicals this emphasis involves an ultimate withering away of the church (Christ's kingdom) as well as of the state, a perfect democratic anarchy in a classless society" (304).

The Father's summation of the event could almost serve as a celestial restatement of the Leveller view: "Love hath abounded more then Glory abounds" (3.312), he declares. Walwyn had also affirmed that, "in all such willing hearts, God is all in all, for all things are from God, through God, and to God, and God is love. But the devil and all impious men [such as Calvinists], hate love, because love is contrary to their nature, and therefore they would overthrow love, by preferring of faith before her" (21). At the end of this scene, the Father then enjoins, "But all ye Gods, / Adore him, who to compass all this dies, / Adore the Son, and honour him as mee" (3.341–3). For the first time in the poem, the angels are addressed as his equals – "ye Gods" – though it will not be the last time. Continuing changes in the forms of social addresss will be our clearest and most enduring sign of the ongoing evolution of political forms in Heaven.[32]

So what had always been latent in this scene now ends in high drama as "The multitude of Angels with a shout / Loud as from numbers without number, sweet" (3.345–6), follow the Son in renouncing "all Power," status, and privilege: "lowly reverent / Towards either Throne they bow, and to the ground / With solemn adoration down they cast / Thir Crowns inwove with Amarant and Gold" (3.349–52). While "[n]either throne" ceases to occupy space, "crowns" seem to have lost their surplus value in Heaven – their greatest worth consists in their renunciation. Even though the "Angels" have just been addressed as "Gods," they, too, re-enact the model of the Father's "abdication," much as they repeat the Son's gesture of a "self-denying ordinance." So the seat where "[thou shalt] sit incarnate, here shalt Reign /

Both God and Man" begins to look more like a site where sovereignty is transferred to man and angels alike. In direct contrast to Satan, God is bent on dispersing power from the One to the Many, and his aim seems to be in keeping with the Leveller attempt to create what Brian Manning calls "a society of self-governing local communities, with a large degree of voluntaryism."[33]

Whether as "the joyning of two free-wils in one" in religion, or whether as elective participation in government, "voluntaryism" was crucial for the Levellers[34] and Milton alike. And yet the former, as David Wootton points out, "never envisaged presenting themselves as a faction for election, or claimed to be the appropriate officers in a new government. They never saw themselves as seeking to concentrate power in their own hands" ("Leveller Democracy," 423–4). They would have doubtless approved of the *dispersed* form of sovereignty championed by Politicus: "The Majesty of *England*, (though now diffused in the hands of many) is the same it was, when in the hands of one; and is indeed much more majestick now, than it hath been for many hundred years past, being regulated and supported by the Arm of heaven, as also by wise Councels, and victorious Armies, free from the check of any *single Tyrant*."[35] So, too, the "positive ambition" of the Levellers, as Philip Baker describes it, "to overhaul the workings and structures of government within the dispersed state"[36] accords with this evolving government of Heaven in *Paradise Lost*. For Milton's God is totally antithetical to Walwyn's "white devil" in the drama of Book 3 where "all Power" devolves, not just on the Son, but on down through the angelic hierarchy to "this Throne," where "Here shalt Reign / Both God and Man." Humankind is destined to share rule in a polity that anticipates the "decentralized, minimally-governed, libertarian England" that Ian Gentles recognizes in the third *Agreement of the People*.[37]

Finally, there is further evidence of Milton's part – whether as a licenser or author – in advocating for a devolution of power in that series of editorials on "Commonwealth principles" that Politicus had issued in the wake of Cromwell's triumph at Worcester:

> We hear not of many Nations in this latter Age, wherein the People have been solemnly acknowledged and declared to be the *Original and Fountain of Supremacy*, or that they have been made thus to understand it; But wherever it hath been so presented to vulgar Apprehensions, it takes such deep Impression, that all the Arts under

> heaven can never wear it out of memory; nor will they ever rest, till they have sipt and tasted of all the sweets of *Soveraignty.*[38]

Two weeks later, Politicus affirmed that the "People never had any reall *Liberty*, till they were possest of the Power of calling and dissolving the supreme Assemblies, changing Governments, enacting and repealing Laws, together with a Power of chusing and deputing whom they pleased to this work, as often as they should judge expedient, for their own well being, and the good of the Publick."[39] Beware indeed of a "single ruler."

The old conundrum of why Milton favoured monarchy in Heaven and republican government on earth[40] is resolved by God himself, who prophesies the end of monarchy, just as Daniel had done in reading King Nebuchadnezzar's dream in Daniel 2.[41] God's support for popular sovereignty – a Leveller idea shared by Nedham and Milton – is deeply antithetical to the political thought of Satan and of Cromwell. For Satan merely pretends to be a democrat to seize a throne, while Milton's God poses as a tyrant to test and confirm the commitment of his creatures to good "Commonwealth principles."

Even so, the threat from those pretending to "Commonwealth principles" in order to pervert them to demagogic ends persists at the end of Book 3. Even "The sharpest sighted Spirit of all in Heav'n" (3.690) is not able to penetrate Satan's disguise as "a stripling Cherube" (3.636) when Uriel first meets him on "the Sun's lucent Orbe" (3.589). The dissembler expresses "Unspeakable desire to see, and know / All these his wondrous works, but chiefly Man, / His chief delight and favour" (3.662–4). It is the closest that Milton will come in the poem to a direct admission that he, too, was deceived for a time, before the great pretender to republican principles claimed the throne in the name of the public good: "So spake the false dissembler unperceivd; / For neither Man nor Angel can discern / Hypocrisie, the only evil that walks / Invisible, except to God alone" (3.681–4).

· 6 ·

"Two of Far Nobler Shape"

NAKED MAJESTY

THE PRESUMPTION OF A "masculinist" ideology at work in *Paradise Lost* has likely done more in recent decades to reduce the poem to "a monument to dead ideas" than the more common error of mistaking Milton's God for Walwyn's "white devil." When Adam and Eve first appear in Satan's field of vision and he explores "thir looks Divine" (4.291) for signs of relative weakness, the *narrator* adds, "though both / Not equal as thir sex not equal seemd; … Hee for God only, shee for God in him" (4.295–6, 299). That dictum continues to underwrite Milton's reputation as the "patriarchal bogey"[1] of English poetry. His sexist sins, it seems, were many: there is his declaration in prose that "it is no small glory" to the man "that a creature so like him, should be made subject to him." He held early on to the dogma that "*St. Paul* ends the controversie by explaining that the woman is not primarily and immediately the image of God, but in reference to the man."[2] Where the apostle had offered complementary images of the man as "*the image and glory of God, she the glory of the man*," Milton added a limiting clause, "he not for her, but she for him." His anti-feminism, as commentators frequently note, is more extreme than most biblical exegetes in the Reformed tradition. Mary Nyquist is no more rigorous than others in her judgment that, "Milton's stridently masculinist, 'Hee for God only, shee for God in him' … goes much further than Calvin in drawing out the masculinist implications of this hermeneutical practice, which forges an identity between the generic and the gendered 'man.'"[3] Adam's primacy, it would appear, is both primal and essential to Milton.

But nothing is ever what it seems on first sight in *Paradise Lost*. If appearances can be deceptive in both Hell and Heaven, then why not in Eden? It bears repeating that our first glimpse of Adam and Eve is focalized through Satan, "where the Fiend / Saw undelighted all delight, all kind / Of living Creatures new to sight and strange" (4.285–7). Long ago, Barbara Lewalski remarked that what we see is limited to Satan's field of vision from the start of his ascent "Of a steep wilderness" (4.135) towards "a landscape with spatial depth presented from a single angle of vision," where "[t]he perspective again is Satan's, now sitting like a cormorant atop the Tree of Life."[4] It beggars belief, of course, to assume that the narrator sees "living Creatures new to sight and strange"; they could only be such to a tourist like Satan in our world. Susan Wiseman complicates this difficulty even more by noting that, "As with other language clustering around Eve, 'seems' poses for the reader the problem of how to respond to implied qualifications of the Edenic state."[5] At the very least, the repetition in consecutive half-lines of this verb "seemd" – "In naked Majestie seemd Lords of all / And worthie seemd" (4.290–1) – makes Satan a dramatic locus of perceptual uncertainty in the scene.[6] We still need to come to a full realization that what we "see" within the Satanic perspective is framed in ways where "seem" can be the very antithesis of reality, and where "new to sight and strange" may involve us as well in a process of defamiliarization. In brief, we are asked to rethink what else is likely to appear "new" and "strange" in this increasingly complex image of traditional authority.

IN *THE FREE-MANS Freedome Vindicated* (23 June 1646), Lilburne added "*A Postscript, containing a generall Proposition*" about the creation of Adam and Eve that on the authority of scripture overturned traditional hierarchy and social privilege. God, Lilburne read in Genesis, had not only created man "after his own image," but had made "*Adam*, a male, or man … out of the dust or clay," and "out of [his] side … made a female, or Woman cal'd *Eve*, which two are the earthly, original fountain … of all and every particular and individuall man and woman." What is revolutionary in Lilburne's reading of the creation is the social levelling that flows from that "original fountain." For all who

> ever breathed in the world since, … are, and were by nature all equall and alike in power, dignity, authority, and majesty, none of them having (by nature) any authority dominion or majesteriall power, one

> over or above another, neither have they, or can they exercise any, but meerely by institution, or donation, that is to say, by mutuall agreement or consent, given, derived, or assumed, by mutuall consent and agreement, for the good benefit and comfort each of other.[7]

Here, the story of the Fall is no longer used to justify the law of patriarchy as punishment merited by and from that lapse; instead, it is a founding text in a discourse that claims social and sexual equality from the first moment of the creation. Neither patriarchal, nor monarchical, nor any other form of "majesteriall power" is really legitimate, Lilburne declares, unless it be by "mutall agreement or consent." For dignity, authority, and majesty are innate to every human being, our original legacy from Adam and Eve.

Nor was the inherent majesty of human beings revoked by the Fall, as authorities are wont to claim. For "any man whatsoever, spirituall or temporall, Cleargy-man or Lay-man" who seeks "to appropriate and assume unto himselfe, a power, authority and jurisdiction, to … raign over any sort of men in the world" without our consent is guilty of "endeavour[ing] to appropriate & assume unto themselves the Office and soveraignty of God." This, Lilburne maintains, "was the sinne of the Devils, who not being content with their first station … would be like God, for which sin they were thrown down into hell" (12). Although he does accept the traditional idea that "*Adams* sin … brought the curse upon him and all his posterity, that he was not content with the station and condition that God created him in, but did aspire unto a better," this is not the end of the story, although it would have "been the everlasting ruin and destruction of him and all his, had not God been the more mercifull unto him in the promised *Messiah*" (12).

What frees mankind from the consequence of original sin is the heretical doctrine of "'free grace,' termed by its opponents antinomianism," not for denying law, but for denying "that any were predestined to salvation."[8] For, if the *possibility* of salvation is open to all, then all are surely equal in God's sight. And, by the original law of creation, none should ever "assume unto himself" an authority "to rule, govern, or raign" over others "without their free consent." Walwyn likewise expresses this idea in *Tyranipocrit*, where he claims that the "*unum necessarium* … is to participate of Gods nature" (25), given that, at the moment of creation, God had "breathed in his face, or in his soule, a quickning spirit, which caused man to be man" (8). Then the only thing "needfull to salvation," Walwyn says, has been and must always be the same: "A man must goe unto God with a willing minde … and in all things to bee ruled by him," and "then is that *unum necessarium* attained" (25–6). We are returned by a union of wills to the first state of the Creation, where no one is privileged to rule over another, but God rules in us.

This first "law" of Adamic equality was also elaborated in Richard Overton's *An Arrow Against All Tyrants* (10 Oct. 1646), issued from Newgate prison, where Overton had been detained for promoting Lilburne's defiance of traditional authority: "For by nature," Overton explains, "we are the sons of *Adam,* and from him have legitimatly derived a naturall propriety, right and freedome, which only we require" (5). But, "as we are delivered of God by the hand of nature into this world" (3), selfhood itself becomes a *property*. So, "every one with a naturall, innate freedome and propriety (as it were writ in the table of every mans heart, never to be obliterated" has a share in that original majesty: "It is but the just rights and prerogative of mankind (whereunto the people of England, are heires apparent as well as other Nations)" (5). Whereas the legacy was simply natural for Lilburne, for Overton it was "writ in the table of every mans heart," the testamentary will of our father Adam entitling us "to live, every one equally and alike[,] to enjoy his Birthright and priviledge" (3). If God was a printer like Overton himself, then his writing in "the table" of our hearts would be legible in this pamphlet held in our hands.

This icon of Adamic equality was further developed by the Leveller author of *Vox Plebis* (19 November 1646) in terms of a logical syllogism: "For as God created every man free in *Adam*: so by nature are all alike freemen born; and are since made free in grace by Christ: no guilt of the parent being of sufficiency to deprive the child of this freedome" (4). If Lilburne had merely assumed the annulment of the curse on Adam in God's offer of mercy in "the promised Messiah," the author of *Vox Plebis* literally spells out the force of "free grace" in Christ. Like Overton envisioning God writing on "the table of every mans heart," Marchamont Nedham, the likely author of *Vox Plebis,*[9] imagines that "it is (as it were) the ingraven Character of the mind & wil of God in the soul of man; not passive nor consisting of bodily substance: therefore it is not to be constrained, or inforced to submit to any other rule, then what the Creator, by his revealed will, according to the Scriptures, hath imprinted in it" (4). For David Wootton, this is a particularly "elegant" (438) formulation of the argument "that men, created free in Adam, born free by nature, had indeed, as *Vox Plebis* put it, been once again 'made free in grace by Christ' after the servitude of the Mosaic law"

("Leveller Democracy," 441). Henceforth, social equality has the authority of divine revelation.

Within seven weeks of *Vox Plebis*, Marchamont Nedham, the likely author[10] once again of *Regall Tyrannie Discovered*, limned two further consequences of this principle of Adamic equality: popular sovereignty and government by consent.[11] Adapting his arguments from Cicero and natural law theory,[12] the Oxford-educated Nedham insists all the same that he "may not raise a Fabrick, without laying a good Foundation" from "a Post-script in the latter end of Lieutenant Colonel *Lilburns* printed *Protestation* against the *Lords*" (6). Quoting verbatim the long passage from *Free-Mans Freedome* on the divine donation of sovereignty to Adam and Eve, he makes only a few small changes in spelling and drops "equal" from the clause[13] "*which two are the earthly, original fountain, as begetters and bringers forth of all and every particular and individuall man, and woman, that ever breathed in the world since*, who are, and were, by nature all [equal and] alike in power, dignity, authority, and majesty" (6–7). Milton, as we already know from his arguments for popular sovereignty and government by consent in *The Tenure of Kings and Magistrates* (1649), knew *Regall Tyrannie* very well.[14] Lilburne's icon was written not only in "the table" of the heart and in the law of Nature, but in the biblical story of creation.

The portrait of Adam and Eve in Book 4 of *Paradise Lost* is too close to this Leveller icon to be coincidence.[15] The narrator describes the couple as "Two of far nobler shape erect and tall, / Godlike erect, with native Honour clad / In naked Majestie" (4.288–90). The terms "native Honour" and "Majestie" are clear echoes of the "dignity, authority, and majesty" of Lilburne's image, even where Milton's "naked Majestie" takes a republican swipe at the costly "majesty" of an over-dressed court. Furthermore, "the Fiend," who still uses regal pomp and artificial majesty to bolster his position, has good reason to see "undelighted all delight" (4.286), as he grieves the loss of his native dignity in Heaven. Even so, it is possible that some of these value judgments are proper to the narrator as much as to Satan. Such descriptors, for example, as "Absolute rule" (4.301) and Eve's "Subjection … Yielded with coy submission" (4.308, 310), do appear to be seconded by some forms of dramatic address – "my Guide / And Head" (4.442–3), "My Author and Disposer," Eve says (4.635) – as if to authorize patriarchal rule and sexual inequality in Eden. Does Milton intend to expose the Leveller icon as false? Or is the "devil" given his due in paradise, much as the White Devil received his due in Heaven? Either sexual inequality is a political reality in Eden, or else patriarchal language itself is on trial here, much as republican language was on trial in Hell, and regal language in Heaven.

Mikhail Bakhtin, who distinguishes between "*double-voiced discourse*" in the "polyglot world" of the novel and the "style, tone, and manner" of "epic discourse," takes the latter to be "infinitely far removed" from the "time and value plane"[16] of the present. But Milton's scenes set in Hell and Heaven are very much about his contemporary world; his modus operandi in representing Hell and Heaven seems more "novelistic" than "epic" in presenting a past that is anything but "absolute and complete" (Bakhtin, 16). In this light, Milton's strategy of "double-voiced discourse" in every scene to date is likely more novelistic than "epic," for novelistic narrative, as Bakhtin insists, carries "the speech of another … introduced into the author's discourse (the story) in *concealed form*, that is, without any of the *formal* markers usually accompanying such speech, whether direct or indirect."[17] Contrary to Satanic hypocrisy, double-voiced discourse is a diagnostic tool in gauging the health of each sociolect in the story.[18] For what Bakhtin calls "heteroglossia … is also diffused throughout the authorial speech that surrounds the characters, creating highly particularized *character zones*" (316). Without fully realizing it, we do see things from the "character zone" of Milton's Satan from the moment of his entrance to Eden.

On this reading, the couple's "naked Majestie" is necessarily qualified by Satan's "character zone" in phrases such as "seemd Lords of all" and "worthie seemd." Now, "two utterances, two speech manners, two styles, two 'languages,' two semantic and axiological belief systems" (Bakhtin, 304) are heard in the same lines, allowing Satan and the narrator both to conclude, though from opposing perspectives, that, "in thir looks Divine / The image of thir glorious Maker shon, / Truth, wisdome, Sanctitude severe and pure" (*PL* 4.291–3). For Satan, having borne the same image, recognizes it even as he grieves its loss. The narrator, by contrast, continues to carry that image by virtue of "free grace," rejoicing in the very terms that leave Satan in regret and despair. As Bakhtin remarks of this sort of "double-voiced discourse," "It frequently happens that even one and the same word will belong simultaneously to two languages, two belief systems that intersect in a hybrid construction" (305). Since Milton's emerging narrative practice is "novelistic," how are we to characterize differing systems of belief encoded in the apposite phrase, "The image of thir glorious Maker shon"? Satan is not likely to say, "Sanctitude severe and pure, / Severe but in true filial freedom plac't; / Whence true autoritie in men" (4.293–5), since, in his soliloquy on Mt Niphates, he had privately admitted to forfeiting that freedom: "Hadst thou the same free Will and Power to stand?" he had asked himself, only to conclude plaintively: "Thou hadst: whom hast thou then or what to accuse / But Heav'ns free Love dealt equally to all?" (4.66–8). The clause "Whence true autoritie in men" thus intersects with Satan's speech; but it also sounds like "direct authorial speech" (Bakhtin, 306).

Then is it *both* or just *one* voice that sounds in the clause, "though both / Not equal, as thir sex not equal seemd" (4.295–6)?[19] Would the verb "seemd" not locate us in Satan's character zone, given his usual preoccupations with status ("seemd Lords"), with corruptibility ("worthy seemd") and relations of power ("not equall seemd")? Even at his first sight of those *other* "Creatures new to sight and strange" – "the Snakie Sorceress" and her son at Hell's gate – Satan was first concerned with "The likeness of a Kingly Crown" on "what seem'd [Death's] head"; second, with the clearly dubious worth of "Hell-born" creatures; and third, with questions of gender and power relations in "What thing thou art, thus double-form'd" (2.672–3, 687, 741). Initially, he had failed even to recognize his lover before Sin comically recalled him to himself: "Thy self in me thy perfect image viewing" (2.764).

Are these not compelling reasons to ask whether the (in)famous description of Adam and Eve belongs to Milton, or whether it expresses the "common language"? For Bakhtin, this latter is "the average norm of spoken and written language for a given social group – [which] is taken by the author precisely as the *common view*, as the verbal approach to people and things normal for a given sphere of society, as the *going point of view* and the going *value*" (301–2). Both Presbyterians and Anglicans would surely agree on *this* "going value" for the "*common* view": "For softness shee and sweet attractive Grace, / Hee for God only, shee for God in him: / His fair large Front and Eye sublime declar'd / Absolute rule" (4.298–301). While Paul's first epistle to the Corinthians made the man "the image and glory of God: but the woman is the glory of the man" (1 Cor 11: 7–9), Lilburne completely ignored that reading. Furthermore, Milton had argued in *Doctrine and Discipline of Divorce* that "we may plainly discover how Christ meant not to be tak'n word for word, but like a wise Physician, administring one excesse against another to reduce us to a perfect mean" (*CPW* 2: 282–3). Thus, as Hugh MacCallum remarks, "Milton evolves a significant theory of Christ's method of teaching. Christ, he argues, employed in his teaching a strategy of indirection ... leaving the work of drawing together his remarks to 'the skilfull and laborious gatherer.'"[20] Since Milton insists that reading scripture "requires a skilfull and laborious gatherer; who must compare the words he finds, with other precepts, with the end of every ordinance, and with the general *analogy* of Evangelick doctrine,"[21] he is likely more inclined than most to ask whether the Leveller icon or the "common view" best reconciles Paul with Genesis by situating them together within "the general *analogy* of Evangelick doctrine."

If Milton expected readers of his prose to be "skilfull and laborious gatherers" in penetrating the veil of the "common language" to match "Evangelick doctrine,"[22] then why not readers of his poetry as well? As Diane McColley has remarked, the narrator's "observations reflect the conventional expectations of his audience with some differences that will take root and grow" (40). As McColley further insists, "In the context of the literary and iconographic tradition, it is unusual for Milton to include Eve in all the qualities enumerated in the first eight lines" (41). For "Here, Eve is clearly a bearer of the divine image, participant in honor, majesty, truth, wisdom, sanctitude, freedom, and authority as one of the lords of all."

More than anyone, Satan should favour "the common view," since he comically hopes that, "up and down unseen," his grotesque mistress will "Wing silently the buxom Air" (2.841–2), as opposed to Sin's expectation to "Reign / At thy right hand voluptuous, as beseems / Thy daughter and thy darling, without end" (2.868–70). Given the priority Milton assigns to the Edenic icon, the "common view" appears to be less congenial to him than the Leveller view. Consider, for example, the ensuing description of Eve: "Shee ... Her unadorned golden tresses wore / Dissheveld, but in wanton ringlets wav'd / As the Vine curles her tendrils, which impli'd / Subjection, but requir'd with gentle sway" (4.305–8). Even the syntactic break in the clause – "which impli'd / Subjection" – hints at the narrator's "fictive solidarity" (Bakhtin, 306) with Satan – "Nor those mysterious parts were then conceald, / Then was not guiltie shame, dishonest shame" (4.312–13).

But the problem of appearance is immediately renewed in direct authorial speech – "Sin-bred [shame], how have ye troubl'd all mankind / With shews instead, meer shews of seeming pure" (4.315–16). Doubtless we are now asked to recall the thrice-used "seemd" of Satan's first view of the couple. And the narrator, to underscore his method, offers a second, otherwise redundant, description of the pair as they pass out of view, in order to complete his vocal break with the "double-voicing" of the prior view.[23] And we are finally left with the unadulterated view of the narrator, free of any trace of power relations and female subordination as Adam and Eve pass beyond Satan's ken where he remains perched in his tree "like a Cormorant" (4.196):[24] "So passed they naked on, nor shund the sight / Of God or Angel, for they thought no ill," the narrator says. "So hand in hand they passd, the lovliest pair / That ever since in loves imbraces met." And the "common view" is left conclusively behind: "*Adam* the goodliest man of men since borne / His Sons, the fairest of her Daughters *Eve*" (4.319–24). It is also this second description that now begins to resonate with Lilburne's depiction of the pair as "equall and alike in power, dignity, authority, and majesty, none of them having (by nature) any authority dominion or majesteriall power, one over or above another."

Nor does Adam make any claim for himself to authority, power, or dominion over Eve in his opening speech, but only to mutuality ("Sole partner and sole part of all these joys" – 4.411), the pun on "sole part" clearly leaving room for individuality as the part that stands apart from the whole. Nor is God a dominating figure in Adam's view, since "needs must the power / That made us, and for us this ample World / Be infinitly good, and of his good / As liberal and free as infinite" (4.412–15). Adam celebrates God's liberal trust in their shared power, "who at his hand / Have nothing merited" (4.417–18). He is not far at all from Overton's claim that "all just humain powers take their original; not immediatly from God (as Kings usually plead their prerogative) but mediatly by the hand of nature … for originally, God hath implanted them in the creature, and from the creature those powers immediatly proceed" (*An Arrow Against All Tyrants*, 4). Adds Overton, "Every man [or human being] by nature being a King, Priest and Prophet in his owne naturall circuite and compasse, whereof no second may partake, but by deputation, commission, and free consent from him, whose naturall right and freedome it is." Recognizing a *liberal* power entrusted in their very nature, Adam asks no more than to be worthy of that trust: "The only sign of our obedience left / Among so many signes of power and rule / Conferrd upon us; and Dominion giv'n / Over all other Creatures" (4.428–31). It is this trust on which "no second may presume without consent; and by naturall birth, all men are *equall, and alike borne to like propriety and freedome*."[25] As Rachel Foxley sees it, Overton has just now "claimed that natural, and consequently, political freedom consisted in a kind of self-ownership (although still one given by God)."[26] In short, it is the trust of free will divinely bestowed on humankind to be self-determining – more (or less) like God himself – to be true to one's own nature.[27]

As Adam sums up this God-like "propriety," he joyously concludes: "But let us ever praise him, and extoll / His bountie, following our delightful task / To prune these growing Plants, and tend these Flours, / Which were it toilsome, yet with thee were sweet" (4.436–9) Eight times in thirty-nine lines, he describes their condition in terms of "we" or "us"; twice, he makes use of the possessive "our"; and three times, he slips into the intimacy of the second-person singular, addressing her as "thy self," and "thou," and "thee." In other words, Adam's view of their estate, like the joint "proprietie" (4.751) of their marriage, is that of a mutual donation. Adam thus speaks in Leveller accents throughout this speech, both in his implied emphasis on equality and in his assumption that they enjoy "an individuall propriety by nature" (Overton, "Appeale," 6). Re-reading his speech in this light, we are obliged to draw three conclusions: first, his discourse is instinctively egalitarian and dialogical: "the power / That made us"; "hee who requires from us no other service"; he "Conferrd upon us"; "Then let us not think hard / One easie prohibition." Secondly, his sense of this liberal trust placed in them underscores his view of their mutual responsibility to God and to each other, "to keep / This one, this easie charge" (4.420–1). Thirdly, his clear sense of limits and bounds ("nothing merited," "our delightful task") is what converts "Toilsom" to "sweet." Indeed, his own ethic of self-denial asserts no power over anyone, least of all over Eve. His is manifestly a good Levelling language that reverbates with a number of echoes of Nedham's (and Milton's) "good *Commonwealth* Language" in *Politicus*, affirming "that the wisdom, the piety, the Justice, and the self-denyal of those Governors in *Free-States*, is worthy of all honor and admiration, who have, or shall at any time as willingly resigne their Trusts, as ever they took them up, and have so far denied themselves, as to prefix Limits and bounds to their own Authority."[28] But Adam does not mistake himself for Eve's governor; he sees his role as being no more than to earn her trust, rather than to put her under governance.

The strong moral objections of Politicus to "the brutish Principles of *Monarchy*" also offer a contrapuntal echo, since monarchy tends to make people "more averse from entertaining Notions of a more noble Form."[29] In contrast, the Edenic portrait of "Two of far nobler shape" (4.288) celebrates the "more noble Form" of our first parents, being made in the image of God ("for in thir looks Divine / The image of thir glorious maker shone" [4.291–2]). Their natural dignity depends only on their mutual exercise of "true filial freedom … / Whence true autoritie in men" (4.294–5). Without freedom, "autoritie" and nobility would both be lost. What Politicus identifies as the "common" objection to "such a Government" in the Commonwealth – that it "would be to set on *Levelling and Confusion*" – is then no more than a smokescreen for preventing people from becoming "sensible of the great benefits they may reap" once they are "put in possession of their *Liberty*" (1458). Since Milton's God constantly affirms the freedom of his creatures – "Not free, what proof could they have given sincere / Of true allegiance, constant Faith or Love" (3.103–4) – Milton's portrait of Adam and Eve depends on a *voluntary* levelling of their differences, as appears in this iconic image: "So hand in hand they passd, the lovliest pair / That ever since in loves imbraces met" (4.321–2). It is the habitual "handedness" of the couple that assures us of their mutual commitment to preserve the dignity, authority, and majesty of the other in a voluntary "joyning of two free-wills."

So why is it that Eve answers Adam in the language of subordination, not of levelling? Doubtless Diane McColley is correct in her claim that "the only character who speaks of Eve's liabilities before the Fall is Eve herself" (29); but there is more in Eve's self-denigration than even so sympathetic a reader as McColley has recognized: "O thou for whom / And from whom I was formd flesh of thy flesh, / And without whom am to no end, my Guide / And Head" (4.440–43), she says entirely submissively. In view of those previous echoes of the Leveller icon of egalitarian marriage, why does Eve insist on her subordination and secondary postion ("enjoying thee / Præeminent by so much odds" [4.446–7])? Why make herself dependent on him for her very existence, let alone for knowledge, moral guidance, and personal authority? Why, in short, does she speak the "common language" when her husband addresses her in a levelling language of equality? Is she describing the way things really are? Or is her husband a wishful thinker?

There are three contextual reasons for Eve to speak as she does. Firstly, the "common language" of her social position has behind it the full weight of Paul's first epistle to the Corinthians. Were Milton to utterly ignore the "authorized version," he would fail in his responsibility to read scripture as "a skilfull and laborious gatherer." Secondly, he would risk alienating the "common" reader for whom a dogmatic reading of Paul was the truth. Thirdly, the possibility that a double-voiced discourse "serves two speakers at the same time and expresses simultaneously two different intentions – the direct intention of the character who is speaking, and the refracted intention of the author" (Bakhtin, 324) – greatly enlarges the scope of Milton's artistry. For, given the dramatic character of Adam's speech, Eve's response is evidently *situational*, and thus dramatic, even dialogical. For her speech is internally dialogized, much like the opening portrait of the couple in the "character zone" of Satan. As such discourse unfolds, "[A]ll the while these two voices are dialogically interrelated, they – as it were – know about each other (just as two exchanges in a dialogue know of each other and are structured in this mutual knowledge of each other); it is as if they actually hold a conversation with each other" (Bakhtin, 324). In these terms, the better question to ask is what recognizable sociolect in Eve's speech engages in dialogue with the Authorized Version? To answer this question, we first need to ask if there are "historical" reasons for Eve to speak as she does?

In naming her husband her "Guide / And Head," Eve clearly expresses the "common view," if outdoing the apostle by half in claiming to enjoy "So farr the happier Lot" than he, who "Like consort to thy self canst no where find" (4.448). In brief, here is writ large the burden of her later dramatic claim: "My Author and Disposer, what thou bidst / Unargu'd I obey; so God ordains, / God is thy Law, thou mine" (4.635–7). Yet what would make her exceed the "common language" of scripture in such egregious fashion? In granting him superiority to a point where he can find no "like" in her, in making Adam her "Author and Disposer," as if he were her God, she obviously distorts Pauline doctrine. Is her excess the point? It does follow catechetical teachings of the era, whether they be the Laudian doctrine of High Church Anglicanism in the 1630s or the Presbyterian Larger Westminster Catechism of 1648. As Andrew Sharp characterizes the former, "The whole social order in the church-state – imitated throughout the counties, towns, boroughs, and hamlets, as at the political centre at Westminster – was buttressed by belief in a divinely ordained series of gradations between all things that existed: from God through the ranks of angels, humans, animate and inanimate creation."[30] Such a world view demanded social deference and even subservience to one's spiritual, political, and social betters. For "Anglican catechismal teaching" impressed on congregations "that the Fifth Commandment, 'honour thy father and thy mother,' provided ('honour' being translated into 'obey' at the appropriate points) a pattern of subordination throughout society. It commanded subordination not only to parents, but to social superiors in general: to teachers, ministers, elders – and above all to ruling magistrates" (xx). To call her husband "Guide and Head" was almost doctrinal for an English wife.

After the downfall of the bishops, Col Thomas Rainsborough had asked a most telling question at Putney: "[With respect to the divine law which says *Honour thy father and thy mother*] the great dispute is, who is a right father and a right mother? I am bound to know who is my father and mother; and – I take it in the same sense you do – I would have a distinction, a character whereby God commands me to honour [them]."[31] Parliament responded[32] the following year that *all* of one's superiors were one's "father and mother," and were owed the deference that was due to one's natural parents. But, much like Eve outdoing Paul, the Larger Westminster Catechism also exceeded by half the Shorter Catechism of 1647. Question 124 demanded, "Who are meant by *father* and *mother* in the fifth commandment." The correct answer was, "not only natural parents, but all superiors in age and gifts; and especially such as, by God's ordinance, are over us in place of authority, whether in family, church, or commonwealth." Question 125 inquired: "Why are superiors styled *father* and *mother*?" Came the rejoinder, "Superiors are styled *father* and *mother* … to work inferiors to a greater willingness and cheerfulness in performing their duties to their superiors, as to their parents." As for Question 127, "What is the honour that inferiors owe to their superiors?" the proper response was "willing obedience to their lawful commands and counsels; due submission to their corrections; fidelity to, defence, and maintenance of their persons and authority, according to their several ranks, and the nature of their places; bearing with their infirmities, and covering them in love, that so they may be an honour to them and to their government."[33] This was more than the familiar social deference of the English class system; social "inferiors" owed their "superiors" all the obedience due to a "natural parent." So Eve is never more "English" than when she tells Adam, "Unargu'd I obey" (4.636).

Less than a month before Parliament ordered the printing (22 September) of the Shorter Westminster Catechism, Marchamont Nedham published a cautionary tale of one William Harris, "taken before two *Iustices* of the *Peace* for the County of *Huntington*, upon the 29. of *July*. 1648 which being a *Rarity*," he chortled, "I must needs publish." The story illustrates the threat to church and state alike from wives who failed to obey their husbands, as well as from "inferiors" who disobeyed their superiors. For Harris "avowes himself to bee *God*, and that there is no *God* besides him, with many other high *Blasphemies*." As Nedham warns, "the whole *Kingdome*" ought to "take notice … what this *Reformation* is come to," as appears in this instance of religious *and* social heresy:

> *Being demanded why he did lately commit Adultery upon the Lords day, with* Lockington's *wife of* Godmanchester, *he confesseth she did come to his Bed's side and kisse him, and then did lie down upon the*

Bed by him, and that he did then kisse her, and that she stay'd above an houre with him. He further saith, she came to him by the will of God, and could not keep away, and that when God extends himself to any man, he must doe whatsoever he would have him, though it be to the committing of Adultery (as some call it) … And he further saith, that which we call Adultery, or any other sin, is no sin, but that it is the suggestion of the Devill, he saith is a mistake of those that are not Called, *there being* no Devill: *But* God *being in him, and he in God, all his Actions (how weak soever seeming to us) are no sin, but his Commands.* Unto which *Examination* he set his *hand*; and both he and his *Adultresse* lie now committed in *Huntington* Goale.[34]

What would have shocked authorities and catachumens more than this story of a woman taken in flagrante delicto was the rationale for it: "This *Lockington's* wife being asked by the *Iustices* why she would break the Bond of *Matrimony* betwixt her and her Husband, she answered, shee *had Idolized her husband too long already*." Nedham, in his current phase as the royal messenger, clearly relished this moment of "I-told-you-so" to the Parliament together with its Assembly: "[S]*ince Superstition* is fled out of *painted windows*, and Surplices into *Sheets*, judge you whether the *Synod* and the rest of them had not best hasten the setling of *Church government*, lest the new *Planters* and *Waterers* make this *Doctrine* spread, and cause poore *Lockington's* Branch of *Reformation*, to sprout forth … upon the *Brow-antlers* of all the *Belweathers* of the *Faction*" (6). Indeed, the iconoclasm of Lockington's wife threatened the social order. For the entire system, from family to church and state, was quite literally "patriarchal."

Patriarcha, Sir Robert Filmer's treatise on monarchy as the true and "natural" state of government, was apparently complete in manuscript by 1648, although it was not published until 1680.[35] John M. Wallace notes that it was "intended to be a public and last minute plea for kingship itself when the monarchy was at stake and the institution of a republic had become a real possibility," although "the reason why it was never published in his lifetime was that history so quickly rendered his whole enterprise vain and useless" (160). Taking monarchy to be that institution derived from the "natural" rule of Adam and the biblical patriarchs over their families,[36] Filmer made the King a "father" of his political family. As the father's rule was grounded in the "natural right" of a parent over what he had begotten, so the monarch had a "natural" right to rule over his kingdom. While Filmer's treatise circulated in manuscript by 1648, as well as after his death in 1653, it was not available in print until royalist apologists used it during the succession crisis[37] to stave off concerns about a Catholic James II; suddenly, even James became a "natural" father to his people. Though not privy to Filmer's manuscript, Salmasius also appealed in his *Defensio Regia* to a monarch's "natural right" as the father of his people.[38] It was this notion that Milton mocked in *Pro Populo Anglicano Defensio* (1651), since "Fathers and kings are very different things: Our fathers begot us, but our kings did not, and it is we, rather, who created the king. It is nature which gave the people fathers, and the people who gave themselves a king; the people therefore do not exist for the king, but the king for the people" (CPW 4.i: 327). Since Milton's *Eikonoklastes* aimed at smashing the royal idol, it begs belief to think that he would now make an idol of "husbands" and "fathers."

By contrast, Eve seems eager to "idolize" her husband. The question is why? Was the iconoclastic apologist for regicide so blind that he thought it no contradiction to deny monarchy in the state, yet defend it in the home?[39] Or can the refracted intention of the author be differentiated from the intention of a character who speaks? In Eve's case, the conflation of "superiors" and governors with "natural parents" is impossible, since Adam is no more her natural parent than he is her "natural" superior. Yet, unlike Lockington's wife, Eve really does "idolize" her husband. Lest God be a tyrant, however, she must be free to misread her status, and so miss the "general *analogy*" between the story of her creation and that of her husband. Yet how on earth could she so misread her situation?

Eve's first speech shows her to be most worthy of the epithet "accomplisht *Eve*" (4.660), for her narrative of waking by the pool is charged with deep significance for her: "That day I oft remember" (4.449) she says, as if to admit that her experience was as formative as it was haunting. As Mark Edmundson says, "Her first sight … is potentially a fiction of her own genesis, a myth that is prior to language, culture, and the law. The 'Shape' that appears in the pool, offering Eve 'answering looks / Of sympathy and love' (464–5), is a self-image invested with maternal tenderness."[40] It is a telling sign that Eve, while "much wondring where / And what I was" (4.451–2), is just as ready to look *beyond* as she is to look *at* herself, since she seeks a mother's "answring looks" of love. Although she depicts her arrival at the pool "With unexperienc't thought" (4.457), she is already a gifted artist, capable of reproducing the kinaesthesia of "A Shape within the watry gleam" which, "Bending to look on me, I started back, / It started back, but pleas'd

I soon returnd, / Pleas'd it returnd as soon" (4.461–4). Ovid's *Metamorphoses* had introduced this "technique of verbal mirroring" (Edmundson, 58) as one of the more comic features of Narcissus's experience beside the pool. But Eve learns, unlike Narcissus, to master her longing for iteration and doubled images to escape the mirror of self-absorption.[41] As Lewalski says, "Eve's autobiography is in fact the antithesis of the Narcissus myth, and also of those narrations common in Renaissance eclogues in which a shepherd complains of his nymph's coyness, or a nymph of her lover's unfaithfulness."[42]

But the unnerving fact for Eve is that "there I had fixt / Mine eyes till now, and pin'd with vain desire, / Had not a voice thus warnd me, What thou seest, / What there thou seest fair Creature is thy self" (4.465–8). Edmundson notes how "The voice insinuates itself into the scene of mirrorings by framing a near repetition. But the interjected word 'there' delicately begins to undo Eve's fascination with pure iteration" (60). He explains how "The intrusion of the voice also summarily asserts the power of speech over image and of the invisible over the seen, relationships of some importance … to the genesis of *Paradise Lost*."[43] Suffice to say that the intervening voice, though unnamed, speaks the "common language" of marriage and motherhood: "hee / Whose image thou art, him thou shall enjoy / Inseparablie thine, to him shalt beare / Multitudes like thy self, and thence be call'd / Mother of human Race" (4.471–5). Eve, who had gone down to the pool in search of a mother, now finds that she must become that which she sought by leaving the pool.

But the Freudian reading is valid only to a point. Edmundson's claim that "the voice leads Eve to Adam, transferring the powers of language to the man" (61) makes too much – in view of Eve's artful telling – of her silence in the scene. For we watch her in the linguistic process of mastering that experience ("That day I oft remember"), even as she continues to express understandable anxiety about her dangerous mistake: "[W]hat could I doe, / But follow strait, invisibly thus led?" Her error is not her disobedience but her disappointment that what she finds is "less faire, / Less winning soft, less amiablie milde, / Then that smooth watry image; back I turnd, / Thou following cryd'st aloud" (4.475–81). Her choice, as Edmundson maintains, likely anticipates what Freud calls "secondary narcissism" (61), but Eve is persuaded by what Adam says about his self-sacrifice to reject her self-love, even if it does sound at first like a parallel obsession with iteration and self-mirroring. The lucky suitor gets off on his best foot in a chance reversal of syntax that performs (and so invites) what is initially voiced in the imperative: "Return faire *Eve*; / Whom fli'st thou? whom thou fli'st, of him thou art." But it is not just an echo, or verbal mirroring, of her own experience that wins her over. It is his apparent concern for her – "to give thee being I lent / Out of my side to thee, neerest my heart / Substantial Life" – that persuades her to be other-directed, to respond with an answering desire "to have thee by my side / Henceforth an individual solace dear" (4.481–6). Whether Eve has remembered Adam's words exactly or not, her phrasing now becomes its own echo of her original hope to find "answering looks / Of sympathie and love."

It is her mastery of language, not her outward silence, that explains how Eve is able to reorient her affections so swiftly from self-directed love to love of the other. Her memory of Adam's language of courting quickly becomes for her an echo of her own yearning at the pool. As she phrases his appeal, Adam cries, "Part of my Soul I seek thee, and thee claim / My other half." And "with that," she adds, "thy gentle hand / Seisd mine, I yielded, and from that time see / How beauty is excelld by manly grace / And wisdom, which alone is truly fair" (4.487–91). Yet this same repetition of "truly fair" suggests that it is also a learned response, and a willed one at that. So "less faire, / Less winning soft, less amiablie milde" all remain as options to be mastered by her "oft remember[ing]" that day, and by her artful telling of that "echoing" scene. If, at the outset, she does protest too much in naming Adam her "Guide / And Head," or if she goes much further than she ought to do in proclaiming her dependence on him – "for whom / And from whom I was formd flesh of thy flesh, / And without whom am to no end" (4.440–3) – it is not all that unusual for someone to compensate, or even overcompensate, for a perceived error. If Eve's submissive posture is excessive, it is voluntary; marriage really is a union of wills.

So Adam's next speech is not the "common" view but the Miltonic one – who else would call for labour in paradise? – for Lewalski says that the work of "restrain[ing] the growth or [*sic*] the Garden is an emblem of the labor required to order the self – pruning unwarranted impulses and ordering the burgeoning growth of human possibilities" (*Rhetoric*, 187). Perhaps Eve does proclaim, as Lewalski thinks she does, "her full understanding of and delight in her hierarchical position of subordination to Adam" (185). And yet, insisting that "God is thy Law, thou mine: to know no more / Is womans happiest knowledge and her praise" (4.637–8), she can't sustain that submissive posture to the end of her speech – "But wherefore all night long shine these, for whom / This glorious sight, when sleep hath shut all eyes?" (4.657–8). Excessive obedience to her husband as the embodiment of Law hints at contradictions in her experience, but it also points to glaring contradictions in the "common language" of Milton's era, cultural blind spots that would even compromise the egalitarianism of a John Lilburne.

Under examination in May 1647 by yet another parliamentary committee, Lilburne protested the recent arrest of his wife for having simply obeyed his orders:

> I shall humbly crave liberty to make one motion to this Committee, for the discharge of my wife, for by vertue of your warrant she is a prisoner, for dispersing some of my bookes … and truly I appeale to every one of your own consciences, whether you would not have taken it very ill at the hands of any of your wives? if you were in my case, and she should refuse, at your earnest desire to doe that for you that she by my perswasions hath done for me, therefore I intreat you to set her at liberty … [S]o with one consent she was discharged, for which I thanked them.[44]

Lilburne clearly relied on parliamentary support for his authority as a husband, whether he assumed as much for himself or not.[45] What Elizabeth Lilburne had to say about her release from prison in these circumstances is not recorded. Was her husband's word her "Law"? Or did she acquiesce in this legal ruse to escape the clutches of the law?

We know that Elizabeth petitioned Parliament a number of times between 1646 and 1649 for her husband's release from prison. As Brailsford comments, "Among the Leveller women, Elizabeth Lilburne was respected for her own sake as well as her husband's, for her courage and strength of character were outstanding." But the chief petitioner among the Leveller women was likely "Mrs Katherine Chidley, the mother of Samuel, one of the party's treasurers, who had made her mark as the author of a pamphlet which advocated the Independent view of church government against the redoubtable Thomas Edwards" (Brailsford, *The Levellers*, 317). Their celebrated "A Petition of Women" was presented on 7 May 1649 to Parliament, requesting the release of the four Leveller leaders charged with high treason. This "petition, which may have come from the practiced pen of Mrs Chidley," is reprinted by Woodhouse in *Puritanism and Liberty* under the condescending subtitle, "The Female of the Species." While the masculinist editor says, "It is improbable that this petition was actually composed by the women" (367, n1), Brailsford thinks there is "no reason for supposing that Lilburne wrote it. He was too much the naïve egotist to think himself easily into a woman's skin."[46] Rather, "The ten thousand women who signed this petition and the thousand who carried it to the House with seagreen ribbons [the colours of the Leveller martyr Thomas Rainsborough] pinned to their breasts" (317), left no doubt that Leveller claims for sexual equality were practical as well as theoretical. "Have we not an equal interest," the female author asks, "with the men of this nation in those liberties and securities contained in the *Petition of Right*, and other the good laws of the land? Are any of our lives, limbs, liberties, or goods to be taken from us, no more than from men, but by due process of law and conviction of twelve sworn men of the neighbourhood?"

One of the petition's questions is of particular interest for those who assume that Eve must be wrong to argue her right in the Separation Scene to leave Adam's side: "Would you have us keep at home in our houses, when men of such faithfulness and integrity as the four prisoners, our friends, in the Tower, are fetched out of their beds and forced from their houses by soldiers, to the affrighting and undoing of themselves, their wives, children, and families?" "Or should we be so basely ungrateful," the Leveller women ask, "as to neglect them in the day of their affliction? No, far be it from us."[47]

As moving and as memorable as these words are as a declaration of female agency in 1649, they are just as memorable and moving for what they say about Eve's rephrasing of two key motifs in the petition. Echoing the women's claim that their men "continually hazarded their lives" and "thought nothing too precious for defense of us," Eve confesses that she was won over by Adam's cry: "to give thee being I lent / Out of my side to thee, neerest my heart / Substantial Life, to have thee by my side / Henceforth an individual solace dear" (4.483–6). She is just as sensible as the Leveller women are of the sacrifices their men have made on behalf of their wives and families. Nor is she "so sottish or stupid as to fail to perceive" (Woodhouse, 367) that "manly grace / And wisdom, which alone is truly fair" (4.490–1) may echo her own sense of "fair" in Adam's noble commitment to "equity" and "justice" as an "individual solace dear."

As for Eve's tone in describing Adam's courtship, her own view of gender roles is not that far from the Leveller women who do identify themselves with what can be called the "Gideon syndrome" of God's ways in scripture: "And therefore again we entreat you to review our last petition in behalf of our friends above mentioned, and not to slight the things therein contained because they are presented unto you by the weak hand of women, it being a usual thing with God, by weak means to work mighty effects" ("A Petition," 369). The paradox of a "gentle seizure" to mark Eve's surrender to Adam – "thy gentle hand / Seisd mine" – further implies a hand that was not forced, even when it recalls that "weak hand of woman" from the Petition. While neither Eve nor Adam yet understands the means by which God works – "by things deemd weak / Subverting worldly strong" (12.567–8) – Eve's story of their courtship ends very tellingly with Adam's grasp of "the weak hand of woman," anticipating the Leveller women's own claim that it is "a usual thing with God, by weak means to work mighty effects."

While Eve is adamant that "God is thy Law, thou mine: to know no more / Is womans happiest knowledge and her praise," she also speaks as a woman in the first bloom of love, delighting in her "sole" possession. And her beautiful love song is "a rhetorically elaborate lyric of eighteen lines, containing one vast sixteen-line epanalepsis."[48] "With thee conversing I forget all time," her song begins; "Sweet is the breath of morn, her rising sweet, / With charm of earliest birds; pleasant the Sun / When first on this delightful Land he spreads / His orient Beams, on herb, tree, fruit, and flour, / Glistring with dew" (4.639–45). But the latter half of her song brilliantly echoes the former part: "But neither breath of Morn when she ascends / With charm of earliest Birds, nor rising Sun / On this delightful land, nor herb, fruit, floure, / Glistring with dew." The mirroring half thus serves to undercut her attraction to the world's beauty, since it fails to match the beauty of her love for her husband. While the song may recall that other verbal mirror she had constructed at the pool, this epanalepsis no longer expresses a desire that she can't even name, much less repress. Rather, it actively masters her fascination with iteration – and her reflected image – by negating the doubling of the image at every point of its iteration.[49] Her categorical refusal of the reflected image simply turns her away from her own self-image. In one final, magnificent suspension, it now turns completely toward the Other ("without thee is sweet"). Playfully though movingly, humbly yet artfully, Eve thus transcends self-love in a disciplined demonstration of her love of Adam above all things else in the world.

Before they retire for the night, both lovers pray in unison in a mutually spontaneous act, projecting their love of each other outward to love of God: "Thou also mad'st the Night, / Maker Omnipotent, and thou the Day, / …

and this delicious place / For us too large," petitioning him to give them offspring "who shall with us extoll / Thy goodness infinite, both when we wake, / And when we seek, as now, thy gift of sleep" (4.724–35). Literally speaking with one voice, the couple both enact and preserve an equality of love that, in "good Commonwealth language," may have begun as a solo, but is now repeated as a duet. This great hymn of love no longer echoes with the "common language" of patriarchal dogma, much less with the subordination of wives who must "idolize" their husbands. In the absence of Satan's contaminating perspective, the poet's investment in sexual equality is heard throughout the beautiful epithalamium which follows: "Haile wedded Love, mysterious Law, true source / Of human ofspring, sole proprietie, / In Paradise of all things common else" (4.750–2). Referring to marriage as their "sole" property, the poet then echoes Adam's words about God's gift to them in Paradise, and Eve's words about the "discipline" of marriage in their mutual "labour" of re-ordering the self.

While Eve's experience at the pool may have unnerved her, leaving her inclined to subordinate herself, the narrator confirms that her marriage to Adam is indeed the "sole proprietie" of equals in Paradise. Even the placement of this word "property" at the end of the line – "sole proprietie, / In Paradise of all things common else" – appears expressly designed to recall the Leveller icon of paradisal marriage, where, "To every Individuall in nature, is given an individuall property by nature" (Overton, *Arrow*, 3). Although some critics fairly read the "handedness" of the couple as a republican icon,[50] the narrator's insistence on marriage as the "sole proprietie / In Paradise" might just as easily suggest that the republican icon has now mutated into a Leveller one. Like religion for Walwyn, marriage is a union of wills, "Founded in Reason" (4.755).

What cannot be in doubt is how the narrator's epithalamium refutes the "common view" of the husband's monarchical rule in its apostrophe to marriage as an equalizing power that drives "adulterous lust … from men / Among the bestial herds to raunge" (4.753–4). It is "Here," in "Relations dear" of marriage, "Founded in Reason, Loyal, Just, and Pure" (4.755–6), that "Love his golden shafts imploies, here lights / … Reigns here and revels; not in the bought smile / Of Harlots … nor in Court Amours" (4.763–7). These lines beg to be read in light of the infamous "Court Amours" of Charles II, whose adulterous affair with "Mrs Palmer"[51] had been a public scandal since the first night of his return to Whitehall in May 1660. Nor was it really "Casual fruition," given that "Mrs Palmer," née Barbara Villiers, future Countess of Castlemaine, bore the King a "bastard" every year from 1661 to 1665, until he, following her husband's example, cast her off.

In view of the "common language" of female inequality in the Restoration era, the "naked Majestie" of Adam and Eve in *Paradise Lost* then offers the contrary hope of an egalitarian marriage, far removed from the "casual fruition" and "Court Amours" of the times, much less ordinary marriages like that of Samuel Pepys and his wife, Elizabeth, whom Sam unfairly suspected of having an affair with her dance teacher. Besotted as he was with "my Lady Castlemayne," where she "stood over against us upon a piece of Whitehall – where I glutted myself with looking on her" (3: 175), Pepys best represents the "common view" of Restoration marriage. Even the title of a play he attended on 5 February 1662 announces as much. It was a comedy by John Fletcher entitled "*Rule a Wife and have a Wife* – very well done; and here also I did look long upon my Lady Castlemayne, who, notwithstanding her late sickness, continues a great beauty" (3: 24).

By contrast, Milton's portrait of the paradisal marriage presents an implicit rebuke to the debauchery of the age, where a king's mistress was hardly more than property to be enjoyed and discarded at the royal pleasure, while his espoused queen appeared in public as nothing more than a regal ornament. The marriage of Eve to Adam, by contrast, is in truth their "sole proprietie / In Paradise," where the absence of all other property renders "all things common else."[52] "Sole partner and sole part," each of the partners in the companionate marriage truly enjoys an "individual property" from "nature," out of which a mutual, yet fluid, partnership emerges. And it is evidently modelled on that Leveller icon of marriage which – for Milton, as for Lilburne and Overton – could only be founded on "an individual property given to us by nature."

So, "Sleep on / Blest pair, and O yet happiest if ye seek / No happier state, and know to know no more" (4.773–5), which – in the shadow of "Court Amours" – is a moving reminder to have and to hold the only property one need ever know in Paradise.

· 7 ·

"The Winged Hierarch"

IRONIES OF DEGREE

RAPHAEL'S ARRIVAL IN EDEN, trailing clouds of divine authority, poses a formidable challenge to the ideal of sexual equality, for his teachings are as inimical to Leveller ideals in the poem as Milton's supposed loyalty to Cromwell. Conservative Miltonists like Paul Stevens (2007) continue to trumpet Raphael's authority as "God's epic poet,"[1] while others argue that the angel's authority derives less from his poetic talent than his skill at dialectics: does he embrace or revise a Neoplatonist metaphsysics? Clay Daniel (2004), for instance, faults Adam for exhibiting a "Neo-Platonic desire for divine ascent," and perverting it into a Ficino-like version of "Neo-Platonic notions of love and ascent." According to Daniel, "Raphael's dialogue with Adam locates problems in Adam that thematically balance those that have been raised in connection with the prelapsarian Eve."[2] By contrast, Feisal Mohamed (2008) continues to valorize Raphael's Neoplatonic metaphysics, concluding that "Adam's is not a misguided attempt at Neoplatonic ascent … so much as it is a fetishization of things extreme and scattering bright."[3]

Mohamed's work is unique in its attempt to situate Milton's angelology in the context of Reformed versions of the "ninefold hierarchy" of the angels, "the most commonly evoked model of the heavenly city in the Middle Ages" (4) originating from the *Mystical Theology* and *Ecclesiastical Hierarchy* of Dionysius the Pseudo-Areopagite. Given that Dionysius's angelic hierarchy, and its distinctive functions for each order, had long served as a political justification for church hierarchy, it is no surprise that Milton's "placement of Archangels at the top of the angelic hierarchy, and of cherubim and Seraphim at the bottom of it, inverts the Areopagite's celestial hierarchy" (111).

What is surprising, however, is Mohamed's assumption that "Raphael demonstrates an entire set of principles that Adam never acknowledges at all, and indeed that he cannot recognize at his point in human history, namely the full significance of the Seraph's portrait of the Triune God" (133). Oddly, Mohamed takes up orthodoxy and its conservative agenda to overwrite Milton, the anti-Trinitarian poet. Milton even comes to resemble Calvin in his "employment of angels in *Paradise Lost*" to instantiate "election and illumination" (104). The more radical implications of Milton's materialist heresy are thus totally eclipsed in this return to a dualist angelology that reaffirms "the ontological superiority of spirit to sense" (121). Equally astonishing is the implication that Milton shares the views of his friend Henry Lawrence, president of the Council of State, for whom "the spiritual communion of Saints and angels lends itself … to an endorsement of the Cromwellian absolutism in which he would play a strong supporting role" (98).

While the resurrection of "dead ideas" is not a bad thing in itself, this deeply misguided notion of "medieval influence" (7) reduces the poem to Walter Raleigh's marble monument by making the angel a reliable expositor of the medieval Chain of Being. Long ago, E.M.W. Tillyard's *The Elizabethan World Picture* (1943) had done something similar in attempting to make the Great Chain of Being a totalizing image of English literary and political culture well into the seventeenth century, where somehow, "Milton against unbelievable odds prolongs their [the Elizabethans'] spirit in a later age."[4] Amidst the social upheavals of a later era, Douglas Bush (1964) furthered this notion of Raphael as an uncomplicated exponent of "the universal doctrine of hierarchical order."[5] A year before him, Marjorie Nicolson (1963) had been insisting that Raphael helped "Adam and Eve learn of the hierarchy everywhere in the universe, governing both Heaven and earth."[6] Angelology, it seems, is the default defence of orthodoxy against changing social norms.

But literary critics ignore at their peril Arthur O. Lovejoy's initial reminder in *The Great Chain of Being* (1936) that Milton was "antipathetic" to two of the three basic principles of Neoplatonism – "plenitude" and "sufficient reason."[7] Even so, Lovejoy had concluded that "The notion of a hierarchical scale of nature is, indeed, not lacking" in *Paradise Lost*. Indeed, the founder of this new academic discipline – *The History of an Idea*, as Lovejoy subtitled his book – concluded that the third principle – Neoplatonism's "law of continuity" – was shared by poet and angel alike.[8] Still, the historian was more keenly aware than most literary scholars are today of the knot of logical contradictions that accompany neo-Platonizing[9] accounts of creation. In all these accounts, the material world proves to be a literal embarrassment of riches – the plenitude of spirit overflowing from an immaterial creator whose "goodness" descends by degrees into solid matter.[10]

Worse yet, the "scale of Nature"[11] that links part to part in the Great Chain of Being serves to *naturalize* hierarchal rule. As Lovejoy demonstrates, Thomas Aquinas made a hash of things in his attempt to reconcile the Neoplatonic principle of plenitude with the Judaic notion of divine volition. Arriving at the logical absurdity of "a divine completion which was yet *not* complete in itself, since it could not be itself without the existence of beings other than itself," Aquinas had to affirm "an Immutability which required, and expressed itself in, Change" (50). In his concerted efforts to defend the deity's freedom by revising Plotinian necessity (the deity helplessly overflowing with goodness), Aquinas inadvertently exposed the hidden politics of plenitude. As Lovejoy quotes Aquinas, "All possible grades of goodness would not be filled up, nor would any creature be like God in having pre-eminence over another" (76–7), *unless* all "grades of goodness" were able to imitate God's "pre-eminence" over each and every grade beneath it. "If there were a dead level of equality in things, only one kind of created good would exist" (77). Inequality was thus built into the nature of things, since the deity's defining attributes had to be inexhaustible plentitude and absolute pre-eminence. On the gossamer wings of medieval angelology, social and political hierarchy thus took flight down to earth and back up to heaven.

It is this *necessary* system of governance and social relations that Milton frames in his middle books through a series of figurative and dramatic ironies that raise troubling questions about Raphael's role as "God's epic poet," and about God's purpose in sending him to meddle in matters about which he knows next to nothing. (It is only in Book 8, for example, as he begins to lecture Adam on marital matters, that Raphael confesses, "I that Day was absent" [8.228–9] when God poured out "his Equal Love" on man and woman.) It is difficult, in fact, to imagine a less informed and more obtuse visitor than the well-intentioned "sociable Spirit" (5.221), a.k.a. "the winged Saint" (5.247), "the god-like Guest" (5.351), "the winged Hierarch" (5.468), and "the affable Arch-Angel" (7.41). For Raphael's supposedly "epic" performance in Milton's poem is more likely to upend than to endorse, or even to adapt, the hierarchical premise of the "Christianizing Platonist" that "the abilities of superior creatures contain those of their inferiors, and knowledge of God moves only downward through the hierarchical ranks" (Mohamed, 3, 4).

IN HIS INITIAL ASSAULT on ecclesiastical hierarchy in *Of Reformation in England* (1641), Milton writes scathingly about the "kind of Pupillage" that monarchs can expect from bishops "under their *Hierarchy*," or why a "provident King ought to suspect a *Hierarchy* in his Realme" (CPW 1: 595). By contrast, if an "*Episcopacy*" were "reduc't to what it should be," he jauntily remarked, "we might call every good Minister a *Bishop*, as every *Bishop*, yea the *Apostles* themselves are call'd Ministers, and the *Angels ministring Spirits*, and the *Mininsters* againe *Angels*" (CPW 1: 606). In this context, it is significant that the angel, instructed by God to converse "as friend with friend" (5.229), is called "the winged Hierarch" (5.468) just as he is about to lecture on the Great Chain of Being. As Mohamed justly reports on Milton's attitude to church hierarchs, "The argument throughout the antiprelatical tracts is that the creation of bishops hierarchically superior to their fellow ministers stems from worldly greed and heathenish ceremony rather than from godly devotion" (Mohamed 104). But Raphael is neither greedy nor heathenish, and is evidently sincere in his "godly devotion"; so why name him "the winged Hierarch" at this point in the story? Is it merely to identify him as one of the "ministering spirits" of a "Reformed model" of celestial hierarchy (91)? Or he does he also preserve the habits of an Anglican bishop, however well-meaning? Given that God expressly advised Adam, "[A]ll the Earth / To thee and to thy Race I give; as Lords / Possess it" (8.338–40), what "kind of Pupillage" should we expect a "Lord" to receive from "the winged Hierarch"?

There are two obvious – and rather portentous – problems linked to these questions. First, why does the archangel, who with his peers had, "lowly reverent" and "With solemn adoration," cast down "Thir Crowns" (3.349, 351–2) in Heaven, suddenly forget on earth that heaven's feudal order was dissolved, and that he himself had renounced hierarchy? And second, why would a God of volition, who praised his Son for his willing humility, send a messenger with a metaphysical bias toward *inequality* and the contradictions of Aquinas to "advise" man "of his happie state, / Happiness in his power left free to will, / Left to his own free Will, his Will though free, / Yet mutable" (5.234–7)? To anticipate a far more complex answer to this question in later chapters, has Raphael been left free, perhaps, to innocently intensify the conditions of trial of free, if still mutable, human wills?[12]

The scope of the present chapter is limited to the former question: does Raphael not see how he is pouring old wine into new bottles?[13] Having cast down his crown, why does "the winged Hierarch" introduce a philosophy of *natural* inequality to paradise, where innocents now live in mutual and equal "Majestie"? Even as the archangel tries to account for their existence through the Neoplatonic doctrine of emanation, or "overflow" of "goodness," he is constrained by the Thomistic premise that inequality has *necessarily* to exist between each grade of existence for the Good to be manifested and all "genuine possibles" to be actualized. Furthermore, instead of dwelling on what Lovejoy calls the "this-worldliness" (45) of Goodness "overflowing" the scale of being down to denser matter, Raphael invokes instead the "otherworldliness" of Neoplatonic doctrine[14] in its reverse phase of *remanatio* – the goal of "Goodness" to flow upwards out of matter in its return to the Good. While this figure was a commonplace in Renaissance thought,[15] there is no escaping the fact that the Great Chain of Being was a doctrine whose contradictions were irreconcilable, even for the "Angelic Doctor" of the Church, Thomas Aquinas.

From the outset, Raphael is implicitly linked to Aquinas,[16] as well as to those Church prelates opposed by Milton in the 1640s. Still, there is nothing untoward in the angel's initial claim that "one Almightie … created all / Such to perfection, one first matter all, / Indu'd with various forms, various degrees / Of substance, and in things that live, of life" (5.469–74). But in describing "various degrees of substance" that flow from the Good in Neoplatonic doctrine and move downward on the "scale of Nature," where things are ranked in order of their excellence,[17] Raphael fails to say that, since these ranks are fixed, individuals cannot move upward on a "this-worldly" scale by "assimilation or approximation to the divine nature" (Lovejoy, 82). Any ascent on the "scale" is merely the ascent of "goodness" itself back to the "Good," rather than "various degrees of substance" rising in this world.[18] The angel's logical categories of "more refin'd, more spirituous, and pure, / As neerer to him plac't or neerer tending / Each in thir several active Sphears assignd" (5.475–7) point toward a static, not dynamic, system.[19] Up to this point, Raphael merely expounds an unexceptional Neoplatonist doctrine of *emanatio*.

But what does the reverse direction of *remanatio* – "Till body up to spirit work, in bounds / Proportiond to each kind" (5.478–9) – entail? In Raphael's analogy of the plant mounting "from the root" to the "lighter … green stalk," and "from thence" to "leaves / More aerie" (5.479–81), there are traces of the deterministic optimism of the twelfth-century theologian Abelard, that *bête noire* of Aquinas, who took "plenitude" to mean that "all things must have been precisely what they are" (Lovejoy, 71). So a root remains a root, the leaf a leaf, each fixed in its place, in the best of all possible worlds, where only "the bright consummate floure / Spirits odorous breathes" (5.481–2). Yet even Aquinas would not say with Raphael that "Your bodies may at last turn all to Spirit, / Improv'd by tract of time" (5.497–8), for spiritual fitness can only be achieved through obedience to superiors by staying in one's rank. On the other hand, Reformed angelology did find its own authority for "the spiritual communion of Saints and angels" in Calvin's doctrine of election (another version of the static system of medieval hierarchy), and thus a parallel emergence of a "spiritual elect" in the government of the church, as Milton's friend Sir Henry Vane seems to have believed (Mohamed, 98, 104). In Raphael's prospect of a new and "improv'd" state of being, does Milton then hint, as Mohamed says he does, at the potential "superiority" of "the spiritually enlightened Saint" (103)?

A potential problem emerges at once out of the category confusions of this angel. Raphael's valorization of "Spirit" over "bodies" is dualist in its ontology, although the Neoplatonic principle of continuity implies monism,[20] not dualism, based on continuous connection between degrees of being from the crudest clod of earth to the lightest form of spirit. Each form holds to its fixed place as the divine "goodness" rises through it toward the Good. Although "Body," or "root" in Raphael's organic analogy, produces "Spirit" as "aerie" fragrance, the "root" remains lower on the "scale," less "excellent" than an "aerie fragrance" which ascends heavenward. What Raphael seems to forget, however, is that the Father had called the Son "a second root" in which "all men … shall be restor'd" (3.287–8). In this levelling image, the Son as "root" is farther from the deity than the angelic "floure." God, it seems, then aims to upend the old assumption that "hierarchy is the divine order by which all creatures are arranged according to their proximity to God" (Mohamed, 5). While Raphael excels at expounding such traditional doctrines – once taught in heaven as now on earth – he is lamentably weak on incorporating "a second root" or "casting down" of "Crowns" into his model of cosmic order. In fact, Clay Daniel concludes that the "Neo-Platonic 'program' clashes with Milton's belief in the 'inherent worth' of a universe that God has created from himself. Indicating something of the problems of this passage, even so careful a scholar as Lovejoy attributes these lines on ascent (5.508–14) to the 'angelic schoolmaster' (89)," rather than the epic poet.[21]

Well before the angel pulls that figurative "Tree of Being" out of his hat, there are indications that he may be unreliable.[22] For one thing, the description of his approach to Eden suggests a sudden *upset* in the natural order at his approach, first as "Nature here / Wantond as in her prime … Wilde above Rule or Art"; then as "the mounted Sun / Shot down direct his fervid Raies to warme / Earthes inmost womb, more warmth then *Adam* needs" (5.294–5, 297, 300–2). The *dramatic* result is the husband's first lapse in marital courtesy: "Haste hither *Eve*, and worth thy sight behold … what glorious shape / Comes this way moving; seems another Morn / Ris'n on mid-noon" (5.308–11). If a superfluous sun ("another Morn") is not sufficient hint of danger at "the mounted Sun" supplying "more warmth then *Adam* needs," there is Adam's new tone of command in addressing his wife: "But goe with speed, / And what thy stores contain, bring forth and poure / Abundance, fit to honour and receive / Our Heav'nly stranger" (5.313–16).

The tone of Eve's response, while gentle, does not hide her implied reproach: "*Adam*, earths hallowd mould, / Of God inspir'd," she says, and her insistence on the customary form of courteous address is not the least expression of her disappointment: "small store will serve, where store, / All seasons, ripe for use hangs on the stalk" (5.321–3). After reminding Adam about the proper terms of their relationship, Eve recalls the painful lesson from her dream about temperance ("small store will serve"), before reminding her husband of the true terms of their relationship to the Deity: their true "giver" is not the angel, but "God," who "hath dispenst his bounties" here on earth, "as in Heav'n" (5.330). The gentle terms of her reproach indicate that Eve now foregoes her submission to Adam, where she had previously named him "My Author and Disposer." In the wake of her dream of evil, she begins to negotiate between two dangerous extremes: one of subordination and one of self-sufficiency. The "fruits" of her dream are thus twofold: she is no longer slavishly dependent on Adam, able to teach now as she is taught; and she rejects the notion of angels as their "givers," of goodness coming from any but God's hand.

The irony of Adam's response to the approach of their visitor, so soon after Eve's dream, is also underscored in two epic similes used to describe the angel's flight as he "Winnows the buxom Air" like "A *Phoenix* … When to enshrine his reliques in the Sun's / Bright Temple, to *Ægyptian Theb's* he flies" (5.272–4). The "reliques" of the Phoenix evidently evoke the ashes of the mythic bird's fiery self-immolation before he rises, in Ovid's comic version of the story, to bear his "father's" ashes to the temple of the Sun.[23] Here is a further reminder, in light of another "bright" Sun, that Raphael brings "more warmth then Adam needs." The context of the scene further underwrites the dramatic irony: Raphael comes to Eden bearing the dead "ashes" of Neoplatonic hierarchy.

The second epic simile is more ominous still for the couple's paradisal marriage. As Raphael alights "on th' Eastern cliff of Paradise" (5.275), "Like *Maia's* son he stood, / And shook his Plumes" (5.285–6). "*Maia's* son" is the name Virgil gives to Mercury in *Aeneid*, when Jove's messenger "tied on / The golden sandals"[24] to descend to earth and warn Aeneas of the dangers of love. To Romans, it was the hero's dangerous love for Carthaginian Dido that threatened to abort his imperial mission to found an "eternal" empire, as Dido's response to the hero's desertion soon confirms. Of course, the divine messenger to Adam has no mission to support an empire; so Raphael has no warrant to teach Adam about the dangers of love. In view of his God-given commission to tell man "withall / His danger, and from whom" (5.238–9), the epithet "*Maia's* son" turns him into a dark omen of the tragedy of "Dido." And as the "imperial" messenger, Raphael further evokes a Leveller memory of Norman empire and its imposition of feudal hierarchy on England, a system which "the winged Hierarch" would appear to be importing to Eden.[25]

When Adam goes out to meet his angelic visitor, the narrator pointedly praises his lack of monarchical pomp and regal retinue, as if to make a republican icon of his quiet progress, "without more train / Accompani'd then with his own compleat / Perfections." Indeed, the narrator says, "in himself was all his state, / More solemn then the tedious pomp that waits / On Princes, when thir rich Retinue long … / Dazles the croud, and sets them all agape" (5.351–7). There sounds as well in this implicit republican image an echo of Nedham's (and Milton's) arguments for the greater "excellencie of a *free-state*," "because under this Government, the People are ever endued with a more Magnanimous, active, & noble Temper of spirit, then under the grandeur of any *standing Power* whatsoever."[26] Evidently, Adam is not yet cowed by external authority; his bearing suggests the dignity and nobility that is truly native to his "naked Majestie."

The image of republican dignity is nonetheless controverted an instant later by what seems feudal obeisance: "Neerer his presence *Adam* though not awd, / Yet with submiss approach and reverence meek, / As to a superior Nature, bowing low" (5.358–60). His "submiss approach" recalls Eve's excess of submission, particulary in view of this comparative construction, "As to a superior Naure." But "bowing low" also evokes a contemporary image of Lilburne standing on his dignity and refusing to bow to the Lords "as incroachers and usurpers upon [his] freedomes and liberties."[27] As Nedham recalls:

> The said *John Lilburn* in contempt and scorn of the said high Court, did not only refuse to kneel at the said Bar; but did also, in a contemptuous manner, then, and there, at the open Barre of the said House, openly and contemptuously, refuse to heare the said Articles read, and used divers contemptuous words in high derogation of the Justice, Dignity, and Power of the said Court.[28]

Yet there was really nothing contemptuous in Lilburne's refusal to betray the "Birth-rights" of "the free-born people of *England*" (*Vox*, 58). He merely "answered that he had learned both better Religion and manners then to kneele to any humane or mortall power how great so ever."[29] The issue, as indicated in his response, was the real idolatry implicit in the teachings of the English church – whether that of the Anglican catechism or of the Westminster Assembly (1648) – that inferiors must remove their hats before superiors, and use "my lord" to their "betters" and the respectful "you," not "thou," to parents.[30] Since Adam is not obligated by "birth" or nature to kowtow to the "sociable Spirit" as a "parent" or even a social "better," it may be no more than native courtesy that prompts him to address the angel as a "Native of Heav'n, for other place / None can then Heav'n such glorious shape contain," and to thank him for "descending from the Thrones above" and "deign[ing] a while" those "happie places … To want, and honour these" (5.361–5).

At first meeting, Raphael is also courteous, if oddly fixated – more so than Adam is – on Eve's body: "Haile Mother of Mankind, whose fruitful Womb / Shall fill the World more numerous with thy Sons / Then with these various fruits the Trees of God / Have heap'd this Table" (5.388–91). By contrast, Adam reaffirms his courtesy to his wife by showing that he has learned the lesson she had imparted about their "givers": "Heav'nly stranger, please to taste / These bounties which our Nourisher, from whom / All perfet good unmeasur'd out, descends" (5.397–9). It is more than polite self-deprecation that causes Adam to add, "unsavourie food perhaps / To spiritual Natures;

only this I know, / That one Celestial Father gives to all" (5.401–3). With touching humility, he has paraphrased Eve's words, "God hath dispenst his bounties." At least the angel now responds with similar humility, confessing that, "food alike those pure / Intelligential substances require / As doth your Rational; and both contain / Within them every lower facultie / Of sense" (5.407–11). With due reverence, he even concludes: "God hath here / Varied his bounty so with new delights, / As may compare with Heaven; and to taste / Think not I shall be nice" (5.430–3).

The irony is not lost on anyone attuned to the damaging contradictions in the idea of the Great Chain of Being. For the archangel, who is indeed able to digest the "coarse" fare of human beings, says with a straight face, "Wonder not then, what God for you saw good / If I refuse not, but convert, as you, / To proper substance" (5.491–3), even as he reminds them that they are as yet too low to "participate" with angels in their fare. But why should Heaven's "too light Fare" (5.495) be difficult for humans to digest if their "grosser" food is not in the least indigestible for him? The inversion of the problem of density leads to a further inversion, although Raphael can hardly be expected to know that "wingd ascend / Ethereal, as wee" creates a troubling echo of the "angel's" words in Eve's dream: "But somtimes in the Air, as wee, somtimes / Ascend to Heav'n" (5.79–80).[31] The reader hears the irony of the "Hierarch's" metaphysical abstractions, while the speaker does not.

And yet, when Raphael turns from philosophical discourse to narrative, his God is more the Hebraic God of will acting in time,[32] as compared to the unchanging God of the Neoplatonist, where "metaphysical necessity," or reason as opposed to arbitrary will, explains the existence of things (Lovejoy, 64–5). And it is evidently this arbitrary divinity that Satan resists, not a metaphysical abstraction of the Good. The Adversary, in fact, pits himself against the will of a personal God whom he accuses of having acted wilfully in altering the laws of their polity. To his "Companion dear," Satan says, "[N]ew Laws thou seest impos'd; / New Laws from him who reigns, new minds may raise / In us who serve" (5.679–81). From the story that Raphael now narrates to warn Adam and Eve against disobedience, it is difficult to see how God's actions can be anything more than the whim of an all-powerful, arbitrary deity, or how the supposed inequality that Satan rejects is either reasonable or just.[33] In a narrow sense, Satan may be a much better Neoplatonist than Raphael insofar as he rejects an "arbitrary" First Cause and denounces the exercise of an Absolute Will (which is only revealed in Hell as the projection of his own will). For Satan clearly assumes an equality in degree between the archangels and the Son that requires the inequality of lower degrees of angels. Yet is Satan really alone in opposing Neoplatonic necessity to Hebrew voluntarism in this account of the "will of Heav'n"?

By Raphael's account – the earliest glimpse we get of the Heaven that used to be – the rule of God is properly that of a feudal state (so why necessarily "Good"?), where "th' Empyreal Host / Of Angels by Imperial summons" is called "before th' Almighties Throne" to "Hear [his] Decree, which unrevok't shall stand" (5.583–5, 602). It sounds like the fiat of an absolute monarch who brooks no disagreement with what he wills. His will is to name a successor, it seems, in defiance of reason and justice. He announces muscular provisions for disinheriting and punishing all who choose to disobey his will:

> This day I have begot whom I declare
> My onely Son, and on this holy Hill
> Him have anointed, whom ye now behold
> At my right hand; your Head I him appoint;
> And by my Self have sworn to him shall bow
> All knees in Heav'n, and shall confess him Lord. (5.603–8)

Issuing out of no apparent cause and provoking a response it means to crush, the absolute decree is also unilateral: "[H]im who disobeyes / Mee disobeyes, breaks union, and that day / Cast out from God and blessed vision, falls / Into utter darkness" (5.611–14).

To be told that the scene is biblical only deepens the voluntarist problem of a deity of will. To be sure, the words of the decree and the tone in which it is spoken do echo the scene from Psalms 2: 4–7:[34] "He that sitteth in the heavens shall laugh: the Lord shall have them in derision. Then he shall speak unto them in his wrath, and vex them in his sore displeasure. Yet have I set my king upon my holy hill of Sion. I will declare the decree: the Lord hath said unto me, Thou art my Son; this day have I begotten thee." The third-century Church father Lactantius had even inferred Satan's envy from Psalm 2, and Protestant theologians of the sixteenth and seventeenth centuries had returned to "envy," rather than the "pride" Augustine took to be his only motive for rebellion.[35] For all that, the words are nothing more nor less than the arbitrary decree of a tyrant.

The Greek account in the Pseudepigrapha *Apocalypsis Mosis* (ca. 1st to 3d century CE; trans. Latin *Vita Adae et Evae*, 3d to 4th century CE) offers no better solution to this problem of a deity of arbitrary volition. Here, Satan's envy and rebellion were only prompted by the arbitrary exaltation of Adam, not the Son. The "Devil" tells Adam, "On account of you I was cast out from heaven." For, "When God blew into you the breath of life and your countenance and likeness were made in the image of God, Michael led you and made you worship in the sight of God." Then "Michael called all the angels saying: 'Worship the image of the Lord God, just as the Lord God has commanded.'" But when Michael "called me and said: 'Worship the image of God Jehovah,' I answered … 'Why do you compel me? I will not worship him who is lower and posterior to me. I am prior to that creature … He ought to worship me.' Hearing this, other angels who were under me were unwilling to worship him."[36]

The broad influence of this account in antiquity appears in surviving manuscripts in Greek, Latin, and fragments of Coptic, as well as in the later variant texts in Armenian, Georgian, and Slavonic.[37] Well into the seventeenth century, poetic dramas like G. Peri's *La Guerra Angelica* (ca. 1612) and J.V. Vondel's *Lucifer* (1654) were tightly focussed on "the reluctance of the angel as a superior creature to bow before an inferior" (Revard, 209). But, while the *Vita* does fill a gap in canonical scripture, it does so by converting Neoplatonism's necessary inequality into a narrative of divine partiality. Nor is circular logic helpful to theodicy; Adam falls because his creation caused Satan to fall.[38] Worse yet for a Neoplatonist, Adam is arbitrarily exalted above the angels, leaving them to worship one less good, in the metaphysical sense, by virtue of being farther from the Good on the Chain of Being. Written in the era of the philosopher Plotinus, the Greek *Apocalypsis Mosis* thus provides a vivid reminder of why the Neoplatonist preferred metaphysical necessity to the contingency of will as his logical explanation for the goodness of things. In the *Vita*, God is not just the Final, but the *efficient* cause of Evil, taunting Satan to rebel against his decree exalting man above the angels.

None of this would be promising for theodicy in *Paradise Lost* were the Son's sudden exaltation to render God nothing more than an *agent provocateur*. Yet Milton's acute revisions to the ancient story[39] have advantages that are both moral and logical, as well as dramatic. Morally, the first advantage is that the Son is not, like Adam, Satan's junior in the creation – not when Milton in his *De Doctrina Christiana*[40] says "it is certain that the Son existed in the beginning, under the title of the Word or Logos, that he was the first of created things, and that through him all other things, both in heaven and earth, were afterwards made."[41] In this scenario, the Son is Satan's *creator* and so is worthy of the angel's reverence. And the logical advantage is that the story no longer turns on divine whim or contingency; instead, it revolves on the issue of angelic will, of whether these beings accept or reject what they are told about their creation, and whether they trust or mistrust the word of "the Father infinite, / By whom in bliss imbosom'd sat the Son" (5.596–7). As the Leveller William Walwyn had insisted, "religion must bee a joyning of two free-wils in one" (*Tyranipocrit*, 9); so, too, the religion of Milton's angels turns on the fidelity of their wills to what is acceptable to reason.

So the ultimate advantage in Milton's account – that of setting the Exaltation in a *dramatic* context – is the considerable authority it gains from scripture. As Milton affirms in his *De Doctrina Christiana*, "[W]e have Heb. i. 5, where it is written of the Son's exaltation above the angels: *for to which of the angels did he ever say, You are my Son, I have begotten you today? And again, I will be to him a Father, and he shall be to me a Son.*" For this particular use of "begetting," Milton is quick to point out, refers not to the Son's "generation" as a creature but to his exaltation to a new dignity in Heaven:

> From the second Psalm it will also be seen that God begot the Son in the sense of making him a king, Ps. ii. 6, 7: *anointing my king, I have set him upon my holy hill of Sion*. Then, in the next verse, having anointed his king, from which process the name "Christ" is derived, he says: *I have begotten you today*. Similarly, Heb. i. 4, 5: *made as superior to the angels as the name he has obtained as his lot is more excellent than theirs*. What name, if not "Son"? The next verse drives the point home: *for to which of the angels did he ever say, You are my Son, I have begotten you today?* (CPW 6: 207)

The new dignity accorded the Son is the Father's revelation to the angels of what had *not* been revealed before: God's instrument in the creation of the angels is honoured as being closer in his nature to the Father. The stage is set for Satan's dramatic rebellion against what could yet prove to be metaphysical necessity rather than whim or contingency, a protest against the very ground of their existence. But at least the *drama* now hinges on the fallibility of the actors as to how far their reason and wills square with reality.

Satan, for example, complains of "New Laws from him who reigns" (5.680). From the perspective of the Neoplatonist, the complaint about change is justified by the necessary precedence of eternal over temporal matters, a situation now reversed by events. For the Eternal Being is supposed to stand outside of and beyond all becoming and change. But, in exalting the Son, God changes all the rules; worse yet, he does so at his pleasure, without *reason*. In *Politicus*, Milton's friend Nedham had rejected this voluntarist account of the origins of human or divine law as it "is managed in the hands of a *particular person*, or continued in the hands of a certain number of *Great men*," for the people then "have no Laws but what *Kings* and *great men* please to give, nor do they know how to walk by those Laws ... because the sense is oftentimes left to uncertainty, and it is reckoned a great mystery of State in those forms of Government."[42] So Satan has some reason to object that the exaltation of the Son is presented as a "mystery of State," enacted at the whim of the Ruler:[43] "Hear my Decree, which unrevok't shall stand." In fact, Satan's reaction to this "mystery" differs little from the observation of Politicus that the discontent of the people is justified "when any of their Fellow Citizens or Members of the Commonweal shall arrogate any thing of Power, and Priviledge unto themselves, or their Families, whereby to grandise or greaten themselves beyond the ordinary size or Standard of the People."[44] God really does appear to "greaten" himself by promoting his Son at others's expense and by arrogating more "Power and Priviledge" unto himself and a royal "family" newly named as such.

The problem, of course, is that Satan has a good deal to gain from category confusions. Protesting a coup in which a Neoplatonic metaphysics of "necessary inequality" appears to work against him, his own mode of address gives him away:[45] "Thrones, Dominations, Princedomes, Vertues, Powers" (5.772), he addresses his subordinates while repeating the very titles God had used to announce the exaltation: "Hear all ye Angels, Progenie of Light, / Thrones, Dominations, Princedoms, Vertues, Powers, / Hear my Decree" (5.600–2). The irony is blatant: Satan merely seeks to preserve *l'ancien régime*, if now in the name of liberty and equality. For that *ancien régime* had always been ordered "Under thir Hierarchs in orders bright" (5.587), where "Standards ... for distinction serve / Of Hierarchies, of Orders, and Degrees" (5.589–91).

The only way for Satan to defend his status – exalted above every title he names – is to construe the Son as a usurper of their ancient titles, a Johnny-come-lately on the ladder of hierarchy. "If these magnific Titles," he scoffs, "yet remain / Not meerly titular, since by Decree / Another now hath to himself ingross't / All Power, and us eclipst under the name / Of King anointed" (5.773–7).[46] A grammarian might want to ask who is this "us" now "eclipst" under the singular "name / Of King anointed"? Instead, Satan turns the focus back on the upstart usurper of their collective rights, though it is now clear that he holds to the notion of the One ruling the Many, not the rule of the Many: "if not equal all, yet free, / Equally free," the sophist reasons, "for Orders and Degrees / Jarr not with liberty, but well consist" (5.791–3). By locating "equality" in "freedom," rather than in rank, he is thus able to cloak his ambition with the regal "pretensions" of another: "Who can in reason then or right assume / Monarchie over such as live by right / His equals, if in power and splendor less, / In freedome equal?" (5.794–7). The rhetorician ultimately fails to conceal his self-interest, arguing for a singular "Monarchie" within this system of "Orders and Degrees," while equating the system alone with "freedome," where all are "free" regardless of status. It is Satan's will that is arbitrary, since unsupported by reason.

A decade before giving Satan these dramatic lines to speak, Politicus had recalled a similar situation in antiquity: "Thus in *Syracusa*, *Dionysius* clothing himself with a pretence of the Peoples Liberty, and being by that means made their *Leader*, and then making use of that Power to other ends then was pretended, became the firebrand of that *State*."[47] Satan thus becomes a clear prototype for the Sicilian demagogue, not to mention an English Lord Protector, in "clothing himself with a Pretence of the Peoples Liberty," while protesting "th' abuse / Of those Imperial Titles which assert / Our being ordain'd to govern, not to serve" (5.800–2). For it is those same "Imperial Titles," he says, which ordained "our" right "to govern." Since "all" are not able to govern and some will be left to "serve," Satan must pretend to defend the "People's" liberty by defending that necessary inequality of "Orders and Degrees" he is so loath to give up; "our" thus turns into the royal "we" as the syllogism ends in "such as live by right / His equals, if in power and splendour less, / In freedome equal."

This is the basis of Abdiel's objection[48] to demagoguery as he breaks ranks to say:

> O argument blasphemous, false and proud!
> Words which no eare ever to hear in Heav'n
> Expected, least of all from thee, ingrate
> In place thy self so high above thy Peeres. (5.809–12)

For Abdiel, there is no hiding the fact that Satan does not speak for his inferiors in his bid to preserve the status quo.[49] Twice in the space of three lines, the narrator describes him as speaking "in a flame of zeale" (5.807), the only one "among the Seraphim ... then whom none with more zeale ador'd / The Deitie" (5.804–6). In his conspicuous "zeal," Abdiel resembles no one in Milton's own era more than John Lilburne in his "zeale to truth and justice," as the latter had characterized himself in *Jonah*[50] in his opposition to Cromwell's injustice. Abdiel is just as singular – and lonely – as Lilburne was, and quite as prescient in recognizing the real tyranny intended by the demagogue: "[U]njust thou saist/ Flatly unjust, to binde with Laws the free / And equal over equals to let Reigne, / One over all with unsucceeded power" (5.818–21). Hinting at the tyrant's veiled hope of unsucceeded power in reigning "over equals," Abdiel begins to untangle Satan's multiple obfuscations about degree by asking whether God has in fact promoted or demoted the Son, and whether the "way up" might be the "way down," whether one chooses it or not?

While Abdiel's defence of God's justice verges on voluntarism – "[S]halt thou dispute / With him the points of libertie, who made / Thee what thou art?" (5.822–4) – he returns to the crux of the matter, exposing the logical and grammatical contradictions in Satan's use of "equal." What is your ground of equality, he asks, and how is it justified? "But to grant it thee unjust, / That equal over equals Monarch Reigne," he gives the devil his due, while keeping the sting for the tail of the argument: "Thy self though great and glorious dost thou count, / Or all Angelic Nature joind in one, / Equal to him begotten Son" (5.831–5). In other words, do you really "count" yourself, no matter how "great and glorious," as "equal to him begotten Son"? Or is it "all Angelic Nature joind in one" that you assume to be "equal to him?" When you speak of "Our being ordain'd to govern," don't you really mean "yourself," not "all" the angels? On this point, Abdiel appears to echo Lilburne in his *Impeachment* of "Lieut: Gen: *Cromwell*, who was once the glory of Englishmen ... (whose name for honesty once rung and eccho'd throughout *England*)" who "should now apostate from his former declared gallantry and honesty ... and now of late become a grand patron, protector and earnest pleader for the preservation of all the grand corrupt and inslaving interests in *England*)."[51] As Cromwell had looked to Lilburne, so Satan appears to Abdiel to be no more than a conservative defender of "inslaving interests."

There is also the question of who had *ordained* Satan "to govern," and to what end? It is the Father, of course, who ordained that rule. But Abdiel's faith in the Father's goodness is grounded on what is for him an unshakeable fact: "As by his Word the mighty Father made / All things, ev'n thee, and all the Spirits of Heav'n / By him created in thir bright degrees" (5.836–8). So if he orders "his Word" to govern them, what can it matter, if "by experience taught we know how good, / And of our good, and of our dignitie / How provident he is, how farr from thought / To make us less" (5.826–9). Abdiel's willed obedience is not blind, since his own "experience" confirms his sense of the goodness of God's will: far from imposing new laws or reducing "our dignitie," he is "bent rather to exalt / Our happie state under one Head more neer / United" (5.829–31). There is just one question to be considered, and the answer is obvious: Did he make "us less" by this exaltation of the Son? or is his "bent rather to exalt" us "under One Head," where we may be "more neer United"? Power before now, it is true, had been distributed geographically; Satan's "Royal seat" is set "High on a Hill" within "the limits of the North" (5.755). But why should a territorial model of governance continue? Why should the Father not bring us into nearer union if he deems it good? Is he not asking the Son to become one of us, "since he the Head / One of our number thus reduc't becomes" (5.842–3)? Why do you say that the Son has clambered up the "chain" of being when he seems to be reduced to "our" level? Is God not proposing – rather like the Levellers – to do away with "aristocratic privilege"[52] by asking the Son to become one with us? Why should we obey you as our Lord? Should we not strive to be more closely united in will with him?

Indeed, Abdiel's reading of events points to a political "humiliation" of the Son long before the colloquy in Heaven, where he volunteers to die in man's stead. There is even a precedent for this reading in the apocryphal *Ascension of Isaiah* (ca. 150 to 200 CE). As Albert C. Labriola has argued, this passage authorizes a "reduction" of the Son to the level of the angels.[53] For, as Isaiah says of his vision, he has heard the voice of the Most High, the Father of my Lord, saying to my Lord Christ who will be called Jesus":

> Go forth and descent [sic] through all the heavens … And thou wilt become like unto the likeness of all who are in the five heavens … And none of the angels of that world shall know that Thou art with Me of the seven heavens and of their angels. And they shall not know that Thou art with Me, till with a loud voice I have called … in order that you mayest judge and destroy the princes and angels and gods of that world, and the world that is dominated by them: For they have denied Me and said: "We alone are and there is none beside us."[54]

When the Son of God passed unrecognized through every level of the angels in his descent, still "they did not praise Him (nor worship Him); for His form was like unto theirs" (10.20). "Subject to the limitations of this lesser nature," Labriola concludes, "the Son is humiliated, but the angelic nature is exalted because it has been assumed by the deity. In this way, too, the deity has chosen to manifest himself more fully to lesser creatures, and by governing the angels through someone who shares their nature, God is thus attentive to their dignity" (32).[55]

The refusal of so many angels in Milton's exaltation scene to praise the Son – since he shares their form and appears to be no more than their equal – helps to clarify what is truly unique and defensible in his account of Satan's fall. For, at its farthest reach, suggests Labriola, the scene enacts a Christocentric theology of humiliation: "[F]or the two begettings – the first in eternity, the second in time – show the continuing humiliation of the deity, first as an angel, then as a man" (33). More to the point,

> After the begetting of the Son as an angel, the previous hierarchical arrangement of angels, though still observed, is less important than their unity in and with the Son. The experience of humiliation in laying aside divinity to become an angel provides a model whereby angels who have presided in the hierarchy should be willing to forgo their status and degree. (Labriola, 36)

In effect, what Milton shows in the exaltation scene is an act of Levelling among the angels that anticipates the abolition of the Lords – or a Levelling of God and man and angels – that was suggested at the end of the colloquy in Heaven. The divine nature, in other words, is being communicated downwards to those who are free to accept it or not; contrary to the Neoplatonic model of a "necessary" descent or "overflow" of goodnesss, each creature must choose how to respond. Those who refuse appear to do so to forestall a threat to their rank, to any levelling of their power in the social hierarchy. Conversely, those who embrace the divine nature take on its burden of humiliation, volunteering to be as selfless as the Servant-Ruler of *Tyranipocrit*. It was exactly in such terms that Politicus had celebrated a "Free Common-weal," because "it is ever the Peoples care to see, that Authority be so constituted, that it shall be rather a Burthen than a Benefit to those that undertake it."[56] In his keen rebuke of Satan, Abdiel likewise remarks the benefit to the angels who accept a celestial version of the Self-Denying

Ordinance, and its burden on the Son, "since he the Head / One of our number thus reduc't becomes." Yet, by stooping to assume their nature, the Son does exalt the angelic nature to equivalence with him. The Exaltation Scene is thus a model for dismantling the old hierarchy of ruler / ruled.

Reading the exaltation scene as drama accomplishes several things at once, not least of which is its calculated ambiguity of events. Abdiel offers a far more reasonable reading of the scene than Satan allows; his will continues to be informed by his reason, thus providing his fellow angels with the opportunity to choose the Good and avoid the loss of goodness.[57] Much as the Son lays his "divinity" aside to become "one of [their] number," every one of the angels could choose to give up hierarchy, to reject status and degree. The scene could even end, as the colloquy in Heaven later does, in a casting down of crowns and the renunciation of power: "So spake the fervent Angel, but his zeale / None seconded, as out of season judg'd, / Or singular and rash, whereat rejoic'd / Th' Apostat" (5.849–52).

In naming Satan "Th' Apostat" at this precise point in the drama, Milton recalls how like to events in Heaven are those on earth. "*O Crumwell, O Ireton*," Overton had lamented. "Was there ever a generation of men so Apostate so false and so perjur'd as these?"[58] And Lilburne repeatedly used the same word to judge Cromwell, as well as his whole faction, inveighing against "the present dissembling interest of *Independents* for the peoples Liberties in generall … merely no more but Self in the highest *and to set up the false saint, and most desperate Apostate murderer and traytor*, Oliver Cromwell."[59] These words from the summer of 1649 have found their echo in Heaven, where Abdiel accuses Satan and his followers of a "dissembling interest" for "the peoples Liberties in generall." What events demonstrate beyond a doubt is that the heavenly "Apostate" can allow no one, not even the Son of God, to claim precedence over him. Against all reason, he insists: "We know no time when we were not as now; / Know none before us, self-begot, self-rais'd / By our own quick'ning power" (5.859–61). Logically, this is the dead end of apostasy, since the Apostate can no longer do more than scoff at the Loyalist's trust in what he has been told, that "by his Word the mighty Father made / All things, ev'n thee" (5.836–7). Yet, in claiming equality with God, the Apostate must finally abandon reason itself to claim his self-creation. But *will* without *reason* leads to tyranny, as Satan shows in his proud insistence that "our own right hand / Shall teach us highest deeds, by proof to try / Who is our equal" (5.864–6). "O alienate from God," Abdiel retorts," O spirit accurst, / Forsak'n of all good; I see thy fall / Determind"

(5.877–9). He sounds like no one in the world so much as Lilburne addressing Cromwell.

Henceforth, it is hard to doubt that civil war in Heaven will be the template for civil war on earth. For Satan, the "humiliation" of the Son requires his own humiliation in an effective abolition of the Lords. This simple model of a divine reduction and decentring of power, so like the Leveller agenda on earth, seems to promise a continuing paradise. Of course, "paradise" would not be realized in seventeenth-century England, any more than it was realized in Hell's "classical" republic. But a huge question remains: why would a loving God greet rebellion in Heaven with a smile? "Heir of all my might," he scoffs, "Neerly it now concernes us to be sure / Of our Omnipotence" (5.720–2).

Once again, Plotinus seems to have been right to prefer necessity – even with its necessary inequality – over the whims of an arbitrary deity. But, as always in *Paradise Lost*, appearances are deceiving. "Mightie Father," the Son says, "thou thy foes / Justly hast in derision, and secure / Laugh'st at thir vain designes and tumults vain" (5.735–7). While the Son never doubts his Father's might, or even presumes on his right as the "Heir of all [God's] might," even he does not recognize the irony of his Father's "doubt" of the outcome, "lest unawares we lose / This our high place, our Sanctuarie, our Hill" (5.731–2). For it is this "high place" that the Father will later ask him to give up in the colloquy of Book 3. In fact, the most dramatic result of the "exaltation" scene is the way that it raises the bar, thus complicating the Son's choice, as "Heir of all my might," to later volunteer his life for those who are supposed to be his inferiors. In his free choice, despite appearances to the contrary, we might begin to grasp a little of God's ways in all these links, given these connections between humility and the diffusion of power.

·8·

"Behold the Excellence"

MIGHT AND RIGHT

GOD IS THE FIRST LITERARY CRITIC to question epic prowess in arms (and the providentialist ethos of the New Model Army[1]) when he praises Abdiel at the beginning of Book 6 for having "fought / The better fight, who single hast maintaind / Against revolted multitudes the Cause / Of Truth, in word mightier then they in Armes" (6.29–32). But the angel's – and the reader's – revaluing of "Armes" is further complicated by the deity's promise that "the easier conquest now / Remains thee, aided by this host of friends" (6.37–8), to turn back on the foe, "and to subdue / By force, who reason for thir Law refuse" (6.40–1). In this supreme authorization of force, we appear to be back to business as usual, where "mightier" in "word" than "they in Armes" denotes "The pen is mightier than the sword."

Nor is a momentary doubt of the divine word relieved by its ensuing commission: "Go *Michael* of Celestial Armies Prince, / And thou in Military prowess next / *Gabriel*, lead forth to Battel these my Sons / Invincible" (6.44–7). God makes a formal declaration of war, sending a force "Equal in number" to meet "that Godless crew" with "Fire and hostile Arms" and "to the brow of Heav'n / Pursuing drive them out from God and bliss" (6.49–52). He sounds like an outraged prince, quite as stern and imperious as the deity in Peri's play *La Guerra Angelica* (ca. 1612), or Vondel's *Lucifer* (1654), or any number of Renaissance poems about Lucifer's rebellion noted in Stella Revard's definitive study of Milton's sources.[2] What she calls the "tradition of Satan's rebellion"[3] is more like a classical war in heaven modelled on the conflicts of Homer's *Iliad* and Virgil's *Aeneid*.[4]

In ancient times, heroic tradition made a virtue of *virtus*[5] (from Latin *vir*, man), the manly strength, fortitude, and skill of the dauntless warrior whose excellence the Greeks called *areté*. For Homer, that excellence ranged from the *furor* (battle-fury) of Achilleus to the cunning of Odysseus, but the moral excellence of the hero was his noble inclination to die in battle.[6] The heroic code of conduct[7] allowed him to be driven by shame (Gk. *aidōs*), if not by the desire for glory. But the poet was similarly bound by a narrative code in which events would follow familiar sequences, or *scripts*,[8] in which the poet's originality appeared in small, though not inconsequential, departures from traditional patterns.

Since the heroic contest was the heart and soul of heroic narrative, the motif of arming for battle was one basic "script" in the heroic tradition. One of its features was a verbal contest[9] prefatory to the martial contest that established, as Ward Parks maintains, "a consistent and rule-governed relationship"[10] between the opponents. The crucial connection between a war of words and bodily combat was the display of personal superiority, not of brawn alone but of wit and mental dexterity. In this literal "theatre" of war, both the war of words and the war of arms will unfold "as the ritualized valorization of selfhood."[11] Above all, it is a public performance, since the quest for glory – "called *kléos* in the Greek, cognate with *klúein*, 'to hear'" – can only be confirmed by "*witnesses*; indeed, the very word *contest* contains the meaning 'witness' in its Latin etymology" (Parks, 61). The scene of performance is as much ritual, then, as it is theatre, since *kléos*, or "personal glory," can only be realized "through formalized public contesting" (62). While Milton's God praises Abdiel, a lowly seraph, for his moral and intellectual *virtus*, it seems that he still wants public proof of his skill in "Armes."[12]

Abdiel's challenge, when he next confronts Satan in the field, proceeds much along the lines of his earlier verbal success: "Proud, art thou met?" (6.131), he taunts, thereby reducing Satan to the name of his sin and belittling[13] the Adversary's reliance on force: "[F]ool, not to think how vain / Against th' Omnipotent to rise in Arms" (6.135–6). What distinguishes his ritual performance of selfhood from the classical model, however, is its genuine humility: "Who out of smallest things could without end / Have rais'd incessant Armies to defeat / Thy folly" (6.137–9). Abdiel, that is to say, seeks only the Father's glory in exposing the "fool's" belief that "Arms" could ever succeed against Omnipotence. With touching modesty, he makes himself a ready example of the "smallest things" that God can use to thwart the

"Proud"; for proof, he points to the whole host of witnesses behind him who had *not* been present at his previous contest of words with his feudal overlord: "[B]ut thou seest / All are not of thy Train; there be who Faith / Prefer, and Pietie to God, though then / To thee not visible" (6.142–5). His "Faith" and "Pietie" are now proved in a very public way: "my Sect thou seest, now learn too late / How few somtimes may know, when thousands err" (6.147–8).

Satan's verbal weapon of choice is cynical relativism.[14] Calling Abdiel a "seditious Angel" (6.152), he first accuses him of disloyalty to his feudal lord (himself), and then describes him as a loser in a democratic vote of "A third part of the Gods" who "can allow / Omnipotence to none" (6.156, 158–9). A skilful politician, Satan manages once again to gerrymander the result of the vote, transforming the dissent of a minority of one-third in Heaven to majority support in his regional kingdom: "At first I thought that Libertie and Heav'n / To heav'nly Soules had bin all one" (6.164–5). And he further belittles Abdiel by reducing him and the faithful angels behind him to "the Minstrelsie of Heav'n" (6.168). As Ward Parks remarks of the verbal contest paradigm, "[E]ven as the heroes vie with one another for personal glory, they are tacitly or explicitly negotiating the terms of a trial of arms that will determine which of them has won" (60). And Satan evidently expects his own performance, both verbal and martial, to define the outcome in terms of his "revolutionary" politics: "Servilitie with freedom to contend" (6.169).

But the logic of Satan's attempt to redefine the terms of combat is fatally flawed. "This is servitude," Abdiel retorts, "To serve th' unwise, or him who hath rebelld / Against his worthier, as thine now serve thee, / Thy self not free, but to thy self enthrall'd" (6.178–81). In much clearer terms than Satan is able to muster, he exposes the fundamental contradiction of the heroic ethos. It is the quest for personal glory that is itself enslaving, a valorization of selfhood that is not meant to set others free or to defend community, but to hold all others thrall. Indeed, the heroic ethos enslaves the hero most of all. So, "Reign thou in Hell thy Kingdom" (6.183), Abdiel unmasks the brutal egotism of the heroic tradition, leaving a vanquished Satan to re-affirm "heroically" later on in Hell his discredited proposition: "Better to reign in Hell then serve in Heav'n" (1.263).

Abdiel's challenge to the heroic tradition is far more, however, than a mere rewriting of the war of words. In the "contest paradigm" described by Ward Parks, "The primary participants are the two adversaries, who are ideally comparable in their standing within their respective communities and in their martial attainments" (61). But Abdiel belongs to the second-lowest rank of angels in Heaven, making Satan's failure in the war of words an omen of the impending collapse of the old feudal hierarchy. As Mohamed suggests, in "demoting the Serpahim and Cherubim to the bottom" of the angelic hierarchy, "Milton creates a heaven where the enactment of divine will is the highest creaturely calling" (*In the Anteroom of Divinity*, 112). So it is hardly the case "that Milton begins to differ sharply from his predecessors" (Revard, 186) only when the inconclusivesness of the first day of battle has degenerated into the chaos of the second day of fighting. From the outset, Milton has undercut the epic "tradition," represented by Vondel and Peri and others, of making the duel a contest between social equals, between, say, the "mighty" archangels Michael and Lucifer.[15]

This departure is more radical than it seems, since it recalls the recent civil wars in England pitting aristocrat against aristocrat, and commoner against aristocrat. In much the same way as the English cavaliers, "The great Seraphic Lords and Cherubim" (1.794) of Satan's "secret conclave" stand on the rebel side with their social inferiors, while the lowly Seraph Abdiel stands on the loyalist side with the archangels Michael, Uriel, Gabriel, and Raphael. No more than the recent war in seventeenth-century England is this "timeless" war in Heaven a war between the classes; rather, it recalls the assault on Troy to uphold an aristocrat's (in this case, Satan's) honour. And yet the script of verbal combat clearly begins a process of social levelling which, as we know from that "later" scene in Book 3, is going to end by overturning age-old hierarchies.

So when the subaltern scoffs, "[M]y Sect thou seest" (6.147), and names his adversary "Apostat" (6.172), the words evoke more than the brutal wars of religion that had plagued the Continent during the Thirty Years War (1618–48), or even the "religious" wars between Anglicans and Puritans, then Presbyterians and Independents, in the English civil wars (1642–46, 1648, 1651). At times, Abdiel seems to be quoting that other war of words between Lilburne and the politician Cromwell, particularly in the former's use of the language of apostasy.[16] Contending in "the present contest of the present dissembling interest of *Independents* for the peoples Liberties in generall," Lilburne had inveighed against Cromwell's party in Parliament as aiming at "no more but Self in the highest" in its attempt "*to set up the false saint, and most desperate Apostate murderer and traytor*, Oliver Cromwell."[17] In his printed "Prayer," Lilburne beseeches God to

> protect and deliver me *from the cruell and bloudy rage, of thy once* SEEMING *servant*, CROMWEL, who if my soul is now able to judge, is visibly become a FALNESTAR, an *Apostate* from thee, an ENEMY to thee, and desperate persecutor of thee, in all those where he meets with the shining splendor and the glory of thine owne bright Image of Justice holinesse, purity, and righteousness.[18]

In Abdiel's war of words with Satan, the echoes of the literary tradition have become secondary to a number of departures from that background by way of historical allegory.

Lilburne, like Abdiel "before" him, engages his quondam military commander in a war of words that Cromwell cannot hope to win. Here is further reason to think that Milton refuses to identify the loyalist armies in Heaven with the "Puritan" cause on earth that he is supposed to have supported; the "Saints" in England are closer to the "Falnestar" Cromwell than they are to the loyalists in Heaven. In his isolation amidst the army of the "Falnestar" Lucifer, Abdiel could easily sound more like Lilburne than anyone from the Rump Parliament or the Council of State. "My Sect, thou seest," the Seraph expresses his disdain for the fallen sectary; "seditious Angel,"[19] Satan retorts with cynical relativism. From this point on, their war of words resounds with the language of *The Second Part of Englands New-Chaines*, where Lilburne recalled how the Levellers were "reproached with the names of Atheists, Hereticks, and seditious Sectaries."[20]

Even in terms of the ancient literary tradition, Abdiel proves to be mightier "in word ... than they in Armes," though the martial duel lasts but an instant: "So saying, a noble stroke he lifted high, / ... ten paces huge [Satan] / back recoild; the tenth on bended knee / His massie Spear upstaid" (6.189, 193–5). And yet, though the word is mightier than the sword, it still requires the sword to put beyond dispute the lie of Satan's refusal "To bow and sue for grace / With suppliant knee, and deifie his power, / Who from the terrour of this Arm so late / Doubted his Empire" (1.110–13). To the Satanic mind impervious to reason, the sword is a last resort by which to expose the emptiness of mere words. God's words, however, are not an empty promise, unless we seek a referent for that ambiguous commission to the "Prince" of "Celestial Armies" to "lead forth to Battel ... my armed Saints ... Fearless assault, and to the brow of Heav'n / Pursuing drive them out from God and bliss" (6.51–2). Because that's not how it happens; Michael and the loyalists win the first day's battle, but they don't win the war; and then things get worse on Day Two.

Remarking Milton's bold departure from tradition, Stella Revard explains that "Most poets move the warfare swiftly from beginning to end; all is concluded in one day with one battle proper"; the tradition requires that "Michael, in single combat with Lucifer, wins the day. What follows in a typical Renaissance poem is the rebels' expulsion from Heaven; what follows in *Paradise Lost*, however, is the realignment of the rebel's [*sic*] forces" (182). Revard also notes that Milton's God "alone (among those Gods portrayed by Renaissance poets) is sending forth an army to carry out a commission he knows perfectly well they cannot complete" (170). Are his agents misled? No more so than the Son and the angels are misled in Book 3 (though Revard does not make this point) when God pronounces judgment on Adam and his race: "Dye hee or Justice must" (3.210). What Revard concludes of this representation of God's ways bears repeating:

> Other Renaissance poets portray a God of straightforward and simple intention. He sends armies forth to conquer and they do conquer; he tells them they will win glory and honor in the fight and they do. But Milton's God dispatches his saints to learn a humbling lesson. Glories of battle they will not win; conventional honor and renown will not be theirs; no spoils of the enemies will they exultingly hang up in triumph. Therefore it is highly significant that Milton's God promises them none of these. The saints will glean a different reward from "heroic" battle. All this, however, is perceived only in retrospect. (170)

What is not clear in retrospect, however, is why the poet who questions tradition from the outset would stick to a script of "arming for battle"? "Milton," Revard remarks, "has not drawn a simple contrast between his rebel and loyal angels. He has shown both as devoted to and exercised in the classical values and trappings of warfare. In this first description of the armies he is perhaps even more deliberately Homeric than his Renaissance followers" (172). Yet Milton needs no more than a few lines to describe the warrior's shield – where Homer lingers over peaceful pictures of Greek life on the shield of Achilleus, for example, and Virgil dwells on images of Rome's future history wrought upon the shield of Aeneas – and even then, it is the "ample Shield" not of Abdiel but of Satan, made "of tenfold Adamant," "A vast circumference" (6.255–6).

Even more telling than Satan's shield is "the Sword of *Michael*," by which he "smote, and fell'd / Squadrons at once, with huge two-handed sway / Brandisht aloft the horrid edge came down / Wide wasting" (6.250–3). One reason for focalizing Michael's sword through Satan's perspective is the imminence of divine judgment connoted by it in the literary tradition. In Erasmo di Valvasone's *Angeleida* (1590), "Michael lifts his sword and cuts through Lucifer's wing and arm into his body. The blood pours forth. Lucifer is defeated and driven from Heaven by the victorious archangel" (Revard, 185). It is also a scene repeated in at least a half-dozen Renaissance poems, where the fight ends in "a single decisive blow by Michael. Milton has closely imitated this scene up to and including the wounding blow at the hands of the archangel. But Michael's duel in *Paradise Lost* proves indecisive" (186).

In fact, Satan's surviving to fight another day culminates in the startling innovation (both literary and military) of rebel artillery on the second day, and the regression of the loyal angels to the Stone Age ethos of Hesiod's Hundred-Arms. As Revard points out, "The loyal angels who bury the cannons with their volley of hills distinctly recall the giants who in service to Zeus overwhelm the Titans with volleys of rock and literally bury them" (192).[21] But here the argument breaks down – essentially it is Arnold Stein's case in "Milton's War in Heaven: An Extended Metaphor," if not acknowledged as such – that the war in Heaven basically concerns the preservation of order and degree[22] ("kingship," in Revard's terminology). Stein thinks that the whole point of the episode is to render Satan's assault on spirit by means of matter (281–2) ridiculous, an assault on reason *by* means of reason (275). But this breakdown in "discipline," supposedly necessary to preserve "order and degree," quickly leads to a "descent of spirit to matter" in good and bad angels alike. Moreover, neither Stein nor Revard can make anything of the fact that the divine "laugh" in Milton's "divine comedy" is that of a god who laughs at himself before anyone else: "Heir of all my might," he addresses the Son, "Neerly it now concernes us to be sure / Of our Omnipotence" (5.720–1). God's self-directed irony alters the landscape of the war in Heaven by forcing us to question the dualist assumption that "chaos" is foreign to the divine nature.[23] For an omniscient deity who laughs at himself invites us to do so as well; we are all required to internalize what others read as "external ridicule" (Stein, 268–9).

If we look again at Milton's handling of the traditional "script" of Michael's sword, we find the poet, like his deity, laughing at himself and his earlier views of "sword-law." Setting out to question the legitimacy of

English kings in 1651, Politicus[24] had reduced their collective "right" to sword-law: "If we look as high as the *Norman Bastard*, the father of them all, and the founder of their *Titular pretences*, we finde him to have no better Title then a good *long Sword*, with which he established a *Tyranny* here by *Conquest*."[25] The history of kingship outlined by Politicus in the very next issue of the newsbook lists an unbroken line of British kings who had "made good their successions by the *Sword*."[26] The collaboration of Milton[27] with Nedham during a series of tutorials in "Commonwealth principles" in 1651, and the congruency of their political attitudes with those expressed by Raphael in *Paradise Lost*, is too significant to go unremarked.

Milton's revisions to the "epic" script of Michael's sword in the poem are more telling still in view of the extraordinary debate that Lilburne published from the Tower. In May 1649, Cromwell's chaplain Hugh Peter had paid a visit to Lilburne in prison, two months after the latter's arrest on charges of high treason. After the Leveller leader's expression of suspicion that his visitor had come as a spy, the latter abruptly stood up:

> Mr *Peter* casting his eye upon my Law-books, takes up one of *Cook's Institutes*, and professed, *I was meerly gull'd in reading or trusting to these books, for there was no Laws in* England.
>
> I answered to this effect, That I did beleeve what he said; for they (meaning his great Masters, *Cromwel, Fairfax, &c.*) had destroyed them all.
>
> *Nay,* saith he, *I tell you, there never was any in* England.[28]

Ever the "lawyer" in search of a legal precedent, Lilburne snatched up his "Statute-book," with which he "turned him to the Petition of right." As he recounts, "I read to him, as followeth: 'The Law is that which puts a difference between good and evill, betwixt just and unjust: If you take away the Law, all things, will fall into confusion, every man will become a law unto himself.' To which the good chaplain unblushingly responds, 'I tell you saith he, for all this, there is no Law in this Nation, but the sword, and what it gives; neither was there any Law or Government in the World, but what the Sword gave and set up'" (5). In what sounds like an epic script of "arming for battle," Lilburne replies:

> But Sir, in short and in plain English, let me tell you, that if there be now no law in *England*, nor never was, that then you and your

great Masters, *Cromwell, Fairfax*, and the Parliament, are a pack of arrant bloody Rogues and Villaines, in setting the people together by the ears, to fight for the preservation of their Laws, in which their Libertie is contained (which is the principall declared cause of the Warre from the beginning to the end of the War never) if there were no such thing in being as Law in *England*. (5)

It is an astounding scene, not merely for Hugh Peter's frank admission that the Commonwealth rested on a foundation of force, but for the self-righteous assurance of one of the "Saints" that the Parliamentary armies supposedly wielded the sword of divine justice. So Lilburne tries to point out to Cromwell's envoy where his logic must end: "But Sir, let me tell you withall, if your reasoning be sound and good, then if six Theeves meet three, or four honest men, and because they are stronger then they, rob them, that act is righteous, sound and good, because their swords are stronger then the others" (5). Does Cromwell's chaplain not see that Might, by this cynical standard, is the only Right there is or ever could be? Say that Cromwell had failed to win a single battle, let alone the war: did that mean that God would then have been on the royalist side?

Lilburne's logic did not convince Hugh Peter of the error of his ways. Nor would it have done better with Politicus two years later. Writing in 1651, the journalist still held with the "Saints" that "The *Sword* is the great *Engin*, used by the hand of God, in erecting, altering, and establishing all the Frames of Government of the world … [I]f there be anything under the Sun, that holds *Jure Divino*, it is the *Sword*."[29] Like other English classical republicans, Politicus had yet to recognize the blind spot that hampered theocratically-minded politicians. "Was it the *Sword* then," Politicus plaintively asked, "that did thus enslave us from time to time, and shall we not free our selves now we have the *Sword* in our own hands?" Clearly, these public defenders of the English republic suffered as much from the tendency to self-contradiction as did other apologists for the Conquest: "Must *Usurpers* ride in triumph, with the *Sword* by their sides, over the heads of the people?" Politicus asks rhetorically. "[A]nd shall not the Patriots of *England*, adorned with all the Priviledges and Liberties of the people, take occasion to secure themselves, and settle us, with much more reason, by the *Power of the Sword*?" (848–9).

By the time that Milton came to write Book 6 of *Paradise Lost*, he seems to have realized the need to unsay his previous misreading of the sword as the revealed law of God. "Lead forth to Battel these my Sons / Invincible," God declares without a flicker of a smile at his equivocal term "Invincible," a word that, if not predicting victory for the loyalists, surely hides the impending humiliation of "Angel on Arch-Angel rowl'd" (6.594). And yet one of the more painful features of the loyalists' predicament in this scene is Satan's savage mockery of their helpless innocence, just before iron balls are belched from the mouth of the cannons, and "down they fell / By thousands" (6.593–4). The devil's cynical perversion of the word in his punning pretence of peaceful motives is an intellectual humiliation as galling as the physical humiliation of being trapped in medieval suits of armour that "help'd thir harm, crush't in and bruis'd / Into their substance pent" (6.656–7). Here, we must recall, was that obvious affront to reason that so offended Dr Johnson, a "confusion of matter with spirit" that Arnold Stein could only explain as "an extended metaphor." To give the devil his due, he must, Stein says, be punished in the form in which he sinned: in Heaven, he sinned against spirit and reason by material means; so we witness his punishment in terms of his descent "down the scale of being" from angels to "a herd of animals" to plants that "have been *rooted* out" (272). But the armour is medieval, an indication, at the very least, of laughably outmoded thinking.

While Stein reads the laughter in Book 6 as "symbolic action" (269) – a *flyting* contest between God and Satan to define the truth of reality and the reality of truth (268) – he ignores the literal effect of ridicule on the loyal angels. "O Friends," Satan taunts,

> why come not on these Victors proud … when wee,
> To entertain them fair with open Front
> And Brest, (what could we more?) propounded terms
> Of composition, strait they chang'd thir minds,
> Flew off, and into strange vagaries fell,
> As they would dance, yet for a dance they seemd
> Somewhat extravagant and wilde, perhaps
> For joy of offerd peace: but I suppose
> If our proposals once again were heard
> We should compel them to a quick result. (6.609–19)

The problem can be called the uncomprehending nature of innocence – the goodness, we might say, of goodness – that leaves the virtuous angels angry and ashamed. For their "open Front" has made them "stupidly good," and truly vulnerable to "terms of weight, / Of hard contents," as Belial jests in "gamesom mood" (6.620), that, "full of force," have "stumbl'd many" (6.621–4). In a word, the angels are humiliated by their literal failure of "intelligence" as much as by their clunky kit. Ethereal spirits are brought down to "earth" by armour designed to make them look ridiculous. So what was it all for? To teach them, like their God, to laugh at themselves, perhaps? And yet how hard that is to do.

The scornful laughter of the foe makes it harder still. The shouts of laughter from the foe are every bit as trying to their sense of justice and decency as they once were to Richard Overton, haled before the House of Lords in 1646 where, with great courage, he had expostulated: "[L]et me have justice, or let me perish. I'le not sell my birth-right for a messe of pottage, for Justice is my naturall right, my heirdome, my inheritance by lineall descent from the loins of *Adam*, and so to all the sons of men as their proper right without respect of persons."[30] Later, Overton protested, "*Gentlemen, I am resolved not to make answer to any Interrogatories that shall infringe my own property, right or freedome in particular, or the rights, freedoms and properties of the Nation in generall.* Whereat the whole House of Lords in a most scornfull deriding manner laughed at me, as I then conceived on purpose to dash me out of countenance, and so to hinder or weaken my just defense."[31] Overton is hardly mistaken in his judgment of the Lords: "*Gentlemen, it doth not become you thus to deride me that am a prisoner at your Barre*" (18). Lords are lordly in their derision *because* their might to mock what they call right is thereby confirmed. So "little brisk Levelling Dick" is left to conclude, "Thus we may see to what a heavie case, and sad condition, all of us are come; that a free Commoners challenging of his own properties, rights and freedoms, must be had in derision thus openly amongst the House of Lords" (18). Caught in the callous grip of social hierarchs, Overton can do little more than suffer the Lords' power — before publishing another pamphlet in the larger war of words where it is "as if the Seat of Justice were a place of derision, mockerie, laughter and sports; and not of Judgement, gravitie and justice" (18). Just as surely as so many Renaissance poets had done before him, Overton follows the traditional script by attempting to redefine the terms of the combat.

Yet the good angels do not suffer nearly so long as the Leveller pamphleteer was forced to do, since Justice in Heaven is not justice withheld. Still, it is apparent from the very first burst of fire from the cannon that the angelic hierarchy has been designed to be "Level'd" (6.591). For the war in

Heaven is more a test of faith,[32] it seems, than it is a military contest. And Michael passes with flying colours, refusing to presume on his own might in the contest with Satan while humbly affirming that "Heav'n casts thee out" (6.272), and warning Satan to repent, "Ere this avenging Sword begin thy doome, / Or som more sudden vengeance wing'd from God / Precipitate thee with augmented paine" (6.278–80).

From this, Revard draws a far-reaching conclusion about the first two days of battle:

> Milton makes his angels take on the demeanor of classical warriors in order to discredit the ethic of heroic battle. Whereas his predecessors built their wars in Heaven with the bricks of Homer and Virgil, Ariosto and Tasso, sure that in so doing they were giving literary quality to their celestial poems, Milton is not so uncritical … He allows the angels to raise heroic battle in Heaven not so that he may have the opportunity to create a splendid tableau of arms and armor, but to demonstrate what is essentially perverse in the ethic of typical heroic poems. (197)

Still, the poet's reason for doing so is more immediate than the arrogance of the heroic tradition, the vaunting boasts and scornful pride so alien to the Christian ethic of humility. For one thing, mortality rates in the English civil wars exceeded those of the Great War – a conflict we mistakenly regard today as the worst to that point. For another, it was clear by 1653 that the sword of the Lord Protector had little to do with *Jure Divino*. And after 1660, "all this wast of wealth, and loss of blood"[33] had clearly been for naught.

In this changed political context, Milton had reason to regret his earlier *Jure Divino* view of the sword. For the lofty contempt he displays in Book 6 for "Might" as proof of "Right" is shared by the deity himself, as Arnold Stein shrewdly points out. As God declares at the end of the second day of battle, "Warr wearied hath perform'd what Warr can do, / And to disorder'd rage let loose the reines" (6.695–6). From this judgment, as well as from the outcome of events, Revard concludes that, "The war waged before us in *Paradise Lost* is Satanic in essence. Rebel and loyal angel alike – even though the loyal are upheld by truth and justice – subscribe to the classical ethic of war making wherein skill and strength determine victory" (196–7). But it is also true that "the loyal angels must learn how vain is their trust in material arms and the glory of material warfare. They are not permitted the glory of sword or spear. They throw down their arms, and in this combat they never resume them" (190–1). At the same time, Revard's evocative phrase, "Satanic in essence," unwittingly exposes the "Father of lies" as the source of the heroic tradition's endless contradictions; for the trouble with *essence* and *archetype* is that they really are *ahistorical* categories. And in view of the tragedy of mid-seventeenth-century British history – all those deaths and mutilations rendered null and void at the Restoration – it would be rather more surprising had Milton *not* rewritten *force* as farce, or sought to revise the literary tradition in the unflattering light of recent history.

So why doesn't Raphael get it? As the archangel narrates the descent of the celestial war into chaos, and his own and other loyalists' descent on the "scale of being" to the level of the mythic monsters Briareos and the Fifty-Headed, Hundred-Armed giants in Hesiod, his tone "rises" nearly to a breathless rapture: "Forthwith (behold the excellence, the power / Which God hath in his mighty Angels plac'd) / Thir Arms away they threw, … Amaze, / Be sure, and terrour seis'd the rebel Host" (6.637–9, 646–7). Amaze, be sure, seizes any reader who asks whether Raphael understands what he has just said about "mighty Angels." Still, on closer examination, one catches an aesthetic regression in Raphael's diction that is almost as archaic as the situation he describes. Accommodating Adam's understanding to the vastness of Heaven, for example, he speaks of battlefields which are "Tenfold the length of this terrene" (6.78). Three lines later, the foe's line is "stretcht / In battailous aspect," before he depicts the rebels' motives in terms of an obsolete verb: "they weend / That self same day by fight, or by surprize / To win the Mount of God" (6.86–8). By this time, terms like "terrene," "battailous," and "weend" were long since out of date. While Raphael's outmoded diction could be nothing more than a "valiant" attempt to "heighten" the style to suit the matter, what his *matter* actually envisions is cultural regression to the Neolithic Age; the outmoded thoughtways appear to belong rather to Raphael's narrative than to the epic narrator, who simply provides a framing narrative for the archangel.

That this cultural regression is proper to the character, not the poet, is beyond dispute by the end of Raphael's account of the duel between Michael and Satan over "The strife which thou call'st evil, but wee," as Satan says, "style / The strife of Glorie" (6.289–90). At which point, Raphael's style lapses back into the Norman French of medieval epic – "They ended parle" (6.296) – effectively pulling rank on his auditors and proclaiming his ethnocentric pride in the "heroic" grandeur of the action: "[F]or who, though with the tongue / Of Angels, can relate, or to what things / Liken on Earth conspicuous, that may lift / Human imagination to such highth / Of Godlike Power: for likest Gods they seemd" (6.297–301). Despite the magnificence of the simile likening Michael and Satan to "Two Planets rushing from aspect maligne / Of fiercest opposition in mid Skie" (6.313–14), there can be no doubt of the angel's chauvinism in his portrait of the war, or of his naive view of the "Godlike Power" of angels, given that he likens *both* Michael and Satan to "Gods." It is as if Raphael were already anticipating Satan's ethnocentric pride in his temptation of Eve, "And what are Gods that Man may not become / As they" (9.716–17).

Such magniloquence does more than just hint at Raphael's comically limited view of things. Firstly, he lets slip his own lust for fame in what, says Satan, "wee style the strife of Glorie" (the "wee" including the angel Raphael as well). Publicly, he professes the opposite: "I might relate of thousands, and thir names / Eternize here on Earth; but those elect / Angels contented with thir fame in Heav'n / Seek not the praise of men" (6.373–6). But he seems to forget that, a mere ten lines earlier, he had recounted how, "On each wing / *Uriel* and *Raphael* his vaunting foe, / Though huge, and in a Rock of Diamond Armd, / Vanquish'd *Adramelec*, and *Asmadai*" (6.362–5). Though "thousands" are worthy to be named on Earth, but are passed over in silence, Raphael still manages to name himself before bringing down the curtain on the deeds of others. His inflated sense of self is thus deflated for the reader, if not for his paradisal auditors, by this inept display of subjectivity that pretends to pass for objectivity. Raphael's braggadocio is no worse, though it is certainly no better, than the heroic posture "Of *Moloc* furious King, who him defi'd, / And at his Chariots wheeles to drag him bound / Threatn'd, … but anon / Down clov'n to the waste, with shatterd Armes / And uncouth paine fled bellowing" (6.357–62.) In that instant, the reader can only laugh at the long-delayed joke dating from Moloch's furious insistence in the Stygian Council on headlong assault against Heaven: "More destroy'd then thus," he says with chagrin, "We should be quite abolisht and expire" (2.92–3). Now his death wish is intelligible; try as he might, Moloch will never outrun that image of himself, "Down clov'n to the waste," bellowing in pain and rage like a neutered bull. By its calculated delay, the comedy is delightfully understated, much as Raphael's "election" to the warrior's hall of fame appears to pass for "objectivity."

While the fallibility of an "heroic" narrator is disconcerting – given the terms of his mission to the Garden – Milton warns us to take the teachings of the angel with a grain of salt, since the next corrective to his perspective comes from the Son of God. On the third day of the battle, the Son arrives to tell the loyalists to "stand onely and behold" (6.810). Satan's fight, like that of all the rebels, he declares, is not with the loyalists but with him. "Therefore to mee thir doom," he declares, the Father "hath assigned; / That they may have thir wish, to trie with mee / In Battel which the stronger proves, ... since by strength / They measure all, of other excellence / Not emulous" (6.817–22). Yet Raphael never stops to ask, What did he just say? Is "strength" not a true "measure" of "excellence"? Are these brave feats not proof of our "Godlike Power"? What "other excellence" are we supposed to emulate? Instead, Raphael fails to see that the new "philosophy" calls in doubt both the tenor and the vehicle of his metaphors. And the irony is even greater for his pretence of simply reporting what he has heard, for getting the "facts" right while failing to grasp their import. As the narrator of a "heroic" epic within an epic, Raphael[34] likely recalls no one so much as Milton himself in his own efforts in *Defensio* and *Defensio Secunda* to construct a prose epic,[35] but where he tends to glorify his own role as teller quite as much as he praises the achievements of his countrymen. As Blair Worden describes his epic writing in prose, "In *Defensio Secunda* he would glory in the tribute that had been accorded him when he, and he alone, was selected by the state to answer Salmasius. For at least until the composition of *Paradise Lost*, the writing of *Defensio* was in his own mind the central event of his life."[36]

At the same time, Raphael has reason to be confused by the number and nature of the conflicting signals given by no less a personage than the Father in his commission to the Son. For, at the end of the second day of battle, Raphael has to admit that all "Had gon to wrack, with ruin overspred, / Had not th' Almightie Father where he sits ... / Consulting on the sum of things, foreseen / This tumult, and permitted all, advis'd" (6.670–4). What follows sounds like a public-service announcement more than the former "Imperial summons" (5.584) of the Exaltation Scene. While the Son's commisioning as a "warrior" takes place without fanfare or evident drama, it does take the form of a public speech, where God, in the presence of the loyal angels, announces his intent "To honour his Anointed Son aveng'd / Upon his enemies, and to declare / All power on him transferr'd" (6.676–8). But the Father doesn't just proclaim, "For thee I have ordain'd it, and thus farr / Have sufferd, that the Glorie may be thine / Of ending this great Warr" (6.700–2); he pointedly adds, "since none but Thou / Can end it" (6.702–3).

Here, God seems to follow the classical script of singling out a solo champion to challenge the foe. Were the analogy to hold, the Son would be another Achilleus setting out to put to flight a second Hektor (if he were not a primordial Samson challenging another Harapha). God even specifies a necessary transfer of *might* – a monopoly on force – as a seeming prerequisite to political authority, declaring that "Into thee such Vertue and Grace / Immense I have transfus'd, that all may know / In Heav'n and Hell thy Power above compare" (6.703–5). In a nutshell, it is God who appears to validate the Greek or Roman conjunction of "Vertue" (*virtus*) with "Power above compare."[37]

If the point, like that of the military stalemate, were merely "To manifest thee worthiest to be Heir / Of all things, to be Heir and to be King / By Sacred Unction, thy deserved right" (6.707–9), then Raphael could be forgiven his confusion about *might* and *right*.[38] For God *did* say, "Go then thou Mightiest in thy Fathers might, / Ascend my Chariot" (6.710–11). And it seems obvious that we are about to witness an actual ceremony of succession in the ancient ritual of kingship. Stella Revard notes how, "When the Son comes" to the battlefield "in book 6, it is to manifest that union proclaimed earlier by the Father and now to be brought to realization. In mounting the chariot, the Son initiates union" (258). The problem, of course, is that this conception of kingship differs little from that of a royalist like Sir Robert Filmer, who, in *Patriarcha* (ca. 1648), had made the government of Adam and the biblical patriarchs over their families the "natural" model for Kings as "fathers" to their political family.[39] Doubtless, it was the duty of fathers to bring their families into closer union but, as Milton had scolded Salmasius, "Fathers and kings are very different things: Our fathers begot us, but our kings did not, and it is we, rather, who created the king. It is nature which gave the people fathers, and the people who gave themselves a king; the people therefore do not exist for the king, but the king for the people."[40] And it is this Salmasian view of kingship that ultimately vitiates Revard's otherwise sensible reading of the war in Heaven, since she makes a needless concession in her introduction that Milton "supported rebellion" in "his own life … and was on the side of the revolutionaries … but in literature he seems to have turned 'royalist' and upheld King Messiah and the divine right" (25–6).[41] Ultimately, this is to accept Raphael's problematical narrative as the "authorized version" and to miss the crucial distinctions between might and right which emerge in the emplotment of Book 6.

In his acceptance of God's commission, the Son begins, "O Father, O Supream of heavn'ly Thrones" (6.723), but then moves to the Pauline conception[42] of a deity who is more properly described as being "All in All" (6.732). The Son sounds a lot like William Walwyn in *Tyranipocrit* discriminating between a hypocritical "white devil" and a loving God who seeks only the "joyning of two free-wils in one."[43] More clearly still, the Son anticipates his later political choices, and so develops his moral character in the direction of Book 3 in Heaven (of which he can have no foreknowledge): "Scepter and Power, thy giving, I assume, / And gladlier shall resign, when in the end / Thou shalt be All in All, and I in thee / For ever, and in mee all whom thou lov'st"[44] (6.730–3). Perhaps the most interesting thing about the renunciation scene that we are witnessing for a second time – from two distinct points, the time of reading as well as the time of action – is that the Son is tested almost as sorely here as he will be in the colloquy in Heaven. For a terrible temptation lurks in this scene, anticipating the more explicit gospel temptation of the kingdoms, where, to possess the kingdoms of this world, Jesus need only bow to Satan.[45] Here is a moral danger that could also lead to failure in the future colloquy: were he to take the word of the Father – "Go then thou Mightiest in thy Fathers might" – as literally as Raphael appears to do, he might later claim exemption from death on the ground that God said he was the "heir of all my might." In that case, he need not endure weakness or death, or be obliged to give his life for the sins of others. That he does accept his Father's might, however, as being neither his nor anything more than a temporary power, suggests that he sees himself in all this as really no more than an instrument of the divine might. And it is precisely this selfless assumption of his Father's power which makes him a true model for "kingship" on earth,[46] following the uncommon coronation "script," which amounts to no more than a temporary assumption and imminent abdication of power.

So when the Son rides out in "the Chariot of Paternal Deitie" (6.750), only God knows that the vehicle – "It self instinct with Spirit" (6.752) – signifies much more than the aweful might of the "divine glory."[47] As Revard suggests, "[W]e should keep in mind that the vision of the chariot symbolized for the seventeenth-century mind the key to the divinity of Christ. So, when the Son mounts the chariot, he reveals to his enemies and friends alike the meaning of his divinity" (259). Just as surely, we need to keep in mind that this vehicle does *not* manifest the glory of Christ the King but that of God the Father. In the context of "gladier shall resign," the Son's act of ascending the chariot instantiates the awful weakness of the incarnate Son that we witnessed in Book 3. While the Son has, or could have, no inkling of the Incarnation upon mounting his Father's chariot, he still shows his genuine excellence (*areté* as moral worth) in the present trial: "Not my will but thine be done," the reader murmurs, knowing more at this point than either Raphael or the Son understands about the trajectory of his "ascent." All the Son can be sure of for the moment is that he resigns his will to the will of his Father, "Whom to obey is happiness entire" (6.741). By his very nature he embodies, as much as illustrates, the "divine" love, that desire of "joyning two free-wils in one" that has, and will continue to, inform the ethic of testing. Even in this scene of Judgment, the Son empties himself out, as if to make himself weak in order to express God's strength.

In this trope of "strength out of weakness,"[48] we should anticipate a type of the future Leveller Jesus we meet in *Paradise Regain'd*. Yet for now we need look no further than the Son's present ascent to the chariot of the Father, a vehicle in which he rides without infantry, without artillery or other luggage of war, to "infix … Plagues" in "thir Soules" (6.837–8). And the real "terrour" of "His countenance" (6.824–5) is derived from a perfect innocence that is willing to be given over to death in order to preserve his Father's justice and goodness. More awful still is the revelation of his moral excellence, through which the divine righteousness appears with terrible clarity. For in the Son's "countenance," the fallen angels may see, if not comprehend, the nature of that perfect obedience by which they are now judged and found wanting. Is it any wonder that they are struck dumb by the "terrour" of "Right"? Or that "they astonisht all resistance lost, / All courage; down thir idle weapons drop'd" (6.838–9)? For the "terrour" of the Son's glance is nothing more, and nothing less, than the "Might" of his selfless absorption into the divine will.

Here, in what may be called the "Gideon syndrome" of God's ways, there appears the pattern of the Few sent out against the Many in a recurring story of the humblest of God's servants, like Gideon, Jephtha, or David the shepherd lad,[49] who manifest the righteous judgments of God by their very weakness. In this humble image of Right – of a righteous hero sent out to confront the Mighty who are without peer in strength and number – there lurks an important, if implicit, contrast between the war in Heaven and the recent wars in England. For, soon after Cromwell's final victory at Worcester, writes Politicus,

> It was a loud *Declaration* from Heaven at *Naisby*, when by a despised Company it pleased God to decide the controversie … But in the year 1648. he spake louder, in the midst of all those Alarms

> and *Insurrections*, when by a small handfull he overthrew *Hamilton's* numerous proud Army in *Lancashire*, re-setled the whole Nation, and brought the *King* to the Bar and Block of Justice … but especially at *Dunbarr*, where by a wearied and sick handfull of men, coop't in a nook of Land … & encompass't with extreme disadvantages, hee was pleased so visibly to make bare his own Arm.[50]

What could still be construed in 1651 as a story of righteous humility in the cause of the English republic had turned by 1667 into a devastating critique of the pride of the mighty, since the difference between Cromwell's "divine" victories at Naseby, Dunbar, and Worcester, and that of the Son taking the field in the war in Heaven, is the simple truth, so obvious but also so painful in retrospect, that the former had not resigned his power once the issue was decided, but strove rather to centre and concentrate it until it was reborn, by another name, as the old discredited form of "kingship."

So what is the point of the war in Heaven? For one thing, to discredit the classical heroic ethos on earth as in Heaven, leaving it without reason or excuse; for another, to level the distinction between spirit and matter, thereby freeing us to envision a God who also comprehends matter; for a third, to offer a larger model of kingship as the temporary assumption and renunciation of power, thus undercutting the usual model of hereditary right; for a fourth, to prepare us to accept a new type of *areté* or *virtus*, the godly ethic of strength out of weakness, and to initiate a movement from "kingly" to domestic – even a "feminized" – heroism; and last, though not least, to teach us the fallibility of all created beings, even of heaven-sent teachers, thus freeing us to test our own perceptions against the muddled perspectives of "authority," and so to be immersed in a "poetics of choice."

After all is said and done, Raphael honours the terms of his commission to relay the substance of his message. Yet God has left it up to him – "and such discourse bring on, / As may advise him of his happie state" (5.233–4) – to choose what else the human couple ought to know. And here, the story turns out to be the unreliable narrator himself, given the confusions of his conflicted attitudes to war and his contradictory signals about excellence.[51] For the moment, we need only notice that an archangel with the best of intentions reports the Son's judgment of the fallen angels' values – "since by strength / They measure all, of other excellence / Not emulous" – without realizing how he now compounds that error by clinging to an outmoded notion of *virtus*. Incredibly, at the end of his account of the war in Heaven, the "sociable Spirit" turns away from a woman who welcomes him into her home to advise her husband to "warne / Thy weaker" (6.908–9).

Once again, Raphael fails to realize that he has implicitly identified the "weak" woman with the Son, although he expressly affiliates her to Satan. But it is a fitting end to the frame narrator's story of "the winged Hierarch," who shows himself to be oddly confused about changing ideas of degree and excellence in Heaven. For the archangel has yet to grasp another principle of virtue on display in his narrative of the war – not the old species of *virtus*, but the divine excellence of "strength out of weaknesse."

· 9 ·

"And Thence Diffuse His Good"

GOD AND MATTER

"THE CONFUSION OF SPIRIT AND MATTER which pervades the whole narration" of the war in heaven exasperated Samuel Johnson more for its aesthetic "incongruity" than for its suspect theology. Had Johnson realized the truly heretical implications of Milton's materialism, he would not have stopped at demoting "the book in which it is related" to the status of a "favourite of children."[1] Two centuries later, Arnold Stein tried to take the sting out of Johnson's strictures by turning the war into "An Extended Metaphor";[2] he totally ignored Milton's materialism in order to ridicule Satan's "materialistic concept of might" (25). For Stein, the episode is a divine comedy, its "symbolic action" based on the "philosophical" view "that regards order as possible only through discipline and therefore regards chaos as the logical alternative to discipline" (35).

Playing the "chaos" card is not unique to Stein, of course. It has long been a ploy of orthodox critics to downplay, if not to disregard entirely, Milton's materialist heresy, since his chaos too much resembles a part of the divine substance, even if it is a fraction of God's being. If matter were instinct with divine life and goodness, it would possess godly attributes of goodness, will, and reason even after its liberation from the Creator's substance. This is one of the key premises of what John Rogers terms "radical science" in Milton's era: "To infuse matter with a rational spirit or motivating force was not only to render unnecessary an omnipotent and directly controlling God. This monistic vitalism could offer as well the evidence, at the very basis of the micro-universe of material parts, for the efficient and harmonious dynamics of an organization – any organization – operating outside the immediate superintendence of a single, centralizing power."[3]

One crucial effect of a decentring tendency in vitalist materialism is that, contrary to "the centralizing logics of Calvinism" and of Hobbesian mechanism, it "secured into the fabric of the physical world a general scheme of individual agency and decentralized organization that we can identify as a protoliberalism" (Rogers, 12). Milton even comes to regard agency itself in *Paradise Lost* as being radically feminine, God declaring of the fallen couple that "no Decree of mine … with lightest moment of impulse" touched "His free Will, to her own inclining left" (10.43–6). Since the syntax of "His free Will" ends in "*her* own inclining left," *will* is then gendered feminine. But if matter – left in the will of its new possessor – is *ontologically* feminine, it becomes so for Milton only by being freed from the will of the "Father." The "symbolic action" of marriage in the poem may thus be described as the deity's desire – in concert with the creature's longing – to be united by "a joyning of two free-wils in one."[4] Will, not reason, is the decisive faculty.

But the question of "feminine" agency in relation to the "symbolic action" of marriage is better left for the next chapter; first, we need to explore Milton's exceptional rendering of creation, tracing the deity's identity with chaos and the liberalizing course of his creation as a key Leveller signature in the poem. The protoliberal politics of Milton's material God achieve the formal logic of a syllogism where: 1) a good God chooses to share his divine substance; 2) this "God-stuff" guarantees the primal goodness of what is liberated from, as well as given form by, the deity; 3) therefore, the primal goodness of matter "secures the natural liberty" of all individuals who possess it.[5] In Milton's vitalist philosophy of matter, we thus witness a logical extension of divine law into natural law.[6]

John P. Rumrich says that, "although Milton scholars generally admit that Milton's metaphysics were monistic and that he considered matter the basis of all good, most of us are still suspicious of chaos as presented in *Paradise Lost*."[7] For much of the twentieth century, in fact, "Milton scholars have argued that the allegorical character of Chaos in *Paradise Lost* represents either a neutral, passive condition or an ominous and evil state of being … A.B. Chambers, for example, insisted in a classic essay that 'Chaos and Night are the enemies of God,' 'opposed to him only less than hell itself'" (118–19). This, at least, is the impression left by the figures of "Chaos and old Night," whom Satan meets on his voyage to earth; but first impressions are meant to be deceiving in *Paradise Lost*, whether in Hell or Heaven or Eden.

Since the narrator remarks early on that "chaos is 'the Womb of Nature'" (*PL* 2.911, 916), "containing the 'dark materials' necessary for divine creation" (Rumrich, 119), it may be worth asking whether Milton's allegory of chaos anticipates our modern understanding of it through quantum mechanics, where it now looks like "order's precursor and partner rather than its opposite."[8]

Assuming Chaos to be a personified enemy of God is clearly fatal to Milton's theodicy. For, "If a disposition toward destruction were latent in the very substance of existence," Rumrich cautions, then "the attempt to justify the Creator's ways toward his creatures would be absurd." Each time that orthodox critics depict Milton's chaos as being "either passively ominous or actively evil," they "not only acquiesce in a narrative impression left by an allegory that occurs early in the epic; they also reproduce – as Milton himself does not – traditional, Western, philosophical and religious attitudes concerning matter" (119). Thus Maurice Kelley sums up this heritage of philosophical dualism as making God and matter into "two distinct, self-existent, and co-eternal principles, with creation resulting from God's working his will on matter." But while Platonic Idealism might have "relieved God of the charge of being the origin of evil," Kelley cautions, "it did so by impugning his attributes of infinity and omnipotence."[9] Seven centuries after Plato and Aristotle, the Manichaeans (ca. 3d to 4th century CE) revitalized this ancient doctrine of pre-existent matter as being eternally opposed to God, thus denying his "goodness and his greatness both," to borrow a phrase from the Son in Book 3. But Augustine's conversion from Manichaean dualism to Christian "monism" tended to obscure the continuing problem of matter. While his theology now rendered matter "good" by having God create it out of nothing (*creatio ex nihilo*), matter for Augustine was ontologically deficient, always a half-step away from lapsing into original nothingness (*naught* being the very root of *naughtiness*). As Rumrich sums up this problem, "Matter was thus deemed acceptable, but only if kept in its place, that of passive stuff created from nothing and ordered into shape by God."

In consequence, Augustinian politics were inherently authoritarian, since matter, like human flesh, was unruly, requiring discipline. As Rumrich claims, Augustinian theology was suited to the "patriarchal government of church and state: its ready resort to coercive force, and suppression of the lower classes generally ... Such doctrine and discipline remained a commonplace of political theory throughout the English Renaissance" (119–20).

For instance, in Hobbes's *Leviathan* (1651), the basis of the social contract was the coercive force required to maintain order in an anarchic state of nature. For Hobbes, an absolute sovereign's rule over the unruly masses was akin to the Christian idea of God taming Chaos. In spite of charges of "atheistic materialism" levied against him, Hobbes's view that "there is nothing in the universe but matter in motion"[10] was merely a logical extension of the occidental prejudice against matter – dating back to the *Enuma elish* in Babylon and to Hesiod's *Theogony* in ancient Greece. Chaos was an existential threat to universal order, particularly the divine "order of kingship." The Babylonian Marduk, for instance, "the heroic creator in the *Enuma elish* … kills and butchers the maternal chaos deity, Tiamat, and builds creation out of the pieces,"[11] thus grounding earthly kingship in the patriarchal order of divine hierarchy. In a similar way, "Hobbes in *Leviathan* invokes 'the first Chaos of Violence, and Civill Warre' to deplore the consequences of rebellion against the divinely sanctioned monarch."[12] Strangely, Hobbes's "atheist materialism" is quite orthodox, at least in terms of its assumptions about an "evil" Chaos that must be suppressed and controlled by divine force.

By contrast, the Leveller view of nature is diametrically opposed to the Western notion of an elemental evil in matter, whether "evil" be conceived in dualist terms as the eternal foe of God, or else in terms of a moral dualism in which matter, suffering from ontological deficiency, is forever on the verge of lapsing into original disorder, where "chaos," as Othello puts it, "is come again." The corollary of this Leveller faith in the goodness of matter is their rejection of the dualist bogey of a threatening chaos. Nicholas McDowell argues in a notable recent essay that Richard Overton's monist materialism[13] is what guarantees the Leveller notion of *natural* rights.[14] McDowell claims that his "*Mans Mortalitie* has been most often discussed in terms of its possible influence on the development of Milton's monism and mortalism as imaginatively represented in *Paradise Lost* and bluntly stated in the *De Doctrina Christiana*" (62); but the mortalist-materialist heresy is more obviously a metaphysical basis as well for natural liberty in *Paradise Lost*.

While historians have partitioned Overton's work into its pre-Leveller and Leveller phases, McDowell insists that there is a "more immediate relationship between the philosophical and theological principles of the tract and the Leveller ideas espoused by Overton in the mid-1640s" (63). His recognition of a fundamental link between Overton's metaphysics and his Leveller politics is helpful for a number of reasons. First, Overton argues from natural philosophy, scripture, and reason that the soul cannot exist apart from the body; ipso facto, there was never a fall *into* matter: "If it be said," Overton counters the orthodox belief that "the soule comes pure from God, and it is the body that corrupteth it. I Answer, that this to excuse God one way, makes him like the tyrant *Mezentius*,[15] that bound living men to dead bodyes, till the putrefaction and corruption of the stincking corps had kild them."[16] Since God could not be both tyrannical and good, the body must then be good, coming as it does from the hand of a material God as a body infused with spirit and a spirit incorporated with body.

Secondly, God himself "is not distinct from the material universe,"[17] since "there is no *beyond*, without it *place* or *being* is impossible"; then "everie place must be materiall, for *non datur vacuum*, and everie matter must imply creation, else it could not be" (33). Anticipating an obvious objection that the soul's abolition also abolishes heaven – so where did Christ go after his bodily resurrection? – Overton denies that it was to some heavenly dimension of spirit. Rather, he who called himself "the light of the world" must still "be in the most excellent glorious and heavenly part thereof, which is the SUN, the most excellent peece of the whole Creation, the Epitome of Gods power, conveyour of life, groweth, strength, and being to everie Creature under Heaven" (33). Simple logical consistency demands as much, for "Reason tels us, that he must be within the compasse of the Creation." Overton's insistence, however, that there is "no beyond" does not at all deny the existence of God; for if "everie place must be materiall," so must every living form be material. God has a body, though he never describes the "'corporeality' of God." Rather, "the claim that '*being* is impossible' outside matter implies that God is not distinct from the material universe. It would seem that for Overton, as for his fellow thnetopsychists Milton and Hobbes, 'all that exists is body'"[18] (McDowell, 65).

"[A]s an implication of his teaching," Hobbes realized "that he must either deny that God exists," as Edwin Curley says, "or affirm that God is a body."[19] Were he to say that God "is identical with the totality of bodies," he then risked "incurring charges of atheism (xxxi, 15)"; conversely, were he to argue, that God "is one body among others," he would "seem to say that he is finite, which again may lead to charges of atheism (xxxi, 18)."[20] But, unlike Overton, the exiled Hobbes was not subject to the draconian measures of the Blasphemy Act of 1650 "against several Atheistical, Blasphemous and Execrable Opinions, derogatory to the honor of God, and destructive to humane Society." Anyone convicted of a first offence would "suffer six moneths imprisonment without Bail … on the Oath of two or more

Witnesses." Publishing "Atheistical, Blasphemous or Execrable Opinions," as Overton had done six years earlier, would be punished by "Banishment ... out of the Commonwealth of England, and all the Dominions thereof."[21]

In this political climate Milton was no more likely than Overton to say that God had a "body," not even in a private book of systematic theology that seems to have been in fair draft at the beginning of the 1660s.[22] Rather, in Book I, Chapter vii, "Of the Creation," Milton says that both scripture and reason[23] teach that God is "the perfect and absolute cause of all things." Weighing Augustine's doctrine of *creatio ex nihilo* against Platonic dualism, let alone a Manichaean God at war with pre-existent matter, Milton assumes that "matter must either have always existed, independently of God, or else originated from God at some point in time. That matter should have always existed independently of God is inconceivable." Like Augustine, he is certainly no Manichaean, believing in a material world independent of God. "But if matter did not exist from eternity, it is not very easy to see where it originally came from. There remains only this solution, especially if we allow ourselves to be guided by scripture, namely, that all things came from God."[24] But, as Nigel Smith points out, "[T]o create out of himself means logically that everything that exists was originally part of God, the matter of God, so to speak."[25] So, in no uncertain terms, everything in the universe derives from "the matter of God."

Conversely, nothing proceeds from nothing. Or, as Maurice Kelley explains, "nothing" is no "cause" at all, least of all for Milton. For he insists that "not even God's virtue and efficiency could have produced bodies out of nothing (as it is vulgarly believed he did) unless there had been some bodily force in his own substance, for no one can give something he has not got."[26] And, lest we doubt what is really meant by "some bodily force in his own substance," Milton glosses it thusly: "since all things come not only from God but *out of God*, no created thing can be utterly annihilated."[27] It is the closest that he comes in his theology to a concrete image of God's material "body," "out of" whose "substance" "all things come." Still, his adherence to the older theory of *creatio ex deo*[28] allows him to avoid "the covert dualism" of the doctrine of *creatio ex nihilo* "that shifts to nothing the onus that overt dualism lays on matter."[29] Just as significantly, it permits him to skirt the "Atheistical" opinion of Hobbes that God must be an agglomeration of bodies or else a finite instance of a body. For Milton's distinctive expression "*out of God*" redefines God as being simultaneously within and without the creation.

As for overcoming the "covert dualism" of *creatio ex nihilo*, Milton's monistic theory of *creatio ex Deo* hinges on "a demonstration of supreme power and supreme goodness," inasmuch as "such heterogeneous, multiform and inexhaustible virtue should exist in God, and exist substantially," because it comes "out of God." For these reasons, "It is, I say, a demonstration of God's supreme power and goodness that he should not shut up this heterogeneous and substantial virtue within himself, but should disperse, propagate and extend it as far as, and in whatever way, he wills" (*CPW* 6: 308). This is where his monism now begins more meaningfully to overlap with Overton's materialism: "For this original matter was not an evil thing," Milton insists, "nor to be thought of as worthless: it was good, and it contained the seeds of all subsequent good. It was a substance, and could only have been derived from the source of all substance. It was in a confused and disordered state at first, but afterwards God made it ordered and beautiful."

If the original matter that came from God "was good, and it contained the seeds of all subsequent good," then a crucial question arises: "How can anything sinful have come, if I may so speak, from God?" (*CPW* 6: 309).[30] Milton's answer is fairly close to Overton's notion of "an individuall property by nature"[31] premised on "the spiritual autonomy of matter."[32] For it is ultimately mankind's spiritualized body, freed from the "body" of God, as Overton sees it, which is the *natural* source of liberty. In essence, Overton's version of Adam's creation assumes that "The *Forme* is so in the *Matter*, and the *Matter* so in the *Forme*; as there-by, and not else, is an *Existence*, or *Humane Entitie*: And their *Being* is in this *Union*, and their *Union* is in this *Being*" (Overton, 13). The same idea underlies Milton's claim that, "When matter or form has gone out from God and become the property of another, what is there to prevent its being infected and polluted, since it is now in a mutable state, by the calculations of the devil or of man, calculations which proceed from these creatures themselves" (*CPW* 6: 309). In agreement with Overton, he then adds, "But, you will say, body cannot emanate from spirit. My reply is, much less can it emanate from nothing. Moreover spirit, being the more excellent substance, virtually, as they say, and eminently contains within itself what is clearly the inferior substance; in the same way as the spiritual and rational faculty contains the corporeal, that is, the sentient and vegetative faculty" (ibid.). Spirit is no more than body's container – not body the container of spirit – by which substance itself is vitalized; though spirit may possess a higher "degree of substance" than the body, there persists between them an "identity of essence"[33] that animates the "whole man." Like Overton's philosophy of vitalized matter, Milton's "animist materialism"[34] affirms the goodness of matter[35] for which its possessor is responsible. An attendant, if implicit, refusal of the hierarchy of soul and body thus entails a rejection of other social hierarchies based on it, such as male/female and ruler/ruled.

As his philosophical foundation in 1644, Overton's vitalism would be further revitalized two years later by Lilburne's arrest, and transformed into political polemic in *An Arrow Against All Tyrants* (10 October 1646). "To every Individuall in nature," Overton now writes, "is given an individuall property by nature, not to be invaded or usurped by any: for every one as he is himselfe, so he hath a selfe propriety, else could he not be himselfe" (*Arrow*, 3). Yet this "individuall property by nature" has nothing to do with the "possessive individualism"[36] of another historiography, one disinclined to value metaphysical and theological arguments. For the abstract idea of *natural* rights is now underwritten by a claim that "we are delivered of God by the hand of nature into this world, every one with a naturall, innate freedome and propriety," and "even so are we to live, every one equally and alike to enjoy his Birthright and priviledge; even all whereof God by nature hath made him free" (3). Creation for Overton is thus the liberation of the creature from the "God-stuff" of the Creator. Such a "liberation" from the divine matter is what guarantees the creature's freedom to make proper use of such "property" granted by a bodily God who had "*breathed in his [Adam's] face the breath of Lives, and Man became a living Soul*" (1). The vitalizing union of body and soul confers "natural rights," literally freeing the owner to choose what use to make of this God-given "property."[37]

Milton's theology similarly affirms the creature's freedom to decide what use to make of "property" received as a gift from God. One's "natural" right to such inalienable "property" is further secured by Milton's Arminian theology[38] of free will, a doctrine to which Overton also subscribed as an Anabaptist.[39] The implicit political significance of "vitalism – the belief that life is a property traceable to matter itself rather than to either the motion of complex organizations of matter or an immaterial soul"[40] – is that it "offered an alternative to traditional theories of hierarchy and absolutism as the natural, divinely-ordained way of things and could thus function as a philosophical analogue for ideas of popular sovereignty and liberty of conscience."[41]

THE RUDIMENTS OF a vitalist philosophy in *Paradise Lost* are immediately evident in Book 7 in God's identification of himself with original matter.

Assuring the heavenly host that "I can repaire / That detriment, if such it be to lose / Self-lost, and in a moment will create / Another World" (7.152–5), the Father defines his means to create more worlds:[42] "My overshadowing Spirit and might with thee / I send along," he assures the Son, "ride forth, and bid the Deep / Within appointed bounds be Heav'n and Earth." Then he adds something just as revolutionary as that other vision of future things, when "thou thy regal Scepter shalt lay by." Only this time, it is new beginnings, not unexpected endings, that are ground-breaking: "Boundless the Deep, because I am who fill / Infinitude, nor vacuous the space" (7.165–9). Affirming his ubiquity in space, God denies that this "Infinitude" of space is "vacuous" (or derived *ex nihilo*). Referring to himself by the familiar scriptural name "I am" – later revealed to Moses in the burning bush (Exodus 3: 14) – he names himself "I am who fill / Infinitude" (7.168–9), thus making himself co-extensive with the "Boundless … Deep"[43] and consequently "the source of all substance."[44]

Even so, Dennis Danielson rightly insists on distinguishing "between Chaos and the deep of Gen. 1: 2" which "first emerges at the beginning of book 3." Much as he says of "that holy light which 'as with a mantle [did] invest / The rising world of waters dark and deep, / Won from the void and formless infinite' (3.10–12)," this matter of chaos for Milton "is consistently acknowledged to be 'infinite,' 'illimitable,' 'immeasurable,' 'without bound,'" although "Heaven and earth are bounded" and "Chaos – the 'deep' referred to here – is boundless."[45] Chaos is thus coextensive with God, though caution is warranted in differentiating "Chaos" from the biblical "Deep," since that "boundless" remnant of chaos is left over from the creation of the world. And the infinity of matter, as Danielson stipulates, cannot "be coextensive with that 'one first matter,' mentioned by Raphael (5.472–4), of which all things, in various forms and degrees, consist." Even so, "it may be the same sort of stuff; and likewise the 'matter unformed and void' that composes the newly circumscribed world contrasts, by virtue of its finite bounds, with 'the void and formless *infinite*' known as Chaos" (47). Yet it is not the created world which is coextensive with chaos; God alone is that existence comprehending the entire created universe *and* the "infinite beyond" of matter – "His dark materials to create more Worlds" (2.916). Simply put, God is "fundamentally material. To allow the seeds of good to grow and bear fruit beyond himself, God had first to make a 'beyond.' Moreover, if all this is conceived spatially, and if the 'beyond' is not to be surrounded by God, then it, like God, will be infinite. As God is its origin, however, no dualism follows" (48).

Some ambiguity remains by virtue of what God cryptically implies of his being: "Though I uncircumscrib'd my self retire, / And put not forth my goodness, which is free / To act or not" (7.170–2). But God does not appear to lessen himself by extracting chaotic matter from his being – a self that remains "uncircumscrib'd" – nor does he curtail his absolute freedom to act: "Necessitie and Chance / Approach not mee, and what I will is Fate" (7.172–3). As Danielson properly concludes, "God's omnipotence is compromised by no pagan fate, no Platonic 'necessity' – not by any internal 'pure actuality,' not even by an infinity which he himself creates (7:168–70)" (Danielson, 48).

So what does God mean by his claim that, "I uncircumscrib'd my self retire / And put not forth my goodness"? Kelley paraphrases his declaration as follows:

> Although uncircumscribed (a statement of God's omnipotence), I retire and do not put forth my goodness (remain at rest and thus set bounds to my goodness by not reducing all matter to form and order), which is free either to act or not (a statement of God's free agency), my dormant state is not contingent on necessity or chance, nor is it compelled by fate, for fate is nothing more than what I myself will. (*This Great Argument*, 211)

What Kelley refers to as God's "dormant state" sounds more like a muddled effort to counter Denis Saurat's theory of creation by "retraction,"[46] whereby "God created finite beings by withdrawing himself from certain of his parts, and thus delivered those parts up to the obscure, latent impulsions that remain in them" (quoted by Kelley, 209). Rather than compromise God's own goodness or his greatness, Kelley shifts the connotations of "retire" from "retraction" to "dormancy," a state of "rest" supposedly natural to God.

And yet the tenor of God's declaration makes "freedom" the central issue – not only the freedom of the Creator but also of the creature. "For the deep is boundless only *because* God himself is both boundless and free, if he chooses, to place certain limits on himself for the sake of putting forth what amounts to a vast ocean of potentiality" (Danielson, 48). In practice, this suggests that God chooses to renounce a portion of his omnipotence to make room for creaturely volition. As Danielson sums up, "God, as it were, provides the matter, and it is up to the creature to give it form. Just as God 'retires' himself in order to provide the matter, the potentiality, which will receive form in his positive act of creation, so creaturely freedom involves a self-limitation of God as a means of providing the stuff of that freedom which man himself is to exercise" (49).

Yet, as Rumrich parses this notion of the deity's self-limitation, "Perhaps the terms 'my self' and 'my goodness' do not refer to all of God, just as 'I am who fill infinitude' or 'Whom thou sought'st I am' do not. Although God's self – his actualized, volitional persona – is absent from Chaos, 'the heterogeneous and substantial virtue' of his material potency remains, filling the infinite."[47] God, in other words, has chosen to withdraw the "goodness" of his *will* – not the "goodness" of his *substance* nor the animating "breath" of his *spirit* but the imposition of his will – thereby freeing the creatures, as God puts it, to "open to themselves at length the way / Up hither, under long obedience tri'd, / And Earth be chang'd to Heav'n, & Heav'n to Earth, / One Kingdom, Joy and Union without end" (7.158–61).[48] "The parts of God thus freed from his will become persons," as Saurat concludes (124), stating the obvious. Saurat's corollary, however, that God, by withdrawing his will, "delivers them up, so to speak, to obscure latent impulsions that remain in them,"[49] is highly doubtful. God himself has indicated something quite the opposite of "latent impulsions" by communicating his material "goodness" to humans even as they are left free to seek his will.

Here, Rumrich's overarching conclusion also has the symmetry of a syllogism: "If God's potential rests latent in unformed matter, chaos should be recognized as the realm that substantiates his sovereignty. Furthermore, where there is potential for good, there is also potential for evil" ("Matter," 1043). For, "Without the indeterminacy, the potential for otherness, that chaos constitutes," Rumrich adds, "Satan could not tempt humankind or even conceive of success. Indeed, the psychological correlative of the potential for otherness that underlies created order is freedom of will, the foundation of Milton's ethical beliefs at least since the composition of *Areopagitica* (Danielson, 49)." So it is perfectly reasonable to say with Milton's God that "Necessitie and Chance / Approach not mee," since it is his omniscience that allows for divine, as well as creaturely freedom. "[A]nd what I will is Fate" means no more than what its etymology declares it to be: "fate or *fatum* is only what is *fatum*, spoken, by some almighty power" (Danielson, 42). And what is truly "spoken" by Providence, as the angels hail it in their hymn of praise, is God's manifest will to "diffuse / His good to Worlds and Ages infinite" (7.190–1). Contrary to the centralized, "fated" universe of Calvin, where everything is eternally determined and limited by divine decree, Milton's angels celebrate an ongoing diffusion of divine goodness, a term which ought to recall for thoughtful readers, even as it anticipates for loyal angels, that astounding conclusion to the colloquy in Heaven – the revelation of a decentralizing, universal politics: "Then thou thy regal Scepter shalt lay by, / For regal Scepter then no more shall need, / God shall be All in All" (3.339–41).

Even so, "th' Omnific Word" (7.217) cannot avoid imposing his physical will on that heedless substance freed from the "body" of God in a way that both engenders the creation and sets in motion the marriage plot. First, "th' Omnific Word" must set "thy just Circumference" to "Matter unform'd and void," where "Darkness profound" still "Cover'd th' Abyss" (7.231–4). Then, "on the watrie calme / His brooding wings the Spirit of God outspred, / And vital vertue infus'd, and vital warmth / Throughout the fluid Mass" (7.234–7). As Nigel Smith insists, "[W]e are witnessing a description of, so to speak, divine sexuality."[50] In retrospect, this was already evident in the invocation to Book 1, where the poet affirms: "Thou from the first / Wast present, and with mighty wings outspread / Dove-like satst brooding on the vast Abyss / And mad'st it pregnant" (1.19–22). Despite freeing matter from himself, "the Spirit of God" must then impose his will on "the Womb of nature" (2.911). Without power of consent,[51] the "Womb of nature," like the poem itself, is henceforth utterly reliant on Eve's agency.

For the moment, it will suffice to draw two conclusions from this explicit image of creation through insemination. First, the "vital vertue" which "infus'd … vital warmth / Throughout the fluid Mass" echoes that "vitalist" philosophy of matter that Milton took from *Mans Mortalitie*.[52] Second, the "pregnant" body from which the cosmos necessarily derives was originally extracted from God's "body," much in the way that Eve was also "Extracted" (8.497), as Adam says, from his "side." Cosmic matter, it seems, is thus born in a *literal* separation of the Father's "spirit" from "her" vitalized matter,[53] while "his" moral agency is symbolically justified through Eve in her act of consensual sex. In such a creation by separation, the traditional hierarchy of male/female is fundamentally undone.

The evidence in Book 7 for a re-gendering of the creation is ubiquitous. Light, the first of created things, is immediately described as feminine:[54] "Let ther be Light, said God, and forthwith Light / Ethereal, first of things, quintessence pure / Sprung from the Deep, and from *her* Native East / To journie through the airie gloom began" (7.243–6; italics added). Even the Sun, though named "of Celestial Bodies first," is not "his" own source of light, not even when "First in the East his glorious Lamp was seen" (7.370). Rather, "the greater part he took" of light "Transplanted from *her* cloudie Shrine, and plac'd / In the Suns Orb, made porous to receive / And drink the liquid Light, firm to retaine / *Her* gather'd beams, great Palace now of Light" (7.359–63; italics added). The traditional hierarchy of a subordinate "Moon" serving as the male Sun's "mirror, with full face borrowing her Light / From him" (7.377–8) is swiftly overturned in the "leveld West" (7.376) by "Her gather'd beams," which journey from "her Native East." As McDowell explains, "the orthodox Augustinian distinction between created or material light (*lumen*) and uncreated or divine light (*lux*)" (67) has just been obliterated by virtue of a feminine *lux* which lends the Sun his "*lumen*." While McDowell takes Milton's unique account of the origin of light to mean that he "agrees with Overton and considers the physical light of the sun as a continuous extension, or emanation in Neoplatonist terms, of the divine substance" (67), McDowell somehow fails to see that the "divine substance" is gendered feminine, and that it instantly undoes Augustine's hierarchy of *lux* and *lumen*.

Aside from reversing the ancient model of woman's creation out of man, this story of sunlight's origin out of the divine essence (*Lux*) of female Light suggests that matter has been vitalized by the feminine goodness inhering in the divine substance. Even the poetic line quickens in this vitalizing hymn to natural fertility,[55] where the verbal movement virtually enacts a type of midwifery, as "The Earth obey'd, and strait / Op'ning her fertil Woomb teem'd at a Birth" (7.453–4). From the maternal body of earth comes "The Tawnie Lion, pawing to get free / His hinder parts, then springs as broke from Bonds, / And Rampant shakes his Brinded main" (7.464–6). The consonants after "pawing to get free" – mostly in the movement of the "*r*" sound from the "hinder" part of the line to its middle in "springs" and "broke," before splitting at the end into "Bonds" and "Rampant," as if to mimic passage through the birth canal – serve verbally to enact the "embodiment" of creation as a joyous act of parturition, quite literally the *liberation of matter* from its maker. The poetic-speech act thus *becomes* the thing that it describes, the poet revealing and simultaneously enabling the "property" of each word-thing much in the manner of God himself in producing creatures out of "his" substance.

While examples abound, three must serve to illustrate the *poetic* fertility of Milton's mimesis of divine creation. "And God said let the Waters generate" (7.387) and,

> Forthwith the Sounds and Seas, each Creek and Bay
> With Frie innumerable swarme, and Shoales
> Of Fish that with their Finns and shining Scales
> Glide under the green Wave, in Sculles that oft
> Bank the mid Sea. (7.399–403)

Here, in lively, quickening monosyllables that come to populate the line in "innumerable swarme," it is alliteration (chiefly "*s*" and "*f*" sounds) that produces an effect of rapid darting to and fro of "Frie" and "Fish" from colourful "Shoales" to "Sounds and Seas" that, "with their Finns and shining Scales," evoke a wider sense of darting movement. In contrast, "part huge of bulk," the seals, the dolphins, and the whales all "Wallowing unweildie, enormous in thir Gate / Tempest the Ocean" (7.410–12), move in ponderous polysllables that mimic the heavy movement of sea mammals. Finally, in the sudden flight of birds, "bursting with kindly rupture" (7.419) from "the Egg," we see

> Thir callow young, but featherd soon and fledge
> They summ'd thir Penns, and soaring th' air sublime
> With clang despis'd the ground, under a cloud
> In prospect; there the Eagle and the Stork
> On Cliffs and Cedar tops thir Eyries build. (7.420–4)

In this case, both the alliteration and the dynamic displacement of *c*'s and *l*'s – from "callow" to "clang" and "cloud" that ends in "Cliffs and Cedar tops" – creates the illusion of flight in these newborn fowl that "summ'd their Penns, and soaring th' air sublime," slip free of the heavy, blended consonants (in the repeated *kl* sounds) to come to rest at the end of the line in solid *see-der* "tops" and *air-ees* "build."

Apart from this joyous, "vitalizing" use of language, the other unique feature of Milton's poetic version of the creation is its silent correction of the Authorized Version of Genesis. In the stately simplicity of the King James translation (1611), "God said, Let the earth bring forth grass, the herb yielding seed, and the fruit tree yielding fruit after his kind, whose seed is in itself, upon the earth" (Genesis 1: 11). In Milton's version, God "said, Let th' Earth / Put forth the verdant Grass, Herb yielding Seed, / And Fruit Tree yielding Fruit after *her* kind; / Whose Seed is in *her* self upon the Earth" (7.309–12; italics added). Similarly, in the Authorized Version, "God said, Let the earth bring forth the living creature after his kind, cattle, and creeping thing, and beast of the earth after his kind: and it was so. And God made the beast of the earth after his kind" (Genesis 1: 24–5). But in Milton's version, "God said, / Let th' Earth bring forth Soul living in *her* kinde, / Cattel and Creeping things, and Beast of the Earth, / Each in their kinde" (7.450–3; italics added). While not precisely restoring the grammatical neuter of Hebrew scripture, Milton's re-gendering does enact a motivated reversal, fulfilling the basic requirement of his materialist metaphysics – that what is freed from God's substance is both *good* and also *other* than God himself, a secret side of the divine being that he has gendered *metaphysically* feminine, and that now gains existence as "his" *substantial* opposite.

The divine injunction further affirms Milton's monist vitalism, so like that of Overton, in rendering matter as a spiritualized substance, given the way that original matter is emphatically liberated ("*Let* there be Light … *Let* th' Earth," etc.) from divine substance, even as it is vitalized by God's animating spirit: "And God said, *let* the Waters generate / Reptil with Spawn abundant, living Soule" (7.387–8; italics added); and "God said, / *Let* th' Earth bring forth Soul living in her kinde" (7.450–1; italics added). Through the cumulative force of all these repetitions, we begin to sense that the totality of living matter is truly instinct with "soule." In this, Milton goes even further than Overton who, in *Mans Mortalitie*, had merely indicated that God "gave that lifelesse Body" of man "a communicative rationall Facultie or property of life, in his kind: And so it became a living Creature" (1). For Milton, not just man but the Earth, the "Waters" and Heavens are each filled with every form of "living Soul" derived from that first matter.

Political equality is the ultimate by-product of this collapse of the soul/body hierarchy. For example, Raphael depicts "The Parsimonious Emmet, provident / Of future, in small room large heart enclos'd, / Pattern of just equalitie perhaps / Hereafter" (7.485–8). While Milton's scriptural source is Proverbs 6: 6 – "Go to the ant, thou sluggard; consider her ways and be wise" – the political source is the political tradition common from Aristotle to Shakespeare that has always "gone to the ant" and the bee to defend monarchy as a "natural" state of government. In *Henry V*, for example, Shakespeare found a model for human government in "the honey bees, / Creatures that by a rule in nature teach / The act of order to a peopled kingdom. / They have a king, and officers of sorts."[56] Hobbes resorts to a similar idea in *Leviathan*, "that certain living creatures (as bees and ants) live sociably one with another (which are therefore by *Aristotle* numbered amongst political creatures)," although Hobbes does not employ the conceit as justification for monarchy, given that, while "the agreement of these creatures is natural; that of men is by covenant only, which is artificial; and therefore, it is no wonder if there be somewhat else required (besides covenant) to make their agreement constant and lasting, which is a common power to keep them in awe, and to direct their actions to the common benefit."[57] But in bypassing Hobbes, Milton rejects both the "natural" and "artificial" justifications for monarchy, substituting the "just equalitie" of "ants" as a "natural" model for his ideal Commonwealth. Here, the lesson is one taught by Overton as well – that matter freed from the divine substance is what confirms the "divine right" not just of kings but of all Commonwealthsmen. For both Milton and Overton, the "divine right" of ordinary human beings clearly originates in God himself by virtue of his gift of spiritualized matter.

What is less clear in Raphael's brief lesson on the "natural" republic is how the narrator – an archangel who had renounced a crown – now fails to grasp the implications of his own narrative. Describing human creation, Raphael repeats in biblical terms how

> [H]e formd thee, *Adam*, thee O Man
> Dust of the ground, and in thy nostrils breath'd
> The breath of Life; in his own Image hee
> Created thee, in the Image of God
> Express, and thou becam'st a living Soul. (7.524–8)

The vitalist pattern of creation now explicitly extends from the sub-human to the human plane, where the "body" is a "living soul." But his startling reduction of Eve's creation to succesive half-lines reduces her to an appendage, only "useful" to Adam in the matter of procreation: "Male he created thee, but thy consort / Female for Race" (7.529–30),[58] the angel declaims like an Anglican bishop. Worse yet, the half-line deflation of "Female for Race" reduces Eve to a function, without affirming that she too "becam'st a living Soul."[59] At best, Raphael appears to hew to "the 'narrow-Augustinian' concentration on woman's procreative function" for which St Augustine had argued in *De genesi ad litteram*, before he modified his views on marriage in *The City of God*. Asking in *De genesi* "for what fitting purpose" Eve had been created as a helpmeet to Adam, Augustine answered with no better than a rhetorical question: "If not to help him produce children, what other sort of help could she have been made for?"[60] But at worst, the archangel's depreciation of Eve's value is uncomfortably close to Aquinas's view that, individually, woman "is naturally 'deficiens et occasionatum,' a product of debility, indisposition, or acccident, and thus 'naturally' in need of domination by a man … But with regard to the species she is not defective, since all generation, Aristotle assures us, requires an active and a passive. Generation, then, is the sole function for which woman was created."[61] Whether he speaks as a Thomist or simply as a "narrow-Augustinian," Raphael all unwittingly sows the seeds of confusion about gender, much as he had previously sown seeds of confusion about the "virtue" of hierarchy and the "excellence" of sword-law.

Beyond challenging the patristic view of male/female hierarchy in woman's functional subordination to her husband, what else has Milton achieved in his Leveller-inspired attempt to rehabilitate the goodness of matter? First and most importantly, creation is re-gendered feminine – in a metaphysical sense – as being fundamentally "other" to, since "freed" from, God the Father. Second, creation proceeds by separation from the divine substance, thus ensuring the goodness of the original matter as well as rendering it the "individuall property" of its recipient. Third, God's act of gifting a particle of the divine substance then frees its recipient from control by the divine will, leaving the property in the "gift" of the receiver to accept or to reject re-union with the divine will. Finally, the gendering of the creature as metaphysically feminine makes the marriage plot essential to the poem, much as it appears to have been in Walwyn's Leveller vision of divine Love – marriage, like "true" religion, requiring "a joyning of two free-wils in one."[62] For will, not reason, is the faculty that determines whether two may become one flesh. Ultimately, this daring revision of the story of creation as "the result of the sex life of God"[63] turns on the deeply positive value that Milton assigns to material being as an aspect of the divine being.

But Rumrich's view of "unformed matter as God's potential" adds a further, crucial stipulation that chaos "be recognized as the realm that substantiates his sovereignty."[64] However paradoxical this idea may seem, it is literally the precondition of divine rule. For "God cannot take complete control of chaos without sacrificing his freedom and sovereignty – without ceasing to be God. At bottom, divine substance is the as yet unrealized capacity for otherness … Milton's deity, for the sake of his sovereignty and omnipotence, must always have access to the realm of possibility, to the well of new life."[65] Nothing in Milton's universe embodies that "realm of possibility" more suggestively and powerfully than Eve, whom even Raphael had found at their first meeting to be disconcertingly like her Creator: "Haile Mother of Mankind," he had blurted out, "whose fruitful Womb / Shall fill the World more numerous with thy Sons / Then with these various fruits the Trees of God / Have heap'd this Table" (5.388–91). In his social faux pas of making a sexual reference about a woman he is meeting for the first time, Raphael reveals what is most unsettling about her being. There is a "perplexing excessiveness" in "Eve's beauty"[66] that puts even the most "sociable" of the archangels out of his depth.

As we shall see in the next chapter, however, the intrinisic vitality of matter is equally vital to the dramatic choices made in paradise. For now, it will suffice to quote Rumrich's answer to the metaphysical question of what "perplexes" Raphael, not to mention Adam, about femininity in general: "In certain respects, chaos is to God as Eve is to Adam. If God has no separate, female other *external* to him, he nevertheless acquiesces in his own feminine otherness – a gender-specific negative capability – and can only exercise sovereignty and creative power by virtue of her."[67] Chaos can rightly be seen, then, as the feminine body of God, *her* "Womb of nature" set free from *his* all-controlling will.

Once we begin to see that God's moral authority derives from his goodness in freeing "her" matter from his creative power and might, both his "goodness" and his "greatness" (3.165) must then derive from his respect for "otherness" – the will of his "feminine" *other* to consent to or to deny "his" sexual advances. The truth that emerges from the profound simplicity of Milton's story of *creatio ex deo* is that, contrary to Hobbes's archaic myth or Hesiod's myth of loveless patriarchy, God's creation of "living Soul" is only ever accomplished through loving sexual union, not through military conquest.[68]

· 10 ·

"Among Unequals What Societie?"

THE REPUBLIC OF LOVE

PHILOSOPHICAL DUALISM HAS LONG been an inveterate enemy of levelling, for its principles impose a "normal" superiority of spirit over matter, mind over body, reason over passion, and man over woman. So when Raphael sternly reproves Adam in Book 8 for "attributing overmuch to things / Less excellent" (8.565–6), and allowing "Reason" to be "sunk in carnal pleasure" (8.593), he only does what is demanded by received ideas, the "common view" of the era: that is, he warns the man (identified with reason) to "take heed least Passion sway / Thy Judgement to do aught, which else free Will / Would not admit" (8.635–7). And yet this sharp rebuke is complicated by a number of issues, not least of which is how his discourse in Book 5 was rooted in a Neoplatonic notion of the Good as "one first matter all" (5.472), thereby avoiding the thorny problem of a God of arbitrary will, while the story thereafter turns into the narrative of a volitional deity. In the last chapter, we also saw how Neoplatonic monism extends the hierarchical world view, since it posits an emanation of matter from the Good down the Chain of Being to become less "spirituous," less "pure, / As [farther from] him plac't or nearer tending" (5.475–6).

Raphael even sounds at times like a younger Milton, who is "torn" in his divorce tracts, as James G. Turner says, "between materialist monism and hierarchic dualism."[1] Nigel Smith likewise says that, "However we approach" his divorce tracts, "the dualism/monism confusion is apparent, and Milton appears to be divided against himself."[2] In fact Milton's first marriage appears to have opened deep fissures in his thinking and feeling about sexuality, as well as about gender and the desiring body. On the one hand, he tried in *Doctrine and Discipline of Divorce* to elevate marriage to a noble union of minds in his railing against "the Canon Law," since it "made such carefull provision against the impediment of carnal performance," although it "had no care about the unconversing inability of minde, so defective to the purest and most sacred end of matrimony."[3] On the other hand, the young Milton's high-minded view of the soul's "inbred desire of joyning to it self in conjugall fellowship a fit conversing soul (which desire is properly call'd love)" (*CPW* 2: 251), quickly turns to disgust at the sight of "an image of earth and fleam, with whom he lookt to be the copartner of a sweet and gladsome society" (*CPW* 2: 254). For, "instead of beeing one flesh," the couple are "rather two carkasses chain'd unnaturally together; or," worse, "a living soule bound to a dead corps, a punishment too like that inflicted by the tyrant *Mezentius*" (*CPW* 2: 326–7). As Turner notes, "It is ironic, given their vivid evocations of sexual disgust, that Milton's divorce tracts should have been so widely denounced as the work of a 'Libertine'" (203). His ideal of marriage as "a cheerfull and agreeable conversation" is all too often juxtaposed to "the channell of concupiscence" (*CPW* 2: 248–9), provoking nausea about "the vessell of voluptuous enjoyment ... when as [it is] the minde from whence must flow the acts of peace and love, a far more precious mixture then the quintessence of an excrement" (*CPW* 2: 248).

Even the counter-claim that "marriage cannot be honorable for the meer reducing and terminating of lust between two; seeing many beasts in voluntary and chosen couples live together as unadulterously, and are as truly maried in that respect" (*CPW* 2: 252), manages to leave an impression that coupling is bestial. For the old dualist separation of body and soul is reinforced in the very next sentence: "But all ingenuous men will see that the dignity & blessing of mariage is plac't rather in the mutual enjoyment of that which the wanting soul needfully seeks, then of that which the plenteous body would jollily give away." Milton's ready recourse to Plato's *Symposium* thus seems to justify Irene Samuel's sober judgment that, "The theory of marriage and divorce that dominates these tracts, and asserts itself again in the treatise *De Doctrina Christiana*, depends upon the Platonic dichotomy of the world into two realms: the material, or that which affects the body, and the spiritual, or that which affects the soul."[4]

Yet, "Despite this strident and dualist attack on sexuality," Stephen Fallon counters, "we are given brief and incomplete indications of a more balanced view"[5] of the union of mind and body in the divorce tracts. For proof,

Fallon turns to *Tetrachordon* (1645), in which Milton recalls the caveat of St Augustine, "that if God had intended other then copulation in Mariage, he would for *Adam* have created a freind, rather then a wife, to convers with" (CPW 2: 739–40). Yet "this cannot but bee with ease conceav'd," Milton objects, "that there is one society of grave freindship, and another amiable and attractive society of conjugal love, besides the deed of procreation, which of it self soon cloies, and is despis'd, unless it bee cherisht and re-incited with a pleasing conversation" (CPW 2: 740). The insistence here and elsewhere[6] on fleeting moments of transfigured desire allows for a more balanced view that Milton, "alone" among thinkers of his era, "argues that a union of minds is *essential* to the couple's becoming one flesh."[7] Far from falling into dualistic thinking about body and soul in the divorce tracts, Fallon thinks that Milton is experimenting "with an early and not fully rationalized version of the monism informing *De Doctrina Christiana* and *Paradise Lost*" (69). To Fallon, what appears to be "aggressively dualistic" (70) in the divorce tracts is no more than a tactical move of "separating his audience into wise monists and blind dualists" (69). On this view, dualists are merely able to provide for the body in marriage, while monists are actually able to achieve "one flesh" by virtue of their sense of spiritualized bodies.

As near as this sounds to the joys of sex in the Edenic marriage of *Paradise Lost*, the "divorcing" Milton was still unable in 1643–45 to imagine a unity of body and spirit, except *in potentia*. Even in more hopeful commentary on Genesis 2: 24 in *Tetrachordon*, the divorcing Milton writes, "*They shall be one flesh*; but let the causes hold, and be made really good, which only have the possibility to make them one flesh. Wee know that flesh can neither joyn, nor keep together two bodies of it self; what is it then must make them one flesh, but likenes, but fitnes of mind and disposition, which may breed the Spirit of concord, and union between them?" (CPW 2: 605). But this ideal holds for no longer than the time it takes to state; more often than not, sexual coupling is likened to the mis-yoking of St Paul's "*Asses and Oxen*," leaving the baffled male to wonder what could "be a fouler incongruity, a greater violence to the reverend secret of nature, then to force a mixture of minds that cannot unite, & to sowe the furrow of mans nativity with seed of two incoherent and uncombining dispositions?" (CPW 2: 270).[8]

It would be naive if not tendentious to assume that what was still "incoherent" in Milton's thought and life in the 1640s could achieve coherence by displacement to an imaginary state, to paradise. As long as Milton had to rely polemically on the dualist assumptions of his culture, he was likely to be trapped by their paralyzing contradictions. With refreshing candour, Fallon then admits that "Milton's first essay in matter-spirit monism is finally incomplete. If he intended the administration of one extreme dualism (spirit over body) to counteract and balance another dualism (body over spirit), his medicine has proved too strong. The monist physician must still heal himself" (82).

What is missing from this reading, however, is the impact of *Mans Mortalitie* on Milton. Overton's little book appeared a mere fortnight before the second edition of *The Doctrine and Discipline of Divorce.*[9] Unless Milton had read it before it went to press, Nigel Smith is surely mistaken about "textual echoes"[10] of *Mans Mortalitie* in *Doctrine and Discipline*; Overton's work simply appeared too late.[11] Later on, it clearly got his attention, though, given the sensational public pairing of Overton's mortalist heresy with "divorce at pleasure." Indeed, the imprint it left on *Tetrachordon* the following year is impressive, if but intermittently visible in fleeting passages where a meeting of minds does lead at times to a union of "one flesh." More often, however, the imperative "to force a mixture of minds that cannot unite" leads only to sowing again "the furrow of mans nativity with seed of two incoherent and uncombining dispositions." In 1645, this was the extent of Overton's impact on the "incipient monism evident in those tracts."[12]

What more likely allowed the "monist physician" to heal himself was his experience of love and loss. If the death of his first wife – Mary Powell, the occasion of the divorce tracts – after the birth of their third daughter, Deborah, and the death of their year-old son, John, within the month, was not soul-destroying for the monist in 1652, the death of his second wife, Katherine, in 1658, followed by the death of their infant daughter, Katherine, was truly determinative. Milton's haunting expression of loss in "Methought I saw my late espoused Saint, / Brought to me like *Alcestis* from the grave"[13] is one of the most moving sonnets in the language. Here, a blind and bereaved husband comes face to face with his lost "Saint," whose "face was vail'd, yet to my fancied sight, / Love, sweetness, goodness in her person shin'd / So clear, as in no face with more delight." And yet the husband's faith in the imminence of an afterlife – "as yet once more I trust to have / Full sight of her in Heaven without restraint" – is crushed by his sense of this second loss with which the poem concludes: "But O as to embrace me she enclin'd, / I wak'd, she fled, and day brought back my night." In his painful awakening to the absent body of his beloved, the poet has awakened to the "truth" that for the moment she is nowhere, at least not until the general resurrection of the dead, and that his loss is now utter and complete. In fact, his beloved exists only in his aching memory of her. And so the life of the body *has* indeed become the life of the mind, as the heavy-hearted monosyllables of the final line of the sonnet register on his very pulse: "I wak'd, she fled, and day brought back my night."

And yet the "love, sweetness, goodness" that was visible in that remembered face is hardly the stuff of what critics so often mistake for Milton's gloomy pessimism about life after the Fall. Nicholas McDowell's conclusion in "Ideas of Creation" is premature at best: "While Overton conceives of human beings as born into a state of grace from which they can fall, in the manner of Milton's Adam, Milton conceives of postlapsarian man as born into sin but with a potentially saving remnant of Adamic perfection – the capacity for rational choice" (77). For Milton, the original goodness of matter continues, as it did for Overton, to inhere in the "mother" substance. Rejecting the orthodox belief that "the soule be a creature infused"[14] at birth by the hand of God, Overton finds his proof-text in "*Luke;* 1.31. *Thou shalt conceive in thy wombe and bring forth a son*." To Overton, this means that the soul, like the body, can only be born of the mother: "[W]hence observe, that what she was to bring forth, she was to conceive, to wit a sonne; and none will deny, Christ was borne complate man, in all things as we are, sinne excepted … So then, the soule as well as the body is *borne*, that is proceedes from the flesh, except we be borne without it: Wherefore, they are no more *twaine, but one flesh*" (55).

Soul is likewise joined to body in *Paradise Lost* in ways that make them indistinguishable. And Adam and Eve are "*one flesh*" in another sense, since Adam, who lent Eve being from his "side," derives from the very "god-stuff" that Milton portrays as a "feminine" potency at work in the story of creation. The "living soul" of the man, like that of the woman, is also born of the divine substance. And these "two," as Lilburne wrote, "are the earthly, original fountain, as begetters and bringers forth of all and every particular and individuall man and woman, that ever breathed in the world since." As Overton explained, this meant not of "natural" bodies alone but of their souls, too. This concept of the soul's origin from the "mother" substance is what seems to have predisposed Overton to agree with Lilburne's revolutionary view that human beings "were by nature all equall and alike in power, dignity, authority, and majesty, none of them having (by nature) any authority dominion or majesteriall power, one over or above another" (*Free-mans Freedome*, 11).

Similarly, it was Eve's *substantial* likeness to the Creator that enabled Milton to imagine Adam daring to contend with his Maker for a mate.[15] Yet the heretical effrontery of Milton's theology of matter was less apparent to orthodox readers than the obvious social effrontery of Adam in his familiarity with God. Marchamont Nedham mocks this type of religious conservative who would be utterly horrified at the prospect of Adam arguing with God for a mate. In his first incarnation as *Britanicus*, Nedham had scoffed at an Anglican curate who had insisted in a sermon preached before the king at Oxford, as "all wise men know, that *Reverence, Obedience, Allegiance*, and *Loyalty*, are *Links* only of that *chain* which is fastned to the *Throne* at *Westminster*."[16] The curate goes on to complain of the grave affront given to royalists by the brashness of sectaries daring to address God as their familiar: "He sayes, *If a Turk had been present, he would have wondred whether it were a Deity, or a Companion, the Preacher were so familiar with.* You see then our Preachers are Gods familiars, his friends, while yours are as strangers, and enemies. And you may guesse how little they understand at *Oxford*, what *walking with God* means, *by* their deriding the *Heavenly familiarity*" (1030).

To modern sensibilities, the portrait of "sectarian" Adam arguing with God for a mate is one of the more endearing features of Milton's version of the creation. As Turner explains, "[W]e learn that Adam's most fervent desire is for an equal – a desire so deeply rooted in his being that it gives him the astonishing ability to argue down the Almighty within minutes of his creation."[17] For Adam, like Walwyn's "Brownist and Anabaptist," really is one of those "rationall examiners of those things they hold for truth, milde discourses" by which they are "able to give an account of what they beleeve," and "by which meanes the weakest becomes in a short time much improved, and every one able to give an account of their tenets, (not relying upon their Pastors as most men in our congregations *doe*)."[18] What seems like lack of reverence to some is a virtue for sectaries whose God even invites his creatures to prove themselves in reasoned debate with him.

Responding to the Creator who gives him at least a hint[19] with respect to his intent – "Not onely these fair bounds, but all the Earth / To thee and to thy Race I give; as Lords / Possess it, and all things that therein live" (8.338–40) – Adam remarks of the beasts he names that they have mates, "but with mee / I see not who partakes. In solitude / What happiness, who can enjoy alone, / Or all enjoying, what contentment find?" (8.363–6). To which the Creator responds: "What call'st thou solitude, is not the Earth

/ With various living creatures, and the Aire / Replenisht," and "know'st thou not / Thir language and thir wayes, they also know, / And reason not contemptibly; with these / Find pastime, and beare rule; thy Realm is large" (8.369–75). But Adam proves to be an attentive listener as well as a "rationall examiner," who, from the instant of his creation, wants to account for what he holds to be true. Given that God says, "To thee and to thy Race I give / As Lords," even when to human solitude "the Universal Lord" had "seem'd / So ordering" (8.376–7), Adam is able to see through appearances, making a very cogent case for the absurdity of obedience, "without knowing other reason," as Milton had put the case in *Areopagitica* for the necessity of rational inquiry.[20] As David Aers and Bob Hodge astutely note of the structural location of this scene, "[T]he effect of placing the debate with God immediately before the debate with Raphael … gives divine sanction for Adam's view of marriage as a mutual relationship between equals."[21]

Adam, however, is still not completely certain that he is asked to give an account of his "tenets," rather than to take his "Pastor's" word for things: "Let not my words offend thee, Heav'nly Power, / My Maker, be propitious while I speak. / Hast thou not made me here thy substitute, / And these inferiour farr beneath me set?" (8.379–82). In the image of "these inferiour," Adam tugs at the one loose thread in God's command: the implicit promise of "thy Race." In fact, the "truth he holds" could well become his heresy were he *not* to object, "Among unequals what societie / Can sort, what harmonie or true delight? / Which must be mutual, in proportion due / Giv'n and receiv'd" (8.383–6). And then he spells out his true wish list: "Of fellowship I speak / Such as I seek, fit to participate / All rational delight, wherein the brute / Cannot be human consort" (8.389–92). As James Turner realizes, "The craving for partnership is so 'deeply graven,' and so energetically maintained throughout the long wrestling-match with God, that it seems to define his whole being; he is unfinished without Eve" (283). Adam can't rest, however, in this mere "truth" of self-definition; he has been asked to "know" God, as well as himself, "aright." Even more provocatively, God asks, "What thinkst thou then of mee, and this my State, / Seem I to thee sufficiently possest / Of happiness, or not?" (8.403–5). Strictly speaking, since it is the Son who creates, it can only be through him that the Father claims to be "alone / From all Eternitie, for none I know / Second to me or like, equal much less" (8.405–7). And yet Adam is still able to refuse the gambit of identifying himself with his Maker, much as he had refused that previous "command" to identify himself with the beasts. Indeed, Adam implies, Just because You have no equal, must I be denied an equal? For "Thou in thy self art perfet," he adds, "and in thee / Is no deficience found; not so is Man, / But in degree, the cause of his desire / By conversation with his like to help, / Or solace his defects" (8.415–19). Demonstrating his acute awareness of his "deficience," Adam proposes a remedy in "conversation with his like."[22]

As much as his proposal reveals a remarkable degree of self-awareness, more notable still is Adam's ability to define his difference from the deity. As he says: "No need that thou / Shouldst propagat, already infinite; / And through all numbers absolute, though One" (8.419–21). Conversely, he understands that "Man by number is to manifest / His single imperfection, and beget / Like of his like." Only in such fashion can "his Image" be "multipli'd, / In unitie defective, which requires / Collateral love, and deerest amitie" (8.423–5). To Adam's credit, he comprehends his need to "propagat" not as a biological but as a metaphysical deficiency. His sense of being "In unitie defective" then anticipates the higher "unitie" of "a hermaphroditic deity"[23] who "through all numbers absolute" is "absolute, though One." But Adam has yet to discover how the Creator had first freed the "other" from "himself" in order to create "his" opposite out of the divine substance. Yet, long before he hears the story of the creation from Raphael, he is filled with an innate longing for "Collateral love" (8.426) – the etymology of "collateral" suggesting a "parallel," or "side by side" love – with his co-equal, "an equal in rank."[24] In defining "the cause of his desire" for "deerest amitie," he sees his difference from God who has no equal. And the deity, as Turner says, even "congratulates Adam for passing this test" (284): "Thus farr to try thee, *Adam*, I was pleas'd, / And finde thee knowing not of Beasts alone, / Which thou hast rightly nam'd, but of thy self, / Expressing well the spirit within thee free" (8.437–40). Adam's daring, while maybe not what the "Pastor" or "Assembly" would urge as pious behaviour, reveals the "meanes" by which, as Walwyn says, "the weakest becomes in a short time much improved," since even a "newborn" such as Adam is "able to give an account of [his] tenets, not relying upon [his] Pastor,"[25] much less his God, to tell him what he should believe.

Nor is the deity a teacher who fails to praise a good student, informing Adam how, "I, ere thou spak'st, / Knew it not good for Man to be alone" (8.444–5). Making it clear that "no such companie as then thou saw'st" was "Intended thee, for trial onely brought, / To see how thou could'st judge of fit and meet," the deity makes a solemn promise to Adam that, "What next I bring shall please thee, be assur'd, / Thy likeness, thy fit help, thy other self, / Thy wish exactly to thy hearts desire" (8.446–51). It sounds "exactly" like the sort of partner that Adam was forced to imagine in a world without women. For the specification of "Thy likeness, thy fit help, thy other self" corresponds exactly to the divine word in Genesis, as Milton glossed the Hebrew word *keneged*[26] in *Tetrachordon*. The Authorized Version, as the younger Milton noted, translates it as "[*Meet for him*.] The original heer is more expressive then other languages word for word can render it; but all agree effectuall conformity of disposition and affection to be heerby signify'd; which God as it were not satisfy'd with the naming of a help, goes on describing *another self, a second self, a very self it self*."[27] Turner remarks that "Female subordination and inferiority are never mentioned in this episode, astonishingly enough. Milton here, however locally, remains true to the orginal text, to the Lutheran vision of primal freedom for both sexes, and to the love of equality proclaimed in his own political writings (though not in his domestic treatises)" (284).

In a wider sense, however, the "irresolvable doubleness" that Turner finds "at the heart of Milton's apprehension of wedded love – a contradiction that lies dormant in Genesis and the Pauline tradition" (286), weakens his otherwise exemplary reading of this narrative of testing in which the scene of Adam's demand for "fellowship … fit to participate / All rational delight" is framed by a prefatory dialogue with the angel about love and the stars that now creates a more complicated test.[28] While Turner understands that "Adam's critical analysis and defence of his own passion comes at the climax of the most idyllic part of *Paradise Lost*; it is the intimate core to which the conversation with Raphael gradually moves" (273), he fails nonetheless to recognize that the "irresolvable doubleness" of egalitarian and subordinationist views of marriage is not Adam's problem.

From the outset of his dialogue with Raphael,[29] Adam concedes that "something yet of doubt remaines" (8.13), even as he admits to a degree of subtlety – first of all in his own voice ("How suttly to detaine thee I devise," [8.207]), and then in acceptance of the Creator's praise of him ("A nice and suttle happiness I see / Thou to thy self proposest" [8.399–400]) – to which the "sociable Spirit" remains oblivious. Adam's "doubt," in fact, has less to do with geocentric or heliocentric systems of astronomy than with this notion of inequality brought to paradise by "the winged Hierarch." Adam's difficulty should be evident to any reader who recalls his earlier assurance in satisfying Eve's curiosity about the stars: "These then, though unbeheld in deep of night, / Shine not in vain" (4.674–5). But here, in response to the teachings of the celestial visitor, he is suddenly left to wonder why the "numberd Starrs" should "rowle" "Round this opacous Earth, this punctual spot, / One day and night; in all thir vast survey / Useless besides" (8.19, 23–5).

There seem to be spaces more "incomprehensible" (8.20) than those "travelled" by the stars in the drift of Adam's thought from "Shine not in vain" to "Useless besides." Yet he surely identifies what he needs to make such "Spaces" comprehensible: a proper understanding of gender relations on earth as in the heavens. But this implication is made "suttly," since he is too polite as a host to name the source of his difficulty: "[R]easoning I oft admire, / How Nature wise and frugal could commit / Such disproportions, with superfluous hand / So many nobler Bodies to create" (8.25–8). These latter, he thinks, must be "Greater so manifold to this one use" than "the sedentarie Earth, / That better might with farr less compass move, / Serv'd by more noble then her self, attaines / Her end without least motion" (8.29, 32–5). He assumes, in other words, that the Ptolemaic system of solar and stellar motion must support Raphael's hierarchical discourse on "degree" and his praise of "excellence" in the War in Heaven. At the same time, Raphael's story of the "god-stuff" of the creation had clearly "levelld" what he had tried to rank in ascending order of "degree." Since God assured him that he was given the equal partner he had requested, Eve can no more be defined as "Female for Race" than she can as "Thy weaker." So which of these two images is false? Is Eve, so much like the Earth itself, and so also like the divine substance of creation, really noble or not? Or is the universe nearly as hierarchical as the archangel has made it out to be? Given "So many nobler Bodies" in the angel's Ptolemaic system of hierarchy, would Eve not then need to be "Serv'd by more noble then her self"?[30]

Eve, by contrast, is more alert – because she is far more accustomed than Raphael – to Adam's practised subtlety. Here, "Perceaving" the evident drift of the conversation, she instantly chooses to absent herself. Doubtless she has her own reasons for preferring "Her Husband the Relater … / Before the Angel, and of him to ask / Chose rather" (8.52–4). "Grateful digressions" and "conjugal Caresses" will surely be welcome to her after the unwitting slights she has borne from the heavenly visitor. But the narrator also supports her at this departure, noting how, "A pomp of winning Graces waited still, / And from about her shot Darts of desire / Into all Eyes to wish her still in sight" (8.61–3). The effect is well summed up in Rumrich's notice of "the depiction of Eve in particular … as a site for the coincidence of opposites" that do unsettle the old binaries of gender by identifying "Apollonian Adam" as "the Earth from which Eve is taken, and the Dionysian Eve" as "shooting darts of desire" that render her "the more brilliantly sunlike in beauty."[31] The narrator thus makes it very clear that Eve transcends traditional gender categories.

Precisely at this point, we get the first unequivocal judgment of Raphael's world view that we have had since the arrival of "the winged Hierarch" in Eden: "And *Raphael* now to *Adam*'s doubt propos'd / Benevolent and facil" (8.64–5). Since the only other instance of "facil" appears in Book 4 – Gabriel dismissing Satan back to "The facil gates of hell too slightly barrd" (4.967) – we have more authority to judge the angel's "benevolent" intentions for what they are: "not harsh or severe; affable, courteous, relaxed"; "easy to use or understand"; yet "easily led, flexible, compliant, yielding, weak-minded."[32] Raphael may indeed be affable and compliant to answer Adam's concerns, at once acknowledging that, "Alreadie by thy reasoning this I guess, / Who art to lead thy ofspring, and supposest / That bodies bright and greater should not serve / The less not bright" (8.85–8). Having touched the root of the problem, however, Raphael forgets his pronouncements on hierarchy in his "weak-minded" vacillation about which is more "excellent" [his own term], or "noble" [Adam's term], in the scheme of things. As Martin Kuester notes, Raphael "seems unable to realize that his position is contradictory, or that his mission is another test of Adam's ability to reconcile the dual terms of God's irony."[33] But these contradictions appear to go deeper than Kuester has realized in his pioneering assessment of the angel's limited "sematology": "[C]onsider first, that Great / Or Bright inferrs not Excellence" (8.90–1), Raphael says, backtracking on his previous insistence, "[B]ehold the excellence," for "likest Gods they seemd." In fact, he now admits, "'T]he Earth / Though, in comparison of Heav'n, so small, / Nor glistering, may of solid good containe / More plenty then the Sun that barren shines" (8.91–4). Without progeny, the angels are obviously "barren," as Rapahel is forced to admit by means of the noble Sun, "Whose vertue on it self workes no effect, / But in the fruitful Earth" (8.95–6). While Adam surely appreciates the angel's generous reversal of value, which better fits the celestial hymn to fertility and "feminine" potency which echoed resoundingly throughout Book 7, it still contradicts the presumed scale of values that Raphael had announced in his Homeric narrative of the War in Heaven: "behold the excellence, the power / Which God hath in his mighty Angels plac'd" (6.637–8).

Now the angel's provisional adoption of a Copernican system – "What if the Sun / Be Center to the World" (8.122–3) – sounds almost concessive in linking the "god-stuff" from the narrative of creation to feminine agency.

For "If Earth industrious of her self fetch Day / Travelling East" (8.137–8), the very cosmos would support Adam's view of his wife – "so well to know / Her own" – in the passionate confession he is about to make to Raphael.[34] And if his revised estimate of "Male and Femal Light" is also "true" of those "two great Sexes" that "animate the World" (8.150–1), then "that light / Sent from her through the wide transpicous aire, / To the terrestrial Moon" must also be "reciprocal, if Land be there" (8.140–4).[35] Whatever the model, "Whether the Sun predominant in Heav'n / Rise on the Earth, or Earth rise on the Sun" (8.160–1), Adam finally has reason to believe that the "winged Hierarch" is no longer quite so dismissive of his spouse, and is ready to hear with sympathy Adam's confession of his instinctive desire for an equal partner.

That their discourse on celestial events is less about heavenly than terrestrial "bodies" is evident in Adam's easy expression of relief at the outcome: "Thee I have heard relating what was don / Ere my remembrance: now hear mee relate / My Storie, which perhaps thou hast not heard" (8.203–5). Adam seems to believe that "the winged Hierarch" will be able to change his mind, or at least to adopt a more human perspective. So he misses the angel's autocratic method of resolving an intellectual impasse: "Sollicit not thy thoughts with matters hid" (8.167). Further signs of trouble ahead are also evident in Raphael's blatant contradictions: "Heav'n is for thee too high / To know what passes there" (8.172–3). Really? So what have you been talking about now for three books? But there is at least a kindly note of advice: "[J]oy thou / In what he gives to thee, this Paradise / And thy faire *Eve*" (8.170–2). While such counsel aims to restore Adam to the legitimate joys of Paradise with his "faire *Eve*," the admonition to "be lowlie wise: / Think onely what concernes thee and thy being; / Dream not of other Worlds" (8.173–5) suggests that the angel now sees that his discourse poses a danger to Adam. For Raphael is about to admit, with respect to Adam's own story of the creation, how much he is out of his depth: "For I that Day was absent" (8.229), he says with facile glibness, admitting he knows next to nothing about Eve's creation, and that at best he has had to rely on hearsay witness in Heaven for the story of her creation, not having seen it himself.

For his part, Adam responds to "the Godlike Power" with true humility,[36] admitting that, "For Man to tell how human Life began / Is hard; for who himself beginning knew?" (8.250–1). He reveals himself to be the polar opposite of Satan, given the latter's claim to "know no time when we were not as now; / Know none before us, self-begot, salf-rais'd / By our own quick'ning power" (5.859–61). Describing himself "As new wak't from soundest sleep" (8.253), Adam gives his first waking moment the character of his earlier charmed response to the angel's story of the creation, where he had "stood fixt to hear; / Then as new wak't thus gratefully repli'd" (8.3–4). In other words, we are alerted from the outset of Adam's narrative to the effect of Raphael's story on him, as if it were another creation, leaving him to wonder yet again "who I was, or where, or from what cause / Knew not" (8.270–1). Almost, but not quite, since Adam recalls each of the answers he had received to each of his prayers: the first for evidence of his Maker who "came, methought, of shape Divine, / And said, thy Mansion wants thee, *Adam*, rise"; the second for reassurance that, "call'd by thee I come thy Guide" (8.295–6, 298). His first heavenly guide, who was indeed "benevolent" but never "facil," had also engaged him in ways that left him "streind to the highth / In that celestial Colloquie sublime" (8.454–5). Forced into a strenuous "sectarian" exercise of giving an "account of what he believe[s]," Adam had received just the answer he was looking for: he has rightly outfaced God's seeming commandment to settle for less than an equal partner. Does he not have equal reason now to trust his abilities in debate with this new celestial visitor?

Adam is never more lyrical than in the tender account he gives of the way God fashioned a mate for him from a "Rib":

> Under his forming hands a Creature grew,
> Manlike, but different Sex, so lovly faire,
> That what seemd fair in all the World, seemed now
> Mean, or in her summd up, in her containd
> And in her looks, which from that time infus'd
> Sweetness into my heart, unfelt before,
> And into all things from her Aire inspir'd
> The spirit of love and amorous delight. (8.470–7)

In giving up a part of his "stuff" to his "other self," he participates in the divine act of self-sacrifice, saying "'Account me woman,' so to speak,"[37] as Stuart Curran remarks.

What God fashions is not just a new "form" in "different Sex," but a "spirit of love" which, until now, had been truly foreign to Adam, "unfelt before," but now world-altering in its demand to revalue *self* and *other*.[38] For, "Grace," he says, "was in all her steps, Heav'n in her Eye, / In every gesture dignitie and love" (8.488–9). Despite Feisal Mohamed's insistence that this use of "grace" is reminiscent of "Milton's terminology in *Eikonoklastes* … rendering her a 'supersititious Image' (3: 343),"[39] Adam finds in the coincidence of "dignitie" (*self-worth*) with "love" (openness to *another*) an echo of God's "Grace."[40] As Rumrich has remarked of Eve's "Beautie, which whether waking or asleep, / Shot forth peculiar Graces" (5.14–15), "These last two words appear together in only one other place in the epic: 'Some I have chosen of peculiar grace / Elect above the rest; so is my will' (3.183–4)."[41] Eve is thus bound, more than Raphael seems to realize, to her Creator as a "spiritualized body"; and Adam strikes exactly the right note by identifying her particular "grace" with God's "Grace." Here is love of a sort that Walwyn identifies with true religion, that "where God is, there is love … and hee hath all that hath God … for all things are from God, through God, and to God, and God is love."[42]

As much as Adam's "love" for Eve may be of God, through God, and to God, it is not yet "reciprocal" love. For, in her recollection of Adam's courtship, Eve had confessed that she found him "Less winning soft, less amiablie milde" (4.479) than her own "faire" image. It was only after he told her what was "lent / Out of my side to thee, nearest my heart" (4.483–4), that she began to take seriously his sense of her being "Part of my Soul … / My other half" (4.487–8). It was exactly at that point she "yielded, and from that time see / How beauty is excelld by manly grace" (4.489–90). But here, the continuing identification of love and "grace" in her person begins to anticipate that larger union of God and humankind by virtue of "free grace,"[43] which, as Walwyn maintained, was "a joyning of two free-wils in one."[44] Fortunately for Adam, Eve's grace truly resembles the divine Grace, although he has likely passed too quickly over some of the difficulties and challenges faced in "joyning two free-wils in one": "I follow'd her, she what was Honour knew / And with obsequious Majestie approv'd / My pleaded reason" (8.508–10).

What Adam says next has confounded Miltonists where it has not confirmed them in their prejudice against "English literature's paradigmatic patriarch."[45] Reading this scene fifty years ago as confirmation of "the universal doctrine of hierarchical order," Douglas Bush accused Adam of "an abdication of his own dignity and responsibility."[46] Millicent Bell even took Adam's passionate confession as evidence that he was already fallen, since "Eve's influence over his judgement is no longer compatible with a state of innocence."[47] More cautiously, Marjorie Nicolson wrote that "Adam has gone so far in his adulation that Raphael warns him against going too far," although she will conclude that Milton subscribes to "the Neoplatonic scale of love" by which the angel admonishes Adam to fulfill "his two-fold responsibility for Eve and for himself."[48] More recently, the same idea reappears in Feisal Mohamed's use of medieval angelology to show why "Adam is a lacklustre pupil" (117–18), and why the angel's "discussion aimed at quickening the spiritual faculty that is Adam's best defence against temptation" fails to deter Adam from his "adulation of Eve that is posing an obstacle to right knowledge of divine order" (131) – the same old same old knowledge of Neoplatonic hierarchy.

Read in dramatic terms as an apologia for love, however, and judged by the standards of classical rhetoric, Adam's speech puts a rather different face on his "weakness," or his presumed "predisposition" to fall. "Thus I have told thee all my State," he says, "and brought / My Storie to the sum of earthly bliss / Which I enjoy" (8.521–3). Were this indeed the "sum" of what he has to say, it might give his auditor reason to question his own notions of hierarchy, since God himself had tested, nay encouraged, Adam to articulate his desire for equality, ultimately granting his request for an equal partner. But when Adam "comes to describe 'the sum of earthly bliss,' the account that should reflect his new awareness of the universe around him," the "winged Hierarch" jumps, like most of his academic counterparts, to the mistaken conclusion that Adam "stumbles significantly when he subordinates the faculties tending most toward God to his physical adulation of Eve" (Mohamed, 132). Adam might even wonder if he is being tested again to defend the love of his life with the same passionate persistence that he had displayed in his colloquy with God. Unfortunately, the "godlike" angel, far from being all-knowing, is more of a "lacklustre" listener whose fatal incomprehension is the true measure of "hierarchy."

Although he has no formal training in the subject, Adam makes brilliant use of epideictic rhetoric, by which the classical orator aims to persuade an audience of the merits of the praise or blame he assigns. Thus, like all good rhetors, Adam begins with ethical proofs of his character and credibility, opening his heart to demonstrate his vulnerability, as well as to prove his virtuous character. Of his passion for Eve, he says,

> but here
> Farr otherwise, transported I behold,
> Transported touch; here passion first I felt,

Commotion strange, in all enjoyments else
Superiour and unmov'd, here onely weake
Against the charm of Beauties powerful glance. (8.528–33)

What Adam *cannot* know is that Raphael has come to Eden with foreknowledge of the Fall, and so is put in the impossible position of rendering mankind without excuse. In Adam's assessment of his "problem," it may be reasonable for the angel to assume that he has now identified the cause of a Fall that he will be powerless to prevent. How could Adam's frank admission – "here onely weake" – *not* be the angel's "Eureka" moment, leading him to think that here he will fulfill his charge? Adam, on the other hand, admits to a weakness that aims to revise Raphael's previous injunction, "Warne thy weaker" (6.908–9). The dynamic at work throughout this scene is that of a conventional drama of mutual incomprehension: the angel and the man are both limited beings; both labour at cross purposes; neither is undeserving of our pity.[49]

Adam, who tries with might and main to persuade his guest of the unintended insult to his wife and his serious misunderstanding of gender, even comes close to blaming his Maker[50] for what seem to be the unsettling effects of "the charm of Beauties powerful glance":

Or[51] Nature faild in mee, and left some part
Not proof enough such Object to sustain,
Or from my side subducting, took perhaps
More then enough; at least on her bestow'd
Too much of Ornament, in outward shew
Elaborate, of inward less exact. (8.534–9)

Like the "Grace" he finds in his Creator, there is a "grace" in sexual love that Adam can't quite explain, putting it beyond reason and lending it a supernal charge of the *mysterium tremundum*. In fact, Rumrich finds in Adam's "misgivings over the excessive appearance of Eve" more, not less, evidence of her likeness to Milton's "hermaphroditic deity," since "it is her very richness of adornment – her cosmetic excess – that ties Eve to the irrational wildness of chaos, another coincidence of opposites pushing us to the edge of paradox."[52]

While Adam admits to an irrational depth of feeling about Eve's nature, linking her "charm" to divine "Grace," he is intelligent enough to realize that he must show his good will by accommodating the teachings of the "God-like Power" to his first-hand experience. And so he systematically repeats the angel's lessons with an enviable clarity:

> For well I understand in the prime end
> Of Nature her th' inferiour, in the mind
> And inward Faculties, which most excell,
> In outward also her resembling less
> His image who made both, and less expressing
> The character of that Dominion giv'n
> O're other Creatures. (8.540–6)

Adam's summation of the "Angelic Doctor's" teachings amounts to little more, however, than strategic repetition of the latter's anti-feminism[53] in "Warne thy weaker" and "Female for Race," as he rehearses Raphael's proofs for the argument that "body" is lower than "spirit" ("Till body *up* to spirit work" [5.478]), or that "Reason," not *body*, is "spirit" (5.487). Even the angel's condescension in his claim, "Your bodies may at last turn all to Spirit, / Improv'd by tract of time" (5.497–8), is recalled in Adam's assurance that "well I understand" what neither God nor man had said, much less implied, at Eve's creation, about "her resembling less / His image who made both." With manifest good will and intelligence, the student leaves it up to his auditor to interpret the disconcerting dissonance between his own "Storie" of Eve's creation, and the angel's version of it.[54]

But Adam also appeals to the reader, if not to the archangel, in pathetic proofs of the levelling effects of love on one "supposed" to be "superior" by virtue of the "excellence" of his reason, and the "character" of his "Dominion": "yet when I approach / Her loveliness, so absolute she seems / And in her self compleat, so well to know / Her own, that what she wills to do or say, / Seems wisest, vertuousest, discreetest, best" (8.546–50). The repetition of "seems" is evocative of the narrator's own description of the couple, viewed from the perspective of fallen Satan, who had just encountered "living Creatures new to sight and strange" (4.287). But the devil's language, like his political judgment in "seemd Lords of all" and "Not equal, as thir sex not equal seemd" (4.290, 296), is now systematically rejected in Adam's confutation of the angel's dogma. In "so absolute she seems" he manages, through the etymology of "absolute" – Latin *absolvere*, "freed from," "forgiven," "absolved" – to sum up that really crucial image in the vitalist philosophy of matter whereby God brought the world into being by "freeing" matter from "himself," in the same way that Eve is "freed" from Adam's "side."[55] With a humility approaching that of Abdiel in his debate with Satan, Adam finally confirms his faith in Eve as being "in her self compleat," since she has literally been freed from "him." Even her hesitation at being wooed, whether or not to join "two free-wils in one," suggests "that what she wills to do or say, / Seems wisest, vertuouest, discreetest, best," since it is ultimately this expression of her will, not her reason, to be joined with him which carries them both to the heart of the greatest mystery in the poem – the "divinity" of love.

For such reasons, Adam throws all caution to the wind in a ringing peroration that plumbs the depths of his love, even as it amplifies the range of Eve's "naked Majesty":

> All higher knowledge in her presence falls
> Degraded, Wisdom in discourse with her
> Looses discount'nanc't, and like folly shewes;
> Authority and Reason on her waite,
> As one intended first, not after made
> Occasionally. (8.551–6)

As Karen Pruitt argues most persuasively, "Hierarchical distinctions are most threatened when Adam theorizes that 'All higher knowledge in her presence falls / Degraded, Wisdom in discourse with her / Loses discount'nanc't, and like folly shows' (551–3). And why? Because 'to consummate all, / Greatness of mind and nobleness thir seat / Build in her loveliest'(556–8)."[56] In the clearest possible terms, Adam thus renounces the claim of superiority bestowed on him by "the winged Hierarch," insisting that neither Raphael's nor his own "higher knowledge" is higher than Eve's "Greatness of mind." As much as Eve, Adam fundamentally unsettles the hierarchical relation of reason to will.

Picking up, then, the thread of his previous question about astronomy – why should "the sedentarie Earth," if she is lower, be "Serv'd by more noble then herself"? – Adam defends his loyalty to Eve with all the humility of Abdiel defending God from Satan. If Raphael means to demote the partner whom God had promised as his equal, then Adam is prepared, like the Son in Abdiel's story, to accept demotion in serving her: "Authority and Reason on her waite, / As one intended first, not after made / Occasionally" (8.554–6). While he does not say so, Adam may even hear an echo of the

"Exaltation" scene in Raphael's demotion of Eve, with the angel assuming the role of the Father in appearing to elevate an "equal" while implicitly "demoting" him, as Abdiel had inferred, to a position of equality as *primus inter pares*.[57] Making no secret of his judgment of Eve's "godlike" nature – having faced a far sterner test already in his request for an equal by knowing both himself and God "aright" – Adam refuses to be persuaded by anyone but God that her equality is only an illusion. Indeed, "[T]o consummate all," he rises to the challenge of this second test from Heaven, "Greatness of mind and nobleness thir seat / Build in her loveliest, and create an awe / About her, as a guard Angelic plac't" (8.856–9). It is not a case of idolatry but respect for what is "divine" in Eve's person that is now reflected back to her – "Greatness of mind and nobleness thir seat." These are godlike qualities, Adam says, that do indeed resemble "a guard Angelic plac't" about her, denying the superiority of "the winged Hierarch" in reducing him to his proper role as a ministering angel.

Raphael's response shows him at his worst,[58] failing to grasp much of consequence from Adam's "Storie" of God's "ways" to "men."[59] Indeed, he sounds almost like Milton in his youthful divorce tracts, writing about bodies that, in the absence of an "apt and cheerfull conversation of man with woman," are forced, "spight of *antipathy* to fadge together, and combine as they may to their unspeakable wearisomnes & despaire of all sociable delight."[60] The haughty angel even sneers at Adam's confession of "too much" delight: "[W]hat transports thee so, / An outside?" (8.567–8). As Nigel Smith says, "Raphael's denial of 'carnal pleasure' does not reveal an adequate understanding of Adam's feelings, which might already as 'passions' be partaking of the higher love that the angel praises" ("Heresy," 516). Still, ever mindful of Eve's higher profession of love in "With thee conversing I forget all time" (4.639), Adam steadfastly refuses the "barren" angel's judgment of him as "attributing overmuch to things / Less excellent" (8.565–6) – all the more so in view of the "winged Hierarch's" egregious error in defining and extolling that previous "excellence" in the War in Heaven (6.637, 821).

In ways that come to resemble Milton's previous projection of his youthful errors onto the angel in defence of "epic" deeds,[61] the poet once again echoes his previous errors in the divorce tracts by means of what this Platonizing angel says to a loving husband:

> But if the sense of touch whereby mankind
> Is propagated seem such dear delight
> Beyond all other, think the same voutsaf't

> To Cattel and each Beast; which would not be
> To them made common and divulg'd, if aught
> Therein enjoy'd were worthy to subdue
> The Soule of Man, or passion in him move. (8.579–85)

In his youthful idealism, Milton had expressed similar disdain at having "to grind in the mill of an undelighted and servile copulation," a bodily act amounting to a "meer reducing and terminating of lust between two: seeing many beasts … live together as unadulterously, and are as truly maried in that respect. But all ingenuous men will see that the dignity & blessing of marriage is plac't rather in the mutual enjoyment of that which the wanting soul needfully seeks, then of that which the plenteous body would jollily give away."[62] Raphael's contempt for such "common" things is only rivalled by the "divorcing" Milton's disgust at what he took to be the common condition of wedlock.

In other ways, the "Hierarch's" ethic of self-esteem recalls Milton's inflated sense of self in autobiographical passages from his early prose. For, "At the centre of the kind of love recommended by Raphael," write Aers and Hodge, "is a simple egoism … It is certain that Milton would at one time have totally endorsed Raphael here; in the *Apology* of 1642 he referred to his own 'self-esteem either of what I was or what I might be (which let envy call pride).'"[63] "[W]eigh with her thyself," the lordly angel advises, "Then value: Oft times nothing profits more / Then self esteem, grounded on just and right / Well manag'd" (8.570–3). Raphael seems to have forgotten everything he heard in the colloquy in Heaven about love and self-sacrifice, substituting in its place an ethic of egoism that effectively produces another Exaltation – of Adam over Eve. For, "of that skill [i.e., self esteem] the more thou know'st, / The more she will acknowledge thee her Head, / And to realities yield all her shows" (8.573–5). It is totally arrogant advice from one who heard the Father commend a godlike disregard of self, elevating it to sublimity: "Therefore thy Humiliation shall exalt / With thee thy Manhood also to this Throne."

Above all else, Raphael's ethic of self-assertion asserts an ethic of power that blatantly contradicts his story of the Creator's refusal to control "feminine" matter in "retiring" his "self" from a portion of "the Deep," making it *absolutely* the property of the "other" to do with as "she" wills. While a reader can sympathize with the angel in his task of warning against an outcome he knows he will not prevent, Raphael exhibits a lack of self-awareness and logical consistency that contributes much more than he knows to the Fall of man.[64] The more's the pity, since "neither Eve nor Adam says a word about subordination or inferiority when they describe the most sacred moment of their lives, when God spoke directly to them and presented them with their mate."[65] The difference of this latest "headship" scene from the exaltation scene could not be more clear: the Son is made "the Head / One of our number" (5.842–3), as Abdiel puts it, but the truth does not emerge until the sequel: "thus reduc't becomes." To be "the Head" is not a promotion but a demotion for the Son who has become "incarnate" as an angel.[66]

While Turner is justified in thinking that Adam "replies to Raphael's charge with a sense of mild superiority derived from the experience of married love,"[67] Adam is also dismayed by the angel's inconsistency, which is why his response is at best "half abash't" (8.595). For, point by point, he gives an experiential, as well as a logical, refutation of the angel's dualistic prejudice against "her out-side formd so fair" and "procreation common to all kindes," insisting that nothing "So much delights me as those graceful acts, / Those thousand decencies that daily flow / From all her words and actions mixt with Love" that declare "Union of Mind, or in us both one Soule" (8.596–7, 600–4). Adam's "in us both one Soule" is the final achievement of a monist union of body and spirit that had escaped Milton in his youthful writings on divorce. For, in the measured decency of his response and his respect for all that is human and humane in Eve's character, Adam demontrates the divine reality of "joyning two free-wils in one," both in a loving marriage and in the love of God. For good measure, he now draws attention to the basic difference between his faithful love of Eve and the promiscuous love of angels, wryly asking, "Love not the heav'nly Spirits, and how thir Love / Express they?" (8.615–16). The event suggests that Adam calls his critic's bluff, the latter forced to beat a hasty retreat: "Let it suffice thee that thou know'st / Us happie," Raphael says, adding, "But I can now no more" (8.620–1, 630). Still, the "Angel," who "with a smile that glow'd / Celestial rosie red, Loves proper hue" (8.618–19) is unable to deny that sexual love is an analogue of divine love, though he is less prepared than Adam to define his need of an Other, or to know himself "aright."

In the end, what Milton offers in a marital union of equals as a model for his "leveller" republic is an accounting of sorts for the failure of the English republic. In his portrait of a Neoplatonic angel whose premise is a *necessary* inequality in the nature of things, and of a "winged Hierarch" who is compromised by ideological contradictions and aristocratic attitudes,

Milton recalls some of his own compromises and contradictions during the republican era. Having bet on the Rump and Council of State, instead of the Leveller *Agreement of the People*, to establish a popular republic, and having "defended" the "English people" from the enemy abroad instead of the enemy within, Milton had actually failed to defend and protect the infant republic. In having retained his position in government after it lapsed from a Republic into a Protectorate, and proposing (even in desperation) a perpetual Senate to forestall the restoration of the perpetual kingdom,[68] Milton had made the classic mistake of all classical republicans – of trusting the few to the exclusion of the many. Perhaps he was able to portray so clearly the limitations of an aristocratic angel because, in part, he had *been* Raphael. And he was able to portray so movingly the egalitarian longings of Adam because they were an expression of his regret at having opted for a classical, rather than a Leveller, republic, free of the ancient class structure.

While Merritt Y. Hughes concludes that, "In spite of Milton's respect for the people collectively as the rightful source of all authority and the masters of their rulers, he was no egalitarian,"[69] it is more accurate to say that an aristocratic Milton belongs to the early Commonwealth period, not to the "short but scandalous night of interruption"[70] of the Protectorate, and certainly not to the Restoration era of the disgraced republican. Despite Hughes's reminder that "Lilburne and the Levellers are never mentioned by name anywhere in Milton's work,"[71] both epic poems do "name" the Levellers, at least by indirection, in their emplotment and surface allsuions, where the outcomes are really determined by what each protagonist says and does. Splitting himself in *Paradise Lost* into "hierarch" and "democrat" in this tense debate about gender equality, Milton finally manages to take a measure of responsibility for the fate of the English republic.

Alternatively, the levelling imperative in God's continued testing of the married couple – in their mutual quest for a "like" or "equal"; in their ongoing efforts to join "two free-wils in one"; in their rupture and repair of that union with the divine will – is equally a measure of Milton's continuing hopes for a true "commonwealth." Indeed, it is this levelling imperative that will finally lead Adam and Eve to a reunion with the divine will, thereby unsettling the hierarchy of reason and will and making the "joyning of two free-wils in one" the seminal moment in bringing about the true "levelling" republic of love.

· 11 ·

"Here Grows the Cure of All"

VIRAL HIERARCHIES

NO ONE HAD OBJECTED in the least when Eve, on leaving Adam and Raphael to discuss "nobler Bodies" in the heavens, "Rose, and went forth among her Fruits and Flours, / To visit how they prosper'd, bud and bloom, / Her Nurserie" (8.44–6). Had she met Satan on that occasion and tasted the forbidden fruit, the angel's interference would have been more obvious, and Eve's deception much less damaging to women as the cause of "all our woe" (1.3). For it was her *weakness*, St Augustine asserted, that gave the devil his opening, since "he, at first, parleyed cunningly with the woman as with the weaker part of that human society, hoping gradually to gain the whole. He assumed that a man is less gullible and can be more easily tricked into following a bad example than into making a mistake himself."[1] Or, as C.S. Lewis plainly glosses Augustine, "Satan attacked Eve rather than Adam because he knew she was less intelligent and more credulous."[2] Why Adam should be absent, and why he would leave Eve alone to face the Tempter, are two questions that are never asked in *De Civitas Dei*. So Lewis feels free to ignore them too, given his facile assumption that "Milton's version of the Fall story is substantially that of St Augustine, which is that of the Church as a whole" (65). Theocrats are uniquely ill-equipped, of course, to understand the dramatic implications of the "winged Hierarch's" anti-feminism, although republican commentary of late has been quite as depressingly authoritarian in its own reading of this scene.[3] For the most arresting development in Milton's subtle and profound rewriting of Genesis is the *dramatic* and deeply human psychology given to the couple in the Separation Scene, one that is without precedent[4] in patristic or even apocryphal commentaries on Genesis.[5]

Criticism since C.S. Lewis has been agonizingly slow to recognize Eve's reasonable motives for leaving Adam in Milton's drama, let alone their advantages for theodicy.[6] In "the aftermath of the unprecedented public activity of Quaker and other women during the Civil Wars,"[7] many traditional social assumptions were no longer taken as axiomatic among sectaries and radicals. That male critics continue to find them axiomatic speaks volumes about the politics of criticism since the end of the Second World War. For instance, A.J.A. Waldock (1947) baldly states that Eve "wakes in independent mood" and "shows a pretty obstinacy, feels her power, gets her way," while "Adam's weakness … is perhaps the one single and specific piece of behaviour having an absolutely critical importance."[8] Waldock's reading of Eve's "mood" or "whim" (31) is surely no better than the emplotment of chance or divine improvidence in the apocryphal *Vita Adae et Evae* to explain the Fall of mankind, while his sexist interpretation of "Adam's weakness" is laughably based on the poor schmuck's failure to "rule" his wife.

Equally sexist is the view of E.M.W. Tillyard (1951) that "The natural hierarchy has already been upset" through Eve's decision to work apart from Adam. Finding her initial "proposal" to be "relatively harmless" if "not sincere," Tillyard trivializes Eve's conduct, claiming that she hopes Adam "will retort that she asks too much and that he cannot bear to lose sight of her." So it is "impossible" to deny "the hard fact that both Adam and Eve have sinned: Eve by assuming the leadership that Milton's age believed belonged in nature to the male, Adam in failing in the authority it was his duty to assert."[9] Tillyard never mentions the fact that Adam had asked God for an equal partner, or that the poet was strongly opposed to Hobbes's principle of "patriarchal right." What "Milton's age believed"[10] is more like Tillyard's own conservative outlook in the postwar era, when men were returning to Britain and jobs occupied by women. Such conclusions at the mid-point of the twentieth century seem as befitting of a royalist audience for Robert Filmer's seventeenth-century *Patriarcha* as they are of a postwar audience.

Somewhat more generously, Joseph H. Summers (1962) hears in Eve's proposal to work alone a genuine desire "to get the job done once for all," since it has become a "source of minor anxiety" to her. Adam, however, is still to blame for his failure of leadership: first, "he changes his tack" in responding to his wife's desire for efficiency; "perhaps she is bored with him," an assumption that Eve finds upsetting. Then, "In his anxiety about

Eve's attitude towards him, in his passion which makes him wish to see her as absolute and superior to himself," Adam "dismisses his knowledge and his reason"[11] both. So the "cause," as ever, is Adam's lamentable failure to govern his wife, a clear violation of the "natural" principle of gender and social hierarchy.

John Diekhoff (1958) is more virulent in his claim that "Eve forgets her proper submission and chooses to separate herself from Adam," hewing as closely to the beliefs of "Milton's age" as Tillyard does: it is Adam's "complaisance" which "is correlative to Eve's willfullness. Overcome here, perhaps, as later, by 'femal charm,' he ignores his duty, ignores Raphael's admonition that he weigh himself with Eve, ignores his own superiority and what is proper to it." Above all, Diekhoff blames Eve for refusing "to demonstrate her obedience. Instead, she fails in obedience ... Her arguments are but the rationalization of her desire – the desire for temptation which, following the dream, is another step toward her ultimate fall."[12] And Lawrence Babb (1970) is almost as patriarchal as Robert Filmer or Thomas Hobbes in his claim that, Adam "knows better than to do what he does. Yet he lets her go. In both an internal and an external sense, he has violated the God-ordained scheme of subordinations: he has allowed the lower faculty (affection or passion) to rule the higher, and he has allowed the inferior creature (woman) to govern her superior." For Babb, Eve's "sin, if she is guilty of any, occurs earlier, at the time when she willfully overrules her husband and goes out alone."[13] For she "is, after all, a second class human being."

In the wake of *The Female Eunuch* (1970), one hardly expects to find a female hewing to this line of criticism in 1989, that resounding year of "reviving liberty." While Joan S. Bennett replaces Filmer and Hobbes with thinkers who are far closer politically to Milton – radical preachers like John Saltmarsh, William Dell, and John Goodwin, whose antinomianism did call the law and "all external authority" into doubt – she arrives at the hoary conclusion "that Adam fails as Eve's governor when he 'lets' her go, because by giving his permission when he does, he substitutes his own authority for her truly free decision."[14] The virtue of Bennett's reading is that it tries to render Eve's debate with Adam meaningful in terms of a question of some importance to Milton – whether "the inner light that supersedes all external authority is Christ *as* the self, speaking directly to the will of the believer, obviating the need for reason," or whether "the inner light is Christ *in* the self, rectifying reason" (109). Although Eve's argument is linked for Bennett to "voluntarist" antinomians (98), who substitute the illumination of the Spirit for the evidence of reason, while Adam's position is tied to arguments for "Right Reason" as a ground of freedom from external authority, she cannot abandon the idea of an external "governor" for Eve. For Bennett, the crux is the "governor's" failure to make Eve grasp his reasons for denying her liberty; the critic has no issue with the concept of Adam as Eve's "natural" ruler.[15] Failing, however, to make it an issue for Eve, Bennett reduces their quarrel to an academic debate about antinomian theology. But since Adam and Eve have immediate experience of God's will, one must ask why, of all people, they would be required to justify their "inner light"? Is the Separation Scene no more than a misplaced, anachronisitc debate about theology? *Why* does *Eve* feel she needs to work apart? Why *now?* The whole of human history hangs on the answer.

J.B. Broadbent (1960) is atypical in recognizing, at the beginning of Book 9, that "Milton clears his stage as for drama … More relics of an actually dramatic version survive here than anywhere else in the poem." And yet, "The shift into drama," he adds, "is incomplete and confusing," with Satan posturing like "a melodrama villain," and the couple forced "into a pattern of this or that general posture," until "the drama tightens into domesticity. Eve suggests dividing their labour. Adam answers sententiously."[16] *Why* Eve suggests working apart at exactly this point is what Broadbent can't explain. Even then, it is only after Adam's first reply that the case for drama begins to emerge: "Eve's second speech, of 'sweet austeer composure,' is superior to Adam's as dramatic poetry because it develops with her emotions within the actual situation, ending on the verge of self-induced tears" (250). Here, the "cause" that Broadbent assigns to the action is at least refreshingly existential: "Her slight despair at the garden's fertility, and her desire for children, are significant … She puts efficiency before community. Thus the limits of their physical powers, the scope of their foresight, and the richness of their environment, have combined to bring them to the moment of choice" (255).

John Peter (1960) offers a slightly larger dramatic reading of Eve's suggestion to work alone as evidence of her "practicality … The proposal is entirely natural and clearly dictated by the least frivolous side of her character: together, she feels, they will waste time in 'Casual discourse,' whereas apart much can be done." Why *now* matters less to Peter, however, than why *this*, although his reading is both dramatic *and* sympathetic to Eve, who "endears" herself to readers by arguing "gently and equably. Surely, she asks (185–9), Adam does not feel doubtful about her ability to stand alone."[17] Ultimately, their passing disagreement is transposed into recognizably personal terms; it is Eve's "gentle persistence" that "has forced [Adam] to acknowledge, to her and to himself, that her complaint at 285–9 is justified. He feels guilty for mistreating her, and tries to make up for it by letting her have her way" (118). Nor does Peter revert to the argument about the violation of "natural" hierarchy in order to render culpable either party to the quarrel: "The most accurate paraphrase for our response to their conversation is thus almost a paradox: both are right, but Adam is righter because events will prove him so." In terms of dramatic form, Peter is even closer to the mark: "[T]he first four hundred lines of the book, a crucial prologue, could hardly be better managed" (119).

Thomas Blackburn (1971) also advances the case for a dramatic reading, arguing that "Adam and Eve before the Fall are no more like 'Adam as he is in the motions' than is the Adam described in *Areopagitica*."[18] Indeed, "[T]he knowledge and survay of vice"[19] available to the couple in Paradise by means of "the account of Satan's rebellion is in many respects the equivalent for Adam and Eve of a book which shows what 'vice promises'" (132). Without any hint of gender bias but with one problematic qualification, Blackburn manages to align Eve's proposal with the true principles of liberty that Milton had limned in *Areopagitica*: "If, when she remains adamant in her decision to labor away from Adam for a morning, she does choose a lesser good over a greater, it is to be known as such only by the outcome (which was not necessitated by her choice to leave), and she departs forewarned by Adam's last 'reassuring words' (IX, 379)" (131).

Diane McColley (1983), who has done the most to rehabilitate Eve's character, wisely reads her argument to work alone as "a succinct compendium of *Areopagitica*."[20] "On the principles of *Areopagitica*," she argues, "and the rest of Milton's prose as well, Eve is right: if they allow the enemy to narrow the scope of goodness, he will have won a major victory" (177). Although McColley painstakingly demonstrates a great number of parallels in logic, in phrasings, and in principles between the prose tract and the poem, her premise remains unexamined: "Milton's Eve is distinguished from all other Eves by the fact that she takes her work seriously" (110). For the evidence of the text does not bear out the claim that "Eve's suggestion that she work on her own for a bit is a part of her response to her callings. God has called her, and the Garden calls her" (111). Her "calling" by a voice at the pool – if "calling" is Eve's motive for separation – ought rather to take her in the opposite direction: "[H]ee / Whose image thou art, him thou shall enjoy / Inseparablie thine" (4.471–3); "inseparability," not "separation," would then be Eve's true "calling." To read "their work in the Garden," as McColley supposes Eve to do, as "a metaphor for marriage" (112), ought as well to make the work of "pruning" her will logically prior to pruning the garden, which is only "a metaphor for marriage."

McColley's refreshing sensitivity, however, to the conditions and terms of debate in the unfolding drama compensates for such deficiencies in her premise. She is virtually alone in noticing how, "On two occasions before the separation for which she is so often blamed, Eve goes forth alone on gracious errands," and how "Adam shows no lack of confidence at these departures" (114). All the evidence supports her remark that, "Of all writers on calling, only Milton gives Eve equal work, equal talent, and equal opportunity for growth and accomplishment" (129), while "explicitly dissociat[ing] Eve from exactly the weaknesses that his predecessors and contemporaries assigned to her and carefully preserv[ing] her unfallen liberty and her delicate yet sufficient adherence to active goodness" (141). Further, McColley's cross-examination of the usual suspects is quite devastating to the orthodox judgment of Eve: "Are Eve's motives vain? Did God make her a free agent? Does subordination mean insufficiency? Are Eve's arguments or Adam's permission products of passion? Does Eve govern Adam? Is she a citizen of God's commonwealth?" (142). It is impossible to deny McColley's conclusion that, "If Eve is not sufficient, with Adam's counsel, to stand without Adam's physical presence, her union with 'God in him' is defective, her faculties are flawed, and her will is not free. If she is flawed, and Adam is to cleave unto her, God has created a predisposition to sin" (147). And yet the fact remains that Eve was never "called" to work alone, or to be simply efficient in her labours; her motives are more immediate and circumstantial.[21]

To McColley's careful reading of the Separation Scene, Phil Gallagher adds "that Eve's argument 'recaptures moral clarity and turns the tide in her favor with a succinct compendium of *Areopagitica*,' 'on the principle of [which] … [she] is right.' *But nothing in Milton's excoriation of prepublication censorship justifies Eve's preference for a solitary, unaided psychomachia*."[22] Assuming that "the blind bard is a noble exponent of human equality," and that he should be counted "among the most powerful allies the modern feminist movement can hope to find in Western culture" (8), Gallagher attempts to prove Milton's "exoneration of Eve from blamable deception" (51), given that "The dialectic that comprises this portentous event enables him … to eradicate misogyny from the deutero-Pauline deception ethic" (68). For it is "Adam's tentative imposition of hidden motives on Eve" that leads him to misread "her concern that 'discourse … intermits / Our day's work'

… as unspoken ennui at conversation itself."[23] Still, Adam's innocent deception fails to explain Eve's reasons for her proposal. *What* prompts her to say what she does? Why *now*? It is the suddenness, and seeming unexpecteness, of her proposal that actually confounds Adam. As he bitterly accuses her at the end of the day,

> Would thou hadst heark'nd to my words, and stai'd
> With me, as I besought thee, when that strange
> Desire of wandring this unhappie Morn,
> I know not whence possessd thee; we had then
> Remaind still happie. (9.1134–8)

Contrarily, a feminist like Christine Froula, takes aim at "the workings of canonical authority in a literary context," more particularly "in *Paradise Lost* – the canonical text par excellence of English literature,"[24] to critique the "authorized" silencing of Eve. Froula says that Eve ought to speak out, if not against Adam, at least against those critics whose cultural authority continues to perform the work of denying Eve a right to speak. For Froula, the poet himself is the first to indoctrinate Eve in a posture of "self-subordination," before his historical accomplices begin to enforce the consignment of "her authority to Adam, and through him to Milton's God, and thence to Milton's poem, and through the poem to the ancient patriarchal tradition" (327). Despite her claim that Eve's "imagination is so successfully colonized by patriarchal authority that she literally becomes its voice" (329), it is Froula who inadvertently silences Eve by simply ignoring the Separation Scene and Eve's dramatic insistence that a cultural "authority founded upon women's silence" (339) is no authority at all.

Most recently and disappointingly, Martin Dzelzainis (2009) ignores the broader historical context in reverting to a biographical textualism that lumps Milton's prose writings from the decade 1643–54 together with a poem composed from 1658 to 1663, in order to convict Adam of undermining hierarchy. For, both "inwardly and outwardly," Dzelzainis opines, "Adam is naturally superior to Eve, and Eve recognizes this. The trouble is that in the event neither of them can sustain this understanding."[25] And yet a relevant document from the historical period strongly suggests that women's exclusion from the public sphere was neither natural nor inevitable. Ten thousand women signed, and a thousand of them marched through the streets of London to the House of Commons on 5 May 1649, to present the self-styled "*A* Petition of Women"[26] to Parliament. In it, they not only objected to the unjust imprisonment of four male Leveller leaders, but mocked traditional cultural attitudes that would keep them at home and reduce them to silent subordination. "Would you have us keep at home in our houses," they complained, "and be quiet about the injustices we have witnessed? And must we keep at home in our houses, as if our lives and liberties and all were not concerned?"[27]

Aside from their claims to have an equal share "in the image of God" and an equal "interest in Christ," as well as in "the freedoms" of the new commonwealth, these women pose the question which, on its face, is Eve's question exactly in the Separation Scene: If the petition's likely author, Mrs Katherine Chidley,[28] was having none of this patriarchal authority in the spring of 1649, patriarchy continues to function in the margins of the text three centuries later, and in much the fashion that Froula has described. In the foremost twentieth-century edition of English republican documents, the editor A.S.P. Woodhouse condescendingly makes *woman* visible in his "authoritative" heading, "The Female of the Species," while, in a note at the bottom of the page, he reassigns authorship of Katherine Chidley's work to an invisible man.[29] But Woodhouse, at least, wrote in 1938; Dzelzainis's masculinist assumptions belong to the twenty-first century.

Despite Froula's tendentious omission of the Separation Scene, it is fair to say that "canonical authority," if not the poet's authority, continues to perform its cultural work of silencing women, in this case Eve. Accepting "Froula's theory … that Eve is being educated into a submissive role and Adam into a dominant one,"[30] Deborah A. Interdonato argues quite persuasively that, "In the prelapsarian Eden of *Paradise Lost*, Adam and Eve assume the traditional postlapsarian gender roles of superiority and inferiority, respectively," and that it is this "[g]ender inequality" which "subversively precludes good-will interpretation of the other, undermining the ability to understand and respond responsibily to the other."[31] Here is an account of the dynamics and outcome of the debate where, as Interdonato sees it, Eve's "desire is not so much to be away from a dominant Adam as to be with an egalitarian one. But tragically, neither Eve nor Adam demonstrates the insightful self-knowledge that would enable them to recognize that their unequal relationship has subtly distanced each, in understanding, from the other" (103).

To Interdonato, Eve's first speech in the Separation Scene shows that her "suggested need for solitude manifests itself suddenly, seeming to be more a contextually provoked rather than a newly realized fact of essential human nature" (97). The problem with this reading is that Interdonato fails to note that Adam's "authoritative condescension" and "patriarchal assumptions and criticisms" (98) are just as sudden and unprecedented as Eve's own sudden desire to be alone. Although Eve, as Interdonato claims, may have begun her life with Adam in a submissive posture, we have nonetheless seen how Adam's "Levelling" language worked to discount, and even to resist, that self-subordination. Nor does the poem, as Interdonato concedes, offer an "identifiable, God-sanctioned basis for a gender-determined unequal relationship" (99). Indeed, Adam's story of contending with God for a mate had from the beginning established sexual equality as his priority. While Interdonato quotes from Eve's early speeches as evidence of gender inequality, the only real evidence she cites for a hierarchical Adam comes from his late dispute with Raphael. Here, his declaration, "For well I understand in the prime end / Of Nature her th' inferiour" (8.540–1), is hardly more than strategic repetition of the angel's teachings, giving Adam a rhetorical jumping-off point for his impassioned defence of Eve's moral "greatness."[32]

Where Interdonato's argument has the ring of truth, however, concerns several passages from the Separation Scene where Adam and Eve both sound anxious. "Each insecure, then," she says, "in mysteriously inscribed gender categories that increasingly belie merit, Adam and Eve are unable to demonstrate the grace to concede in argument that they so notably lack, for such grace can only emerge from secure knowledge and honest evaluation of self and other" (101). But gender categories are not "mysteriously inscribed" in the poem – not if God had initially refused to authorize them, not if Adam had continually rejected them, at least until after the departure of the archangel.[33] In other words, there are more immediate, more dramatic, reasons for Eve's evident unease and sudden proposal without making gender inequality the prerequisite of life in Paradise.

Eve gives Adam fair warning of a particular incitement in her second speech of the Separation Scene. As McColley says, she "tactfully mentions" that she "has overheard 'the parting Angel … As in a shadie nook I stood behind, / Just then returnd at shut of Evening Flours'" (9.276–8). But, "What she has heard the Angel say to Adam – who has just been wrestling aloud with his passion for Eve – is 'take heed lest Passion sway / Thy Judgment'" (8.635–6).[34] Sadly, it is an issue that drops from sight in McColley's reading of the drama. For Eve – the point cannot be overstated – longs to find Adam's "Judgment" unchanged. She does not insist (at least not yet) on her own compentency, as McColley seems to think (171), in order to prove herself equal to Raphael's parting injunction to Adam to be "Perfet within, no outward aid require" (8.642).

Nor is Eve another Polonius, who hid himself in order to overhear Hamlet's conversation with his mother; she is simply a loving wife looking for reassurance that her husband's feelings for her are not altered by what the angel has said to him. Nor is this the first time Eve addresses him by name – "*Adam,* well may we labour still" (9.205) – though it is the first time she omits the ceremonial form of address that had personalized her previous speeches: for example, "*Adam*, earths hallowd mould, / Of God inspired, small store will serve" (5.321–2). An attentive husband would recall the mild tone of reproach which had accompanied that first use of his name, when he was tactfully reminded of his proper relationship to God (and to his wife).

Were Adam to listen carefully, he might even hear an echo of his own words[35] in the halcyon days of their marriage, and be reminded of the bliss he enjoyed in gardening with his spouse, before the advent of their heavenly guest. In the space of seven and one-half lines, Eve manages to conjure up that idyllic scene of recuperable bliss:

> *Adam,* well may we labour still to dress
> This Garden, still to tend Plant, Herb and Flour,
> Our pleasant task enjoyn'd, but till more hands
> Aid us, the work under our labour grows,
> Luxurious by restraint; what we by day
> Lop overgrown, or prune, or prop, or bind,
> One night or two with wanton growth derides
> Tending to wilde. (9.205–12)

"Still," she says over and over, "still to dress" and "still to tend," not, to be sure, out of weariness with him, but in the conditional mood of "may," hoping for continuity. Or, as a young generation says today, "Are we still good?" *Are things still the same between us?*

So begins Eve's catechism of love's labours: "Our pleasant task" ought to recall Adam to his former delight in and with her "at our pleasant labour" (4.625); "till more hands / Aid us" ought to revive his thrilling hope of "More hands then ours" (4.629); and Eve's "what we by day / Lop overgrown" should remind him of his prior description of the "branches overgrown / That mock our scant manuring" (4.627–8), a salient detail that Eve repeats in "wanton growth derides" (9.211), as if to recall Adam to his former hope of "More hands then ours to lop their wanton growth" (4.629). Throughout her prologue, both these speeches are so clearly intertwined that they form a spoken analogue of their gentle garden labours, where "they led the Vine / To wed her Elm" (5.215–16). And the "Vine," it would seem, "still" tends lovingly "To wed her Elm."

At this point, a slight change of tone in Eve's echoing "song" could be reassuring, since it is expressed conditionally, even hypothetically: "Thou therefore now advise / Or hear what to my minde first thoughts present, / Let us divide our labours" (9.212–14). For someone with the native subtlety that Adam had evinced in his colloquy with the Creator, here is a challenge that need not be too difficult: "[F]irst thoughts," Eve says, stressing the provisional nature of what she says, making it clear that she leaves him room, if he so wishes, still to lead: "Thou therefore now advise." Eve could not do more to reassure him of her love, let alone her continuing good will, although her choice of diction in "what to redress till Noon" (9.219) hints at her need to "repair (an action); atone for (a misdeed)," to "remedy or remove (trouble or distress)," or even to "set (a person or thing) upright again," to "bring back (a person) to the right course," to "set in the right direction."[36]

That Eve does not intend to mislead Adam with respect to her hopes and concerns is spelled out in what amounts to no more than mild anxiety: "[W]hat wonder," she says with a charming air of self-deprecation, perhaps intended to alleviate any suspicion that Adam may have about her ulterior motives, "if so near / Looks intervene and smiles, or object new / Casual discourse draw on, which intermits / Our dayes work brought to little" (9.221–4). Eve could not do more to ease Adam's concerns in her effort to recall him to himself and this way of life they have shared before "the winged Hierarch" came to interrupt their blissful labours. And besides, she suggests – after her explicit confession that she did overhear (how much of it?) his conversation with the angel – the Creator's test of your desire didn't dampen your feelings … did it? She has good reason to believe that Adam will come through in spades for her, and tell her what she longs to hear: that Raphael's "contracted brow" (8.560) has not cooled his ardour in the least, that he "still" delights in working at her side in their mutual bliss of "near looks" and "smiles."

Nevertheless, Tillyard says, Adam "proceeds to make two mistakes. Instead of being personal, he is vague and lectures [Eve] on the abstract principle of recreation … And then, not noticing her disappointment and her consequent deafness to argument, he chooses the wrong moment to advance his really important plea of danger and the folly of being separated," ending "earnestly but on the wrong note" (*Studies in Milton*, 17). Adam begins well enough in his "mild answer," striking the right note in a ceremonious form of address: "Sole *Eve*, Associate sole, to me beyond / Compare above all living Creatures deare" (9.227–8). Nothing, it seems, has changed; she is as ever his "Sole partner and sole part of all these joyes" (4.411). Had Adam stopped at this point, all might have ended well; had he not sounded like a sententious "Hierarch" in what follows, she could have taken his compliment at face value, along with his concerns about a skulking enemy. But something else lurks in his words, threatening to corrupt his love: "nothing lovelier can be found / In Woman, then to studie household good, / And good workes in her husband to promote" (9.232–4). So when did he start reading the *Oxford Dictionary of Proverbs*? And what other wives, or what other husbands, can there be who stand in need of such *sententiae*? Adam, it seems, is straining for authority; worse yet, he tries to make himself her standard of reference. For what "the" wife does, he suggests, matters most for how it will reflect on her husband. *Thoughts, which how found they harbour in thy brest, /* Adam, *misthought of her to thee so dear?* Though Eve doesn't say as much just yet.

Worse is to come, however, since Adam fails to realize that he has just confirmed the source of the "thoughts" which do "harbour" in his breast. Even if he still sounds like himself in recalling their "sweet intercourse / Of looks and smiles" (9.238–9), he instantly spoils the effect with language reminiscent of the supercilious angel: "[F]or smiles from Reason flow," Adam qualifies his passion, speaking now to Eve as he had not spoken to Raphael, "To brute deni'd, and are of Love the food, / Love not the lowest end of human life" (9.239–41). Adam could not say more plainly that his spontaneity *has* been checked by Raphael's reproof that Love "hath his seat / In Reason, and is judicious, is the scale / By which to heav'nly Love thou maist ascend, / Not sunk in carnal pleasure, for which cause / Among the Beasts no Mate for thee was found" (8.590–4). For now, instead of "Those thousand decencies that daily flow / From all her words and actions mixt with Love" (8.601–2) – those loving words he had nobly used to defend her – Adam forgets himself to an extent that, "to short absence I could yield," were it not that, of a sudden, "other doubt possesses me, least harm / Befall thee sever'd from me" (9.248, 251–2).

Worst of all, Adam ends not just in another authoritative proverb, but in the blunt imperative of a command, even if he does his utmost to make it sound like a plea:

> [L]eave not the faithful side
> That gave thee being, still shades thee and protects.
> The Wife, where danger or dishonour lurks,
> Safest and seemliest by her Husband staies,
> Who guards her, or with her the worst endures. (9.265–9)

Is it any wonder that "the Virgin Majestie of *Eve*, / As one who loves, and some unkindness meets, / With sweet austeer composure thus replyd" (9.270–2)? Finding fault with Joan Bennett for reducing Eve's metaphoric "as" to a simile, with its "distancing effects," Deborah Interdonato seizes on "its identifying power" to explain "how Adam has unintentionally, but nonetheless irresponsibly, hurt Eve" (98). But there is much more here than Eve's sense "that Adam has underrated her, i.e., felt her to be inferior." Our first clue (*and* Adam's, it should be noted) is her confession, just *here*, just *now*, "[T]hat such an Enemie we have, who seeks / Our ruin, both by thee informed I learne, / And from the parting Angel over-heard / As in a shadie nook I stood behind, / Just then returnd at shut of Evening Flours" (9.274–8). The question is whether Eve had "just" returned at that moment, as she says, or whether, in "such an Enemie we have" that "from the parting Angel over-heard," she admits that she has heard far more. The last time Raphael spoke of the external "enemie" (8.234) was at the end of his starry speculation; the only enemy mentioned at parting was the *internal* foe: "[T]ake heed least Passion sway / Thy Judgement to do aught, which else free Will / Would not admit" (8.635–7).

So Eve may have reason to fear that Adam now regards his passion for her as the enemy. She even speaks as if he has confirmed her worst fears: "But that thou shouldst my firmness therefore doubt / To God or thee, because we have a foe / May tempt it, I expected not to hear" (9.279–81). She does not exaggerate. From his stirring defence of her in the face of the angel's "contracted brow," Eve had expected much better than this puling display of "authority." For such reasons, it is beside the point to ask with Nigel Smith, "Is not Milton associating Eve with (female) radical Puritan piety and castigating it?"[37] It is only for *dramatic* reasons that she now insists,

"His fraud is then thy fear, which plain inferrs / Thy equal fear that my firm Faith and Love / Can by his fraud be shak'n or seduc't" (9.285–7). The syntax of "plain infers / Thy equal fear" more pointedly recalls the issue of equality, and Adam now reneging on his original request for a mate. While "Eve's language, e.g., 'plain *infers*,' and earlier '*expected* not to hear,'" does show that "she is reading between the lines of their discourse, feeling for effects in an attempt to hear what else is being said,"[38] she is doing more than "feeling for effects." She is telling Adam that she understands "what else is being said," framing her conclusion, like that confession about what she has overheard, to convict him of treacherous "Thoughts, which how found they harbour in thy brest?" (9.288). She no longer bothers to hide her feelings about the "winged Hierarch," who had praised a hero who was "Unshak'n, unseduc'd, unterrifi'd / His Loyaltie he kept, his Love, his Zeale" (5.899–900).[39] For Adam is failing in his loyalty, "his Love, his Zeale" to her. To her sorrow, he is no Abdiel, "unshak'n, unseduc'd, unterrifi'd." Though still innocent, Adam gives signs of being all too human.

At least he is sensitive enough to recognize the effect, if not the source, of the hurt he has given his wife, doing his best, with "healing words" (9.290), to make amends. Now her problem is not with the name he uses to reassure her – "Daughter of God and Man, immortal *Eve*" (9.291) – but with those other phrases that recall the contretemps of man and angel: "Not diffident of thee," Adam tries to allay the hurt, "do I dissuade / Thy absence from my sight" (9.293–4). But his choice of words makes him sound all the more like he is parroting the angel: "[B]e not diffident / Of Wisdom" (8.562), Raphael had said. It is as if the voice of her "enemie," the "Hierarch," now sounds in her husband's voice.

Adam ends as badly as he began, making not God but himself "best witness of thy Vertue tri'd" (9.317). He is back to where he was at first sight of their visitor, when, in his exictement, Adam had forgotten, and Eve had needed to remind him, that God, not the angel, was their Giver (5.317, 330). He is thus faithless to her, to himself, and to his former language in twisting the sense of words that once comforted her – "Evil … / May come and go, so unapprov'd, and leave / No spot or blame behind" (5.117–19). Now taking the opposite position, he counsels her "to avoid / Th' attempt it self, intended by our Foe. / For hee who tempts, though in vain, at least asperses / The tempted with dishonour foul" (9.294–7). Few readers have failed to register Adam's denial of the basic premise of Milton's *Areopagitica* – "I cannot praise a fugitive and cloister'd virtue."[40] Yet few have noticed that Adam contradicts *himself* here. In the wake of the angelic doctor's teachings, he is mired in self-contradiction, as if he no longer knows how to be true to himself.

Although "her reply with accent sweet renewd" (9.321) cannot hide her real disappointment, Eve does not fail to name him now or to speak with ceremonious respect. She merely lets him know that she hears the language of her oppressor in his words. On two counts, she convicts him of lapsing from his stated convictions. Both in her assertion, "But harm precedes not sin," and in her claim that "foul esteeme / Sticks no dishonor on our Front" (9.329–30), she reminds Adam of his former profession that "Evil … May come and go," yet leave "No spot or blame behind," if it is not "approv'd" by the will. Her gentle reminder that "Heav'n, our witness from th' event" (9.334) further recalls her earlier caveat that God, not the angel, is their true "Giver." It is a mistake that Adam had tried to correct in offering "unsavourie food perhaps / To spiritual Natures; only this I know, / That one Celestial Father gives to all" (5.401–3). Eve may be subtle, but she is not opaque about the source of her discontent: "If this be our condition, thus to dwell / In narrow circuit strait'nd by a Foe" (9.322–3), she says, not to gainsay their Creator but only her husband who has "misthought" of God and her alike in reducing paradise to her prison. "Let us not then suspect our happie State / Left so imperfet by the Maker wise" (9.337–8), she warns him of his incipient blasphemy. For good measure, she asks him to recall his former ethic of testing, as well as that test of desire by which he had won her as his equal: "And what is Faith, Love, Vertue unassaid / Alone, without exterior help sustaind?" (9.335–6) she pointedly insists. Surely Eve has done her part to "redress" Adam's errors; is it not time for him to "redress" his wrongs to her?

And here is where Adam fails her most. Not only does he drop all pretense of courtesy; he literally reduces her to her gender: "O Woman!" he berates her "fervently." It is as if he has now become a different person, fraught with contradiction, quite as oblivious to his flaws as the angel had been: "[B]est are all things as the will / Of God ordain'd them, his creating hand / Nothing imperfet or deficient left / Of all that he Created" (9.343–6). How could he forget that story he had told her of contending with God for a mate (or was she simply reduced to overhearing his account to Raphael?): "Supream of things; / Thou in thy self art perfet, and in thee / Is no deficience found; not so is Man" (8.414–16). And what about that other deficiency, the very existence of which he now denies? Does he not hear that echo of the angel's voice in those words, "within himself / The danger lies" (9.348–9)?

Much less that horrid echo of the "Hierarch's" syntax – "[W]eigh with her thyself / Then value" (8.570–1) – in his cold imperative to her – "Wouldst thou approve thy constancie, approve / First thy obedience" (9.367–8)? The echo of Raphael's words reverberates above all in Adam's injunction, "God towards thee hath done his part, do thine" (9.375). Obviously, she had heard the angel bristle at Adam's confession – "here onely weake" – as he then had scolded him: "Accuse not Nature, she hath don her part; / Do thou but thine, and be not diffident / Of Wisdom" (8.561–3). And now he harangues her in the very terms that the archangel with "contracted brow" had first used against him.

For good measure, the narrator gives his new behaviour a name: "So spake the Patriarch of Mankinde" (9.376). For Adam has never spoken more like a patriarch than in this last speech to his still-innocent wife: "Not then mistrust but tender love enjoynes," he says, "That I should mind thee oft, and mind thou me" (9.357–8). In the shift of his verb mood from the conditional ("should mind") to the imperative ("mind thou me"), Adam signals the completion of the ideological shift that Raphael had "enjoyned" on him:

> [W]eigh with her thy self;
> Then value: Oft times nothing profits more
> Then self esteem, grounded on just and right
> Well manag'd; of that skill the more thou know'st,
> The more she will acknowledge thee her Head,
> And to realities yield all her shows. (8.570–5)

While Adam has yet to sin, he has yet to recognize the damage that he now inflicts on his wife by failing to treat her as an equal. All those distressing echoes of the Hierarch in this speech advise her that he has latterly succumbed to the angel's view of her as his "weaker." And yet how "weakly" he manages the problem of authority himself! For he now subordinates the deity's egalitarian definition ("thy other self") to the angel's hierarchical assumptions ("The more she will acknowledge thee her Head").

Joan Malory Webber notes that "It is one of the most remarkable things about the poem that seemingly insignificant domestic quarreling, set side by side with traditional epic endeavor, achieves such obvious, overwhelming importance. Human relationships are at the center of cosmic loss and gain."[41] It is a concise epitaph to human innocence, for the condition that is necessary to the Fall (its *sine qua non*) has emerged from this needless assertion of power. While neither is yet fallen, Adam does "sin" in a way against Eve, as she will sin against God *and* him. But for now, "*Eve* / Persisted, yet submiss, though last, repli'd" (9.376–7). And what she says, in her touching innocence, proves that Raphael's estimate ("Warn thy weaker") has become self-fulfilling prophesy: "With thy permission then, and thus forewarnd / ... that our trial, when least sought, / May finde us both perhaps farr less prepar'd, / The willinger I goe" (9.378, 380–2). The sad fact is that the intergenerational debate among critics over Adam's "Go"[42] – whether he revokes the exercise of her liberty by giving her permission – is entirely academic. It is Adam's anxious, unwarranted assumption of Headship, not his "Go," that creates the necessary conditions for Eve to fall. Nothing but mindless submission to the changed conditions of her marriage could spare her from deception where she is now so vulnerable.

Eve's vulnerability to temptation only *becomes* intelligible by virtue of this dramatic prologue to her scene of trial. Is it casuistry to insist with Phil Gallagher that the question, "When does Eve sin?" (*Milton, the Bible, and Misogyny*, 78), may be central to understanding her failure? To say with Augustine and Aquinas (and most Milton critics) that Eve sins before she eats the fruit is to assert that she sinned before she sinned, and thus to valorize a misogynistic tradition of making Eve corrupt – predisposed to sin before the fact. Take Augustine's assertion that "our first parents only fell openly into the sin of disobedience because, secretly, they had begun to be guilty."[43] While the Church Father's diction is inclusive ("our first parents" and "them" instead of "her"), his handling of motive ("pride") works to exonerate only Adam,[44] since the husband transgresses "the law of God, not because he was deceived into believing that the lie was true, but because in obedience to a social compulsion he yielded to Eve, as husband to wife, as the only man in the world to the only woman."[45]

Looking back to Augustine's reading of 1 Timothy 2: 14 in his eleventh chapter of Book 14, one finds no mention of a parallel "pride" in his account of Adam's fall: "It was not without reason that the Apostle wrote: 'Adam was not deceived but the woman was deceived.' He means, no doubt, that Eve accepted the serpent's word as true, whereas Adam refused to be separated from his partner even in a union of sin – not, of course, that he was, on that account, any less guilty, since he sinned knowingly and deliberately."[46] So it continues to matter in the patriarchal tradition that Eve was deceived, because it is supposedly her pride that proves her "evil will" before her "evil work": "Thus, there is a wickedness by which a man who is self-satisfied, as if he were the light turns himself away from that true Light which, had man loved it, would have made him a sharer in the light; it was this wickedness which secretly preceded and was the cause of the bad [evil] act which was committed openly."[47] It was clearly the preceding corruption of her will that allowed Eve, Augustine insists, to believe the serpent's lies as truth.

So when did Eve fall? An Augustinian like C.S. Lewis convicts her of pride from the first words out of the serpent's mouth, when "Satan approaches Eve through her Pride: first by flattery of her beauty," and secondly, through his "direct appeal to the finite creature's desire to be 'on its own', *esse in semet ipso*. At the moment of eating 'nor was godhead from her thought' (IX, 790)" (*A Preface*, 68). It is against this prejudicial judgment of her that Gallagher argues that "the beguiling of Eve merely occasions her disobedience" (75). Indeed, "Contrary to Augustine and Aquinas, Eve is without fault even after she has been deceived, flattered, and led by Satan, in a willed but innocent surrender of initiative, 'to the tree / Of prohibition' (644–5)" (*Misogyny*, 76).

There is, for instance, the devil tempting Eve to "vanity," recalling a variety of distinct advantages he enjoys in being able to repeat both the circumstance and the syntax of her dream temptation. For the "Serpent Tongue / Organic" (9.529–30) should easily catch her off-guard, more so than the tongue of "One shap'd and wing'd like one of those from Heav'n" (5.55), whose dream technique of verbal mirroring had merely aimed to tempt her by means of her supposed vanity. So the Tempter begins anew: "Wonder not, Sovran Mistress … sole Wonder … Fairest resemblance of thy Maker faire, / Thee all things living gaze on … and thy Celestial Beautie adore / With ravishment beheld, there best beheld / Where universally admir'd" (9.532–3, 538–42). The mirroring inversions of "Wonder not … sole Wonder" and "Fairest resemblance of thy Maker faire" are designed to recall her to the pool of "Narcissus," about which Satan had overheard her telling Adam. Attempting to alienate her from Adam, he reverses her first impressions ("methought less faire"), as well as her learned response to "manly grace / And wisdom, which alone is truly fair" (4.478, 490–1). And he does so by attempting to estrange her from the earth itself, his overpraise of her "Celestial Beautie" drawing her back into the dream-state, where "Heav'n wakes with all his eyes, / Whom to behold but thee" (5.44–5), "fair Angelic *Eve*," who, "happie though thou art, / Happier thou mayst be" (5.74–6).

Although he is not privy to Eve's latest feelings about her husband and his recent, ruinous, attempt at "Headship," Satan's words ought to find traction with her, given how she feels that her own "fair" is not valued fairly, not when, "one man except, / Who sees thee? (and what is one?)." In any event, her husband *has* failed to appreciate her, "who shouldst be seen / A Goddess among Gods, ador'd and serv'd / By Angels numberless, thy daily Train" (9.545–8). The lucky devil has hit the nerve of her resentment: if Eve *should* be adored and "Serv'd by more noble then her self" (8.34), then why not "Angels numberless," not least of which would be that "winged Hierarch"? And "what is one" man anyway, if he can't recognize real virtue when it looks him in the face?

In spite of Adam's failure to respect and honour his wife's virtue, the epic narrator insists on "the Virgin Majestie of *Eve*" in the instant of her supposed vanity.[48] Unimpressed and not at all inclined to seduction, Eve responds quite practically: "What may this mean? Language of Man pronounc't / By Tongue of Brute, and human sense exprest?" (9.553–4). She not only asks very sensibly, "How camst thou speakable of mute," but "how / To me so friendly grown above the rest / Of brutal kind, that daily are in sight?" (9.563–5). Despite a slight twinge of hurt that shows in her implied need of a friend ("To me so friendly grown"), Eve gives no other sign of a bad or "evil will" which Augustine had surely assumed to precede her "evil deed." Nor is it her "sinful pride," as Thomas Aquinas says in his own echo of Augustine, "that corrupted Eve into deception":

> According to Augustine (*Gen. ad Lit.* xi.), *the woman had not believed the serpent's statement that they were debarred by God from a good and useful thing, were her mind not already filled with the love of her own power, and a certain proud self-presumption*. This does not mean that pride preceded the promptings of the serpent, but that as soon as the serpent had spoken his words of persuasion, her mind was puffed up, the result being that she believed the demon to have spoken truly.[49]

Nothing is further from the mind of Milton's Eve than "love of her own power and a certain proud self-presumption." Nor is she "puffed up" at the adulation of a serpent in whom she has no reason to suspect the agency of "the demon." As Gallagher declares, "In a revisionary critique of his biblical source and the tradition it spawned, [Milton] insists that the beguiling of Eve merely occasions her disobdence. How indeed could it be otherwise, since prelapsarian deception, as Uriel discovers, is inevitable?" (75).

Eve might wish rather to think that the serpent speaks truth when he says, "Easie to mee it is to tell thee all / What thou commandst, and right thou shouldst be obeyd" (9.569–70). At this point, how could she not recall the conditional mood of Adam's "That I should mind thee oft," followed by the imperative, "mind thou mee" (9.358)? Yet the serpent's falsehood about the magical efficacy of the fruit does nothing to inspire in her a "love of her own power." According to him: "Thenceforth to Speculations high or deep / I turnd my thoughts, and with capacious mind / Considerd all things visible in Heav'n, / Or Earth, or Middle, all things fair and good" (9.602–5). Of course he will try to make her believe that "United I beheld" all that was "fair and good in thy Divine / Semblance." In fact, "no Fair to thine / Equivalent or second" appears, leaving him to "worship thee of right declar'd / Sovran of Creatures, universal Dame" (9.608–12). But Eve, though "more amaz'd unwarie," is having none of it: "Serpent, thy overpraising leaves in doubt / The vertue of that Fruit, in thee first prov'd" (9.614–16). She has a particularly painful reason, of course, to mistrust flattery, since her husband had tried to manipulate her affections by calling her "Daughter of God and Man, immortal *Eve*" (9.291), just before he let slip the mask to reveal the face of the patriarch, snapping at her in total frustration, "O Woman!"

So when does Eve fall? Has her curiosity now made her culpable in asking, "[W]here grows the Tree, from hence how far" (9.617). Evidently not. When the narrator says, "the dire Snake … into fraud / Led *Eve* our credulous Mother, to the Tree / Of prohibition, root of all our woe" (9.643–5), as if to invite condemnation, her response defeats our expectation: "Serpent, we might have spar'd our coming hither, / Fruitless to mee, though Fruit be here to excess" (9.647–8). At this point, Gallagher judiciously observes that, "Whereas in the Bible temptation begins with certain words of the serpent (1b), *Paradise Lost* reverses the potentially damaging implications of this fact: Eve sees the prohibited tree and *she* speaks first, confirming her inner rectitude and momentarily recapturing lost initiative by informing the snake that she cannot eat the bad fruit" (77). Moreover, Eve identifies *herself* with the divine law, since "God so commanded, and left that Command / Sole Daugher of his voice" (9.652–3). Her loyalty and her obedience to her Creator thus continue firm and unshaken, as the narrator shows by her swift response to the notion that God has contradicted himself in forbidding "these Garden Trees," and "Yet Lords declar'd of all in Earth or Aire" (9.657–9). "To whom thus *Eve*," he pointedly adds, "yet sinless. Of the Fruit / Of each Tree in the Garden we may eate, / But of the fruit of this fair Tree amidst / The Garden, God hath said, Ye shall not eate" (9.659–62).

So the issue does turn on deception, if more on the side of the devil's hypocrisy than on Eve's credulity.[50] As we recall of Satan's encounter with Uriel, even "The sharpest sighted Spirit of all in Heav'n" (3.691) was easily deceived: "For neither Man nor Angel can discern / Hypocrisie, the onely evil that walks / Invisible, except to God alone" (3.682–4). Milton, of course, had witnessed an unpleasant decade of public hypocrisy, and seen the republican cause betrayed by devilish means. In Satan's response to Eve's steadfast will, the sting of duplicity that had doomed the English republic sounds as if it were just now given again: "She scarse had said, though brief, when now more bold / The Tempter, but with shew of Zeale and Love / To Man, and indignation at his wrong, / New part puts on" (9.664–7). These words are a strong echo of Walwyn's prophetic warning about Cromwell: "Let not faire shewes or pretences of zeale, religion, or reformation of whatsoever kinde any longer delude you, but observe him for a traitor to his Countrey."[51] Moreover, the characterization of Satan's "shew of Zeale and Love" echoes Overton's portrait of Cromwell, Ireton, and the rest of the generals: "Was there ever a generation of men so Apostate so false and so perjur'd as these? did ever men pretend an higher degree of Holinesse, Religion, and Zeal to God and their Country than these?"[52] Even the peculiar timing of Eve's deception seems to run parallel to that bitter betrayal of English republicans. Would Milton's misplaced faith in a devilish hypocrite not teach him, then, to pity the woman deeply, though not to extenuate her evil doing?

It is actually to the creature's show of indignation at the slights she has suffered that Eve hearkens at last, even if his argument shows no knowledge of particular wrongs. The apple, as it were, has fallen into his lap. Now he presents her with specious proof: "Queen of this Universe, doe not believe / Those rigid threats of Death; ye shall not Die" (9.684–5); "[L]ook on mee, / Mee who have touch'd and tasted … / And life more perfet have attaind then Fate / Meant mee, by ventring higher then my lot" (9.687–90). By now, Eve is likely to hear no more than that pretended sympathy,[53] failing to catch the fallacy of his syllogism. For the major premise *is* logical: "God therefore cannot hurt ye, and be just; / Not just, not God" (9.700–1). But there follows his questionable minor premise – "Why then was this forbid? Why but to awe, / Why but to keep ye low and ignorant" (9.703–4). This is her feeling exactly about Adam's intervention. And the serpent says effectively, He wants to hurt you. Now, from this faulty minor premise he obtains his "logical" conclusion: So he can't be God. Or, in the devil's words, "The Gods [plural] are first, and that advantage use / On our belief, that all from them proceeds" (9.718–19). Were Eve to recall Raphael's discourse about the Tree of Being, before he had managed to alienate Adam's affections from her, she could object, Not so! "[O]ne Almightie is, from whom / All things proceed" (5.469–70). Yet Raphael's words are the last thing she wants to hear right now.

Inadvertently, Satan recalls something more congenial to her in words that echo Adam's challenge to the archangel about "nobler Bodies" and "the sedentarie Earth," "Serv'd by more noble then her self" (5.32, 34): "I question it," Satan unknowingly sides with Adam in her favour, "for this fair Earth I see, / Warm'd by the Sun, producing every kind, / Them nothing" (9.720–2). Here, if anywhere, Satan's words are most "impregn'd / With Reason" (9.737–8), for he sounds like the man her husband had once been, before he pulled rank and began to order her about. No wonder that her interest is now piqued by a sliver of reason in his final appeal: "[T]hese, these and many more / Causes import your need of this fair Fruit. / Goddess humane, reach then, and freely taste" (9.730–2).

While Gallagher does "not essay detailed exegesis of Eve's monologue," I will do so, since I depart at this point from his view that "the woman's musings are absolutely sinless" (81). Eve's apostrophe to the fruit "inferrs the good" for her, "By thee communicated, and our want" (9.754–5). But it is that "want" – what the serpent calls "your need" – that marks the beginning of the declension of her will. Now she puts her feelings (or "need") ahead of any other, in order to traduce God and her husband both: "[W]hat forbids he but to know, / Forbids us good, forbids us to be wise?" (9.758–9). Sudden doubt of God's goodness swiftly turns to blasphemy as she accepts the serpent's faulty syllogism that, "He wishes to hurt you." And scepticism about the serpent's motives turns into praise of his daring: "How dies the Serpent? hee hath eat'n and lives" (9.764). So Eve's trust in his friendship, rather than her love of God and Adam, shades into tragic irony: "yet that one Beast which first / Hath tasted, envies not, but brings with joy / The good befall'n him, Author unsuspect, / Friendly to man, farr from deceit or guile" (9.769–72). Only at this late point does Milton give credence to the commonplace that an "evil will" preceded Eve's "evil deed." For she has managed for some time now to hold the innocent fort of her will very stoutly against the Tempter. And the wall of that will only crumbles at precisely the point where Adam had undermined it (because of the unfallen angel's "innocent" meddling), "to keep ye low," thereby violating the equivalence (or equality) between will and reason in Milton's schema. The lucky devil has actually stumbled on the sole weak point in her defences. It is hard to imagine a more sympathetic victim of tragedy than Milton's Eve, much less to conceive of one who is *less* tainted by obstinacy, perversity, credulity, and simple-mindedness than the patristic tradition has usually made her out to be.[54]

At the point at which the declension of her will turns to active trangression, Milton's Eve says, "Here grows the Cure of all" (9.776). While her words gesture toward the tradition of a "magic" fruit, the narrator's stress falls on "Cure," as in the need to treat the virus of hierarchy that the angel brought unwittingly to the garden. Also unmagically, "Earth felt the wound" at her taste, "and Nature … gave signs of woe, / That all was lost" (9.782–4), thereby confirming the metaphysical identity of Eve's will with an *essentially* feminine creation.[55] "Puffed up" with the sort of pride that Aquinas and Augustine had accused Eve of harbouring, "nor was God-head" then "from her thought" (9.790). But this pride is only born *after* she eats the fruit, and only because of her husband's tragic failure to soothe her fears in the Separation Scene. "Though her reasoning does suggest a selfish desire to gain an opportunistic advantage over Adam," as Interdonato expresses it, the provisional "seemingly" can here be dropped from the claim that, "it is a desire that emerges from a seemingly genuine sense of incompleteness and inferiority."[56]

Eve falls because Adam followed the advice of a well-intentioned, if meddling, angel, rather than trusting the reasons of his heart. With some justice, a fallen Eve now begins to think of giving him his comeuppance:

> But to *Adam* in what sort
> Shall I appeer? shall I to him make known
> As yet my change, and give him to partake
> Full happiness with mee, or rather not,
> But keep the odds of Knowledge in my power
> Without Copartner? (9.816–21)

That she begins to express her relationship in terms of power may be the most bitter fruit of Adam's innocent temptation – one that neither man nor angel had foreseen at the time as a possible temptation. But Eve leaves no doubt that this is the natural result, leaving her to think she might yet "add what wants / In Femal Sex, the more to draw his Love, / And render me more equal" (9.821–3). Given her precarious situation, even equality may not be enough; better to be "somtime Superior; for inferior who is free?"

(9.824–5). She has now caught the virus of hierarchy from Adam who was infected by Raphael, and the "Cure" she imagines will only spread the infection. For her desire to be "more equal" is about to end in the loss of her innocence, her dignity, and her "naked Majestie." No matter; she is determined to enjoy the "freedom" of her superiority, even if it means giving Adam his just deserts.

Eve's problem, however, is that she cannot forget her promised punishment: "[B]ut what if God have seen, / And Death ensue?" (9.826–7). From this point, she sees herself as a character in a soppy melodrama: "[T]hen I shall be no more / And *Adam* wedded to another *Eve*, / Shall live with her enjoying, I extinct; / A death to think" (9.827–30). Her rapid swings of emotion from self-exaltation to self-pity, obsessively repeated as the *image* of herself, suggests that Eve is now stage-acting, creating a counter-drama as it were, to the Separation Scene. She is feeding off a sudden surfeit of emotion that leads to her self-deluding assertion that "*Adam* shall share with me in bliss or woe: / So dear I love him, that with him all deaths / I could endure, without him live no life" (9.831–3). She is not, of course, thinking of him at all now, but only of the actor who bears his name, the one who has his own sad part to play in her little melodrama.[57]

So we are hardly surprised to find her belated return described in theatrical terms: "To him she hasted, in her face excuse / Came Prologue, and Apologie to prompt" (9.853–4). She joins those other hypocrites (serpent-Cromwells all) pretending to noble sentiments and principles that they do not hold, who play their part simply to seduce an innocent audience. "Thee I have misst," she insists, "and thought it long, depriv'd / Thy presence, agonie of love till now / Not felt" (9.857–9). None of it is true in quite the way that she pretends, since she wishes to manipulate him to a terrible end, careless of the "death to think" that her husband must share with her.[58] But Adam is not fooled nearly as much as Eve fools herself. Now that it is too late, he senses what must have driven her to this desperate act. "Thou therefore also taste," she urges him, "that equal Lot / May joyne us, equal Joy, as equal Love" (9.881–2). At some level, even he can't miss the sad fact, in this threefold repetition of "equal," of what had wrought her Fall. He had denied her the very equality he had demanded of God; now it is he who must live or die with the result.

Adam's "inward silence" fails to hide the decision he has taken in the instant: "[S]om cursed fraud / Of Enemie hath beguil'd thee, yet unknown, /

And mee with thee hath ruin'd, for with thee / Certain my resolution is to Die" (9.904–7). Nor is he mistaken in his recognition of her state: "How art thou lost, how on a sudden lost, / Defac't, deflourd, and now to Death devote? / Rather, how hast thou yeelded to transgress / The strict forbiddance" (9.900–3). And yet, for all his clear-sighted analysis, he can't imagine an alternative: "How can I live without thee, how forgoe / Thy sweet Converse and Love so dearly joyn'd, / To live again in these wilde Woods forlorn?" (9.908–10). So he converts to necessity what he assumes is now beyond help: "Should God create another *Eve*, and I / Another Rib afford, yet loss of thee / Would never from my heart" (9.911–13). But it is himself, not her, who is uppermost in his mind. She has ceased to exist independently of him: "no no, I feel / The Link of Nature draw me: Flesh of Flesh, / Bone of my Bone thou art, and from thy State / Mine never shall be parted, bliss or woe" (9.913–16). The stages of Adam's rational decline, like the declension of his will, are as clearly marked as the deterioration of Eve's will, ending in the same logic of necessity. "The Link of Nature" is a frail invention to deny himself the possibility of choice: not "I," but "Nature in me," does this. Yet, no more than Eve before she eats the fruit, is his will forced to crumble; there is still a chance to do things differently. What if he were to call on the Creator and volunteer himself to pay the price of her sin? What if he were to love Eve more than this image of himself as a romantic Lover, doomed to share the fate of his beloved?[59] But nothing of this sort occurs to "domestick Adam." His "fate" is finally sealed in the comment of the narrator: "So having said, as one from sad dismay / Recomforted, and after thoughts disturbd / Submitting to what seemd remediless" (9.917–19). This final "seemd" reminds us that there are choices that he simply fails to see.

Adam doesn't stop, however, to consider those better options which we recall from those scenes set in both Heaven and earth. Instead, he rationalizes his acceptance of a pagan Fate that stands apart from God: "But past who can recall, or don undoe? / Not God Omnipotent, nor Fate" (9.926–7). In extenuating Eve's crime, he contradicts his own admission that she is "now to Death devote," insisting rather, "Perhaps thou shalt not Die; perhaps the Fact / Is not so hainous now, foretasted Fruit, / Profan'd first by the Serpent" (9.928–30). Hopelessly, he seizes on the same evidence that Eve had taken for hope – "How dies the Serpent? hee hath eat'n and lives" (9.764) – to rationalize his lapse from grace: "[H]e yet lives, / Lives, as thou saidst, and gaines to live as Man / Higher degree of Life" (9.932–4). Here, Milton does not quite escape Augustine or Aquinas in showing that an "evil will" precedes an "evil deed," though, with respect to Eve, Milton does manage to delay the crumbling of her will far longer than he does with Adam.

By contrast, the husband seeks to mitigate his wife's offence by means of arguments that unwittingly parody the Son's challenge to the Father in Book 3. There, the latter had dared to question the efficiency of inflexible Justice: "[W]ilt thou thyself / Abolish thy Creation, and unmake, / For him, what for thy glorie thou hast made?" (3.162–4). Says Adam, "God shall uncreate, / Be frustrate, do, undo, and labour loose" (9.943–4). The Son had asked provocatively, "Or shall the Adversarie thus obtain / His end, and frustrate thine, shall he fulfill / His malice, and thy goodness bring to naught?" (3.156–8); Adam argues that God "would be loath / Us to abolish, least the Adversary / Triumph and say; Fickle their State whom God / Most Favors, who can please him long? Mee first / He ruind, now Mankind; whom will he next?" (9.946–50). But where the Son had spoken in the conditional mood, intending to uphold the Father's "goodness" and "greatness," Adam argues nothing of the sort with respect to God, and "proves" his love in a merely negative sense by choosing to die *with*, not *for* her. However "noble" Adam's sacrifice may seem at first, he is unable to conceal his self-absorption in his use of the possessive case: "So forcible within my heart I feel / The Bond of Nature draw me to my owne, / My own in thee, for what thou art is mine" (9.955–7). His repeated phrasings of "My own in thee" show how far he has in truth declined from God's promise to give him a mate who is "Thy likeness, thy fit help, thy other self" (8.450). Instead, he effaces all sense of a genuine "other self" in confessing what had been his greatest fear in the Separation Scene: "[T]o loose thee were to loose my self" (9.959). And so he perverts the very promise he had made to win his bride – "And they shall be one Flesh, one Heart, one Soule" (8.499) – into "One Flesh" as no more than a bodily extension of himself.

Eve, who is "nothing loath" (9.1039) to be reduced to the possessive case, is equally blind about his "glorious trial of exceeding Love" (9.961), or "This happie trial of thy Love, which else / So eminently never had bin known" (9.975–6). Ironically, her words hark back to that unhappy trial of his love in the Separation Scene, where he so miserably had failed to speak the words of love she needed to hear. So she speaks them now herself, even when he doesn't – "And gladly of our Union heare thee speak / One Heart, one Soul in both" (9.966–7). Her completion of the formulaic "One Flesh" thus renders totally ironic his expression of anti-dualist sentiments to the angel apropos "those graceful acts, / Those thousand decencies that daily flow / From all her words and actions mixt with Love / And sweet compliance, which declare unfeign'd / Union of Mind, or in us both one Soule" (8.600–4). Those were the very words she had longed to hear from him; but now, when it is too late, she blithely speaks them herself, if only to put a better gloss on his corrupt affirmation that "we are one, / One Flesh; to loose thee were to loose my self."

Too late, Adam does the "right" thing in "sacrificing" himself, as she "Tenderly wept, much won that he his Love / Had so enobl'd" (9.991–2). Nothing, as the narrator plainly says, could be further from the truth: "Against his better knowledge, not deceav'd, / But fondly overcome with Femal charm" (9.998–9). Adam has been lying to himself all along, but now he lies to his wife as well. As if to demonstrate the nature of his deceit, he will "possess" her in deed, as well as in word ("One Flesh," though not "one Soule"), reducing her to an object of his possession: "For never did thy Beautie … so enflame my sense / With ardor to enjoy thee, fairer now / Then ever, bountie of this vertuous Tree" (9.1029–33). So the language of innocence is perverted as each word – "Beautie," "perfection," "fairer," and "virtuous" – degrades into its opposite. But, as "They sate them down to weep" after the perversion of their love, all those ironic reversals of their lexical jugglings soon reappear in "high Winds," as "worse within / Began to rise, high Passions, Anger, Hate, / Mistrust, Suspicion, Discord" (1121–4).

Nor is it an accident that the aftermath of the Fall should constitute an ironic reversal of the Separation Scene. Only this time it is Adam who speaks first, in bitter tones of reproach: "Would thou hadst heark'nd to my words, and stai'd / With me, as I besought thee, when that strange / Desire of wandring this unhappie Morn, / I know not whence possessd thee" (9.1134–7). Like so many of Milton's critics, Adam is much too eager to condemn his spouse, failing to grasp what has really happened, let alone to grapple with her disappointment and eventual alienation. Ironically, his profession of ignorance – "I know not" – does touch on the root of the difficulty – "possessd thee" – even as he fails to see how possessiveness was in truth the catalyst for what followed.

Eve bridles at his gross injustice in blaming her, in imputing "to my default, or will / Of wandring, as thou call'st it" (9.1145–6). Having obtained the proof of the "love" she had sought, she is now chary of revealing too much. Instead, she goes over the same argument again that had started with his failure to repeat to her his words to Raphael in defence of their "Union of Mind, or in us both one Soule." Now what is there left to say? "Was I to have never parted from thy side?" (9.1153). For good measure, she repays him in kind: "Being as I am, why didst not thou the Head / Command me absolutely not to go?" (9.1155–6). It is the unkindest cut of all, and why not? To concede, after the fact, the justice of Raphael's advice to "weigh with her thy self" (8.570), so forcing her to "acknowledge thee her Head" (8.574), is to invert the terms of their quarrel, to shift all responsibility to him for failing to control her, to be the "Patriarch" he was told to be. Ironically if not sarcastically, she then "submits" to him as the patriarch, though more in the breach than in the observance. In turning his argument back on him, she is finally most cruel.

Of course Adam is incensed and righteously indignant: "Is this the Love, is this the recompence / Of mine to thee, ingrateful *Eve*" (9.1163–4). He has no way of knowing that he now speaks the language of an angry God ("ingrate, he had of mee / All he could have," 3.97–8), of a deity whose irony brings good out of evil, enabling "Heav'nly love" to "outdoo Hellish hate" (3.298). Yet it is Adam's hate, more than his self-pity, that leads him to protest, "And am I now upbraided, as the cause / Of thy transgressing? not enough severe, / It seems, in thy restraint?" (9.1168–70). He has a right to be bitter; for he *had* left her free, though he compromised her liberty by first declaring, then unsaying, that he was her Head. "[B]eyond this," he says, had indeed "bin force, / And force upon free will hath here no place" (9.1173–4). And yet he is about to descend into something worse than self-pity; his bathos makes him sound like a sententious "Patriarch," fatuously generalizing from the example of one woman about all "women" in all time to come:

> Thus it shall befall
> Him who to worth in Women overtrusting
> Lets her will rule; restraint she will not brook,
> And left to her self, if evil thence ensue,
> Shee first his weak indulgence will accuse. (9.1182–6)

Adam, who blames Eve for letting "her will rule," is now the one who fancies himself an actor, cast in the role of Petruchio in *The Taming of the Shrew*. The husband has only to demand, "Katharina, I charge thee, tell these headstrong women / What duty they do owe their lords and husbands," and Kate, who has learned with much comic difficulty to be a submissive wife, repeats the catechism taught her by her domestic Prince: "Thy husband is thy lord, thy life, thy keeper, / Thy head, thy sovereign." And Kate goes on to answer for faithful wives and loyal subjects everywhere:

> Such duty as the subject owes the prince
> Even such a woman oweth to her husband.
> And when she is froward, peevish, sullen, sour,
> And not obedient to his honest will,
> What is she but a foul contending rebel
> And graceless traitor to her loving lord?[60]

It is clear from Adam's sententious speech at the end of Book 9 that he has learned almost nothing from the viral effects of patriarchy, arguing like the Church Fathers for the suppression of female will by superior male reason. He accepts blame only for his failure to be Eve's lord when she proposed to leave his side. His blame of her, on the other hand, now gives him reason to desert her, leaving her without a prop or consolation for her "sin" of wanting to be his likeness, his fit help, his other self, his wish exactly to his heart's desire. Failing to see himself as having been mistakenly "exalted" above her through the myopic advice of "the winged Hierarch," he chooses instead to identify her with Satan as merely another "graceless traitor to her loving lord."

· 12 ·

"To Her Own Inclining Left"

JUDGMENT AND REGENERATION

"TH' ETHEREAL PEOPLE"[1] who run "towards the Throne Supream" in Book 10 "to hear and know / How all befell" (10.27–8) the quarrelling couple in paradise bear little resemblance to the "mighty Angels" of Raphael's account of the War in Heaven. Nor does the present heavenly throne much recall the absolute centre of power that the "winged Hierarch," who must have come running with the other "ethereal People," had once sketched for Adam. Heaven is changed out of recognition: the feudal king of the Exaltation scene has given way to the kindly "familiar" of Adam's creation story. And the devolution of centralized power that had begun in Book 3 continues to evolve toward this heavenly polity of "People." Even in God's mode of address, no trace remains of what Feisal Mohamed calls "the most commonly evoked model of the heavenly city in the Middle Ages," the "ninefold hierarchy" of Dionysius the Pseudo-Areopagite (*In the Anteroom of Divinity*, 4). Evidently, the old system of "Thrones, Dominations, Princedoms, Vertues, Powers" has been dissolved as the deity now speaks in "levelling" fashion to a *popular assembly*: "Assembl'd Angels, and ye Powers return'd / From unsuccessful charge, be not dismaid, / Nor troubl'd at these tidings from the Earth" (10.34–6). Heaven's feudal polity has evidently evolved into a Commonwealth.

So Raphael can breathe a little easier to hear that God will not hold him personally responsible for what his "sincerest care could not prevent" (10.37). The deity also gestures toward an an implicit theodicy by which his own motives become explicable in sending a fallible messenger to warn about a Fall from Grace which all Heaven regrets.[2] As he says: “I told ye then he should prevail and speed / On his bad Errand, Man should be seduc’t / And flatter’d out of all, believing lies / Against his Maker” (10.40–3). But he no longer needs to clear his foreknowledge from a suspicion of necessity; for his reason in sending the “sociable Spirit” to man was to reveal something else about mankind’s “free Will, to her own inclining left / In eevn scale” (10.46–7). Much as Adam had implicitly admitted in the Separation Scene that Eve must be left “to her own inclining” to exist as a free agent, God explicitly declares that man’s “free Will” has been left “to her own inclining.” And we begin to see why the faculty of Will has been gendered metaphysically feminine: this human creature made in God’s image is both distinct from, but also derived from, him as God’s true “other.” “Feminine” freedom of the will is thus fundamental to a male God’s goodness, inasmuch as “creaturely freedom involves a self-limitation of God as a means of providing the stuff of that freedom which man himself is to exercise.”[3]

In the final analysis, creation exists by virtue of God’s separation of his will from her divine matter. Yet the *feminine* substance – its goodness guaranteed by divine origins – is clearly unable to inseminate itself. The “Womb of nature” (2.911), though freed from the divine will, has no power of reason and thus no power of consent to be impregnated by “th’ Omnific Word” (7.217). The Creator had no other way but to impose his will on the heedless body of feminine matter. But Eve, the “sole” rational female in all creation to embody this “feminine” will, does have the power to consent to union with the divine will. That consent was first given by Eve in her marriage to Adam, “joyning,” as Walwyn would say, “two free-wils in one” in their symbolic union with God. But in her fall, Eve was unfaithful to God before she was unfaithful to Adam; she thus broke the sacred union of Heaven and Earth in violating her bond of love with Adam. In a sense, Eve “divorces”[4] the entire “female” creation from God by eating the Fruit: “So saying, her rash hand in evil hour / Forth reaching to the Fruit, she pluck’d, she eat: / Earth felt the wound, and Nature from her seat / Sighing through all her Works gave signs of woe, / That all was lost” (9.780–4). The very cosmos loses “her” virginity through Eve’s rash act.

Far more than he knows, Adam was already implicated in “her” loss: “How art thou lost, how on a sudden lost, / Defac’t, deflourd, and now to Death devote?” (9.900–1). While “Earth trembl’d from her entrails” at his first eating of the Fruit, “as again / In pangs, and Nature gave a second groan” (9.1000–1), his act, both temporally *and* metaphysically, was secondary. Notwithstanding familiar assumptions about Eve’s “secondariness,”[5]

Milton's monist materialism actually requires the secondariness of Adam. For it is Eve's agency, by virtue of her gender, that takes precedence over his will.[6] God himself defends her freedom to choose, whether for good or evil, whether for ultimate union or disunion with God, at each of the two great crises of the poem: her "divorce" and her later reunion with Adam. She alone has the power of consent for earthly matter; she answers for all "Nature" in a way that Adam can never hope to do.[7]

Like Adam, however, Eve has to answer for herself after the Fall, although the couple is not yet privy to God's pronouncement that both will face judgment: "But whom send I to judge them?" the Father answers his own question, "whom but thee / Vicegerent Son, to thee I have transferr'd / All Judgement, whether in Heav'n, or Earth, or Hell" (10.55–7). As in all the other scenes of testing, God's tone is gently ironic – his irony serving to preserve the creature's freedom by means of epistemic distance. But the Son still divines the Father's intent; he will go to judge the fallen couple not in power and wrath but as "Mans Friend, his Mediator, his design'd / Both Ransom and Redeemer voluntarie, / And destin'd Man himself to judge Man fall'n" (10.60–2). The Son understands what this mediation means – that he must pronounce the criminal sentence on himself as much as on them, since "thou knowst, / Whoever judg'd, the worst on mee must light" (10.72–3). Still, this is a less rigorous test for the Son than what he faced in the colloquy of Heaven, where he couldn't be sure of the outcome until the Father's prophetic revelation. Now he has merely to act on those same prophesies to bring the promised future into being.

John Peter is not mistaken in *A Critique* about the Son's response, although, as usual, he is deaf to God's tonal ironies: "Unlike his Father the Son is 'milde' ([10.]67, 96) and quite devoid of 'wrauth' (95); he has to 'appease' God (79); and he tactfully persuades him to permit the judgement to be delivered in private, so that Adam and Eve may be spared unnecessary humiliation (80–2)."[8] More largely, Hugh MacCallum observes how "The Son's manner throughout the judgment scene is stern, and while he does remove the stroke of death into the future … his emphasis is not encouraging as he reveals the pain and labour that will characterize man's life until his eventual return to earth."[9] Yet even MacCallum misses the deeper irony of this scene in which the Son appears to institute the hierarchical order that was first introduced to the Garden by the patriarchal Raphael.

Marjorie Nicolson rightly remarks in *A Reader's Guide* that, "In the Judgment Milton follows Genesis closely, making no attempt to develop or embroider the Scriptural account,"[10] though the second part of her claim is patently false. In Genesis 3 the Lord God "said, Who told thee that thou wast naked? Hast thou eaten of the tree, whereof I commanded thee that thou shouldest not eat? And the man said, The woman whom thou gavest to be with me, she gave me of the tree, and I did eat."[11] Milton, however, writes eighteen lines for Adam before arriving at the one line assigned to him in scripture: "Shee gave me of the Tree, and I did eate" (10.143). Where the biblical Adam shifts his guilt onto God and his wife, Milton's Adam goes much farther in accusing God of having bargained in bad faith: "O Heav'n! in evil strait this day I stand / Before my Judge, either to undergoe / My self the total Crime, or to accuse / My other self, the partner of my life" (10.125–8). In this phrase "My other self," Adam pointedly recalls the promise the Creator had made that she would be "Thy likeness, thy fit help, thy other self, / Thy wish exactly to thy hearts desire" (8.450–1). Implicitly, he accuses God of criminal entrapment in having assured him that she would be his "likeness." Although simple love and human dignity would require him to "conceal, and not expose to blame / By my complaint" (10.130–1) the "partner of my life," Adam retreats to an argument which is quite as fatalistic as the one about "the Link of Nature": "[B]ut strict necessitie / Subdues me, and calamitous constraint / Least on my head both sin and punishment … be all / Devolved" (10.131–3, 134–5).

Adam's strategy is not only to blame Eve, but rather – by means of his extensive embroidery of Genesis – to make his blame of the Creator as explicit as possible:[12]

> This Woman whom thou mad'st to be my help,
> And gav'st me as thy perfet gift, so good,
> So fit, so acceptable, so Divine,
> That from her hand I could suspect no ill,
> And what she did, whatever in it self,
> Her doing seem'd to justifie the deed;
> Shee gave me of the Tree, and I did eate. (10.137–43)

Carefully quoting each clause in his marriage contract with God – "my help," "so fit," "so acceptable" – and then adding terms like "Divine" that he had used with Raphael to characterize Eve, Adam attempts to make God more guilty than anyone, except perhaps, his defective female creation. He even lies brazenly by inserting the phrase, "from her hand I could suspect no ill," to cover up his private admission that she was "Defac't, deflourd, and now to Death devote" (9.901). His diction signals his desire to distance himself from "This Woman," but also to distance his "innocence" from the divine deal-maker. Milton's fallen Adam, it turns out, is more ignoble than the biblical Adam, willing to sacrifice the goodness of God and the love of his life to keep his own "righteousness."

Both for reasons of character and of dramatic testing, Milton interpolates a passage of stinging rebuke into the biblical scene. The Judge asks: "Was shee thy God, that her thou didst obey / Before his voice, or was shee made thy guide, / Superior, or but equal, that to her / Thou didst resigne thy Manhood" (10.145–8). It is a devastating reproach, for it appears to confirm the idea that Adam had adopted, if fitfully at first in the Separation Scene, before his vehement embrace of it in his recriminations at the end of Book 9. The bite of the Judge's questions is terribly painful: *Was shee thy God?* Certainly not, and yet he *had* made an idol of her, setting her above his God. *Was shee made thy guide?* Not any more than he was hers, had he known himself aright. Yet, apart from such obvious answers to these questions, a shadow of doubt lurks in the grammatical constructions, especially around the either / or alternative of "*Superior, or but equal.*" No, she was not his "superior"; he had asked for an "equal." Apart from a niggling doubt that creeps into this reproach, Adam has to admit that he did "resigne [his] Manhood" in the process of trying to assert it. As for "the Place / Wherein God set thee above her" (10.148–9), where had that clause ever appeared in his Maker's contract with him? Nowhere. Nothing of the sort had been indicated, much less intimated, when, "guided by his voice, nor uninformed / Of nuptial Sanctitie and marriage Rites," Eve had come toward him, when "Grace was in all her steps, Heav'n in her Eye" (8.486–8).

In that initial colloquy with the Creator, Adam had been able to detect a creative dissonance, enough to make him wonder, perhaps, if what the Judge now says should be taken literally. Of course, on that first occasion, the "vision bright" had spoken to him "As with a smile more bright'nd" (8.367–8), to give him non-verbal cues. But this time, "The gracious Judge," at first "without revile" (10.118), is most stern and censorious. But how much was true? The Lord made her "of thee, / And for thee"; but was it true that his "perfection farr excell'd / Hers in all real dignitie" (10.149–51)?[13] Adam might be tested again, if more severely than before, to determine where and when the Judge speaks literally, and where his contradictions signal a space of interpretation. At least the reader of Milton's prose has this advantage over Adam of being told "how Christ meant not to be tak'n word for word, but like a wise Physician, administring one excesse against another to reduce us to a perfect mean."[14] And this is the position in which Adam now finds himself, treated homeopathically, as it were, with "one excesse against another." But such a trial seems to be almost as great a test of Adam's comprehension as the Son's own comprehension of the Father in the colloquy of Book 3.

Given that Adam had confessed to Raphael, "[W]hen I approach / Her loveliness, so absolute she seems, / And in her self compleat" (8.546–8), his Judge specifically asks him to recall how "Adornd / Shee was indeed, and lovely to attract / Thy Love, not thy Subjection" (10.151–2). Did Adam go too far, then? Had he idolized her "loveliness"? Or had he at least qualified his feelings in his ambiguous "seems" – "so absolute she seems"? Might his Judge even be using Adam's rhetoric against him, claiming that "her Gifts / Were such as under Government well seem'd" (10.153–4)? After all, no one had ever told her – or him, apart from Raphael – that he was supposed to be her governor!

Still, it was "Unseemly," indecent, indecorous, even unbecoming for Eve "to beare rule" (10.155) over him. But did that mean that it was really his "part / And person" to rule, had he known himself "aright" (10.155–6)? The last time his Maker had asked him to know himself aright, he had been teaching the contrary truth: "Thus farr to try thee, *Adam*, I was pleas'd, / And finde thee knowing … of thy self, / Expressing well the spirit within thee free" (8.437–40). Should Adam now forego his reason, ceasing to express "the spirit within [him] free" by refraining from further questions? He is more likely to be tempted to mistrust Eve completely now, to reject her advice and so avoid her "unseemly" rule over him. And yet here she is, "with shame nigh overwhelm'd, / Confessing soon, yet not before her Judge / Bold or loquacious," quietly responding in the restrained language of Genesis 3: 13: "The Serpent me beguil'd and I did eate" (10.159–62). In her deep shame and humiliation, as much as in her undisguised brevity, Eve – "to her own inclining left / In eevn scale" – is already closer than Adam is to repentance and regeneration.

The judgments which are passed – on the serpent, on the woman, and on the man – come verbatim from the Authorized Version of Genesis 3: 14–19. Milton's fidelity to scripture contrasts sharply with his handling of Adam's part in the Judgment Scene. There, his scriptural additions highlight the dignity of Eve and dramatize the ignobility of Adam. But there is more here than a narrative judgment of fallen Adam; fallen readers are also judged, rather like Christ's disciples, by how well they interpret the master who "speaks oft in Monosyllables … scattering the heav'nly grain of his doctrin like pearle heer and there, which requires a skilfull and laborious gatherer." His hermeneutics apply, as ever, to Milton's own poetry as much as to his reading of scripture, since we too "must compare the words [we find], with other precepts, with the end of every ordinance, and with the general *analogy* of Evangelick doctrine."[15] So, after comparing "the end of every ordinance" with "other precepts" found in the poem, we would be ill-advised to read the Son too literally in his judgement of Eve: "Thy sorrow I will greatly multiplie / By thy Conception; Children thou shalt bring / In sorrow forth, and to thy Husbands will / Thine shall submit, hee over thee shall rule" (10.193–6). It is neither disregard for scripture nor special pleading to ask how, if "her Gifts" were already "such as under Government well seem'd," it is now a punishment to be subjected to her "Husbands will," where "hee over thee shall rule"? Such logical dissonance recalls that other judgment of God in Book 3.[16]

In the brief tableau that follows the sentence of the Judge, we may catch a glimpse of something else that had been latent in the stern address of the Judge: "So judg'd he Man, both Judge and Saviour sent, / And th' instant stroke of Death denounc't that day / Remov'd farr off" (10.209–11). It is the clearest sign we have that all is not lost, that the Judge is more a "Saviour" or "Father of his Familie" than his language declared him to be. For, "pittying how they stood / Before him naked to the aire," he "disdain'd not to begin / Thenceforth the form of servant to assume, / As when he wash'd his servants feet so now / As Father of his Familie he clad / Thir nakedness with Skins of Beasts" (10.211–17). Although Adam is not yet able to read this sign, it appears that "hee over thee shall rule" means something more than its literal sense, since it modulates into "the form of servant," this startling role assumed right before their eyes by the stern Judge.

In this surprising outcome of the scene, there is a deeper congruity with the colloquy in Heaven, where God said of the rule of the Son, "Then thou thy regal Scepter shalt lay by, / For regal Scepter then no more shall need" (3.339–40). For the ruler's "Scepter" – which was just used as a rod of correction – is now "laid by" as well. Here, the Judge who stoops to clothe his "naked" children begins to enact God's prophecy that "[T]hy Humiliation shall exalt / With thee thy Manhood also to this Throne" (3.313–14). To the reader, the implicit promise is that man may yet ascend to that "Throne," which is no ordinary throne, much less a regal centre of power. The closest thing, in fact, to this most unusual "Throne" is figured in Walwyn's unmasking of the Tyrant Hypocrite, when he puts the humble servant-Redeemer on the throne in his stead: "[T]hou knowest that Christ ruled as a servant, and tooke the burden of the people upon him, but our Rulers do rule like Lords, and cast their burden upon the poor people, and thou knowest that to rule as dictators, and not directors by their own examples, that is contrary to the rule of Christ, and repugnant to reason."[17] To this extent, Walwyn and Milton both incline to the argument in Augustine's *City of God* that "[T]wo societies have issued from two kinds of love. Worldly society has flowered from a selfish love which dared to despise even God [for instance, Adam in the Judgment Scene], whereas the communion of saints is rooted in a love of God that [witness Eve] is ready to trample on self."[18]

Conversely, Satan's Sin is a negative instance of such feminine agency, a complete contrary to Eve, who alone enjoys power of consent for feminine matter to be reunited with God. Sin, who is no part of God's creation, is in a way faithful to her father Satan in consenting to incestuous union with him. But that union is a narcissistic love, since Sin sees no more than herself in Satan, as she remarks of him as well: "Thy self in me thy perfect image viewing / Becam'st enamour'd" (2.764–5). If Satan finds himself unable to repent, it may be because his "likeness" and "fit help," while springing from his thoughts as much as Eve from Adam's dream of her, is not truly an "other self." Sin has no real agency apart from him, and so no power to consent to his advances. Unlike Eve, who is totally free to be her own person, Sin has no true existence apart from Satan, and must will what he wills. Satan is thus cut off from all possibility of repentance – or reunion with God – because he loves nothing other than himself. Redemption is out of reach of this demonic couple because they are unable to love the "other" as much as the self. Or, as Walwyn so well expressed this trope, "But the devil and all impious men, hate love, because love is contrary to their nature, and therefore they would overthrow love."[19]

More tellingly, Milton reintroduces Sin with Death immediately after the Judgment Scene to encounter Satan winging his way across Chaos, where he finds them building a "new wondrous Pontifice" (10.348) from Hell to Earth. It is Sin, in fact, who resorts unwittingly to Adam's fatalistic language of "the Link of Nature": "[B]ut straight I felt / Though distant from thee Worlds between, yet felt / That I must after thee with this thy Son; / Such fatal consequence unites us three" (10.361–4). Apart from their status as a devilish inversion of the Trinity, these mock-creators are also portrayed materially as now binding Chaos without its consent. Contrary to God's intent to liberate matter from "himself," Sin and Death seek to dominate it: "[O]n either side / Disparted *Chaos* over built exclaimd, / And with rebounding surge the barrs assaild, / That scorn'd his indignation" (10.415–18). John Rumrich recognizes how "Satan's successful mission on earth impairs chaos … The Satanic suppression of chaos" makes Death appear "as the ultimate silencing of ironic determinacy,"[20] that final source of God's creative potency.

Assuring Satan that God will "henceforth Monarchie with thee divide / Of all things" (10.379–80), Sin is praised by her father, since, "with this glorious Work," she has "made one Realm" of "Hell and this World, one Realm, one Continent" (10.391–2). Satan thus parodies God's great purpose that "Earth be chang'd to Heavn'n, & Heav'n to Earth, / One Kingdom, Joy and Untion without end" (7.160–1). Upon his return to Pandemonium, "There kept thir Watch the Legions, while the Grand / In council sate" (10.427–8), the "Grand" appearing to be counterparts of Politicus's and Lilburne's "Grandees" of scornful fame. Now, Satan's royal mode of address gives added sharpness to the fixity of the demonic hierarchy as compared to that popular "assembly" of angels that we had recently glimpsed in God's mode of address. Here, Satan's ritual repetition of the ancient formula of fealty speaks for an outmoded system of overlapping jurisdictions of the feudal hierarchy: "Thrones, Dominations, Princedoms, Vertues, Powers" (10.460). It is all illusion, of course; the "dismal universal hiss, the sound / Of public scorn" (10.508–9) that greets Satan is a satiric hiss of judgment on his monarchy, reducing "triumph" to a Pyrrhic victory. First, his "shew" of "Plebeian Angel militant / Of lowest order" (10.442–3) is exposed as his habitual hypocrisy, since it is little more than a magic trick, meant to reveal him as a "shape Starr bright" (10.450) to credulous followers. When he gloats, "[T]he more to increase / Your wonder" that his victory over universal power was achieved by means of "an Apple … worth your laughter" (10.487–8), what we hear is only the laughter of Heaven as Satan himself is cast, with the host of his admirers, "down … / A monstrous Serpent on his Belly prone" (10.513–14).

Forced to take the literal shape of his instrument of evil, Satan is "punisht in the shape he sin'd" (10.516). The phrase is evocative, for it is the same trope that Overton had used in 1649, waiting in the Tower to be tried for treason, when he wrote a scathing satire that anticipates this comic judgment of Satan. Reducing Cromwell to the "Town-Bull of Ely," Overton punishes the adversary "in the shape he sin'd." Casting his scene in the form of a drama, "brisk Levelling Dick" has Lilburne say, "Be sure to *tye* him fast, that he get not *loose*; for 'tis a dangerous Beast that has goar'd to death the best men in *England*; nay, in the world."[21] *In propria persona*, Overton laughs that "he has so *Bull'd* poor *England*, that she lies *calving* and *labouring* in most bitter *panges* of *Calamity* and *Poverty*, whilst he Junkets, Feasts, and Kings it in his Chariot with six *Flanders Mares*" (4). Cromwell is reduced to a beast whose lusts are insatiable; he is "still hungery, though he has fed on the flesh of King and Nobles, and drunk their *bloud*; has devoured a Crown, a Kingdom, a People, whole Churches, Chansels, Steeples at a *morsell*."

In most respects, the satiric deflation of Satan in Book 10 closely follows this brisk type of Leveller deflation of Cromwell who "no sooner" found himself "in the House of *Commons*, but he was like *Belzebubb* amongst the inferior *Devils*," where "he hath taken the Oath of his Allegiance, Supremacy, the Solemn League and Covenant; look'd up to Heaven, call'd God to behold his Hypocrisie, and the Angels to witness his perjury; he hath broken all Oaths himself, and caused others to do the like" (6). Like Milton's Satan, Cromwell has also "erected a Popular Government of himself, his hired Servants, and combined Creatures," and, "having usurped *Gods Authority*, as well as the *Kings*, hath establisht a Monstrous *Government*, without *head* or *tayle; rule* or *President*; *law* or *Reason*; and commanded all *People* under pain of *high treason*, to acknowledge just, and be subject unto it" (7). Monstrous as it is, this is a "government" that is powerless to escape the satirist's scourge. For, while there is an obvious element of wish-fulfillment in having Satan-Cromwell "punisht in the shape he sin'd," it is also a God's-eye view of human history, with its ever-present reminder that earthly triumph is short-lived, no more than marking time before the Last Judgment. In this sense, the comic "Judgment" of Satan attempting to re-ascend his "Throne" only shows how those who humble themselves are likely to be exempt from "This annual humbling" (10.576).

While it offers an abrupt tonal contrast to the human scene of Judgment with its hint of "sonship" and its promise of renewal, Satan's comic scene of Judgment anticipates another lesson in Levelling that Adam has yet to learn: that God is "Mercifull over all his works, with good / Still overcoming evil, and … by things deemd weak / Subverting worldly strong, and worldly wise / By simply meek" (12.565–9). Here is powerful evidence of Milton's sympathy, belated or not, for the cause of the defeated Levellers. For his mockery of Satan's triumph says more about the justice of the Leveller cause than anything to be found in his prose. Here, for the first time, we see Augustine's City of Man in all its false glory; here as well, we anticipate the emergence of the City of God – what in Milton's terms is more like Walwyn's republic of Love, founded "in all such willing hearts," than that Augustinian sense of a willingness to "trample on self."

Yet after his own Judgment Scene, Adam is as far from love as it is humanly possible to be. In "one of the loneliest scenes in literature,"[22] Adam sits "hid in gloomiest shade / To sorrow abandond" (10.716–17) and to hopeless despair. Calling himself "Accurst of blessed," he calls on some unknown power to "hide me from the face / Of God" (10.723–4). Although Kester Svendsen describes his soliloquy as "the great justification scene of the poem,"[23] it does less to justify God's ways than the scene of Judgment, since it ends not in the mercy of the "Father of his familie," but in the terror of a condemned parent whose only identity is with Satan. In Adam's tortured recollection of a "voice once heard / Delightfully, *Encrease and multiply*" (10.729–30), another question sounds that haunts every attempt to justify himself, or, failing that, to justify his Maker who has left him "miserable of happie!" (10.720). Adam's variations on the question of justice are agonizingly simple: Why be a father at all? Why create that which suffers and dies? But Adam is not yet free of self-pity when he asks, "[W]hat can I encrease / Or multplie, but curses on my head?" For, "Who of all Ages to succeed, but feeling / The evil on him brought by me, will curse / My Head, Ill fare our Ancestor impure, / For this we may thank *Adam*" (10.731–6). And yet it is more than pride – or its inverse image, shame – that prompts his despairing cry, "[A]ll from mee / Shall … on mee redound, / On mee as on thir natural center light" (10.738–40). He can see no way to free his heirs from the vicious circle that will inevitably redound on his head. Reason is impotent without will.

Like his imagined sons, Adam blames his Maker in a self-fulfilling prophecy that lays bare the deeper problem of paternity: why propagate misery without end? "Did I request thee, Maker, from my Clay / To mould me Man?" (10.743–4). Adam's shocking question poses a problem that filial gratitude, let alone human deceny, forbids: Why did you bring me into a world like this? For *this* is the world that Adam himself has spoiled; *this* is what logically disables him from begetting children. Yet he is also that ungrateful child: "[A]s my Will / Concurd not to my being, it were but right / And equal to reduce me to my dust, / Desirous to resigne, and render back / All I receav'd, unable to performe / Thy terms too hard" (10.746–51). Augustine says that, "God had not burdened man with many precepts that were heavy and hard, but had propped him up with a single precept that was momentary and utterly easy and that was meant merely as a medicine to make man's obedience strong, and as a reminder that it was good for man who is a creature to give his service freely to God who is his Master."[24] But God *knew* what he would do, yet made him anyway. Why must the creature forever suffer "his" maker's fault? "To the loss of that, / Sufficient penaltie," he says, "why hast thou added / The sense of endless woes?" (10.752–5), concluding not unjustly that "inexplicable / Thy Justice seems" (10.755–6).

Nor does he find a "justification" of God's ways in an analogical turn of argument to ask, "[W]hat if thy Son / Prove disobedient, and reprov'd, retort, / Wherefore didst thou beget me? I sought it not" (10.760–2). The fifth commandment is no more than a smokescreen for what cannot be helped: "[Y]et him not thy election, / But Natural necessity begot" (10.764–5). Modern readers of Harold Pinter's *The Homecoming* (1965) sense the justice of Lenny's question to his father Max: "That night … you know the night you got me … that night with Mum, what was it like? Eh? When I was just a glint in your eye. What was it like?"[25] Yet neither Adam nor Milton's whole epoch would have countenanced the outrage to honour and decency in the "Lenny"-question: "Wouldst thou admit for his contempt of thee / That proud excuse?" (10.763–4). As a human father, what choice does Adam have? Given his biology, he is hardly free of "Natural necessity." Yet God is not bound by his biology: "God made thee of choice his own, and of his own / To serve him, thy reward was of his grace, / Thy punishment then justly is at his Will" (10.766–8). The answer is almost as terrifying as the question: if God knew the outcome, why did he act on his "choice"? Adam has reached a logical dead end, suggesting that reason alone is insufficient to save him: "Thy punishment then justly is at his Will. / Be it so, for I submit, his doom is fair" (10.778–9). Convicted by conscience, he accepts his just deserts, although, contrary to Calvin, he will not say "what God wills is just." For a voluntarist philosophy of the will only reifies God's power, not his goodness; it cannot not dispel a suspicion of malice in a Creator who has full foreknowledge.

What is far more compelling than the dead end of Adam's logic is the dialectical drama of his technique. As Svendson describes it, "The strategy of the passage is debate: Adam divides against himself; reason struggles with passion; he calls up excuses and evasions, only to to argue them down, his reason gradually emerging to keep him honest" (329). As prescient as Svendsen's judgment may be about the technique of Adam's "dramatic monologue" (328), it mistakes the effect. For this self-division is linguistic as much as it is psychological. Arriving at the conclusion that God's terms are just, Adam switches from first- to second-person speech: “Thou didst accept them; wilt thou enjoy the good, / Then cavil the conditions?” (10.758–9). This technique persists in several first-person questions about his seeming stay of execution: “[W]hy delayes / His hand to execute what his Decree / Fixd on this day? why do I overlive, / Why am I mockt with death, and length’nd out / To deathless pain?” (10.771–5). Even a meditation in the first-person ends in Adam’s fear “That Death be not one stroak” (10.809), that he may in fact be condemned to live in a paradoxical state where “both Death and I / Am found Eternal” (10.815–16). The collapse of the plural subject into the singular verb “am” marks his total alienation from himself, where he identifies himself singularly with Death and disappears grammatically into his deathly “other,” as if Death alone could speak for him.

Adam is riven by conscience to an extent that he is split into accuser and defender both. But even his turn away from self-pity to pity for his unborn children does not restore him to psychological unity, for no better “Patrimonie” awaits “ye, Sons” (10.818–19), he says, than this endless misery bequeathed by their father “Death.” Adam’s dramatic monologue thus leads him into the same abyss in which Satan found himself in his dramatic monologue in Book 4, soon after his arrival on Earth. For Adam’s grammar, like that of Satan on Mt Niphates, fatally divides him, even in his promise to absolve God by taking all the blame on himself: “Him after all Disputes / Forc’t I absolve: all my evasions vain, / And reasonings, though through Mazes, lead me still / But to my own conviction” (10.828–31). Even as he accepts responsibility for his crimes – “On mee, mee onely, as the sourse and spring / Of all corruption, all the blame lights due” (10.832–3) – the weight proves unbearable, “though divided / With that bad Woman” (10.836–7). Alienated from his wife and the sons he can’t even imagine, Adam ends not just in alienation from God but in the alienation of his reason from his will, as if to say that the Restoration had indeed destroyed Milton’s faith in reason. “Thus what thou desir’st / And what thou fearst, alike destroyes all hope / Of refuge,” he says, “conclud[ing] thee miserable / Beyond all past example and future, / To *Satan* only like both crime and doom” (10.837–41).

Even his apt use of simile fails to put distance between him and Satan, because his use of the familiar second-person pronoun leads him into a metaphorical identity with the devil, whom he unknowingly echoes in his apostrophe to his accuser: “O Conscience, into what Abyss of Fears / And horrors hast thou driv’n me; out of which / I find no way, from deep to deeper plung’d” (10.842–4). He has not even heard, and yet he echoes, what we heard before in Satan’s monologue in Book 4: “Which way I flie is Hell;

my self am Hell; / And in the lowest deep a lower deep / Still threatning to devour me opens wide, / To which the Hell I suffer seems a Heave'n" (4.75–8). But Adam's choice of diction, like his self-dividing grammar, only serves to identify him all the more with the fallen angel. As Marshall Grossman comments, "Because he lacks an adequate conviction of God's mercy, Adam turns from 'that bad Woman' (X.837), Eve, to Satan for the *other* in whom he finds his image reflected."[26] And Adam is no more able, in and of himself, to "at last relent" (4.79) than the Adversary was able to do. His reason must be united with his will.

While Adam's logic may defend God's justice, it fails to provide an answer to his anguished question, *Did I request thee, Maker, from my Clay / To mould me Man?* Adam continues to be as far from answering that question as he is from having children by himself. For his logic is impotent to effect a reunion with the divine will, let alone to reunite him with "the partner of [his] life." In fact, it is he, not Eve, who is like Narcissus, wallowing at the end of this self-damning monologue in self-pity and hopeless nostalgia: "O Woods, O Fountains, Hillocks, Dales and Bowrs, / With other echo late I taught your Shades / To answer, and resound farr other Song" (10.860–2). For all these reasons, he is unable, when Eve does approach him, to see the true "likeness" that God had promised him: "Out of my sight, thou Serpent" (10.867), he divorces her by savagely projecting his identity with Satan – "To *Satan* only like" – onto her instead. Historically, Adam's evasion has continued to function in Christian iconography like an article of faith. The icons of the tradition are still visibile in Masolino/Masaccio's fresco (ca. 1427) in the Cappella Brancacci in Florence, with its muted colours and bright skin tones depicting an Eve-faced serpent in the tree directly above her head. In the darker skin tones of Raphael Sanzio's otherwise brilliant gold mosaic of Eve (1509) – gracing to this day a wall in the Vatican apartments – the image of the woman's serpent-double emerges out of the tree above her brow, as if, Athena-like, springing from her own thoughts.[27] And yet, since Adam is so greatly mistaken in view of what follows, Milton offers a profoundly original revision to the traditional image of Eve's narcissism, making it a passing mistranslation of "serpent," which has yet to find its true signified in "our grand Foe" (10.1033).

For the moment, however, Adam is the sole source of this misogynistic belief:

But for thee
I had persisted happie, had not thy pride
And wandring vanitie, when lest was safe,

Rejected my forewarning, and disdain'd
Not to be trusted, longing to be seen
Though by the Devil himself. (10.873–8)

His previous inclination to take the blame on himself was more generous, if sentimental and insincere. But now, his rage at her appearance shows why he is locked in the dungeon of his will: he sees her as little more than a blight on his own "perfection," which his Judge had said "farr excell'd / Hers in all real dignitie" (10.150–1). So he succumbs once more to the latent temptation that had lurked in a literal "reading" of the Judge's sentence: to shut his ears to his wife, to mistrust whatever she may chance to say.

Adam's misogyny, however, is so extreme – and so obviously ludicrous – that it fairly bids to outdo Masolino and Raphael both in assigning blame not just to her but to God: "O why did God / Creator wise, that peopl'd highest Heav'n / With Spirits Masculine, create at last / This noveltie on Earth, this fair defect / Of Nature?" (10.888–92). It is a moment of shocking forgetfulness, in which Adam not only carries the angel Raphael's motif of "self-esteem" to its logical absurdity, but in which he ignores his own role in ensuring that the "World" was not filled "With Men as Angels without Feminine, / Or find some other way to generate / Mankind?" (10.893–5). Adam even anticipates Euripides' Jason in *Medea*, whose anti-feminist tirade ends in like vituperation: "There ought to have been some other way for men to beget their children, dispensing with the assistance of women. Then there would be no trouble in the world."[28] Lest there be any doubt of Milton's distaste for this venerable tradition of misogyny, he now has Adam rant that a man "never shall find out fit Mate, but such / As some misfortune brings him, or mistake, / Or whom he wishes most shall seldom gain / Through her perverseness" (10.899–902). Such lugubrious "generalizations" are "ridiculous, and properly so"; Adam "moves from the particular to the general; he is blustering, generalizing from a single example which even his experience will not support, much less confirm."[29]

Even so, it is difficult to credit the notion that "The effect of such a speech is to suggest both lack of judgment in Adam and his ripeness for persuasion by Eve."[30] A far stronger case can be made that it is his lack of judgment that leaves Adam trapped, like Satan, in the prison of his will, unable to save himself, much less his mate. Without Eve – and his spite could hardly be more clear to her – he is no more than a lost soul, doomed to eternal alienation from the Creator and all of his creation. Adam's emotional sterility, like his barren logic, cuts him off from everyone and everything around him.

His will, "to her own inclining left," finds nothing but "infinite calamitie" in woman's being, which must surely "household peace confound." He has nothing left to say to Eve, "and from her turn'd" (10.908–10) as if to underscore his vicious words – "Out of my sight, thou Serpent" – that declare he can't stand the sight of her, pronouncing their divorce final.

And it is here that Eve answers in the most moving way possible his ludicrous question, *O why did God … create at last / This noveltie on Earth, this fair defect / Of Nature?* Divorced from God and Adam both, and left with neither help nor influence, Eve's lonely being is evidently central to the cosmic drama. For in her total isolation, she is free to choose herself or Adam, or else God. And we begin to see why Eve's agency matters so very much, why she has to be free – at the farthest possible remove from her Creator – to consent for "feminine" matter, and thus to answer for all Nature:

> Forsake me not thus, *Adam*, witness Heav'n
> What love sincere, and reverence in my heart
> I beare thee, and unweeting have offended,
> Unhappilie deceav'd; thy suppliant
> I beg, and clasp thy knees; bereave me not,
> Whereon I live, thy gentle looks, thy aid,
> Thy counsel in this uttermost distress,
> My onely strength and stay. (10.914–21)

Few readers are unaffected by these words, and fewer still are unable to say why; it is the depth of her love that makes Eve's plea so very moving and compelling.[31] To others, her humility is foremost, her ability to forego pride in admitting her need of him.[32] For her pleading resonates with the most moving words of poetry in the entire narrative.

When Eve cries, "On me exercise not / Thy hatred for this miserie befall'n, / On me alreadie lost" (10.927–9), one hears Adam's despairing cry: "[F]irst and last / On mee, mee onely, as the sourse and spring / Of all corruption, all the blame lights due" (10.831–3). But Adam's acceptance of the blame, as his actions later show, is at best provisional, at worst hypocritical: "Out of my sight, thou Serpent" is a better sign of what blame he accepts. By contrast, Eve's assumption of responsibility is as absolute as it is sincere:

> [B]oth have sin'd, but thou
> Against God onely, I against God and thee,
> And to the place of judgment will return,

> There with my cries importune Heaven, that all
> The sentence from thy head remov'd may light
> On me, sole cause to thee of all this woe,
> Mee mee onely just object of his ire. (10.930–6)

As Diane McColley concludes with proper sympathy, "The beginning of her resumption of responsibility is marked by lines that echo Adam's creation for no less than 'God only' and hers for no less than 'God in him'" (210).

And yet the most powerful echoes in Eve's speech do not come from the narrator's double-voicing of the problem; they derive rather from the rich range of echoes of the Son's speech in Book 3 where he volunteers his life for the sins of mankind. No one has described the echo-chamber effects of this scene better than Joseph Summers: "For, as we read it within its context, we are sure that this speech involves more meaning than its immediate surface indicates; and we feel, as in dreams, that this has all happened before."[33] While Eve has no idea that she speaks the language of the Redeemer, the sound patterns of her speech forge a genuine link between her offer to take Adam's punishment on herself and the selfless action of "the true Redeemer … of which Eve's [action] is only the imperfect, if unconscious, imitation: the loving offer that all the sentence justly due to man should light 'on me.'"[34] As Summers demonstrates, with keen sensitivity to effects:

> In the speech itself we hear the continual recurrence of the long *e*'s. The repetitions of the sound are emphasized by the frequent stressing of the syllables in which it occurs and by the frequency with which it appears in the initial or final foot of a line or immediately before or after a caesura. Despite some clusters ("clasp thy knees; bereave me not" or "let there be peace," for example), we hear the long *e* chiefly in the many repetitions of the simple "me" and "thee." The climax of Eve's speech is also the climax of this pattern of sound. (178–9)

Of course, this moving rhetoric works more powerfully at first on readers than it does on Adam, who is not privy to the scene of the Son's offer. Adam is still ignorant of the divine "redeemer-hero" who "acts not at all from self-interest; he avoids self-aggrandisement, and he is the servant of the highest good and the highest love" (180).

Even so, Adam is helpless to resist the power of love and mercy shining through Eve's tears when she volunteers to take his punishment on herself, "that all / The sentence from thy head remov'd may light / On me, sole cause to thee of all this woe, / Mee mee onely just object of his ire" (10.933–6). The Son had said, "Behold mee then, mee for him, life for life / I offer, on mee let thine anger fall; / Account mee man" (3.236–8). There sounds in Eve's plea a willingness, if lesser efficacy, to be the substitute for Adam's sin. "It is in this speech," Svendsen comments, "that Eve teaches Adam what he could not learn in his soliloquy; for she rouses his pity by offering to take all the punishment on herself" (332). But there is more in Eve's speech than just this model of mercy. We still need to divine

> the whole truth: that Eve is also the embodiment of humility and of uncalculating love, that she is the mother both of the highest perfection of human love and, justly, of the Divine Redeemer – whereby all men are blessed. Whether we are conscious of Milton's complex structure is, perhaps, unimportant; the poem has planted the images of the ways of love within our minds and has related those images to the sounds of the Redeemer's speech which it has fixed within our ears. (Summers, 183)

Summers rightly says that, "The greatness of Eve's speech to Adam in Book X is largely the result of the enormous pressure which the rest of the poem brings to bear on it … The reader who troubles to read the poem aloud finds himself often in the position of the unfallen Adam in at least one respect: he feels that he is happier than he knows" (185). For in the reunion of her reason with her will, the possibility of redemption emerges.

Adam, of course, cannot hear (as we can) the voice of the Redeemer in Eve's speech; his response is more grudging, though her "lowlie plight" and sincere concern for him do move him: "As one disarm'd, his anger all he lost" (10.937, 945). Yet he responds with petulance, even condescension: "Unwarie, and too desirous, as before, / So now of what thou knowst not, who desir'st / The punishment all on thy self" (10.947–9). In thus chiding her –"Beare thine own first, ill able to sustaine / His full wrauth whose thou feelst as yet lest part" (10.950–1) – he is finally able to see what is most divine in her, this humble love which is even willing to "trample on self," as Augustine had expressed it. "If Prayers / Could alter high Decrees," Adam's sour criticism blossoms on the instant into sudden hope, "I to that place / Would speed before thee, and be louder heard, / That on my head all might be visited" (10.952–5). Still, he cannot resist a final accusation – "Thy frailtie and infirmer Sex forgiv'n " – before he grasps the possibility of true forgiveness, of both forgiving and being forgiven. And then he adds the crucial concession: "Thy frailtie and infirmer Sex forgiv'n, / To me committed and by me expos'd" (10.956–7). In his first halting step towards humility, Adam feels a sudden rush of love: "But rise, let us no more contend, nor blame / Each other, blam'd enough elsewhere, but strive / In offices of Love, how we may light'n / Each others burden" (10.958–61). It is surely Eve's humility and generosity that have put him back on this path to love, to a genuine love of God and of each other. Yet Eve's plea also recalls him to his better nature, by which he not only takes pity on her, but also on their "Seed (O hapless Seed)" (10.965).

And here is where Eve makes her most serious error since she mistook the Fruit as "the Cure of all." While grateful to be "Restor'd by thee, vile as I am, to place / Of new acceptance, hopeful to regaine / Thy love" (10.971–3), she is blinded by her own rush of feeling for this man who shows pity for their unborn children and grieves the prospect of their mutual mortality. As a solution she proposes abstinence, forgetting that they were commanded to *Encrease, and multiply and fill the earth.* Fortunately, Eve is engaged in genuine dialogue – the sort of provisional suggestion that she floated in the Separation Scene – to which Adam responds more intelligently this time. To fail to create would be to fail in their likeness to the Creator, to rupture yet again their union with the divine will. Although Eve knows next to nothing about her likeness to Chaos, or the way she forms a living bridge to the Creator through her dialogue with the "other,"[35] she is instinctively open to dialogue, and so to dialectical discovery. And she doubts the "virtue" of celibacy: "But if thou judge it hard and difficult, / Conversing, looking, loving, … / And with desire to languish without hope, / Before the present object languishing / With like desire … Let us seek Death" (10.992–3, 995–7, 1001). In her divorce from God and her alienation from Adam, Eve had come dangerously close to a permanent alienation of "feminine" matter from the divine will. Now, in spite of her loving reunion with Adam, she comes close to aborting the whole creation.

This time, it is Adam's grace, like the prophet Isaiah urging, *Come now, and let us reason together* (Isaiah 1: 18), to propose a real solution to the problem that has plagued him since the terrifying alienation of his own soliloquy: "To better hopes his more attentive minde / Labouring had rais'd" (10.1011–12). While praising Eve's stoic contempt of life, he finds in their dialectic the very thing that was missing in his solitary, ever-so-private reasoning: "But self-destruction … refutes / That excellence thought in thee, and implies / Not thy contempt, but anguish and regret / For loss of life and pleasure overlov'd" (10.1016–19). This calling to mind that "Part of our Sentence, that thy Seed shall bruise / The Serpents head; piteous amends, unless / Be meant, whom I conjecture, our grand Foe / *Satan*" (10.1031–4) is the second time that Adam has struggled to translate "Serpent" into its proper signified; this time he gets it right. Crediting Georgia B. Christopher for the recognition, Diane McColley argues that "it is with Adam's comprehension of the *prot[o]evangelium* uttered at the Judgment that regenerate life begins."[36] And Marshall Grossman notes of Adam's sudden burst of recollection and comprehension: "Through his judgment on the meaning of the promised revenge and the choice that issues from that judgment, Adam participates, of his own free will, in the creation of a divinely ordained human history."[37] Even so, Christopher concludes that "Eve's loving gesture of reconciliation (which is far more self-serving than selfless, anyway) has no direct bearing upon Adam's return to faith. At best, Eve serves as an unwitting but providential stimulus to memory."[38] Not memory, however, and not reason, but *will* is the deciding factor. Adam has learned that reason without will is dead.

While Adam's openness to contextual and comparative interpretation is close to Milton's own method of reading scripture in *The Doctrine and Discipline of Divorce*,[39] his will is what truly matters. For it is the actual softening of what God had called "stonie hearts" in the colloquy of Heaven (3.189) that now opens his mind and memory to the promise hidden in the *protoevangelium*, or implicit "gospel" of the future saviour: "Remember with what mild / And gracious temper he both heard and judg'd / Without wrauth or reviling; wee expected / Immediate dissolution" (10.1046–9). But instead of death, "to thee / Pains onely in Child-bearing were foretold" (10.1050–1). Given that *Paradise Lost* is shaped at its deepest level by a philosophy of will[40] – ultimately a divine will that refrains from imposing on the creature's will to seek reunion with that divine will – it is fair to say that it is the gift of Eve's will that enables Adam to exercise his own gift of reason in bringing about the marriage of Heaven and Earth. It is no accident that Adam recalls just now the non-verbal message that had followed the *protoevangelium*, how "his hands / Cloath'd us unworthie, pitying while he judg'd; / How much more, if we pray him, will his ear / Be open, and his heart to pitie incline" (10.1058–61).

The narrative redundancy of repeating verbatim seven lines of poetry just spoken by Adam underscores the deeper design of this poem about a larger union of wills. Adam advises: "What better can we do, then to the place / Repairing where he judg'd us, prostrate fall" (10.1086–7). What follows is a penitential formula for the two of them: "Humbly our faults, and pardon beg, with tears / Watering the ground, and with our sighs the Air / Frequenting, sent from hearts contrite, in sign / Of sorrow unfeign'd, and humiliation meek" (10.1089–92). But what follows merely sounds at first like slavish repetition: "[T]hey forthwith to the place / Repairing where he judg'd them prostrate fell / Before him reverent, and both confess'd / Humbly their faults" (10.1098–1101). Every detail is repeated in the third person now as, "Watering the ground, and with thir sighs the Air / Frequenting," they "sent from hearts contrite, in sign / Of sorrow unfeign'd, and humiliation meek" (10.1102–4). It is the clearest sign we could have that we are called, along with the narrator, to join our wills to those of our first Parents, speaking in union with them as we unite our wills to the divine will, until "Earth be chang'd to Heav'n, & Heav'n to Earth, / One Kingdom, Joy and Union without end" (7.160–1).

· 13 ·

"Brought Down to Dwell on Eeven Ground"

FATHERS AND SONS

"IT WAS PERHAPS FROM NEWTON," Joseph Summers remarks of the final books of *Paradise Lost*, "that the custom developed of considering the last two books as the work of an old and tired Milton."[1] But long before Bishop Newton (1796) opined "that the two last books fall short of the sublimity and majesty of the rest,"[2] Joseph Addison (1712) wrote that they were "not generally reckoned among the most shining books of this poem."[3] Modern readers have been even less charitable in their judgments, J.B. Broadbent censuring the "decay of the poetry" – even remarking at one point "that the verse becomes arthritic" – while elsewhere recalling, that "Paul used Adam as a doctrinal symbol," whereas "Milton makes him a living being and then treats him as a hostage to dogma."[4] John Peter likewise finds a "strain in the poetry which is turgid and tortuous," a judgment that does not surprise, given what he calls "the artistic problem of anticlimax"[5] in the close of the poem. Even David Loewenstein, who reads these last books as an eloquent summation of Milton's polemical prose, has "to concede that these remain artistically problematic books in which Milton is struggling with his imaginative responses to history as a tragic process."[6]

Worse than any of these, however, is the harsh judgment of C.S. Lewis that the poem "suffers from a grave structural flaw." For "Milton, like Virgil, though telling a short story about the remote past, wishes our minds to be carried to the later results of that story. But he does this less skilfully than Virgil." Blaming him for being too traditional, the old-style critic and orthodox Anglican finds Milton guilty not only of "following his master in the use of occasional prophecies, allusions, and reflections," but of making "his two last books into a brief outline of sacred history from the Fall to the Last Day. Such an untransmuted lump of futurity, coming in a position so momentous for the structural effect of the whole work, is inartistic."[7] Taking for gospel this "untransmuted lump of futurity" at the end of *Paradise Lost*, Charles Martindale complains that it works "in a manner that is comparatively dry and undernourished," and merely contents himself by repeating Samuel Johnson's judgment of the poem that "No one ever wished it longer than it is."[8]

These unfavourable comparisons of the design of Milton's epic to the prophetic design of Virgil's *Aeneid* are surprising, given Addison's informed judgment that "the plan of *Milton's* poem is in many particulars greater than that of the Iliad or Æneid. Virgil's hero, in the last of these poems, is entertained with a sight of all those who are to descend from him; but though that episode is justly admired as one of the noblest designs of the whole Æneid, every one must allow that this of Milton is of a much higher nature."[9] Rare is the critic like Lawrence Sasek who rates Milton's achievement as superior to that of Virgil, because Milton renders dramatically what Virgil's eighth book had merely treated descriptively in a hundred lines on the shield of Aeneas.[10] Martindale, on the other hand, allows that he outdoes "his master if only because the Christian concept of eternity overtops in imaginative splendour Virgil's vision of empire without end" (144–5).

While Louis Martz seeks to atone for a prior judgment in *The Paradise Within*, where he had expressed "considerable disappointment with Milton's performance in his finale," he leaps too quickly – rather like Sasek thinking Adam is disciplined through vision to accept God's ways – to the stoical conclusion that "Milton's lowered style refuses to be heroic: the style itself scorns the distentions of empire and leads toward the firm and quiet closing words of Adam and the angel."[11] As a good Latinist, Martz ought to have remembered that the true benchmark for Adam's visions was always Virgil's *Aeneid*, not Camoëns's *Lusiads*, the great sixteenth-century Portuguese poem of empire.[12] Yet Sasek, who at least got the source right, failed to see beyond the "static" (345) description of the shield of Aeneas to what Addison took in at a glance: the descent of Aeneas into the Underworld as the main object of Milton's poetic reversal.

Virgil's structure, like his lofty style, is part and parcel of an imperial design, whereby the Roman hero, meeting in the Underworld the ghost of his father, Anchises, sees face to face "What famous children in your line will come, / Souls of the future, living in our name."[13] As Father Anchises hastens "in the telling" to "Teach you your destiny" (186), his filial survivor comes, a thousand years in advance of that "empire without end," to gaze upon the face of the Roman "Caesar, and all the line of Iulus, / … this is the man, this one, / Of whom so often you have heard the promise, / Caesar Augustus, son of the deified, / Who shall bring once again an Age of Gold / To Latium"[14] (187–8). In fact, the great vision of Aeneas comes at the precise midpoint of the Roman epic (near the end of the sixth of twelve books), after Troy's survivor has made landfall in Italy and descends into Avernus with Apollo's Sibyl through the cave at Cumae. His vision of future things is what ultimately inspires Aeneas to become the Roman founder who is symbolically reborn from the Underworld as the Roman hero, a true prototype of Augustus.[15]

What Lewis called an "untransmuted lump of futurity" in Milton is literally a "lump of futurity" in Virgil's poem; even its stasis is iconic, where Milton's future is dramatic. And if Martindale is right to see Virgil's handling of time as superior to Milton's, it is only in the limited sense of giving temporal depth to local places, the "most telling instance" of which "in the *Aeneid* occurs in Book VIII when Aeneas visits the future site of Rome."[16] Still, what Martindale fails to say is that Virgil's structure, with all its temporal depth, is designed to make Rome the centre of world history, the true pivot of Latin power and imperial might. And these are values that Milton's God opposes.

At the very centre of the historical design of *Paradise Lost* is the folly of Satanic empire set over against the glory of God's creative power.[17] Far from being the narrative reification of a centralized and centralizing power, Milton's poem advances structures of thought and language (what Martz calls Milton's "lowered style") that aim to decentre and diffuse all power in Heaven and on earth. The structure of that history, like the narrative itself, requires radical openness to the future. Nor can there be any doubt of the immediate consequence of the political decentring that Michael prophesies: "this had been / Perhaps thy Capital Seate, from whence had spred / All generations, and had hither come / From all the ends of th' Earth, to celebrate / And reverence thee thir great Progenitor" (11.342–6). Contrary to a static, hierarchical, centralized society, the Fall has brought about a social levelling: "But this præeminence thou hast lost, brought down / To dwell on eeven ground now with thy Sons" (11.347–8). It might be Adam's personal misfortune to have lost that "præeminence," but it is no real misfortune for his heirs to have escaped the sway of patriarchal power, thus avoiding subject status at his "Capital Seate." Here, if anywhere, Milton could have found the political ground for a "fortunate Fall," were the *felix culpa* required to achieve that radical renunciation of power that has already begun in Heaven's casting down of crowns (3.351–2), and is refigured (no matter the vagueness of Raphael's understanding of it), in prophecy where "Earth be chang'd to Heav'n, & Heav'n to Earth, / One Kingdom, Joy and Union without end" (7.160–1).

The very description of the father "brought down / To dwell on eeven ground now" with his sons appears to signal a change in Milton's own thinking about patriarchal rule in the Commonwealth era and thereafter. Before the Lord Protector had yet risen to semi-absolute power, Politicus[18] reported the view of a social majority who believed that

> our *first Parent* ruled by a plenary Power and Authority, in himselfe only, as did also the *Patriarchs* before, and after the *Floud* too for some time, becoming Princes by vertue of a Paternall right, over all the Families of their own Generation and extraction; so that the Fathers by reason of their extraordinary long lives, and the multiplicity of wives, hapned to be Lords of Kingdomes or Principalities of their own begetting. And so some deriving the pedigree or Government from this Paternal Right of Soveraignty, would by all means conclude; That the original of Government, neither was, nor ought to be in the People.[19]

Contrary to received opinion, Politicus concluded that "This Form of government was only temporary, and took an end not long after the flood, when *Nimrod* changed it, and by force combining numbers of distinct Families into one Body, and subjecting them to his own Regiment, did by an arbitrary power, seated in his owne Will and Sword, constrain them to submit unto what Lawes and Conditions himself pleased to impose upon Them. Thus the *Paternal* form becam changed into a *Tyrannical*" (1538).

Contrary to royalist dogma, Politicus had insisted in 1652 that sovereignty derived from the people; yet Milton at the time could still believe in the right of Adam to rule his sons. But when he came, after the Restoration, to write the final books of *Paradise Lost*, he now rejected unequivocally that paternal right. Neither "our *first Parent*" nor God's anointed "Princes" could claim to rule "by vertue of a Paternall right." Patriarchal power, which for Hobbes and Filmer had for all time justified the rule of princes, ended for Politicus with Nimrod, the biblical usurper. Even more remarkably, the "vertue of a Paternall right" had for the aging poet ceased at the Fall. Patriarchal "right" in *Paradise Lost* is a stillborn idea that only ever held sway *by means of force*, and only after the Fall.

On this point, the evolution of public discourse in Heaven over the course of the poem is even more telling. In the primal scene in Book 5, God had addressed the angelic host in terms of his absolute power and their feudal dependence for their very titles on him: "Thrones, Dominations, Princedomes, Vertues, Powers," he declaims, "Hear my Decree" (5.601–2). Satan, "Affecting all equality with God" (5.763), chooses to repeat the same titular forms: "Thrones, Dominations, Princedomes, Vertues, Powers, / If these magnific Titles yet remain / Not meerly titular" (5.772–4). Yet God adopts an inclusive form of address to announce his intention to create new worlds: "Mean while inhabit laxe, ye Powers of Heav'n, / And thou my Word, begotten Son" (7.162–3). Oddly enough, this last vestige of hierarchical address is more relaxed after the Fall of Man: "Assembl'd Angels, and ye Powers return'd / From unsuccessful charge, be not dismaid" (10.34–5). Most telling of all, the Father sounds a distinctly new public note after the contrite prayers of Adam and Eve and the Son's intercession: "O Sons, like one of us Man is become" (11.84). Only after the restoration of human beings to grace and the restoration of God's image within them by virtue of the Son's imputed sacrifice, does the Father unveil his program of inclusive sonship.[20] It is his "first-begotten" who shows what it means to be a "Son" of God, and what that filiation implies, given how "All my redeemd may dwell in joy and bliss, / Made one with me as I with thee am one" (11.43–4).

Both theologically and narratively, what the Son models for other "Sons of God" is his oneness in will with the Father. As Hugh MacCallum notes, "Their unity is one of mind and will, as the Son emphasizes with characteristic humility: 'this I my Glorie account, / My exaltation, and my whole delight, / That thou in me well pleas'd, declarst thy will / Fulfill'd, which to fulfil is all my bliss' [6.726–9]."[21] "The Son is united to the Father through obedience and love, and thus provides a living paradigm of the wisdom, holiness, and righteousness which are" originally "reflected in Adam. This filial Adam lives in freedom and not under a covenant of works, for he has the law of nature within him."[22]

After the Fall, however, the filial image is obscured, if not extinguished, by the broken unity of wills, and is only restored by means of the Mediator whose grace it is to model that perfect unity of wills. In other words, it is not the fruit that brought Adam to "know both Good and Evil," as one assumes God had really said – as if to be "like one of us" required knowledge of actual evil. It is through filial freedom – the choice to be contrite, to be open to love, to eschew the Evil of the faithless angels – that Man "is become like one of us," as the Father says, honouring the fidelity of those who chose to shun Evil, as well as him who "sorrows now, repents, and prayes contrite" (11.90–1) to regain a state of filial love and unity. "Only by thinking of God in this way," MacCallum remarks, "can man realize the godlike elements within himself" (62). Or, as the Son phrases it most memorably, man is "Made one with me as I with thee am one." In the final analysis, to become a Son of God is to love and live for that time when "thou thy regal Scepter shalt lay by, / For regal Scepter then no more shall need, / God shall be All in All" (3.339–41). Here, indeed, exists that Kingdom of Grace where, as Walwyn had described it, "Faith is a mercenary, but love is a voluntary souldiour … for in all such willing hearts, God is all in all, for all things are from God, through God, and to God, and God is love."[23]

If we need to extend, we also need to modify what Thomas Amorose finds in the final visions in *Paradise Lost* – how "God's miraculous intervention in history" is "an indication of God's process in history for leading man back to him: the last two books of *Paradise Lost* show God producing his desired results through the annihilation of patterns of behaviour that obstruct his freeing mankind from fallen history."[24] Amorose reads these last books as being entirely iconoclastic, their dissonance of "epic, history, and prophecy" working "to subvert belief in imprisoning forms of action. For this and other reasons, Books XI and XII should be considered an apocalyptic, indeed a millenarian presentation of history."[25] David Loewenstein, on the other hand, sees the outcome of history as tragic in *Paradise Lost*, claiming that Milton's "iconoclasm is simultaneously literary and historical: historical transformation involves 'casting down imaginations,' a powerful and destructive act that for Milton is nevertheless poetic and theatrical."[26]

For Loewenstein, the outcome differs little from the supposed emplotment of history as tragedy in Milton's *Second Defense*, the *History of Britain*, and *The Readie and Easie Way*, even where "The various historical configurations which emerge in these troubled books – degenerative, cyclical, apocalyptic, typological – represent a series of imaginative and conflicting responses to Milton's revolutionary years and writings."[27] Exploring the governing pattern of "the 'one just Man'" (11.818, 890), which Amorose sees as introducing "a new, anti-epic hero, the prophet-hero,"[28] Loewenstein concludes that "The just man of Michael's visions *would like* to be radically involved in the social order – to be an activist agent in the turbulent process of history – but instead finds himself radically alienated from the historical process itself" (104; italics in original).

To a significant extent, this reading of Milton's epic historiography repeats the critical cliché of "an old and tired Milton," particularly in the way that the "polemical Milton had experienced a similar dilemma" to that of Adam. As Loewenstein sees it,

> [O]n the one hand, he continued to involve himself actively in the historical drama, as he desperately urged the Commonwealth to reform itself; on the other hand, his late revolutionary tracts registered his sense of radical alienation from the relapsing nation, with its lust for royalist authority, and his desire to disengage himself from the tragic historical process altogether … This powerful tension, unresolved in the flurry of late pre-Restoration polemics, finds renewed dramatization in Michael's depiction of Noah and other isolated godly men caught up in the midst of a world perverse. (105)

On this view, God alone can be a successful iconoclast, meaning that "Adam and Eve essentially walk into the history envisioned throughout much of Milton's revolutionary prose works and major poems" – a world in which "historical characters do indeed often act, as they do in the *History of Britain*, like 'little more then mute persons in a Scene'" – a future that insists on "the drama of history as a tragic and difficult process, where human progress and reform are far from assured."[29]

But what each of these iconoclastic readings – the tragic as much as the millenarian – leaves out is the governing ethic of testing that informs *Paradise Lost*, from the Exaltation Scene through the colloquy in Heaven to Adam's dialogue with Raphael, to Eve's debate with Adam in the Separation Scene, right down to the motivated ambiguities of the Judgment Scene. For Joseph Summers, this ubiquitous ethic of testing suggests that "The final books provide for both Adam and the reader the final temptations."[30] Summers only falters in establishing what might be at stake in this culminating series of temptations.

In his first vision, Adam watches as "A sweatie Reaper," enraged by "a Shepherd next / More meek" – because the herder's offering is accepted by Heaven where the tiller's sacrifice is not – "Smote him into the Midriff with a stone / That beat out life" (11.434, 436–7, 445–6). Adam is "Dismai'd," crying out, "O Teacher, some great mischief hath befall'n / To that meek man, who well had sacrific'd; / Is Pietie thus and pure Devotion paid? [11.450–2]." Instead of assuming the poet's pessimism,[31] however, Summers says that "Adam is too involved in his personal fate to respond to" a comforting promise that "the bloodie Fact / Will be aveng'd, and th' others Faith approv'd / Loose no reward, though here thou see him die, / Rowling in dust and gore" (11.457–60).[32] There is even reason to condemn Adam for his self-concern: "But have I now seen Death? Is this the way / I must return to native dust? O sight / Of terrour, foul and ugly to behold" (11.462–4). And yet Adam has witnessed more than a violent murder; for the first time, he looks Death in the eye and blinks, his natural instinct being to ensure his own survival.

Adam, however, is not lacking in sympathy. In the vision after Cain and Abel, "Before his eyes appeard, sad, noysom, dark, / A Lazar-house" (11.478–9), where for the first time he beholds every disease that flesh is heir to, and sees the "heart-sick Agonie" (11.482) of those dying from natural causes, a "natural" result of his own evil: "Sight so deform what heart of Rock could long / Drie-ey'd behold?" Of course, "*Adam* could not, but wept, / Though not of Woman born; compassion quell'd / His best of Man, and gave him up to tears / A space" (11.494–8). Such sympathy, however, is also the occasion of another temptation. In despair, Adam now cries out: "O miserable Mankind, to what fall / Degraded, to what wretched state reserv'd! / Better end heer unborn" (11.500–2). In this delayed reaction, he begins to recoil from the agony of knowing that one of his sons will grow up to kill his brother. Better, he assumes, not to give his sons life at all than to allow their fratricide to come to pass. For Adam now despairs of more than life; he suddenly despairs of the promise of the *protoevangelium*, that faith he had first expressed to Eve in the Reconciliation Scene, "that thy Seed shall bruise / The Serpents head; piteous amends, unless / Be meant, whom I conjecture, our grand Foe / *Satan*" (10.1031–4).

In both of these painful encounters with Death, Adam stands in danger of losing not only his faith in life but in a benign Providence. In the ensuing visions, there lurks again the unvoiced leitmotif of "Better end here unborn." It now persists as a latent threat to the great design of Creation, whereby a liberal God seeks reunion with "her" substance freed from "his" being. "Better end here unborn" threatens to repeat the error against which Adam had warned Eve so strongly in the Reconciliation Scene – of stoic contempt for life that "refutes / That excellence thought in thee, and implies, / Not thy contempt, but anguish and regret / For loss of life and pleasure overlov'd" (10.1016–19). Should Father Adam refuse to accept fatherhood, the Son's warning to the Father could yet come to pass: "[S]hall the Adversarie thus obtain / His end, and frustrate thine," allowing Satan to "fulfill / His malice" (3.156–9)? In spite of being levelled by the common human fate, Adam's sympathy for his sons actually threatens to return the creation to square one.

Even so, Summers is justified in his view that a stoic form of acceptance which Adam next embraces – "Henceforth I flie not Death, nor would prolong / Life much … patiently attend[ing] / My dissolution" (11.547–8, 551–2) – is radically insufficient: "Michael's two-line reproof summarizes what is wrong with it and indicates the limitations of Adam's responses to the initial visions: 'Nor love thy Life, nor hate; but what thou liv'st / Live well, how long or short permit to Heav'n' (553–4)" (201). Yet what Summers fails to say is that stoic resignation really involves a choice of self over God, making it hardly more than an expression of indifference to life. It can even be taken for the reverse face of Adam's despairing cry, "Better end here unborn."

While Adam finds new hope in the next vision "Of Arts that polish Life" (11.610), he is warned that the "fair femal Troop" associated with these arts is "empty of all good," and is "Bred onely and completed to the taste / Of lustful appetence, to sing, to dance, / To dress, and troule the Tongue" (11.614, 616, 618–20). Adam's response shows why he is not yet fully regenerate, slipping, as he does, back into the misogyny that had nearly pre-empted Eve's humility in their reconciliation. There are further signs of his previous mistrust of "This noveltie on Earth, this fair defect / Of Nature" (10.891–2), as he renews his laughable complaint: "But still I see the tenor of Mans woe / Holds on the same, from Woman to begin" (11.632–3). In effect, Michael's tactic is to mock Adam out of self-conceit: "From Mans effeminate slackness it begins / … who should better hold his place / By wisdome, and superiour gifts receav'd" (11.634–6). *Should* is the marker of Adam's self-importance, a sign of what he could say were his presumptions justified. Yet despite a pervasive weariness in these visions, it is not weariness in the narrative; it is the reader's own weariness at Adam taking two steps back for each forward one he makes.

In the vision of Enoch and that monstrous "Oppresion" against which "one Just man" is moved to speak out, we finally witness the emergence of

Adam's better nature in the way he begins to respond to scenes of troubling violence, "and Sword-Law / Through all the Plain," where "refuge none was found" (11.672–3). Understandably, "*Adam* was all in tears, and to his guide / Lamenting turnd full sad; O what are these, / Deaths Ministers, not Men?" (11.674–6). His judgment, as Michael admits, is astute. Although such warriors can "be styl'd great Conquerours, / Patrons of Mankind, Gods, and Sons of Gods," they are "Destroyers rightlier call'd and Plagues of men" (11.695–7). One may be forgiven for finding Milton railing here like another Enoch against the ancient heroic ethic that the poet had from the outset promised "to soar / Above" (1.14–15).

Yet Milton takes aim at more than literary targets in this scene. For Cromwell is one of those "great Conquerours" and "Patrons of Mankind" who "rightlier" should be called "Destroyers … and Plagues of Men." Particularly in the phrase "Sword-Law," one hears the echo of what Cromwell's preacher Hugh Peter had said to John Lilburne in his prison cell in 1649. Scoffing at Lilburne for being "*meerly gul'd in reading or trusting to these Books*" of law, Peter sneered that "*there was no Laws in* England." As he pontificated, "[T]here is no Law in this Nation, but the sword, and what it gives; neither was there any Law or Government in the World, but what the Sword gave and set up" (5). To which Lilburne, like another Enoch, had responded in the manner of the "one just Servant":

> But Sir, in short and in plain English, let me tell you, that if there be now no law in *England*, nor never was, that then you and your great Masters, *Cromwell, Fairfax*, and the Parliament, are a pack of arrant bloody Rogues and Villaines, in setting the people together by the ears, to fight for the preservation of their Laws, in which their Libertie is contained (which is the principall declared cause of the Warre from the beginning to the end of the War).[33]

Lilburne was also to condemn "your new Sword Tyranny, called a Common-wealth"[34] in *Strength out of Weaknesse.* In "Sword-Law," Milton turns Lilburne into something close to a biblically-inspired prophet. Nor is the poet himself sunk in despair, given how much these last two books are subversively designed to carry on the radical cause.

That cause is still complicated by what Adam sees next – a vision of the Flood that, for all its concision, breadth of vision, and precise diction, far surpasses that of a world drowned in Ovid's *Metamorphoses*. On this point,

Addison's judgment is most instructive: "As it is visible that the poet had his eye upon Ovid's account of the universal deluge, the reader may observe with how much judgment he has avoided every thing that is redundant or puerile in the Latin poet. We do not here see the wolf swimming among the sheep, nor any of those wanton imaginations, which Seneca found fault with, as unbecoming the great catastrophe of nature."[35] Equally instructive is his modulation of Ovid's satiric portrait of the hypocrisy of Roman deities and rulers[36] into a tragic key. For Milton now envisions a God who is just as "Griev'd at his heart" (11.887) as Adam, who is left "comfortless, as when a Father mourns / His Children, all in view destroyed at once" (11.760–1). Even the epic narrator comes to share in Adam's inconsolable grief, stepping aside from the narrative for a few lines to speak directly to our first parent, much as Virgil had used this subjective form of narration to express a deeply human, if not filial, sympathy with the grieving or dying protagonist:[37] "How didst thou grieve then, *Adam*, to behold / The end of all thy Ofspring." Indeed, "another Floud, / Of tears and sorrow a Floud thee also drown'd, / And sunk thee as thy Sons" (11.754–8). That even the narrator turns aside to grieve for Adam now implicates the reader in the chain of mourners extending up to God himself; the price of free-willed creatures is divine loss.

Most of all, Adam's lament says that he, too, must bear the burden of foreknowledge: "O Visions ill foreseen! better had I / Liv'd ignorant of future, so had borne / My part of evil onely" (11.763–5). For he feels how "The burd'n of many Ages, on me light / At once, by my foreknowledge gaining Birth / Abortive, to torment me ere thir being, / With thought that they must be" (11.767–70). It is as moving a threnody as anything in the genre, including Milton's great lament in *Lycidas*, for it expresses anguish not just for the universal loss of the Flood, but for all those losses yet to come, for the cataclysmic loss that will encompass the entire world. As Summers notes, "Adam laments both the future event and his knowledge of it; his speech dramatizes the burden of foreknowledge more movingly than any other in the poem" (203). And it is God's burden as much as it is his.

Where Adam grieves his heirs, Aeneas rejoices at the prospect of bearing on his shoulders the whole glorious future of Rome pictured on the shield of Vulcan: "All these images on Vulcan's shield, / His mother's gift, were wonders to Aeneas. / Knowing nothing of the events themselves, / He felt joy in their pictures, taking up / Upon his shoulder all the destined acts / And fame of his descendants."[38] Whether he understands it or not, Adam, by contrast, stands in much the same pained relation to the future as God does by virtue of his foreknowledge. While Adam fails to ask about this parallel, and Michael offers no comment, the narrative is suggestive. Adam is forced to lament his foreknowledge, since it renders "Abortive" the birth of all his "Sons"; he is "tormented," even before "thir being, / With thought that they must be." Yet *must* implies his final acceptance of paternity, and so a commitment to some sort of history beyond himself; still, the Flood threatens what Adam has had to accept. "Knowing the worst," Summers says, "he must be willing to live, to conceive life as possible and as possibly blest" (190).

Adam's foreknowledge has no other correlate, apart from the divine decision to create, since the Father had always foreknown the cost of liberating others from his substance, allowing them to seek or not to seek reunion with him. The costs are so great, in fact, that God could have chosen to forego the creation of free beings. For God, it seems, had two stark choices – to create or not to create; to be alone from all eternity, or to share his gift of life in spite of its waste. His only paternal difference from Adam is that God foresees what Adam cannot: an effective means of reconciliation. Without it, the Father would also be "Brought down / To dwell on eeven ground now" with his sons. For God suffers sinlessly what sinful Adam deserves to suffer. Indeed, as Stuart Curran remarks, "God would not have had to lose a third of the heavenly angels if he had not decided that his original heaven was not all it could be." Yet this process of divine and terrestrial evolution is no easy thing: "God's willing self-sacrifice is the heart of the logic of creation."[39]

Ultimately, the poem – with its radically decentred visions – moves in an opposite direction from Virgil's *Aeneid*. The Roman epic is a triumphalist account of the divine plan of history, where the clock stops with Augustus as the goal and end of history – eternity brought down to earth in the human face of a divine ruler. For Aeneas, the prototype of the imperial ruler, enacts the will of Heaven in founding an *imperium sine fine*. As Jupiter tells his daughter Venus, mother of Aeneas: "For these I set no limits, world or time, / But make the gift of empire without end." And Venus is assured that Juno "Will mend her ways, and favor them as I do, / Lords of the world, the toga-bearing Romans. / Such is our pleasure"[40] (13). Even Virgil will not spare the Roman hero, however, from enormous trial and psychological suffering before he completes his great undertaking: "For years / They wandered as their destiny drove them on," the narrator sings,

"From one sea to the next: so hard and huge / A task it was to found the Roman people"[41] (4). But the task is minimal, and the suffering rather little, in comparison to the endless "torment" borne by Adam, who foresees the death of all his sons. Where Aeneas is ultimately left to rejoice in his vision of descendants who will "live in his name," Adam is left to grieve his heirs in a way that is almost unimaginable.

And yet, by the close of the eleventh book, Adam begins to demonstrate his true capacity for fatherhood, for showing concern for those whose existence is still precarious. At sight of "the Ark hull[ing] on the floud" (11.840), Adam for the first time comprehends the deep love and concern of the Father for his Creation: "Whereat the heart of *Adam* erst so sad / Greatly rejoyc'd" at the "Covn'nant new" (11.867–9). Unable to contain himself, "his joy broke forth": "I revive / At this last sight, assur'd that Man shall live / With all the Creatures, and thir seed preserve" (11.871–3). In a flash, he comes to see the true continuity of the present with the future, and a greater continuity still of the Creator with his creation. Reading the rainbow in the sky as a type of legal contract, as well as a familial covenant, Adam can finally rejoice: "Farr less I now lament for one whole World / Of wicked Sons destroyd, then I rejoyce / For one Man found so perfet and so just, / That God voutsafes to raise another World / From him" (11.874–8). In asking, "[W]hat mean those coloured streaks in Heavn" (11.879), he even intuits God's covenant to spare the human race from another universal deluge. While the angel properly commends the pupil – "Dextrously thou aim'st" (11.884) – Adam has yet to see deeper implications in this act of "binding" Heaven to earth, much less the revolutionary manner in which the Incarnation demands a deeper levelling still between fathers and sons.[42]

· 14 ·

"So God with Man Unites"

A LEVELLING INCARNATION

WHILE JOSEPH ADDISON ADMITS OF *Paradise Lost* "that these two last books can by no means be looked upon as unequal parts of this divine poem,"[1] the neoclassical critic is frustrated nonetheless by the modal shift in Book 12 from vision to narration:

> [D]oubtless the true reason was the difficulty which the poet would have found to have shadowed out so mixed and complicated a story in visible objects. I could wish, however, that the author had done it, whatever pains it might have cost him. To give my opinion freely, I think that the exhibiting part of the history of mankind in vision, and part in narrative, is as if an history painter should put in colours one half of his subject, and write down the remaining part of it. If Milton's poem flags any where, it is in this narration, where in some places the author has been so attentive to his divinity, that he has neglected his poetry.[2]

Were the final book actually to descend to dogma or even to an orthodox "history" of the Incarnation, one could agree that the poem "flags" where it most needs to soar. Yet it is difficult to credit the notion that Milton, always the Independent in religion and politics, would recant his great heresies with the goal in sight, particularly when, the next year, he defiantly faced down a question "why the Poem Rimes not" with this radical retort: "*This neglect then of Rime so little is to be taken for a defect, though it may seem so perhaps to vulgar*

Readers, that it rather is to be esteem'd an example set, the first in English, *of ancient liberty recover'd to Heroic Poem from the troublesome and modern bondage of Rimeing*"[3] (italics in original). The fault, then, has to be in the neoclassical reader, not the poem, for Addison to assume that it ends as tamely as he thinks.

Michael, for one, leaves no doubt of the radical design of Book 12 in its swerve from a vision of "the world destroy'd" to a narrative of the "world restor'd" (12.3), only to show how soon the "restor'd" world relapses into renewed fratricide, like that initial vision of Cain and Abel, where humankind no longer "spend thir dayes in joy unblam'd, and dwell / Long time in peace by Families and Tribes / Under paternal rule"[4] (12.22–4). For brother shall overthrow brother as another "one shall rise," a kingly usurper, "Of proud ambitious heart, who not content / With fair equalitie, fraternal state, / Will arrogate Dominion undeserv'd / Over his brethren." The advent of a single ruler will do more than put an end to *liberté, egalité*, and *fraternité*; it will "quite dispossess Concord and law[5] of Nature[6] from the Earth" (12.25–9). Despite Michael's narrative inconsistency (did Adam exercise "paternal rule" or not?), the archangel insists that antediluvian societies were republican, and that "fair equalitie" and "fraternal state" were initially the political norm. It is only after the Flood that "A mightie Hunter" – not named here, but evidently referring to the biblical Nimrod[7] – usurps power and sets himself, like Satan, as monarch over equals, "from Heav'n claiming second Sovrantie" (12.33–5).[8]

Writing in 1650, shortly before Milton was to join him as his licenser and fellow contributor to *Mercurius Politicus*, Marchamont Nedham had expressed precisely this view:

> The World, after the *Floud*, in time grew more populous, and more exceeding vitious, being inclined to Rapin, Ambition, &c. so that the *Pater-familiar* way of Government being found insufficient to correct those grand Enormities, there was need of some one more potent than the rest of his Neighbors, that might restraine Them by Force.
>
> Upon which Ground it was, that *Nimrod*, first of all men, complotted a new and arbitrary way of Government, backing it with Power by a Party of his own, and introduced the *Political* Form, by reducing diverse Cities and Countries into an intire combination, under one head or Monarch. And thus you see the Power of the *Sword* to be the

Originall of the first *Monarchy*, and indeed, of the first *politick form* of Government that ever was.[9]

A year later, Politicus (if not Nedham and Milton together) resurrected this idea that the paternal "Form of government was only temporary, and took an end not long after the flood, when *Nimrod* changed it."[10] Lilburne, in 1646, had already popularized this trope of "the incroaching usurpations of some great and mighty *Nimrods* of the world, made so by wayes and means, more immediatly and properly flowing from the Divell, then God."[11] By the summer of 1649, when Parliament and the Council of State had reneged on implementing the second *Agreement of the People*, Lilburne dared to name the current Nimrod of the English Revolution, inveighing from his prison cell in the Tower "against this great and mighty (apostasizing) hunting *Nimrod*, CROMWELL, and solely at thy feet cast his contest with him, earnestly imploring for that glorious and unparallel'd riches sake that shines in Jesus Christ."[12]

Much as Michael responds to Adam, "Justly thou abhorr'st / That Son, who on the quiet state of men / Such trouble brought, affecting to subdue / Rational Libertie" (12.79–82), William Walwyn likewise expressed the "hope to see this Nation governed by reason, and not by the Sword."[13] In the angel's brief history of Nimrod's usurpation, one thus finds the subtext of two key Leveller ideas dating from the Commonwealth period: that Adam's "fatherly" displeasure echoes the Levellers' displeasure at this "execrable Son" for daring "to aspire / Above his Brethren, to himself assuming / Authoritie usurpt, from God not giv'n" (12.64–6); and that only the Son of God – yet to be identified by the angel – offers hope of returning to "faire equality" through his "humiliation." What remains to be seen is how the Incarnation itself comes to embody these two principles (or types of "sonship") in the final book of the epic, thereby showing how the poet is every bit as attentive to his poetry as he is to his "divinity" in setting up these dramatic parallels between divine and human fathers who graciously give way to their offspring.

The unity of vision attained by Adam in the organizing trope of sonship begins to coalesce around his repeated attempts to read the sign of "the Woman's Seed," the *protoevangelium* that has haunted him since the Judgment Scene, and which he vaguely begins to comprehend, being informed "by types / And shadows, of that destind Seed to bruise / The Serpent, by what means he shall achieve / Mankinds deliverance" (12.232–5). One reason for Addison's qualified impression, shared by most readers, that the poem "falters" here is because it does seem more doctrinal than dramatic. Were it to turn entirely on the doctrine of "the Woman's Seed," such an impression would be justified: for "from him" – Father Abraham – God "will raise / A mightie Nation," the archangel says, "and upon him showre / His benediction so, that in his Seed / All nations shall be blest" (12.123–6). It is a lesson taught from Christian pulpits down through the centuries, "that all Nations of the Earth / Shall in his Seed be blessed." And "by that Seed," Michael explains somewhat elliptically, "Is meant thy great deliverer, who shall bruise / The Serpents head; whereof to thee anon / Plainlier shall be reveald" (12.147–51). Read as a Sunday-morning sermon, or even a child's Sunday-school lesson, the poetry of Book 12 grows numbing, "informing them, by types / And shadows, of that destind Seed to bruise / The Serpent" (12.232–4). As the chosen "Nation" wanders in the wilderness, God simply "voutsafes / Among them to set up his Tabernacle, / The holy One with mortal Men to dwell" (12.246–8). And the tedium turns palpable.

Read as drama, however, a rather different story emerges, leaving one to marvel at the tremendous compression achieved in the poet's choice of biblical episodes, as well as the precision of Adam's responses to the angel: "[N]ow first I finde / Mine eyes true op'ning, and my heart much eas'd, / Erewhile perplext with thoughts what would becom / Of mee and all Mankind" (12.273–6). Ever since Summers first drew attention to this passage,[14] countless readers have remarked how Adam's vision has improved from his myopic view of that "Beavie of fair Women" who led him to exclaim, "True opener of mine eyes, prime Angel blest, / Much better seems this Vision" (11.582, 598–9). Indeed, he begins to foresee "His day, in whom all Nations shall be blest" (12.277). Still, most readers fail to notice the humility of Adam's assumption of blame – becoming more like his partner, "much-humbl'd *Eve*." For in this phrase, "Favour unmerited by me" (12.278), there is a clear echo of Eve, who did take full responsibility for their lapse from grace, parrying her husband's fatuous praise of her in Book 11 with sincere self-deprecation: "Farr other name deserving" than "Mother of all Mankind" (11.171, 159). What at that time had still sounded like Adam's anthropocentrism – "since by thee / Man is to live, and all things live for Man" (11.160–1) – is finally corrected here by his genuine expression of humility.

What Adam fails to understand, however, is why "a long succession must ensue" (12.331) before the *protoevangelium* is realized, when "of the Royal Stock / Of *David* (so I name this King) shall rise / A Son, the Womans Seed to thee foretold, / Foretold to *Abraham*" (12.326–8). Why is it "that the true / Anointed King *Messiah* [must] be born / Barr'd of his right" (12.358–60)? The beginnings of an answer emerge in a telling series of images constellating the removal of "paternal" and "kingly" power over the course of human history. In the place of a human "father" appears "The Power of the most High" (12.369); in effect, the fate of "Father Adam" is his own disappearance from the "union" of Heaven and Earth, given that a woman's role is much more immediate and natural than anything in his experience. To his lasting credit, however, Adam does find a way to participate in the union of "two free-wils in one," as Walwyn had defined religion, or as Milton emplots it as the marriage of God the Father with the "lost" matter of his Creation. "O Prophet of glad tidings," Adam is scarcely able to contain his sudden surge of joy,

> finisher
> Of utmost hope! now clear I understand
> What oft my steddiest thoughts have searcht in vain,
> Why our great expectation should be call'd
> The seed of Woman: Virgin Mother, Haile,
> High in the love of Heav'n, yet from my Loynes
> Thou shalt proceed, and from thy Womb the Son
> Of God most High; So God with man unites. (12.375–82)

It is Adam, not the angel,[15] who in a flash has found his proper place in the "Family of God"[16] as "grandfather" to "the Woman's Seed," or, more daringly, as "father-in-law" to "The Power of the most High." As MacCallum remarks of this compressed scene *in Milton and the Sons of God*, "There is in this passage an extraordinary sense of things falling into place. Adam's comprehension of the heart of the mystery of the Incarnation is contained in the brief statement 'so God with man unites'" (198). Yet Milton goes well beyond most Christian exegetes in seeking to demystify the "mystery of the Incarnation." In what is the first and most important sequel to the original story of the Creation, Adam sees why "a long succession must ensue," and why the Creator has to distance himself from Adam's generation to avoid the taint of incest. "*So God with man unites*": the poem literally turns on the sexual union of God the Father with one of Eve's "daughters." And yet Adam has a right to boast that it is "from my Loynes" that God the Father's partner "shalt proceed." From everything he learns from both archangels, Adam is able at last to see himself as a type of the "Father" renouncing power in favour of his successors, thereby allowing himself to be "brought down / To dwell on eeven ground now with [his] Sons." MacCallum likely says more than he intended, then, in his summative judgment that, "The thrust of the historical revelation has been the rediscovery, in a new context, of the God already known" (198).

At the same time, Adam is mistaken in his first impression of the character of the incarnate Son. Recalling the story of the War in Heaven, Adam leaps to the conclusion that the advent of the Son will end in martial combat, where "Needs must the Serpent now his capital bruise / Expect with mortal paine: say where and when / Thir fight,[17] what stroke shall bruise the Victors heel" (12.383–5). Michael is surely qualified to correct him, having failed as a military general to quash the proud rebel in Heaven: "Dream not of thir fight, / As of a Duel, or the local wounds / Of head or heel: not therefore joynes the Son / Manhood to God-head" (12.386–9). Still, Adam has no true sense of how it is supposed to happen, "Not by destroying *Satan*, but his works / In thee and in thy Seed" (12.394–5).

More tellingly, what Michael says about the Crucifixion is kept to a minimum, beyond the fact that "his obedience / Imputed becomes theirs by Faith, his merits / To save them, not thir own, though legal works" (12.408–10). Although Adam is told that "For this he shall live hated, be blasphem'd, / Seis'd on by force, judg'd, and to death condemnd / A shameful and accurst, naild to the Cross / By his own Nation, slaine for bringing Life" (12.411–14), the Passion as a drama dwindles to an event of no more than fifteen lines. About this passage, Christopher Hill opines that the heretical sect of "Familists rejected the theology of the Atonement,"[18] as if this could explain Milton's pointed refusal to dwell on the fact of Christ's bodily suffering and death. The form of Michael's narration appears more to recall the style, however, of Foxe's *Actes and Monuments*, or the so-called "Book of Martyrs" (1563), in which "The privileging of the textual body over the physical one is a version of the general Christian privileging of the spiritual world over the corporeal one."[19] As Gretchen Minton notes more generally of the verbal form of Foxe's martyrology, "We are never allowed to dwell upon the body because the body becomes text as soon as its story is recorded in written form."[20]

Foxe's project,[21] which had grown before his death in 1583 to four massive editions,[22] is another key document in charting the seismic shift from the medieval culture of the Mass as a vehicle of the "Real Presence" – where a hierarchical form of mediation was the sole means of salvation – to a technologically mediated, "bibliographic form of real presence,"[23] where the flesh is made word in and through the textualized body as it is democratically distributed to communicants (that is, readers) widely dispersed in time and space.[24] Christopher Mead describes the process of this shift as Foxe "[e]ucharistically transforming" an "ineffable" history "into a revivified textual present ... materializing it as a thing that can be endlessly called up by readers"[25] in the present tense of reading.

Michael's use, for example, of the present-tense verb in his narrative of Christ's death recalls the "Eucharistic method" of *Actes and Monuments*, which transubstantiates the martyr's death into "a mechanically reproduced text distributable to a vast community of readers" (Mead, 57–8) by rendering the scene of "burning" not as a participle but as a gerund, which "exists as a present tense phenomenon free of both past and future participle" (Mead, 34). The temporal doubling of the gerund "burning" now makes it far more difficult to separate the "nounal and verbal qualities of burning," since, "Considered as a noun, 'burning' is [the] historical moment materialized as a specific place" in Foxe's book, while, "Considered as a verb activated in the moment of reading, 'burning' revivifies the scene, allowing the flames to continue to sear the martyr's body" (Mead, 34). Michael likewise speaks of Christ in this ongoing present tense: "[S]o he dies, / But soon revives, Death over him no power / Shall long usurp" (12.419–21). Grammatically, the verb unites past and future in the present tense of Adam's hearing as well as in our own present tense of reading. So the act of reading resurrects the broken body of the Saviour, now moving in the space of three words – from "dies" to "revives" – to facilitate simultaneously Adam's and our own revivification of the Word.

When Michael assures Adam, "[T]his God-like act / Annuls thy doom, the death thou shouldst have dy'd, / In sin for ever lost from life" (12.427–9), it virtually cancels the death even before it occurs. So Adam is left, along with Milton's "fit audience," in the present tense of a narrative where the gift of life is communicated equally to each communicant in the act of reading. *Now*, the Son, whose body is literally communicated both in speech and in print, comes "Proclaiming Life to all who shall believe / In his redemption, and that his obedience / Imputed becomes theirs by Faith" (12.407–9). The efficacy of this faith turns on the manner in which the Word is eucharistically distributed to readers and auditors across time and space, endlessly reproducing himself on each reading. Adam even recognizes, as much as he extends, this sense of the "Real Presence" of the Word in his succinct summation of the effects of its reception: "Henceforth I learne, that to obey is best, / And love with fear the onely God, to walk / As in his presence, ever to observe / His providence, and on him sole depend" (12.561–4). How Michael leads him to this expression of loving obedience, however, works to recapitulate Leveller doctrines as much as to mimic Foxe's radical theology of reading.

What Michael says is mostly personal at first, offering an admonitory reminder to Adam that "hee, who comes thy Saviour, shall recure, / Not by destroying *Satan*, but his works / In thee and in thy Seed" (12.393–5). While Adam's fault is foregrounded, he is reassured that "The Law of God exact he shall fulfill / Both by obedience and by love, though love / Alone fulfill the Law" (12.402–4). The Leveller William Walwyn had said as much, if rather more diffusely, in admonishing those who "taught thee to pay God with an external show of holinesse, when he will have internall holinesse," and "to show him the figure of the law, without the substance and meaning of the law, and to maintaine lovelesse law, when the whole law is love."[26] Walwyn also warned that "the devil and all impious men, hate love, because love is contrary to their nature, and therefore they would overthrow love, by preferring of faith before her" (21). Michael similarly advises Adam that the Saviour "shall live hated" for "bringing Life; / But to the Cross he nailes thy Enemies, / The Law that is against thee, and the sins / Of all mankinde" (12.411, 414–17). At this point, Adam can now look beyond death to fix his gaze on transcendent love: "O goodness infinite, goodness immense! / That all this good of evil shall produce, / And evil turn to good." That he sees it as "more wonderful / Then that which by creation first brought forth / Light out of darkness" (12.471–3) indicates that he sees it as a second creation. For Adam has glimpsed the power of perfect love to undo his own disobedience.

Summers is right to claim that "This is the climax. Another poet would have ended the narrative here," though not quite for the reason that Summers gives – that Adam "has not yet been made the reader's equal."[27] Rather more like Foxe, who had begun his ever-expanding project soon after the accession of Elizabeth in that unprecedented age of Protestant triumphalism, yet whose vision grew more apocalyptic as he "systematically interpret[ed] historical events as the fulfillment of the prophecies of

Revelation."[28] Milton is likewise forced by historical events to turn away from the triumphalist hopes of the Commonwealth to his own apocalyptic vision of post-Restoration history.[29]

Like his Leveller sons in a far-off future, Adam still finds it difficult to understand why human institutions, both sacred and civic, should be so untrustworthy, especially after the age of the apostles. Yet this is precisely what Michael warns him to beware: "Wolves shall succeed for teachers, grievous Wolves." Indeed, he foresees how such "wolves" shall "the truth / With superstitions and traditions taint, / Left onely in those written Records pure, / Though not but by the Spirit understood" (12.508, 511–14). Once they begin "to avail themselves of names, / Places and titles, and with these to joine / Secular power, though feigning still to act / By spiritual," it should be clear that "to themselves" they have appropriated "The Spirit of God, promisd alike and giv'n / To all Beleevers" (12.515–20). David Loewenstein concludes that, "Here, within some forty lines of narrative poetry, Milton has managed to condense and evoke the convoluted, bleak course of history that he had taken some four hundred pages of dense, weary prose to chart in the *History of Britian.*"[30] But Michael's anti-prelatical warning appears to be focused rather on the reader's role in receiving and recovering the true meaning of "those written Records pure" (12.513).[31] The idea will continue to echo in the final words that Adam speaks in the poem, "that suffering for Truths sake / Is fortitude to highest victorie, / And to the faithful Death the Gate of Life; / Taught this by his example whom I now / Acknowledge my Redeemer ever blest" (12.569–73).

Even so, what emerges from his final reading lesson is more than what Sharon Achinstein thinks: "Milton urges his fellow countrymen not to give up faith in their cause; he seeks a fit audience, 'though few' (7.31), to prepare and keep watch … In his aim to transform his own readers into a 'fit audience,' Milton made the 'revolutionary' content of the poem not an overt political statement, but the very process of training readers."[32] What Milton's "fit" audiences[33] are more surely trained to read is something closer to the Foxean tradition of active suffering than this alert passivity of "keeping watch." As early as 1641, Milton had in *Of Reformation* celebrated the "reviving joy" of Christians when "the sweet Odour of the returning *Gospell*" had dispelled

> the black and settled Night of *Ignorance* and *Antichristian Tyranny* … Then was the Sacred BIBLE sought out of the dusty corners where

> prophane Falshood and Neglect had throwne it, the *Schooles* opened, *Divine* and *Humane Learning* rak't out of the *embers* of *forgotten Tongues* … the *Martyrs*, with the unresistable *might* of *Weaknesse*, shaking the *Powers* of *Darknesse*, and scorning the *fiery rage* of the old *red Dragon*. (CPW 1: 524–5)

In effect, it is this "unresistable *might* of *Weaknesse*" that Adam begins to identify as the way "to highest victorie, / Taught" by the example of "my Redeemer ever blest."

Like Milton, Lilburne had repeated the same lesson from Foxe, stating it most explicitly in the title of his pamphlet, *Strength out of Weaknesse*, a "finall and absolute Plea" of the "prisoner in the Tower of *London*, against the present Ruling Power siting at *Westminster*."[34] Here, Lilburne's narrative of suffering follows most closely the "Eucharistic method" of his hero John Foxe. Writing mere weeks before his capital trial, Lilburne evidently expected to be convicted on the charge of high treason and thus to die a martyr to the Leveller cause.[35] Even so, he insists on bearing witness to the martyred "truth" that is communicated to every faithful reader of the *Actes and Monuments*,

> that if I should die in this contest (for putting them in mind of their promises) [i.e. Cromwell and the Commons' promise to implement the *Agreement of the People*] … that this *Epistle* may live, and many Thousands of them be re-printed, and seeing by their new pretended Act about Printing they cannot be sold, they may be thrown away, and given, and sent all up and down the Nation; So with my true love presented to you all, I commit you to the safe Protection of the Lord God omnipotent.[36]

This is my body, Lilburne effectually says, *take and eat*; or, more precisely, *This is my textual body duplicated exactly and distributed universally by print. Take it and read.*[37]

As Gretchen Minton recognizes, this powerful vision of a textualized body distributed by means of the book to a dispersed community is the essence of a Protestant theology of the Incaration, though its "normal" direction is reversed. Instead of "the Word made flesh," the pivotal narrative movement in the *Actes and Monuments* is from "*Flesh to Word*," where Foxe "highlights the written record in his martyr accounts, giving prominence to the letters and written testimonies of the martyrs both before and after the description of their physical deaths." By such means, "The mutable bodies of the martyrs are transferred into immutable texts that will survive, precisely because the martyrologist has monumentalized them in such a way" (Minton, 729–30).

Adam has no way of knowing that the lesson he learns about suffering – of "Accomplishing great things, by things deemd weak / Subverting worldly strong" (12.567–8) – anticipates the experience of the five soldiers drummed out of the Army for supporting Lilburne's *Englands New Chains Discovered* (26 February 1649), given that their weakness will "confound the mighty." Much as Foxe had presented "many of his martyrs on trial in courtroom scenes" in a new genre amounting to a "divinely directed courtroom drama" (Minton, 726, 727), the Leveller martyrologist in "*The Examination and Answers of* ROBERT WARD, *before the Court Martiall*, March 3 164[9]," presents Ward's "martyred" flesh as proof of the "strength of weakness," insofar as his accusers "told him, he had not wit sufficient to compose such a Letter: He answered, The Letter he did own; and as for worldly wisdom, he had not much; but he told the Court, he hoped he had so much honesty as would bear him out in this action; and desired them to remember what *Paul* spake, how that God did chuse the foolish things of the world to confound the mighty."[38] Similarly, the great lesson learned by Adam about "the Seed of Woman" has indeed revealed, by "his example whom I now / Acknowledge my Redeemer ever blest" (12.572–3), the continuity of Adam's present with the future of his descendants. For Adam comes to see himself, like God the Father, as a parent giving over his power to his Son – who is clearly Adam's "son" by a future "daughter" as much as he is *the* Son of God – ceding control of the future to him, where Heaven is to be joined apocalyptically to Earth and Earth to Heaven, "One Kingdom, Joy and Union without end" (7.161).

Of course, there are no "worldly strong" waiting to attack Adam outside the gates of Paradise, where he will make his new home.[39] Notwithstanding David Loewenstein's conclusion that "the apocalypticism in the final books underscores powerful and unresolved tensions in Milton's historical thought – between responding to history dramatically and envisioning its decline tragically, between an impulse to reshape its convoluted course and an impulse to retire inwardly from its conflicts" (*Milton and the Drama of History*, 119–20), Adam's final speech is a salutary reminder that neither he nor the poet has withdrawn from, much less will refuse, engagement with the world.

In the main, Adam's stirring vision of the weak things of this earth "subverting wordly strong" anticipates other writings of the Levellers from their prison cells throughout the spring and summer of 1649. Much like Father Adam, Lilburne, Overton, and Walwyn assume the burden of all those who are "deemd weak" in order to hold the mighty to account. So, too, the Leveller women bear out this truth in their petition of May 1649, reminding, even as they warn the Parliament and Council of State, "not to slight the things therein contained because they are presented unto you by the weak hand of women, it being a usual thing with God, by weak means to work mighty effects."[40]

So it is utterly appropriate that Eve has the last dramatic words in the poem, not just because of their theme of subverting "worldly strong" by "things deemd weak," but more largely in terms of the cosmic "marriage" plot, where the female will is left free to choose or to reject the Creator. Michael has no more idea than Adam that, during their hours of absence, Eve is tutored by God in matters that are more intimate and private than anything Adam learns. "[G]o, waken *Eve*," the angel says, acknowledging the value of education for women, but failing to recognize the increasing marginalization of the male:

> Her also I with gentle Dreams have calm'd
> Portending good, and all her spirits compos'd
> To meek submission: thou at season fit
> Let her with thee partake what thou hast heard,
> Chiefly what may concern her Faith to know,
> The great deliverance by her Seed to come. (12.594–600)

In joy and expectation of bearing the promise of the Annunication to his wife, Adam "ran before, but found her wak't" (12.608), so gaining another lesson in humility. For Adam has had to go to school to learn what Eve learns immediately from God himself:

> Whence thou returnst, and whither wentst, I know;
> For God is also in sleep, and Dreams advise,
> Which he hath sent propitious, some great good
> Presaging, since with sorrow and hearts distress
> Wearied I fell asleep; but now lead on;
> In mee is no delay; with thee to goe,

> Is to stay here; without thee here to stay,
> Is to go hence unwilling; thou to mee
> Art all things under Heav'n, all places thou,
> Who for my wilful crime art banish hence. (12.610–19)

As Hugh MacCallum concludes, "Milton achieves a remarkable effect of beauty and fulfilment by giving the last speech of his great story to Eve … The last voice of *Paradise Lost* is that of a woman in love who is confident that her descendant will renew the world" (201). Eve's measured rhythms, her balanced phrasings, and her inverted parallels – "Whence thou returnst … whither wentst"; "with thee to goe is to stay," "without thee … to stay is to go … unwilling" – help to make this one of the most tender and moving professions of love in the language. But it is more than merely the assurance of a woman secure in her love; it is also a moving reminder of God's promise to the Son that "Thy humiliation shall exalt," a promise already shared by Eve in her closing words: "though all by mee is lost, / Such favour I unworthie am voutsaft, / By mee the Promis'd Seed shall all restore"[41] (12.621–3).

The closing lines of the poem are breathtakingly beautiful for the way they renew the original hope of "faire equality" (12.26) that, until the Flood, is supposed to prevail outside of Paradise. The traditional view of the couple's exile, contained in the terrible beauty of Masaccio's painting[42] of "The Expulsion" (1428), is that a "winged Hierarch" comes to harry the couple out of Paradise, hovering in the air above the retreating husband and his agonized wife, the angel's bright scarlet robes and his black sword contrasting violently with the skin tones of the splotchy white and starkly naked couple. In shame and grief, Adam hides his face in both his hands while Eve howls, her mouth agape and her arms stretched desperately to cover her "shameful" parts. Roland Mushat Frye justly describes this image as "the most devastating of all renderings of the Expulsion," since "there is and can be no looking back – only a bleak and desolate facing ahead, a wailing entry into the future."[43]

This idea of postlapsarian despair persists in the folio edition (1688) of *Paradise Lost*, where the engraver, likely "Henry Aldrich, Dean of Christ Church, a college known as a hotbed [!] of Anglicanism,"[44] barely alters the hierarchical figuration of the Middle Ages and early Renaissance – the archangel now on terra firma holding his sword firmly in one hand, the other pushing before him the shoulder of a naked Adam, the man's face engulfed in both hands. Behind him, the angel stands on the bottom step of a stairway to Heaven, from which a half-dozen lesser angels peer down, as if to remind the viewer of the presence of the hierarchy of priests and prelates set over them to pass judgment on lay persons. While covering her sexual organs with both hands, Eve would do better to cover that sottish expression on her face as she stares vacantly ahead like a dumb animal.

By contrast, Milton's beautiful lines assign a unique position to each figure, including the sword: "High in Front advanc't, / The brandisht Swórd of God before them blaz'd / Fierce as a Comet" (12.632–4), as if brandishing itself, like that "pillar of fire" which will accompany the Israelites on their way out of Egypt. What each of these novel figurations points to is the true first fruit of a "levelling" Incarnation, by which, God has promised, "Thy Humiliation shall exalt / With thee thy Manhood also to this Throne." For Heaven itself will one day stoop to become human flesh. For now, however,

> In either hand the hastning Angel caught
> Our lingring Parents, and to th' Eastern Gate
> Led them direct, and down the Cliff as fast
> To the subjected Plaine; then disappeer'd. (12.637–40)

There is no longer any "hierarch" to hover overhead, much less behind or above, our "first Parents." To the contrary, Milton's Angel occupies the same level plane as his human charges, pacing like a parent between them while holding the hand of each, until he simply disappears, leaving the couple to walk "hand in hand," as in that original glimpse we caught of them passing beyond the view of Satan, who sits like a cormorant[45] in the Tree of Life. Gendered differences are once again "levelled," as lingering doubts or angry accusations are finally dispelled. The final image we are afforded of Adam and Eve is that of "our first Parents" setting foot outside the Garden as figurative equals, fully committed to each other as they were in the first halcyon days of Paradise.

The final impression left by the epic narrator who has brought us all this distance is of a "Father"-author revealing himself in this final act of letting go of his great creation,[46] handing over his divine story and its liberal design to readers, who are left to participate in an infinity of choices, both inside and outside the poem, in their own readerly process of recovering lost Eden. Ultimately, it is the readers who must complete the act of reunion with the author-"god,"[47] to fulfill the cosmic plot, much in the way that the

Son has described it, of being "Made one with me as I with thee am one." The entire poem, in this sense, turns into a narrative act of surrendering the "creation" to readers who have yet to realize, and so to complete, its revolutionary design. And we get the creation we deserve by virtue of the choices we make in our reading.

The poet is thus revealed as a type of God the Father, together with Adam the father, each of whom hands over the process of restoration to be completed in others. In this sense, *Paradise Lost* may be best described as the epic of print culture itself – from the expanding martyrologies of Foxe to the Leveller martyrologies of Lilburne, to the continuing response of each new reader of Milton's work – this form of epic designed to complete the historic shift from older, hierarchical forms of mediation to the primacy of every reader interpreting for *her*self the great "Unless be meant" of history – that eternal desire of the Creator to be rejoined in loving union with his Creation.[48]

So God with man unites.

PART III

Paradise Regain'd

· 15 ·

"Searching What Was Writ"

THE FOXEAN READER

ITS VERY TITLE declares *Paradise Regain'd* to be a sequel[1] to the epic story of cosmic loss and recovery in *Paradise Lost* through the promised "seed of Woman" (12.379). The subject of the "brief epic,"[2] of course, is the long-awaited fulfillment of the Incarnation, already hailed by Adam in Book 12 as the ultimate design of Providence: "Virgin Mother, Haile, / High in the love of Heav'n, yet from my Loynes / Thou shalt proceed, and from thy Womb the Son / Of God most High; So God with man unites" (*PL* 12.379–82). Yet, nothwithstanding its high theme, the later poem has disappointed most readers.

Public disenchantment was already evident in Milton's lifetime. In the "Life" of his uncle, Edward Phillips recalls Milton's impatience with plodding readers who expressed indifference to "his other poem call'd *Paradice Regain'd*," a narrative

> which doubtless was begun and finisht and Printed after the other was publisht, and that in a wonderful short space considering the sublimeness of it; however it is generally censur'd to be much inferiour to the other, though he could not hear with patience any such thing when related to him; possibly the Subject may not afford such variety of Invention, but it is thought by the most judicious to be little or nothing inferiour to the other for stile and decorum.[3]

Yet the style and decorum of *Paradise Regain'd* are actually the major sources of difficulty for readers today, including "the most judicious." The language is too plain and terse, the "action" anything but "epic." In the parlance of television, it consists for the most part of "talking heads." Consequently, the author's notorious impatience with his critics can only be taken for peevishness, or downright arrogance.

Even its chief defenders find that the poem is lacking in drama. "In *Paradise Regained*," Northrop Frye remarks, "as to some extent in *Comus* … the tempted figures are either motionless or unmoved and have only the ungracious dramatic function of saying No." Worse yet, "Christ's ability to reply 'Why art *thou* solicitous?' to every temptation destroys all opportunity for narrative suspense," with the result that, "*dramatically* Christ becomes an increasingly unsympathetic figure, a pusillanimous quietist in the temptation of Parthia, an inhuman snob in the temptation of Rome, a peevish obscurantist in the temptation of Athens."[4] To Frye, the sole saving grace of a "suspenseless" plot – and thus a failed drama – is its typological function of separating the gospel "from the law. Judaism joins classical wisdom as part of the demonic illusion, as the center of religion passes from the temple Christ is standing on into the true Christian temple, the body of Christ above it" (444). As for the poem's "inaction," its chief "poetic effect is that of a negative clarification of Christ's own thoughts. The climax of the temptation corresponds to the death of Moses in the Exodus; it is the point at which Jesus passes from obedience to the law to works of faith, from the last Hebrew prophet to the founder of Christianity" (432). Yet dogma is a poor substitute for drama.

On behalf of a later generation of critics, Alan Fisher bluntly asks, "Why Is *Paradise Regained* So Cold?"[5] His answer turns on a species of reception theory. To Fisher, the poem patently lacks drama; although "*Paradise Regained* is almost wholly speeches[,] epic action, in the usual sense, is at a minimum. The way to recover Paradise is to say no in the face of an 'impact' that insists on yes. No is said, again and again, until suddenly and miraculously the need to say it disappears." But even Fisher has to admit, "Critics complain about this, and with reason: listening to someone else – even Jesus – say no is not exciting" (199). What interests him most is the "subjective drama" (205), where "the reader's feelings" are "the poem's most interesting battleground" (201). The "heroism of denial" (206) demonstrated by Jesus in his expression of a perfected humanity is more like "an endurance test" (207), not only for him but for a reader who feels impatience with this poem that negates, rather than fulfills, our humanity. Yet, since "Milton has designed this temptation deliberately," and asks "his reader to face it, reject it, and continue to endure" (207), one has to accept that "Endurance ... is a mode of faith" (209). In effect, "Milton makes Jesus distant because he believes that people must have room to breathe, space of their own through which to reach toward God" (215). A lack of subjectivity in the poem thus frees us to live our "subjective drama" of faith, although the poem by now is really beside the point.

Conversely, it is the audience that is beside the point for Laura Lunger Knoppers in a drama where "the Son's true witness is private," "unobserved" by anyone outside of his "divine audience."[6] And the reason for this lack of a public audience, Knoppers says, is not theological but historical: "Milton's Son of God recalls the *Eikon Basilike* and the martyrologies of Charles I precisely to critique the claims of one who suffers for the preservation of an earthly monarchy" (212). Doubtless Milton had laboured to no avail in his *Eikonklastes* (1649) to expose the trumped-up theatricality of the royal martyr. For the "King's Book" (207), and the flood of "martyrologies" that followed it, did "recast the alleged justice of Charles's public trial and execution as a false, theatrical reeanactment of Christ's trial and crucifixion" (208). The appropriation of the discourse of martyrdom, enabling "Charles's assimilation of himself to the Christ of the Gospels – suffering for the people and unjustly put to death – was ... so brilliantly successful that Milton could no longer use this discourse" (219). That is why, Knoppers assumes, his "poem is deliberately antitheatrical, or, rather, it links theatricality with Satan, who has a full complement of props, costumes, scenery, and dramatic ploys" (214). By "virtue" of the historical success of "Charles's false kingly witness ... the Son's true witness is" then necessarily "private" (218). Although the demands of historical context for Milton's "brief epic" are unlikely to make the poem popular, or even to reconcile readers to its lack of drama, it could explain why "Paradise is regained not by theatrical suffering but by an intellectual debate in the wilderness; the genre is not tragedy but brief epic, the protagonist not the crucified, kingly Christ but the constant, unmoved Son of God" (214).

Could explain, I say, because this welcome turn to the poem's historical context is weakened from the outset by a faulty definition of its genre. Knoppers mistakenly conflates the "King's Book" with Foxe's "Book of Martyrs" (205), assuming that the former "draws on and dramatically revises the Foxean tradition in its compelling portrait of the martyr-king" (206). Indeed, these traditions are antithetical. Because it is modelled on the gospels and the Psalms of King David, the "King's Book" assimilates the martyr to the *Passion* of Christ the King. Downplaying the Passion, Foxe draws on the trials in the book of Acts, and on the courtroom dramas of lower-class martyrs who died under the thumbs of those same kings and emperors.[7] To the majority of Foxe's readers, kings were the persecutors, not the persecuted, which explains why Milton's Jesus is never once called "Christ" (or "anointed one," that is, Christ the King) in the poem.[8] In other words, no reader of *Eikon Basilike* was likely to confuse "the royal image" of Charles the martyr with the humble martyrs of Foxe's anti-hierarchical myth-making.

Even Foxe's title declares his radical purpose to extend the record of the Acts of the Apostles, of the stirring deeds of humble heroes who, as he writes in his "Preface," had so often died at the hands of "the heathen Emperours of Rome, who hauing the whole power of the world in their hands, did what the world could do, to extinguish the name and church of christ. Whose violence continued the space of 3. hundreth yeares."[9] For such reasons, the *Actes and Monuments of these latter and perillous dayes, touching matters of the Church* (1563) also aims to extend the *Historia ecclesiastica* of Eusebius, the "Father of Church History," a genre which evidently "attracted Foxe, who likewise wanted to assert the authority and antiquity of his church."[10] Eusebius (d. 339 CE) had already "found a precedent for chronicle and narrative history in the Bible itself – in Old Testament books such as 1 and 2 Chronicles, and in the New Testament Acts of the Apostles."[11] But, more than anything, Foxe's own "Acts of the Apostles" narrated the deeds of humble men and women used by God to confound the mighty in bearing witness to His truth by their suffering of persecution and death. They are the true narrative heirs to the protomartyr Stephen, "a man full of faith and of the Holy Ghost" in the Book of Acts who saw "the heavens opened, and the Son of man standing on the right hand of God." And the high priest and his followers "cast him out of the city, and stoned him: and the witnesses laid down their clothes at a young man's feet, whose name was Saul."[12] So it is that Saul, the notorious persecutor of Christians and the "chief of sinners," set off on the road to Damascus that ended in his conversion to Paul, surnamed the Apostle.[13]

Contrary to the intensely *public* career of Foxe's martyrs, however, Milton's Jesus is led almost invisibly into "the wast Wilderness" (*PR* 1.7), out of which, the narrator concludes, "hee unobserv'd / Home to his Mothers house private return'd" (4.638–9). Of course, the "patient suffringes of the worthy martyrs" in the Marian persecutions would have been scattered with their ashes had the printing press not been available to memorialize their witness: "I thought it not to be neglected," Foxe adds in his Preface of 1583, "that so precious Monumentes of so many matters, meet to be recorded and regestred in books, should lie buried by my default vnder darkenes of obliuion."[14] In this new and revolutionary context of print culture, Milton's epic narrator ventures similarly "to tell of deeds / Above Heroic, though in secret done, / And unrecorded left through many an Age, / Worthy t' have not remain'd so long unsung" (1.14–17). For Milton, so much like Foxe in extending the Book of Acts, aims to expand on scripture by recovering a "lost" gospel, in order to supplement the "Actes" of these latter-day apostles.[15] But the Passion and the Crucifixion are left outside his dramatic frame; Milton limits the martyr's trials to the temptation in the wilderness, so that Jesus may be brought "thence / By proof the undoubted Son of God" (1.10–11), *the* one true witness to God's truth, if by "deeds ... in secret done."

Bearing witness, of course, is "the original meaning of the word 'martyr,'"[16] which is why the Son's lonely trial does make *dramatic* sense as a transcript of a courtroom trial in camera, given that the "connection between martyrdom and the law was apparent to Christian martyrologists from the beginning."[17] In Foxe, such "witness" invariably takes the form of a transcript of the "martyr's" examination before a secret[18] ecclesiastical court. For example, in "The Martyrdome of Thomas Haukes," Foxe quotes from an unpublished narrative left by the martyred Haukes, while converting it to dramatic form and attaching names to speeches, as well as stitching events together into a first-person narrative. Even the legal warrants of Edmund Bonner, Bishop of London, for the close confinement and eventual condemnation of Haukes, are inserted at the end of Foxe's *dramatic* transcript, after a brief rehearsal of Haukes's death by burning. Thereafter, Foxe appends a public codicil composed of letters sent by the gentleman himself – formerly an employee in the household of the Earl of Oxford – to believers from his congregation in Essex, and to his wife and those left to oversee his son's education. "Thus Foxe, like Eusebius, highlights the written record in his martyr accounts, giving prominence to the letters and written testimonies of the martyrs both before and after the description of their physical deaths. Despite the sensationalism of the portions of the book dealing with the actual executions, Foxe's greater attention is turned to the textual memorialization of these events."[19]

Above all, the story of Haukes's martyrdom is a record of the Church's secret abuse of power in examining an honest man for refusing to christen his newborn son. As Haukes explains to the Bishop of London, "Because we be bound to do nothing contrarye to the word of God,"[20] he will not consent to infant baptism. His story thus takes the form of a trial transcript as a layman teaches his bishop from scripture the true gospel meaning of baptism: "Go teach all nations, baptizing them. &c," which is hardly applicable to infants unless they can be taught. To which the bishop says, "Thou speakest that because I am no Preacher" (1609). Haukes is thus the better *witness* by virtue of his quoting Christ as the Word. As he writes to comfort his fellow parishioners:

> [W]e are as Pilgrimes and straungers, following the footesteps of Moses, among many vnspeakeable daungers ... of that dreadfull dragon, and his sinnefull seede ... casting abroad his apples in al places, times, and seasons, to see if Adam will be allured and entised to leaue the liuing God ... & set at naught, the euerlasting kingdome of heauen ... for though the world rage, and blaspheme the elect of God, ye knowe that it did so vnto Christ, his Apostles, and to all that were in the primitiue Church, and shalbe vnto the worldes end.[21]

In terms of this written tradition that aims to compensate for, if not to undo, Adam's sin, it is not surprising, then, to hear Milton's God say that the Son has been sent "forth / To conquer Sin and Death the two grand foes, / By Humiliation and strong Sufferance: / His weakness shall o'recome Satanic strength" (1.158–61). Even God appears to take his dramatic cue from Adam at the end of *Paradise Lost* – "[B]y things deemd weak / Subverting worldly strong" (*PL* 12.567–8) – a maxim likewise used by Lilburne in *Strength out of Weaknesse*. This is the plot of most of the stories in the *Actes and Monuments* (1583), as Foxe explains: "[W]e haue a much more assured and playne witnes of God both in whose liues and deathes appeared suche manifest declarations of Gods diuine working, whiles in such sharpnes of tormentes we behold in them strength, so constant aboue mans reach, such readines to aunswere, such patience in imprisonment."[22] Indeed, the English martyrs bear witness to a distinctly Foxean Jesus, one found in Milton's poem as well, where the trials he faces do bear out God's prediction that "men hereafter may discern, / From what consummate vertue I have chose / This perfect Man, by merit call'd my Son" (*PR* 1.164–6).

So we encounter yet again what was said in far different circumstances in *Paradise Lost*, where the Son, as God declares, is "found / By Merit more then Birthright Son of God, / Found worthiest to be so by being Good, / Farr more then Great or High" (*PL* 3.308–10). That trial in Heaven was the supreme test of anyone in the previous poem, including Adam and Eve. But in view of a radically different trial in Milton's "brief epic," one recalls that image of Jesus in the Arian Baptistery in Ravenna (ca. 500 CE) – a stripling youth on whom the dove descends as the apostles look down from the circle of eternity upon this earthly scene where Jesus has been left to win his way back to that empty throne in Heaven.[23] If God insists in this poem on his *earthly* drama of testing and trial – "But first I mean / To exercise him in the Wilderness, / There he shall first lay down the rudiments / Of his great warfare" (*PR* 1.155–8) – we ought to take him at his word, reading Milton's poem in the light of a "divinely directed courtroom drama"[24] so familiar to the readers of Foxe and Eusebius as an in-camera proceeding.

Nor is the Father the only one to insist that this is an initiatory drama[25] to be privately played out "in the Wilderness." Satan begins the earthly drama by recalling the Exaltation in *Paradise Lost*, that originary moment in the previous poem which had sparked the War in Heaven: "And what will he not do to advance his Son? / His first-begot we know" (*PR* 1.88–9). But, "Who this is we must learn," Satan urges, "for man he seems / In all his lineaments, though in his face / The glimpses of his Fathers glory shine" (1.91–3). Lacking the grandeur and high language of the former rebel-hero, this Satan "To Councel summons all his mighty Peers" (1.40). But his "gloomy Consistory" (1.42) lacks all pretense of democratic debate; Satan is the only one who speaks in this scene, letting the devils know they have no choice now but to leave the "management of this main enterprize / To him their great Dictator" (1.112–13).

While Satan is desperate to prolong "our freedom and our being / In this fair Empire won of Earth and Air" (1.62–3), the setting is no longer the epic architectural grandeur of Pandæmonium. The naked ambition of Satan, "High on a Throne of Royal State" (*PL* 2.1), once the motor of the action, is now reduced to a bare mention of those "ancient Powers of Air and this wide world," preferring "This our old Conquest" to having to "remember Hell / Our hated habitation" (*PR* 1.44–7). Nor does the great dictator even try, as he formerly did, to rouse his troops with "heroic" language – "New Laws from him who reigns, new minds may raise / In us who serve" (*PL* 5.680–1). Rather, he speaks in the tone of a self-confessed neurotic, "With dread attending when that fatal wound / Shall be inflicted by the Seed of *Eve*" (*PR* 1.53–4). Pretense is beside the point; not even the rash and suicidal

Moloch needs to round out this portrait of collective neurosis as Satan now confesses: "His Birth to our just fear gave no small cause, / But his growth now to youths full flowr, displaying / All vertue, grace and wisdom to atchieve / Things highest, greatest, multiplies my fear" (1.66–9).

Satan's Socinian hope is that this present, "perfect" man – singled out by a familiar voice from Heaven at the River Jordan pronouncing, "This is my Son belov'd, in him am pleas'd" (*PR* 1.85) – bears no relation to the celestial Son who drove them from "the happy Realms of Light" (*PL* 1.85) into the vast, unbottomed deep. Cyncially, he tells of having witnessed the "Heav'n above the Clouds / Unfold her Crystal Dores, thence on his head / A Perfect Dove descend, what e're it meant" (*PR* 1.81–3), as if this sneer can keep the "Truth" at bay. "His Mother then is mortal," Satan declares; but what if "his Sire" is "He who obtains the Monarchy of Heav'n" (1.86–7)? What lies ahead for Satan can only be conceived of as a drama of identity;[26] as he insists, "Who this is we must learn." Is this Son merely a man, or is he the "first-begot," that other, celestial Son whom they have every reason to rue?

Even the sequence of events in Book 1 follows the sequence of the first three books of *Paradise Lost*, inviting comparison with all three scenes in the "grand consult" in Hell, the colloquy in Heaven, and the human dialogue in Eden. As Satan now ends his speech, the narrator cuts away to God in Heaven, who "in full frequence bright / Of Angels, thus to *Gabriel* smiling spake" (1.128–9). As the Father's interlocutor, Gabriel is *dramatically* appropriate, since he has recently appeared on earth to the Virgin Mary and "toldst her doubting how these things could be / To her a Virgin, that on her should come / The Holy Ghost, and the power of the highest / O're-shadow her" (1.137–40). But the angel's role as a sounding board also signals the Son's absence from Heaven, reminding us that, for Milton at least, the Son is neither co-essential nor co-eternal with the Father. What had been a crucial prerequisite to actual drama in *Paradise Lost* during the colloquy in Heaven – to avert the spectacle of "all that play-acting of the persons of the godhead" (*CPW* 6: 213) – is no longer required on earth to underwrite a drama of initiation. For, as MacCallum notes, the Son "is absent from the councils of the Father in heaven, and clearly does not, like Calvin's Son, continue to exercise divine power in the government of the universe during the period of his Incarnation" (*Milton and the Sons of God*, 238).

Like his protagonist, the poet must also lay "down the rudiments" of his dramatic "warfare" in reprising the order of events and speakers from *Paradise Lost*. As they had celebrated the outcome of the colloquy in Heaven, the angels also sing again, as if to dispel any further notion of "play-acting" in "the persons of the godhead": "The Father knows the Son; therefore secure / Ventures his filial Vertue, though untri'd" (1.176–7). MacCallum rightly notes that "This could not be said of the pre-existent Son, whose virtue was put to the test in such trials as the war in heaven, the creation, and the decision concerning man's redemption. There is no sense in which the pre-existent Son could be describ'd as 'untri'd'" (239–40). No more than Satan can the heavenly angels be sure that this Son of God is identical to "his first-begot." *Who this is we must learn* indeed. But if *Paradise Regain'd* takes the form of a drama of identity, it is not so merely for onlookers.

Jesus' opening soliloquy, which points to his new conditions of trial, is extraordinarily revealing of his changing conceptions of himself from childhood to manhood. He admits to "a multitude of thoughts at once / Awakn'd in me" (1.196–7) by both the baptism and that sudden voice from Heaven; but this "swarm" of ideas also reveals his uncertainty – not the doubt of a Hamlet about some visible ghost, but of a deep discrepancy between what this extraordinary human person feels and "my present state compar'd" (1.200). Jesus has not yet lost all his boyish desire "to learn and know, and thence to do / What might be publick good" (1.203–4). Yet, even as a child, "Born to that end, born to promote all truth" (1.205), he had known exactly where to look in scripture[27] for his proper means: "The Law of God I read, and found it sweet, / Made it my whole delight, and in it grew / To such perfection" that he could enter the Temple as a stripling boy of twelve and teach "The Teachers of our Law" (1.207–9, 212). And yet nothing he has learned to date has equipped him to act.

His autobiography closely follows the stages of his growth: "victorious deeds" first "Flam'd in my heart, heroic acts" (1.215–16), as he once envisioned himself as a latter-day Samson, "rescu[ing] *Israel* from the *Roman* yoke" (1.217). Later, he saw himself as a Hebrew Aeneas who should "subdue and quell o're all the earth / Brute violence and proud Tyrannick pow'r, / Till truth were freed, and equity restor'd" (1.218–20). Youthful idealism was never far, either, from the education of the Roman hero in Virgil's epic, published just five decades before this present trial. In the Underworld, Aeneas had learned about his Roman mission "To pacify, to impose the rule of law, / To spare the conquered, battle down the proud."[28] Or, as Jesus glosses those Virgilian lines, "[I] held it more humane, more heavenly first / By winning words to conquer willing hearts, / And make perswasion do the work of fear" (1.221–3). Jesus almost sounds like another Aeneas when he adds, "[T]he stubborn only to subdue" (1.226). This, as Anchises had taught his son in Elysium, was the Roman hero's world-changing destiny: "pacisque imponere morem / parcere subiectis et debellare[29] superbos" (*Aeneid* 6.852–3); "to impose the habit of peace, by sparing the humble and warring down the proud" (my translation). Much as Aeneas had learned to exchange the arts of war for the arts of peace and law, the younger Jesus has dreamed of becoming a universal champion of civility and "equity."

But he was disabused of this notion by his mother, who soon redirected his "high" thoughts toward a higher throne: "By matchless Deeds express thy matchless Sire. / For know, thou art no Son of mortal man, / Though men esteem thee low of Parentage" (1.233–5). It is his sense of lowly birth – the incompatability of his "present state" with his inward "promptings" – that is the real catalyst of his growth. For his mother insisted, "Thy Father is the Eternal King," instilling in him a sense that "Thou shouldst be great and sit on *David's* Throne, / And of thy Kingdom there should be no end" (1.236, 240–1). Yet a mother's love is also a snare. Mary's stories of the Annunciation, the angelic choir at his nativity, the adoration of the humble shepherds and kingly Magi, the prophecies of Simeon and Anna: all still threaten to obscure the will of Heaven and his part in it.

Here, Milton's Jesus most resembles the Foxean hero in the way he turns to scripture to confirm his mother's witness and to ground her soaring ambitions for him: "This having heard, strait I again revolv'd / The Law and Prophets, searching what was writ / Concerning the Messiah, to our Scribes / Known partly" (1.259–62). Significantly, it is not in oral testimony but in the book that he "soon found of whom they spake / I am; this chiefly, that my way must lie / Through many a hard assay even to the death, / E're I the promis'd Kingdom can attain" (1.262–5). Yet this is hardly reassuring, since his titles as "king" are not limited to such prepossessing images as "Counsellor, The mighty God, The everlasting Father, The Prince of Peace," destined to sit "upon the throne of David" (Isaiah 9: 6–7). For he is first destined to be Isaiah's "man of sorrows," the man who "is despised and rejected of men; a man of sorrows, and acquainted with grief … Surely he hath borne our griefs, and carried our sorrows: yet we did esteem him stricken, smitten of God, and afflicted. But he was wounded for our transgressions, he was bruised for our iniquities: the chastisement of our peace was upon him; and with his stripes we are healed" (Isaiah 53: 3–5). This all-too-human Jesus finds little comfort, then, in his mother's witness, knowing he has first to die to enter "his kingdom, to order it, and to establish it with judgment and with justice from henceforth even for ever" (Isaiah 9: 7).

What should strike readers of *Paradise Lost* is the *dramatic* requirement that the Son now make the same leap of faith on earth that he once made in heaven, even if he no longer even recalls that scene in which he volunteered to die for the sake of sinful man, trusting that "thou hast givn me to possess / Life in my self for ever." In the immediate presence of his Father, and fully present to his "goodness," it was not difficult to believe that "Thou wilt not leave me in the loathsom grave" (*PL* 3.243–4, 247). Yet here below, his limited knowledge derives from hearsay and the Father's word in scripture. The only direct evidence he has of a future kingdom comes from that offstage voice, "Audibly heard from Heav'n," from that speaker who "pronounc'd me his, / Me his beloved Son" (1.284–5). Even his repetition of "me" suggests his amazement at being singled out for what he only knew about from reading Isaiah's "man of sorrows" – that he must endure "many a hard assay even to the death, / E're I the promis'd Kingdom can attain." He is thus reduced to a bookman with little more than the written word to realize his destiny.

MacCallum has outlined "the new terms and conditions of choice arising from the Incarnation," and rightly concludes, at least theologically, that "The divine and human nature are united in the Son through the act of choice, the man realizing in a human mode the will of the divine being" (240). Yet this is to make Jesus' own emphasis rest on his "divine" nature more than on his "human mode" of being. While his mother had told him that "men esteem thee low of Parentage," she had also filled his head with ideas of royal power and "Eternal" glory. What he finds instead in Isaiah is something closer to the idea of the servant-ruler. Walwyn for one reminds us: "[T]hou knowest that Christ ruled as a servant, and tooke the burden of the people upon him; but our Rulers do rule like Lords, and cast their burden upon the poor people." And this, the Leveller insisted, "is contrary to the rule of Christ, and repugnant to reason; for the world subjecteth reason to tyranny, and thou knowest that the glory of the world and the devil, are one."[30] Here is something that, in Milton's time, was fairly close to the self-understanding of Jesus after "searching what was writ / Concerning the Messiah, to our Scribes / Known partly" (1.260–2).

His trial in the wilderness would be considerably less difficult were Milton's Jesus able to read the English Walwyn along with the Hebrew Isaiah. For "nothing," the Leveller wrote, "can bee more rediculous to the world, then the rule of Christ. Who will give his coat after his cloake, and turn one cheek to bee smitten, after the other? Who will sell all to follow Christ?"[31] Here is the "Humiliation and strong Sufferance" of which God had also spoken in predicting to Gabriel how "His weakness shall o'recome Satanic strength" (1.160–1). In fact, it is this humility that will be his chief *dramatic* reason for refusing wealth and power. And his soliloquy shows that even the angels know more than he does. So the essence of his humanity is not just, or even merely, his mortality: it is also the human limits set on his knowledge as a *reader*. And that unmediated assurance on which he was still able to rely in Heaven – the promise of his Father in the Exaltation scene – is far beyond the ken of this very human Son. There, God had commanded, "Under his great Vice-gerent Reign abide / United as one individual Soule / For ever happie" (*PL* 5.609–11). But here, he has no memory of a Father he has never seen, whom he knows merely by hearsay and by writing, and who promises only to see him "Through many a hard assay even to the death, / E're I the promis'd Kingdom can attain" (1.264–5). A far greater leap of faith is then required of him on earth than the leap he does not even remember making in the colloquy of Heaven.

The drama of *Paradise Regain'd* literally turns on his acts of reading – like that of Foxe's heroes – by which Jesus learns "of whom they spake / I am" (1.262–3). Yet none of these "hard assays" is spelled out; nor is the *where* or *when*. Even John's gospel, by which the scriptural Jesus had also staked his claim to an eternal identity – "I say unto you, Before Abraham was, I am" (John 8: 58) – is now inverted. Milton's Jesus makes no claim at all to identity with the heavenly "Messiah," at least no more than in his present identity; he does not call himself the eternal "I am." While the voice that spoke from heaven had signalled a fulfillment of the scriptures, all it literally said was that "the time" is "Now full, that I no more should live obscure, / But openly begin, as best becomes / The Authority which I deriv'd from Heaven" (1.286–9). Without presumption, he is led "by some strong motion … / Into this Wilderness, to what intent / I learn not yet, perhaps I need not know; / For what concerns my knowledge God reveals" (1.290–3). The only continuity of this man with the pre-existent Son – about which he knows nothing, while the reader of *Paradise Lost* knows a lot – is his perfect trust in God. If he can wait on God for "what concerns my knowledge," then readers should be prepared to wait as well.

When, for example, the young man meets "an aged man in Rural weeds" (1.314) in the desert, his knowledge is much less than our own – we who possess the gospels he lacks. Nor is he abrupt or rude in responding to a stranger's questions, since the subtext of the question is encouragement to self-pitying distrust: "Sir, what ill chance hath brought thee to this place /

So far from path or road of men?" (1.321–2). Should he not expect better, since the prophet "call'd thee Son / Of God; I saw and heard … / Fame also finds us out" (1.329–30, 334)? Satan's concern actually cloaks a dangerous assumption that "ill chance," rather than God's will, is what has brought him to these dire straits.

In a similar way, Foxe's devilish tempter Bishop Bonner assures Thomas Haukes that the churchman acts in good faith, wanting no more than to set him on the right path. The confession that he asks him to sign signifies no more than, "I Thomas Haukes haue talked with my sayd Ordinary, with certayne good, godly, and learned men. Notwith-standing I stand still in myne opinion." To which Haukes replies, "Shall I graunt you to be good, godly, and learned men, and yet graunt my selfe to stand in a contrary opinion? No, I will not graunt you to be good, godly and learned men."[32] Milton's Jesus is not as abrupt or "short"[33] as Haukes admits to being. Jesus says, "Who brought me hither / Will bring me hence, no other Guide I seek" (1.335–6). The issue, as he sees it, is simply trust.

But Satan's voice of worldly experience dismisses "naïve" trust out of hand: "By Miracle he may, reply'd the Swain, / What other way I see not" (1.337–8). What follows shows his solicitous demeanour to be no more than rank hypocrisy. The tempter scoffs and steps in to trip up the "witness" whatever way he can: "But if thou be the Son of God, Command / That out of these hard stones be made thee bread; / So shalt thou save thy self and us relieve / With Food, whereof we wretched seldom taste" (1.342–5). To a Foxean reader, it is a speech heard before as in a dream. The inquisitor Fecknam had in very similar terms mocked the martyr Haukes, devilishly twisting the facts to claim that "Ridley hath preached at Paules Cross openly, that the deuill beleueth better then you: for he beleueth that Christ is able of stones to make bread, and ye will not beleue that Christes body is in the Sacrament, and yet thou buildest thy faith vpon them."[34]

But Milton's Jesus has access to the same proof-text, by which he is now able to identify his Tempter and to situate himself in another version of the story told in the Law:

> Think'st thou such force in Bread? is it not written
> (For I discern thee other then thou seem'st)
> Man lives not by Bread only but each Word
> Proceeding from the mouth of God; who fed
> Our Fathers here with Manna. (1.347–51)

For Jesus recalls, as any reader of Foxe would be able to do, the corresponding scene in scripture where Israel had grumbled, only to be chastised by God who "led thee these forty years in the wilderness, to humble thee, and to prove thee, to know what was in thine heart, whether thou wouldest keep his commandments, or no. And he humbled thee, and suffered thee to hunger, and fed thee with manna, which thou knewest not, neither did thy fathers know; that he might make thee know that man doth not live by bread only, but by every word that proceedeth out of the mouth of the Lord doth man live" (Deuteronomy 8: 2–3). Milton's Jesus, in brief, finds himself reliving the difficulties of "Our Fathers here with Manna," as well as "in the Mount" with "*Moses*," who "was forty days, nor eat nor drank, / And forty days *Eliah* without food / Wandred this barren waste, the same I now" (1.351–4). Never more sure of himself than when walking in the ink-marked footsteps of his ancestors, Milton's Jesus has good reason to be "short" with the Adversary: "Why dost thou then suggest to me distrust, / Knowing who I am, as I know who thou art?" (1.355–6). And the reader begins to see that this is no ordinary drama of identity: Jesus is able to determine his identity only from each scene in scripture that corresponds to his temptation. So the *literary* threat to drama does prove to be the academic disputation, which was the actual experience of the Foxean martyrs.[35]

Suffice to say that Satan displays more self-control than Bishop Bonner musters in the story of the Marian martyr, asking Haukes, "Haue ye not reade in the eyght of Iohn, where hee sayd, he would send his comforter which should teach you all thinges?" To which Haukes replies, "I graunt you it is so, that he woulde sende hys comforter, but to what ende? forsooth to this ende, that hee should lead you into all truth and verity, and that is not to teach a new doctrine." Outfaced by the martyr's superior grasp of scripture, Bonner snaps: "A Syr, ye are a right scripture man. For ye wyll haue nothing but the scripture. There is a great number of your countrey men of your opinion."[36] Far more urbane and polished than an English bishop, Milton's Satan is well-enough versed in scripture to let him see that two can play at this game. Satan even shows his cards in such a manner as to win pity from the man, though the man steadfastly refuses to pity himself: "'Tis true, I am that Spirit unfortunate, / Who leagu'd with millions more in rash revolt / Kept not my happy Station, but was driv'n / With them from bliss to the bottomless deep" (1.358–61). Satan is looking for some sort of recognition from "the Son," some sign, perhaps, that he does recall the primal event in their careers, to grasp what he now faces.

Recalling that "I came among the Sons of God, when he / Gave up into my hands *Uzzean Job* / To prove him, and illustrate his high worth" (1.368–70); or, again, "when to all his Angels he propos'd / To draw the proud King *Ahab* into fraud / That he might fall in *Ramoth*, they demurring, / I undertook that office" (1.371–4), Satan pretends, like a true believer, to be a faithful servant of God: "For what he bids I do" (1.377). But he also pretends to be a competent reader of scriptures; the litany of loss that follows is surely calculated to make *him* look like the "man of sorrows," as he names his deprivations, not least of which is his lost proximity to goodness. For "What I see excellent in good, or fair, / Or vertuous" (1.381–2), is now denied him forever. And, to consummate all, he says, "This wounds me most (what can it less) that Man, / Man fall'n shall be restor'd, I never more" (1.404–5). But perhaps Satan lets slip more than he intends in his appeal for pity; if his counterpart really were the Son of old, the latter would now be on his guard against the Adversary who had attempted to destroy Job. But, although Jesus gets at least a glimpse of the sinister power he faces, he shows no sign of knowing what to do, aside from exposing Satan as a liar: "Deservedly thou griev'st, compos'd of lyes / From the beginning, and in lies wilt end" (1.407–8). He knows only that his reading of Job and 1 Kings has taught a different truth from the one proposed to him. Only the Adversary enjoys "leave to come / Into the Heav'n of Heavens"; as Jesus says on the basis of his reading, "[T]hou com'st indeed, / As a poor miserable captive thrall, / Comes to the place where he before had sat / Among the Prime in Splendour, now depos'd" (1.409–13). But he gives no sign of recalling that deposition, much less of being the deposer. Indeed, his entire reproof is little more than what could be offered by any good reader of scripture:

> What but thy malice mov'd thee to misdeem
> Of righteous *Job*, then cruelly to afflict him
> With all inflictions, but his patience won?
> The other service was thy chosen task,
> To be a lyer in four hundred mouths. (1.424–8)

At this point, the Foxean reader expects Satan to burst into a rage, much as Edmund Bonner had done, infuriated by Haukes who has forced him, over and over, to repeat his catechism: "Do ye not beleue that there remaineth in the blessed Sacrament of the aultar after the wordes of consecration be spoken, no more bread, but the very body and bloud of Christ." But

Haukes rejects the dogma, saying, "I do beleue as Christ hath taught me." In exasperation, Bonner sneers: "Well, we will make you to know it, and beleue in it too, ere euer we haue done with you." But Haukes is immovable, retorting simply, "No, that shall ye neuer do." At which the Bishop snaps, "Yes a Fagot will make you do it."[37] So now it is both Satan and Milton who are dramatically disadvantaged. For the Adversary cannot, like Foxe's bishop, simply "rid you awaye and then we shall haue one hereticke lesse."[38] By murdering a perfect man, the Adversary would only hasten the work of the Redeemer. He dare not destroy Jesus until – or *if* – he shows a lack of trust in the Father. Similarly, the poet has to find some novel way to overcome the dramatic difficulty of portraying this disputant who, ever ready with a good proof-text, will not be disposed of on the stake, since he is not a fallen son of Adam – unlike the Marian martyr who, although a faithful witness, has in his human nature been corrupt since birth.

This is the crux of a plot that could easily turn into an aporia, without possibility of resolution. For even Satan doesn't know what to do next. At first, he merely professes admiration for this paragon of "Vertue," of whom he asks nothing more than access: "To hear thee when I come (since no man comes) / And talk at least, though I despair to attain" (1.484–5). Nor does Jesus know what to do. In the tone of Haukes responding to the threat of the "Fagot" – "What God thinketh meete to be done, that shall ye do, and more shall ye not do"[39] – "our Saviour" answers "with unalter'd brow": "Thy coming hither, though I know thy scope, / I bid not or forbid; do as thou find'st / Permission from above; thou canst not more" (1.493–6). It is the poet, as much as Satan, who still needs "more" to realize the *drama* of recovered Paradise, and so "to tell of deeds / Above Heroic, though in secret done, / And unrecorded left through many an Age" (1.14–16).

· 16 ·

"Also It Is Written":

THE FLESH MADE WORD

POTENTIAL DISCIPLES WHO were certain that they had spoken with "Jesus Messiah, Son of God declar'd" (2.4), yet "missing him thir joy so lately found," "Began to doubt, and doubted many days" (2.9, 11). Indeed, "His words, his wisdom full of grace and truth" had left them with a strong conviction that, "Now, now, for sure, deliverance is at hand, / The Kingdom shall to *Israel* be restor'd" (2.34–6). But then Messiah's abrupt disappearance had cast them down almost as far as his sudden advent had raised them up.

Frustration of this sort was familiar to the Levellers in the 1640s, as it also had been to republicans and sectaries, whose hopes of deliverance were permanently dashed at the Restoration. Like some of these revolutionaries, Milton's "Plain Fishermen" entreat the "God of *Israel*," nay, *command* him: "Send thy Messiah forth, the time is come; / Behold the Kings of the Earth how they oppress / Thy chosen" (2.43–5). Their longing for liberation is palpable: "[V]indicate / Thy Glory, free thy people from thir yoke" (2.47–8). Just as tangible are the echoes of Lilburne, Overton, and Walwyn at the end of the First Civil War. Seizing upon the myth of the Norman Yoke – the fiction of Saxon liberties before the Conquest – Lilburne had challenged lordly prerogative in his demands for social equality: "Againe, my Lord, that which is the greatest mischiefe of all, and *the oppressing bondage of England* ever since the *Norman yoke*, is this, I must be tryed before you by a Law (called the Common Law) that I know not, nor I thinke no man else, neither do I know where to find it, or reade it; and how I can in such a case be punished by it, I know not."[1] Four weeks later, Overton and Walwyn issued their *Remonstrance* against "the Illegall and Barbarous Imprisonment of that Famous and Worthy Sufferer for his Countries Freedoms, Lieutenant Col. JOHN LILBURNE." The seminal document of the Leveller movement, the *Remonstrance* affirmed that "[W]e remain under the *Norman* yoke of an *unlawfull Power*, from which wee ought to free ourselves; and which yee ought not to maintaine upon us, but to abrogate."[2] From Newgate Prison, where he was now incarcerated for his defence of Lilburne, Overton sought to open "darkned eyes" by "endeavour[ing] to discover & break the *Norman* yoke of cruelty, oppression, and tyranny from off their necks, and set their heels at liberty from the Prerogative fetters of the House of Lords, (by opening the Cabinet of their machivilian policy, against the peoples Liberties, that those Usurpers might be discovered in their deceit)."[3]

In a fragment of autobiography remarkable even for Lilburne, the Leveller claims to have "continually spent" his youth "in reading the Bible, the Book of Martyrs,"[4] and Luther and Calvin, as if he were consciously preparing to martyr himself for the principle that God created "every particular and individuall man and woman ... equall and alike in power, dignity, authority, and majesty."[5] A similar dramatic challenge from Jesus' disciples for God to "vindicate / Thy Glory, free thy people from thir yoke" shades into a type of "Leveller" protest in *Paradise Regain'd*, although Messiah's followers are not as likely to dictate terms to God: "But let us wait ... he will not fail / Nor will withdraw him now, nor will recall, / Mock us with his blest sight, then snatch him hence" (2.49, 54–6). And yet these biblical radicals, who went out seeking Jesus "in *Jerico* / The City of Palms, *Ænon*, and *Salem* Old" (2.20–1), are no more resigned than the Levellers were to wait on God's choice of a time to begin the work of deliverance. For the hope of each is to instantly overthrow the Roman or Norman yoke; each begs God to answer prayer as each sees fit. By contrast, Milton's Jesus asks no more of God at the end of his second soliloquy than, "Where will this end?" (2.245). While he knows that the *end* must be his death, he is willing to live in suspense about the *where* and *how*, much as he is willing to endure physical hunger, all the while "hungring more to do my Fathers will" (2.259).[6]

This manifestly human Jesus is shown to be his mother's child as she asks, quite as patiently as he, at the beginning of Book 2, Where will this end? For Mary is just as certain as her son that the *end* of her "Exaltation" is "to Afflictions high"; yet, like him, she still adds, "Afflicted I may be, it seems, and blest" (2.92–3). Their resemblance becomes even more pronounced in her conclusion: "But I to wait with patience am inur'd" (2.102). Mary seems to have read her fate as well in the prophetic narrative of the Man of Sorrows: "Hale highly favour'd, among women blest; / While I to sorrows am no less advanc't" (2.68–9). Although her son wishes to spare her certain knowledge of the yoke he bears – "Through many a hard assay even to the death, / E're I the promis'd Kingdom can attain" (1.264–5) – she has reached the same conclusion, "that through my very Soul / A sword shall pierce, this is my favour'd lot" (2.90–1). Her understanding of the prophecy that "Thou shouldst be great and sit on *David's* Throne" (1.240) thus comes at most points to parallel the psychological development of her son. And yet, though his *end* is shadowed by his death, "I will not argue that," she says, "nor will repine" (2.94).

This perplexing resignation of mother, son, and disciples alike makes for "a reading experience," Stanley Fish claims, "that can fairly be characterized as frustrating."[7] For the reader faces a depth of resignation, amounting to a "declaration of passivity" (31) on the part of all three – most of all the Son – that is nearly "as exasperating for us as it is for Satan" (35). Fish admits, "There is the same felt disparity between the presentation of the problem and the egregious passivity of the (non) response. Just at that moment when we expect an issue to be met head on, the speaker wraps himself in a piety and says in effect, 'Let God worry about it.'" And yet such a "deliberate refusal to act" (35) is the whole point, Fish argues, since the Son's only motive is to do "the Father's will," a state of mind that "requires the relinquishment of one's own [will], the most difficult of all acts, although its visible manifestations are necessarily unimpressive. 'What dost thou in this world?' I do my Father's will, and therefore *I* do nothing" (37). That is why, for Fish, "Nothing happens" in the poem, because "the pattern of temptation-rejection which constitutes the whole of the poem's plot is itself patterned in such a way as to defuse the dramatic thrust it potentially embodies" (29). As a result, the "impulse behind Milton's art – to lose the self in a union with God" – requires us "to exchange our (human) values for his" (27). "A successful reading of the poem must then be marked by a *re*valuing of the Son's passivity, which implies of course a *de*valuing of assertive action and self-expression" (38). A less passive reader, however, might suspect a cynical ploy in such a critical position: to do nothing and so to abstain from choice.

In the poem, Milton's Jesus is just as active as Foxe's Thomas Haukes is in his defiant answers to Bishop Bonner. For the task of the Foxean martyr is to refute every claim of the Tempter to power, thereby exposing the circumscription of the Adversary by a greater power. For instance, Satan conjures up a banquet attended by "Tall stripling youths rich clad" and "Nymphs of *Diana*'s train" (2.352, 355), only to inquire, "What doubts the Son of God to sit and eat? / These are not Fruits forbidden, no interdict / Defends the touching of these viands pure" (2.368–70). Unctuously, he describes the attendants as "Thy gentle Ministers, who come to pay / Thee homage, and acknowledge thee thir Lord" (2.375–6). Yet Jesus is quick to catch the contradiction in the Tempter's words: "Said'st thou not that to all things I had right? / And who withholds my pow'r that right to use?" (2.379–80). Although Fish links the "insufficiency" (30) of his response – "And with my hunger what hast thou to do?" (2.389) – to his habitual evasion of "the immediate problem" that "is left behind, not even dismissed but simply unattended to" (34–5), it is the right *dramatic* response if one has glimpsed how the Tempter *works*.

On his return to tempt the Son of God who has "dream'd, as appetite is wont to dream, / Of meat and drinks, Natures refreshment sweet" (2.264–5), Satan virtually emerges out of Jesus' dream about Elijah, to see "his Supper on the coals prepar'd, / And by the Angel was bid rise and eat" (2.273–4). Of course, Satan cannot read his mind or his dreams; he merely picks up where he left off in the previous temptation ("stones to bread"), if unable any longer to perfectly conceal his dialectical method.[8] The resulting dialectical drama is far more dangerous than Fish allows: "With granted leave officious I return," Satan says, "But much more wonder that the Son of God / In this wild solitude so long should bide / Of all things destitute" (2.302–5). Here is where his method is most devilish: "Others of some note, / As story tells," he insinuates, "have trod this Wilderness" (2.306–7), presuming in this way to identify himself with the "providing Angel" of "The Fugitive Bond-woman with her Son / Out cast *Nebaioth*," or "all the race / Of *Israel*," which "here had famish'd, had not God / Rain'd from Heaven Manna, and that Prophet bold / Native of *Thebez* wandring here was fed / Twice by a voice inviting him to eat" (2.308–14). More insidiously, Satan now reprises the scene of stones-to-bread to deny that he had ever incited mistrust.

Jesus had immediately recognized the first scene in which he was cast – the devil tempting the Israelistes who began to murmur that God left them in the wilderness to starve. Citing the divine word of admonition, the Son had entered on the instant into the scene in scripture: "[I]s it not written / … Man lives not by Bread only, but each Word / Proceeding from the mouth of God; who fed / Our Fathers here with Manna" (1.347, 349–51). It was he who first cited "Moses" and "Eliah" as his true exemplars of trust in

God; so Satan returns to these stories – adding for good measure a third one of Hagar and her infant, Ishmael, dying of thirst in the desert – in order to portray himself in each crisis in the desert as God's "providing Angel." But this appropriation is also exposed as the active hinge of the drama, since any time that Jesus quotes scripture – like Foxe's martyr refuting his torturers – Satan instantly writes himself into the story, rendering it unusable.

"Where will this end?" is thus the real question of moment, creating suspense in the character and reader alike; for Milton's devil is far more able to quote an apt verse of scripture than the Catholic bishop Bonner. At some point, the reader begins to fear that Jesus, like Foxe's martyrs, will exhaust all possibility of reply. Haukes, on the other hand, finds the way clearly marked out to his martyrdom. Waiting in confinement under immediate threat of dying, he has nothing more to worry about than being faithful unto death; he does not bear the burden of universal salvation, needing only to quote the right scripture to prove his faith in God. But the *way* for Milton's Jesus is not at all clear. Like the Foxean martyr, he is bound to die; yet the Adversary proves to be far more devious and insidious than his own agent in the Marian persecutions. Jesus knows only that Satan aims to turn his faith in scripture against him in a way that must abort the redemption of mankind. *Where will this end?* is less a question for him of bodily death than of mental sufficiency to withstand this nearly impossible trial. If Satan manoeuvres him into a situation where he momentarily forgets, or else misreads, however slightly, the authority of scripture, both he and the work of human salvation will be fatally compromised.

When Satan, for instance, mentions Hagar led by "a providing Angel" to a well in the desert, he now denies Jesus this defence from scripture, since it has been appropriated to the devil's domain. Yet Jesus is not "inactive" in his response, since he claims new authority from the messianic prophecies of the Psalms, which appear to authorize him to summon his own providing angels. Satan has even assured the Son that, as "thir Lord," he has a right to expect his angelic attendants at the banquet to do his bidding. To which the Son replies: "Saidst thou not that to all things I had right? / And who withholds my pow'r that right to use?" (2.379–80). Here, Jesus responds quite as curtly as Haukes replies to Bishop Bonner.[9] At the same time, he makes no claim for himself, not even speaking in his own voice as he paraphrases two Davidic Psalms: "Thou preparest a table before me in the presence of mine enemies" (Psalms 23: 5); and, "[H]e shall give his angels charge over thee, to keep thee in all thy ways. They shall bear thee up in their hands, lest thou dash thy foot against a stone" (Psalms 91: 11–12). *If* he is the Messiah, as Satan insists, should Messianic prophecy not refer to him? "I can at will, doubt not, as soon as thou, / Command a Table in this Wilderness, / And call swift flights of Angels ministrant / Array'd in Glory on my cup to attend" (2.383–6). He is never more the Foxean reader than here and in similar acts of lateral reading where he confutes the devil's "Word."

By contrast, Satan is more formidable than Foxe's Adversary in his ability to present himself as the mouthpiece of the divine Word. Compare Satan's abilities with the scholastic handicap, say, of Edmund Bonner in his scriptural duel with Thomas Haukes:

> *Boner.* Do ye not beleue that there remaineth in the blessed Sacrament of the aultar after the wordes of consecration be spoken, no more bread, but the very body and bloud of Christ? And at that word he put of his cap.
>
> *Haukes.* I do beleue as Christ hath taught me.
>
> *Boner.* Why? Did not Christ say: Take: eate, this is my body?
>
> *Haukes.* Christ sayd so: but therefore it foloweth not, that the Sacrament of the aultar is so as you teach, neither did Christ euer teach it so to be.
>
> *Boner.* Why? The Catholicke Church taught it so, and they were of Christes Church.
>
> *Haukes.* How proue ye it? The Apostles neuer taught it so. Read the Actes, the second, and the twenty. Neither Peter nor Paule euer taught it, neither instituted it so.[10]

The bishop, who is less well versed than an ordinary Protestant in reading scripture, has no good answer aside from his insistence on orthodox dogma.

Conversely, Satan is as capable as Jesus of moving from a story of hunger in the desert (Israel, stones, and bread) to another story of providing angels, making his every success a mortal danger to the Son. Satan is so cunning, in fact, that for the time being he eschews the blatant opening given him by that first proof-text. Letting go the biblical injunction, "Man lives not by Bread only, but each Word / Proceeding from the mouth of God," Satan waits until the next morning to quote it when he returns as a providing angel.

Cunning devil that he is, he also aims, as far as possible, to conceal his dialectical method from the Son (as well as from Milton critics) by distracting sidebars. One of these sidebars underlies the temptation to riches.

While it is a legitimate temptation – *Who is going to follow you if you can't offer anything in return?* – it leaves the broader field of contending scriptures for the nonce to probe instead for hidden weaknesses, while holding in reserve the Son's allusion to "swift flights of Angels ministrant" (2.385). For the moment, it is simply enough to insist: "Thou art unknown, unfriended, low of birth, / A Carpenter thy Father known, thy self / Bred up in poverty and streights at home; / Lost in a Desert here and hunger-bit" (2.413–16). In effect, he asks, what "Authority" (2.418) from above can you claim if you are lacking in "quality" here below? Without means, what do you hope to achieve? Even were you able to attract the notice of malcontents, why should they be inspired by your plebeian origins? "What Followers, what Retinue canst thou gain, / Or at thy heels the dizzy Multitude, / Longer then thou canst feed them on thy cost" (2.419–21)? Even a youth, "Bred up in poverty and streights at home," has to understand that, without riches, "Virtue, Valour, Widsom sit in want" (2.431).

Yet Jesus remains unapologetic about his humble beginnings, let alone his current state of abject poverty. Has the Tempter not read in scripture of poor men who, because they *were* "endu'd with these [Virtue, Valour, Wisdom] have oft attain'd / In lowest poverty to highest deeds" (2.437–8). By way of illustration, he names "*Gideon* and *Jephtha*, and the Shepherd lad, / Whose off-spring on the Throne of *Juda* sat / So many Ages, and shall yet regain / That seat, and reign in *Israel* without end" (2.439–42). For good measure he is able to name, like any good Commonwealthsman, those memorable heroes of the Roman republic – "*Quintius, Fabricius, Curius, Regulus*" (2.446) – who *were* renowned for their unimpeachable integrity. Had not Lucius Quintius Cincinnatus quietly returned to private life after the expiration of his emergency term as Rome's *dictator*? Each of the others was likewise notable for his incorruptibility, whether refusing to keep the spoils of war or spurning bribes (much as Lilburne, in Milton's time, claimed to have done).[11]

Jesus goes out of his way, in fact, to "esteem those names of men so poor / Who could do mighty things, and could contemn / Riches though offer'd from the hand of Kings" (2.447–9). His sympathy for hardscrabble effort recalls Lilburne's expression of pity for those men who "have spent all they have in the world, and done the Kingdom good service," who "have not a bit of bread to put in their mouths, but what they borrow money to buy withall, and many poor Widdows & Fatherlesse children, that have lost their husbands & fathers in the publick service," and yet are left to cry at the door of the Lords, "Bread, Bread, and [the latter] ready to curse them all to their faces," since the latter "have no bowells of compassion towards them."[12] Milton's Jesus is equally sensible of the great hardships and feeble hopes of the poor, to the point of confessing that he *shares* in their aspirations: "And what in me seems wanting, but that I / May also in this poverty as soon / Accomplish what they did, perhaps and more?" (2.450–2).

Jesus does not rest his case on merit alone, but also on human pity. For it is not *natural* equality that invalidates "the office of a King" (2.463), given that the office itself is based on a false notion of natural hierarchy; rather, it is "he who reigns within himself, and rules / Passions, Desires, and Fears, [who] is more a King" (2.466–7). Yet higher than this Stoic type is that human being who has the grace "To know, and knowing worship God aright," which "[i]s yet more Kingly" (2.475–6). "Besides" this, "to give a Kingdom hath been thought / Greater and nobler done, and to lay down / Far more magnanimous, then to assume" (2.481–3). Milton had long ago suggested as much in *Defensio Secunda*, when Queen Christina of Sweden showed true queenliness in wanting to renounce her crown.[13] On this scale of values, Richard Cromwell is more noble than his father, Oliver, and greater than any king, since he abdicated that "throne" he inherited from his father the Protector. But Jesus, like Walwyn, has read 1 Samuel 8: "[T]hou knowest that God gave the office of a King in his wrath, and that Kings and Priests are Jewish ceremonies, and thou knowest … the glory of the world and the devil, are one."[14]

After his deep expression of sympathy for men risen from "lowest poverty" to serve their people, Jesus' sudden diatribe against the "miscellaneous rabble" (3.50) comes as a shock, for it threatens the work of *universal* atonement. Why would the "saviour of mankind" be so disdainful of the very people he was born to save? The answer is not far to seek, given that Jesus reflects back to him, as in a looking-glass, the Adversary's own contempt for "the dizzy Multitude" (2.420) during the previous temptation to riches. By now, at the outset of the temptation to glory, Jesus has begun to pick up on the devil's method by turning his own dialectical strategy against him: "For what is glory but the blaze of fame, / The peoples praise, if always praise unmixt?" Most readers can't help but flinch when he asks, "And what the people but a herd confus'd, / A miscellaneous rabble, who extol / Things vulgar, & well weigh'd, scarce worth the praise" (3.47–51). In fact, he only flings Satan's own words back at him. It is a stunning display, not of passive indifference to worldly values, but of an active mind ready and able to turn the devil's best weapons against him. Since Satan shows that he does regard the common sort as "the dizzy Multitude," then "miscellaneous rabble" is exactly the right response to empty out Satan's worldly value of *fame* among those he would reduce to "a herd confus'd."[15]

In redefining "glory" by the light of eternity, where things "scarce worth the praise" – the brutal wars, for example, of "*Macedonian Philip*" and "young *Scipio*," and "Great *Julius*, whom now all the world admires" (3.32, 34, 39) – are revealed as vanity, Jesus is just as adept as Socrates[16] had been in distinguishing between true and false values. Implicit in his scornful critique of the conqueror is his sympathy for the suffering masses of mankind who still endure the misery of Sword-law. By contrast, "This is true glory and renown, when God / Looking on the Earth, with approbation marks / The just man, and divulges him through Heaven / To all his Angels" (3.60–3). And he clinches the point of "true glory" with a key example from scripture: "[T]hus he did to *Job*" (3.64). It is not the first time that Jesus reminds Satan of his failure with this man of faith.[17] But what is revealing is the likeness he finds between biblical and pagan heroes: "Who names not now with honour patient *Job*? / Poor *Socrates* (who next more memorable?)." The reason for that likeness should be familiar to a reader of Foxe: "By what he taught and suffer'd for so doing, / For truths sake suffering death unjust, lives now / Equal in fame to proudest Conquerours"[18] (3.95–9). For Socrates genuinely matters to the Son as much as he does to Milton in bearing witness against false gods. To Jesus, Socrates was a true "martyr" in the etymological sense of *witness*, "For truths sake suffering death unjust." Indeed, Socrates stands second only to Job in Jesus' own pantheon of martyrs.

Satan, of course, cannot accept death and defeat as a sign of glory, any more than he can hide his longing for transcendent glory: "Think not so slight of glory; therein least / Resembling thy great Father; he seeks glory, / And for his glory all things made" (3.109–11). But the Son of God, who gives no sign of recalling his former life in Heaven, responds as he had done in the colloquy in Heaven, where he had asked, "[W]ilt thou thy self / Abolish thy Creation, and unmake, / For him, what for thy glorie thou hast made? / So should thy goodness and thy greatness both / Be question'd and blaspheam'd without defence" (*PL* 3.162–6). At this point, neither Satan nor Jesus knows what only the reader can see – that the Son exhibits an unconscious continuity[19] with his previous identity in his willingness to upbraid anyone who dares to call the Father's goodness into question:

To whom our Saviour fervently reply'd.
And reason; since his word all things produc'd,
Though chiefly not for glory as prime end,
But to shew forth his goodness and impart
His good communicable to every soul. (*PR* 3.121–4)

Abandoning the temptation to glory, Satan now seeks, through appeals to "Zeal and Duty" (3.172), to tempt the Son to be the author of his own story by forcing a distorted version of it on him: "So shalt thou best fullfil, best verifie / The Prophets old, who sung thy endless raign" (3.177–8). The Son's response proves his acceptance of "many a hard assay," though he likely reveals too much of what he knows about the *end* of that story: "What if he hath decreed that I shall first / Be try'd in humble state, and things adverse" (3.188–9). The danger is that he might let the Adversary discover what he holds sacred, thereby giving him means to replay other scenes from scripture, where "he may know / What I can suffer, how obey? who best / Can suffer, best can do; best reign, who first / Well hath obey'd" (3.193–6). At the same time, what Jesus says is nothing that the Tempter hasn't already realized. Later, he will even admit to having read the same story written in the stars – "Sorrows, and labours, opposition, hate, / Attends thee, scorns, reproaches, injuries, / Violence and stripes, and lastly cruel death" (4.386–8).

One of the lasting illusions of Satan's power, of course, is that he always feels able to control events. By contrast, Jesus exhibits a counter-model that later martyrs will follow in their reading of the Book of Acts, of Eusebius and, ultimately of Foxe, since even "the early martyrs see God or Christ himself as the agent of their martyrdom, rather than the various governors that decree their deaths. This is, in other words, a performance orchestrated by God. It must have been a comforting thought."[20] Claiming, "[W]ho best / Can suffer best can do," Jesus appears to comfort himself with the thought that suffering and death are in God's hands. Like Haukes in the *Actes and Monuments*, he might well insist on his own willingness to die for his profession of his faith. But he chooses rather to prove his constancy by grace of God's providence, bearing witness to a higher court than that of Satan, who, after all, is still one of the "mighty Peers" and "ancient Powers of Air and this wide world" (1.40, 44). The danger, then, is not just that he may have given the Adversary licence to kill him, since this is the necessary *end* of the story. Rather, the danger concerns *where* this may end, since Satan has only to find a way to make his fall from innocence simultaneous with Jesus' death to thwart the work of redemption.

Satan's handicap is that he can't yet make use of state power, unlike Bishop Bonner, who has simply to get Haukes to confirm his heresy to claim civil authority over him:

> *Bonor.* How say you to Confiteor?
> *Haukes.* I say it is abhominable & detestable, ye and a blasphemy agaynst God and his sonne Christ, to call vpon any, to trust to any, or to pray to any, saue only to Christ Jesus …
> *Boner.* Wyll you haue no body to pray for you, when you be dead?
> *Haukes.* No surelye except you can prooue it by the Scriptures.[21]

In his exercise of ecclesiastical *and* state power, the bishop still holds all the cards: "And he said to me: Syr, it is tyme to begin with you: we will rid you awaye and then we shall haue one hereticke less." His contest with a fallen son of Adam is only a legal formality; for *where this must end*, if Hauke will not recant, is in a fiery death. Were he to kill a sinless man, however, Satan would merely hasten the work of redemption; Jesus has to be brought into bondage to sin *before* he is put to death. The devil's dramatic dilemma is then how to prolong the trial just long enough to bring the Son down to his own level of corruption. While Jesus evinces a readiness like every Foxean martyr to die in God's good time, his repeated answer to the question, *Where will this end?* ought to give Satan pause. For the Son of God reads the Messianic prophecies in a way that cannot help but heighten the devil's sense of urgency: "Know'st thou not that my rising is thy fall, / And my promotion will be thy destruction" (3.201–2). *Where will this end indeed?*[22]

The temptation of the kingdoms, in the devil's successive offers of Parthia, Rome, and Greece, builds towards acute doubt about martyrdom as a proper means to realize the promise of the Messianic prophecies. Satan urges, for example, with respect to Rome: "Aim therefore at no less then all the world, /Aim at the highest" (4.105–6). In purely logical terms, he is right: "[W]ithout the highest attain'd / Will be for thee no sitting, or not long / On *David*'s Throne, be propheci'd what will" (4.106–8). Highest is best in the effort to gain, let alone to hold, any high throne. As he now cautions Jesus, concerning Parthia: "[T]hy Kingdom though foretold / By Prophet or by Angel, unless thou / Endeavour, as thy Father *David* did, / Thou never shalt obtain" (3.351–4). But Satan is merely the first to criticize the Son's "passivity." Time and again, he says, *Do something, you have to do something, lest all those heady predictions be for naught.*

The answer that Satan receives could confirm Stanley Fish in his view of a "willess" hero who, "By this point … is less angry than bored."[23] Yet Jesus proves every bit as strong-minded and succinct as the Foxean martyr in his confession of faith, let alone his willingness to die in order to prove the truth of the Messianic prophecies: "Know therefore when my season comes to sit / On *David's* Throne, it shall be like a tree / Spreading and over-shadowing all the Earth" (4.146–8). In his grasp of the ancient prophecies of Daniel, he sounds almost like a Fifth Monarchist. But, unlike these English millenarians, he is keenly aware of what the cost to him will be: "Means there shall be to this, but what the means, / Is not for thee to know, nor me to tell" (4.152–3). Jesus thus maintains what every future "witness" – from Eusebius to Foxe – will claim in his turn: the martyrologies are invariably the story of a reading contest, in which the drama turns on the martyr finding his proper opening to step into the pages of scripture.[24] Turning the Mass into mass communications[25] is what Lilburne meant by his plea that "this *Epistle* may live, and many Thousands of them be re-printed"[26] and given away. Bodies turning into text, or the flesh made word, is the last flourish of Milton's Leveller signature in the poem.

Of course, Satan is enraged by this martyr who refuses to explain the means by which he might step into the pages of the Word. The stoic mask of the Tempter begins to crack as he retorts that he offers him the world only "On this condition, if thou wilt fall down, / And worship me as thy superior Lord" (4.166–7). But "our Saviour" is no more willing than his future followers – Lilburne for one – to kneel to the Lords of this earth: "I never lik'd thy talk, thy offers less, / Now both abhor, since thou hast dar'd to utter / The abominable terms, impious condition" (4.171–3). In what he says next, some readers still hear nothing more than passivity: "But I endure the time, till which expir'd, / Thou hast permission on me" (4.174–5). Yet the Son needs to resist the devil's claim that he is the author of the story in which they find themselves, that of the first commandment: "Thou shalt have no other gods before me." Like the locution "It is written,"[27] which so often prefaces the martyr's climactic arguments in *Actes and Monuments*, Jesus rebuffs Satan for presuming to be God: "It is written, / The first of all Commandments, Thou shalt worship / The Lord thy God, and only him shalt serve" (4.175–7). But in his rebuke he claims for himself no more than what scripture says of him: "And dar'st thou to the Son of God propound /

To worship thee accurst[?]" (4.178–9). MacCallum notes that "[H]e clearly refers to the Father and not himself" (260) in this quotation of Deuteronomy 6: 13: "Thou shalt fear the LORD thy God, and serve him, and shalt swear by his name."

It is equally clear that Jesus has taken his cue from Satan, who had told him, "But thou art plac't above me, thou art Lord" (1.475). So now he does no more than defend the truth of scripture: "Wert thou so void of fear or shame, / As offer them to me the Son of God, / To me my own, on such abhorred pact, / That I fall down and worship thee as God?" (4.189–92). Yet his injunction "Get thee behind me; plain thou now appear'st / That Evil one, Satan for ever damn'd" (4.193–4) says that what is "plain" to him comes from his reading, not from any recollection of the War in Heaven. Lest we should doubt, Milton even reverses the syntax of Luke's gospel.[28] The latter reads: "Get thee behind me, Satan: for it is written, Thou shalt worship the Lord thy God, and him only shalt thou serve" (Luke 4: 8). By contrast, Milton's Jesus rebukes the devil only *after* he has quoted the condition, "It is written," as if to ground his rebuke on the Word, not on his own will.

Satan, though "abasht" (4.195), does not recognize his antagonist of old from the War in Heaven, trying to mollify this very angry man whose identity is still opaque to him:

> Be not so sore offended, Son of God;
> Though Sons of God both Angels are and Men,
> If I to try whether in higher sort
> Then these thou bear'st that title, have propos'd
> What both from Men and Angels I receive. (4.196–200)

What Satan offers next is the Socratic knowledge that Jesus says is second only to Job in importance: "Be famous then / By wisdom … All knowledge is not couch't in *Moses* Law, / The *Pentateuch* or what the Prophets wrote" (4.221–2, 225–6). And yet the answer Jesus gives is deeply disconcerting – not only to Satan but to a host of Milton's admirers.

Marjorie Hope Nicolson reports the dismayed reactions of most critics of her generation to the crabbed response of the Son: "Robert Adams speaks of 'that provincial contempt for the classics, which resounds throughout *Paradise Regained*.' Malcolm Ross sees Christ denying 'the philosophic spirit, the searching mind of the Greeks (once so dear to Milton).' Douglas Bush refuses to believe 'that in old age the puritan had conquered the humanist,' though he finds it 'painful to watch Milton turn and rend some main roots of his being.'"[29] But in fairness to the leading humanist of his generation, Bush did change his mind, or at least tempered his deep misgivings, admitting that

> This whole exchange has shocked and pained many readers. Satan's eulogy of Athens, we feel sure, came from Milton's heart; did Christ's repudiation of Greek culture come from the same heart? Is the aged Puritan turning and rending the literature and thought that had done so much to make him an artist and a lover of virtue and liberty? But second thoughts should remove the grounds for dismay. The gist of the matter is that, if there must be a showdown between the light of nature, which may nourish irreligious pride, and the light of Christian truth, on which man's earthly and eternal welfare depend, the choice is clear. Milton had always ranked the Bible far above the classics.[30]

But this is to lose sight of "our Saviour's" former pairing of "patient *Job*" with "Poor *Socrates* (who next more memorable?)" (3.95–6), thereby letting slip an occasion to explore the *dramatic* character of the action. Nicolson, to her credit, reminds us of "the perversity of reading an author's personal position and convictions into a particular speech of his characters" (342). Milton also reminded readers of his prose "that all places of Scripture wherin just reason of doubt arises from the letter, are to be expounded by considering upon what occasion every thing is set down: and by comparing other Texts."[31] Even so, most critics continue to blame the poet, not his characters, for his glaring contradictions; the a priori assumption seems to be that, by definition, a "dogmatic" poet cannot be a dramatic poet.

It is Jesus' self-contradiction that finally exposes the true hinge of the drama. Having celebrated Socrates above all other men except for Job, and having declared him to be a true martyr – "For truths sake suffering death unjust" – he is now forced to reverse his field when Satan offers him what he had most admired in "poor Socrates" – "Whom well inspir'd the Oracle pronounc'd / Wisest of men" (4.275–6). Moreover, the Tempter now links wisdom to Stoic "rules" that "will render thee a King compleat / Within thy self, much more with Empire joyn'd" (4.283–4). But it was Jesus who had first claimed as much in refusing the temptation of riches: "Yet he who reigns within himself, and rules / Passions, Desires, and Fears, is more a

King" (2.466–7). Yet the cunning Adversary contrives to absorb *both* of these basic classical positions. So the Son is denied the "wisdom" of human reason as much as he is forced to forgoe the stoic mastery of passions, desires, and fears. All of his successes are now turned against him, forcing him to reduce "poor Socrates" to little more than a method without substance – "The first and wisest of them all profess'd / To know this only, that he nothing knew" (4.293–4) – and to dismiss even self-mastery as "Philosophic pride, / By him call'd vertue" (2.300–1). Jesus has won every battle only to "lose" the war.

Satan now has only to absorb Jesus' retreat to his refuge of "our native Language" and "All our Law and Story strew'd / With Hymns, our Psalms with artful terms inscrib'd, / Our Hebrew Songs and Harps in *Babylon*" (4.334–6). In fact, the "Psalms" and "Hebrew Songs" soon turn, by virtue of the Tempter's dialectical method, into the ground of a still more devastating attack. For the moment, however, "all his darts were spent" (4.366), and Satan reveals little more than his passing exasperation with this man:

> Since neither wealth, nor honour, arms nor arts,
> Kingdom nor Empire pleases thee, nor aught
> By me propos'd in life contemplative,
> Or active, tended on by glory, or fame,
> What dost thou in this World? (4.368–72)

The answer to this question seems to alarm the fiend, since he tries at once to solve it by himself. There must be a "fulness of time," he says, "When Prophesies of thee are best fulfill'd[,] / Now contrary, if I read aught in Heaven, / Or Heav'n write aught of Fate" (4.380–3). Yet what the Satanic astrologer finds written in the stars is only "Sorrows, and labours, opposition, hate," not to mention "scorns, reproaches, injuries, / Violence and stripes, and lastly cruel death" (4.386–8). While Satan admits that he has always known where the story tends, there is still one thing that he can't make out: "A Kingdom they portend thee, but what Kingdom, / Real or Allegoric I discern not" (4.389–90). Unlike Bishop Bonner or Foxe's other inquisitors, however, he is truly desperate to *prevent* the death he sees written in the stars – until he knows *what* kingdom it signifies.

This is the point of the violent storm to which he subjects the man, leaving him to bear the psychological violence of a second night of troubled sleep. As MacCallum remarks, "Having finally understood that the Son intends to accept hard assays, he is making a last minute effort to suggest the futility and horror of suffering" (265). In the morning, Satan returns to clinch this point exactly: "Did I not tell thee, if thou didst reject / The perfet season offer'd with my aid / To win thy destin'd seat" (4.467–9), that all would come to naught? Insisting that "no man knows when, / For both the when and how is no where told" (4.471–2), he seeks more information about the promised kingdom: "Thou shalt be what thou art ordain'd, no doubt; / For Angels have proclaim'd it, but concealing / The time and means" (4.473–5). From the outset, each has occupied the same ground; the *end* was also apparent to both. "If thou observe not this," Satan warns in language close to that of Jesus in his opening soliloquy, "be sure to find, / What I foretold thee, many a hard assay / Of dangers, and adversities and pains, / E're thou of *Israel's* Scepter get fast hold" (4.477–80). *Many a hard assay.* So the end is clear; only the when and how are yet in doubt.

As Satan begins to absorb the premise of this last argument used against him, he gives a virtuouso performance in composing a biography that we also read as *auto*biography. Point by point, Satan recalls the narrative of the "Son of *David*, Virgin-born," if with a very different purpose – to confess how "Son of God to me is yet in doubt" (4.500–1). After hearing "thee pronounc'd the Son of God belov'd," he admits, "Thenceforth I thought thee worth my nearer view / And narrower Scrutiny" (4.513–15). And yet all his surveillance has come to naught, though his confession of motive touches the heart of the drama. He still needs to know "In what degree or meaning thou art call'd / The Son of God, which bears no single sence" (4.516–17). He does not dissemble when he says, "The Son of God I also am, or was, / And if I was, I am; relation stands; / All men are Sons of God" (4.518–20). Here is his final concession to the truth he had denied at the Exaltation, where he was hell-bent on preserving the ancient system of hierarchy. *All men are Sons of God.* In the end, even the devil is forced to concede the Leveller premise.

So were the royalists right? Was Levelling an invention of the devil?[32] Likely not, since Satan aims by his concession to diminish the image of God in this man whom even he must "confess have found thee / Proof against all temptation" (4.532–3). He finds him "proof," that is to say, "To the utmost of meer man both wise and good, / Not more, for Honours, Riches, Kingdoms, Glory / Have been before contemn'd, and may agen" (4.535–7). Even so, it is a remarkable testament to the Son's "meer" humanity, as well as a strong model for future martyrs to bear witness to him as the Word of God. Some of them will even step into the Word with him through narratives of their own martyrdom.

At this true crisis of the action, however, Satan is mistaken to think that he has finally found out how to turn the Son's own "Hebrew Songs" against him, robbing him of his last prop: "Therefore to know what more thou art then man, / Worth naming Son of God by voice from Heav'n, / Another method I must now begin" (4.538–40). A stunning dramatic reversal is about to take place on the needle point of the Temple Pinnacle, where the literal ground of Jesus' support is removed, and the Son is left "free" to stand revealed as "God" or fall like a "meer man" to his death. Yet what Satan "fails to understand" is "that the mystery of the Incarnation is meaningful because it involves an act of accommodation, that the divinity of the man he has been tempting is expressed through his perfect humanity."[33] Satan is so certain that the Son will not escape the horns of this dilemma that he dares, with characteristic *hybris*, to taunt him, much as he had taunted the loyal angels in the War in Heaven, with double entendres about having "stumbl'd many," so that they "walk not upright" (*PL* 6.624, 627). "There stand, if thou wilt stand," he says, "to stand upright / Will ask thee skill" (*PR* 4.551–2). In placing him "highest," the fiend even taunts:

> Now shew thy Progeny; if not to stand,
> Cast thy self down; safely if Son of God:
> For it is written, He will give command
> Concerning thee to his Angels, in thir hands
> They shall up lift thee, lest at any time
> Thou chance to dash thy foot against a stone. (4.554–9)

The Adversary thus plays his trump card – which he has held in reserve from the second day, when the Son rebuffed his claims to power with the promise of Psalms 23 and 91: "I can at will, doubt not, as soon as thou, / Command a Table in this Wilderness, / And call swift flights of Angels ministrant" (2.383–5). And so his bluff, if that is what it is, has been called. As MacCallum remarks, "Satan has finally devised a situation by which he expects to show that the Son is either man or God" (255). The "meer man" will be exposed as a poseur, falling to his death; conversely, *the* Son of Heaven will be forced to do the devil's bidding, summoning angels from Heaven to his rescue. Either way, the Son will "fall," physically if not morally. It is a trap from which there is no escape.

There isn't time to pity the poor Son, since everything happens on the instant: "To whom thus Jesus: also it is written, / Tempt not the Lord thy God, he said and stood" (4.560–1). And Satan, "smitten with amazement fell," while "strait a fiery Globe / Of Angels on full sail of wing flew nigh" and "receive'd him soft / From his uneasie station" (4.562, 581–4). So what really happens in these few lines? Far from claiming to be God, Jesus, with an inveterate reader's command of scripture, recalls the distinctive biblical scene in which he is cast, and quotes the one verse of scripture that could save him.[34] It comes from the story of the Exodus, where Israel, on receiving the Decalogue, fell into muttering against Providence, for which God took them to task: "Ye shall not tempt the LORD your God as ye tempted him in Massah" (Deut. 6: 16). At Massah, the Israelites had "thirsted there for water," and "because of the chiding of the children of Israel … they tempted the LORD, saying, Is the LORD among us or not" (Exodus 17: 3, 7). Here again, Satan asks the same ancient question in the same instant that he lets go of Jesus, leaving him to fend for himself upon the needle point of the pinnacle: "Is the LORD among us or not?"

Whatever miracle occurs, it cannot rival the uncanny ability of this man to locate himself immediately in the biblical scene, answering the Tempter with the single passage from scripture that could save him. Although Satan's dialectical method has succeeded in depriving Jesus of the promise – "I can command" – let alone its prophetic assurance – "He shall give his angels charge over thee, to keep thee in all thy ways" – he nonetheless manages to answer with the sole verse of scripture that can fend off his fatal "fall."

The author of *Vox Plebis* (1646) had come to a similar dramatic recognition about the devil's method. In a Leveller pamphlet written to expose the cunning of Lilburne's enemies, Marchamont Nedham[35] had repeated the story of the trial on the pinnacle, where "the *Divell*, when he tempted our blessed Saviour, as you may read, *Matth. 4.6.* could cite this part of the Scripture, *Cast thy selfe down, for it is written, He shall give his Angels charge over thee*: But concealed another part of the Scripture which made against his ends, to wit, *It is written, Thou shalt not tempt the Lord thy God*: So deales this Lieutenant or *Grand Goaler, West*, with his prisoners."[36] Milton was as concerned as Nedham to expose the devil's strategy of concealing "another part of the Scripture." For Satan's act of concealment[37] is antithetical to the Son's attempt, as Calvin read it, to conceal his divinity, since Jesus has no inkling of his pre-existence. Concealment is just Satan's strategy to hide the truth of God's purpose. By attempting to make Jesus despair of Providence,

Satan expects he will act to save himself. Instead, the Son recalls the one story in scripture that speaks to his "uneasie station," not even presuming to answer with his own voice, but with that of the divine Word: *Tempt not the Lord thy God, he said and stood.* It is a profession of faith that *performs* the act that it describes. Although the Son may speak it with a human voice, it is really the Word of the Father that speaks through him, that is manifested in frail human form. But it is in such fashion his flesh is literally made *Word*, as Jesus steps into this future public narrative that he comes to embody.

Indeed, the flesh made Word is precisely the opposite of the Word made Flesh, or what Barbara Lewalski describes as a "miracle of full illumination" of the Son who "has now become again (as before in heaven) the conscious agent of the divine power in working the defeat of Satan."[38] Instead, he is left to learn from the song of the angels, not from some miraculous moment of inward illumination, of having once exercised that *divine* power in another life. At no point in the poem – not even at the close – does he ever enjoy more than *human* power; he merely receives "wisdom from above," as Elijah and Daniel had acquired such knowledge, by organs of human sense. As MacCallum insists, "His assumption of humanity is simply the acceptance of new conditions of trial," with the result that "The divine and human nature are united in the Son [only] through the act of choice, the man realizing in a human mode the will of the divine being" (240).

There is another sense, however, in which the flesh does become Word.[39] Like the martyrs who follow him, Jesus "speaks apparently as a reader of scripture rather than as a being who in another life acted as the Word."[40] In that sense, he steps into the pages of the Word like an actor entering a script[41] in performance, or better, as a "publisher" of "mass" communications. Gretchen Minton recalls how "Ordinary Marian martyrs" in Foxe "become transformed into Scriptural figures, and all the drama of their lives has become, in a way, a Scriptural event, itself a part of, and a continuation of, the sacred story" (732). The larger drama of the Foxean martyr serves to repeat and reconfirm this deeply human trial of the Son unto death and beyond. The result, Minton argues, is that "The mutable bodies of the martyrs are transferred into immutable texts that will survive, precisely because the martyrologist has monumentalized them in such a way" (730). In point of fact, "The relationship between the body of the martyr and the text is central to Foxe's narrative strategy in the *Acts and Monuments*. Foxe 'reads' the bodies of the martyrs and, through an allegorical movement from body to Word, encases events and people within an arena defined by Scripture.

Foxe's martyrs are named, memorialized, and textually remembered" (731). But the telling difference in Milton's martyrology is that the body is actually sublimated into text *before* the death of the body. Because Jesus *is* the Word – though he does not recall and dare not rely on that circumstance – he must first learn how to embody it in life for it to be a life-giving "script for the martyrs to follow."[42] Only then does the Real Presence re-emerge from the page.

Conversely, Milton's epic similes, which describe Satan's fall, suggest that even the pagan stories had pointed to this presence of the Son of God,[43] although Satan had failed to heed them. Recalling the scene where "Earths Son *Antæus* (to compare / Small things with greatest) in *Irassa* strove / With *Joves Alcides*" (4.563–5), the epic narrator likens Satan's strength to the earth-bound monster in order to show how, couched in the ancient Greek story, there lurks the figure of a half-human, half-divine hero, however imperfectly shadowed forth in Hercules. As for the story of "that *Theban* Monster" (4.572) who once held a Greek city-state in thrall, the answer that Oedipus gives to the Sphinx's riddle – Man – is also the answer to the riddle of the Son's identity. Jesus thus proves himself to be his mother's son even in the instant he is revealed as the Son of God. Nowhere is this fact more movingly affirmed than in the final lines of the poem, where "hee unobserv'd / Home to his Mothers house private return'd" (4.638–9).

At the same time, the song of the angels as they bear him to earth, notes MacCallum, tells him "emphatically that his nature as the image of God is not altered by these changes of state, since it consists in his perfect fulfilment of the will of the Father" (240):

> True Image of the Father, whether thron'd
> In the bosom of bliss, and light of light
> Conceiving, or remote from Heaven, enshrin'd
> In fleshly Tabernacle, and human form,
> Wandring the Wilderness, whatever place,
> Habit, or state, or motion, still expressing
> The Son of God. (4.596–602)

MacCallum properly concludes that this song "does not serve as a gloss upon some flash of illumination by which Jesus has realized his identity with the pre-existent Son. Rather it is confirmation and restatement in apocalyptic language of the understanding he has reached through meditation on scripture" (262). Yet even this is not the whole truth.

The angelic hymn also fills gaps of knowledge that had remained outside the ken of the Son's personal history in Book 1, and that he is hearing about now for the first time. These gaps include what readers of *Paradise Lost* are sure to recall – that "with Godlike force indu'd / Against th' Attempter of thy Fathers Throne, / … him long of old / Thou didst debel, and down from Heav'n cast / With all his Army" (4.602–6). Readers of *Paradise Lost* are finally able to join the song of the angels, that "thou hast aveng'd / Supplanted *Adam*, and by vanquishing / Temptation, hast regain'd lost Paradise" (4.606–8). Readers, moreover, are meant to recall the "one greater Man" of the opening of *Paradise Lost*, who will "Restore us, and regain the blissful Seat" (*PL* 1.4–5). The narrator of the "brief epic" has surely kept his promise "to tell of deeds / Above Heroic, though in secret done, / And unrecorded left through many an Age" (*PR* 1.14–16).

The joyous salutation of the angels at the end of the hymn further echoes what the Leveller Walwyn had claimed about the Kingdom of Grace: that "Faith is a mercenary, but love is a voluntary soldiour, that knoweth no why nor wherefore, but faith with Christ, *Behold, here I am, ready to do thy will, O God.*"[44] So it is in the Son of God that we see how it is, "in all such willing hearts," that "God is all in all, for all things are from God, through God, and to God, and God is love." What indeed is the love of God but "a joyning of two free-wils in one"?[45] This was the whole burden of the Father's praise at the end of the colloquy in Heaven: "Love hath abounded more then Glory abounds" (*PL* 3.312). Is this not the burden of the words of the angels' song now at the end of *Paradise Regain'd*? "Hail Son of the most High, heir of both worlds, / Queller of Satan, on thy glorious work / Now enter, and begin to save mankind" (4.633–5)?

CONCLUSION

IN THE END, Milton's choice of Foxe's *Actes and Monuments* as a dramatic model for *Paradise Regain'd* looks inevitable for political as much as for theological reasons. In doctrinal terms, the Book of Martyrs was perfectly consistent with his theology of testing and choice as the likeliest means of binding readers together into a godly unity of wills.[1] Foxe's martyrology was further predisposed to support his Christology up to a point, at least, where Milton required the Son to be tried as a "perfect Man" in order to achieve unity with the Father in this uniquely *dramatic* vision of "two free-wils" joined in one.

Just as surely, Foxe's work was the ideal choice for a poet whose imagined republic was authorized by a "Levelling" deity. In the same way that "the vernacular Bible served as a great and irresistible leveller," so, too, the Book of Martyrs was a hugely popular social leveller. As Richard Helgerson recalls, "The printed Bible in English served to constitute a new social reality in which unlearned commoners were able to argue on an equal footing with doctors of the church, a new social reality that Foxe represents and that Parsons and Shakespeare resist." Indeed, "In *Acts and Monuments*, wives, widows, and maidens, merchants and craftsmen, husbandmen, laborers, and servants are subjected to the same interrogations, answer with the same articulate and informed conviction, die with the same fortitude, as their social betters. And many of them proudly call attention to their humble station."[2] Of course, "This reversal of hierarchy did not go unnoticed by Foxe's detractors. In the words of the Jesuit Robert Parsons, the martyrs of *Acts and Monuments* are a 'contemptible and pitiful … rabblement,' rags and rotten clouts cast out to the dunghill, as they well deserve.'"[3]

Sixty years ago, *The Pelican Guide to English Literature*[4] – celebrating *The Age of Chaucer* and *The Age of Shakespeare* before delimiting a third "age" *From Donne to Marvell* – may not have intended, in its snub to Milton, to widen the cultural divide that had so gravely troubled the early modern era. But Shakespeare's snub of Foxe was almost certainly meant to police that cultural divide by turning the Lollard martyr Sir John Oldcastle into the sack-swilling Falstaff of *Henry IV*, Part 1, clown prince to the crown Prince Hal.[5] For, as Helgerson sees it, "Turning an aristocratic Lollard martyr into a fat, festive, clownish, Bible-quoting thief and lord of misrule was part of a strategy of rhetorical debunking that Shakespeare shared with bishops, archbishops, and a host of clerical and lay supporters of episcopacy" (251). With some justice Helgerson concludes, "It is as though Shakespeare set out to cancel the popular ideology with which his cycle of history plays began, as though he wanted to efface, alienate, even demonize all signs of commoner participation in the political nation. The less privileged classes may still have had a place in his audience, but they had lost their place in his representation of England" (214). And so the essential question for Helgerson comes down to a political choice: "What interests are we preferring when we prefer Shakespeare? Shakespeare's history plays are concerned above all with the consolidation and maintenance of royal power" (234). By contrast, "Foxe's apocalyptic narrative" – as opposed to Shakespeare's "apologetic" narrative – achieved a more folk-oriented "displacement" by setting "martyrs in the place of kings."[6] More largely, Milton's apocalyptic narrative put the "humiliated" and "levelled" Son, perpetually "Barr'd of his right" (*PL* 12.360), in the place of those same hierarchs and kings.

Like Foxe's Book of Martyrs, both of Milton's epics helped to form and sustain a community of readers that was in part (but only ever in part) precipitated by the vernacular bible. Such reading communities are a species of what Benedict Anderson calls *Imagined Communities*,[7] an emergent political form that became the *nation*, the origins of which Anderson would locate in the eighteenth century. Its true pedigree, however, reaches two centuries farther back to the fierce and bitter culture wars fought first around the martyrology of Foxe,[8] and then around the pamphlets and newsbooks of the English Civil Wars.[9] In these ephemeral print forms, as well as in the popular narratives of Foxe and the timeless magnificence of Milton's epic poems, we witness a rapid growth of "levelling" imaginings that continue, even today, to underwrite Western liberal democracy. For these days, such "imagined communities" are largely composed of readers and viewers of newer media who "do not know and have for the most part never seen one another but who nevertheless have a strong sense of belonging together."[10] And most of them share a culture that they do not – perhaps need not – know was once the imaginative creation of writers who dared to put martyrs in the place of kings.

For their daring, these same writers ended their lives, like the poet Milton and the printer Overton, marginalized and disgraced by the "nation" they had served – even when they did not, like Lilburne at the age of forty-three, actually die as martyrs to the ideal of an English republic. Such a community had to wait a century or more after their deaths – still among readers of English,[11] if now an ocean away from Old England – where means were found to rid themselves of kings and hierarchs, at least for another century or two.

NOTES

PREFACE

1 Walter Raleigh, *Milton* (London: E. Arnold, 1900), 88.

2 F.R. Leavis, "Milton's Verse," *Scrutiny* (September 1933): 124.

3 "Milton I" (1936), in *Selected Prose of T.S. Eliot*, ed. Frank Kermode (London: Faber & Faber, 1975), 261, 263. Eliot's obtuse refinement is best answered by Christopher Ricks in *Milton's Grand Style* (Oxford: Clarendon Press, 1963). Eliot's notorious rejection of Satan's first speech as "rhetoric" (262) is particularly rich, given that the speech occurs in a dramatic scene.

4 William Empson, *Milton's God* (London: Chatto & Windus, 1961), 50.

5 J.B. Broadbent, *Some Graver Subject: An Essay on "Paradise Lost"* (London: Chatto & Windus, 1960), 144.

6 C.S. Lewis, *A Preface to "Paradise Lost"* (London: Oxford University Press, 1942).

7 William B. Hunter, C.A. Patrides, and J.H. Adamson, *Bright Essence: Studies in Milton's Theology* (Salt Lake City: University of Utah Press, 1971).

8 William B. Hunter, *Visitation Unimplor'd: Milton and the Authorship of "De Doctrina Christiana"* (Pittsburgh: Duquesne University Press, 1998).

9 Denis Saurat, *Milton, Man and Thinker* (New York: The Dial Press, 1925).

10 Maurice Kelley, *This Great Argument: A Study of Milton's "De Doctrina Christiana" as a Gloss upon "Paradise Lost"* (Princeton: Princeton University Press, 1941).

11 Dennis Danielson, *Milton's Good God: A Study in Literary Theodicy* (Cambridge: Cambridge University Press, 1982).

12 Hugh MacCallum, *Milton and the Sons of God: The Divine Image in Milton's Epic Poetry* (Toronto: University of Toronto Press, 1986).

13 John P. Rumrich, *Milton Unbound: Controvery and Reinterpretation* (Cambridge: Cambridge University Press, 1996).

14 Nigel Smith, *Is Milton Better Than Shakespeare?* (Cambridge, MA: Harvard University Press, 2008), 7.

15 Benjamin Myers, *Milton's Theology of Freedom* (Berlin: Walter de Gruyter GMBH & Co., 2006), 5.

16 Paul Rahe argues in his admirable study *Against Throne and Altar: Machiavelli and Political Theory Under the English Republic* (Cambridge: Cambridge University Press, 2008), that "Milton was that rarity of rarities in mid-seventeenth-century England: a genuine, fully conscious classical republican" (105).

17 See, e.g., Murray Tolmie, *The Triumph of the Saints: The Separate Churches of London, 1616–1649* (New York: Cambridge University Press, 1977).

18 For his statement of intent, see *Defensio Secunda* (1654), in *Complete Prose Works of John Milton*, vol 4.i, and vol. 4.ii: *1650–1655*, ed. Don M. Wolfe. (Vol. 4 had to be split into two volumes numbered 4i, and 4ii.) (New Haven and London: Yale University Press, 1966), 624–6 (hereafter cited as *CPW* 4.i, etc).

19 Ernest Sirluck cautions in *"Paradise Lost": A Deliberate Epic* (Cambridge: Heffer, 1967) that "The essential nature of the poem as written is incompatible with the nature of the theatre," and that "Milton's God ... cannot be staged" (11). But Sirluck makes an honourable exception to the rule that Miltonists are immune to a dramatic Milton, finding a "dormant, five-act structure" (13) in a poem that becomes somewhat conventional.

20 Nicholas von Maltzahn, "John Milton: The Later Life, 1641–1674," in *The Oxford Handbook of Milton*, ed. Nicholas McDowell and Nigel Smith (Oxford: Oxford University Press, 2009), 45.

21 "*De Doctrina Christiana*," in *The Compete Prose Works of John Milton*, vol. 6: *Christian Doctrine*, ed. Maurice Kelley (New Haven: Yale University Press, 1973), 213 (hereafter cited as *CPW* 6).

22 *The Riverside Milton*, ed. Roy Flannagan (Boston and New York: Houghton Mifflin, 1998), 683. Subsequent quotations from Milton's poetry refer to this edition.

23 See Joseph Anthony Wittreich, *Feminist Milton* (Ithaca and London: Cornell University Press, 1987).

INTRODUCTION

1 Elliot Vernon and Philip Baker, in their "Introduction" to *The Agreements of the People, the Levellers and the Constitutional Crisis of the English Revolution*, ed. Philip Baker and Elliot Vernon (London: Palgrave Macmillan, 2012), recall how "a range of contemporaries" in England of the late 1640s "looked to a written constitution, in the form of an *Agreement of the People*, as a solution to the protracted constitutional crisis initiated by the Civil Wars," and how "designs for a settlement were not limited only to the three 'Leveller' *Agreements* but also produced a number of closely related pamphlets and texts, as well as alternative versions of the document" (20).

2 Ian Gentles, "'*The Agreements of the People*' and Their Political Contexts, 1647–1649," in *The Putney Debates of 1647: The Army, the Levellers and the English State*, ed. Michael Mendle (Cambridge: Cambridge University Press, 2001), 148.

3 David Wootton, "The Levellers," in *Democracy: The Unfinished Journey, 508 BC to AD 1993*, ed. John Dunn (Oxford and New York: Oxford University Press, 1992), 71.

4 *Mercurius Pragmaticus* 8 (9 November 1647): 61.

5 *Pace* Elliot Vernon, "'A Firme and Present Peace; Upon Grounds of Common Right and Freedome': The Debate on the *Agreements of the People* and the Crisis of the Constitution, 1647–59," in *The Agreements*, ed. Baker and Vernon (2012), who argues that, "The *Agreements* were not untimely documents advocating a democratic constitutionalism that was at least 125 years ahead of its time; rather, they were proposals advancing the fundamentals of settlement at a time when the English constitution was perhaps undergoing its greatest crisis" (195–6). While the *Agreements* were a timely response to a specific historical crisis, they were *untimely* in the sense that they did not gain wide acceptance for centuries.

6 Catherine Gimelli Martin, *Milton among the Puritans: The Case for Historical Revisionism* (Farnham, Surrey: Ashgate, 2010), 11.

7 Paul Stevens approvingly quotes this passage from David Masson's *Life of John Milton* (London, 1875–88), vol. 5, 398, in "Milton's 'Renunciation' of Cromwell: The Problem of Raleigh's 'Cabinet-Council,'" *Modern Philology* 98, no. 3 (February 2001): 81.

8 Rachel Foxley, "Freedom of Conscience and the *Agreements of the People*," in *The Agreements*, ed. Baker and Vernon (2012), argues that "it was 'conscience,' rather than 'liberty,' which was the key notion in 'liberty of conscience'" (121), for reasons that expose the innate "relationship between political and religious life" (117): "In religion, we are forced to own our consciences and not give them away; in politics, we are forced to own our basic physical security and political freedom and not give it away" (125).

9 *Areopagitica*, in *The Complete Prose Works of John Milton*, vol. 2: *1643–48*, ed. Ernest Sirluck (New Haven: Yale University Press, 1959), 514, 527 (henceforth CPW 2: 514, etc.)

10 *The Riverside Milton*, ed. Roy Flannagan (Boston: Houghton Mifflin, 1998), 419. Subsequent quotations from Milton's poetry refer to this edition.

11 *The Complete Prose Works of John Milton*, vol. 1: *1624–1642*, ed. Don M. Wolfe (New Haven: Yale University Press, 1953), 543–4 (hereafter CPW 1: 543–4, etc).

12 *The Complete Prose Works of John Milton*, vol. 3: *1648–1649*, ed. Merritt Y. Hughes (New Haven: Yale University Press, 1962), 198–9 (hereafter CPW 3: 198, etc).

13 Elliot Vernon is right to suppose that, "The term 'Leveller' as used in the [autumn] of 1647" was "deployed by propagandists to evoke the fear of the lowly heretics' revolution that had been nurtured by the myth-making of the Civil War's heresiographers" ("The Debate," *The Agreements*, 200).

14 Nigel Smith, "*Paradise Lost* and Heresy," in *The Oxford Handbook of Milton*, ed. Nicholas McDowell and Nigel Smith (Oxford: Oxford University Press, 2009), 524.

15 *The Poetical Works of John Milton*, vol. 1: *The Minor Poems*, ed. David Masson (London and New York: Macmillan, 1890), 227.

16 John Lilburne, *The Legal Fundamental Liberties of the People of England* (8 June 1649): 35, 39. Except where noted, all Leveller documents are from the British

Library, accessed online between 2009 and 2016 through EEBO (Early English Books Online) at: http://eebo.chadwyck.com.proxy2.lib.umanitoba.ca/

17 Frances Henderson, "Drafting the Officers' *Agreement of the People*, 1648–49: A Reappraisal," in *The Agreements*, ed. Baker and Vernon (2012), provides evidence that the general council of officers met as early as 11 December at Whitehall to consider the draft *Agreement* submitted to them by the Committee of Sixteen (167), making substantial but thoughtful changes to the draft *Agreement* that ultimately included a reserve denying the Representative power "to Compell ... or to Restraine any person" from the "exercise of religion according to his Conscience" (182).

18 As David Wootton claims, the Levellers refused "during the Whitehall Debates which followed hard on Pride's Purge (December 1648) to retreat from the principle of freedom of conscience." See Wootton, "Leveller Democracy and the Puritan Revolution." *The Cambridge History of Political Thought, 1450–1700*, ed. J.H. Burns (Cambridge: Cambridge University Press, 1991), 434.

19 Barbara Taft, "From Reading to Whitehall: Henry Ireton's Journey," in *The Putney Debates of 1647: The Army, the Levellers and the English State*, ed. Michael Mendle (Cambridge: Cambridge University Press, 2001), 191–2.

20 Ian Gentles, "The New Model Army and the Constitutional Crisis of the Late 1640s," in *The Agreements*, ed. Baker and Vernon (2012), 156.

21 In particular, two articles in the Officers' *Agreement* would have been obnoxious to members of the Rump: the demand in Article 1 that "this present Parliament end and desolve upon or before the Last day of Aprill in the yeare of our Lord 1649"; and the stipulation in Article 6, that "noe Member of a Counsell of State nor any officers of any Sallary Forces in Army or Garrison ... shall (while such) bee elected to bee of a Representative" (Henderson, "Drafting," 178, 181). According to Article 6, Lt-Gen. Cromwell, MP, soon to be a member of the Council of State, would be in a double conflict of interest. As for Article 1, the Rump was not about to "desolve" itself.

22 Don. M. Wolfe finds many parallels between Miltonic and Leveller arguments for liberty in his *Milton in the Puritan Revolution* (1941; London: Cohen & West, 1963), though he insists on the aristocratic leanings of "university men" like "Milton, Williams, Peters, Goodwin, Ireton, [and] Cromwell himself" (139).

23 Nigel Smith, *Is Milton Better Than Shakespeare?* (Cambridge, MA: Harvard University Press, 2008), 4.

24 David Norbrook, *Writing the English Republic: Poetry, Rhetoric, and Politics, 1627–1660* (Cambridge: Cambridge University Press, 1999), 130.

25 Rachel Foxley, "John Lilburne and the Citizenship of 'Free-born Englishmen,'" *The Historical Journal* 47, no. 4 (2004): 851. Accessed online 15 June 2016 at: http://journals.cambridge.org/HIS. Lilburne carried his campaign for the rights of "free-born Englishmen" from religion into politics in *The Copy of a Letter* (9 August 1645), where he defied a Committee of Examinations, saying: "*I am a free-man, yea, a free-borne Denizen of* England" (2).

26 *CPW* 2: 485.

27 Paul Rahe, *Against Throne and Altar: Machiavelli and Political Theory under the English Republic* (Cambridge: Cambridge University Press, 2008), 25.

28 The assumption of Milton's "aristocratic" leanings in *Areopagitica* and his general commitment to "classical republicanism" have been the dominant view since Wolfe's *Milton in the Puritan Revolution* (1941), although both ideas have found their largest expression in Norbrook's study, as well as in important scholarly work by Paul Rahe ("Preface," n16 above); Martin Dzelzainis (n40 below), Blair Worden (n37), Jonathan Scott (n29 below), as well as Quentin Skinner, David Armitage, and others.

29 Jonathan Scott, *Commonwealth Principles: Republican Writing of the English Revolution* (Cambridge: Cambridge University Press, 2004), 9.

30 *CPW* 4.i: 383.

31 Aristotle, *The Politics*, ed. Stephen Everson (Cambridge: Cambridge University Press, 1988), 1281a42–1281b9, was of the opinion that "the many, of whom each individual is not a good man, when they meet together may be better than the few good, if regarded not individually but collectively, just as a feast to which many contribute is better than a dinner provided out of a single purse. For each individual among the many has a share of excellence and practical wisdom, and when they meet together, just as they become in a manner one man, who has many feet, and hands, and senses, so too with regard to their character and thought. Hence the many are better judges than a single man of music and poetry; for some understand one part, and some another, and among them they understand the whole" (66).

32 Lilburne denied authorship of *Regall Tyrannie* soon after its appearance (*The Oppressed Mans Oppressions declared* [30 January 1647]), 13. There is reason to think that Marchamont Nedham, the journalist whose newsbook *Mercurius Politicus* was later licensed by Milton, either contributed to or was the primary author of this Leveller tract, starting from its scriptural reminder that God gave Israel "a King in his anger, and took him away in his wrath" (14), a principle wittily recalled by Nedham several years later in *Mercurius Politicus*: "As it was said of Old concerning *Israel*, That *God gave them a King in his wrath*; so we may say of our own Nation" (4 September 1651: 1029). The same sort of joke had appeared in *The Case of the Commonwealth* (1650) – "as it hath been long since observed in print" (93) – referring to Nedham's royalist work, *The Case of the Kingdom Stated*. Thereafter, he resumes the history of tyranny since the Norman Conquest, begun in the previous issue of *Politicus*, to show, as he had likewise asserted at the end of *The Case*, "that there is no difference between king and tyrant" (127). See also Chapter 6, n10, below.

33 Sarah Mortimer, *Reason and Religion in the English Revolution: The Challenge of Socinianism* (Cambridge: Cambridge University Press, 2014), says that "Perhaps the most ambitious use of the natural law argument by Parliamentarian polemicists came from the pen of Henry Parker," starting with "the claim that power was

inherently in the people and that government must have been established for their benefit," and so "taking it for granted that the law of nature could – and must – override any written or positive laws" (93).

34 Ann Hughes, "Milton, *Areopagitica*, and the Parliamentary Cause," in *The Oxford Handbook of Milton*, ed. Nicholas McDowell and Nigel Smith (Oxford: Oxford University Press, 2009), 209.

35 Merritt Y. Hughes, "Introduction," *CPW* 3: 37.

36 *CPW* 3: 190.

37 Blair Worden, *Literature and Politics in Cromwellian England: John Milton, Andrew Marvell, Marchamont Nedham* (Oxford: Oxford University Press, 2007).

38 Anthony à Wood, *Fasti Oxonienses; or Annals of the University of Oxford* (1691), in *The Early Lives of Milton*, ed. Helen Darbishire (1932; New York: Barnes and Noble, 1965), 44.

39 C.H. Firth, "Needham or NEDHAM, Marchamont (1620–1678)," *Oxford Dictionary of National Biography* Archive (1894), online edn. September 2015; accessed 11 June 2016 at http://www.oxforddnb.com.

40 Martin Dzelzainis evidently begs the question when he asks, "If to be a republican at all was to be a classical republican, then what exactly was the classical element in Milton's republicanism?" (7). See his "Milton's Classical Republicanism," in *Milton and Republicanism*, ed. David Armitage, Armand Himy, and Quentin Skinner (Cambridge: Cambridge University Press, 1995), 3–24.

41 David Norbrook, *Writing the English Republic*, 440–1; 473–4. Rahe flatly contradicts Norbrook's case for Milton's "reduction to first principles" of state and church: "At no time did John Milton allow the thinking of Niccolò Machiavelli to shape in any fundamental way the manner in which he wrote about, defended, and surreptitiously tried to guide the nascent English republic in stricitly political affairs" (*Against Throne and Altar*, 104).

42 Joad Raymond, "Marchamont Nedham," in *The Oxford Handbook of Literature and the English Revolution*, ed. Laura Lunger Knoppers (Oxford: Oxford University Press, 2012), 375–93. Nedham's support of religious toleration further "explains his sympathy with the Levellers, and his support of the radicals in the early days of the Rump" (378).

43 Stevens, "Milton's 'Renunciation' of Cromwell," 364.

44 Martin Dzelzainis, "Milton and the Protectorate in 1658," in *Milton and Republicanism*, ed. David Armitage, Armand Himy, and Quentin Skinner (Cambridge: Cambridge University Press, 1995), 201.

45 Ibid., 205.

46 Paul Stevens, "Intolerance and the Virtues of Sacred Vehemence," in *Milton and Toleration*, ed. Sharon Achinstein and Elizabeth Sauer (Oxford: Oxford University Press, 2007), 265.

47 Paul Stevens, "Milton and National Identity," in *The Oxford Handbook of Milton*, ed. Nicholas McDowell and Nigel Smith (Oxford: Oxford University Press, 2009), 359, 358.

48 Paul Stevens, "How Milton's Nationalism Works: Globalization and the Possibilities of Positive Nationalism," in *Early Modern Nationalism and Milton's England*, ed. David Loewenstein and Paul Stevens (Toronto and Buffalo: University of Toronto Press, 2008), 276.

49 Stevens, "Milton and National Identity," 349, 358.

50 Typical is Don Wolfe's assumption that, apart from the author of *Areopagitica*, no other "aristocratic lover of liberty had called for freedom of the press and freedom of speech in *all* fields as the *sine qua non* of progress" (*Milton in the Puritan Revolution*, 121).

51 Stevens, "Milton's 'Renunciation' of Cromwell," 364.

52 Worden's reading of *Defensio Secunda* in two central chapters of his *Literature and Politics*, 262–325, suggests that Milton's break with Cromwell took place in 1653–54, the year of the Lord Protector's ascension. In my reading of the newsbook *Mercurius Politicus*, I see strong indications that Milton and Nedham began agitating against Cromwell soon after his return from Worcester in September 1651.

53 This particular reader, an historian of the English Revolution, perhaps of the Levellers, asked some of the more stimulating questions that I have encountered in a decade of work on this project. I am particularly grateful for this reader's efforts to hold a literary scholar accountable to the demands of history.

54 Plato, *Timaeus*, vol. 7, The Loeb Classical Library, 1929. Trans. Rev. R.G. Bury (London: William Heinemann, 1966), 127.

55 Nicholas McDowell, "Ideas of Creation in the Writings of Richard Overton the Leveller and *Paradise Lost*," *Journal of the History of Ideas* 66, no. 1 (January 2005): 61.

56 See Chapter 1, n44.

57 See Chapter 9, 232–8.

58 Paul Rahe, *Against Throne and Altar*, 46. For the influence of Lucretian atomism on Machiavelli's political thought, see Rahe, 30–55.

59 Cicero affirms something similar in *De legibus*, "that all nature is ruled by the force, nature, reason, power, mind, majesty – or whatever other word there is by which I may signify more plainly what I want – of the immortal gods," I.21 ("*On the Republic*"*and* "*On the Laws*," trans. David Fott [Ithaca and London: Cornell University Press, 2014], 137). Milton's monotheism is not the only thing, however, that makes his God distinct from Cicero's "immortal gods"; a material deity gives a unique inflection to nature's divinity in his creation of the universe out of his own substance. See Chapter 9, 232–8.

60 Historians have attributed *Vox Plebis* to other writers, although Rachel Foxley finds "good reasons" in *The Levellers: Radical Political Thought in the English Revolution* (Manchester and New York: Manchester University Press, 2013) "for linking him [Nedham] to the *Vox Plebis* pamphlets from the 1640s" (213). Perhaps the best reason for attributing *Vox Plebis* to Nedham, as Jonathan Scott argued in *Commonwealth Principles* (2004) is "the first systematic English public use" in

the 1640s "of Machiavelli's *Discourses*" (83), itself the best signature of Nedham's political theorizing.

61 Wootton, "Leveller Democracy," 437.

62 Rachel Foxley, "Freedom of Conscience and the *Agreements of the People*," in *The Agreements*, ed. Baker and Vernon (2012), maintains nonetheless "that the Levellers' accounts of the origins and nature of government display an optimism that humans can use their God-given reason – not, at least with the help of Christ, ruined beyond repair by the Fall – to achieve modes of government that approximate to a prelapsarian and rational ideal" (130).

63 *Tyranipocrit* (14 August 1649), 9.

64 Wolfe, *Milton in the Puritan Revolution*, 343.

65 See Chapter 7, "'The Winged Hierarch': Ironies of Degree," 191–201.

66 Ernest Sirluck, "*Paradise Lost*": *A Deliberate Epic* (Cambridge: Heffer, 1967), 15.

67 Similarly, the "imagined community" of the Levellers could only be realized in their writings. See Philip Baker, "The Levellers, Decentralisation, and the *Agreements of the People*," in *The Agreements,* ed. Baker and Vernon (2012), for evidence that "the past the Levellers appealed to – that of a nation of self-governing local communities free from political and religious compulsion – was not a real but an imagined one" (106).

68 "Lycidas," *The Riverside Milton*, ed. Roy Flannagan, 101.

69 See Benedict Anderson's *Imagined Communities: Reflections on the Origin and Spread of Nationalism*, rev. ed. (London and New York: Verso, 1991), for a useful discussion of the joint roles of print capitalism and readers in the rise of nationalism.

70 Early in his career, Worden penned a sardonic review of Christopher Hill's *Milton and the English Revolution* (London: Faber & Faber, 1977). Hill, Worden argued, had waxed eloquent about Milton's "'permanent dialogue' with 'the plebeian radical thinkers of the English Revolution': Levellers, Diggers, Seekers, Ranters, Quakers, Baptists, Fifth Monarchists, Muggletonians, Behmenists, Familists" (*TLS*, 2 December 1977: 1394). Yet, despite his vast knowledge of the sectaries, Hill was "lacking a single piece of evidence to show that Milton ever met any member of the radical underground," much less shared in their political philosophy.

71 See Chapter 2, "Milton and Politicus: Deposing Cromwell," 64–102.

72 Scott's detective work has established Nedham as the Leveller author of *Vox Plebis*, although he still accepts the attribution of *Regall Tyrannie* to Lilburne: see n32 above.

73 Wootton, "Leveller Democracy," 437.

74 See, for example, Worden's striking catalogue of reciprocal echoes between Milton and Nedham in Chapter 9 of *Literature and Politics*, "Milton in Journalism," 201–17.

75 John Lilburne, *Foundations of Freedom; or An Agreement of the People of England* (15 December 1648): 3, 4. EEBO Online. University of Manitoba. Accessed 13 October 2014.

76 Recalling "the *Annuall Consuls in Rome*" [*Londons Liberty* (2 November 1646), 2], Lilburne made annual elections a *sine qua non* of Leveller demands until Putney in 1647. Perhaps as a concession to army demands, the first two *Agreements* allowed for biennial parliaments (Foxley, *Levellers*, 176–7); in their third *Agreement* of 1 May 1649, the Levellers reverted to annual parliaments. Their deep mistrust of power persisted onward to Thomas Jefferson's proposal to the Continental Congress of 1789 for biennial elections to the House of Representatives. See Gentles, "The Agreements of the People," 168–74.

77 Ian Gentles, "The New Model Army and the Constitutional Crisis of the Late 1640s," in *The Agreements*, ed. Baker and Vernon (2012), makes the compelling argument that, "the idea of powers reserved by the governed to themselves has come to be adopted by one country after another, in the shape of bills, or charters, of rights" (147).

78 On tithes and liberty of conscience, see Foxley, *The Levellers* (2013), 132–43.

79 *An Agreement of the Free People of England* (1 May 1649), 3.

80 As Don Wolfe describes this elemental political divide of the early modern era, "The typical Elizabethan leader was a landed aristocrat … The citizen rising to new commercial power in London usually had little in common with the feudal aristocrat" (*Milton in the Puritan Revolution*, 2, 4).

81 John Gingell, Adrian Little, and Christopher Winch, eds., *Modern Political Thought: A Reader* (London and New York: Routledge, 2000), 22–42.

82 Hugh Jenkins, "Shrugging off the Norman Yoke: Milton's *History of Britain* and the Levellers," *English Literary Renaissance* 29, no. 3 (1999): 310.

83 *CPW* 2: 338.

84 Rachel Foxley, "The Levellers," in *The Oxford Handbook of Literature and the English Revolution*, ed. Laura Lunger Knoppers (Oxford: Oxford University Press, 2012), 272–86.

85 Jonathan Scott maintains that there is a greater confluence of classical and biblical influences in English republicanism than most historians allow. He sees it as "a broader function of both Milton's and Nedham's writing during the 1640s to underline the close relationship between Leveller and republican ideas. This is easier to see now that we can acknowledge the classical content of Leveller, and the religious content of republican thought" (*Commonwealth Principles*, 248).

86 Title-page spelling of Part 1 is *Englands New Chains*; Part 2 is *Englands New-Chaines*.

87 H.N. Brailsford, *The Levellers and the English Revolution*, ed. Christopher Hill (London: The Cresset Press, 1961), 475, 512–19, 564, 577.

88 Tim Harris, "The Leveller Legacy: From the Restoration to the Exclusion Crisis," in *The Putney Debates of 1647*, ed. Michael Mendle (Cambridge: Cambridge University Press, 2001), 219.

89 Stanley Fish, *Surprised by Sin: The Reader in "Paradise Lost"* (New York: St Martin's Press, 1967), ix.

90 Sharon Achinstein, *Milton and the Revolutionary Reader* (Princeton: Princeton University Press, 1994), 221.

91 See my *Imagined Nations: Reflections on Media in Canadian Fiction* (Montreal and Kingston: McGill-Queen's University Press, 2003), particularly the section "The Nation in Theory," 5–73, for a revision of Benedict Anderson's model in a world of digital media.

92 See Christopher Mead, *Mass Communication: The Eucharist and Authorship in Early Modern England* (PhD diss., University of California, Berkeley, 2015), for a discussion of the cultural significance of this seismic shift by means of technological mediation.

93 In *Legal Fundamental Liberties* (8 June 1649), Lilburne confesses that, as a youthful apprentice, he "had spare time enough, yet I never misspent it, but continually spent it in reading the Bible, the Book of Martyrs, *Luthers, Calvins, Bezaes, Carwrights, Perkins, Molins, Burtons*, and *Rogers* Works" (25).

94 John Foxe, *The Actes and Monuments Online* [TAMO] (1583), Book 11: 1612. HRI Online Publications, Sheffield, 2011. Accessed 27 November 2015 at: http//www.johnfoxe.org.

95 *The Perfect Weekly Account* (17–24 January), 357–8.

CHAPTER ONE

1 Merritt Y. Hughes, ed., *The Complete Prose Works of John Milton*, vol. 3: *1648–1649*, (New Haven: Yale University Press, 1962), 36 (hereafter cited as CPW 3).

2 J. Milton French, *The Life Records of John Milton*, vol. 2: *1639–1651* (New Brunswick, NJ: Rutgers University Press, 1950), 239.

3 In fact, it is the second such order to appear next to his name in the Order Book of the Council of State in the Public Record Office (French, *Life Records*, 2: 238–9), after his appointment as "Secretary for fforeigne Tongues" (2: 236).

4 Martin Dzelzainis, "History and Ideology: Milton, the Levellers, and the Council of State in 1649," *Huntington Library Quarterly* 68, nos. 1–2 (March 2005): 276, 279.

5 See H.N. Brailsford, *The Levellers and the English Revolution*, ed. Christopher Hill (London: The Cresset Press, 1961), for evidence that the "mutineers, who, of course, supported the Agreement of the People, were also 'for the bringing in of Prince Charles' … Many civilian Levellers are said to have rallied to them, but not one troop or company of any other regiment" (564).

6 In *The Engagment Vindicated and Explained* (22 January 1650), Lilburne tells of his family's move from Southwark to London, "where by the affection of diverse Inhabitants, I was put in nomination for the year ensuing to be one of their *Common Counsell*; and when the question was put for me according to your custome, I withdrew, and afterwards found, that my election by majority of hands was clear, without all manner of dispute; whereupon according to the Act you tendered me the *New Engagement* in these words, *I doe Declare and promise, that I will be true and faithfull to the Common-wealth of* England, *as the same is now established,*

without a King or House of Lords" (1–2). For the sequel, see Brailsford, *Levellers*, 608.

7 See Samuel R. Gardiner, *History of the Commonwealth and Protectorate, 1649–1656*, 4 vols. (London and New York: Longmans, Green & Co., 1903), 1: 37. Milton's nineteenth-century biographer David Masson had, in *The Life of John Milton*, vol. 4: *1649–1654* (London: Macmillan, 1877), likewise suspected that the Latin Secretary "deferred his 'observations … till they were no longer necessary'" (4:97).

8 French, *Life Records*, 2:54, is clearly mistaken in his assumption that the Overton praised in *Defensio Secunda* ("Te, Overtone, mihi multis abhinc annis") was the Richard of Leveller fame; rather, Robert Overton, soldier and scholar, and later Cromwell's prisoner after he rejected the Protectoral regime, was the friend to whom Milton referred.

9 Ibid., 2:108. The damning sentence comes from Prynne's *Twelve Considerable Serious Questions touching Church Government* (1644), 7.

10 Barbara Kiefer Lewalski, *The Life of John Milton* (Oxford: Blackwell, 2003), 202.

11 The *Officers' Agreement* was consistent, from the draft submitted by the Committee of Sixteen to the interim agreement to the final version, in its provision in Article 5 for "a council of state" to be appointed "within twenty days" of an election, and to be "under the direction of the Representative, to act until the first day of each succeeding Representative." See Frances Henderson, "Drafting the Officers' Agreement," in *The Agreements*, ed. Baker and Vernon (2012), 172.

12 In *The Fountain of Slaunder Discovered* (30 May 1649), Walwyn writes "That I could not but wonder (considering how well I was known) that I should be sent for by Souldiers, when there was not the meanest civil Officer but might command my appearance: That I thought was a thing not agreeable to that freedom and liberty which had been pretended" (11–12).

13 *Fountain of Slaunder*, 13. Walwyn's decision to publish a separate defence seven weeks after the other three is in part because he had neither attended meetings nor discussed the Levellers' attack on the legitimacy of the regime in either part of *Englands New-Chaines Discovered*.

14 Lewalski, *Life of John Milton*, 240.

15 *CPW* 2: 559.

16 Don M. Wolfe, *Milton in the Puritan Revolution* (1941; London: Cohen & West, 1963), cites the second edition of Walwyn's *Compassionate Samaritan*, thus leaving an impression, in his rather sketchy notice of its similarities to Milton's work, that "The *Samaratane*" (134) was influenced by *Areopagitica*. But influence clearly runs the other way, from Walwyn to Milton.

17 Walwyn, *The Compassionate Samaritan* (29 July 1644), 58–9. Huntington Library. EEBO Online. University of Manitoba. Accessed 8 July 2013. "The Second *Edition*, corrected, and enlarged" of Walwyn's tract (British Library, EEBO) is dated "Jan: 5th London" in the familiar hand of the bookseller George Thomason. Where the first edition runs to seventy-six pages, the second edition – in the same font and type-size – ends on page seventy-nine. Milton's *Areopagitica* appeared 118 days after the first edition of *The Compassionate Samaritan*, on 23 November 1644.

18 Wolfe remarks that "Of the three Leveller leaders Walwyn believed most strongly in triumph of truth in a free and open discussion" (133). Yet, after a brief survey of their views on censorship, he says, "One looks … in vain among Milton's liberal contemporaries for a resourceful champion of a free press comparable with Milton himself" (*Milton in the Puritan Revolution*, 135).

19 For a discussion of Milton's "Rhetoric and Strategy" in *Areopagticia*, see Sirluck, CPW 2: 170–8.

20 Marcus Tullius Cicero, "*On the Republic*" *and* "*On the Laws*," trans. David Fott (Ithaca: Cornell University Press, 2014), 1: 23.

21 Fred D. Miller, Jr, "The Rule of Reason in Cicero's Philosophy of Law," *University of Queensland Law Journal* 33, no. 2 (2014): 326.

22 More generally, Lilburne's writings make it clear that "'monopolies' of private interest were diametrically opposed to the Leveller ideal of the common good as exemplified in the equal freedoms of individuals" (Foxley, *The Levellers: Radical Political Thought in the English Revolution* [Manchester and New York: Manchester University Press, 2013], 94).

23 Walwyn, *Gold tried in the fire, or The burnt Petitions revived* (14 June 1647), 4.

24 Milton would not publish his sonnet by that name, written in 1646, until 1673.

25 Barbara Taft doubts Walwyn's authorship of this pamphlet in *The Writings of William Walwyn* (Athens, GA, and London: University of Georgia Press, 1989), 532–5, although she has to admit that her co-editor, Jack R. McMichael, "discerned ideas shared by Walwyn and the author of *Tyranipocrit* and detected a Walwyn-like irony in the style" (533). But McMichael died five years before their book appeared, leaving his co-editor to conclude that "*Tyranipocrit*'s all-out attack on the doctrine of predestination as 'blasphemous' is unlike Walwyn's inclusive tolerance" (533), supposedly making it antithetical to the gospel of love in *The Compassionate Samaritan*. Yet Taft does not deny the "sweeping severity" (38) of Walwyn's attack on Independents in *The Vanitie of the Present Churches* (12 March 1649), penned a few months before the appearance of *Tyranipocrit* (14 August 1649). For evidence that Walwyn wrote *Tyranipocrit*, see Chapter 5, n1 below.

26 Stanley Fish, "Driving from the Letter: Truth and Indeterminacy in Milton's *Areopagitica*," in *Re-membering Milton: Essays on the Texts and Traditions*, ed. Mary Nyquist and Margaret W. Ferguson (New York and London: Methuen, 1987), offers a brief, but fairly accurate, summary (234–5) of the positions taken by critics over the second half of the twentieth century.

27 Sirluck, "Introduction" to *Areopagitica* in CPW 2: 158–83.

28 Thomas Edwards, *Gangraena; or a Catalogue and Discovery of many of the Errours, heresies, Blasphemies and pernicious Practices of the Sectaries of this time*, 3 parts (London: Ralph Smith, 1646), 3:156.

29 "House of Commons Journal, Volume 3: 26 August 1644," *Journal of the House of Commons*: vol. 3: *1643–1644* (1802), 606–8. Accessed 10 January 2013 at: http://www.british-history.ac.uk/report.aspx?compid=11391.

30 Published in *The Picture of the Councel of State* (11 April 1649), 25–45.

31 H.N. Brailsford, in *The Levellers and the English Revolution*, ed. Christopher Hill (London: The Cresset Press, 1961), remarks on "The profound belief of the Anabaptists in human equality, including the equality of the sexes," as one of the reasons for "their faith in toleration" (33). Richard Overton, like John Lilburne, was a practising Baptist.

32 Merritt Y. Hughes notes that, "In *The Tenure* there is much that recalls the political slogans and thinking of the Levellers," although he goes on to exclude Leveller influences, finding other antecedents instead for Milton's arguments (CPW 3: 36–8).

33 Lilburne, *The Oppressed Mans Oppressions Declared* (30 January 1647), 13.

34 Barbara Lewalski, *Life of John Milton*, 237.

35 Richard Lee Bradshaw, *God's Battleaxe: The Life of Lord President John Bradshawe* (Bloomington, IN: Xlibris, 2010), 96.

36 *Tenure*, CPW 3: 222.

37 Ibid., 204.

38 Ibid., 220.

39 While Stephen Fallon recognizes that Milton's arguments from "natural liberty" in *Tenure* derive from the Levellers, he makes Lilburne's "Postscript" to *The Freemans Freedome* Milton's likely source; *Regall Tyrannie* and its verbal resonances in *Tenure* are never mentioned. See Fallon, "Nascent Republican Theory in Milton's Regicide Prose," in *The Oxford Handbook of Literature and the English Revolution*, ed. Laura Lunger Knoppers (Oxford: Oxford University Press, 2012), 309–26.

40 *Regall Tyrannie discovered* (6 January 1647), 38.

41 In his introduction to *The Tenure* (CPW 3), Merritt Y. Hughes remarks that "To see the resemblance between Lilburne's 'political primitivism' and Milton's survey of men's efforts to control predatory kings since rulers first became necessary after the loss of the perfect law of God in Eden, it is only necessary to turn to the paragraph beginning with the words, 'No man who knows ought …' on p. 198 below. In spite of Milton's respect for the people collectively as the rightful source of all authority and the masters of their rulers, he was no egalitarian" (27–8). What follows is meant to attenuate that judgment.

42 Flannagan, *The Riverside Milton*, 1057.

43 Nedham, if he was indeed the author of *Regall Tyrannie* (see "Introduction," n32), was an Oxonian, who would have been familiar with Cicero's natural law theory; even so, he appeals, like "Leveller writings" in general, "to both native and natural rights" (D. Alan Orr, "Constitutionalism: Ancient, Modern, and Early Modern in the *Agreements of the People*," in *The Agreements*, ed. Baker and Vernon, 85).

44 In *De republica*, Cicero claims that, "True law is correct reason congruent with nature, spread among all persons, constant, everlasting"; and that there is "but one law both everlasting and unchangeable" which "will encompass all nations and for all time" (trans. David Fott, 98–9). In *De legibus*, he starts from the premise "that all nature is ruled by the force, nature, reason, power, mind, majesty – or whatever other word there is by which I may signify more plainly what I want – of the immortal gods" (Fott, 137). "Since that is law," Cicero adds at another point in Book

1 of *De legibus*, "we should also consider human beings to be united with gods by law. Furthermore, among those who have a sharing in law, there is a sharing in right" (1:23).

45 See, for example, "least of all to be endured by free born men" (CPW 3: 204); "merely by the liberty and right of free born Men" (206); "why among free Persons" (199), etc.

46 CPW 3: 199–200.

47 *Regall Tyrannie*, 8.

48 Ibid., 13.

49 See Paul Rahe, *Against Throne and Altar: Machiavelli and Political Theory under the English Republic* (Cambridge: Cambridge University Press, 2008), 233–8; and see my "Introduction," 9–10.

50 Barbara Lewalski, *Life of John Milton*, 232.

51 See above, "Introduction," 8–10.

52 *Regall Tyrannie* offers further support for Jonathan Scott's identification of "the classical content of Leveller" thought, and "the religious content of republican thought" (Scott, *Commonwealth Principles: Republican Writing of the English Revolution* [Cambridge: Cambridge University Press, 2004], 248).

53 Stephen M. Fallon, "'The Strangest Piece of Reason': Milton's *Tenure of Kings and Magistrates*," in *The Oxford Handbook of Milton*, ed. Nicholas McDowell and Nigel Smith (Oxford: Oxford University Press, 2009), 250.

54 "Introduction," *John Milton: Political Writings*, ed. Martin Dzelzainis (Cambridge: Cambridge University Press, 1991), xviii–xix.

55 Go Togashi, "Milton and the Presbyterian Opposition, 1649–1650: The Engagement Controversy and *The Tenure of Kings and Magistrates*, Second Edition (1649)," *Milton Quarterly* 39 (2005): 59–81.

56 Nicholas von Maltzahn, *Milton's "History of Britain": Republican Historiography in the English Revolution* (Oxford: Clarendon Press, 1991), 209.

57 French Fogle, the modern editor of the *History*, concludes, after surveying a range of possible dates, "that Milton began the writing of his *History* during the period from 1645 to 1647, and probably toward the end of that period." See French Fogle ed., *Complete Prose Works of John Milton*, vol. 5: *1648?–1671*, Part 1 (New Haven and London: Yale University Press, 1971): xxxix (hereafter, CPW 5.i: etc.)

58 The myth of the Norman Yoke, put to such effective use by Overton and Walwyn in *A Remonstrance of Many Thousand Citizens* (7 July 1646), first appeared in *The Just Mans Justification* (10 June 1646), where "that which is the greatest mischiefe of all, and *the oppressing bondage of England* ever since the *Norman yoke*, is this," writes Lilburne, that "I must be tryed before you by a *Law* (called the Common Law) that I know not, nor I thinke no man else, neither do I know where to find it, or reade it; and how I can in such a case be punished by it, I know not" (11). And so he exhorts Parliament "*forever to annihilate this* Norman *innovation, and reduce us back to that past of the ancient frame of government in this Kingdome, before the* Conquers *dayes*" (15).

59 *CPW* 5.i: 49.

60 Cf. Tacitus, *The Annals of Imperial Rome*, 12.34, trans. Michael Grant, 1956 (London: The Folio Society, 2006): "Caratacus [*sic*], as he hastened to one point and another, stressed that this was the day, this the battle, which would either win back their freedom or enslave them forever. He invoked their ancestors, who by routing Julius Caesar had valorously preserved their present descendants from Roman officials and taxes – and their wives and children from defilement" (232).

61 David Loewenstein, *Milton and the Drama of History: Historical Vision, Iconoclasm, and the Literary Imagination* (Cambridge: Cambridge University Press, 1990), 83.

62 See my treatment of Geoffrey's justification for Norman Empire in *Imagined Nations: Reflections on Media in Canadian Fiction* (Montreal and Kingston: McGill-Queen's University Press, 2009), 10–11.

63 Martin Dzelzainis, "History and Ideology: Milton, the Levellers, and the Council of State in 1649," *Huntington Library Quarterly* 68, nos. 1–2 (March 2005): 287.

64 Hugh Jenkins, "Shrugging Off the Norman Yoke: Milton's *History of Britain* and the Levellers," *English Literary Renaissance* 29, no. 3 (March 1999): 310.

65 See Chapter 6 below, 180–3.

66 Ian Gentles, "The New Model Army and the Constitutional Crisis of the Late 1640s," in *The Agreements*, ed. Baker and Vernon (2012), says that Cromwell and Ireton had already realized at Putney that "the *Agreement* proposed a bill of rights guaranteeing freedom of religion" and "freedom from military conscription," not to mention "a written constitution" that would be "unalterable by any future parliament or government" (147), both of which ideas were prejudicial to the rights of the landed class and England's "natural" rulers.

67 Blair Worden, *Literature and Politics in Cromwellian England: John Milton, Andrew Marvell, Marchamont Nedham* (Oxford: Oxford University Press, 2007), 262–88; see Chapter 2 below, 99–101.

68 Fogle writes, "We can, then, place the resumption of writing certainly after 1652, when Simeon of Durham became available [as a source for the last fifteen pages of the Fourth Book], and probably after 1655, when Milton had done with the Defences" (*CPW* 5.i: xli). Most Miltonists concur; e.g., see von Maltzahn, *Milton's "History of Britain,"* 169–70, and Worden, *Literature and Politics*, 321.

69 Worden, *Literature and Politics*, 293.

70 Worden finds no reason to doubt Edward Phillips that it was after "the publication of *Pro Se Defensio* in August 1655" when Milton resumed his *History* (413).

71 Nicholas von Maltzahn plausibly suggests that Milton withdrew his critique of the Rump and the Westminster Assembly after the censor had cut his portrait of the Saxon bishops as being too nearly modelled on Restoration episcopacy (*Milton's "History of Britain,"* 14).

72 Thanks to the work of of Blair Worden, *Literature and Politics*, 387–8, 410–26; and to Austin Woolrych, "Dating Milton's *History of Britain*," *The Historical Journal* 36, no. 4 (1993): 929–43, the traditional date of "The Digression" has become

untenable. Woolrych now dates it plausibly to March 1660, "probably soon after General Monck's readmission of the secluded members" (943); while Worden argues more daringly that "The Digression," and possibly the preamble to Book 3, are "late work" (420), composed ca. 1669–70.

73 Fogle, *CPW* 5.i: 426–35.

74 Ibid., 441.

75 Worden, *Literature and Politics*, 412.

76 Hugh Jenkins, "Shrugging Off the Norman Yoke: Milton's *History of Britain* and the Levellers," *English Literary Renaissance* 29, no.3 (1999), finds a parallel with "fit audience … though few" (*PL* 7.31), suggesting that "Milton's appeal to the judicious reader in the *History* ultimately moves the locus of that history, the text to be read, from without to within" (324). As a restatement of the traditional view of Milton retreating from worldly affairs to "A paradise within thee, happier far" (12.587), this reading is finally at the opposite pole of the view advanced in this book.

77 Fogle, *CPW* 5.i: xl.

78 As Woolrych comments, "'So many years doeing and undoeing' is a natural way of describing the changes of the regime in the 1650s," which, *pace* von Maltzahn, "is meaningless in the context of February 1649" ("Dating Milton's *History*," 938).

79 Hugh Jenkins comes to a similar conclusion about Milton and Lilburne's similar verdicts in favour of the people and against their rulers ("Shrugging Off the Norman Yoke," 317).

80 *Englands New Chains Discovered* (26 February 1649), 15.

81 My best estimate is thirty months, based on evidence presented in Chapter 2.

82 Scott, *Commonwealth Principles*, 241; for his dating of "Digression," see 240.

83 Paul Rahe takes the opposing view of Milton's "Digression," arguing that, "As for those who were 'more prudent,' they were not even permitted to convey what they had in mind. There was no point, therefore, in blaming 'the *saniores*' – England's more reasonable, sounder, saner men" (*Against Throne and Altar*, 126).

84 *The Likeliest Means*, in the revised edition *of The Complete Prose Works of John Milton*, vol 7: *1659–1660*, ed. Robert W. Ayers (New Haven and London: Yale University Press, 1980), 274 (hereafter cited as *CPW* 7: 274, etc.).

85 Worden, *Literature and Politics*, 262–88.

86 Milton, writes Worden, "would discover the fullness of his poetic powers only when he had found, in the subject of *Paradise Lost*, the scope for a new kind of heroic song … The writing of the *History of Britain* has an essential place in that transition" (*Literature and Politics*, 389). Worden measures that transition by the common failure of Englishmen and Adam to respond wisely to "the strenuousness of freedom" (397); conversely, I believe, it is the writer who ultimately blames himself in each work for having failed, like Adam, to choose "aright."

87 *Englands New Chains* (26 February 1649), 14 (although unpaginated).

88 *Englands New Chains*, title page.

89 *The Second Part of Englands New-Chaines* (24 March 1649), 10.

90 Elliot Vernon, "The Debate," in *The Agreements*, ed. Baker and Vernon (2012), 212.

91 *Englands New Chains* (26 February 1649), 6.

92 See Chapter 2, "Milton and Politicus: Deposing Cromwell," where I find evidence that he did so in 1651–52.

93 An echo of Lilburne would confirm Milton's claim in *Defensio Secunda* that he "had already finished four books [of a *History*] when the kingdom of Charles was transformed into a republic, and the so-called Council of State ... summoned me" (CPW 4.i: 627–8).

94 *The Second Part of Englands New-Chaines*, 4.

95 Lieut. Col. John Lilburne, Mr Thomas Prince, and Mr Richard Overton, *The Picture of the Councel of State, Held forth to the Free people of England* (11 April 1649), 11–12.

96 *To the Hon[ble]. The House of* Commons *now Assembled in the high Court of* Parliament, *The humble Petition of* John Lilburne. *Liet Colonel* (1646), 1.

97 *The Picture of the Councel*, 13. Lilburne quotes himself in this speech.

98 Ibid., 15. Lilburne introduces the speech as follows: "I laid my eare to their doore, and heard *Lieutenant General Cromwell* (I am sure of it) very loud" (14).

CHAPTER TWO

1 *Jonahs Cry out of the Whales Belly* (26 July 1647). Lilburne had published some of his previous correspondence with the Lt-General, most notably in *The Copy of a Letter* (9 August 1645), in which Cromwell bids Parliament, on behalf of "*Lie. Col.* Lilburne, *who hath done both you & the Kingdom good service*," to make "*repairation according to their Votes, for his former sufferings and losses* [under the tyranny of Star Chamber], *and some satisfaction for his Arrears for his* [military] *service of the State*" (20).

2 The date of writing is 25 March 1647.

3 H.N. Brailsford, *The Levellers and the English Revolution*, ed. Christopher Hill (London: The Cresset Press, 1961), 88.

4 A year before writing this letter, Lilburne had written publicly of Manchester that he had "treacherously, betrayed and delivered *Lincoln* last up to the enemy, without striking one stroke, or staying till so much as a Troope of Horse, or a Trumpeter came to demand it," thereby renewing the threat of impeachment "that makes him he cannot be quiet, till Lieut. Gen. *Crumwels* Charge against him, fully proved in the *House of Commons*, be revived" (*The Free-mans Freedom Vindicated*, 23 June 1646), 8. Tellingly, Manchester would not seek legal redress through the courts, but rather through the House of Lords, where he abused his role as Speaker to summon Lilburne before the Lords and to convict him summarily of contempt.

5 Wildman, *Putney Projects: or The Old Serpent in a New Forme* (30 December 1647), 7.

6 This letter is dated 10 April 1647.

7 Walwyn, *Englands Weeping Spectacle: or, The Sad Condition of Lieutenant Colonell* John Lilburne (29 January 1648), 9. Although Barbara Taft rejects Walwyn's authorship of this pamphlet in *The Writings of William Walwyn*, ed. Jack R. McMichael and Barbara Taft (Athens, GA, and London: University of Georgia Press, 1989) for its "sentimentalism and stylistic extremism" (531), the tenor of its narrative of Lilburne's refusal to kneel before the Lords is close to that of a similar account in *The Just Man in Bonds* (29 June 1646), which she does attribute to him; its "harsh attacks on Cromwell and Ireton" also fit the mood of frustration and anger in the wake of the Putney-Ware failure, while anticipating his bitter accusations against "Politicians" in *The Fountain of Slaunder* (30 May 1649), 2–4.

8 Edward Vallance, "Oaths, Covenants, Associations, and the Origins of the *Agreements of the People*: The Road to and from Putney," in *The Agreements*, ed. Philip Baker and Elliot Vernon (London: Palgrave Macmillan, 2012), argues more largely that "the idea of an *Agreement of the People* ... was drawn from the example of the Long Parliament's oaths and covenants" (42), and that "Lilburne appealed to medieval charters and communal oaths, at the same time as invoking reason and natural law" (43).

9 Rachel Foxley makes it clear, however, that in *Jonahs Cry*, it is the *army*, not the government or nation, that Lilburne sees dissolved "into the originall law of Nature" (*Jonahs Cry*, 13; Foxley, *The Levellers: Radical Political Thought in the English Revolution* [Manchester and New York: Manchester University Press, 2013], 75).

10 Rachel Foxley, *The Levellers*, 22–8.

11 Foxley nonetheless denies that the Levellers believed the social contract had been abrogated and men were returned to a state of nature to construct a new constitution *ab novo*: "The passage most often cited as an explicit statement that government had dissolved and England had returned to the state of nature in fact says nothing of the kind: it is talking about the army only, not the nation or government" (75). It is worth noting that the Army's assumed right of reserving power of disbanding to themselves is a very likely precedent for the reservation of powers in the *Agreements of the People*.

12 Walwyn, *Englands Weeping Spectacle* (29 January 1648), 12.

13 For the arguments of Scott and others making Nedham the author of the Leveller pamphlet *Vox Plebis* (17 November 1646), see my "Introduction," n60; for my attribution of the Leveller pamphlet *Regall Tyrannie discovered* to Nedham, see "Introduction," n32; and Chapter 6, n10.

14 *Mercurius Pragmaticus* 17 (11 January 1648): 9 [although unpaginated].

15 *Englands New Chains Discovered* (26 February 1649), 1, 2.

16 *Mercurius Pragmaticus* 44 (5 March 1649): 5 [although unpaginated].

17 Scott, *Commonwealth Principles: Republican Writing of the English Revolution* (Cambridge: Cambridge University Press, 2004), 246.

18 Lilburne, *To all the Affectors and Approvers in* England (17 July 1649), 8. He used almost exactly the same words three weeks later in *An Impeachment of High*

Treason Against Oliver Cromwell, and his son in Law Henry Ireton (10 August 1649), 8.

19 *Mercurius Pragmaticus* 3 (6 October 1647): 22, 23.

20 Today, it is a commonplace among historians of English republicanism to describe Milton's Satan in terms that the Levellers and Nedham used to describe the "apostate" Cromwell. As these historians remind us, however, Milton did not repent of his republican sentiments by situating them in Hell; rather, as Jonathan Scott insists, "Satan is Cromwell, speaking the language of a noble cause, while hypocritically leading its followers to destruction. In this, too, there is an echo of Lucan's Caesar, who speaks the same language to the same effect" (Scott, *Commonwealth Principles*, 320). There is some danger, however, in Scott's (and Norbrook's) telescoping of the Levellers' "apostate" into the antagonist of the Roman republic. For the classical label obscures a more significant drama in *Paradise Lost*, in which "the monarchy of Heaven" evolves toward popular sovereignty. What the mask of Calvin really hides in Milton's poem is a divine democrat. This is not a view that is shared, however, by republican historians. Indeed, as Austin Woolrych says of Milton, "There is no sign that he felt drawn to such genuine political radicals as Henry Marten or Thomas Chaloner, or to the Levellers, whose serious threats to the Commonwealth's stability in the spring of 1649 he probably deplored, and whose egalitarianism ran counter to his own elitist brand of classical republicanism." See Woolrych, "Dating Milton's *History of Britain*," *The Historical Journal* 36, no. 4 (December 1993). See also David Norbrook's *Writing the English Republic* (1998) for Milton's evolving blueprint of a "classical" English republic, based on a Greco-Roman model informed by classical virtues of civic education, public probity, and private rectitude – in short, an aristocracy of virtue.

21 *Mercurius Pragmaticus* 12 (20 June 1648): 6 [although unpaginated].

22 *Mercurius Pragmaticus* 47 (27 March 1649): 5 [although unpaginated].

23 J. Milton French, "Milton, Needham, and *Mercurius Politicus*," *Studies in Philology* 33, no. 2 (1936): 236. Accessed 2 June 2016 at http://www.jstor.org/stable/4172321.

24 J. Milton French, *The Life Records of John Milton*, vol. 2: *1639–1651* (New Brunswick, NJ: Rutgers University Press, 1950), 2: 270.

25 *The Oxinden and Peyton Letters*, ed. Dorothy Kempe Gardiner (London: Sheldon Press, 1937), 161. Cited by Blair Worden, "Milton and Marchamont Nedham," in *Milton and Republicanism*, ed. David Armitage et al. (Cambridge: Cambridge University Press, 1995), 162.

26 Lewalski, *The Life of John Milton* (Oxford: Blackwell, 2003), 245.

27 Nedham, *The Case of the Commonwealth, Stated*, ed. Philip A. Knachel. The Folger Shakespeare Library (Charlottesville: University Press of Virginia, 1969).

28 Scott, *Commonwealth Principles*, 177.

29 This passage is repeated in slightly revised form in Nedham's *The Excellencie of a Free State* (London: Thomas Brewster, 1656), 18–19.

30 Wolfe, *Milton in the Puritan Revolution* (1941; London: Cohen & West, 1963), 343.

31 See my "Introduction," 9–11; also see Paul Rahe, *Against Throne and Altar: Machiavelli and Political Theory under the English Republic* (Cambridge: Cambridge University Press, 2008), 118–23.

32 Vernon, "The Debates," in *The Agreements*, ed. Baker and Vernon (2012), 207.

33 Ibid.

34 *Paradise Lost* pretends to confirm, but totally ironizes, the classical republican idea of masculine *virtus*, as we will see in Book 4 of *Paradise Lost* (Chapter 6 below). The idea suffers a frontal assault in Heaven (Chapter 5), where "Love hath abounded more then Glory abounds" (*PL* 3.312), a trope that echoes the gospel of Love in *Tyranipocrit*, another Leveller tract, where "religion must bee a joyning of two free-wils in one" (9). The logic of love that informs the story of creation in *Paradise Lost* amounts to a late, if thorough-going, repudiation of the whole ethos of classical republicanism, which is shown to be foreign to the "feminine" – read divine – ethos of love in Milton's "Republic of Love."

35 Cicero, *De inventione*, II.53.159, trans. H.M. Hubbell. Loeb Classical Library (Cambridge, MA: Harvard University Press, 1949)."Virtue may be defined," Cicero affirms, "as a habit of mind in harmony with reason and the order of nature. Therefore when we have become acquainted with all its parts we shall have considered the full scope of honour, pure and simple. It has four parts: wisdom, justice, courage, temperance" (327).

36 Paul Rahe, *Against Throne and Altar*, 236.

37 Lilburne denied authorship of "those two notable discourses called, *Vox Plebis*, and *Regall Tyranny discovered*" "which some of my friends, or well-wishers have done it excellent well for me" (*Oppressed Mans Oppressions*, 13). This further strengthens Jonathan Scott's case for Nedham "as one probable author of *Vox Plebis*" (*Commonwealth Principles*, 84).

38 Lilburne's lumping together of both treatises is another reason to regard Nedham as a likely contributor to *Regall Tyrannie* (see my "Introduction," n32 above, and Chapter 6, n10 below).

39 See Chapter 1, 43–8.

40 Scott, *Commonwealth Principles*, 83, 84.

41 French, *Life Records* 2: 309.

42 Ibid., 2: 311. The abrupt mingling of Latin, Greek, and English in this sentence is of Nedham's doing.

43 J. Milton French, "Milton, Needham, and *Mercurius Politicus*," *Studies in Philology* 33, no. 2 (1936), notes that there "is no definite proof that Milton did not have the oversight of this paper during the whole two years in which its editorials appeared" (238).

44 In *The Life Records of John Milton*, vol. 3: *1651–1654* (New Brunswick, NJ: Rutgers University Press, 1954), J. Milton French catalogues thirty-nine weekly entries from *The Stationers' Register* "by order of" or under "the hand of Master MILTON" as the licenser of "a pamphlet called, *Mercurius Politicus*" (*passim*). The first entry is dated 17 March 1651, "Entred … by order of Master MILTON, 6 Pamphletts"

(9). His retroactive permission thus reaches back to 10 February 1651, while the next entry "under the hand of Master MILTON" on 17 April is for "5 pamphletts" (21), followed on 28 April "by permission of authority 3 pamphletts called, *Mercurius Politicus*" (23). Assuming that this "authority" of 28 April refers to Milton, his belated licence to publish could extend at least as far back as 23 January 1651. Conversely, the last multiple entry on 22 May for "4 Pamphletts" (32) brings the licenser fully up to date. Thereafter, all entries "under the hand of Master MILTON" appear on the date of publication, with the notation "the same day" recorded weekly from 12 June to 9 October, excepting only the entry of 4 September (70). From 16 October until 22 January 1652, after which Milton's "hand" in *Politicus* disappears from the record, "the same day" is dropped, whether due to changes in the style of notation or to irregularities in the timing of "authority" is impossible to say.

45 French, "Milton, Needham, and *Mercurius Politicus*," 244, 237.

46 David Masson, *The Life of John Milton*, 4: 335.

47 French, "Milton, Needham, and *Mercurius Politicus*," 244.

48 Foxley, *The Levellers*, 197–8.

49 French, "Milton, Needham," 242.

50 As Worden notes, "Nedham had no need to alter those passages of *Politicus* when he reproduced them in *The Excellencie.* They had stood still while Cromwell's usurpation had given them an altered context" (*Literature and Politics*, 308).

51 Elmer A. Beller, "Milton and *Mercurius Politicus*," *Huntington Quarterly* 5, no. 4 (1942): 479–80.

52 Worden, *Literature and Politics*, 204.

53 William Riley Parker, *Milton: A Biography*, vol. 1, 1968. Rev. ed. Gordon Campbell (Oxford: Clarendon Press, 1996), 1: 390–1.

54 *The Early Lives of Milton*, ed. Helen Darbishire (1932; New York: Barnes & Noble, 1965), 71; citation corrected from Worden, *Literature and Politics*, 216.

55 Worden, *Literature and Politics*, 93.

56 See Rahe, *Against Throne and Altar*, 235–44.

57 *Mercurius Politicus* 77 (27 November 1651): 1222.

58 See Rahe, *Against Throne and Altar*, 235–9.

59 Such distinctions between liberty and virtue, or between liberty and licence, are one of the hallmarks of 1650s republicanism in its fear of the ungovernable mob: "License they mean when they cry libertie" (Flannagan, *Riverside Milton*, 252), Milton had inveighed in 1646 against Presbyterians like Thomas Edwards (*Gangraena*), who were hardly populists, although they were willing to use the "mob" in support of "virtuous" or "aristocratic" interests.

60 Rahe (*Against Throne and Altar*, 195) cites Nedham's source in Machiavelli's *Discorsi* 1: 16–18, but fails to specify that his epistological assumptions remain Platonic.

61 Scott, *Commonwealth Principles*, 152.

62 Cicero, who called Socrates the greatest of all philosophers, claims in *De legibus* that "this thing [the law] has been called [from] the Greek name for 'granting to

each his own,' whereas I think it comes from our word for 'choosing.' As they put the effect of fairness into law, we put the effect of choice into it," I: 19 (*On the Laws*, trans. David Fott [Ithaca and London: Cornell University Press, 2014], 136). *Choice* and *law* may also be cognate for Milton.

63 In fairness to Cromwell, it ought to be noted that, after Worcester, he did press the Rump to dissolve and call new elections; to pass a bill of oblivion meant to reconcile royalists to the regime; and to enact measures for poor relief and law reform. Was his reforming image of 1651–52 as "the champion of the radicals" genuine? Blair Worden, in *The Rump Parliament, 1648–1653* (Cambridge: Cambridge University Press, 1974), admits to "his policy of radicalism on the public stage and conservatism behind the scenes," yet wonders "whether he could square his behavior with the conflicting demands of his conscience" (275, 278). What seems like ambivalence to one may look like hypocrisy to others; witness Lilburne's strident accusations and Politicus's veiled warnings of Cromwell's growing hypocrisy.

64 Cromwell's regal ambition is already hinted at in his choice of a residence after his return from Worcester. Until he became Lord Protector and moved to Whitehall Palace, he made his home at Hampton Court (French, *The Life Records*, 3: 69), Henry VIII's palace, where the Army had kept Charles I under house arrest from early June until 11 November 1647, at which point the king fled "into *Cromwells* mouse trap in the Isle of *Whight*" (Lilburne, *The Prisoner's Plea for a Habeas Corpus* [4 April 1648], 12).

65 In *Literature and Politics*, Worden modifies his earlier view of Cromwell in *The Rump Parliament* as a radical reformer after Worcester: "Bradshaw championed the radical cause … His principal antagonist in the winter of 1650–1 was Cromwell … The conflict of Bradshaw and Cromwell, which opened up in the wake of Dunbar, represented the opposing directions in which the Commonwealth might move" (195–6).

66 Rachel Foxley recalls that Nedham had warned in *The Case of the Commonwealth, Stated* of "the people's proneness to be gulled by anyone promising excessive liberty," meaning "that a democracy could very easily tip over into a tyranny" (*The Levellers*, 212). This is the usual stance of classical republicans throughout the 1650s. But in *Politicus* 72 (23 October 1651), Nedham's sympathies are with the gulled "people," not with the anti-populists.

67 In *Jonahs Cry* (26 July 1647), Lilburne addresses Cromwell for the first time as a "Grandee," recalling "much opposition from your selfe and others of your fellow Grandees in the Army" (9). In *Londons Liberty in Chains discovered* (2 November 1646), he had previously spoken of "the ancient customes and practices of the Grandees of *London*" (41), a colloquialism reserved for the political elite, although Marchamont Nedham had recently used it in *Mercurius Britanicus* to describe royalist military officers as "the *Grandees*, like *Rats* in an *old house* ready to fall" (20 April 1646: 1079). Nedham most likely transliterated the epithet from Machiavelli's *grandi* (on whom see Rahe, *Against Throne and Altar*, 49–52), the nobles or "great ones" in the state.

68 In *A Whip for the Present House of Lords* (27 February 1648), 2. Lilburne's tactic was to turn the accusation of "levelling" back on his accusers, identifying Cromwell and his "Grandees" seven times as such in this pamphlet, to which he and his own party stand as contraries: "*I againe christen your forementioned tribe, the true and reall Levellers*, and those that you nick name *Levellers*, the *supporters and defenders of liberty and propriety, or Anti Grandees, Anti Imposters, Anti-Monopolists, Anti-Apostates, Anti-Arbitrarians, and Anti-Levellers*" (3).

69 *The Prisoners Plea* (4 April 1648), 1. The epithet "Grandee" is used six times in this pamphlet, in typical expressions such as "the Grandees of the Army" (7); "*Cromwell* and his Grandees" (8); "*Cromwell and his grandee faction*" (9).

70 *Mercurius Pragmaticus* (18 April 1648), 2–3. Pragmaticus returns repeatedly, if not as often as Lilburne, to mocking the "Grandees" for their ambition, as he does in the issue immediately following Pride's Purge: "Upon the same *Termes* that the *Houses* quarrel'd with the *King*, doe the Army now with the Houses, in defyance of their *authority*: And if it should happen (which God forbid) that the *Grandees* of the Army can establish themselves in the intended *Tyranny* (be it an *Oligarchy*, or a *Democracy*, or what you please) then admit the same *Principle* of changing *Government* at the pleasure of the *People*, and it will be made use of in a short time by persons of the same *aspiring humor*, to cashire them likewise: And so instead of a *peaceable Government* under *hereditary Kings*, the Land shall groan under the burden of *successive Tyrants*, and be tormented with *Usurpation* upon *Usurpation*, and Rebellion upon Rebellion *in Infinitum*" (*Pragmaticus*, 12 December 1648, 2).

71 C.H. Firth, "Needham or NEDHAM, Marchamont (1620–1678)," *Oxford Dictionary of National Biography* Archive (1894), online edn. September 2015; accessed 11 June 2016 at: http://www.oxforddnb.com.

72 Joad Raymond, "Nedham, Marchamont (*bap.* 1620, *d.* 1678)," *Oxford Dictionary of National Biography* (Oxford: Oxford University Press, 2004), online edn. September 2015; accessed 18 May 2016 at: http://www.oxforddnb.com/view/article/19847.

73 Darbishire, *Early Lives*, 74.

74 *A Complete Collection of the Historical, Political, and Miscellaneous Works of John Milton*, ed. Thomas Birch (London: A. Millar, 1738), adds an interesting gloss to the modern translation, immediately following the word "Senate" in the Yale edition, that "the Authority of the Senate reduced them all, tho' they struggled to retain their Government" (513).

75 The eighteenth-century translation is from the Thomas Birch edition. Lilburne's incitement of the Army to mutiny, in the second part of *Englands New-Chaines Discovered* (24 March 1649), was direct and explicit, and therefore far more dangerous than the many alarms sounded by Politicus or Milton in the autumn of 1651.

76 W.R. Parker, *Milton: A Biography*, vol. 1, 1968. Rev. ed. Gordon Campbell (Oxford: Clarendon Press, 1996), 403.

77 Worden, *Literature and Politics*, 196.

78 See the end of Chapter 1 above, "The Levellers and the Council of State," and *The Picture of the Council of State* (11 April 1649), 15.

79 French, *Life Records*, 3: 115.

80 *Politicus* (1 January 1652), 1304.

81 Lilburne, *As You Were* (Amsterdam: May 1652), 15–16. The subtitle represents with some accuracy its contents: "Or The Lord General *CROMWEL* and the *Grand Officers* of the *Armie* their REMEMBRANCER. Wherein, as in a glass they may see the *faces of their Soules* spotted with *Apostacy, Ambitious breach of promise*, and hocus-pocus-*juggeling* with the honest *Soldiers*, and the rest of the *Free-people of England.*"

82 In his lengthy introduction to the third volume of the Yale edition of Milton's prose, Merritt Y. Hughes makes a similar evaluation of the significance of Lilburne's comment, noting how, "In Wolfe's evidence that as late as 1652 Lilburne publicly expressed his friendship for Milton there is proof that the Levellers had some reason to feel grateful for Milton's forbearance" in not writing his "observations" against them, as the Council of State had ordered him to do (*CPW* 3: 36–7).

83 David Norbrook, *Writing the English Republic: Poetry, Rhetoric, and Politics, 1627–1660* (Cambridge: Cambridge University Press, 1999), 24.

84 *Politicus* 85 (22 January 1652).

85 Here is another Miltonic note that jars with Nedham's Machiavellian argument that ordinary folk are "bounded within a more lowly pitch of desire and imagination," and are thus better guardians of their liberty "than the grandees" (Rahe, *Against Throne*, 236).

86 See, among many other examples, Parker, *Milton: A Biography*, 1: 395; Lewalski, *Life*, 284–5; Worden, *Literature and Politics*, 242–3.

87 J. Milton French remarks that this note "may have been addressed to the Council of State, to the printer, or to someone else; it may have been in commendation or condemnation" (*Life Records*, 2: 321).

88 The pace at which the Council of State, like any government body of the era, moved is evident under the date of "April 2," 1652, in *The Life Records*, where "Mr. *Millington* reports from the Committee to whom the *Racovian* Catechism was referred." Millington reported as well on "the Examination of" "Mr. *Wm. Dugard* … the Printer of the Book," and on "the Examination of Mr. *John Milton*; and a Note under the Hand of Mr. *John Milton*, of the 10th of *August* 1650" (French, *Life Records*, 3: 212).

89 In March 1649, it took three days, if not more, to pass a resolution in Council to arrest those dangerous enemies of the state, Lilburne and his followers, for announcing Cromwell's broken faith and proclaiming the illegality of the new government in the second part of *Englands New-Chaines Discovered* (24 March 1649).

90 Lewalski, *Life*, 279. The explanation given by every biographer is that the Council had to divide up Milton's duties after his blindness became total at the end of February or the beginning of March 1652. Was his eyesight that much better on

15 January, when he still served as state censor of *Politicus*, than it was on 2 February, when Lewis Rosin assumed responsibility for French correspondence? Or have Milton critics been misled by another coincidence like the one involving the printer William Dugard?

91 My phrase "blind guides," which anticipates the royalist Roger L'Estrange's title *No Blind Guides* (1660), is intended to be anachronistic, suggesting the affinities between differing sorts of conservatives at either end of this decade.

92 Worden, *The Rump Parliament*, 282–3.

93 J. Milton French long ago reached a similar, if more tentative, conclusion, that Milton "writes a bit for *Mercurius Politicus* (?)" on "March 4," quoting the sentence that begins, "First for *Kings*, give me leave to shew (what I once published upon another occasion) that tis no new thing for Kings to be deprived, or punish't with death for their crimes in government" (*Life Records*, 3: 205).

94 John S. Smart, *The Sonnets of Milton* (Oxford: Clarendon Press, 1966), 78.

95 Flannagan, *Riverside Milton*, 290–1.

96 *Milton's Sonnets*, ed. E.A.J. Honigmann (New York: St Martin's Press, 1966), 146–7.

97 By now, it will be obvious that I am more than a little sceptical of opinions like those of Austin Woolrych (*Historical Journal* 36, no. 4 [December 1993]) that "The men he most trusted held commanding positions of power in February–March 1649" (937).

98 Their number would not include Cromwell. His "hostility to the war, marked after the dissolution of the Rump, was also in evidence by the last few weeks of the Rump period" (Worden, *Rump Parliament*, 302).

99 *Politicus* 104 (3 June 1652): 1628.

100 Whitelocke, *Memorials of the English Affairs* (1682), iii, 445–6; qtd in Worden, *Rump*, 286.

101 *Politicus* 92 (11 March 1652): 1458.

102 *Politicus* 1 (13 June 1650): 16.

103 "Every mans right" typically connotes the right of every "man," in the Leveller conception of that term, to freedom of conscience, to freedom of opinion and expression, and to freedom to acquire and dispose of property. In one of many examples, Lilburne insists, in *The Legal Fundamental Liberties*, that "Propriety cannot be maintained if Liberty be destroyed; for the Liberty of my person is more neer to me then my Propriety, or Goods: And he that contrary to Law and Justice, robs or deprives me of the Liberty of my Person, the nighest to me, may much more by the same reason, rob and deprive me at his will and pleasure of my Goods and Estate, the further off from me, and so Propriety is overthrown and destroyed" (11).

104 War was finally declared on 8 July 1652.

105 *Politicus* 93 (18 March 1652): 1459, misnumbered from *Politicus* 92.

106 "The Nominated Assembly," *British Civil Wars Project*. Online. Accessed 6 June 2016. http://bcw-project.org.

107 *Mercurius Pragmaticus* (12 October 1647), 4.

108 *History of Britain*, 5.i: 451.

CHAPTER THREE

1 *The Early Lives of Milton*, ed. Helen Darbishire (1932; New York: Barnes & Noble, 1965), 13. Entered beside the combined titles "Paradise lost 4to" and "regained 4to" is the name "Edw. Philips his cheif Amanuensis" (9). While it is in Phillips's own hand, the second claim is unlikely, since he moved to Deptford in Essex on 24 October 1663 to serve as "preceptor" to John Evelyn's son (Parker, *Milton: A Biography*, 1595–6). The end date for the composition of *Paradise Lost* is thereby rendered less certain, although Phillips's faulty memory for dates was surely strengthened by his 1663 departure from London.

2 Austin Woolrych, "Introduction," *CPW* 7: 3.

3 Martin Dzelzainis, "Milton and the Protectorate in 1658," in *Milton and Republicanism*, ed. David Armitage, Armand Himy, and Quentin Skinner (Cambridge: Cambridge University Press, 1995), 205.

4 In *Milton and the Revolutionary Reader* (Princeton: Princeton University Press, 1994), Sharon Achinstein gives several examples of "the Parliament of Hell" genre used by defeated royalists to enact a judgment on their foe. Of these pamphlets belonging to the late 1640s and 1650s, *The Famous Tragedie of King Charles I* is most "emblematic because it presents not only the hellish deeds but the men who were behind them, in no uncertain terms, as Cromwell is represented as Satan himself" (192). This is not to say that Milton presents himself in royalist terms, or even aims at avoiding the censor later on.

5 "John Milton, Englishman, Defense of the English People against Claudius Anonymous alias Salmasius, his Defense of the King. Corrected and enlarged edition, newly revised by the author" [my translation]. *Politicus* 443 (25 November 1658): 29.

6 Diplomats disputing their order of precedence (see Evelyn, n8 below) delayed the procession long enough that it was not completed until after dark, making it impossible to do much of a public nature in the unlit Abbey save deposit the effigy on the great catafalque, say a prayer, and go home.

7 Pauline Croft, *King James* (Basingstoke and New York: Palgrave Macmillan, 2003), 129, cites a letter by John Chamberlain.

8 *The Diary of John Evelyn*, vol. 3, ed. E.S. de Beer (Oxford: Clarendon Press, 1955), 224.

9 See Blair Worden, *Literature and Politics in Cromwellian England: John Milton, Andrew Marvell, Marchamont Nedham* (Oxford: Oxford University Press, 2007), 41, 47, 181, 207–8, 215, 217, 348; and see above, Chapter 2: 82–98.

10 In ascending order behind "Richard Gerald, Deputy Marshall, on horseback" and "Marshall's men, 13, on horseback, with the Knight Marshall," and "Two conductors more, with black staves," were "Poor men in gowns, two and two, in number 82"; "Servants to Gentlemen, Esquires, Knights, Baronets, two and two," and so on down to "Messengers of the Committee of the Army, 4; of the Committee of the Admiralty, 2; Keepers of the Council Chamber and Privy lodgings, 5; Messengers

of the Council Chamber, 15"; and on to "Aldermen, 20"; "Masters of the Chancery, 9"; "Public ministers of foreign states, commonwealths, princes, and kings," etc. See "Cromwell's death and funeral order," *Diary of Thomas Burton, Esq., Vol. 2: April 1657–February 1658* (1828), 516–30. Accessed 3 October 2013 at: http://www.british-history.ac.uk/report.aspx?compid=36889.

11 The traditional social order is preserved in the hierarchical presentation of participants. In ascending order, the name "John Milton" is number 201, the name of his friend "John Bradshaw," former Lord President of the Council from 1649 to 1651, is number 281, and "John Thurloe," the current Secretary of State and Milton's boss, is number 329 among 380 named dignitaries, the latter of whom include "Edward Earl of Manchester, Henry Lord Lawrence, President of the Council: all their trains borne" (ibid.).

12 *Samson Agonistes* (1671), ll. 40–1; *The Riverside Milton*, ed. Roy Flannagan, 803.

13 *Defensio*, CPW 4.i: 457.

14 *Mercurius Politicus* 443 (25 November 1658): 30.

15 *Pro Populo Anglicano Defensio*, CPW 4.i: 303–4.

16 Richard Overton, *The Hunting of the Foxes* (21 March 1649), 12.

17 "Like Lucan's Hell," Norbrook aptly reminds us, "Milton's is a disconcerting mixture of political discourses, so that it is hard for the republican reader to know when to applaud" (*Writing the English Republic: Poetry, Rhetoric, and Politics, 1627–1660* [Cambridge: Cambridge University Press, 1999], 452).

18 Hughes, CPW 3: 199, n42: "Milton expected his readers to recognize his authority as Aristotle's discussion of the merits and origin of the various kinds of kingship in the *Politics*, III, ix and x."

19 *Mercurius Aulicus* (1 April 1644), 917.

20 Ibid. (27 September 1644), 543.

21 Richard Overton and William Walwyn, *A Remonstrance of Many Thousand Citizens* (7 July 1646), 3.

22 William Empson, *Milton's God* (London: Chatto & Windus, 1961), 55.

23 Michael Bryson, *The Tyranny of Heaven: Milton's Rejection of God as King* (Newark: University of Delaware Press; London: Associated University Presses, 2004), 25.

24 CPW 3: 212.

25 Ibid.: 204.

26 John Rushworth, "Appendix: Charles I's Declaration on the dissolution of Parliament, 1628," in *Historical Collections of Private Passages of State*, vol. 1, *1618–29* (London, 1721), 1–11. Accessed 10 May 2015 at: http://www.british-history.ac.uk/rushworth-papers/vol1/pp1-11. The rhetoric of the preamble is designed to confirm the sovereign's graciousness in explaining to his subjects his motives in the quarrel with Parliament which resulted in the *Petition of Right*, while simultaneously upholding the theory of Divine Right by insisting on his accountability to none but God.

27 *A Remonstrance of Many Thousand Citizens* (7 July 1646), 5.

28 *An Anatomy of the Lords Tyranny* (9 November 1646), 4.

29 *Politicus* 92 (11 March 1652): 1457. This is the key issue on which Nedham (and Milton, as I argue in Chapter 2 above) defended the Levellers as "Commonwealthsmen."

30 *Eikonoklastes*, in CPW 3: 362.

31 Merritt Y. Hughes, "Introduction," CPW 3: 160.

32 CPW 3: 361.

33 Foxley says only that Walwyn "quite possibly had a hand in the *Remonstrance*," though it was certainly "printed, if not authored by Overton" (*The Levellers: Radical Political Thought in the English Revolution* [Manchester and New York: Manchester University Press, 2013], 154).

34 *Politicus* 17 (3 October 1650): 278.

35 *Mercurius Britanicus* 108 (8 December 1645): 953.

36 In *The Legal Fundamental Liberties* (8 June; 2nd ed., 4 August 1649), Lilburne claimed that both Cromwell "and his son in Law *Ireton*, were at that time, both openly in your House, and in the General Councel at *Putney, nay, and gave him leave to peruse and correct with his own hands, their Proposals and Declarations, before they published them*: And yet when the King would be no longer subservient to *Oliver* and his sons designs, they as the principal instruments, caused his head to be chopt off as a Traytor, and Tyrant" (4).

37 Virgil, *Aeneid*, trans. Robert Fitzgerald (1983; New York: Vintage, 1985), 219.

38 *Eikonoklastes*, CPW 3: 601.

39 *The Readie and Easie Way*, in rev. ed. CPW 7: 463.

40 *The Likeliest Means*, in rev. ed. CPW 7: 274.

41 *Politicus* 91 (4 March 1652): 1442.

42 Norbrook rightly holds that, "In giving a semi-republican rhetoric to Satan … Milton was linking him more closely with Cromwell than with either Charles. Like Lucan, he demonstrates how republican ideals can become corrupted by personal ambition" (*Writing the English Republic*, 442).

43 *Politicus* 69 (2 October 1651): 1093.

44 Richard Overton, *The Hunting of the Foxes* (21 March 1649), 2.

CHAPTER FOUR

1 James A. Freeman, *Milton and the Martial Muse: "Paradise Lost" and European Traditions of War* (Princeton, NJ: Princeton University Press, 1980), links "the Great Consult" to contemporary English history, remarking that, "During the spring term of 1647, the Long Parliament allowed an innovation: two representatives elected from each squared regiment were allowed to appear on behalf of the army. No doubt competent spokesmen, these 'Agitators' brought into Parliament the acrid smell of powder" (99–100). By such means, "the speaking soldier was familiar to Englishmen before they read *Paradise Lost*" (100). He does not connect the debate in Hell with the autumn's extra-parliamentary debates at Putney, though he does link "Leveller agents" to the Agitators.

2 J.M. French, *Life Records* 2: 286. "Die Martis [Tuesday] the 8th of Ianuarij 1649 [1650] … That Mr Milton doe prepare something in answer to the Booke of Saltmatius, and when hee hath done itt bring itt to the Councell."

3 "Selections from Salmasius' *Defensio Regia*," trans. Kathryn A. McEuen. *CPW* 4.ii: 988. While I follow Don Wolfe's lucid and compelling analysis of "Milton's Reply to the Great Salmasius," I differ from him in seeking to historicize Milton's concept of the "Army," limiting it, that is to say, to a justifiable conflation of the "people" with the "Army" in 1647 that increasingly became a lost ideal to be recovered.

4 Rachel Foxley makes the reasonable observation that, "The army did not have to struggle to identify with the rights of Englishmen: they were their own rights, and it was for those rights that they had fought in the first place." Furthermore, "The army's growing sense of themselves as Englishmen among other Englishmen, whether soldier or civilian, was spurred by the very urgent realization that they would soon lose any special protections they could expect while part of an army" (*The Levellers: Radical Political Thought in the English Revolution* [Manchester and New York: Manchester University Press, 2013], 166–7).

5 *Englands Birth-Right Justified Against all Arbitrary Usurpation* (10 October 1645), 1. For a full discussion of Lilburne's strategy of taking at their word the declarations of Parliament in its struggle with the King published in March 1643, see Andrew Sharp, "John Lilburne and the Long Parliament's Book of Declarations: A Radical's Exploitation of the Words of Authorities," *History of Political Thought* 9, no. 1 (1988): 19–44.

6 Lilburne, *A New Complaint of an old Grievance* (23 November 1647), 2.

7 Austin Woolrych, "The Debates from the Perspective of the Army," in *The Putney Debates of 1647: The Army, the Levellers and the English State*, ed. Michael Mendle (Cambridge: Cambridge University Press, 2001), 55.

8 H.N. Brailsford, *The Levellers and the English Revolution*, ed. Christopher Hill (London: The Cresset Press, 1961), 175.

9 Quoted in Woolrych, "The Debates," 57.

10 Brailsford, *The Levellers*, 176–7.

11 "A Representation of the Army," *Puritanism and Liberty: Being the Army Debates (1647–49) from the Clarke Manuscripts with Supplementary Documents*, ed. A.S.P. Woodhouse (London: J.M. Dent & Sons, 1938), 404.

12 Woolrych, "The Debates," 63.

13 Rachel Foxley offers a salutary reminder, however, that none of these documents "aspire[d] to constitute a polity from scratch. The wording of the first two Agreements and their associated documents certainly gave no hint of any such grandiose intention. There was no principled assertion of the original power of the people to create a polity; no statement of the purposes of society or government; no assertion that this was an originary moment and the foundation of something new" (*The Levellers*, 79).

14 Richard Overton, *Eighteene Reasons Propounded to the Soldiers of the Body of the Army* (13 August 1647), 3.

15 Brailsford, *The Levellers*, 248. The fleeing Independents were to return the favour on 6 December 1648, in Colonel Pride's Purge. But that was still fifteen months in the future, after the bitterness of a second Civil War.

16 Foxley, *The Levellers*, 169–70.

17 By now, most historians have rejected the claim of Barbara Taft that William Walwyn was its silent author, and have recognized John Wildman either as the sole author or else collator of the first *Agreement*. See Elliot Vernon and Philip Baker, "Introduction," in *The Agreements*, ed. Baker and Vernon (2012), 3–4.

18 *Putney Projects: Or the Old Serpent in a new Forme*" (30 December 1647), 2.

19 The block lettering in *Putney Projects* appears in the original.

20 Ian Gentles, "The New Model Army and the Constitutional Crisis of the Late 1640s," in *The Agreements*, ed. Baker and Vernon (2012), rightly points out that "*The Heads of the Proposals* was constitutionally innovatory in providing for biennial parliaments" as well as for "a long list of social reforms" (143), although he is silent on Wildman's furious complaint about Ireton's double-dealing in favour of the king.

21 This page is misnumbered 18, on a second sheet following another numbered 18–19. Block letters are in the original.

22 Barbara Donagan, "The Army, the State and the Soldier in the English Civil War," in *The Putney Debates of 1647*, ed. Michael Mendle (Cambridge: Cambridge University Press, 2001), 79.

23 Ian Gentles, "The New Model Army," believes that "the likely draughtsman" was "the agitator Edward Sexby" (145).

24 "Extracts from 'The Case of the Army Truly Stated,'" in *The Putney Debates: The Levellers*, ed. Philip Baker (London: Verso, 2007), 31–2.

25 Ian Gentles, "The New Model Army," 146.

26 John Wildman, *A Cal to all the Souldiers of the Armie* (29 October 1647), 4.

27 Baker, ed. "Case of the Army," in *The Putney Debates*, 35.

28 Foxley, *The Levellers*, 170.

29 Blair Worden, "The Levellers in History and Memory, c. 1660–1960," in *The Putney Debates of 1647*, ed. Michael Mendle (Cambridge: Cambridge University Press, 2001), 280–1.

30 Lilburne, *The Charters of London* (18 December 1646), 4.

31 Edward Vallance, "The Origins of the *Agreements*," in *The Agreements*, ed. Baker and Vernon (2012), very reasonably asks whether, "Rather than talking about elections, as is usually assumed, was Rainborough speaking of the moment when the *Agreement* would be tendered to the nation for subscription, when all men would choose whether to put themselves 'under that government'?" (42).

32 Col. Thomas Rainsborough, quoted in *Puritanism and Liberty: Being the Army Debates (1647–49) from the Clarke Manuscripts with Supplementary Documents*, ed. A.S.P. Woodhouse (London: J.M. Dent & Sons, 1938), 53.

33 Michael Mendle, "Putney's Pronouns: Identity and Indemnity in the Great Debate," in *The Putney Debates of 1647*, ed. Michael Mendle (Cambridge: Cambridge University Press, 2001), 137–8.

34 Foxley, *The Levellers*, 92–9. She adds that, "while Ireton could not concede to Englishmen any direct connection to the state" at Putney, "the radicals had a way of connecting individuals directly with their nation and polity," which "must surely be due to Lilburne's influence" (112).

35 Foxley insists that, contrary to "the standard revisionist historiography," "The Putney debates and the promotion of the Agreement marked not the end but the beginning of a potentially fertile alliance between civilian Levellers and army radicals" (*The Levellers*, 158).

36 S.R. Gardiner, *History of the Great Civil War*, 4 vols. (1894; New York: AMS Press, 1965), 4:16.

37 Ian Gentles, "*The Agreements of the People* and Their Political Contexts, 1647–1649," in *The Putney Debates of 1647*, ed. Michael Mendle (2001), 155.

38 Overton, *A New Bull-Bayting* (7 August 1649), 7.

39 *Mercurius Politicus* 70 (9 October 1651): 1109.

40 Overton, *A New Bull-Bayting*, 6.

41 See above, Chapter 2, 76–99.

42 See above, Chapter 2, 99–101.

43 Wildman, *A Cal to all the Soldiers of the Army by the Free People of England* (29 October 1647), 4.

44 *Mercurius Pragmaticus* 12 (7 December 1647): 2 (although unpaginated).

45 Ibid. 3 (6 October 1647): 20.

46 Ibid. 4 (12 October 1647): 4 (although unpaginated).

47 Foxley, *The Levellers*, 53.

48 *Mercurius Pragmaticus* 1 (21 September 1647): 3.

49 See above, Chapter 2, 64–6; see also Lilburne's *Englands Birth-Right Justified* (October 1645), 17–18, 32; *Innocency and Truth Justified* (6 January 1646), 22, 26, 41–3, 46; *The Just Mans Justification* (10 June 1646), 2–5, 17–19; and *The Free-mans Freedome Vindicated* (23 June 1646), 8.

50 Lilburne, *Londons Liberty in Chains discovered* (2 November 1646), 67.

51 Robert Baillie, *Letters and Journals* (Edinburgh: William Creech & William Gray, 1775), 2:60.

52 Sir Philip Warwick, *Memoires of the Reign of King Charles I*, 3d. edn. (1701; London: Richard Chiswell, 1703), 246.

53 Milton was not likely to know what Lilburne heard in the aftermath of the Battle of Newbury (27 October 1644), when Manchester infamously defended his policy in a Council of War, "That if we beat the King 99 times yet he is King still, and so will his posterity be after him, but if the King beat us once we shall all be hanged, and our posterity be made slaves." See *Calendar of State Papers of the Reign of Charles I: 1644–1645*, ed. William Douglas Hamilton (London: The Queen's Printer, 1890), 151.

54 Lilburne, *The Copy of a Letter* (9 August 1645), 11, misnumbered 15.

55 Jason Peacey, "The People of the *Agreements*: The Levellers, Civil War Radicalism and Political Participation," in *The Agreements*, ed. Baker and Vernon (2012),

believes that Wildman is the likely author of the Putney *Agreement* of October–November 1647, where he argues "for a radical reconstitution of political society" (58), and where his "anonymous *Cal to all the Souldiers* represented little less than an incitement to mutiny" (71, n47).

56 Lilburne, *The Just Mans Justification* (10 June 1646), 11.

57 *A Remonstrance of Many Thousand Citizens* (7 July 1646), 4.

58 *The Free-mans Freedome Vindicated* (23 June 1646), 8.

59 *An Alarum to the House of Lords* (31 July 1646), 5.

60 What Mammon advocates, writes Martin Dzelzainis, "is, in almost every respect, unmistakably a version of Milton's classical republic," save for the fact that Mammon "is the very personification of wealth, the great enemy of republics," and that he "conspicuously fails to mention what alone could give it some hope of success: the virtues" that are the absolute prerequisite to a classical republic in the thought of Milton's favourite Latin historian, Sallust ("Milton's Classical Republicanism," in *Milton and Republicanism*, ed. David Armitage et al. [Cambridge: Cambridge University Press, 1995], 23–4).

61 The point is that Milton now rejects classical republicanism in the person of Mammon.

62 See my "Introduction" above, 7–14.

63 See my Chapter 2, 71–5.

64 Lilburne, *The Legal Fundamental Liberties of the People of* ENGLAND, 2nd ed. (4 August 1649), 39.

65 There is nothing to have prevented, but also nothing to confirm, his presence at the Whitehall debates, which, as Frances Henderson, "Drafting," in *The Agreements*, ed. Baker and Vernon (2012), points out, were "very well attended, not only by army officers but also, particularly in the early days, by a large number of civilians" (169).

66 David Norbrook helpfully remarks that Milton's "Satan has very pronounced associations with Lucan's Caesar, and had the poem appeared in a period of republican revival, it is likely that readers would have looked back to Cromwell as the last instantiation of the general principle of the corruptions inherent in rule by a single person" (*Writing the English Republic: Poetry, Rhetoric, and Politics, 1627–1660* [Cambridge: Cambridge University Press, 1999], 442).

67 His failure to account for this line reveals the apparent disingenuousness of Empson's critique of "omnipotence," if not his actual gerrymandering of the evidence.

68 Dzelzainis nicely sums up the "outcome of this debate, in which a republican moment yields to the adventure of a single person" ("Milton's Classical Republicanism," 24).

69 Lilburne, *Legal Fundamental Liberties*, 64.

70 Ibid., 31.

71 Lilburne, *As You Were* (Amsterdam: May 1652), 15; Wildman, *Putney Projects* (30 December 1647), 6.

72 Ian Gentles, "*The Agreements of the People* and Their Political Contexts, 1647–1649," in *The Putney Debates of 1647*, ed. Michael Mendle, 153.

CHAPTER FIVE

1 The subtitle of *Tyranipocrit, Discovered with his wiles* (14 August 1649) is Walwyn's retort to his attackers in *Walwins Wiles* (23 April 1649) for his "great Hypocrisie" in using "Religion … to mussle the understandings of over-credulous and flexible men" (3). *Walwins Wiles* was the work of John Price and six other London Baptist and Independent ministers who had vilified him "as the brains of the Leveller movement: the subtle framer and manager of their petitions; the smooth beguiler and persuader, more crafty than his colleagues," who was "the real author of the treasonable *Second Part of Englands New-Chaines Discovered*" (Don M. Wolfe, *Milton in the Puritan Revolution* [1941; London: Cohen & West, 1963], 175). *Tyranipocrit*, in fact, is Walwyn's third defence of himself in as many months – the first in *The Fountain of Slaunder Discovered* (30 May 1649), the second in *Walwyns Just Defence* (June/July 1649) – and bears thematic signatures from previous works, such as "al you proud tyrants, which have your dinners served in with trumpets, and wil have men kneele to you, and wil bee drawne in costly coaches, with six or eight horses, as though you triumphed over the poore people" (22), when it would be far more Christian "if all men did love their poore neighbours as themselves" (38). With Overton in *A Remonstrance* (7 July 1646), Walwyn had chided: "Nay, yee suffer poor Christians, for whom Christ died to kneel before you in the street, aged, sick and cripled, begging your halfe-penny Charities, and yee rushe by them in your Coaches and silkes daily, without regard, or taking any course for their constant reliefe" (16). There is likewise Walwyn's signature theme of Christian love in *Tyranipocrit* – e.g., "the whole law is love" (8); "love respecteth both God and man, but faith doth not so respect his brother, and therefore faith is not so perfect as love is" (20); "hee that loveth God, and not man, hee hateth them both" (42). This is the entire burden of his *Compassionate Samaritan* (29 July 1644), where "the love of God appears most in doing good for others" (4). Regarding his other unsigned writings, Rachel Foxley comments that "Walwyn's contributions to co-authored Leveller works may be quite extensive, but until he was imprisoned with the other Leveller leaders in 1649 he avoided putting his name to political works" (*The Levellers* [Manchester University Press, 2013], 9). In *Tyranipocrit*, he reverts to anonymity, saying, "I have concealed my name, because the Readers shall consider what is written, and not who wrote it, because partiality, if the Author were knowne, might make the worke hatefull" (6). It was certain in any event to be hateful to the authors of *Walwins Wiles*, who, "by their most uncharitable Book, raising up a whole legion of scandals and slanders against me, a necessity was upon me, to shew these men as they are not as they labour by hypocrisie to appear unto the world" (*Just Defence*, 33).

2 *Calvin: Institutes of the Christian Religion*, ed. John T. McNeill; trans. Ford Lewis Battles. *The Library of Christian Classics*, vol. 21 (Philadelphia: The Westminster Press, 1960), 3.23.2. (Hereafter cited by *Institutes*, book, chapter, section, as in 3.23.2).

3 William Empson, *Milton's God* (London: Chatto & Windus, 1961), 146.

4 J.B. Broadbent, *Some Graver Subject: An Essay on "Paradise Lost"* (London: Chatto & Windus, 1960), 144.

5 Michael Lieb, "Milton's 'Dramatick Constitution': The Celestial Dialogue in *Paradise Lost*, Book III," *Milton Studies* 23 (1987): 225.

6 On this topic, see Michael Bryson, *The Tyranny of Heaven: Milton's Rejection of God as King* (Newark: University of Delaware Press; London: Associated University Presses, 2004), 112–25.

7 Calvin, *Institutes*, 3.23.7 (956 n18), citing Augustine, *On Rebuke and Grace*, *x*. 27.

8 This is a point first made by A.J.A. Waldock, *"Paradise Lost" and Its Critics* (1947; Cambridge: Cambridge University Press, 1962), 102–3.

9 See my "Introduction," 19–20.

10 Walwyn, *Englands Lamentable Slaverie* (October 1645), 5.

11 This idea is found as well in Cicero, *De inventione*, trans. H.M. Hubbell, Loeb Classical Library (Cambridge, MA: Harvard University Press, 1949), II.53.159; see my discussion above in Chapter 2, 74–5.

12 This sense of the Father as *eiron* is my irreducible point of difference from Bryson, who maintains that, "Whereas Satan means to overthrow the Father and take him down from a heavenly throne, the Son adopts an end more radical than Satan's (and closer to Milton's) while employing means hitherto unseen in Milton's Heaven: he fights – through reason, self-sacrifice, and self-denial – to overturn heavenly kingship, to refuse thrones both earthly and heavenly, and to abolish kingship itself by reclaiming a Miltonic, internal definition of glory, heroism, and true government" (Bryson, *The Tyranny of Heaven*, 115).

13 Irene Samuel, "The Dialogue in Heaven: A Reconsideration of *Paradise Lost*, III, 1–417," *PMLA* 72 (1957): 605.

14 Bryson's reading in *The Tyranny* of the Son's career throughout *Paradise Lost* and *Paradise Regained* shares a debt that I also acknowledge to Samuel's pioneering reading.

15 Hugh MacCallum, *Milton and the Sons of God: The Divine Image in Milton's Epic Poetry* (Toronto: University of Toronto Press, 1986), 108.

16 See my "Introduction," n60, for an initial discussion of the authorship of this pamphlet.

17 *Vox Plebis* (19 November 1646), 4. The pamphlet contains excerpts from Machiavelli's *Discourses* "which allow us to identify as one probable author of *Vox Plebis* Nedham himself" (Jonathan Scott, *Commonwealth Principles: Republican Writing of the English Revolution* [Cambridge: Cambridge University Press, 2004], 83–4).

18 David Wootton, "Leveller Democracy and the Puritan Revolution," in *The Cambridge History of Political Thought, 1450–1700*, ed. J.H. Burns (Cambridge: Cambridge University Press, 1991), 438, 437.

19 Martin Dawes makes this point with respect to the Father in "Milton's Ironic God: *Paradise Lost* and the Trials of History" (MA thesis, University of Manitoba, 2004, dir. Dr David Williams), 79.

20 Empson reads the colloquy in Heaven, like the council in Hell, as another "political trick rigged up to impress the surviving angels; the Son is free to remark (III.

245) that he knows the Father won't let him stay dead, so that the incantationary repetition of the word *death* comes to seem blatantly artificial" (*Milton's God*, 124).

21 Here, Empson rightly remarks "that he does not know what is going to happen, except for a triumph at which he can rejoice" (Ibid., 126).

22 MacCallum, *Milton and the Sons of God*, 30, makes this point in a context concerning the differences between Calvin and Milton on the identity of the Son.

23 On the land-sea route between Florence and Venice stands the Arian Baptistery of Ravenna, a monument in mosaic tiles to the Christology of Arius that King Theodoric completed ca. 500 CE. It would be satisfying to say that Milton passed that way (he likely did not) on his way from Florence to Venice in 1639. The startling relevance of the image emerges in its difference from that of the Orthodox baptistery across town, where the twelve apostles similarly peer down from the circle of eternity on the scene of baptism in the River Jordan. What is tacitly "heretical" in the Arian image is the empty throne directly above Jesus' adolescent body, neatly intersected by the descent of the Dove. Here is a remarkably graphic image of the anti-Trinitarian theology of the Son, who, cut off from his heavenly origins, must somehow win his way back to that throne.

24 Subscribing to David Norbrook's notion of a Machiavellian reduction to first principles in this scene, Paul Stevens remarks that "The Son reduces himself by becoming mortal in order to restore humankind to its original condition." But in the caveat that, "for whatever reason Norbrook chooses not to emphasize the degree to which Milton's Cromwell in the *Defensio Secunda* anticipates the Son's reduction," there is more than a hint of admiration for the political strongman. The suggestion that "the Son's response to the Father in *Paradise Lost*" finds its precedent in Milton's faithful challenge to the Lord Protector in the *Second Defense* is without peer as a defence of political oligarchy. See Stevens, "Milton and National Identity," in *The Oxford Handbook of Milton*, ed. Nicholas McDowell and Nigel Smith (Oxford: Oxford University Press, 2009), 359, 361.

25 See *De Doctrina Christiana*, I, v: "Of the Son of God," for Milton's blunt rejection of the argument of an essential identity among the persons of the Holy Trinity. God, he writes, "was in a real sense Father of the Son, whom he made of his own substance. It does not follow, however, that the Son is of the same essence as the Father. Indeed, if he were, it would be quite incorrect to call him Son. For a real son is not of the same age as his father, still less of the same numerical essence: otherwise father and son would be one person" (CPW 6: 209).

26 Here, the theology of universal atonement has its political analogue in what Jason Peacey, "The People of the *Agreements*," in *The Agreements of the People*, ed. Baker and Vernon (2012), calls "a fairly remarkable degree of political openness" in later Leveller versions of the *Agreements of the People*, and "the accessibility of the system to more than merely a narrow political elite, or a community of saints" (67–8).

27 "As Empson observed," recalls Bryson, "'Milton did expect God to abdicate.' While not going so far as Empson, David Norbrook raises the issue of divine abdication when he refers to the episode at 3.312–19 as being 'closely parallel to a king's

abdicating and showing solidarity with his people'" (Bryson, *The Tyranny of Heaven*, 130).

28 This is my basic difficulty with Bryson's reading, which holds that "the Father is aware of his position, and his plans for the Son indicate his desire to relinquish power," and yet completely ignores the necessity of divine irony in ensuring the liberty of the subject. Thus, Bryson concludes, "Milton's dilemma is how to create a poetic God who is a dictator but who can 'feel himself justified in stopping being a dictator'" (Ibid., 130–1).

29 In his *Milton: A Structural Reading* (London: Edward Arnold, 1974), Donald F. Bouchard relies as much on Empson as he does on Roland Barthes's "The Death of the Author" to argue that God envisages "his own eradication before man's freedom," and that "the real import of the epic" is its Nietzschean design to prove that "God is dead that man may live" (64). See Brian Johnson, "Sacred Silence: The Death of the 'Author' and *Paradise Lost*," *Milton Quarterly* 29, no. 3 (October 1995): 65–76.

30 Recalling Milton's praise of Queen Christina of Sweden in *Defensio Secunda* (1654), David Norbrook says that it "comes in retrospect to seem something less than a digression. For it has gone as far as Milton is prepared to go in defence of monarchy, only to suggest that the best monarch is one who is ready to abdicate" (*Writing the English Republic: Poetry, Rhetoric, and Politics, 1627–1660* [Cambridge: Cambridge University Press, 1999], 335). Richard Cromwell's meek acceptance of his ouster as Lord Protector on 25 May 1659 likely contributed as well to Milton's portrait of divine "abdication" in Book 3.

31 Hill notes that "At Servetus's trial in 1553 the prosecution had strongly emphasized the socially subversive consequences of his heresy. Pacifism and rejection of oaths tended to be associated with the same group of heresies. A ballad about John Lewis, burnt in 1583 for anti-Trinitarianism, adds the interesting detail that he 'did thou each wight,' that is, he employed the outward symbol of insistence on human equality which was later to be adopted by the Quakers" (*Milton and the English Revolution* [London: Faber & Faber, 1977], 288).

32 The established view is that of Don Wolfe, who has argued that "The government of heaven, as described by Milton, accords ideally with the pattern of his commonwealth principles … When the Son is appointed by God to reign as the active head of Heaven's hierarchy, the angelic hosts, though they have had no voice whatever in his selection, pay their homage in joyful song." Wolfe, in other words, turns this scene into Exhibit A of Milton's increasingly aristocratic "conception of the rule of the virtuous" (*Milton* in *the Puritan Revolution* [1941; London: Cohen & West, 1963], 343) after the fall of the Commonwealth, rather than an Areopagitican argument for liberty, or a 1640s-style "Self-Denying Ordinance" and divine decentring and diffusion of power.

33 Brian Manning, *The English People and the English Revolution, 1640–1649* (London: Heinemann, 1976), 306.

34 Philip Baker, "The Levellers, Decentralisation, and the *Agreements of the People*," in *The Agreements*, ed. Baker and Vernon (2012), argues that "The Levellers' belief in individual liberty of conscience, free from human control by either a coercive national church or a persecuting civil magistrate, was integral to their notion of self-government within the dispersed state" (105). This, as I repeatedly point out, was Milton's belief as well.

35 *Politicus* 39 (6 March 1651): 623.

36 Baker, "The Levellers, Decentralisation, and the *Agreements*," 104–5.

37 Ian Gentles, "The New Model Army and the Constitutional Crisis of the Late 1640s," in *The Agreements*, ed. Baker and Vernon (2012), 157.

38 *Politicus* 71 (16 October 1651): 1125.

39 Ibid. 73 (30 October 1651): 1157.

40 Roger Lejosne, for one, insists "that Milton's treatment of God's heavenly kingship and Satan's rebellion can be viewed as complementary elements in his republican strategy," and "that he made monarchy in Heaven justify republicanism on earth." See his "Milton, Satan, Salmasius, and Abdiel," in *Milton and Republicanism*, ed. David Armitage, Armand Himy, and Quentin Skinner (Cambridge: Cambridge University Press, 1995), 106.

41 Milton, Hill writes, "had been a radical millenarian long before an organized Fifth Monarchist movement existed … The Fifth Monarchists shared many of Milton's views, including condemnation of tithes and a state church. But they were a plebeian semi-anarchist group, and as they saw Christ's cause foundering in the fifties, some of them were goaded into direct action by a combination of impatience and despair, both of which Milton repudiated" (*Milton and the English Revolution*, 283–4). My own sense is that the reading strategies required by *Paradise Lost* turn Fifth Monarchist beliefs into the equivalent of performative verbs adapted to views that Milton apparently shared with Walwyn of "religion as two free-wils joyned in one."

CHAPTER SIX

1 Sandra M. Gilbert, "Patriarchal Poetry and Women Readers: Reflections on Milton's Bogey," *PMLA* 93, no. 3 (May 1978): 368–82.

2 *Tetrachordon*, CPW 2: 589.

3 Mary Nyquist, "The Genesis of Gendered Subjectivity," in *Re-membering Milton: Essays on the Texts and Traditions*, ed. Mary Nyquist and Margaret W. Ferguson (New York and London: Methuen, 1988), 107.

4 Barbara Kiefer Lewalski, *"Paradise Lost" and the Rhetoric of Literary Forms* (Princeton: Princeton University Press, 1985), 178–9.

5 Susan Wiseman, "Eve, *Paradise Lost*, and Female Interpretation," *The Oxford Handbook of Milton*, ed. Nicholas McDowell and Nigel Smith (Oxford: Oxford University Press, 2009), 541.

6 James Grantham Turner, *One Flesh: Paradisal Marriage and Sexual Relations in the Age of Milton* (Oxford: The Clarendon Press, 1987), remarks that, "Even the first description of the couple, a dramatic and didactic *tableau vivant* of Genesis 1 and 2, is framed by the presence of Satan," so "that the only observer, the only subject to whom these qualities 'seemed' a product of 'their sex,' is Satan himself. Indeed, the subjective impression of the couple receives an emphasis unusual even in Milton – 'seemed' is repeated three times in the sentence introducing them, each time as a main verb" (266).

7 Lilburne, *The Free-Mans Freedome Vindicated* (23 June 1646), 11.

8 David Wootton, "Leveller Democracy and the Puritan Revolution," in *The Cambridge History of Political Thought, 1450–1700*, ed. J.H. Burns (Cambridge: Cambridge University Press, 1991), 437.

9 See my "Introduction" n60 and n72; see also Chapter 2, n37.

10 *Regall Tyrannie discovered* is dated in the customary hand of George Thomason (6 January 1647); beneath the title, in the same hand, is written, "*by Lilburne*," although Lilburne had attributed it to "some of my friends" (see "Introduction," n32, above). Like Merritt Y. Hughes in his "Introduction" to CPW 3: 27, Jonathan Scott is willing to take Thomason's word for it, noting that, "Like Nedham later, Lilburne's *Regall Tyrannie discovered* (January 1647) collapsed the (Aristotelian) distinctions between tyranny and monarchy, subjection and slavery" (*Commonwealth Principles*, 248). Scott's notice of Marchamont Nedham's reliance on the same argument, together with his similar usages of legal precedent and English history, ought to have led him to identify Nedham as the likely author of *Regall Tyrannie*.

11 See above, Chapter 1, 44–8.

12 See above, Chapter 1, n44.

13 Given the omission of Lilburne's repeated phrase "by nature" in this clause – "none of them *having* [by nature] *any authority, dominion, or magisterial power, one over, or above another, but by institution, or donation*" (7) – the absence of "equal" in *Regall Tyrannie discovered* is most likely a printer's error.

14 Milton knew equally well such ancient arguments for equality as that of Tacitus, who, in *The Annals of Imperial Rome*, trans. Michael Grant, 1956 (London: The Folio Society, 2006), claimed (3.26) that "Primitive man had no evil desires ... But when men ceased to be equal, egotism replaced fellow-feeling and decency succumbed to violence. The result was despotism" (103). The primal equality imagined by the Roman historian, however, was androcentric and thus contrary to the gender equality inherent in the Leveller icon.

15 In *Feminist Milton* (Ithaca and London: Cornell University Press, 1987), Joseph Wittreich offers incontrovertible evidence that women readers, for more than a century after its publication, found in *Paradise Lost* "an acculturating narrative – a forging ground for their own ideal of educated and responsible womanhood, an ideal then founded upon sexual equality rather than, as today, upon sexual difference" (4). While Wittreich observes the circumstance of the poem's composition

at a time when "the Quakers were awarding women equality with men and crediting both sexes with the capacity for prophesying" (108), he fails to note how this discourse of equality, shared by Quakers, Anabaptists, and Ranters, first acquired its political form in the Leveller icon of marriage.

16 Mikhail Bakhtin, *The Dialogic Imagination*, ed. Michael Holquist, trans. Caryl Emerson and Michael Holquist (Austin: University of Texas Press, 1981), 324, 12–14.

17 Ibid., 303. For a full-scale discussion of Bakhtinian techniques in the poem, see Luann Hiebert, "Milton's *Paradise Lost* as a Proto-Novel" (MA thesis, University of Manitoba, 2007, dir. Dr David Williams), esp. Chapter 2, "The Double Voice of the Divine Word: New Political Worlds in the Making" (40–73); and Chapter 3, "New Social Worlds in the Making," (74–120).

18 Bakhtin's sociolinguistics are not that far from the structuralist linguistics of my friend and former student Martin Kuester in *Milton's Prudent Ambiguities: Words and Signs in his Poetry and Prose* (Lanham, MD: University Press of America, 2009), where he argues that, "In our – and Milton's – times, the description of the prelapsarian world and language is not possible in any but our own 'fallen' language that is geared to our fallen sensibilities. However, this fallen linguistic sensibility also opens up a whole range of creative and artistic possibilities of using language, and *Paradise Lost* itself depends on the limitations and possibilities of fallen language" (75).

19 In *Milton's Eve* (Urbana and Chicago: University of Illinois Press, 1983), Diane Kelsey McColley, taking the narrator at his word, contextualizes "Not equal, as thir sex not equal seemd" in terms of "Richard Hooker's explanation of the 'subalternation' between them: woman, he says, 'was even in her first estate framed by Nature, not only after in time, but inferiour in excellency also unto man, howbeit in so due and sweet proportion, as being presented before our eyes, might be sooner perceived then defined'" (22).

20 Hugh MacCallum, *Milton and the Sons of God: The Divine Image in Milton's Epic Poetry* (Toronto: University of Toronto Press, 1986), 201.

21 *CPW* 2: 338.

22 Similarly, McColley notes that "the narrator tells us only what even Satan, with his vestiges of heavenly percipience limited by his lost sense of process and response, is able to discern. And, as is often true, we the readers are expected to be more perceptive not only than Satan, to whom Adam and Eve are a 'sight tormenting,' but than the narrator also, who at this point has adopted his persona of the excellent conventional observer" (*Milton's Eve*, 40).

23 In *One Flesh*, James Turner remarks that "The effect of continual discovery is generated by the narrative design itself, which builds up a texture of overlapping viewpoints" in a manner "that anticipates the epistolary novel" (266).

24 As a "cormorant," Satan appears to bring the threat of monarchy to a paradisal democracy, given that James I had made the bird emblematic of the house of Stuart. For example, an "expense account" of John Wood, "Master of the Cormorants" to

James I (his son Robert would serve Charles I in the same capacity), "explains why the birds of Fontainebleau in 1625, 'which all have been sent by the King of England to the King of France as a present, along with the trainers and intructors of these birds,' only obeyed English commands" (3). See Marcus Beike, "The History of Cormorant Fishing in Europe," *Vogelwelt* 133 (2012): 1–21. Accessed 30 September 2016 at: http://www.vogelwelt.com/cms/red/download/Beike-Kormoran-engl.pdf.

25 Overton, *An Appeale From the degenerate Representative Body* (17 July 1647), 6.

26 Rachel Foxley, "Freedom of Conscience and the *Agreements of the People*," in *The Agreements*, ed. Baker and Vernon (2012), 125.

27 Don Wolfe has argued more generally that "Milton consistently assumed that the law of nature was a code of abstract justice superior to the law of the state; by the law of nature individuals had reserved to them certain just privileges which the state had no right to abrogate. This assumption was, of course, inherent in the *Agreements of the People* promulgated by the Levellers" (*Milton* in *the Puritan Revolution* [1941; London: Cohen & West, 1963], 328).

28 *Politicus* 79 (11 December 1651), 1257.

29 Ibid. 92 (11 March 1652), 1457.

30 Andrew Sharp, "Introduction: The English Levellers, 1645–1649," in *The English Levellers*, ed. Andrew Sharp (Cambridge: Cambridge University Press, 1998), xx.

31 A.S.P. Woodhouse, ed., *Puritanism and Liberty: Being the Army Debates (1647–49) from the Clarke Manuscripts, with Supplementary Documents* (London: J.M. Dent & Sons, 1938), 61.

32 "An Order for printing the shorter Catechism, and the Title thereto, were read; and agreed unto, with the Addition of a Proviso for the Continuance of restraining the Printing of this Catechism, that it shall continue for a Twelvemonth, and no longer," House of Commons *Journal*, Volume 6: 22 September 1648. *Journal of the House of Commons*, vol. 6: *1648–1651* (1802): 27–8. British History Online. Accessed 11 December 2013 at: http://www.british-history.ac.uk/report.aspx?compid=25475&strquery=catechism.

33 *The Westminster Larger Catechism … with the Proofs from the Scripture.* Accessed 11 December 2013 at: https://puritanseminary.org/wp-content/uploads/2013/09/Larger_Catechism.pdf.

34 *Mercurius Pragmaticus* (29 August 1648): 5–6 (although unpaginated).

35 John M. Wallace, "The Date of Sir Robert Filmer's *Patriarcha*," *The Historical Journal* 23, no. 1 (March 1980): 155–65.

36 Christopher Hill, *The Century of Revolution, 1603–1714* (Edinburgh: Thomas Nelson & Sons, 1961), 251.

37 Ibid., 234.

38 Thomas Hobbes, who knew Filmer and had read his work in manuscript, made this principle of "patriarchal right" central to his argument in *Leviathan* (1651).

39 In "The Politics of Poetry: Feminism and *Paradise Lost*," *Milton Studies* 14 (1980), Joan Malory Webber remarked how "*Paradise Lost* is the first epic whose scene is,

in effect, the home, woman's traditional sphere, rather than the world of warfare and quest outside" (12). In rereading the work of one who died too soon, with so many gaps left to fill in her extraordinarily capacious vision, I find that, for several decades, I have been brooding on the larger reaches of this essay without being fully conscious of it.

40 Mark Edmundson, *Towards Reading Freud: Self-Creation in Milton, Wordsworth, Emerson, and Sigmund Freud* (Princeton: Princeton University Press, 1990), 58.

41 Edmundson fairly describes this stage of her development in Freudian terms of "primary narcissism," which, because it "is self-love prior to self-consciousness," is also "self-love that, because it is confined within images (or the imaginary, as Lacan would have it), cannot name itself" (ibid., 59).

42 Lewalski, *The Rhetoric of Literary Forms*, 186.

43 Cf. Christine Froula, "When Eve Reads Milton: Undoing the Canonical Economy," *Critical Inquiry* 10, no. 2 (December 1983): "The invisible voice that guides Eve away from the visible image of herself in the world to him whose image she is allegorizes what is literally the *secret* not only of spiritual and literary authority in Milton's poem but of cultural authority as such," where "invisibility is a *definitive* attribute of authority: the power of the voice and of the church fathers, like that of the Wizard of Oz, resides in and depends upon invisibility" (330).

44 *The resolved mans Resolution* (24 May 1647), 11–12.

45 More than a decade later, patriarchal authority was to be reconfirmed in more ribald fashion in the Cavalier Parliament. Remarking on "the simple light discourse that sometimes is in the Parliament-house," Samuel Pepys recounts "how in the late business of Chymny-money, when all occupyers were to pay, it was questioned whether women were under that name to pay, and somebody rose and said that they were not occupiers, but occupied." See the entry for 7 May 1662, *The Diary of Samuel Pepys*, vol. 3, ed. Robert Latham and William Matthews (Berkeley and Los Angeles: University of California Press, 1970), 78.

46 As Brailsford adds in *The Levellers and the English Revolution*, ed. Christopher Hill (London: The Cresset Press, 1961), "The most likely author was, surely, Mrs Chidley," 318, n8.

47 Woodhouse, *Puritanism and Liberty*, 367–8.

48 Lewalski, *The Rhetoric of Literary Forms*, 187.

49 Turner, *One Flesh*, describes Eve's song as "eighteen lines of blank verse with the grace and recapitulative pattern of an Elizabethan sonnet" (245). Indeed, "Her 'Air' captures what the whole description of unfallen Eden suggests – the hypnotic strangeness of being in love, the mood of intense subjectivity in which time itself is almost suspended, becoming sweet and thick with 'amorous delay'" (246).

50 Christopher Hill gives at least a nod in this direction in *Milton and the English Revolution*, 130.

51 Pepys, *The Diary* 3: 234 (24 October 1662).

52 Here, the idea of marriage as "property" may differ from the iconic image of it in *Free-Mans Freedome*, but not in Overton's *Arrow*. One recalls how Lilburne was

forced after Putney to defend himself against Ireton and other Army Grandees who claimed "that I am the head and chiefe of a generation or faction of men that are altogether for Anarchy and confusion, and would have no government at all in the Kingdome, but have every man to doe what he list, and have all things common, and so distroy all law and property," whereas, "I am for *meum & tuum*; liberty and property" (*The additionall Plea of Lieut. Col. Iohn Lilburne* [1 November 1647], 19). For the developing link between liberty and property in his thought, see also *The oppressed mans importunate and mournfull cryes* (2nd ed., 18 April 1648), where Lilburne celebrates "all the true hearted patriots of *England*" who "were ready to lay down their lives, for the preservation of their laws and liberties … In the destruction of which we become beasts, and are no more men … And all liberty and property of *meum and tuum* is therby totally levelled, destroyed, and confounded" (1–2); and ultimately, *The Legal Fundamental Liberties of the People of England*, 2nd ed. (4 August 1649), where he repeats that "Propriety cannot be maintained if Liberty be destroyed; for the Liberty of my person is more neer to me then my Propriety, or Goods" (11). In *A Whip for the present House of Lords,* OR *The Levellers Levelled* (27 February 1648), Lilburne had already turned the tables on those who identify "Leveller" with the levelling of property, arguing "that you and your tyrannical *Lords*, and masters *Cromwel and Ireton*, and the rest of their confederat, *Grandees of the Armie, and in both Houses* … are the true and *perfect Levellers that are in being*, in the *Land of England*, having already *filled up all the ditches, and puld down all the hedges* that should be as a fence to preserve our *lives, liberties, and proprieties*, and have already *de facto, levelled* them, and all our just lawes to their *tyrannicall wills*" (2).

CHAPTER SEVEN

1 Paul Stevens, "Intolerance and the Virtues of Sacred Vehemence," in *Milton and Toleration*, ed. Sharon Achinstein and Elizabeth Sauer (Oxford: Oxford University Press, 2007), 245.

2 Clay Daniel, "Milton's Neo-Platonic Angel?" *Studies in English Literature, 1500–1900* 44, no. 1 (Winter 2004): 179, 174, 175.

3 Feisal Mohamed, *In the Anteroom of Divinity: The Reformation of the Angels from Colet to Milton* (Toronto and Buffalo: University of Toronto Press, 2008), 128.

4 E.M.W. Tillyard, *The Elizabethan World Picture* (London: Chatto & Windus, 1943), 108.

5 Douglas Bush, *John Milton: A Sketch of His Life and Writings* (New York: Collier, 1964), 162.

6 Marjorie Hope Nicolson, *John Milton: A Reader's Guide to His Poetry* (New York: The Noonday Press, 1963), 250.

7 Arthur O. Lovejoy, *The Great Chain of Being: A Study of the History of an Idea* (1936; Cambridge, MA, and London: Harvard University Press, 1964), 164.

8 Two years before Lovejoy's *The Great Chain of Being*, George Coffin Taylor published *Milton's Use of Du Bartas* (Cambridge, MA: Harvard University Press, 1934), which takes "the general philosophical principle announced by both Du Bartas and Milton" to be a "definite declaration on the part of both" of faith in "the terms of neo-Platonism" (100).

9 In the entry on "Neoplatonism in Milton" in *A Milton Encyclopedia*, vol. 5, ed. William B. Hunter et al. (Lewisburg, PA: Bucknell University Press, 1979), Jack Ashley is very careful to distinguish between "Neoplatonism" as a direct influence and the "Neoplatonic tradition," which is more eclectic by virtue of its indirect transmission (194).

10 "[A]lthough Milton is often quoted as a proponent of the Great Chain of Being," Dennis Danielson reminds us "that the main thrust of his thought is directed away from such a conception. In particular he rejects both the body-and-soul dualism that accompanies Neoplatonist theology and the suggestion that creation was accomplished by necessity or in accordance with a necessary pattern" (*Milton's Good God: A Study in Literary Theodicy* [Cambridge: Cambridge University Press, 1982] 101).

11 William G. Madsen, *From Shadowy Types to Truth: Studies in Milton's Symbolism* (New Haven and London: Yale University Press, 1968), maintains that "In his set piece on the scale of nature Raphael seems to echo … Neoplatonic doctrine," but has to concede that "The passage is heavily charged with ambivalence" (119–20).

12 This is the view of Martin Kuester in "The End of Monolithic Language: Raphael's Sematology in *Paradise Lost*," *English Studies in Canada* 15, no. 3 (1989): 275, where he suggests that "Raphael is not aware of his part as a pedagogical instrument in the prime example of instruction through irony and the continuing incarnation of the Word in *Paradise Lost.*" In *Milton's Prudent Ambiguities* (2009), he later derives this pedagogical strategy from the "godgames" of early baroque literature that appear to culminate "in the Father's method in *Paradise Lost* of turning Adam and Eve into responsible and independent human beings who are 'Sufficient to have stood, though free to fall' (*PL* III.99)" (127).

13 Clay Daniel, in "Milton's Neo-Platonic Angel," properly points out how the "homely stooping" of "heavenly grace" in *A Mask*, "like the Son's descent" in *Paradise Lost*, "ironically questions the Neo-Platonic notions of love and ascent" (174). But if Adam's love of Eve's "soul" in Book 8 exhibits a "Neo-Platonic desire for divine ascent" (179), it is really Raphael who has initiated this discourse on "ascent" (which Daniel largely ignores) in Book 5, while actively skirting the phase of "descent."

14 Jack Ashley describes a "monistic ontology" and "a process of emanation" in Raphael's doctrine "that is descending and deteriorating but cyclical" (*A Milton Encyclopedia*, 196), although he fails to note that the phase of "descent" is extremely brief in Raphael's formulation ("one Almightie is, from whom / All things proceed"), while the process of "ascent" ("and up to him proceed") is central and

more detailed ("But more refin'd, more spirituous, and pure / As nearer to him plac't ... Till body up to spirit work").

15 See E.M.W. Tillyard, *The Elizabethan World Picture*; and Marjorie Hope Nicolson, *The Breaking of the Circle* (New York and London: Columbia University Press, 1960), Chapter 1.

16 In *The War in Heaven: "Paradise Lost" and the Tradition of Satan's Rebellion* (Ithaca and London: Cornell University Press, 1980), Stella Purce Revard summarizes what Milton owes to the Thomistic tradition of Satan's motivation (46–7), although she ignores or is unaware of its logical association with necessary inequality. Ultimately, she sees the Great Chain as "an illustration of the continuity of parts" (53), and not the principle of continuity itself as the necessary ground of hierarchy. "[B]ecause his teacher Raphael had succeeded" where Satan failed in "approach[ing] the infinitude of good in his Creator," she insists, "we may know that Adam is being led in the paths of light" (52).

17 Plotinus, as Lovejoy remarks, treated "[d]ifference of kind ... as necessarily equivalent to difference of excellence, to diversity of rank in a hierarchy" (*The Great Chain of Being*, 64). More specifically, Plotinus had asked, "How, if there is to be a multiplicity of forms, can one thing be worse unless another is better, or one be better, unless another is worse?" (64). In the translation that Lovejoy (65) gives from the Greek, "Thus the Reason did not make gods only, but first gods, then spirits, the second nature, and then men, and then animals, in a continuous series – not through envy, but because its rational nature contains an intellectual variety. But we are like men who, knowing little of painting, blame the artist because the colors in his picture are not all beautiful – not seeing that he has given to each part what was appropriate to it. And the cities which have the best governments are not those in which all citizens are equal" (Plotinus, *Enneads*, III.2.11, ed. R. Volkmann [Leipzig: B.G. Teubner, 1883]).

18 Even for the monist Proclus, to whom Milton appears to be indebted, "Emanation is a necessity of the One and is eternal, deteriorating, and cyclical. The One does not elect to emanate; it is part of its nature. The levels of being deteriorate as they achieve distance from the One until the emanation reaches the farthest deterioration in matter. Then it begins a retracing of its course back to the One; hence it is cyclic and the power of the One flows in a circle back to its origin" (Ashley, *Milton Encyclopedia*, 195).

19 Madsen, *From Shadowy Types*, helpfully itemizes these tensions of change and fixity as follows: "Some words suggest that the scale of nature is dynamic – 'tending,' 'Till body up to spirit work,' 'Springs,' 'aspire,' and 'ascend' – but at the same time, it appears to be static: 'plac'd,' 'assign'd,' 'bounds'" (120).

20 Neoplatonism, as D. Bentley Hart insists, is really a "metaphysical variety of monism – the belief that the hierarchy of Being is a system of divine emanation and return, or at least that the creation is ontologically continuous with the divine," but "whether Milton embraced the metaphysical variety of monism ... is altogether more uncertain, despite a seeming abundance of evidence to that effect"

("Matter, Monism, and Narrative: An Essay on the Metaphysics of *Paradise Lost*," *Milton Quarterly* 30, no. 1 [March 1996]: 16).

21 Clay Daniel, "Milton's Neo-Platonic Angel," 188n23.

22 More generally, Martin Kuester remarks that "the archangel Raphael plays a more important role than has generally been accorded to him" in "a growing linguistic 'arbitrarization,' as the switch from prelapsarian linguistics to another linguistic system that offers a necessary but not necessarily sufficient explanation of Adam and Eve's 'Fall'" (*Milton's Prudent Ambiguities: Words and Signs in His Poetry and Prose* [Lanham, MD: University of Press of America, 2009], 81).

23 Ovid, *Metamorphoses* 15.386–407, trans. A.D. Melville (Oxford and New York: Oxford University Press, 1986), 363.

24 Virgil, *The Aeneid*, trans. Robert Fitzgerald (1983; New York: Vintage, 1985), 104.

25 See, e.g., Richard Overton's *An Alarum to the House of Lords* (31 July 1646) on the subject of lordly titles: "But if *Titles* were of any value, or *Honour* of any esteeme, hee deserveth the Title of *Lieutenant Collonell*, and the honor he hath gotten in the field in defence of his Countreys *Liberties*, as well as any of you, your Titles or Honours, if not better and more Worthily; for by what meanes some of you came by yours, is very uncertaine, but this is certaine, that most of you gained no part of it your selves: and the common wayes your Auncesters gained it for you, was generally by adhering to Kings, in subduing and oppressing the *Commons*" (4).

26 *Politicus* 85 (22 January 1652): 1349.

27 Reported in *Vox Plebis*, most likely by Marchamont Nedham (19 November 1646): 29.

28 *Vox Plebis*, 32.

29 Walwyn, *The Iust Man in Bonds* (29 June 1646), 4.

30 H.N. Brailsford, *The Levellers and the English Revolution*, ed. Christopher Hill (London: The Cresset Press, 1961), 43–4.

31 William Empson, *Milton's God* (London: Chatto & Windus, 1961), 150.

32 After carefully showing how Milton departs from the traditions of "metaphysical monisim," D. Bentley Hart concludes that Milton "was not simply a 'metaphysical,' or even a 'material,' but a narrative monist," fundamentally committed to a concept of "the creation" as "an event in the life of the eternal, an episode in the endless successiveness of the divine narrative," where "all of Being is joined in one great story" ("Matter, Monism, and Narrative," 25).

33 David Norbrook is doubtless right to claim that "Milton politicized the story of the fall of the angels further than any predecessor" (*Writing the English Republic: Poetry, Rhetoric, and Politics, 1627–1660* [Cambridge: Cambridge University Press, 1999], 445).

34 Revard quite properly remarks that Milton's translation of Psalms 2 in 1653 "reads almost like a resumé of Raphael's account in Book 5 of *Paradise Lost*" (*War in Heaven*, 99–100).

35 Ibid., 67–85.

36 *Apocalypsis Mosis* 13.1–2; 14.1, 3; 15.1. Trans. Gary A. Anderson and Michael E. Stone, *The Life of Adam and Eve: The Biblical Story in Judaism and Christianity.* "Synoptic Presentation of the Text." Based on "Vita Adae et Evae," ed. Wilhelm Meyer. *Abhandlugenn der koeniglichen Bayerischen Akademie der Wissenschaften Philosophische-philolgische Klasse* 14.3 (Munich 1878), 185–250. Accessed 29 December 2014 at: http://www2.iath.virginia.edu/anderson/vita/english/vita.lat.html#per5.

37 "Introduction," *An Electronic Edition of the "Life of Adam and Eve,"* ed. Gary A. Anderson and Michael Stone. Accessed 17 April 2014 at: http://www2.iath.virginia.edu/anderson/iath.report.html.

38 Hugh MacCallum, *Milton and the Sons of God: The Divine Image in Milton's Epic Poetry* (Toronto: University of Toronto Press, 1986), notes that Milton "appears to be the first to envisage such a scene, and his doing so may be taken in part as evidence of his powers as a dramatist" (79).

39 Stella Purce Revard observes that, "Of the two motives available to him [resentment either of the Son's or else man's advancement], Milton chose the one less current in the Renaissance" (*War in Heaven*, 210). She sees several advantages of this choice for characterization, if not for theodicy.

40 "Milton's interpretation of the second psalm … remains clearly within the confines of seventeenth-century orthodox opinion" (Revard, *War in Heaven*, 76).

41 *De Doctrina Christiana*, I, v: "Of the Son of God," CPW 6: 206.

42 *Politicus* 86 (29 January 1652): 1365–6.

43 Revard points out that Milton is unique among Renaissance poets in having "Satan stand alone" (*War in Heaven*, 164) to foment rebellion: "In lonely ambition and pride he forges the rebellion, using the numbers of supporters to carry out what he alone has conceived, needing only silent approval and supportive strength" (165). This characterization sounds rather like Cromwell returning in devious ambition from Worcester. See above, Chapter 2, n64.

44 *Politicus* 95 (1 April 1652): 1489.

45 Revard judiciously remarks how "Milton's emphatic denial that envy of the Son's coming Incarnation in any way influenced Satan either in his initial revolt or in his attempt against Adam is all the more remarkable in that Protestant theologians so frequently speculated that it had" (*War in Heaven*, 78).

46 Norbrook is somewhat mistaken in his claim that "Satan's language becomes more monarchist the further he falls from heaven" (*Writing the English Republic*, 446). Initially, Heaven's rebel speaks the language of a royalist, seeking to preserve *l'ancien régime* by appealing to the "liberties" and "franchises" of titled privilege. He shifts to a pseudo-republican language only after Abdiel reminds him that their titles still depend on the "throne" of Heaven.

47 *Politicus* 95 (1 April 1652): 1490.

48 Among Reniassance poets, says Revard, Milton is also unique in depicting a challenge to Satan's authority from "within the rebel camp"; in Peri's *La guerra angelica*

(ca. 1612) and in Vondel's *Lucifer* (1654), the challenge comes from an *outside* emissary (*War in Heaven*, 164–5).

49 Satan may sound like a Lilburne defending native liberties; but he is more of a Leveller version of those "Lords," who "had, since the time of the Norman Conquest, diminished and in part abrogated, but not entirely destroyed, the native liberties of the freeborn people of England." See D. Alan Orr, "Constitutionalism: Ancient, Modern, and Early Modern in the *Agreements of the People*," in *The Agreements*, ed. Baker and Vernon (2012), 90.

50 Lilburne, *Ionahs Cry out of the Whales Belly* (26 July 1647), 9.

51 Lilburne, *An Impeachment of High Treason* (10 August 1649), 29.

52 D. Alan Orr, "Constitutionalism," in *The Agreements*, ed. Baker and Vernon (2012), notes that "The abolition of aristocratic privilege in legal matters would become a feature of all subsequent *Agreements*" (80) in the Levellers' struggle to restore "native" rights. But increasingly, as Ian Gentles remarks, Parliament's failure to address regal and lordly prerogative allied the New Model with the Levellers, as appears in the Officers' *Agreement*, which "assumed the abolition of the monarchy and the House of Lords" (Gentles, "The New Model Army," in *The Agreements*, ed. Baker and Vernon [2012], 155).

53 Albert C. Labriola, "'Thy Humiliation Shall Exalt': The Christology of *Paradise Lost*," *Milton Studies* 15 (1981): 29–42.

54 *Early Christian Writings*, "The Ascension of Isaiah," 10.8–9, 11–13. Accessed 18 April 2014 at: http://www.earlychristianwritings.com/text/ascension.html.

55 Dennis Danielson makes a similar observation in *Milton's Good God*, "that Milton presents a kind of prelapsarian Incarnation" that has already established "a Christocentric universe," resulting "in a greater manifestation of the glory of God, in a gracious condescension of the Son toward God's creatures, in those creatures being united under the headship of the Messiah and thereby receiving greater benefits than could otherwise be obtained" (223, 224).

56 *Politicus* 77 (27 November 1651): 1222.

57 Rejecting "Abdiel's brave example[,] they have chosen to rebel against God of their own accord, and rejected opportunties for obedience and repentance" (McColley, *Milton's Eve* [Urbana and Chicago: University of Illinois Press, 1983], 190).

58 Richard Overton, *The Hunting of the Foxes* (21 March 1649), 11–12.

59 Lilburne, *To all the Affectors and Approvers in England* (17 July 1649), 6.

CHAPTER EIGHT

1 See Ian Gentles, "The New Model Army," in *The Agreements*, ed. Baker and Vernon (2012), 158.

2 See Stella Purce Revard, *The War in Heaven: "Paradise Lost" and the Tradition of Satan's Rebellion* (Ithaca and London: Cornell University Press, 1980), Chapter 5, esp. 137–52.

3 Ultimately, Revard suggests, "The war waged before us in *Paradise Lost* is Satanic in essence" (ibid., 196). For a reading of Milton's depiction of "holy war" modelled on the Hebrew scriptures, see Michael Lieb, *The Poetics of the Holy: A Reading of "Paradise Lost"* (Chapel Hill: University of North Carolina Press, 1981), 246–312. For a rejection of the idea that Milton sided with those who believed "that men's most strenuous efforts should end in a holy war or, at least, a just war" (4), see James A. Freeman, *Milton and the Martial Muse: "Paradise Lost" and European Traditions of War* (Princeton, NJ: Princeton University Press, 1980).

4 More broadly, Revard argues that sixteenth- and seventeenth-century "poets turned from the Bible to those poems, both ancient and modern, that had most persuasively and skilfully described human and superhuman warfare: the epics of Homer, Hesiod, and Virgil, the mythological poems of late Greek and Latin writers like Nonnos and Claudian, and the chivalric poems of Ariosto, Tasso, and others. Particularly valuable were Homer and Hesiod, whose works were becoming popular in the printed editions of the sixteenth century, in which the Latin translation faced the original Greek" (*War in Heaven*, 148). The latter point is crucial, since the Homeric poems were not available to poets and audiences in Western Europe through most of the Middle Ages.

5 Virgil transforms the Greek notion of *areté* (L. *virtus*), however, when Anchises announces to his son Aeneas in the Underworld, "*Hic vir, hic est*" – "This is the man, this the one" (*Aeneid*, vi.1062), trans. Robert Fitzgerald (New York: Vintage, 1985), 187. Father Anchises points to Augustus, one of the "Souls of the future, living in our name" (6.1018), as the "man" who will become the model of a new type of hero, sacrificing his *virtus* to the notion of a just "empire without end" (1.375). As Brooks Otis concludes in *Virgil: A Study in Civilized Poetry* (Oxford: Clarendon Press, 1963), Virgil "uses platonic dualism … in order to validate an essentially *historical* scheme of values" (301). Virgil is just as likely, however, to be thinking of Cicero's Stoic understanding of *virtus* as "a habit of mind in harmony with reason and the order of nature"; see above, Chapter 2, n35.

6 In *Iliad* 22, Hektor foresees his death in combat with Achilleus, yet has to admit, "I feel shame before the Trojans and the Trojan women with trailing / robes, that someone who is less of a man than I will say of me: / 'Hektor believed in his own strength and ruined his people'" (*Iliad*, trans. Richmond Lattimore [Chicago: University of Chicago Press, 1951], 22.105–7). Similarly, the yet-to-be-reborn Aeneas confesses to Dido his being overcome by *furor* (mad battle-fury) at seeing Troy in flames ("So fury drove me, and it came to me / That meeting death was beautiful in arms" – 2.425–6), while *aidōs*, or shame at witnessing the death of his father, Priam, makes him cry out, "Men, bring my gear … Give me back to the Greeks" (2.874), even though it would mean his death.

7 For discussion of the heroic code of Homer's *Iliad*, see my *Media, Memory, and the First World War* (Montreal and Kingston: McGill-Queen's University Press, 2009), 65–71; for the differing uses of "scripts" in Homer and in Virgil, see *Media, Memory*, 73–8.

8 David C. Rubin, *Memory in Oral Tradtions: The Cognitive Psychology of Epic, Ballads, and Counting-out Rhymes* (New York: Oxford University Press, 1995), describes a script as "a predetermined, stereotyped sequence of actions that defines a well-known situation" (24), thereby helping oral audiences "to preserve the order of events" (26). As formative elements, scripts can be "a way of organizing a story for easier recall and performance for the singer," as well as for "the audience" (210). "Common scripts in the tradition," Rubin says, "include the sequence of concrete actions taken in arming a hero or the hero's horse, assembling an army, joining battle" (11), etc. But while "The order of arming," for example, "is stable, as are the items used … [e]ach arming scene is different from the others and is adapted to its context in the epics in sophisticated ways" (212). Overall, then, "the scripts of Homeric epic can serve as the background of expectations from which deviations can be noted" (ibid.).

9 Albert B. Lord, *The Singer of Tales* (New York: Atheneum, 1965), 86–91.

10 Ward Parks, "The Flyting Contract and Adversarial Patterning in the Alliterative *Morte Arthure*," in *Traditions and Innovations: Essays on British Literature of the Middle Ages and the Renaissance*, ed. David G. Allen and Robert A. White (Newark: University of Delaware Press, 1990), 61.

11 Ibid.

12 It is fair to say with David Norbrook that "These tensions mark Milton's most problematic episode, the war in heaven" (*Writing the English Republic: Poetry, Rhetoric, and Politics, 1627–1660* [Cambridge: Cambridge University Press, 1999], 447).

13 Arnold Stein, "Milton's War in Heaven – An Extended Metaphor," *ELH* 18 (1951), 201–20; rpt. in *Milton: Modern Essays in Criticism*, ed. Arthur E. Barker (London: Oxford University Press, 1965), 264–83, makes "belittling" a central motif in this war where "mind," for its sin against reason in using matter to overthrow the hierarchy of spirit over matter, is punished by a climactic "descent of spirit to matter" (272).

14 Here, Satan may recall Cromwell on the floor of the Commons in early 1648, denouncing "the king as a dissembler, thundering, 'thou shalt not suffer an hypocrite to reign'" (quoted in Gentles, "The New Model Army," in *The Agreements*, ed. Baker and Vernon [2012], 151).

15 While Satan justifies the War in Heaven as resistance to the Son's usurpation, Abdiel sees it much as the Levellers viewed recent English history. For the latter, notes D. Alan Orr, "The Civil Wars arose from a series of noble and regal usurpations since the Norman Conquest, which had abrogated the birthright of all freeborn Englishmen to be self-governing" ("Constitutionalism," in *The Agreements*, ed. Baker and Vernon [2012], 84). God for Milton is the true source of "native" rights among all the "freeborn" Sons of Heaven.

16 The language of apostasy appears frequently in Lilburne's polemics of 1649. For the earliest example, see *A Whip for the present House of Lords,* OR *The Levellers Levelled* (27 February 1648), 3, 4, 5, 18. Later notable examples appear in *The Second*

Part of Englands New-Chaines (24 March 1649), 7, 14; *A Discourse betwixt Lieut. Col. JOHN LILBURN ... and Mr HUGH PETER* (29 May 1649), 8; *Strength out of Weaknesse* (30 September 1649), 3, 4; and *As You Were* (May 1652), 15, 22.

17 Lilburne, *To all the Affectors and Approvers in England* (17 July 1649), 6.

18 Lilburne, *An Impeachment of High Treason Against Oliver Cromwell* (10 August 1649), 17 [misnumbered 15].

19 Stein remarks of Satan's scornful epithet, "Reason is the most important means of destroying reason, and it is a major weapon of the intellectual cynic. When Satan calls Abdiel 'seditious Angel,' he is relishing his own humor; but he is also, shrewd relativist that he is, undermining the possibility of judgment" ("Milton's War in Heaven," 275).

20 Lilburne, *The Second Part of Englands New-Chaines Discovered* (24 March 1649), 2.

21 In his edition of Hesiod's *Theogony* (Indianapolis: Bobbs-Merrill, 1953), N.O. Brown reads the Greek Titanomachia as an allegory of the revolutionary overthrow of matriarchy and the establishment and consolidation of kingship during Europe's pre-history (42–6).

22 Stein regards the war as a defence "of traditional Elizabethan political philosophy," although "Milton personally breaks with some of the implications" ("Milton's War in Heaven," 281).

23 See Chapter 9 below.

24 Whether or not Milton was a contributor to this issue of Nedham's newsbook, he undoubtedly gave it his imprimatur.

25 *Politicus* 52 (5 June 1651): 832.

26 *Politicus* 53 (12 June 1651): 847–9.

27 See above, Chapter 2, 76–95.

28 Lilburne, *A Discourse betwixt Lieut. Col. John Lilburn, close prisoner in the Tower of London, and Mr Hugh Peter* (25 May 1649), 4.

29 *Politicus* 53 (12 June 1651): 849.

30 Richard Overton, *A Defiance Against All Arbitrary Usurpations* (9 September 1646), 6.

31 Ibid., 17

32 Countless commentators have remarked as much, from Arnold Stein ("Milton's War in Heaven," 217–20) to Stella Revard (*War in Heaven*, 126–7).

33 Sonnet 12: 14 (Flannagan, *Riverside Milton*, 252).

34 Blair Worden claims that "Milton, the reverer of lonely heroes, made a lonely hero of himself" in *Defensio Secunda* "as the 'single-handed' defender, by his 'single efforts' in 'single combat,' of English liberty: as the Abdiel of the Puritan Revolution, defiantly and incorruptibly alone" (*Literature and Politics in Cromwellian England: John Milton, Andrew Marvell, Marchamont Nedham* [Oxford: Oxford University Press, 2007], 39). But this is to maintain a focus on the combat per se, rather than on the narrative act and its multiple ironies.

35 "I might almost say," Milton writes at the end of *Defensio Secundo*, "I have erected a monument that will not soon pass away, to those deeds that were illustrious, that

were glorious, that were almost beyond any praise, and if I have done nothing else, I have surely redeemed my pledge," a contract with the reader that he likens to the time-honoured conventions governing "the epic poet" (CPW 4.i: 685).

36 Worden, *Literature and Politics*, 156.

37 Here is the closest Milton comes in the poem to the politics of a classical republican. As David Norbrook puts his case, "The Son's ascent marks the high point of the poem's iconoclasm, its exultant destruction of corrupt forms" (*Writing the English Republic*, 468).

38 John P. Rumrich, *Milton Unbound: Controvery and Reinterpretation* (Cambridge: Cambridge University Press, 1996), remarks, however, "that 'the stately ease' with which the peace-wishing Son achieves victory" belies the appearance of a traditional creation myth "as the beginning of a continuing battle against 'the chaos monster'" (124).

39 Christopher Hill, *The Century of Revolution, 1603–1714* (Edinburgh: Thomas Nelson & Sons, 1961), 251; see as well Chapter 6 above.

40 *Pro Populo Anglicano Defensio*, CPW 4.i: 327.

41 In her review of Revard's book *War in Heaven* in *Renaissance Quarterly* 34, no. 2 (Summer 1981), Miriam K. Starkman offers this shrewd caveat: "Nor is it politically astute to urge that Milton 'was on the side of the revolutionaries,' though 'in literature he seems to have turned "royalist" and upheld King Messiah and the divine right.' Politics aside, however, Revard's is a valuable piece of work" (292).

42 See 1 Corinthians 15: 28, together with the discussion in Chapter 5 above.

43 See Walwyn, *Tyranipocrit*, 9, 44, and discussion of this point in Chapter 5 above.

44 The difference between this version of "union" and the one enunciated by Revard seems minimal, but it is in fact the difference between a renunciation of, and the full assumption of, kingship.

45 See Luke 4: 5–8.

46 Revard offers this apt, if partial, distinction between two starkly different conceptions of "kingship" in the poem: "Satan's rationale of kingship is radically different from Messiah's. First of all, he alters the function of kingship; no longer does it 'serve' to unify God's creatures by conveying the love and care of God to all. Satan's kind of kingship exists only to transmit the care and service of others to itself" (*War in Heaven*, 82).

47 Revard identifies this particular chariot with that of the prophet Ezekiel, citing the Puritan preacher and Cambridge Platonist Peter Sterry, who "calls the chariot of Ezekiel the appearance of 'our Saviour as He descends in a Divine Glory'" (*War in Heaven*, 257).

48 See Lilburne's *Strength out of Weaknesse* (30 September 1649); and "Introduction," 28, above.

49 In *Paradise Regain'd* (*The Riverside Milton*, ed. Roy Flannagan), Jesus recalls these three in particular, "*Gideon* and *Jephtha*, and the Shepherd lad" (PR 2.439) during the initial phase of the temptation of the Kingdoms.

50 *Politicus* 66 (11 September 1651): 1045–6.

51 Herman Rapaport notes in passing the alienating effects of "Raphael's instruction" that "serves mainly to perplex and estrange Adam by developing a speculative thought process that alienates the individual." See "*Paradise Lost* and the Novel," in *Approaches to Teaching Milton's "Paradise Lost,"* ed. Galbraith M. Crump (New York: MLA, 1986), 141.

CHAPTER NINE

1 *Johnson's Lives of the English Poets*, ed. G. Birbeck Hill (Oxford: The Clarendon Press, 1905), 185.

2 Stein, "Milton's War in Heaven – An Extended Metaphor," *ELH* 18 (1951), 201–20; rpt. Arnold Stein, *Answerable Style: Essays on "Paradise Lost"* (Minneapolis: University of Minnesota Press, 1953), 17–37.

3 John Rogers, *The Matter of Revolution: Science, Poetry, and Politics in the Age of Milton* (Ithaca, NY, and London: Cornell University Press, 1996), 12.

4 Walwyn, *Tyranipocrit*, 9.

5 Nicholas McDowell, "Ideas of Creation in the Writings of Richard Overton the Leveller and *Paradise Lost*," *Journal of the History of Ideas* 66, no. 1 (January 2005): 77, 61.

6 While this does not exclude natural law theory derived from Cicero (see Chapter 1, n44), it supplements it with the "natural" being of the Christian deity.

7 John Rumrich, *Milton Unbound: Controversy and Reinterpretation* (Cambridge: Cambridge University Press, 1996), 121.

8 N. Katherine Hayles, *Chaos Bound* (Ithaca, NY: Cornell University Press, 1990), 9; quoted in Rumrich, *Milton Unbound*, 145.

9 Maurice Kelley, "Introduction," *De Doctrina Christiana*, *CPW* 6: 89.

10 Quoted in Stephen M. Fallon, *Milton among the Philosophers: Poetry and Materialism in Seventeenth-Century England* (Ithaca, NY: Cornell University Press, 1991), 60–1.

11 Rumrich, *Milton Unbound*, 124.

12 Ibid., 125.

13 Overton had "matriculated at Queen's College, Cambridge in 1631" (McDowell, "Ideas of Creation," 61), which could explain his skill at metaphysics. Wolfe was evidently mistaken in his belief that "The attitude of both Levellers and Independents toward the *Agreement* was colored inevitably by their social and economic status. The Independents were men of the upper middle class, born into families not rich but prosperous, families accustomed to send their sons to Oxford and Cambridge" (165–6). Add to the list of Leveller sympathizers the name of Marchamont Nedham, an Oxford graduate, and it is quite impossible to say that "Of the Leveller spokesmen only Wildman had had any university training" (Wolfe, *Milton in the Puritan Revolution* [1941; London: Cohen & West, 1963], 166).

14 Overton's matriculation at Queen's College, Cambridge, likely made him aware, as Milton and Nedham more certainly were, of Cicero's natural law theory as the classical basis for "natural rights"; see Chapter 1, nn43, 44.

15 Six months later, Walwyn referred in *The Compassionate Samaritan* to Mezentius as the wicked tyrant, who, like the current forcers of conscience, "would fit all men to one bed" (42). His error is silently amended in the second edition to "the wicked *Procrustes* (mentioned by *Plutarch*)" (42), making it conceivable that he had read *Mans Mortalitie* by the end of 1644.
16 *Mans Mortalitie* (19 January 1644), 44.
17 McDowell, "Ideas of Creation," 65.
18 McDowell quotes this latter phrase from Fallon, *Milton among the Philosophers*, 98.
19 Edwin Curley, ed. "Introduction" to Thomas Hobbes, *Leviathan* (Indianapolis and Cambridge: Hackett, 1994), xii.
20 Ibid., xiii.
21 "*Commons Journal*, August 1650." Accessed 29 May 2014 at: http://www.british-history.ac.uk/report.aspx?compid=56410.
22 Kelley, *This Great Argument: A Study of Milton's "De Doctrina Christiana" as a Gloss upon "Paradise Lost"* (Princeton: Princeton University Press, 1941), 23. Recent attempts to dispute Milton's authorship of *De Doctrina* can be likened to the dying gasp of orthodox souls desperate to save *Paradise Lost* for mainstream Christianity; they ought to be pitied though not indulged.
23 In his "Introduction" to *De Doctrina Christiana*, Kelley specifies in particular "Milton's interpretation of the Bible and his Ramean logic" (CPW 6: 88).
24 Ibid., 307.
25 Nigel Smith, "*Paradise Lost* and Heresy," in *The Oxford Handbook of Milton*, ed. Nicholas McDowell and Nigel Smith (Oxford: Oxford University Press, 2009), 513.
26 CPW 6: 309.
27 Ibid., 310, italics added.
28 The *ex deo* theory of creation, as Maurice Kelley remarks in his "Introduction" to *De Doctrina Christiana*, was "one advanced among others by Plotinus and Gregory of Nyssa" (CPW 6: 89).
29 Ibid.
30 As Kelley remarks, the theory of *creatio ex deo* "is open to charges of making God the origin of evil and of attributing materiality to the Deity. To the first of these charges, Milton replies that evil results from free will … The second charge Milton admits and explains by way of eminence" ("Introduction," CPW 6: 89–90).
31 Overton, *An Arrow against all Tyrants* (10 October 1646), 3.
32 McDowell, "Ideas of Creation," 71.
33 Kelley, *This Great Argument*, 126.
34 Fallon, *Milton among the Philosophers*, 98.
35 J.B. Broadbent, *"Some Graver Subject": An Essay on* Paradise Lost (London: Chatto & Windus, 1960), notes how "the Platonic separation of soul from body is explicitly rejected" in *Paradise Lost* "in favour of the Hebrew psychology, which identified them. Nothing exists except matter, infused with life in varying degrees. Since that vitality is divine, matter is intrinsically holy" (209).

36 See C.B. Macpherson, *The Political Theory of Possessive Individualism: Hobbes to Locke* (Oxford: Clarendon Press, 1962).

37 Rachel Foxley, "Freedom of Conscience and the *Agreements of the People*," in *The Agreements*, ed. Baker and Vernon (2012), adds that "The Leveller notion of liberty of conscience, and its inclusion as a 'reserve' in the *Agreements*, is profoundly political. The premise on which it rests is simple: *if* the magistrate has any power over the people, that power must derive from the people. For the Levellers, this applies just as much to powers in matters of religion as in secular life" (122).

38 See Dennis Danielson, *Milton's Good God: A Study in Literary Theodicy* (Cambridge: Cambridge University Press, 1982), for the definitive account of Milton's Arminian theology in *Paradise Lost.*

39 See McDowell for dating of Overton's "Baptist confession of faith" ("Ideas of Creation," 61). See Brailsford for the more general social implications of the Baptist confession (*The Levellers and the English Revolution*, ed. Christopher Hill [London: The Cresset Press, 1961], 32–4; 45–6); as well as for specific implications of his Baptist faith for Overton (50–6).

40 Fallon, *Milton among the Philosophers*, 111.

41 McDowell, "Ideas of Creation," 71.

42 Following Rumrich, David Norbrook concludes that "Milton departs from nearly every theological and poetic precedent, and even risks charges of materialist heterodoxy, to insist that Chaos is essential to creation, that creation was not out of nothing but out of prime matter" (*Writing the English Republic*, 472). Ultimately, however, God and his "divine reduction" are identified with "the Machiavellian legislator" (469), not with the liberating "womb of Nature," thus instantiating a top-down model of aristocratic republicanism rather than one of popular sovereignty – here, the choice of liberated creatures to rejoin or refuse that divine "body."

43 Rumrich remarks that, "The Hebrew word for *Tiamat* [the mother substance of Babylonian 'Chaos'] is the grammatically feminine *tehom*, rendered in English translations of Genesis as 'the deep'" (*Milton Unbound*, 124).

44 In *This Great Argument*, Kelley elaborates as follows: "It is matter because God fills it. It is boundless because God is infinite. It is confused because from it God has chosen to retire – to withdraw into his normal state of rest – rather than to put forth his goodness and give it form and order … God's statement, therefore, may be paraphrased thus. 'The deep is boundless because I fill infinitude (an assertion of God's infinity), nor is the deep empty (a denial, by implication, of the doctrine of *creatio ex nihilo*)'" (211).

45 Danielson, *Milton's Good God*, 46–7.

46 Denis Saurat, *Milton, Man and Thinker* (New York: The Dial Press, 1925), 124.

47 Rumrich, "Milton's God and the Matter of Chaos," *PMLA* 110 (October 1995): 1043.

48 This is to resurrect, if ultimately to transform, one element of what Maurice Kelley had found so objectionable in Saurat's theory of "retraction" (Saurat, *Milton, Man and Thinker*, 124). As Kelley summarizes, "According to his eternal plans, God

withdraws his will from certain parts of Himself, and delivers them up, so to speak, to obscure latent impulsions that remain in them; through this 'retraction,' matter is created; through this retraction, individual beings are created" (quoted in *This Great Argument*, 205).

49 Ibid.

50 Nigel Smith, *Is Milton Better Than Shakespeare?* (Cambridge, MA: Harvard University Press, 2008), 60.

51 Kelley vigorously denies Saurat's idea that "Milton considered creation the result of the sex life of God" (*This Great Argument*, 129), but his refutation is based solely on marginal evidence: the lack of reference in *De Doctrina Christiana* to this supposed divine "sex life"; and Saurat's own tendentious reading of Wisdom "playing" (291–2), in the sexual sense suggested by the *Zohar*, "In presence of th' Almightie Father." Direct evidence of the "vital vertue infus'd" that "mad'st it pregnant" is ignored in Kelley's quibble with Saurat, who may in fact have gotten the right idea for the wrong reasons.

52 Cf. Christine Froula, "When Eve Reads Milton: Undoing the Canonical Economy," *Critical Inquiry* 10, no. 2 (December 1983): "Milton's image heightens the procreative 'hovering' or 'brooding' of the Hebrew text but in such a way as to annihilate its female aspect: the maternal – and *material* – life-giving waters of Genesis 1: 2 become, in Milton, darkenss and silence, an 'Abyss'" (338).

53 For the counter-view, cf. Froula: "The male Logos called upon to articulate the cosmos against an abyss of female silence overcomes the anxieties generated by the tension between visible maternity and invisible paternity by appropriating female power to itself in a parody of parthenogenesis" ("When Eve Reads Milton," 338).

54 See George Coffin Taylor, *Milton's Use of Du Bartas* (Cambridge, MA: Harvard University Press, 1934), 93, for evidence that Du Bartas gendered the first "Light" feminine, calling her "*God's eldest Daughter*." While Du Bartas had influenced Milton through Joshua Sylvester's translation of *Du Bartas His Divine Weekes and Workes* (1608), neither Taylor the critic, nor the French poet, nor his English translator realizes anything remotely like Milton's monist philosophy of matter, let alone this metaphysical gendering of the divine substance of the creation.

55 A.J.A. Waldock, *"Paradise Lost" and Its Critics* (Cambridge: Cambridge University Press, 1947), is typical of an inveterate critical prejudice that makes "Milton's feeling for feritility" beside the point when "talking about the theme of *Paradise Lost*" (128).

56 William Shakespeare, *King Henry V* 1.2.ll.187–90, ed. Andrew Gurr (Cambridge: Cambridge University Press, 1992), 84.

57 Hobbes, *Leviathan* (xvii.6, 12), ed. Edwin Curley (Indianapolis and Cambridge: Hackett, 1994), 108–9.

58 In *Re-membering Milton: Essays on the Texts and Traditions*, ed. Mary Nyquist and Margaret W. Ferguson (New York and London: Methuen, 1987), Mary Nyquist, in "The Genesis of Gendered Subjectivity" (116–19), reads "Female for Race" as the

fault not of the angel but the poet, who seeks, as he had previously done in the Divorce tracts, to subordinate the more inclusive account of creation in Genesis 1 to a far more masculinist version in Genesis 2.

59 James Grantham Turner, *One Flesh: Paradisal Marriage and Sexual Relations in the Age of Milton* (Oxford: Clarendon Press, 1987), admits that "Raphael is by no means an infallible guide," recalling how "Book VII has already established that his knowledge is limited to the 'Priestly' part of Genesis, to the biological rather than the human aspect of creation" (278–9).

60 Quoted in Turner, *One Flesh*, 104, 99.

61 Turner, *One Flesh*, 101–2.

62 Walwyn, *Tyranipocrit* (1649), 9.

63 Maurice Kelley, *This Great Argument*, 129, seeks to disparage Saurat's kabbalistic view by *reductio ad absurdum*, although the idea contains possibilities not dreamt of in the philosophy of either commentator.

64 Rumrich, *Milton Unbound*, 143.

65 Ibid., 144–5.

66 Ibid., 139.

67 Ibid., 145.

68 Rumrich remarks that "despite the erotic pulse of the creation … and despite Milton's plain identification of it as a womb or a pregnant deep, Milton scholars have ignored the link between chaos and sexual fruition. Like Chambers before her, Schwartz [Regina Schwartz, *Remembering and Repeating: On Milton's Theology and Poetics* (University of Chicago Press, 1988)] describes the ongoing threat of Chaos entirely in military terms" (*Milton Unbound*, 130).

CHAPTER TEN

1 James Grantham Turner, *One Flesh: Paradisal Marriage and Sexual Relations in the Age of Milton* (Oxford: The Clarendon Press, 1987), 200.

2 Nigel Smith, *Is Milton Better Than Shakespeare?* (Cambridge, MA: Harvard University Press, 2008), 49.

3 *Doctrine and Discipline of Divorce*, 2nd ed. (1644), *CPW* 2: 248.

4 Irene Samuel, *Plato and Milton* (1947; Ithaca, NY: Cornell University Press, 1965), 157.

5 Stephen M. Fallon, "The Metaphysics of Milton's Divorce Tracts," in *Politics, Poetics, and Hermeneutics in Milton's Prose*, ed. David Loewenstein and James Grantham Turner (Cambridge: Cambridge University Press, 1990), 71.

6 In *Doctrine and Discipline*, Milton arrives near its end at something like a potential redemption of the flesh through verbal intercourse, as compared to "fleshly accustoming without the souls union and commixture of intellectual delight" which "is rather a soiling then a fulfilling of mariage-rites" (*CPW* 2: 339).

7 Fallon, "Metaphysics," 69.

8 In fairness to Fallon, his argument is designed to conclude with the "instability" ("Metaphysics," 77) of a monistic position that is unable to escape its own residual dualism. Ultimately, "Milton's intention to separate himself from dualism is thwarted, not by the strategic dualism of his arguments for spiritual union, but by a moral dualism secreted at the heart of his ontological monism" (81).

9 While the title page of *Mans Mortalitie* claims that it was printed in Amsterdam in 1643, "Amsterdam" is crossed out by a pen-stroke and "London" substituted in the hand of George Thomason the bookseller. The date "Jan: 19" has also been added to the year "1643," allowing us to date the pamphlet to the beginning of 1644 New Style.

10 Nigel Smith, *Is Milton Better Than Shakespeare?* 51.

11 The first edition of *The Doctrine and Discipline* was published on 1 August 1643; and the second edition "came from the press not later than February 2, 1644," as dated by Lowell W. Coolidge, "Preface and Notes," CPW 2: 217.

12 Nicholas McDowell, "Ideas of Creation in the Writings of Richard Overton the Leveller and *Paradise Lost*," *Journal of the History of Ideas* 66, no. 1 (January 2005): 62.

13 Flannagan, *The Riverside Milton*, 259.

14 Overton, *Mans Mortalitie* (19 January 1644), 42.

15 In "The Genesis of Gendered Subjectivity" in *Re-membering Milton: Essays on the Texts and Traditions*, ed. Mary Nyquist and Margaret W. Ferguson (New York and London: Methuen, 1987), Mary Nyquist argues that "The egalitarian sentiments expressed, sporadically, throughout the divorce tracts," like those of Adam demanding a mate from God in *Paradise Lost*, "cannot finally obscure Eve's secondary status as a 'gift' from one partriarch to another" (106).

16 *Mercurius Britanicus* 117 (9 February 1646): 1029.

17 Turner, *One Flesh*, 280.

18 Walwyn, *The Compassionate Samaritan* (29 July 1644), 8, 10. Luther had disparaged "the garden-brothers [Anabaptists were reputed to meet in gardens], the Anabaptists that maintain no marriage but mix among themselves like animals, this one and that" (*Luther on Women*, ed. and trans. Susan C. Karant-Nunn and Merry E. Wiesner-Hanks [Cambridge: Cambridge University Press, 2007], 123); but Walwyn thought better of them (his fellow Leveller Richard Overton being an Anabaptist), both for their rationality and their moral decency.

19 As Martin Kuester reads this scene, God openly "rejects Adam's plea for a companion only to admit later, after having provoked Adam to come forward with a convincing argument, that his uncooperative behavior had been nothing but a pedagogical strategy," meaning that the Creator "had only played the role of the Socratic *eiron* trying to elicit a certain behavior from his pupil" (*Milton's Prudent Ambiguities: Words and Signs in His Poetry and Prose* [Lanham, MD: University of Press of America, 2009], 83).

20 "A man may be a heretick in the truth," Milton had written in *Areopagitica*; "and if he beleeve things only because his Pastor sayes so, or the Assembly so determins,

without knowing other reason, though his belief be true, yet the very truth he holds, becomes his heresie" (*CPW* 2: 543).

21 David Aers and Bob Hodge, "Milton on Sex and Marriage," *Milton Studies* 13 (1979), 23–4.

22 This is the first hint Adam gives to Raphael that "Female for Race" does not begin to explain the reason for her creation, any more than Luther's doctrine of "procreation" is able to do so.

23 Rumrich, "Milton's God and the Matter of Chaos," *PMLA* 110 (October 1995): 1044.

24 "*collateral*: adj.": def. A1, "situated or placed side by side"; noun (E-M17th century): def. B2, "An equal (in rank)." *Shorter Oxford English Dictionary*, 6th ed., vol. 1 (Oxford: Oxford University Press, 2007), 450.

25 Walwyn, *The Compassionate Samaritan*, 10.

26 Nyquist, "Gendered Subjectivity," 104. Discussing the Hebrew word *keneged* – though ignoring another connotation which can be rendered "equal to" – Nyquist remarks that, "The very phrase 'meet for him' is said by Calvin to suggest in the Hebrew *keneged*, the quality of being 'like or answerable unto' (*quia illi respondeat*) the man and to indicate vividly that psychological rather than physical likeness founds marriage as an institution" (103). The problem for Nyquist is the seeming priority given to a "lonely Adam" *for* whom Eve remains a secondary being, created only in answer to *his* needs.

27 *CPW* 2: 600.

28 Aers and Hodge claim that Adam's debate with the deity also "gives a precedent for God's official spokesman giving out an inadequate ethic in order to 'try' Adam, relying on Adam's 'man-centred' ethic to prevail in argument" ("Milton on Sex and Marriage," 24). Raphael, however, does not seem aware of his role in testing Adam in the manner of the Creator's test; his unwitting inadequacy is nonetheless useful to God in ways that will emerge in discussion of Book 10 in Chapter 12 below.

29 I share the conviction of Kristin A. Pruitt, *Gender and the Power of Relationship: "United as One Individual Soul" in "Paradise Lost"* (Pittsburgh: Duquesne University Press, 2003), "that Raphael is the masculinist and that God, and Milton, are not" (117). But I take the damage caused by the "winged Hierarch" to be exponentially greater than she thinks; for me, it is a "feminine" metaphysics of matter and the whole project of re-union of the creature with the Creator that, far more than Raphael knows, serve as the real guarantees of the Father's promise that, "I can repair / That detriment" (7.152–3).

30 In *Milton Unbound*, Rumrich reads "the Ptolemaic model" as being "most clearly linked with chaotic excess and confusion," whereas "The Copernican model better suits Adam's desire for a nature that does not exceed rational expectations" (135–6). Rumrich thereby finds support for Milton's profound revaluation of chaos in *Paradise Lost*, even as he deflects criticism of those "aligning Eve with the errors of geocentrism," and even reviving "the clichéd critique of Milton as the epic prophet of a phallogocentrism so totalizing that it stretches from human relations to celestial motions" (137).

31 Rumrich, *Milton Unbound*, 138, 137.

32 "*facile*: adj." def. 3, 1, 2. *Shorter Oxford English Dictionary*, 6th ed., vol. 1 (Oxford: Oxford University Press, 2007), 916.

33 Kuester, "The End of Monolithic Language: Raphael's Sematology in *Paradise Lost*," *English Studies in Canada* 15, no. 3 (1989): 271.

34 Rumrich makes this point in *Milton Unbound*, 137.

35 Karen Pruitt notes of "two great Sexes" that "Milton posits a more reciprocal, egalitarian basis for gender than many of his contemporaries" (119), while recognizing "that the archangel is a limited being" (*Gender*, 54).

36 John Peter, *A Critique of "Paradise Lost"* (New York: Columbia University Press, 1960), notes that Raphael "stands as the representative of that heavenly polity around which nebulous prejudices have been steadily gathering, and this means that his deficiences are much more likely to be exaggerated than ignored" (106). Peter, however, makes it less a matter "of Milton's unconscious mistrust of angels" than of "the surge of his imagination, reaching out to embrace the human figure" that he understands and for which he feels human sympathy.

37 Stuart Curran, "God," in *The Oxford Handbook of Milton*, ed. Nicholas McDowell and Nigel Smith (Oxford: Oxford University Press, 2009), 530.

38 By constrast, see Christine Froula, "When Eve Reads Milton: Undoing the Canonical Economy," *Critical Inquiry* 10, no. 2 (December 1983): "Adam's dream of Eve's creation from his rib fulfills his wish for an organ that performs the life-creating function of Eve's womb … Adam's fantasy of Eve's subordinate creation dramatizes an archetypal womb envy as constitutive of male identity" (332).

39 Feisal Mohamed, *In the Anteroom of Divinity: The Reformation of the Angels from Colet to Milton* (Toronto and Buffalo: University of Toronto Press, 2008), 126.

40 Adam's identification of Eve's "grace" with God's "Grace" also carries overtones of Nedham's antinomian conception of "free grace" in *Vox Plebis*: "For as God created every man free in *Adam*: so by nature are all alike freemen born; and are since made free in grace by Christ" (4), which only deepens the paradisal connotations of "grace" in Adam's understanding of what is most God-like in Eve.

41 Rumrich, *Milton Unbound*, 140.

42 Walwyn, *Tyranipocrit* (14 August 1649), 20–1.

43 See my "Introduction," 19–20; and Chapter 6, 174–5.

44 Walwyn, *Tyranipocrit*, 8.

45 Nyquist, "Gendered Subjectivity," 101.

46 Douglas Bush, *John Milton: A Sketch of His Life and Writings* (New York: Collier, 1964), 162.

47 Millicent Bell, "The Fallacy of the Fall in *Paradise Lost*," PMLA 68, no. 4 (Fall 1953): 867.

48 Marjorie Hope Nicolson, *John Milton: A Reader's Guide to His Poetry* (New York: The Noonday Press, 1963), 279. Conversely, Barbara Lewalski, *"Paradise Lost" and the Rhetoric of Literary Forms* (Princeton: Princeton University Press, 1985), reads Adam as playing "the role of the young lover still caught up in the life of

the seasons, while Raphael is the strict Neoplatonist" whose "Neoplatonic ladder of love based on the dichotomy of matter and spirit must necessarily take quite another form in a [*sic*] Milton's monistic universe" (215).

49 Here, Pruitt judiciously observes that Raphael's "reaction is not only inadequate; it is, in certain respects, seriously flawed" (*Gender*, 55).

50 Turner remarks in *One Flesh* that "His blame of 'Nature' for not making him more superior seems unduly fallen, especially when we notice that, even earlier in his narration, he had equated 'Nature' with the possibility of sinful thoughts in Eve" (276).

51 That is to say, "Either … or."

52 Rumrich, *Milton Unbound*, 138.

53 Pruitt finds Adam "[c]asting off the principle of reciprocity in favor of hierarchy," but then happily "adds a series of qualifications that undercut this assertion and suggest its opposite" (*Gender*, 52). I maintain that it is Eve's proposal to work apart, which triggers, as if by delayed reaction, Adam's confusion about gender that is the lasting legacy of the angel's visit.

54 Aers and Hodge focus the effects of this logical dissonance on readers more than on the characters in the drama: "Neo-Christian critics are so awed by authority that they assume the archangel must be right, or more right than Adam. Since Raphael argues a strict antifeminist line, which Adam resists, Milton must endorse Raphael and be dramatizing Adam's fatal propensities to uxoriousness" ("Milton on Sex and Marriage," 23).

55 Here, Christine Froula refers to "Adam's sense of inadequacy in face of what he sees as Eve's perfection." In her view, "Adam's 'perfet' God enables him to contend with the self-sufficiency he sees and fears in Eve, precisely by authorizing Adam's possession of her" ("When Eve Reads Milton," 331–2).

56 Pruitt, *Gender*, 52–3.

57 Diana Benet, "Abdiel and the Son in the Separation Scene," *Milton Studies* 18 (1983): 129–43, sees Eve as identifying with "The zealous angel" in her dispute with Adam in the Separation Scene, while Adam speaks and acts on the example of the Son. Once we have discussed the Separation Scene, however, the reader may have reason to see Adam being influenced by Raphael, to a point that Eve resists negative identification with Abdiel.

58 Waldock, "*Paradise Lost*" *and Its Critics* (1947; Cambridge: Cambridge University Press, 1962), assumes that "Raphael in what he says here is obviously Milton's spokesman" (42), but concludes more perceptively of Adam "that a man who speaks like this has already had his thoughts refined and his heart enlarged," and thus "is already passing Raphael's tests tolerably well" (45).

59 John Peter finds Raphael to be less sympathetic than Adam, and so less worthy of "our regard" (*Critique of "Paradise Lost,"* 108), but assumes nonetheless that Adam speaks only metaphorically about "higher knowledge in her presence" falling "Degraded," thereby failing to see the real critique of "higher" and "lower" that Adam mounts against his interlocutor.

60 *Doctrine and Discipline of Divorce*, 2nd ed. CPW 2: 235, 236.
61 See above, Chapter 8, nn34, 35, 36.
62 CPW 2: 258, 252.
63 Aers and Hodge, "Milton on Sex and Marriage," 26.
64 An omniscient deity, of course, would foresee what his messenger will contribute to that outcome, although his theodical intention cannot be understood until the poem's end.
65 James Turner, *One Flesh*, 282.
66 Albert C. Labriola, "'Thy Humiliation Shall Exalt': The Christology of *Paradise Lost*," *Milton Studies* 15 (1981): 32–3, 36.
67 Turner, *One Flesh*, 278.
68 *The Readie and Easie Way to Establish a Free Commonwealth*, CPW 7: 370–5.
69 Hughes, "Introduction," CPW 3: 27–8.
70 *Considerations Touching the Likeliest Means to Remove Hirelings* (1659), CPW 7: 274.
71 Hughes, "Introduction," CPW 3: 36.

CHAPTER ELEVEN

1 St Augustine, *The City of God*, Books VIII–XVI. *The Fathers of The Church*, vol. 7, trans. Gerald G. Walsh, SJ, and Grace Monahan, OSU (Washington: The Catholic University Press of America, 1952), XIV, xxvii (Book 14, chapter 27), 377–8.
2 C.S. Lewis, *A Preface to "Paradise Lost"* (1942; London and Oxford: Oxford University Press, 1960), 67.
3 See, for example, Martin Dzelzainis, "The Politics of *Paradise Lost*," in *The Oxford Handbook of Milton*, ed. Nicholas McDowell and Nigel Smith (Oxford: Oxford University Press, 2009), 547–68.
4 See Diane McColley, *Milton's Eve* (Urbana and Chicago: University of Illinois Press, 1983), 148–66, for an excellent survey of apocryphal versions of the Fall in antiquity, the Middle Ages, and the early Renaissance that elaborated on the cryptic nature of Genesis 1–3.
5 The Greek pseudepigrapha *Apocalypsis Mosis* and Latin *Vita Adae et Evae* tried to paper over gaping cracks in the biblical account of the Fall: 1) by having God institute a division of labour to keep the couple apart in their work; 2) and by scheduling the angelic guards to depart at appointed hours for divine worship, which the devil remarked at once. See Gary A. Anderson and Michael E. Stone, *The Life of Adam and Eve: The Biblical Story in Judaism and Christianity.* "Synoptic Presentation of the Text": 33.1–3. Accessed 2 January 2015 at: http://www2.iath.virginia.edu/anderson/vita/english/vita.lat.html.
6 Dramatic advantages aside, the question of theodicy cannot be usefully treated before Book 10, and will become more fully evident only in discussion of Books 11 to 12.

7 Susan Wiseman, "Eve, *Paradise Lost*, and Female Interpretation," in *The Oxford Handbook of Milton*, 540.

8 A.J.A. Waldock, *"Paradise Lost" and Its Critics* (1947; Cambridge: Cambridge University Press, 1962), 30–1, 34.

9 E.M.W. Tillyard, *Studies in Milton* (London: Chatto & Windus, 1951), 16, 17, 20.

10 "What Milton's age believed" on this point is largely what Aquinas's age believed: "The subjection of the woman to her husband is to be understood as inflicted in punishment of the woman, not as to his head-ship (since even before sin the man was the head and governor of the woman), but as to her having now to obey her husband's will even against her own." *Summa Theologica* 2.2.164.2, in *The 'Summa Theologica' of St. Thomas Aquinas, Second Part of the Second Part* QQ. CXLI–CLXX. Literally translated by the Fathers of the English Dominican Province (London: Burns Oates & Washbourne, 1921), 270–1.

11 Joseph H. Summers, *The Muse's Method: An Introduction to "Paradise Lost"* (London: Chatto & Windus, 1962), 170–1, 174.

12 John S. Diekhoff, *Milton's "Paradise Lost": A Commentary on the Argument* (New York: Humanities Press, 1958), 66, 67.

13 Lawrence Babb, *The Moral Cosmos of "Paradise Lost"* (East Lansing: Michigan State University Press, 1970), 49–50.

14 Joan S. Bennett, *Reviving Liberty: Radical Christian Humanism in Milton's Great Poems* (Cambridge, MA, and London: Harvard University Press, 1989), 112.

15 The authority of Aquinas would not have mattered much to Milton, although it underwrites Bennett's "governing" assumption. See n10 to this chapter.

16 J.B. Broadbent, *Some Graver Subject: An Essay on "Paradise Lost"* (London: Chatto & Windus, 1960), 248–9, 250.

17 John Peter, *A Critique of "Paradise Lost"* (New York: Columbia University Press, 1960), 116–17.

18 Thomas H. Blackburn, "'Uncloister'd Virtue': Adam and Eve in Milton's Paradise," *Milton Studies* 3 (1971): 133.

19 *Areopagitica*, CPW 2: 516.

20 Diane McColley, *Milton's Eve*, 172.

21 Deborah A. Interdonato, "'Render Me More Equal': Gender Inequality and the Fall in *Paradise Lost*, 9," *Milton Quarterly* 29, no. 4 (December 1995), also notes that "there is the sense in Eve's reasoning that intentions for increased work efficiency are not the most convincing ones for her desire to separate from Adam" (96–7).

22 Philip J. Gallagher, *Milton, the Bible, and Misogyny*, ed. Eugene R. Cunnar and Gail L. Mortimer (Columbia and London: University of Missouri Press, 1990), 71.

23 Ibid., 69. Some three decades earlier, J.H. Summers had noted that Adam "changes his tack: perhaps she is bored with him" (*The Muse's Method*, 171).

24 Christine Froula, "When Eve Reads Milton: Undoing the Canonical Economy," *Critical Inquiry* 10, no. 2 (December 1983): 326.

25 Martin Dzelzainis, "The Politics of *Paradise Lost*," 561.

26 H.N. Brailsford, *The Levellers and the English Revolution*, ed. Christopher Hill (London: Cresset Press, 1961), 317.

27 A.S.P. Woodhouse, *Puritanism and Liberty: Being the Army Debates (1647–9) from the Clarke Manuscripts with Supplementary Documents* (London: J.M. Dent & Sons, 1938), 367–8.

28 See Brailsford, *The Levellers*, 318, n18.

29 "It is improbable that this petition was actually composed by the women. Its principles are none the less interesting" (Woodhouse, *Puritanism and Liberty*, 367). On *invisibility*, see Froula: "The invisible voice that guides Eve away from the visible image of herself in the world to him whose image she is allegorizes what is literally the *secret* not only of spiritual and literary authority in Milton's poem but of cultural authority as such … [T]he power of the voice and of the church fathers, like that of the Wizard of Oz, resides in and depends upon invisibility" ("When Eve Reads Milton," 330).

30 Interdonato, "'Render Me More Equal,'" 100.

31 Ibid., 99, 101.

32 See above, Chapter 10, 263–6.

33 Nor is this the fallacy of *post hoc, ergo propter hoc.*

34 McColley, *Milton's Eve*, 146.

35 Joseph Summers, *The Muse's Method*, offers a rare critical instance here of echo recognition: "When we first see Adam and Eve on the morning of the fatal day, Eve recollects Adam's remarks with a difference: for her they have become the source of minor anxiety" (170).

36 "redress, *v.*" *Shorter Oxford English Dictionary*, 6th ed., vol. 2 (Oxford: Oxford University Press, 2007), defs. 1–4. All four senses of the word were current from late Middle English to the latter part of the seventeenth century.

37 Nigel Smith, *Is Milton Better Than Shakespeare?* (Cambridge, MA: Harvard University Press, 2008), 81.

38 Interdonato, "'Render Me More Equal,'" 99.

39 In "Abdiel and the Son in the Separation Scene," *Milton Studies* 18 (1983), Diana Benet argues that Eve's phrasing in "shak'n or seduc't" is influenced by Raphael's story: "Abdiel appeals to her because he withstood Satan's guiles so heroically and because his status vis-à-vis the tempter and other high-ranking angels corresponds to her own in relation to Adam's" (132). My point is the reverse – that it is Adam who is unconsciously influenced by Raphael, forcing Eve to resist a negative identification with Abdiel.

40 *Areopagitica*, CPW 2: 515.

41 Joan Malory Webber, "The Politics of Poetry: Feminism and *Paradise Lost*," *Milton Studies* 14 (1980): 12.

42 See Summers, *The Muse's Method*, 174–5; Bennett, *Reviving Liberty*, 95, 113–14; Gallagher, *Milton, the Bible, and Misogyny*, 73–4.

43 Augustine, *City of God*, XIV, xiii: 380.

44 C.S. Lewis silently recognizes the force of this emplotment in glossing Augustine as follows: "Adam was not deceived. He did not believe what his wife said to him to be true, but yielded because of the social bond (*socialis necessitudo*) between them (*De Civ. Dei*, XIV, 11)" (*Preface to "Paradise Lost,"* 67).

45 Augustine, *City of God*, XIV, xi: 378.

46 Ibid.

47 Ibid., XIV, xiii: 383.

48 McColley likewise says that, "There is no evidence that Eve responds to the Serpent's flattery in her first reply, and in her second she very sensibly rejects it" (*Milton's Eve*, 196).

49 *Summa Theologica* 2.2.163.1; in *The "Summa Theologica" of St. Thomas Aquinas, Second Part of the Second Part* QQ. CXLI–CLXX: 254.

50 As Gallagher insists, "[H]ypocrisy is therefore a real and insurmountable problem for Eve's intellect (not her will), for the potency of satanic deceit prevents her from exposing fraud at this or at any later prelapsarian juncture" (*Milton, the Bible, and Misogyny*, 77).

51 Walwyn, *The poore Wise-mans Admonition Unto All the plaine People of London and the Neighbour-Places* (10 June 1647), 9.

52 Overton, *The Hunting of the Foxes ... Or The Grandie-Deceivers Unmasked* (21 March 1649), 12.

53 Her failure to remark Eve's need of sympathy and support against the prejudice of Raphael leaves Diane McColley to make "trusting goodness" the cause of her moral failure, thereby accepting, however implicitly, the misogynistic tradition of Eve's credulity: "She is, the narrator says, 'amaz'd' and 'unwarie,' but her mistake is not that she believes the flattery – she does not – but that she believes the story" (*Milton's Eve*, 197).

54 This is true in spite of McColley's claim that it is really Eve's passivity that brings about her fall from grace: "The material of Satan's conquest, then, is not in Eve's 'feminine' weaknesses, which might still have been repaired; not in lack of virtue or education; but in her failure to 'summon all'" (*Milton's Eve*, 204).

55 See Chapter 9 above, 242–8; see Chapter 12, 301–2.

56 Deborah Interdonato, "'Render Me More Equal,'" 95.

57 Joseph Summers observes that Eve "had acted only from self-interest; Adam had been farthest from her thoughs when she ate the Fruit" (*The Muse's Method*, 180).

58 C.S. Lewis is hardly mistaken to say, "I am not sure that critics always notice the precise sin which Eve is now committing, yet there is no mystery about it. Its name in English is Murder" (*A Preface to "Paradise Lost,"* 121).

59 Summers is both perceptive and most relevant on this point: "Adam at the moment of the Fall becomes the embodiment of the romantic rather than the redeeming lover. Like the traditional literary lover, Adam is moved less by his Lady's than by his own plight" (*The Muse's Method*, 181).

60 William Shakespeare, *The Taming of the Shrew* 5, ii: ll.146–9, 155–60, ed. Ann Thompson (Cambridge and New York: Cambridge University Press, 2003), 160.

CHAPTER TWELVE

1 This shift from designated ranks of "hierarchs" to angelic "people" hints at an evolution in Heaven towards populism, if not precisely a heavenly *Agreement of the People.*

2 John Peter, *A Critique of "Paradise Lost"* (New York: Columbia University Press, 1960), takes the contrary view that "God's first reaction to the Fall, in Book Ten, might almost be one of pleasure … Determined that his angels shall not misunderstand him he summons them all from their 'fellowships of joy' into his presence, points out to them just where he stands, and then apparently sends them about their business once again. The episode seems doubly inept. In the first place God is going to inordinate trouble to defend himself, so that one is tempted to imagine the angels' soldierly comments; in the second, the defence he offers is far from conclusive, so that the whole manoeuvre appears to be a waste of time" (144–5).

3 Dennis Danielson, *Milton's Good God: A Study in Literary Theodicy* (Cambridge: Cambridge University Press, 1982), 49.

4 See *The Doctrine and Discipline of Divorce*, CPW 2: "God and nature signifies and lectures to us not onely by those recited decrees, but ev'n by the first and last of all his visible works; when by his divorcing command the world first rose out of Chaos, nor can be renew'd again out of confusion but by the separating of unmeet consorts" (273). Divorce from God is that crucial liminal state in *Paradise Lost* where the Creator will not impose on his intelligent "feminine" other, but where in consequence "she" is left free to prefer "herself" to him, although he remains ever open to reunion with "her."

5 Mary Nyquist, "The Genesis of Gendered Subjectivity," in *Re-membering Milton: Essays on the Texts and Traditions*, ed. Mary Nyquist and Margaret W. Ferguson (New York and London: Methuen, 1987), offers a formidable critique of Eve's "secondariness" in what for her is an "ideologically motivated" manoeuvre in both the divorce tracts and *Paradise Lost*. "Why," Nyquist asks, "if Adam was formed first, then Eve, does Adam tell *his* story to Raphael *last*, in Book VIII?" (115). Because, she concludes, "[B]y associating Eve with the vicissitudes of courtship and marriage, and by emphasizing her voluntary submission both to the paternal voice and to her 'author' and bridegroom, Adam, *Paradise Lost* can *first* present the practice for which Adam *then*, at the epic's leisure, supplies the theory" (123).

6 In *The City of God*, XIV, xxvii, St Augustine had established the orthodox position that, "God preferred not to use His own power, but to leave success or failure to the creature's choice. In this way, God could show both the immense evil that flows from the creature's pride and also the even greater good that comes from His grace" (410).

7 Nyquist suggests that "Milton's Eve tells her story first because the domestic sphere with which her subjectivity associates itself will soon be in need of novels whose heroines are represented learning, in struggles whose conclusions are almost always implicit in the way they begin, the value of submitting desire to the

paternal law" ("Gendered Subjectivity," 123). I find this a prescient observation for reasons other than female indoctrination into the paternal law. Eighteenth- and nineteenth-century women novelists appear to have intuited something of the cosmic significance that Milton ascribes to Eve's choices, thereby making a woman's marriage choices the crucial scene, for two more centuries at least, of cosmic, as well as domestic, gain or loss.

8 Peter, *A Critique of "Paradise Lost,"* 147.

9 Hugh MacCallum, *Milton and the Sons of God: The Divine Image in Milton's Epic Poetry* (Toronto: University of Toronto Press, 1986), 175.

10 Marjorie Hope Nicolson, *John Milton: A Reader's Guide to His Poetry* (New York: The Noonday Press, 1963), 292.

11 St Augustine notes in *The City of God* XIV, xv, that "There is a worse and more execrable kind of pride whereby one seeks the subterfuge of an excuse even when one's sin is manifest ... The pride of the woman blames the serpent; the man's pride blames the woman" (384). And Aquinas argues in *Summa Theologica* 2.2.163.4 that "The woman was deceived because she was first of all puffed up with pride. Wherefore her ignorance did not excuse, but aggravated her sin, in so far as it was the cause of her being puffed up with still greater pride" (260). While pride has little to do with the fall of Milton's Adam, it proves to be the keynote of his postlapsarian self-defence. Eve, by comparison, is less proud, more honest, and more dignified than her husband in his garrulous blame of God and her together.

12 By contrast, Aquinas says that "The man's reliance on God's mercy did not reach to contempt of God's justice, wherein consists the sin against the Holy Ghost, but as Augustine says (*De. Civ. Dei* XIV.xi), it was due to the fact that, *having had no experience of God's severity, he thought the sin to be venial*, i.e., easily forgiven" (261).

13 Readers would assume the truth of this claim because Aquinas said as much in *Summa Theologica*, 2.2.164.2: "Likewise the subjection of woman to man results from the perfection of the male, and the imperfection of the female sex" (267).

14 "Doctrine and Discipline of Divorce," *CPW* 2: 282–3.

15 Ibid., 338.

16 Here, it is difficult to credit McColley's reading of the outcome: "That Eve is now to be ruled by Adam is typologically fitting, since apprenticeship to the Law will prepare God's people for the freedom that the 'Seed of Woman' will restore. Yet Eve is never demeaned by coercion or loss of mutuality" (*Milton's Eve*, 211).

17 Walwyn, *Tyranipocrit* (14 August 1649), 3.

18 *The City of God*, XIV, xxviii: 410.

19 Walwyn, *Tyranipocrit*, 21.

20 Rumrich, "Milton's God and the Matter of Chaos," *PMLA* 110 (October 1995): 1040.

21 Richard Overton, *A New Bull-Bayting* (7 August 1649), 3.

22 Kester Svendsen, "Adam's Soliloquy in Book X of *Paradise Lost*," in *Milton: Modern Essays in Criticism*, ed. Arthur Barker (London: Oxford University Press, 1965), 329.

23 Ibid., 329.

24 St Augustine, *The City of God*, 385.

25 Harold Pinter, *The Homecoming* (London: Methuen, 1965), 36.

26 Marshall Grossman, *"Authors to Themselves": Milton and the Revelation of History* (Cambridge: Cambridge University Press, 1987), 157.

27 See Roland Mushat Frye, *Milton's Imagery and the Visual Arts: Iconographic Tradition in the Epic Poems* (Princeton, NJ: Princeton University Press, 1978), 104; Plates 185 and 198.

28 "Medea," *The Plays of Euripides*, trans. Moses Hadas and John Harvey McLean (New York: The Dial Press, 1936), 76.

29 Svendsen, "Adam's Soliloquy," 331.

30 Ibid.

31 Georgia B. Christopher, "The Verbal Gate to Paradise: Adam's 'Literary Experience' in Book X of *Paradise Lost*," *PMLA* 70, no. 1 (January 1975), offers a concise, if somewhat misguided, challenge to the "romantic notion that it is Eve's love that leads Adam back to God" (69).

32 As Diane McColley remarks, "Eve's part as the first to repent and seek reconciliation is the one act for which she is generally given her due, if not more" (*Milton's Eve*, 210).

33 Summers, *The Muse's Method*, 176.

34 Ibid., 179.

35 See Rumrich, "Milton's God and the Matter of Chaos," 1040, for discussion of Sin as Eve's antithesis, since the fixed bridge Sin builds over the abyss denies any possibility of freedom to Chaos.

36 McColley, *Milton's Eve*, 210; see also 69–76.

37 Marshall Grossman, *"Authors to Themselves,"* 160.

38 Christopher, "The Verbal Gate to Paradise," 69.

39 "First therefore let us remember as a thing not to be deny'd, that all places of Scripture wherin just reason of doubt arises from the letter, are to be expounded by considering upon what occasion every thing is set down: and by comparing other Texts" (*CPW* 2: 282).

40 For a very different reason, William Kerrigan remarks similarly of Milton's last great poems that "Will is the faculty of moment in these works, not reason." See Kerrigan, "The Irrational Coherence of *Samson Agonistes*," *Milton Studies* 22 (1986): 218.

CHAPTER THIRTEEN

1 Joseph H. Summers, *The Muse's Method: An Introduction to "Paradise Lost"* (London: Chatto & Windus, 1962), 186.

2 Thomas Newton, 226. *Paradise lost, by John Milton; with notes, selected from Newton and others, to which is prefixed, the life of the author. With a critical dissertation, on the poetical works of Milton, and Observations on his Language and*

Versification. by Samuel Johnson, L.L.D., vol 2 (London, 1796). Eighteenth Century Collections Online. Gale. University of Manitoba. 14 August 2014.

3 Joseph Addison, *The Spectator* 363 (Saturday, 26 April 1712): 735. *The Spectator … Volume 5. London,* MDCCXCIII. *[1793]*. Eighteenth Century Collections Online. Gale. University of Manitoba. 14 January 2015.

4 J.B. Broadbent, *Some Graver Subject: An Essay on "Paradise Lost"* (London: Chatto & Windus, 1960), 268, 279, 267.

5 John Peter, *A Critique of "Paradise Lost"* (New York: Columbia University Press, 1960), 139, 140.

6 David Loewenstein, *Milton and the Drama of History: Historical Vision, Iconoclasm, and the Literary Imagination* (Cambridge: Cambridge University Press, 1990), 93.

7 C.S. Lewis, *A Preface to "Paradise Lost"* (1942; London and Oxford: Oxford University Press, 1960), 125.

8 Charles Martindale, *John Milton and the Transformation of Ancient Epic* (London and Sydney: Croom Helm, 1986), 148, 149.

9 Addison, *The Spectator* 363 (Saturday, 26 April 1712): 734. This judgment is supported, however, by little more than a generality: "Adam's vision is not confined to any particular tribe of mankind, but extends to the whole species." Addison was unlikely, in the early years of the British Empire, to disapprove of Virgil's politics or the imperial design of his epic; rather, he seems to have approved of Milton's universalism more than anything else.

10 Lawrence A. Sasek, "The Drama of *Paradise Lost*, Books XI and XII," in *Milton: Modern Essays in Criticism*, ed. Arthur E. Barker (London and New York: Oxford University Press, 1965), 342–56. As Sasek rightly observes, "[T]he differences between Milton's biblical pageant and the analogous epic scenes of his predecessors are fundamental" (345), although his reading tends toward didactic orthodoxy, where Adam is schooled into "acceptance," rather than justification of God's ways.

11 Louis Martz, *Poet of Exile: A Study of Milton's Poetry* (New Haven and London: Yale University Press), 169.

12 See "A Poem Written in Ten Books," Chapter 9 of Martz, *Poet of Exile*, 155–68.

13 Virgil, *The Aeneid* (vi.1017–18), trans. Robert Fitzgerald (New York: Vintage, 1985), 186.

14 For the Latin original, see *Virgil*, vol. 1, trans. H. Rushton Fairclough, Loeb Classical Library (Cambridge, MA: Harvard University Press, 1940): "hic Caesar et omnis Iuli / progenies, magnum caeli ventura sub axem. / hic vir, hic est, tibi quem promitti saepius audis, / Augustus Caesar, Divi genus, aurea condet / saecula qui rursus Latio regnata per arva / Saturno quondam, super et Garamantas et Indos / proferet imperium (iacet extra sidera tellus, / extra anni solisque vias)" (vi.789–96).

15 Brooks Otis, *Virgil: A Study in Civilized Poetry* (Oxford: The Clarendon Press, 1963), remarks of Aeneas that he "has finally seen the true *telos* or goal, finally realized what it means to be the Augustan prototype. There can be no further

faltering" (302). For, "It is to Rome, Augustus, the *imperium sine fine* that" Anchises "points as the goal, the true meaning of human action and *pietas*" (301).

16 Martindale, *Transformation of Ancient Epic*, 147.

17 As Summers reads "The Pattern at the Centre" of Milton's epic, "The publication of the poem in twelve books [1674] seems to have been the result of a change in Milton's perception of what he had already made, rather than of a decision to make something new." The structural change shifted the poem's emphasis from "the pattern of the 'one just man,' the individual saving remnant in the midst of evil, the angel who resists temptation and conquers trial" (*The Muse's Method*, 112), to "the war in Heaven and the Creation of the world," and "God's ways at their most providential" (113).

18 See Chapter 2 above for evidence of Milton's continuing collaboration with Marchamont Nedham as the political journalist "Politicus."

19 *Politicus* 98 (22 April 1652): 1537–8.

20 This theology of sonship, if not its political analogue, finds its definitive treatment in Hugh MacCallum's *Milton and the Sons of God: The Divine Image in Milton's Epic Poetry* (Toronto: University of Toronto Press, 1986).

21 Ibid., 75.

22 Ibid., 127.

23 Walwyn, *Tyranipocrit*, 21.

24 Thomas Amorose, "Milton the Apocalyptic Historian: Competing Genres in *Paradise Lost*, Books XI–XII," *Milton Studies* 17 (1983): 141.

25 Ibid., 146, 141.

26 Loewenstein, *Milton and the Drama of History: Historical Vision, Iconoclasm, and the Literary Imagination* (Cambridge: Cambridge University Press, 1990), 5.

27 Ibid., 93.

28 Amorose, "Milton the Apocalyptic Historian," 156.

29 Loewenstein, *Milton and the Drama of History*, 125.

30 Summers, *The Muse's Method*, 191.

31 Cf. Christopher Hill, *Milton and the English Revolution* (London: Faber & Faber, 1977): "At first man's inhumanity to man fills Adam with the naive horror felt by many of the English revolutionaries when they had to face the apparent injustice of the Resoration. 'Is piety thus and pure devotion paid?' Adam cries when he is shown Cain murdering Abel" (380).

32 Summers, *The Muse's Method*, 199.

33 Lilburne, *A Discourse Betwixt Lieutenant Colonel Iohn Lilburn, Close Prisoner in the Tower of* London, *and Mr Hugh Peter* (25 May 1649), 4–5.

34 Lilburne, *Strength out of Weaknesse* (30 September 1649), 12.

35 Addison, *Spectator* 363: 734–5.

36 See Brooks Otis, *Ovid as an Epic Poet* (Cambridge: Cambridge University Press, 1966), for a full discussion of the Flood as satire. As Otis says, "It is almost as if Ovid were insisting on the epic character of his poem; like Virgil, he is bringing in Jupiter at the start, and, like Virgil, he is indicating the solemnity of crisis

by a formal council of the gods. *Dignas Iove concipit iras* – here is a proper epic rage; here is a god whose wrath befits his august power. But in the next few lines (168–80) Ovid does something very un-Virgilian. He modernizes the whole scene and brings it right down to the level of his own, contemporary Rome" (97). Rhetorically, Otis asks, "Is Ovid saying that the Augustan *maiestas* is only a sham and that the 'gods' of Rome are, after all, as amorous and comically human as anybody else – as himself for example?" (126).

37 See Otis, *Virgil: A Study in Civilized Poetry*, 65–96, for discussion of the poet's "subjective style" throughout *Aeneid*. For an example of direct narrative address to a dying hero, see *Virgil in Two Volumes*, rev. ed., vol. 2, *Aeneid VII–XII* (London: William Heinemann, 1942): "Fortunati ambo! si quid mea carmina possunt, / nulla dies umquam memori vos eximet aevo" (*Aeneid*, ix, 446–7): ["Fortunate pair! If my song is able, no day shall ever blot you from the memory of time" (my translation)].

38 Virgil, *The Aeneid* (viii.1017–18), trans. Robert Fitzgerald (New York: Vintage, 1985), 256. For the original, see *Aeneid*, viii, 729–31: "Talia per clipeum Volcani, dona parentis, / miratur rerumque ignarus imagine gaudet, / attollens umero famamque et fata nepotum."

39 Stuart Curran, "God," in *The Oxford Handbook of Milton*, ed. Nicholas McDowell and Nigel Smith (Oxford: Oxford University Press, 2009), 530, 531.

40 *Virgil*, vol. 1, *Aeneid*, i, 278–3: "hic ego nec metas rerum nec tempora pono; / imperium sine fine dedi. quin aspera Iuno, / quae mare nunc terrasque metu caelumque fatigat, / consilia in melius referet, mecumque fovebit / Romanos, rerum dominos, gentemque togatam. / sic placitum."

41 Ibid., 31–3: "multosque per annos / errabant, acti fatis, maria omnia circum. / tantae molis erat Romanam condere gentem."

42 MacCallum, *Milton and the Sons of God*, makes a similar observation that "The understanding which Adam reaches at this point is far from complete: he still thinks in terms of restoration to an outward paradise through justice. Yet the language he is learning is capable of sudden transfiguration when the truth is finally revealed, and the reader is aware that Adam is being prepared without his knowledge for the Incarnation" (196).

CHAPTER FOURTEEN

1 Joseph Addison, *The Spectator* 363 (Saturday, 26 April 1712): 735.

2 Addison, *The Spectator* 369 (Saturday, 3 May 1712): 744–5. *The Spectator … Volume 5. London, MDCCXCIII. [1793].* Eighteenth-Century Collections Online. Gale. University of Manitoba. 14 January 2015.

3 This, according to the first publisher of *Paradise Lost*, Samuel Simmons, concerning both the second and third impressions of the poem in 1668. See Roy Flannagan, *The Riverside Milton*, "The Verse," 352, n6.

4 Here, Michael contradicts his earlier claim that Adam is not to enjoy "paternal rule," but will be "brought down / To dwell on eeven ground now with thy Sons" (11.347–8), although the inconsistency is likely Milton's own, given the substantial length of Michael's denial of "paternal rule" in Book 11 as compared to his brief phrase here.

5 Cicero's "law of Nature" differs from Milton's law of Nature mostly by virtue of the "nature" of Milton's material deity that renders matter instinct with reason, and "correct reason congruent with nature" (*De republica*, trans. David Fott [Ithaca and London: Cornell University Press, 2014], 98). People thus have a natural right to resist tyranny, to choose or reject their rulers, to receive justice, etc. For "Milton and natural right" see Chapter 9 above, 237–8; for Cicero, see Chapter 1 above, 45, and n44.

6 Don Wolfe concludes that "it is Milton's peculiar emphasis on sin which removes him from the extreme democratic theory as embodied in the law of nature. By the law of nature, in Milton's opinion, men are born free, but having rejected God, they may rightfully be subject to a tyrant against their will" (*Milton in the Puritan Revolution* [1941; London: Cohen & West, 1963], 331). But Michael's formulation of the problem – to "dispossess / Concord and law of Nature from the Earth" – really describes a dispossession rather than a punishment, not unlike that "fair equalitie, fraternal state" (*PL* 12.26) which *had* persisted after the Fall, suggesting that the "*law* of Nature" has not been abrogated, in spite of those Nimrods who "will arrogate Dominion undeserv'd."

7 For a view of Nimrod in relation to the topos of tyranny and slavery in the poem, see Mary Nyquist, "Slavery, Resistance, and Nation in Milton and Locke," in *Early Modern Nationalism and Milton's England*, ed. David Loewenstein and Paul Stevens (Toronto and Buffalo: University of Toronto Press, 2008), 356–97. Equating Milton's views on political liberty with those of Locke, Nyquist argues that each uses "slavery" analogically to give European males – at the top of a hierarchy of three distinct modes of servitude – the right of resistance to tyranny, while denying the same right to "African" sons of Ham, thereby defending the institution of "chattel slavery" that she takes to be implicit in Adam's discourse with Michael. Despite its brilliant deconstruction of liberal ideology in the rhetorical figures of each writer, Nyquist's argument ultimately turns on a strained reading of a single phrase – "no wrong" (368) – and finally founders on its curious failure to identify Nimrod as the grandson of Ham and son of the "cursed" Canaan. Is the "racialized" curse of "those who become 'servant of servants'" (368) not bound to fall on Nimrod's race for the colossal injustice of having made servants of everyone else?

8 David Loewenstein, *Milton and the Drama of History: Historical Vision, Iconoclasm, and the Literary Imagination* (Cambridge: Cambridge University Press, 1990), remarks that, for Milton, "Nimrod is a figure of political ambition, defiance, and strife, setting his power directly against the power of God: like Satan he acts 'as in despite of Heav'n' and claims 'second Sovranty' (XII.34–5); like Charles

he attempts to subvert a more progressive historical period, characterized by 'fair equality' and 'fraternal state' (XII.26)" (110).

9 *Politicus* 26 (5 December 1650): 423.

10 *Politicus* 98 (22 April 1652): 1538.

11 Lilburne, *Londons Liberty in Chains discovered* (2 November 1646), 19.

12 Lilburne, *An Impeachment of High Treason against Oliver Cromwell* (10 August 1649), 18 [misnumbered 16].

13 William Walwyn, *The Fountain of Slaunder* (30 May 1649), 15.

14 Summers, *The Muse's Method*, 212–13.

15 MacCallum makes the important point that, "It is Adam who first uses the title 'Son of God,' recognizing in a sudden flash that … [this] is none other than the divine being known to him through Raphael's accounts of the war in heaven and the creation" (*Milton and the Sons of God: The Divine Image in Milton's Epic Poetry* [Toronto: University of Toronto Press, 1986], 198).

16 This is not to suggest that Milton was a member of the Familist sect, but that he gave a new, and fundamentally metaphysical, emplotment to this narrative of the "gathered" Family of God. See Hill, *Milton and the English Revolution* (London: Faber & Faber, 1977), for Milton's affinities with this heretical sect (70–3, 299–302); see Alistair Hamilton, *The Family of Love* (Cambridge: Cambridge University Press, 1981), for a history of the sect in England.

17 John Rogers, "*Paradise Regained* and the Memory of *Paradise Lost*," in *The Oxford Handbook of Milton*, ed. Nicholas McDowell and Nigel Smith (Oxford: Oxford University Press, 2009), 589–612, tends to overread Michael's revelation of a Christology that progresses from adoptionism to Socinianism to low-key Arianism. Adam's sense of a "fight," or what Michael calls a "duel," suggests that he has already made an intuitive identification between this "Seed of Woman" and the Son of Raphael's War in Heaven.

18 Hill, *Milton and the English Revolution*, 73.

19 Gretchen E. Minton, "'The Same Cause and Like Quarell': Eusebius, John Foxe, and the Evolution of Ecclesiastical History," *Church History* 71, no. 4 (December 2002): 729.

20 Ibid., 730.

21 Recalling how the "*Acts and Monuments* asserted the importance of the monarchy and the Protestant episcopacy, and showed God working through such established individuals as Constantine and Elizabeth – the latter-day Constantine – to combat and overcome the powers of Antichrist," David Loewenstein concludes that Milton's "view of Foxe in *Of Reformation*" was ambivalent, an outlook which he attributes to Milton's "uneasiness regarding this conservative apocalypticism, which lacks the emphasis upon dramatic and violent renovation inspired by revolutionary millennialism. By encouraging a reverent approach towards the regime of Elizabeth and the reformed Church of England, Foxe's work made the apocalyptic sense of history an essentially orthodox vision" (*Milton and the Drama of History*, 10). Foxe, however, had already "omitted the explicit comparison between

Constantine and Elizabeth ... in later versions of the *Acts and Monuments*," so that "his changing attitudes toward the Elizabethan church and state can be seen even in subsequent editions of the *Acts and Monuments*" (Minton, "The Same Cause," 717, 737, n33). Furthermore, the posthumous editions of 1596, 1610, 1631–32, and 1641 reflect Foxe's later views. Don Wolfe notes how Milton's "references to Foxe in *The Judgement of Martin Bucer* fit ... the seventh English edition of *Acts and Monuments* (1631–32)," and that Milton "may have used" this edition in *Of Reformation* where, though he "does not mention Foxe by name, he is indebted to him ... on many pages of *Of Reformation*" (CPW 1: 524, n24).

22 In "*Paradise Regained* and the Politics of Martyrdom," *Modern Philology* 90, no. 2 (November 1992), Laura Lunger Knoppers suggests that, while "Foxe writes to support Elizabeth and the established church, to advise the queen in her destined role as true sovereign; yet the martyrdoms he most vividly and elaborately recounts" in his continually expanding editions of the martyrology "are those of middle- and lower-class subjects under conformity proceedings mandated by another monarch – bloody Queen Mary" (206).

23 Christopher Mead, *Mass Communication: The Eucharist and Authorship in Early Modern England* (PhD diss., University of California, Berkeley, 2015), 3.

24 Calvin's "Short Treatise on the Lord's Supper" (1541) offers a trenchant reason for the "False Opinion of the Bodily Presence of Christ in the Supper," in *Tracts and Treatises on the Doctrine and Worship of the Church*, vol. 2, trans. Henry Beveridge (Grand Rapids, MI: Wm. B. Eerdmans, 1958), 186–7. To Calvin, the bread and the wine are no more than "visible signs" (171–2) of the Real Presence which is communicated by the Word.

25 Mead, *Mass Communication*, 26.

26 Walwyn, *Tyranipocrit* (14 August 1649), 8.

27 Summers, *The Muse's Method*, 218.

28 Gretchen E. Minton, "'The Same Cause and Like Quarell,'" 738.

29 Apropos of Foxe's movement from triumphalism to apocalypticism, Minton makes the point that "history for Protestants was inherently a history of persecution and struggle against a consistently defined 'other' that was usually named the Roman Catholic Church. Once the identification of the Pope with the Antichrist became commonplace, Revelation was instilled as an indispensable part of Protestant polemic" ("The Same Cause," 740). In Milton's case, it was evidently an indispensable part of republican and Protestant polemic alike.

30 Loewenstein, *Milton and the Drama of History*, 116.

31 Here, Summers finds something of the same pessimism that Loewenstein will later read into this passage: "The bleakness of Michael's account of post-Apostolic history has disturbed readers from the eighteenth to the twentieth centures. (The eighteenth-century readers were more disturbed than their successors by the fact that Michael makes no mention of the Reformation)" (*The Muse's Method*, 219).

32 Sharon Achinstein, *Milton and the Revolutionary Reader* (Princeton, NJ: Princeton University Press, 1994), 221, 224.

33 Rachel Foxley says something similar about the Levellers' expected readership, where, "indeed, when Lilburne appealed to free-born Englishmen there was a … sense that only a minority would heed the call, at least at first" (*The Levellers: Radical Political Thought in the English Revolution* [Manchester and New York: Manchester University Press, 2013], 141).

34 Lilburne, *Strength out of Weaknesse* (30 September 1649), title page.

35 Three weeks later – barely a fortnight before his trial and unexpected acquittal by a jury of his peers – Lilburne was to put on the public record a complete listing of his literary remains, admitting for the first time, in *The Innocent Man's second-Proffer* (22 October 1649), to authorship of forty-five unauthorized publications for which he had previously refused to answer.

36 Lilburne, *Strength out of Weaknesse*, 25.

37 Lilburne, as Stephen Strehle observes in *The Egalitarian Spirit of Christianity: The Sacred Roots of American and British Government* (New Brunswick, NJ: Transaction Publishers, 2009), was following the example "set forth in Foxe's *Acts and Monuments* (the so-called *Book of Martyrs*), which Lilburne and much of England read with pious devotion and incarnated within their very lives … His ultimate goal was to die for the Lord and have his tombstone engraved with the simple words, 'A faithful Martyr of Our Liberties'" (46).

38 Richard Overton, *The Hunting of the Foxes* (21 March 1649), 20.

39 See Christopher Hill, *Milton and the English Revolution*, 389.

40 *A Petition of Women* (7 May 1649), 369; see Chapter 6 above, 186–8.

41 In formal as well as historical terms, rather than the dramatic and metaphysical ones which I emphasize, David Norbrook remarks in *Writing the English Republic: Poetry, Rhetoric and Politics, 1627–1660* (Cambridge: Cambridge University Press, 1999) how "Her 'restore' (xii.623) refers us back to the 'greater Man' of the poem's opening who will 'Restore us.' By the time the poem was published, the word could be taken as a direct, polemical contrast with Charles's Restoration. In the context of the poem's origins, however, it would have retained a more radical, republican meaning, one that looked back to a pristine liberty and revived a longing for its return" (490).

42 As Roland Mushat Frye, *Milton's Imagery and the Visual Arts: Iconographic Tradition in the Epic Poems* (Princeton, NJ: Princeton University Press, 1978), remarks of this "terrible beauty," although without the use of Yeats's phrase: "No one could expect, or even hope, in the paintings of Masaccio and Michelangelo that the tears of Adam and Eve could be wiped away soon, or that their despair could give place to the muted optimism of Milton's closing lines" (314).

43 Ibid., 313.

44 Roy Flannagan, "The 1688 Illustrations," *The Riverside Milton*, 333.

45 This is to recall the political implications of the cormorant as an image of monarchy that threatens the democratic equality of paradise. See Chapter 6, n24 above.

46 Here is my irreducible point of difference from Loewenstein, who believes that "The just man of Michael's visions *would like* to be radically involved in the social

order – to be an activist agent in the turbulent process of history – but instead finds himself radically alienated from the historical process itself" (*Milton and the Drama of History*, 104).

47 See Brian Johnson, "Sacred Silence: The Death of the 'Author' and *Paradise Lost*," *Milton Quarterly* 29, no. 3 (October 1995): 65–76.

48 This is to reverse the established twentieth-century judgment pioneered by Don Wolfe that "it was by the harsher strain of Calvinistic coloring, the 'retributive justice of the Deity,' that Milton interpreted the crashing of his hopes for England's salvation … Not Milton the pagan humanist, or Milton the tolerationist, but Milton the stern prophet pronounced judgment upon sinning man in *Paradise Lost*" (*Milton in the Puritan Revolution* [1941; London: Cohen & West, 1963], 342–3).

CHAPTER FIFTEEN

1 For John Rogers, Milton's literally incomparable "sequel depends for its culminating truth on the interdependence of the two works," where "the original epic comes to depend on the sequel for the verification of the quasi-scriptural status of its own most daring mythology" ("*Paradise Regained* and the Memory of *Paradise Lost*," in *The Oxford Handbook of Milton*, ed. Nicholas McDowell and Nigel Smith [Oxford: Oxford University Press, 2009], 608). But Rogers reads its dialectics as didactic rather than dramatic, its purpose being to mount, "in the register of poetic fiction, a powerful, dialectically structured attack on the orthodox Christianity with which we know he so vigorously took issue" (611).

2 See Barbara Kiefer Lewalski, *Milton's Brief Epic: The Genre, Meaning, and Art of "Paradise Regained"* (Providence: Brown University Press, 1966), for a definitive history of the literary tradition of Job as an epic poem (10–36), and as a neoclassical model for the brief biblical epic (68–101). More generally, she interprets the biblical allusions typologically in their function to manifest the Son as prophet, king, and priest.

3 Edward Phillips, "The Life of Mr John Milton," *The Early Lives of Milton*, ed. Helen Darbishire (1932; New York: Barnes & Noble, 1965), 75–6.

4 Northrop Frye, "The Typology of *Paradise Regained*," *Modern Philology* 53 (1956): 227–38. Reprinted in *Milton: Modern Essays in Criticism*, ed. Arthur E. Barker (London: Oxford University Press, 1965), 439, 440.

5 Alan Fisher, "Why Is *Paradise Regained* So Cold?" *Milton Studies* 14 (1980): 195–217.

6 Laura Lunger Knoppers, "*Paradise Regained* and the Politics of Martyrdom," *Modern Philology* 90, no. 2 (November 1992): 218–19.

7 Gretchen Minton leaves little doubt that Eusebius and other "martyrologists were following a precedent set by Jesus' insistence that no earthly ruler (for example, Pilate or Herod) could control this divinely directed courtroom drama" ("'The Same Cause and Like Quarell': Eusebius, John Foxe, and the Evolution

of Ecclesiastical History," *Church History* 71, no. 4 [December 2002]: 727). The Foxean tradition, however, does not construct an image of King Jesus, royal heir to the House of David, but rather the "man of sorrows" who "was in all points tempted like as we are" (Hebrews 4: 15).

8 As Knoppers admits, "He is the 'Son of God' (thirty-six times), the 'Son' (fifteen times), 'our Saviour' (eighteen times), 'Jesus' (five times), 'Messiah' (seven times), but never Christ, the one in whom the kingly line of David had been fulfilled" ("Politics of Martyrdom," 214).

9 John Foxe, *The Unabridged Acts and Monuments Online* [TAMO] (1583), "Preface," 11. HRI Online Publications, Sheffield, 2011. Accessed 24 September 2014 at: http//www.johnfoxe.org.

10 Gretchen E. Minton, "'The Same Cause," 720.

11 Ibid., 718–19.

12 *AV*, Acts 6: 5 and Acts 7: 56, 58.

13 *AV*, 1 Timothy 1: 15.

14 John Foxe,. *TAMO* (1583), "Preface," 15. HRI Online Publications, Sheffield, 2011. Accessed 24 September 2014 at: http//www.johnfoxe.org.

15 This is the semi-serious conclusion of Laura Knoppers's compelling argument: "Milton's highly politicized redaction of the temptation of Christ in the wilderness, fully implicated in the contemporary politics of martyrdom, might be better named the (new) gospel according to John" ("Politics of Martyrdom," 219).

16 Minton, "The Same Cause," 725.

17 Ibid.

18 This secret ecclesiastical court is exactly opposite to the very public trial of Charles I.

19 Minton, "The Same Cause," 730.

20 John Foxe, *TAMO* (1583), Book 11, 1609. HRI Online Publications, Sheffield, 2011. Accessed 25 September 2014 at: http//www.johnfoxe.org.

21 Ibid., 1617.

22 Ibid., "Preface," 15.

23 See Chapter 5, n23, for a discussion of the Arian iconography preserved in Ravenna.

24 Minton, "The Same Cause," 727.

25 "Initiation in the Wilderness" is the title of MacCallum's final chapter on *Paradise Regain'd* in *Milton and the Sons of God: The Divine Image in Milton's Epic Poetry* (Toronto: University of Toronto Press, 1986), 226–67.

26 Lewalski reads the poem as a drama of identity not only for Satan but also for Jesus: "He is in the process of winning back the understanding which he previously possessed by means of the teaching of the Father – 'For what concerns my knowledge God reveals.' Though Christ's claim is unambiguous, Satan, the embodiment of the literal mind of evil, cannot fully understand it. Satan shifts ground again and presents himself as a Baalam figure – a miserable liar who yet desires to hear truth in Christ's company" (*Milton's Brief Epic*, 214).

27 Aside from a much greater possibility of drama in Luke's account (ending on the pinnacle) rather than in Matthew's version (ending with the kingdoms), Milton has an equally compelling reason to choose the former for his model: at the end of Luke's version, Jesus returned to Nazareth, and stood up in the synagogue to read aloud from "the book of the prophet Esaias … where it was written, The Spirit of the Lord is upon me, because he hath anointed me to preach the gospel to the poor; he hath sent me to heal the broken-hearted, to preach deliverance to the captives, and recovering of sight to the blind, to set at liberty them that are bruised; To preach the acceptable year of the Lord" (Luke 4: 17–19). The biblical Jesus returns from the wilderness, much like Milton's Jesus, to begin his mission on earth as a *reader* of scripture.

28 Virgil, *Aeneid*, 6.1153–4, trans. Robert Fitzgerald, 190.

29 The Miltonic narrator uses the rare word "debel" (from "debellare superbos," *Aeneid*, 6.853) at the end of the poem – "him long of old / Thou didst debel" (4.605–6) – to signal the advent of the true Prince of Peace, and not some impostor of the *pax Romana*.

30 William Walwyn, *Tyranipocrit* (14 August 1649), 3.

31 Ibid., 40.

32 John Foxe, TAMO (1583), Book 11: 1615. HRI Online Publications, Sheffield, 2011. Accessed 25 September 2014 at: http//www.johnfoxe.org.

33 Ibid., 1615.

34 Ibid., 1613. In the "Apparatus," the editors note in their "Commentary on the Text" that "This is the only record of this sermon, but undoubtedly this is a distorted version of what Ridley actually said." Foxe's readers were more likely to view it as another of the devil's lies.

35 "The account of the disputations at Oxford in April 1554 is the heart of Book 10" of the 1583 *Actes and Monuments* (TAMO, "Apparatus," Block 17). These academic debates pitted the Anglicans Cranmer, Ridley, and Latimer against "the Diuines & learned men of both the Vniuersities, Oxford and Cambridge, about the presence, substance, and sacrifice of the sacrament" (TAMO [1583], Book 10, 1452).

36 Ibid., Book. 11, 1609–10.

37 Ibid., 1611.

38 Ibid.

39 Ibid.

CHAPTER SIXTEEN

1 Lilburne, *The Iust Mans Iustification* (10 June 1646), 11.

2 Overton and Walwyn, *A Remonstrance of Many Thousand Citizens* (7 July 1646), 13.

3 Richard Overton, *A Defiance against all Arbitrary Usurpations* (9 September 1646), 2.

4 Lilburne, *The Legall Fundamental Liberties*, rev. edn. (4 August 1649), 25.

5 Lilburne, *The Free-Mans Freedome Vindicated* (23 June 1646), 11.

6 In *Milton and the Sons of God: The Divine Image in Milton's Epic Poetry* (Toronto: University of Toronto Press, 1986), Hugh MacCallum notes that "his expression of the will of the Father does not make him hypostatically one with the Father: his divine nature does not consist in essential identity with the Godhead," but in obedient conformity to the Divine will. "The moral and spiritual perfection which enables him to fulfill God's will would be undercut if he were, in fact, the same being as God" (261).

7 Stanley Fish, "Inaction and Silence: The Reader in *Paradise Regained*," in *Calm of Mind: Tercentenary Essays on "Paradise Regained" and "Samson Agonistes" in Honor of John S. Diekhoff*, ed. Joseph Anthony Wittreich (Cleveland: The Press of Case Western Reserve University, 1971), 32.

8 MacCallum sees only an inner dialectic at work in the Son's development: "The first soliloquy shows the operation of this characteristic pattern in the past: a dialectical movement leads from the desire to promote all truth and righteousness by reading the law, through the aspiration to restore true liberty to earth by heroic deeds, to the recognition that persuasion may be more effective than fear, then on through the reinterpretation of all in the light of revelation to the concluding idea of a redeemer who must act heroically by suffering and persuade men to embrace life by his death" (*Milton and the Sons of God*, 246).

9 "Haukes: To be short with you, I will knowe whether ye wil recant anye more or no, before I talke with you, credite you, or beleue you." John Foxe, TAMO (1583), Book 11: 1615. HRI Online Publications, Sheffield, 2011. Accessed 20 January 2015 at: http//www.johnfoxe.org.

10 Ibid., 1611. Accessed 9 October 2014.

11 Lilburne claimed in *An Impeachment of High Treason against Oliver Cromwell* (10 August 1649) "*That my Lord* Wharton … did beleeve money was not very plentifull with me," and "that he hath in readinesse a very considerable token for me" if Lilburne would only drop his suit. "*But for me to receive his money, I could not in the least do it*, … (as he was now a Patentee prerogative Lord, and exercised a Legislative and arbitrary power by vertue thereof, which I looked upon as altogether destructive to the very being of the Liberties and Freedoms of the Commons of *England*) *I could not in the least do it: but was absolutely resolved to professe open War with his arbitrary Prerogative-Lordship as long as I had breath in my body*, and never to be reconciled unto it" (41–2).

12 Lilburne, *The Copy of a Letter* (9 August 1645), 16 [misnumbered 61].

13 See Chapter 5, n30.

14 Walwyn, *Tyranipocrit* (14 August 1649), 3.

15 Milton's patrician bias in the Commonwealth period is well known, as in the comeuppance he gave to Salmasius in *Defensio* (1651): "You must attack the populace as 'blind and brutish, without skill in ruling, the most fickle of men, the emptiest, the unsteadiest, and most inconstant.' This description best fits yourself. It may be true of the dregs of the populace, but hardly of the middle class, which produces the

greatest number of men of good sense and knowledge of affairs" (CPW 4.i: 471). "A miscellaneous rabble" and "a herd confus'd" might be evidence of a middle-class prejudice in *Paradise Regain'd*, were it not for the fact that Satan's attack on Jesus as one of those "dregs," together with "our Saviour's" mission of *universal* atonement, and the dramatic occasion for a *dialectical* retort, all point to a more plebeian Milton in the Restoration era.

16 Elaine B. Safer, "The Socratic Dialogue and 'Knowledge in the Making' in *Paradise Regained*," *Milton Studies* 6 (1975), argues that "The Socratic need to question the assumptions of mankind parallels Christ's questioning of the worldly values presented by Satan, values which are so close to those of most readers" (218). My argument moves in a parallel direction, where the dialectical drama also makes Satan into a Socratic figure who negates every stance and position taken by Jesus on worldly values.

17 See Barbara Kiefer Lewalski, *Milton's Brief Epic: The Genre, Meaning, and Art of "Paradise Regained"* (Providence: Brown University Press, 1966), for his use of biblical typology in making the wilderness temptation a "reprise of the past," especially that of Job's temptation (e.g., 164–6, 179, 292–5, 307–8).

18 In this context, the phrase "proudest Conquerours" could allude to Lilburne's rejection of "common law practices in *Westminster* Hall" which "came in by the will of a Tyrant, namly *William* the Conqueror, who by his sword conquered this Kingdome, and professed he had it from none but God and his sword" (*The Iust Mans Iustification* [10 June 1646], 13).

19 As MacCallum expresses it, "Continuity is established by the way the new identity is chosen by the pre-existent Son; discontinuity is introduced by the new terms and conditions of choice arising from the Incarnation" (*Milton and the Sons of God*, 240).

20 G.W. Bowersock, *Martyrdom and Rome* (Cambridge: Cambridge University Press, 2002), 52.

21 John Foxe, *TAMO* (1583), Book 11: 1611. HRI Online Publications, Sheffield, 2011. Accessed 6 October 2014 at: http//www.johnfoxe.org.

22 Lilburne had his own keen sense of *where this will end* – "that if I should die in this contest (for putting them in mind of their promises [to implement the *Agreement of the People*]) that you will improve your utmost interest, that this *Epistle* may live, and many Thousands of them be re-printed, and seeing by their new pretended Act about Printing they cannot be sold, they may be thrown away, and given, and sent all up and down the Nation" (*Strength out of Weaknesse* [30 September 1649], 25).

23 Fish, "Inaction and Silence," 40.

24 As Gretchen Minton defines this action, in "Foxe's narrative, the martyrs can be transformed into the Word precisely because they act in accordance with the Scripture. John Knott observes that Foxe's martyrs 'often appear to be acting out a drama learned from the New Testament' … By acting out the drama of the first martyrs, these Protestant martyrs became an integral part of God's plan; at the

moment of their deaths, it seems that these Protestant martrys have become the protomartyrs whom they represent. The exemplary stories of the Bible provide a script for the martyrs to follow" ("'The Same Cause and Like Quarell': Eusebius, John Foxe, and the Evolution of Ecclesiastical History," *Church History* 71, no. 4 [December 2002]: 731).

25 See Christopher Mead, *Mass Communication: The Eucharist and Authorship in Early Modern* England (PhD diss., University of California, Berkeley, 2015).

26 *Strength out of Weaknesse* (30 September 1649), 25. See n22 above.

27 A search of the online edition of the 1583 *Actes and Monuments* yields 134 instances of "It is written" in 12 volumes. Foxe quotes it *in propria persona* in his story the "Blinde Superstition of Monkes": "What is this, but for mans traditions and commaundmements, to transgresse the commaundement of God, which saith: Thou shalt do no murther. Thou shalt not tempt the Lord thy God?" (Book 3: 177). In the drama of Thomas Haukes contending with Bishop Bonner and Archdeacon Harpsfield, the latter exhorts: "Beware of pride brother, beware of pride." To which "*Haukes*: 'It is written: Pride serueth not for men, nor yet for the sonnes of men'" (TAMO [1583], Book 11: 1611. HRI Online Publications, Sheffield, 2011. Accessed 7 October 2014 at: http//www.johnfoxe.org).

28 Michael Bryson, *The Tyranny of Heaven: Milton's Rejection of God as King* (Newark: University of Delaware Press; London: Associated University Presses, 2004), sees the value of "following the temptation order of Luke, rather than that of Matthew," since it allows Milton to "put the temptations in an ascending scale" (167). But in his rush to "dethrone" the deity, Bryson occludes the poem's emphasis on the faculty of will in its redemptive movement *beyond* the self ("Mee hungring more to do my Fathers will," PR 2.259), much as he makes the marriage in *Paradise Lost* of no account, failing to read it as a trope of reunion with the deity.

29 Marjorie Hope Nicolson, *John Milton: A Reader's Guide to His Poetry* (New York: The Noonday Press, 1963), 342.

30 Douglas Bush, *John Milton: A Sketch of His Life and Writings* (New York: Macmillan, 1964), 189.

31 CPW 2: 282.

32 See, for example, *Mercurius Pragmaticus* 24 (29 February 1648): "[B]ut from levelling of *Alters*, and *Railes*, they proceede to levelling of *Churches*, for edification in *Stables*; and in the end will fall to levelling of *Palaces, Persons*, and *Estates*; that all *Orders* of men may be mingled among the *Litter of Brethren*" (4).

33 MacCallum, *Milton and the Sons of God*, 255.

34 Bryson's valiant attempt to bring Milton's poetic design to rest in a "new-model Divinity" (*The Tyranny of Heaven*, 169) is vitiated by his Gnostic relocation of an external deity to an immanent one that is "within" every human being; it is further hollowed out by his valorization of "a life that has no part in the external government of affairs either earthly or heavenly" (170).

35 The pamphlet contains excerpts from Machiavelli's *Discourses*, "which allow us to identify as one probable author of *Vox Plebis* Nedham himself" (Scott,

Commonwealth Principles: Republican Writing of the English Revolution [Cambridge: Cambridge University Press, 2004], 83–4). The only other probable candidates for authorship of this work are Walwyn or Overton, but the preponderance of evidence points to Nedham.

36 *Vox Plebis, or The Peoples Out-cry* (19 November 1646), 50.

37 "In all this," MacCallum remarks, "there is nothing of Calvin's characteristic emphasis on kenosis as concealment" (*Milton and the Sons of God*, 221). For a discussion of Calvin's concept of concealment, or "veiling" of the Son's divinity, see MacCallum, 30, 219–21.

38 See Lewalski, *Milton's Brief Epic*, 317.

39 In his *Orality and Literacy: The Technologizing of the Word* (London and New York: Methuen, 1982), Walter J. Ong, SJ, inadvertently exposes the impassable gulf between medieval and early-modern cultures: "The spoken word is always an event, a movement in time, completely lacking in the thing-like repose of the written or printed word. In Trinitarian theology, the Second Person of the Godhead is the Word, and the human analogue for the Word here is not the human written word, but the human spoken word. God the Father 'speaks' to his Son: he does not inscribe him. Jesus, the Word of God, left nothing in writing, though he could read and write (Luke 4: 16)" (73). In *Paradise Regain'd* and the *Actes and Monuments*, there is nothing "thing-like" about the "written or printed word." To Foxe (a Protestant Trinitarian) and to Milton (an anti-Trinitarian), God continues to "speak" his Son, while the Son "speaks" the Word of the Father; yet the latter's speech-act is fulfilled in the act of reading – not in the Real Presence of the Mass but in the Real Presence of the Book. In both works, one witnesses the unfolding of a historical drama in which this older, hierarchical oral culture is superseded by the thoughtways and values of a modern democratic culture which is henceforth mediated by the printed word.

40 MacCallum, *Milton and the Sons of God*, 238.

41 John Rogers, "*Paradise Regained* and the Memory of *Paradise Lost*," in *The Oxford Handbook of Milton*, ed. Nicholas McDowell and Nigel Smith (Oxford: Oxford University Press, 2009), comes at the question of identity from an opposite direction, making the reader the object of the poet's action of disproving "an inimical Christological orthodoxy by ignoring it entirely" (611).

42 Minton, "The Same Cause," 731.

43 Cf. Exodus 17: 7, "Is the LORD among us, or not?"

44 Walwyn, *Tyranipocrit*, 21.

45 Ibid., 46.

CONCLUSION

1 Rachel Foxley remarks similarly "on the need" expressed in Leveller writings "for people to search out the truth for themselves, rather than take anything on trust – a characteristic Lilburnian and Leveller theme" (*The Levellers: Radical Political*

Thought in the English Revolution [Manchester and New York: Manchester University Press, 2013], 119).

2 Richard Helgerson, *Forms of Nationhood: The Elizabethan Writing of England* (Chicago and London: University of Chicago Press, 1992), 266, 264.

3 Ibid., 265.

4 *The Pelican Guide to English Literature*, vol. 1: *The Age of Chaucer* (1954); vol. 2: *The Age of Shakespeare* (1955); vol. 3: *From Donne to Marvell* (1956), ed. Boris Ford (Baltimore: Penguin). Of the ten essays printed in Volume 3 on individual poets and prose writers and poetic schools of the seventeenth century, only one concerns Milton.

5 Helgerson maintains that, "'While Shakespeare tends to legitimate heredity and the preservation of an aristocratic order,' plays put on by the newly organized Worcester's Men, plays like *Sir Thomas Wyatt* (1602), *The Royal King and the Loyal Subject* (1602), and *Sir John Oldcastle* (1599), 'offer as hero a man of the people at odds with the monarchy . . . Here, after all, is an English history play written specifically to correct a play by Shakespeare in which Kemp himself had taken the offending part. *Sir John Oldcastle* aims to restore the reputation of the proto-Protestant martyr whose name had been used by Shakespeare for the character who became Falstaff" (*Forms of Nationhood*, 230).

6 Ibid., 294.

7 Benedict Anderson, *Imagined Communities: Reflections on the Origin and Spread of Nationalism*, rev. ed. (London and New York: Verso, 1991).

8 See my discussion of Foxe and universal literacy in *Imagined Nations* (2003), particularly the idea that the "invisible fellowship" felt by readers of Foxe "'with thousands of other readers' (Helgerson, *Forms of Nationhood*, 266) produced an image of readerly communion in the real time of English history as well as in the ideal time of eternity" (15).

9 Rachel Foxley indicates something similar about print culture and readerly involvement in any "imagined community" in remarking that "Lilburne's imagined audience was made up of these 'true hearted,' 'true bred' and 'honest' Englishmen. For example, he appealed 'to every true hearted Englishman that desires a speedie end of these warres'; published information for the benefit of 'all true hearted English-men'; and addressed his message only to those 'True bred Englishmen, that have a life to lay down, for the defence of your just Liberties and Freedomes'" (*The Levellers*, 108–9).

10 Helgerson, *Forms of Nationhood*, 266.

11 See George F. Sensabaugh, *Milton in Early America* (New York: Gordian Press, 1964).

INDEX